ADVANCED TOPICS IN REVENUE LAW

Advanced Topics in Revenue Law

Corporation Tax; International and European Tax; Savings; Charities

John Tiley, CBE, QC (Hon), FBA, LLD

Emeritus Professor of the Law of Taxation
and Fellow of Queens' College,
University of Cambridge

and

Glen Loutzenhiser, DPhil

Pinsent Masons University Lecturer in Tax Law
and Fellow of St Hugh's College,
University of Oxford

·HART·
PUBLISHING

OXFORD AND PORTLAND, OREGON
2013

Published in the United Kingdom by Hart Publishing Ltd
16C Worcester Place, Oxford, OX1 2JW
Telephone: +44 (0)1865 517530
Fax: +44 (0)1865 510710
E-mail: mail@hartpub.co.uk
Website: http://www.hartpub.co.uk

Published in North America (US and Canada) by
Hart Publishing
c/o International Specialized Book Services
920 NE 58th Avenue, Suite 300
Portland, OR 97213-3786
USA
Tel: +1 503 287 3093 or toll-free: (1) 800 944 6190
Fax: +1 503 280 8832
E-mail: orders@isbs.com
Website: http://www.isbs.com

British Library Cataloguing in Publication Data
Data Available

ISBN: 978-1-84946-423-9

Typeset by Hope Services, Abingdon
Printed and bound in Great Britain by
TJ International Ltd, Padstow, Cornwall

MIX
Paper from
responsible sources
FSC® C013056

Preface

In the preface to the companion *Revenue Law* seventh edition volume, I recorded the help I had received from Glen Loutzenhiser in this and other editions. He has worked tirelessly and with amazing speed to carry out the task of splitting the work into two volumes. He and I now put this second part before our readers. That it appears at all is due to the wonderful work and support of all those listed in the other volume. As before Jillinda and I are very pleased to announce the arrival of twin granddaughters, Georgina Rose and Isobel Grace. The parents are Chris and Cerian (our son and daughter in law) who live in Mevagissey.

JT

Recent years have seen major changes—both in substance and in form—to the taxation of domestic and foreign companies, brought on by the final work of the Tax Law Rewrite project, the continuing influence of EU law, and the Coalition Government's stated aim to make the UK the most competitive country for business in the G20. The result has been a steady decline in the main rate of corporation tax, a broadening of the tax base, a more territorial approach to the taxation of foreign profits, a new low rate of tax on patent income, and a revamped controlled foreign company regime. I also note with great interest that at the time of writing, the (low) level of UK corporation tax paid by some very well-known multinational companies is the subject of an unprecedented level of media attention, public debate and parliamentary scrutiny. The pace of reform of the taxation of pensions and preferred savings vehicles has continued unabated as well. I am very pleased to have been a part of the launch of this new text, focusing on the policy and legal issues raised in these especially challenging aspects of the UK tax regime. Thanks go out again to John, to Richard Hart and his dedicated staff, and to my wife Eleanor, son Toby, and my family back in my native Canada. I am also very grateful to Judith Freedman, with whom I teach on the Oxford-taught masters BCL course, and from whom I have learned (and continue to learn) so much.

GL

Contents

List of Abbreviations

AAP	annuity and annual payment
ACE	allowance for corporate equity
ACT	advance corporation tax
AESS	all-employee share scheme
AFR	alternative financial return
AIA	annual investment allowance
AIM	Alternative Investment Market
APSS	approved profit-sharing scheme
AQE	available qualifying expenditure
AR	applicable rate
ASB	Accounting Standards Board
ASP	alternatively secured pension
BES	business expansion scheme
CAA	Capital Allowances Act
CBA	chargeable business assets
CCCTB	common consolidated corporate tax base
CD	certificate of deposit
CDFI	community development finance institution
CDT	capital disposals tax
CEN	capital export neutrality
CFC	controlled foreign company
CfD	contract for differences
CGT	capital gains tax
CGTA 1979	Capital Gains Taxes Act 1979
CIN	capital import neutrality
CIOT	Chartered Institute of Taxation
CIT	comprehensive income tax
CJEU	Court of Justice of the European Union
CON	capital ownership neutrality
CPM	comparable profits method
CPS	Crown Prosecution Service
CSOP	company share option plan scheme
CTA	Corporation Tax Act
CTT	capital transfer tax
CUP	comparable uncontrolled price
CVS	corporate venturing scheme
DB	defined benefit
DDS	deeply discounted security
DTR	double taxation relief
ECHR	European Convention on Human Rights and Fundamental Freedoms 1950
ECJ	European Court of Justice
EEA	European Economic Area

EEIG	European Economic Interest Grouping
EFTA	European Free Trade Association
EIS	enterprise investment scheme
EMI	enterprise management incentive
EMU	European Monetary Union
ER	entrepreneurs' relief
ESC	extra-statutory concession
ESOP	employee share ownership plan
ET	expenditure tax
F(No 2)A	Finance (No 2) Act
F(No 3)A	Finance (No 3) Act
FA	Finance Act
FID	foreign income dividend
FIGs	foreign income and gains
FII	franked investment income
FOREX	foreign exchange
FRS	financial reporting standard
GAAP	generally-accepted accounting practice
GAAR	general anti-avoidance rule
GAAT	General Agreement on Tariffs and Trade
GDP	gross domestic product
GNP	gross national product
HMRC	HM Revenue and Customs
IAS	International Accounting Standard
IASB	International Accounting Standards Board
ICAEW	Institute of Chartered Accountants in England and Wales
ICT	information and communication technology
IFS	Institute for Fiscal Studies
IHT	inheritance tax
IHTA 1984	Inheritance Tax Act 1984
ILGs	index-linked gilts
IP	intellectual property
IRC	Internal Revenue Code (US)
IRS	Internal Revenue Service (US)
ISA	individual savings account
ITA 2007	Income Tax Act 2007
ITEPA 2003	Income Tax (Earnings and Pensions) Act 2003
ITTOIA 2005	Income Tax (Trading and Other Income) Act 2005
LLP	limited liability partnership
LLPA 2000	Limited Liability Partnership Act 2000
LTR	long-term resident
MNE	multinational enterprise
MPS	money purchase scheme
MSC	managed service company
NAFTA	North American Free Trade Agreement
NICs	National Insurance Contributions
NON	national ownership neutrality
OECD	Organisation for Economic Co-operation and Development
OEIC	open-ended investment company
OTS	Office of Tax Simplification
PACE 1984	Police and Criminal Evidence Act 1984

PAYE	pay as you earn
PCTA 1968	Provisional Collection of Taxes Act 1968
PE	permanent establishment
PEP	personal equity plan
POEM	place of effective management
PR	personal representative
PRP	profit-related pay
PSC	personal service company
QCB	qualifying corporate bonds
QUEST	qualifying employee share trust
RBC	remittance basis charge
R&D	research and development
RDS	relevant discounted security
REIT	real estate investment trust
RIA	relevant intangible asset
RRA	rate of return allowance
SAO	senior accounting officer
SE	*Societas Europeae* (or European Company)
SERPS	State Earnings Related Pension Scheme
SFA	Structured Finance Arrangement
SIP	share incentive plan
SIS	share incentive scheme
SME	small or medium-sized enterprise
SORP	Statement of Recommended Accounting Practice
SP	Statement of Practice
SSAP	Statement of Standard Accounting Practice
STRGL	statement of recognised gains or losses
TA 1988	Taxes Act 1988
TCA 2002	Tax Credits Act 2002
TCGA 1992	Taxation of Chargeable Gains Act 1992
TDR	total disposal receipts
TDV	total disposal value
TEC	Treaty Establishing the European Community
TESSA	tax exempt special savings account
TEU	Treaty on European Union
TFEU	Treaty on the Functioning of the European Union
TIOPA 2010	Taxation (International and Other Provisions) Act 2010
TMA 1970	Taxes Management Act 1970
TSI	transitional serial interest
TSS	terminal salary scheme
UET	universal expenditure tax
UITF	Urgent Issue Task Force
UnASOS	unapproved share option scheme
USM	Unlisted Securities Market
VAT	value added tax
VATA	Value Added Tax Act
VCT	venture capital trust
VRS	variable rate security

Table of Cases

PART I

Corporation Tax

1

Corporation Tax—Introduction, History and Policy

1.1 Structure of UK Corporation Tax

Companies resident in the United Kingdom (UK) are subject to corporation tax on their profits; the term 'profits' includes both income and capital gains.[1] The general rate of corporation tax is now normally 24%[2]; a 30% rate still applies to certain 'ring fence' profits,[3] and lower rates apply where profits are below £1.5 million.[4] These rates are charged by reference to 'financial years' which begin on 1 April each year and end on 31 March the following year; they are charged on the company whether it distributes or retains its profits. Corporation tax was introduced in 1965. Before that time corporations were subject to income tax, but not surtax, on their income, with further taxes (profits taxes) also charged on their income to make up for the absence of surtax.

1.1.1 The Legislation and the Rewrite

While the Capital Allowances Act (CAA) 2001 and Income Tax (Earnings and Pensions) Act (ITEPA) 2003 have effect on both corporation tax and income tax, neither the Income Tax (Trading and Other Income) Act (ITTOIA) 2005 nor the Income Tax Act 2007 does.

---

[1] CTA 2009, ss 2 and 5, ex TA 1988, s 6; on non-residents, see below at §2.9; on gains, see TCGA 1992, s 8(3).
[2] FA 2012, s 5. The rate will drop to 23% for the financial year 2013; see FA 2012, s 6.
[3] FA 2007, s 2.
[4] See below at §2.5.

ITTOIA 2005 expressly preserved Schedule A and the Cases of Schedule D for corporation tax; it did not preserve Schedule F as that applied only for income tax.

Since 2009 nearly all of the remaining corporation tax legislation has been rewritten. The rules formerly in the Taxes Act (TA) 1988 are now spread across, primarily but not entirely, the Corporation Tax Act (CTA) 2009, the Corporation Tax Act (CTA) 2010 and the Taxation (International and Other Provisions) Act (TIOPA) 2010. CTA 2009, Part 2 contains the basic charge to corporation tax in respect of both income and chargeable gains. It then follows the ITTOIA 2005 model dealing with Trading Income (Part 3) and Property Income (Part 4), before going on to Loan Relationships (Parts 5 and 6), Derivative Contracts (Part 7), Intangible Fixed Assets (Part 8), Intellectual Property (Part 9), Company Distributions (Part 9A) and Miscellaneous Income (Part 10). Parts 11–21 deal with other matters. The capital gains rules are still primarily found in the Taxation of Chargeable Gains Act (TCGA) 1992.

1.1.2 Tax Credit on UK Dividends

Where a company is subject to corporation tax, ie is resident in the UK, shareholders are liable to income tax on dividends (and other distributions) received from the company and pay tax under ITTOIA 2005, Part 4, Chapter 3.[5] A dividend therefore comes with a tax credit attached to it; this tax credit is currently one-ninth of the dividend, so a dividend of £90 comes with a credit of £10. Assuming that the shareholder is entitled to use the credit, the income of the shareholder is the sum of the dividend (£90) and the credit (£10), or £100. Basic-rate and savings-rate shareholders pay tax at the dividend ordinary rate of 10% so that there is no further income tax to pay; this has been so for many years. Higher-rate taxpayers pay at the special dividend upper rate of 32.5%, which means that after the £10 credit the taxpayer will have to pay another £22.50. The additional dividend rate of 42.5% plus credit applies to taxpayers in the 50% income tax bracket; from April 2013 those rates will drop to 37.5% and 45%, respectively.[6] It is a fundamental feature of the current system that the shareholder cannot, subject only to very limited exceptions, claim any repayment of the tax credit from the Revenue—and never from the company. Another fundamental feature is that a company subject to UK corporation tax generally is not subject to corporation tax on dividends received from another company.[7]

1.2   A Brief History of UK Company Taxation

1.2.1 Before 1965

The UK corporate tax system has suffered major shifts of policy in its (relatively) recent past. In the 19th century the system charged companies, like other persons, to income tax;[8] this lasted until 1965. Until that year dividends were not subject to *income* tax but were

---

[5] Ex TA 1988, s 20.

[6] FA 2012, s 1.

[7] CTA 2009, Pt 9A, ex TA 1988, s 208.

[8] For an explanation, see Royal Commission on the Taxation of Profits and Income, *Final Report*, Cmd 9474 (1955), ch 2.

grossed up to give a figure for *surtax*,[9] whether or not the company paid income tax on its profits. This system was subject to two major modifications. First, the fact that a company was subject to income tax, but not to surtax, meant that it was advantageous for a high-rate taxpayer to leave income behind the veil of a company where it would be taxed at lower rates and so multiply more rapidly. Legislation was therefore introduced in 1922 to deal with 'one-man' companies, which took the form of a surtax direction treating the income of the companies as if it were the income of its owners and so liable to surtax.[10] The legislation continued in substance, but in a new form, as part of the modern close company legislation from 1965–89.

The second modification was the introduction in 1937 of the National Defence Contribution, which in due course became profits tax.[11] This was an extra tax on the profits of the company, which, not being income tax, could not be recovered by the shareholder. This device could be used to levy tax at differential rates on distributed and retained profits, and was so used between 1947 and 1958.[12] The two-tax system was subject to a number of disadvantages separate from the issue of whether it should encourage the retention of profits. First, since the basic tax on the company was income tax, not only was it subject to all the complexities of matters such as the commencement and cessation provisions, but the rate would also alter whenever the Government thought it right to alter the rate in the personal sector. Secondly, profits under the two taxes were computed differently. Not only was profits tax levied on a current as opposed to a preceding year basis, but some items were deductible in computing profits for profits tax which were not deductible for income tax, thus necessitating two sets of calculations; consequently, until 1952 profits tax was itself deductible for income tax. Further, companies whose profits were less than £2,000 were exempt from profits tax.

1.2.2 1965–73

This untidy system was ended in 1965 when corporation tax replaced the previous income and profits taxes; this was a classical system. Dividends were taxed under Schedule F, which was entirely separate from corporation tax on the profits. This system was based on a view that corporations should be encouraged to retain their profits rather than distribute them to their shareholders (see further §1.4).

1.2.3 1973–97

For these years the tax system emphasised the close relationship between the shareholder and the corporation by allowing the shareholders to use a part of the corporation tax paid by the company to offset their own liability to Schedule F income tax. This was known as the imputation system because of the way in which the corporation tax paid by the company was imputed to the shareholder. Technically it was a 'partial imputation' system,

---

[9] However, where dividends fitted in with the Schedular system was obscure but Sch D, Case VI was the prime candidate; see Heyworth Talbot [1962] BTR 394.

[10] See Royal Commission on the Income Tax, *Final Report*, Cmd 615 (1920), para 1021(2).

[11] See Royal Commission (1955), *op cit*, ch 20. This tax was precedented not only in the excess profits duty of the First World War, but also in the general corporation profits tax introduced in 1920 and repealed in 1924.

[12] For figures, see Singh and Whittington, *Growth, Profitability and Valuation* (CUP, 1968), 4.

since only part of the corporation tax paid by the company was imputed to the shareholder. In order to ensure that the tax used as a credit by the shareholder represented tax actually paid by the company, the company, when paying the dividend (or any other qualifying distribution), had to pay advance corporation tax (ACT) to the Inland Revenue. Liability to pay ACT arose whether or not the company was itself liable to pay corporation tax, eg through lack of taxable profits. ACT could, within limits, be set against the company's liability to corporation tax.

In 1973 the choice lay between the imputation system and a two-rate system (also called a split-rate system), whereby corporation tax would be charged at one rate on retained profits and another on distributed profits, the difference between the two rates being that of the basic rate of income tax. In a closed economy there would be little practical difference between the two; it would not matter to resident shareholders whether the distributed profit of the company was taxed at 50%, but shareholders were allowed to take three-fifths of that tax as a credit against their own liability (the credit or imputation system), or the tax on the company was 20% and there was no credit.

The imputation system was preferred for international reasons.[13] Under a two-rate system the lower rate of tax on distributed profits could not distinguish between resident and non-resident shareholders without risking complaints of discrimination from tax treaty partners.[14] However, the imputation system could restrict the income tax credit to residents. Non-residents requesting the tax credit were turned away; when they requested double tax relief for the ACT paid by the company on the dividend, they were denied this on the basis that ACT was a tax on the company in respect of its profits and not a tax on their dividends. It followed that no UK tax was payable on the dividend, and so there was no such tax to be used as a foreign tax credit against the non-residents shareholders' liability to income tax in their own country. The UK could protect its own revenue without great risk of discouraging foreign private investment. This was designed to lead to the renegotiation of double tax treaties and the second reason for the imputation system. The two-rate system would, for the reasons given above, give rise to a lower tax take by the UK Government. This could be adjusted by a double tax treaty with the other country. However, the United States was firmly wedded to the classical system and so saw no reason to grant a different rate of withholding tax to the other country just because that other had moved to a two-rate system; it was therefore unwilling to negotiate agreements other than those giving identical rates of withholding tax for both countries. Thus the attraction of the imputation system was that by being so nasty to US shareholders, the UK could encourage that government to come to the negotiating table.[15]

The imputation system as implemented in the UK was found to have a serious flaw, in that surplus ACT could arise (see below at §3.6). As implemented in the UK and in most other countries, it was also found, eventually, to be incompatible with EU law; the very discrimination which lay at the heart of the system was contrary to EU discrimination law (see below at §§1.3 and 21.3.1).[16]

---

[13] See Green Paper, *Reform of Corporation Tax*, Cmnd 4630 (1970); *Report of the Select Committee on Corporation Tax*, HC 1970–1971, No 622; and Prest [1972] BTR 15. In 1973 the basic rates of income tax and corporation tax were 30% and 50%, respectively.

[14] TA 1988, s 231, ex FA 1972, s 86.

[15] For US retaliation, see Kaplan [1978] BTR 206.

[16] Case C-319/02 *Manninen v Finland* [2004] ECR I-07477.

1.2.4 1997—New Labour

The reforms which began in 1997 and which were completed in 1999 retained the shell of the imputation system. Shareholders receiving dividends still received a tax credit on account of some of the corporation tax paid by the company. However, two major changes were made. The first was the restriction of the use of the tax credit. Until 1997 a tax credit might be used by the shareholder not only as an offset against an actual UK tax liability on the dividend but also where the circumstances allowed (eg where there was little other income to use the personal relief) to be repaid, the claim being made to the Revenue and not to the company. After 1997 there was virtually no right to a repayment, whether the shareholder was a UK pensioner with low income, a charity, a pension fund or most types of non-resident (see §3.3.1). On this last point, the 1997 change had one thing in common with 1973—a wish to attack the foreign shareholder and so the foreign fisc. One effect was to reduce to a minimum a non-resident's right to recover, under the relevant double tax treaty, part of the UK tax withheld on the dividend. The second major change was the abolition of ACT. To make up for the Government's loss of cash flow from ACT, a new scheme of quarterly payments of corporation tax in advance was introduced. The overall effect was a system which for most individual shareholders was much the same as a two-rate system. Later the New Labour Government decided to offer a starting rate initially of 10% then of 0% if profits were below £10,000. Many thought this unwise as it over-encouraged incorporation. However, others thought it an important part of an overall scheme of tax for small businesses.[17]

The professed objective behind the 1997–99 changes was to encourage long-term investment. Companies had to be encouraged to make long-term investment decisions with confidence; hence, part of the money taken by ending the repayment of the credit was returned as a cut in corporation tax rates. Companies were also expected to retain more earnings instead of paying them out by way of dividend, a point achieved by making dividends for investors, such as pension funds, more expensive. It was believed that many pension funds were in substantial surplus and that many companies were enjoying pension holidays, but that proved to be a very short-term view. What was true was that a pension fund had an incentive to ask for profits to be distributed, in that if the dividend came out of the company with a credit which could be reclaimed, there was more money to reinvest, perhaps in that very company, than if the money had been simply left in the company.

The attack on short termism was based on the hypothesis that fund managers, especially pension fund managers, take a short-term view of investments and that this is a bad thing for the economy as a whole.[18] It is thus a mixture of facts, and assessment of those facts. The facts asserted are that there is excess volatility in the investment behaviour of managers; this may, in turn, be due in part to the next fact which is the practice under which trustees regularly monitor their managers' handling of funds in their care against the performance of other managers and the various stock indices. Managers who feel threatened in this way will tend to favour opportunities for short-term gains. This leads to the undervaluation

---

[17] For a wide-ranging policy view, see Chittenden and Sloan [2007] BTR 58.

[18] For critical discussion of the short-term hypothesis, see Walker (1985) 25 *Bank of England Quarterly Bulletin* 570–75; and Marsh, *Short Termism on Trial* (Ifma, 1993). For an examination of pension funds investment practices—and much else—see Davis, *Pension Funds* (OUP, 1995); and LSE Financial Markets Group, *Special Paper No 107* (LSE, 1999).

of firms with good earning prospects and a willingness by managers to sell shares in the event of a threatened takeover when there is no real business advantage to be gained from that takeover. In turn, this leads to a discouragement of long-term investment in research and development rather than paying dividends because the company wants the shortest pay-off period possible, and leads to fund managers wanting to sell out rather than help when a company hits bad times. It may also lead to pension funds being bad at investing in small and medium-sized enterprises. This last point may have other explanations; it may be because (a) the shares may not be marketable, (b) funds have difficulty in researching firms without track records and/or (c) there may be limits on the amount of equity which may be held. These objections may be met by the development of small share markets such as the Alternative Investment Market (AIM). It should also be said that some of the UK's entrepreneurs, such as Richard Branson and Alan Sugar, have not liked dealing with 'The City', regarding it as very expensive and unhelpful. The 'market discipline' exercised by the threat to sell out in the event of a hostile takeover must be balanced against the often negative effects of such takeovers.[19]

1.2.5 2010—Coalition Politics

The Conservative–Liberal Democrat Coalition, led by Prime Minister David Cameron, that formed the Government following the general election in May 2010 is looking to business as the driver of future economic growth and innovation in the UK. To that end, the Government released a Roadmap for Corporate Tax Reform, which included plans to reduce the headline rate of corporation tax and create the most competitive tax system for business in the G20.[20] The main rate of corporation tax has already dropped from 28% to 24% (for the financial year commencing 1 April 2012) since the election, with further cuts planned to take it down to 21% for the financial year commencing 1 April 2014. Even with these planned tax rate cuts, however, research by the Oxford University Centre for Business Taxation suggests that the UK is a long way off its G20 competitiveness goal.[21] In 2011 the Government also introduced a new levy on UK banks.[22]

Simplification is another key aim of the Government's tax reform agenda. In 2010, the Coalition created the Office of Tax Simplification (OTS) to provide the Government with independent advice on simplifying the UK tax system. In its first report, the OTS recommended abolishing some 47 tax reliefs and simplifying others. The OTS has since released other reports on simplifying small business taxation and employee share schemes.[23]

---

[19] Eg Deakin and Slinger (1997) 24 *Journal of Law and Society* 124. See also Singh, 'Corporate Takeovers' in *The New Palgrave Dictionary of Money and Finance* (Palgrave Macmillan, 1992).

[20] See <http://www.hm-treasury.gov.uk/corporate_tax_reform.htm>. See also *The Coalition: our programme for government*, at <http://www.direct.gov.uk/prod_consum_dg/groups/dg_digitalassets/@dg/@en/documents/digitalasset/dg_187876.pdf>.

[21] See <http://www.sbs.ox.ac.uk/newsandevents/news/Pages/UKcorporatetax.aspx>. The UK is at the bottom of the G20 for allowances on capital expenditure, so the fairly competitive corporation tax rate applies to a broad base of profits.

[22] FA 2011, Sch 19, and commentary by Cummings and Gall [2011] BTR 454.

[23] See the OTS's website at <http://www.hm-treasury.gov.uk/ots.htm>.

1.2.6 Small is Beautiful

One other trend deserves mention. This is the granting of special reliefs for small and medium-sized enterprises. In the financial year 2012, special reliefs are available in the form of:

(1) lower rates of corporation tax;
(2) exemption from payments of corporation tax by quarterly instalments;
(3) special capital allowances for machinery and plant;
(4) a special tax credit for research and development; and
(5) exemption from the transfer pricing rules.

The status as qualifying companies is determined for (1) and (2) on the basis of taxable profits, and for (3), (4) and (5) on a more complex formula taking account also of assets and turnover. Other rules designed to benefit small companies include the generous rules for share options under the enterprise management incentive (EMI) scheme.

Some see these incentives as necessary assistance for a sector of the economy which suffers disproportionately from compliance costs while also providing substantial new employment opportunities. Others point out that statistics can show that small companies provide lower productivity, lower wages and less secure employment than large companies, or wonder why a large company should be entitled to some of these benefits just because it makes low profits.[24] A system might be preferred which distinguishes on the basis of newness and growth, or sees all done away with in the name of tax neutrality and the efficient allocation of resources by the market. The Institute for Fiscal Studies (IFS)-led Mirrlees Review recommended against blanket support for all small businesses on the basis that it is unlikely to be an efficient policy response, and concluded:

> There may be some justification for targeted forms of tax support that would tend to favour some kinds of smaller businesses—for example, those undertaking significant expenditures on investment or research and development—more than a typical large company. However, it seems difficult to rationalize the nature and scale of generalized tax advantages for all small businesses that we see in the UK and in many other developed countries.[25]

1.3 The EU Dimension[26]

It is understandable that the European Union (EU) should take an interest in tax matters with a view to harmonisation either with regard to the structure of the corporate tax system, or at least with regard to the tax base. Tax systems and their differences represent significant

---

[24] See Chennells, Dilnot and Emmerson (eds), *Green Budget 2000* (Institute for Fiscal Studies, 2000) §8.1.

[25] Mirrlees *et al* (eds), *Tax by Design: The Mirrlees Review* (OUP, 2011) 455. The Review, chaired by Nobel Laureate Professor Sir James Mirrlees and drawing on the work of leading international experts in economics and tax law, undertook the most comprehensive study of the UK tax system since the 1978 Meade Committee: see www.ifs.org/uk/mirrleesReview.

[26] Literature (with citations) includes Gammie [2001] BTR 233; Haufler (1999) 20 *Fiscal Studies* 133; and Devereux (1999) 20 *Fiscal Studies* 155. For lessons to be learnt by EU Member States from explicitly federal systems, see Daly and Weiner (1993) 46 *National Tax Jo* 441. See also chapter 21.

obstacles to a free market across the EU. The various proposals on corporate tax structure show how difficult it is to reach agreement on any of the underlying economic or commercial principles.[27] The Neumark Report, in 1962, recommended the two-rate system; the Van den Tempel Report, in 1967, recommended the classical system; and the Simonet Report, in 1973, recommended the imputation system.[28] A White Paper was anticipated in 1987, but nothing materialised.[29] Subsequently, there were proposals for harmonisation on particular aspects, eg the draft directive of 1984 concerning the carry-over of losses and a report in 1980 on the possibility of convergence, but nothing much was achieved until 1990 and the arrival of Mme Scrivener. She abandoned the search for the holy grail of harmonisation in favour of a series of highly specific proposals to attack specific problems of discrimination. However, at the same time she set up the Ruding Committee to see how seriously tax problems led to distortions affecting the functioning of the internal market. The report accepted that distortions arose from the interaction of the different tax systems, but that other considerations argued not for heroic action on a broad front but for specific (ie piecemeal or targeted, depending on the point of view) removal of the major distortions. These reasons included the need to allow Member States much flexibility to collect revenue through direct taxes and the principle of subsidiarity.[30] In the new millennium efforts have switched to trying to achieve agreement on a common consolidated corporate tax base (CCCTB).

As discussed below in chapter twenty-one, the European Court of Justice (ECJ) has proved to be an unpredictable body, especially when invoking its non-discrimination jurisdiction. Until 2000 many of the corporation tax rules which follow were confined to entities resident in the UK, and it was uncertain when those would be found to be incompatible with EU law and when not. Thus, Lodin, writing in 1998,[31] suggested (and as it happened suggested very correctly) that because imputation systems imposed heavier burdens on foreign dividends than on domestic dividends, they must be incompatible with EU law. In the 2005 case of *Manninen*, the Court said that Member State A might use an imputation system only if it gave its resident shareholder taxpayers a credit for the tax paid in another Member State.[32] Similar problems emerged from cases involving the UK itself (see below at §21.3.1). Although this was not something Member States wanted to do, some have granted partial dividend relief with respect to foreign dividends. So Germany grants the same half exemption for foreign dividends as domestic dividends. The UK has followed suit, to a point, by, for example, exempting dividends received by a company from corporation tax irrespective of whether the payer is a UK or a foreign company. It is the hope of

[27] See Easson (1992) 40 *Can Tax J* 600. There is a broader analysis in Radaelli, *The Politics of Corporate Taxation in the European Union* (Routledge, 1997), esp chs 5 and 6.

[28] See [1975] BTR 422; and [1976] BTR 39.

[29] See [1987] *Simon's Tax Intelligence* 423.

[30] Ruding (chair), *Report of the Committee of Independent Experts* (EC Commission, 1992); for discussion, see (1992) 13(2) *Fiscal Studies* 85. Dr Ruding's rather brief Tillinghast lecture for 1999 is printed in (2000) 54 *Tax L Rev* 101 and is followed by a longer comment by Stewart at 111. See also comments by members reported in (1993) 33(1) *European Taxation*; Daly (1992) 40 *Can Tax J* 1053 (Daly was Secretary to the Committee); and, more generally, (1991) 1 *EC Tax Review* 12 and (1991) 2 *EC Tax Review* 116.

[31] (1998) 7 *EC Tax Review* 229.

[32] AG Kokott in Case C-319/02 *Manninen v Finland* [2004] ECR I-07477.

some that this very unpredictability may persuade the Member States to try to harmonise their tax rules in this area. The choice was well put by Vanistendael in 1996[33]:

> 1) Further unplanned destruction of national tax systems by successive decisions of the ECJ which has to fulfil its mandate and cannot refuse to do so. 2) Approximation of the basic structure of income tax thereby legitimising and defining the place of national tax systems in the EC legal order and giving guidance to the ECJ about what types of income tax are compatible with the treaty. 3) Full restoration of national sovereignty of income tax which means the beginning of the end of the EU because full national tax sovereignty is incompatible with EMU and a single currency.

Developments from 2000 to 2005 provided more examples of this 'unplanned destruction' of national systems, but there are signs of a more sophisticated approach more recently (see §21.2.2 below).

1.4 Theory and Practice[34]

1.4.1 Significance of Corporation Tax

In most OECD economies companies pay several forms of tax. In addition to a national tax on their profits, they may also pay a regional or local tax, one or more local property taxes (in the UK the business rate is charged on all businesses whether in corporate or unincorporated form), a payroll tax, an annual wealth tax and some minor forms of tax—as well as paying social security contributions as employers.[35] For the countries concerned, of these forms of tax the national tax on company profits is often much less important as a source of revenue than social security contributions.[36] It may therefore be that the tax on corporate profits is significant rather than critical.

1.4.2 Should Companies be Taxed?[37]

The first question is whether companies should be taxed at all. On a benefit theory approach, the company should be taxed because it has legal personality and receives benefits, such as the protection of its property and the privilege of limited liability. This is

---

[33] (1996) 5 *EC Tax Review* 122.

[34] The literature on this topic is prodigious. Among many books and articles, see Gammie [1992] BTR 148 and Gammie [1992] BTR 243; McLure, *Must Profits be Taxed Twice?* (Brookings Institute, 1979); Cnossen, *Corporate Taxes in the European Community* (IBFD, 1992); Cnossen in Sandford (ed), *Key Issues in Tax Reform* (Fiscal Publications, 1993); King, *Public Policy and the Corporation* (Chapman and Hall, 1977), reviewed [1978] BTR 321; Ballantine, *Equity, Efficiency and the US Corporate Income Tax* (Brookings Institute, 1980); and McLure (1975) 88 *HLR* 532. For older material, see Whittington, *IFS Lecture Series No 1* (Institute for Fiscal Studies, 1974), a review of the then economic literature; Royal Commission (1955), *op cit*, ch 2; Carter (chair), Canada Royal Commission on Taxation, *Report*, vol 4 (Queen's Printer, 1966), ch 19; Reamonn, *The Philosophy of Corporate Taxation* (Institute of Public Administration, 1970); Chown, *The Reform of Corporation Tax* (Institute for Fiscal Studies, 1971); Coyle [1964] BTR 408, 417; Wheatcroft [1964] BTR 416. For a fascinating, fresh view see Snape, *The Political Economy of Corporation Tax* (Oxford, Hart Publishing, 2011).

[35] See annual guides by OECD—'OECD in figures'.

[36] For 2009, in the OECD countries corporation tax yielded an average of 8% of the tax take and social security yielded 27% (OECD, Tax Stuctures in the OECD-area, Table C); the UK percentages were 7% and 19% (HM Treasury, *Budget 2010*, Table C11: Current receipts).

[37] A good starting point is the Mirrlees Review, 408–12. See also the Green Paper, *Reform of Corporation Tax*, Cmnd 8456 (1982), Pts I and II.

generally considered a weak argument since there is no systemic relationship between the tax on profits and the benefits received.[38] Other reasons may be that taxing companies is politically more acceptable than taxing individuals, being less personal, and that companies occupy so important a place in the economy that governments cannot afford not to tax them.[39] One suggestion is that companies should be taxed because they lock in capital which should reach the shareholders.[40]

If a tax system had a truly comprehensive income tax (CIT) at shareholder level it would not be necessary to tax companies, although a tax may be charged on a basis other than profits along the lines of one of those just listed in §1.4.1. Under a CIT, shareholders would be taxed each year on any dividends received and on the change in the value of their interest in the company. Since profits of the company would be taken into account in valuing those interests, they would be taxed in the hands of the shareholders. Under a universal expenditure tax (UET) the return on savings is taxed only when consumed and, since profits retained by the company are not consumed, there is no tax charge on such profits. Under a CIT, there is therefore a tax charge on the shareholder in respect of the change in value due to the retained profits, while under a UET there is no charge at all.[41]

However, neither a CIT nor a UET is feasible. The problems with a UET are those relevant to any UET. The obvious problems with a CIT include the difficulty of identifying the shareholder to which the retained profits may be attributed,[42] especially in a world of volatile stock markets and nominee companies, and the liquidity issues for a shareholder who has to pay the tax but has not money to do it with. Exempting corporate entities from tax opens up opportunities for tax avoidance by accumulating profits in the company and then selling the shares—opportunities which are not wholly corrected by having a capital gains tax.[43] Therefore a tax on companies may be needed to protect the individual income tax.

1.4.2.1 Profits or Turnover?

A related question is whether the tax should be on the profits of the company or on its turnover.[44] The argument in favour of the latter is that it can be shown that a tax on some companies enters into the company's pricing process and so is shifted forward to the consumers of the company's products rather than falling on the shareholders—or backwards on the employees of the company through lower wages or other suppliers. If this view is correct or, more accurately, partially correct, a tax on companies is in effect an indirect tax, and a tax on the profits of profit-making companies is simply an erratic and therefore inequitable tax which penalises the profitable companies and subsidises the inefficient. This argument has rarely found favour. First, the shifting of the tax by companies is a matter of great speculation and it is less than clear that taxes are shifted on to consumers. Secondly, a turnover tax would presumably have to apply to individual businesses as well as companies in order to avoid too great a gap between the incorporated and unincorporated business, thus, in turn, making a further division between the self-employed and others.

---

[38] Messere, *Tax Policy of OECD Countries* (IBFD, 1993) 325.
[39] Eg Blough (1943) 10 *Law and Contemporary Problems* 108, 110.
[40] Bank (2004) 30 *Journal of Corporation Law* 1.
[41] See Gammie [1992] BTR 148, 149.
[42] On significance of accruals basis versus receipts basis, see *ibid*, 154.
[43] Bagchi (1990) *IBFD Bulletin* 243.
[44] See Richardson (chair), Committee on Turnover Taxation, *Final Report*, Cmnd 2300 (1964), which rejected the idea of a VAT on companies.

1.4.2.2 Profits and Shareholders

If the tax falls on the profits of the company rather than on its turnover, it is easy to begin to design an ideal tax system; however, it is less easy to complete the task. This is because there are major disagreements over how the corporation tax works, not only as to whether it is 'shifted', ie the burden falls not the company and its shareholders but on others, but also on the corporate finance implications and the role of equity finance in comparison with other sources. Moreover, the topic cannot be taken in isolation from decisions about taxation of savings in general. These problems multiply when other countries are considered, not as a source of ideas but as trading partners—if individual nations find it hard to settle on a coherent tax policy in a purely domestic setting, it is very unlikely that two or more nations will agree on their policy objectives. Under these conditions one nation's tax policy may be cancelled out by another's.[45]

1.4.3 Profits Taxation: Classical Systems Versus Imputation Systems

If the tax falls on the profits of the company rather than on its turnover, the next question is whether that tax is to be regarded as separate from the taxation of the shareholder.[46] The polar starting points are that the two systems should be treated as entirely distinct or as completely identical—however, at least seven models may be discerned. The first, *model 1*, usually called the 'classical system',[47] was part of the UK system from 1965–73, and has been in force in the United States and other countries for much longer.[48] (The model numbering system used in this and the next paragraph are taken from a major OECD Report of 1991.[49])

Under the classical system, corporation tax is levied on the profits of the company and a separate income tax on any dividends paid to the shareholders. This gives rise to what is called economic double taxation of corporate income. The total tax taken from distributed profits is greater than that from undistributed or retained profits. It also discriminates between equity finance and debt finance, the latter being cheaper.[50]

Other models (*models 2–7*) provide some degree of relief from double taxation.[51] The opposite pole from model 1 (*models 6 and 7*) treats company and shareholder as identical.[52] Double taxation may be eliminated either by abolishing the tax on dividends at the shareholder level (*model 7*), or by giving a full tax credit to the shareholder for the tax paid at the corporate level (*model 6*). The US Treasury report refers to model 7 as dividend

---

[45] See, generally, Gammie [1992] BTR 148, Gammie [1992] BTR 243 and *Taxing Profits in a Global Economy* (OECD, 1991), ch 2, part D.

[46] See, generally, Gammie [1992] BTR 148 and [1992] BTR 243; Cnossen in Sandford (ed), *op cit*, 40; and Cnossen (1996) 17(4) *Fiscal Studies* 67.

[47] See Royal Commission (1955), *op cit*, 382 (Memorandum of Dissent). As Cnossen in Sandford (ed), *op cit*, points out, the classical system is actually more recent than some of the imputation systems.

[48] For a 2003 survey, see IFA Cahiers LXXXVIIIa (International Fiscal Association, 2003).

[49] *Taxing Profits in a Global Economy*, Table 3.1.

[50] However, see Andrews (1984) 30 *Wayne LR* 1057–71, pointing out that shareholders gain by not having their income taxed until the profits are distributed by way of dividend.

[51] Cnossen (1996) 17(4) *Fiscal Studies* 67, 81.

[52] Full integration was recommended by the Canadian Royal Commission in 1966, the US Treasury in 1979 and the Campbell Committee in Australia in 1981, but was rejected as impracticable by the US Treasury in 1992; on the United States see, generally, McLure, *Must Corporate Income be taxed Twice?* (Brookings Institute, 1979); and US Department of the Treasury, *Integration of the Individual and Corporate Tax Systems: Taxing Business Income Once* (1992); for US colloquium on 1992 proposals, see (1992) 47 *Tax L Rev*.

exclusion, and to model 6 as shareholder allocation.[53] The difference between the two is that it will be possible to apply progressive taxation to shareholders under model 6, but not under model 7. Model 6 (the shareholder allocation model) is likely to break down at international level.[54]

Models 2–5 are intermediate positions seeking to reduce rather than eliminate double taxation. The difference between some of these models may seem insignificant but becomes critical when considering the position of foreign shareholders, and especially their rights under double tax treaties. The reduction may be effected at the corporate level—by having a split-rate system in which the tax on corporate profits is charged at one rate on retained earnings and another (lower) rate on distributed earnings (*model 2*), or by allowing the company to claim a partial deduction for dividends paid (*model 3*).

There are two ways to reduce double taxation at the shareholder level. One (*model 4*) gives the shareholder a partial credit for the corporate tax paid, eg the UK; the other (*model 5*) gives a partial credit for domestic shareholders only.

1.4.3.1 Hybrids

Variations of these models start with the classical system but then apply a special (flat rate) tax on dividends separate from normal progressive rates. This has become fashionable in EU countries and examples of it may be found in Austria, Belgium, Denmark, The Netherlands and Sweden.[55]

1.4.3.2 The Role of Capital Gains Tax

One other point of comparison should be made—the burden of capital gains tax (CGT) on shares. In the UK we are used to having this charge, although it may, in practice, be softened by the annual exemption, or by the use of intermediaries such as personal equity plans (PEPs) or individual savings accounts (ISAs). In the UK there is now a corporation tax exemption for substantial shareholdings held by companies (§4.3.3). This charge may also be found in France, Ireland, Italy, Spain and Sweden, as well as in the United States, Canada and Australia. However, it is not found in The Netherlands, Austria, Belgium, Greece, Luxembourg or Switzerland (in some of these countries the sale of a substantial holding will attract tax). The lesson to be drawn is that comparison is hazardous unless complete and detailed; the more so since local taxes, a wealth tax or other taxes on businesses, such as social security or payroll taxes, have not been considered. It is therefore appropriate to turn to the arguments used in the debates on the choice of model.

1.4.4 The Arguments

1.4.4.1 Classical Versus Imputation Systems

The debate over the two poles of the classical and imputation systems is long and unresolved, and has been governed by a mixture of rhetoric and business. Critics of the classical system regard the interests of shareholders and those of companies as being one and the

---

[53] See Gammie [1992] BTR 243; on shareholder allocation model, see *ibid*, 256–57.
[54] *Ibid*, 248.
[55] See Cnossen (1996) 17(4) *Fiscal Studies* 67, 87–89; and Gammie [1992] BTR 243, 252.

same; its defenders point to the role of the equity market and claim that most investors take little interest in management, provided their dividends continue to be paid. In the 1970s fundamental problems arose over the virtues of the free market system; these problems are thought to be less important now, but memories are short.

The classical system is favoured by those who believe that the company is not the alter ego of the shareholders but is run instead by managers for their own interests[56] and by those who believe that the burden of the tax is not borne by the shareholders, ie that it is shifted to employees or customers. The classical system also has attracted support from those who believe in the 'new' view of dividends, ie that the form of corporate tax is completely irrelevant to a company's dividend decisions.[57]

Behind the rhetoric are debates over various 'distortions' or examples of discrimination. As with all these situations there are two reactions: one is to find a countervailing device to correct the distortion; the other is to try to remove the bias which underlies the distortion. The classical system means a higher burden of tax on incorporated business than on unincorporated business; in turn, this means that, assuming distribution, the rate of return required by a company to make a profit is higher than that for an unincorporated business.[58] The classical system discriminates in favour of retained, as opposed to distributed, profits. This is not necessarily efficient since it makes it more expensive for a company to maintain its net flow of dividends to its shareholders. This, in turn, makes it more expensive for the company to raise the money for its needs, and especially its growth, from the equity market; instead it must look to borrowing or its own income. On this view a shift away from a classical system and to integration will provide more funds for the corporate sector.[59]

Critics of the classical system assert that an investment financed from outside may be looked after more closely than one funded purely from within. They also suggest that a tax which discriminates against distributions means that companies are encouraged to retain money which could be used better by other companies and so encourages businesses which already have adequate reserves at the expense of those which wish to expand faster than their present profitability will allow. If a company is not expanding, managers should not be encouraged to keep liquid reserves for their own sake; reducing retentions would limit the financial discretion of—and so potential misuse by—management.

Supporters of the classical system approve of the use of borrowed money to expand a business[60]; the right to deduct interest but not dividends in computing profits encourages the practice of high gearing. This practice is beneficial because lenders have an incentive to monitor the activities of the managers.[61] Whether the double tax (on profits and dividends) makes investment more expensive for the corporate sector than for the unincorporated

---

[56] See, generally, Bratton (1989) 1 *Stanford LR* 1471, reprinted in Wheeler, *A Reader on the Law of the Business Enterprise* (OUP, 1995), 117. For an historical account see Bank, *Anglo-American Corporate Taxation* (CUP, 2011).

[57] Bagchi (1990) *IBFD Bulletin* 244, considering the views of Bradford. For an explanation of Bradford's views by himself, see *Untangling the Income Tax* (Harvard University Press, 1986), ch 6.

[58] *Report of the Select Committee on Corporation Tax, op cit,* §259; see also Bittker and Lokken, *Federal Taxation of Income, Estates and Gifts* (Warren, Gorman & Lamont, 1989) §§95–96.

[59] Eg the Department of the US Treasury (1992), *op cit,* 138.

[60] On the importance of non-tax aspects for preferring equity to debt, eg the costs of financial distress and bankruptcies, see Department of the US Treasury (1992), *op cit,* ch 1, 115.

[61] See Department of the US Treasury (1992), *op cit,* 115 *et seq*, where it is pointed out that this might be an ineffective way of improving performance, especially as it did not work where the variation in the firm's cash flow was the same as that of other firms.

sector depends on whether the 'optimistic' view of corporate tax is accepted. This view argues that because companies rely on debt-finance at the margin, the tax is neutral or even mildly beneficial. This is highly controversial.[62] However, it remains true that since most countries not only allow a full deduction for interest payments but also allow inflation to erode the value of corporate debt, they give an artificial stimulus to debt.

These arguments were much debated in the UK in the 1970s at and around the time of the switch from the classical system to the imputation system.[63] The perceived view of dividends at that time (the 'old' or 'traditional' view) was that tax had a major influence on company pay out rates. A classical system, combined with preferential tax on capital gains,[64] made dividends more expensive than retentions. This led people to ask why companies continued to pay dividends when other devices were cheaper in tax terms, and why they preferred to try to raise new equity to finance new investment in order to prevent dividends being lowered even though the effect of this might be that the investment would not be made at all. The explanation seemed to be that a company paying a dividend saw itself as sending a signal that it was in a healthy state and its future earnings prospects were good; critics thought this an expensive way of making such an announcement.

The modern view of dividend taxation suggests that shareholders should, as rational people, prefer lightly taxed capital gains to heavily taxed dividends, and that corporations should therefore retain as much as possible. On this view retained earnings are a much more important source of investment than a new share issue. The new view also asserts that dividend taxes do not affect the profitability of investments funded from retained earnings and so do not distort investment choices; this is because a tax on the shareholder may reduce the value of the shareholding and so the value of the firm, but this will not affect the company's decision whether or not to invest. Since dividend taxes must eventually be paid, they are capitalised into the share values, reducing share prices to compensate for those taxes. In effect, a dividend tax is a lump-sum tax on equity existing when the tax is imposed or new equity is issued.[65] However, this view contains two assumptions and one caveat. First, it assumes that capital gains will be lightly taxed in the hands of the shareholders. Secondly, the non-distortion argument assumes that the tax on dividends remains unchanged. Thirdly, the new view applies only to mature businesses; new businesses will not have enough retained earnings and so will need external finance in the form either of loans or shares.

In 1991 the OECD Report reached the dull conclusion that there was some truth in both views, but highlighted the more interesting point that the differences in policy implications should not be exaggerated.[66] By contrast, Cnossen states that most empirical studies support the old or traditional view,[67] and the US Treasury 1992 Report states that the tax policy implications are different.[68] The US Report argues that, on the new view, reducing the tax on dividends would increase the value of the shares and so benefit existing

---

[62] See Stiglitz (1973) 2 *Journal of Public Economics* 1.
[63] These paragraphs draw unashamedly from *Taxing Profits in a Global Economy*, ch 2, and Messere, *Tax Policy of OECD Countries* (IBFD, 1993), ch 12, section D, 365–66.
[64] UK CGT was charged at a maximum of 30% until 1988.
[65] Department of the US Treasury (1992), *op cit*, 116.
[66] *Taxing Profits in a Global Economy*, 29.
[67] Cnossen (1996) 17(4) *Fiscal Studies* 67, 93, citing, eg, Zodrow (1991) 44 *National Tax Jo* 497.
[68] Department of the US Treasury (1992), *op cit*, 116.

shareholders, and that companies would not pay more dividends. The old view asserts that shares values would not go up just because of a change in the law, making dividends less disfavoured, and that making the tax system more neutral between retentions and distributions would increase distributions and so economic efficiency. These (Treasury) views thus deal with the effect of the transition, itself as well as the long term.

Three concluding points may be noted on the dividend debate. First, the attractiveness of shares is affected by many matters other than tax. Secondly, although the imputation system discriminates less strongly than the classical system in favour of retained profits, it may (and in the UK still does) discriminate to some extent against them. Thirdly, it may be a mistake to tax all companies, other than close companies, in the same way, regardless of size and function. In fact, the present UK structure, by withholding capital allowances from most buildings, does discriminate substantially against property companies, and by giving lower rates of tax (and exemption from payment of tax in advance) on low profits, tries, however unsuccessfully, to distinguish large companies from small (see below at §2.5).

1.4.4.2 International Matters

The policy issues have so far been considered primarily in the domestic context. However, companies operate increasingly in the international economy, and the cosy fireside view is no longer appropriate. Cross-border investment brings its own problems; thus why is it that tax systems almost invariably make international investment more expensive than purely domestic investment[69]—and what can be done about it? What is to be done about those differences between tax systems which cause distortions and, in extreme cases, naked tax competition between countries,[70] or about those domestic souls who can make use of foreign entities, legally or illegally? We also have new problems of equity and neutrality—as between resident and non-resident shareholder and between resident and non-resident company.

1.4.5 Cash Flow Tax

In 1978 the Meade Committee developed ideas for taxing companies on cash flow rather than profits.[71] This might simply total receipts and deduct payments other than those made to banks and others for finance, including shareholders, and pay tax on the resulting figure. It would also universalise capital allowances, and abolish the difference between capital and income. It would have the advantage of taxing property companies, but would initially cause difficulties for highly geared companies. Special provision would have to be made for banks, which could be taxed under the then existing system. There are several variant forms.

---

[69] *Taxing Profits in a Global Economy*, ch 2, part D, and ch 5. See also the slighty more recent Chennells and Griffith, *Taxing Profit in a Changing World* (Institute for Fiscal Studies, 1997), 102.

[70] A good starting place is the Mirrlees Review, *op cit*, ch 18 and below at §19.1. For a view of the problem in the corporate as opposed to the tax field, see Charney (1991) 32 *Harvard Journal of International Law* 423; reprinted in Wheeler, *A Reader on the Law of the Business Enterprise* (OUP, 1994), 365.

[71] See Meade, *The Structure and Reform of Direct Taxation* (Allen & Unwin, 1978), ch 12. The idea is supported on administrative and economic grounds by McLure and Zodrow (1996) 3 *International Tax and Public Finance* 97.

1.4.6 Tackling the Bias Against Equity[72]—Widening the Deductions

1.4.6.1 The IFS and Mirrlees Review ACE Proposals[73]

In so far as the debate concerns the different treatments of debt and equity finance (ie the deductibility of debt and the non-deductibility of dividends), one solution is to allow the deduction of dividends at corporate level either completely (*model 6*) or in part (*model 3*). An alternative approach is to have an allowance for corporate equity (ACE). The essential idea is simple—a company would be entitled to deduct an allowance based on the value of the shareholder's equity employed in the business for the period. A set percentage representing the normal rate of return, as determined by the Government, is applied to the value of the shareholders' funds. Those funds would consist of the sums of: (a) funds from the previous period; plus (b) any new equity contributed; plus (c) the ACE allowance for the previous period; plus (d) taxable profits. From this total would be deducted: (a) the tax paid on those profits and dividends; and (b) distributions to shareholders and capital repaid. In order to avoid a double allowance, adjustments would have to be made when one company invested in another. The allowance would leave most of the UK system of corporation tax exactly as it was. The result is that tax is levied only on 'excess' returns above the normal rate of return.

Three advantages in taxing the company are seen to flow from the idea:

(1) neutrality as between debt and equity finance—since a full allowance would be given for the costs of finance, whether debt or equity, and without regard to the level of dividends actually paid, the treatment of equity finance would be assimilated to that of debt finance;

(2) neutrality as between realised and unrealised profit—realisation of profit will lead to more funds and so a higher rate of allowance; deferral of profit means deferral of tax but a lower rate of allowance; and

(3) inflation—as shareholders' funds rise in response to inflation, so the value of the allowance would also rise.

In addition, the ACE proposal would be economically neutral in terms of its effect on decisions on scale of investment, since only excess returns are taxed.[74]

The system would have to face the familiar problems of interaction between corporate and shareholder levels.[75] The favoured solution is to adopt a classical system for the taxation of dividends, since the effect of the ACE system is that the company's finance costs are fully deductible and so there is no need for imputation. The system can, however, work

---

[72] For a good review of methods of tackling the debt-equity distinction, see Wood (1999) 47 *Can Tax Jo* 49.

[73] See the Mirrlees Review, *op cit*, ch 17. Earlier work includes the influential Gammie (chair), Report of the IFS Capital Taxes Group, *Equity for Companies; A Corporation Tax for the 1990s* (Institute for Fiscal Studies, 1991). For a summary of the 1991 IFS report, see Gammie (1991) 31 *European Taxation* 238–42; there is another summary in Devereux and Freeman (1991) 12(3) *Fiscal Studies* 1.

[74] See Auerbach, Devereux and Simpson, 'Taxing Corporate Income' in Mirrlees *et al* (eds), *Dimensions of Tax Design: The Mirrlees Review* (OUP, 2010); the Mirrlees Review, *op cit*, chs 17–19; Devereux and de Mooij, 'An applied analysis of ACE and CBIT reforms in the EU' (2011) *International Tax and Public Finance* 118, 93–120.

[75] See Report of the IFS Capital Taxes Group (1991), *op cit*, paras 2.4.12–2.4.16; and Cnossen (1996) 17(4) *Fiscal Studies* 67, 85.

perfectly well in conjunction with an imputation system. More problems arise over the taxation of capital gains, but these are seen as arising from the nature of the personal tax system—if the corporate tax system is neutral but the personal tax system is not, an overall neutral system cannot be created simply by dealing with the corporate side. The Mirrlees Review recommended taxing capital gains on shares (and dividends) at a lower rate than earned income to reflect in part tax paid at the corporate level.[76]

Although the ACE proposal has been generally admired rather than widely implemented, it was the inspiration behind a reform in Croatia lasting from 1994 to 2001, and more recent relief for equity finance offered in Belgium.[77] Like other reforms which increase the amount that may be deducted, the change would mean that the same amount of tax would have to be raised from a smaller amount of net profits—assuming that the change is to be revenue neutral.[78] On this basis, ACE would mean both an increase in the rate of corporation tax if the change were to be revenue neutral (Isaac suggested an increase of 10% under an imputation system, say, from 35% to 45%[79] for the years 1973–91, with a 25% rate under a classical system) and a major increase in the burden of tax between different companies, with successful companies paying more tax and less successful companies enjoying a tax reduction.

It is likely that the rate of ACE would be set at a level which would protect a certain amount of real profit. There would be problems on the taxation of capital gains in the hands of companies, in that these ought to be taxed at the same rate without indexation relief; such a high rate would be vulnerable to weakening as a result of either political pressure or avoidance, or both. Furthermore, the ACE does not solve, and may exacerbate as a consequence of its potentially high tax rate, economic distortions related to location of discrete investment projects (especially for more profitable projects) and location of taxable profit (ie profit shifting to lower-tax jurisdictions).[80] There would be the further question whether the principle—that the opportunity cost of capital should not be taxed—should be extended to income tax. In fact, the Mirrlees Review recommended a rate of return allowance (RRA) for income tax as a 'natural counterpart' to the ACE for corporation tax.[81] As with all fundamental changes, there may also be international tax problems in implementing such a change unilaterally. Cnossen agrees that there are attractive neutrality aspects, but suggests that these are best achieved if capital markets are perfect.[82]

---

[76] The Mirrlees Review, *op cit*, 489. The RRA is discussed in detail *ibid* chs 13–14.

[77] Keen and King (2002) 23 *Fiscal Studies* 401–18 (on Croatia), and the Mirrlees Review, *op cit*, 449 (on Belgium).

[78] The Mirrlees Review did not support revenue neutrality, opting instead for lower corporation tax revenues, principally on international competitiveness grounds: 'If a source-based tax on the normal return component of corporate profits is undesirable, and the current UK corporate tax rate is considered more or less appropriate, the implication is that less revenue should be raised from the corporate tax' (Mirrlees *Review*, *op cit*, 450).

[79] Isaac (1997) 18 *Fiscal Studies* 303, 305. Contrast Bond, Devereux and Gammie (1996) 12 *Oxford Review of Economic Policy* 109–19.

[80] See Auerbach, Devereux and Simpson, *op cit*; Mirrlees Review, *op cit*, chs 17–19; Devereux and de Mooij, *op cit*, 93–120.

[81] Mirrlees Review, *op cit*, 496.

[82] Cnossen (1996) 17(4) *Fiscal Studies* 67, 85.

1.4.6.2 The American Law Institute Proposal[83]

The American Law Institute (ALI) had other ideas for reforming the US system so as to reduce the bias against distributed earnings in a classical system. One would be to allow a company to deduct dividends paid on new capital up to a certain percentage geared to the long-term interest rate plus 2%. It differs from the ACE, *inter alia*, in that it applies only to new equity.

1.4.7 *Tackling the Bias Against Equity—Narrowing the Deductions*[84]

A second way to reduce the bias against equity is to look at the company rather than the shareholder, and at the company's inability to deduct dividend payments. Why not reduce or remove the company's right to deduct interest? In 1992 the US Treasury issued a report on integration which suggested a comprehensive business income tax (CBIT).[85] Under this scheme, all company earnings would be taxed at the company level, and there would be no deductions for either dividends or interest paid to shareholders and debt holders; these items would not be taxed as the recipient's income. This would make the debt/equity distinction irrelevant and reduce the retained/distributed distinction; whether the distinction is abolished would depend on what happened to capital gains rates. The attack on the debt/equity distinction means that many familiar problems would disappear, eg thin capitalisation. The idea has the further attraction of benefiting growing firms at the expense of existing ones—one person's benefit is another person's distortion. Another advantage of the CBIT is that it has a wider base than the ACE and thus lends itself to a lower tax rate than the ACE, all else being equal. This would in turn mean a reduced level of economic distortions related to location of discrete investment projects and location of taxable profit compared to an ACE, but the CBIT would not be neutral in terms of decisions on scale of investment (unlike the ACE).[86]

1.4.8 *The Cashless Corporate Tax*

A sharply different view is that governments should receive tax in the form of shares in companies.[87]

---

[83] Andrews, *Reporter's Study Draft for the ALI Federal Income Tax Project, Subchapter C* (American Law Institute, 1989). See also Department of the US Treasury (1992), *op cit*, 108–09; and American Law Institute, *Federal Income Tax Project, Tentative Draft No 2, Subchapter C—Corporate Distributions* (American Law Institute, 1979). The 1979 proposals were criticised as unworkable by Warren (1981) 94 *HLR* 719 and Warren, *ALI Federal Income Tax Project: Integration of the individual and corporate income taxes, reporter's study of corporate tax integration* (American Law Institute, 1993).

[84] See Gammie [1992] BTR 244, esp 246. This paragraph is based on the summary by Cnossen (1996) 17(4) *Fiscal Studies* 67, 86–87.

[85] For comment, see Gammie [1992] BTR 244, esp 257–61; and, for a comparison with ACE, see *ibid*, 273–75. See also Goode (1992) *Tax Notes* 1667; and, for an economic viewpoint, Sunley (1992) 47 *Tax L Rev* 621.

[86] Devereux and de Mooij, *op cit*, 93–120.

[87] Schlunk (2001) 55 *Tax L Rev* 1.

2

Structure

2.1 The Charge

Corporation tax is chargeable on the profits of companies.[1] 'Profits' means income and chargeable capital gains, so, importantly, the same rate of tax is now charged on all profits, whether income or capital gain.[2] Chargeable gains are computed in accordance with the CGT rules in TCGA 1992.[3] The charge to corporation tax excludes any charge to income tax and CGT.[4] Profits in the form of a distribution by another company generally are excluded from corporation tax.[5] There is no charge to corporation tax where profits accrue to a company in a representative or fiduciary capacity.[6] Where profits accrue in the course of winding up, corporation tax is payable notwithstanding the fact that various

---

[1] CTA 2009, s 2(1), ex TA 1988, s 6(1).
[2] CTA 2009, s 2(2), ex TA 1988, s 6(4). From 1973 to 1987 only a certain fraction (six-sevenths for the financial year 1986) of capital gains was included in the computation (see below at §2.3). This meant, in effect, a lower rate of tax on capital gains but avoided the inelegance of two rates.
[3] TCGA 1992, s 8(3).
[4] CTA 2009, ss 3 and 4, ex TA 1988, s 6(2), (3).
[5] CTA 2009, Pt 9A, ex TA 1988, s 208.
[6] CTA 2009, s 6, ex TA 1988, s 8(2).

fiduciary obligations are also owed to the shareholders. Where profits accrue to the company under a trust or partnership, the company is chargeable to corporation tax.[7]

For the financial year 2012, which began on 1 April 2012, the rate of tax is 24%; there is also a lower small profits rate of 20%; a 30% rate applies to ring-fence profits.[8] As discussed in *Revenue Law*, chapter five, it is axiomatic that the UK does not have a general anti-avoidance rule (GAAR). However, the Government is now consulting on a narrow, general anti-abuse rule along the lines recommended by a study group led by Graham Aaronson QC, with a view to its introduction in the Finance Act 2013. One reason for the current lack of a UK GAAR is that the Revenue have not been willing to provide a clearance service. It is therefore well worth noting the number of parts of the corporation tax system which now have their own mini anti-avoidance rules in the form of rules forbidding deductions, etc where the transaction is entered into for a non-allowable purpose—and the list of non-allowable purposes will include avoidance. Such a list includes avoidance involving charges on income (§4.4), tax arbitrage (§4.7) and rules on the use of foreign tax credit relief (§19.6). Thus the UK in any event is getting a form of GAAR by stealth—and still normally without the protection of clearance procedures.

Nearly all of the corporation tax rules formerly in TA 1988 have been rewritten, and are now found primarily, but not exclusively, in a combination of the CTA 2009, CTA 2010 and TIOPA 2010. References to the old rules are included in the footnotes throughout this book to assist readers with the transition, and because the old rules are relevant for the discussion of the cases.

2.2   A Company

A company means[9] any body corporate or unincorporated association,[10] but does not include a partnership,[11] a local authority or a local authority association.[12] Individuals who invest in a joint account, eg as members of an investment club, are not treated as a company carrying on business together. For problems of identifying a company when considering a foreign entity, see below at §15.3.2. On the European Company, see below at §2.14.

---

[7]   CTA 2009, ss 6 and 7, ex TA 1988, s 8(2).

[8]   FA 2012, ss 5-7.

[9]   CTA 2010, s 1121, ex TA 1988, s 832(1), (2). Contrast the more detailed definition in TCGA 1992, s 170. On charitable bazaars, see ITA 2007, s 529, CTA 2010, s 484 and ESC C4. On thrift funds and holiday funds, see former ESC C3.

[10]   *Blackpool Marton Rotary Club v Martin* [1988] STC 823, (1988) 62 TC 286. On liability of officers, see TMA 1970, s 108(2), (3).

[11]   On whether there is a partnership, see *Engineer v IRC* [1997] STC (SCD) 189.

[12]   There is an exemption from income tax (ITA 2007, s 838) and corporation tax (CTA 2010, s 984, ex TA 1988, s 519) for a local authority and local authority association, as defined in CTA 2010, ss 1130 and 1131, ex TA 1988, s 842A, as amended by FA 1995, s 144. TCGA 1992, s 271(3) provides an exemption from CGT.

In *Conservative and Unionist Central Office v Burrell*,[13] Lawton LJ said that an unincorporated association arose where:

(1) two or more persons bound together for one or more common purposes, not being business purposes, by mutual undertakings;
(2) each having mutual duties and obligations;
(3) in an organisation which had rules which identified in whom control of it and its funds rested and on what terms; and
(4) which might be joined or left at will.

He went on to hold that the structure of the Conservative Party was such that it lacked elements (2) and (3); rather, it was, as it described itself, an amorphous combination of elements, with the result that the Party was not liable to corporation tax on its investment income. The Revenue had accepted that the Party's 'Central Office' was not an unincorporated association, but argued that 'the Party' was such an association, comprising all the individual members of the local constituency associations and the parliamentary party. The individual constituency associations can be unincorporated associations.[14]

Authorised unit trusts are treated as if they were companies.[15] Special rules apply for various special companies such as friendly societies[16] and trade unions.[17] Securitisation companies are also the subject of special rules; these are to take the form of statutory instruments rather than primary legislation.[18] The London Organising Committee for the Olympic Games is given exemption.[19] The Treasury is given a power to exempt the International Olympic Committee and any subsidiaries from any liability to income tax, CGT or corporation tax, and to treat the Committee as not having a permanent establishment in the UK. A similar power arises in connection with competitors and staff.

2.3 Associated Companies

Companies are associated if at any time one company has control of the other, or both are under the control of the same person or persons.[20] The definition of 'control' is taken in two stages. First, there is the broad rule[21] that a person has control of a company ('C') if he

---

[13] [1982] STC 317, (1982) 55 TC 671, CA. See also *Re Koeppler's Will Trusts* [1985] 2 All ER 869, 874, where Slade LJ described an unincorporated association as an association of persons bound together by identifiable roles and having an identifiable membership.

[14] Hence, TCGA 1992, s 264 (change of constituency bodies).

[15] CTA 2010, s 617, ex TA 1988, s 468. See below at §23.3.

[16] TA 1988, s 463 (not rewritten).

[17] CTA 2010, s 981, ex TA 1988, s 467.

[18] CTA 2010, Pt 13, Ch 4, formerly regulations made under FA 2005, s 84.

[19] FA 2006, ss 65 and 66.

[20] CTA 2010, s 25, with further elaboration in ss 26–30 and referring to the meaning of 'control' in ss 450 and 451; ex TA 1988, s 416(1). On shareholdings by different trusts with common trustees, see *IRC v Lithgows* (1960) 39 TC 270; for small companies relief, see ESC C9; and, for close companies, see Statement of Practice SP C4.

[21] CTA 2010, s 450(2), ex TA 1988, s 416(2).

exercises or is able to exercise, or is entitled to acquire[22] 'direct or indirect control over C's affairs', a phrase which could mean:

(1)   the power to carry a resolution at a general meeting, including the power to elect C's board of directors; or

(2)   more narrowly, the power to run C's affairs, ie power at director level, the point being that the general meeting cannot usually tell its directors how to manage the day-to-day affairs of the company.

In *Steele v EVC International NV*,[23] the Court of Appeal preferred (1) to (2), concluding that control of the affairs of a company meant control at the level of general meetings of shareholders, as control at that level carried with it the power to make the ultimate decisions as to the business of a company and, in that sense, to control its affairs.

Secondly, control is declared to exist in defined circumstances, which are without prejudice to the broad principle.[24] These circumstances are where a person possesses or is entitled to acquire:

(1)   the greater part of the share capital or issued share capital of the company, or of the voting power of the company;

(2)   such part of the share capital as would entitle him to the greater part of the income of the company were it all distributed, ignoring any loan capital; or

(3)   such rights as would entitle him in the event of the winding up of the company to the greater part of the assets of the company.

Where two persons together satisfy any of these tests, they are taken to have control of the company.[25] The purpose behind these rules is to enable the Revenue to establish that control exists without having to make the detailed enquiries that might be required by the broad rule.

In determining these matters, the rights of associates may be taken into account under various alternative tests. If the Revenue form the view that other persons are indeed associates, they have a duty to attribute those rights to those other[26] persons; they have no discretion in the matter.[27] There is no underlying policy restricting the concept of control to those who might actually benefit from companies over which they were deemed to have control.[28]

Examples

(1)   If L and M each have 50% of the shares of A Ltd, they have control of A Ltd. If they also have control of B Ltd, then A Ltd and B Ltd are associated.

(2)   If L and M each have 50% of the shares of A Ltd but each has 25% of the shares in C Ltd, A and C are not associated since L and M do not have control of C Ltd.

---

[22]   CTA 2010, s 451(2) provides guidance on the meaning of 'entitled to acquire' for the purposes of s 450.

[23]   [1996] STC 785, (1996) 69 TC 88.

[24]   CTA 2010, s 450(3), ex TA 1988, s 416(2).

[25]   CTA 2010, s 450(5), ex TA 1988, s 416(3).

[26]   *Per* Lord Hoffmann in *R v IRC, ex parte Newfield Developments Ltd* [2001] STC 901 (HL), para 19.

[27]   *R v IRC, ex parte Newfield Developments Ltd* [2001] STC 901 (HL). On the (limited) function of the very closing words of s 416(6), see Lord Hoffmann at para 32.

[28]   *Per* Moses J, [1999] STC 373, at 380a.

(3)   If the remaining 50% of the shares in C Ltd are divided equally between N and P, and N transfers his 25% to L, the companies now become associated since L and M together have 75% of the shares in C Ltd. The fact that M might vote with P and block L is irrelevant. If, however, M then transferred his 25% holding in C Ltd to P, the companies would cease to be associated since, while L and M still control A Ltd, they no longer have control of C Ltd.

For the purposes of small profits relief (only), the Revenue will[29] usually disregard common control arising when companies are controlled by a common trustee, such as a trustee company of a clearing bank, by a common commercial loan creditor or by a common shareholder by virtue of fixed rate preference shares. This means that the companies are not associated either with each other or with the company with control.

In applying these rules, there is to be attributed to a person any rights held by a nominee[30] or an associate,[31] a wide term[32] including any relative[33] or partner. There may also be attributed to him all the powers of any company which he controls, whether by himself or with an associate. The effect of these rules is to attribute rights and powers of persons over whom he may in real life have very little control.[34] Partly in response to such concerns, the Finance Act 2011 relaxed the rules somewhat in order to ensure that companies are not held to be associated by mere accident of circumstance, but only where the level of commercial interdependence between companies is substantial.[35] The Treasury may by order prescribe factors that are to be taken into account in making this determination.[36]

Despite these still rather wide attributions, it is possible for companies not to be associated. Thus, if L controls A Ltd and M controls B Ltd, the companies are not, without more, associated, and in practice this is so even if L controls A Ltd and L and M together control B Ltd.[37] If the companies agree to pool their profits or a percentage of them, they will still not be associated unless the Revenue succeed in arguing that they have become partners. However, if the companies were to put themselves under a holding company, they would become associated since they would each be controlled by the holding company.

In *Holland v Revenue and Customs Commissioners and another*,[38] at issue was whether companies were associated and whether the directors had failed to make proper provision for a charge to corporation tax when authorising payment of dividends. The Revenue took the view that certain composite companies were associated and so liable to higher-rate corporation tax for which no provision had been made. Each composite company had a corporate director as its sole director. Dismissing the Revenue's appeal, a bare majority of the Supreme Court held that HMRC had failed to recognise that a *de jure* director of the

---

[29] ESC C9.

[30] CTA 2010, s 451(3), ex TA 1988, s 416(5).

[31] CTA 2010, s 451(4), ex TA 1988, s 416(6).

[32] CTA 2010, s 448, ex TA 1988, s 417(3).

[33] Relatives other than spouses and minor children are generally ignored, but this is no longer so if there is any substantial commercial interdependence; see ESC C9.

[34] *Per* Lord Hoffmann in *R v IRC, ex parte Newfield Developments Ltd* [2001] STC 901 (HL) at para 11, applied in *Gascoine's Group Ltd v Inspector of Taxes* [2004] EWHC ChD 640, [2004] STC 844.

[35] CTA 2010, s 27, as amended by FA 2011, s 55.

[36] CTA 2010, s 27(3), and see the Corporation Tax Act 2010 (Factors Determining Substantial Commercial Interdependence) Order 2011 (SI 2011/1784).

[37] *Simon's Direct Tax Service*, Pt 2, D 109.

[38] [2010] UKSC 51, [2011] STC 269.

corporate director was also de facto director of composite companies. Many will see good sense in the dissenting views of Lord Walker and Lord Clarke.

2.4 Financial Years—Accounting Periods and Periods of Account

2.4.1 Financial Years

Corporation tax is charged on the profits of the corporation during the financial year.[39] The 'financial year' is the year starting on 1 April.[40] Hence 'financial year 2012' is 1 April 2012 to 31 March 2013.[41] The rates of corporation tax are set for the financial year but assessments are made by reference to accounting periods.[42] Where the accounting period does not correspond with the financial year, the profits of the period are apportioned to compute the tax liability.

Where the rate changes from one financial year to the next, each rate is applied to that portion of the accounting period falling within it. So suppose that the rate is 26% in financial Year 1 and 25% in financial Year 2. The company makes up its accounts to 30 June and the total profit for the accounting period ending on 30 June Year 2 amounts to £1,830,000. For Year 1 the share of the profits will be 274/365 × £1,830,000 or £1,373,753, and so corporation tax will be 26% of that, ie £357,176; for Year 2 the share will be 91/365 or £456,247, and so corporation tax at 25% will be £114,062, making a total of £471,238 or 25.75%.

The financial year is relevant only to the rate of tax. If the method of computing income or capital gains and so corporate profits changes from one year to the next, the accounting period is treated as if it were a year of assessment,[43] although various provisions (eg change of ownership) may require an accounting period to be split for specific purposes.

2.4.2 Accounting Periods and Periods of Account

Accounting periods are usually the successive periods for which the company makes up its accounts. An accounting period cannot exceed 12 months. A period of account is simply the period taken by the company in computing its accounts.[44] Where the period of account exceeds 12 months, the fiscal accounting period will end after 12 months and a new one will begin; so where a company's period of account is 16 months, there will be a fiscal accounting period of 12 months, followed by one of four months. Where, as here, one set of accounts covers more than one period, an apportionment is made on a time basis unless

---

[39] CTA 2009, s 2(1), ex TA 1988, s 6(1).
[40] Interpretation Act 1978, Sch 1.
[41] CTA 2010, s 1119, ex TA 1988, s 834(1).
[42] CTA 2009, s 8, ex TA 1988, s 8(3).
[43] CTA 2009, s 8, ex TA 1988, s 9(1).
[44] On the position where a company makes up its accounts both yearly and six-monthly, see *Jenkins Productions Ltd v IRC* [1943] 2 All ER 786, (1943) 29 TC 142. On accounts for an unauthorised period, see *BFP Holdings Ltd v IRC* (1942) 24 TC 483.

a more accurate method can be established.[45] This apportionment is carried out on the basis of days, not months.[46]

When a company draws up accounts, the accounting date to which the accounts are drawn determines the accounting periods for assessment of the company's profits. The Revenue have no power to substitute an accounting period they would prefer. Once an assessment is made for an accounting period, that assessment cannot be revised by virtue of the inspector wishing to use a different period as the accounting period.[47] Where, however, at the time of making an assessment, the date on which an accounting period begins or ends appears to the inspector to be uncertain, the inspector is empowered to make an assessment for such period 'as appears to him appropriate'[48]; these tests are subjective. The inspector may be required to identify an 'appropriate' period only if the rules in TA 1988, section 12 fail to identify a period.[49]

2.4.2.1 Start

An accounting period begins because the previous accounting period has ended and the company remains subject to charge, or if the company, not then being within the charge to corporation tax, comes within it, whether by the company becoming resident or acquiring a source of income.[50] A UK resident company which has not yet commenced business may not yet be within the charge to corporation tax.[51]

2.4.2.2 End

An accounting period ends[52] on the expiration of 12 months from its beginning or, if earlier, any of the following:

(1)   the end of the company's period of account;
(2)   if there is a period during which no accounts have been taken, at the end of that period;
(3)   the company begins or ceases to trade or to be within the charge to corporation tax in respect of the trade, as where a non-resident company continues to trade but no longer through a branch or agency in the UK; if the company carries on more than one trade, the charge to tax must cease in respect of all of them if the period is to end;
(4)   the company begins or ceases to be resident; or
(5)   the company ceases to be within the charge to corporation tax.

2.4.2.3 Two Trades

The scheme of tax is designed so that the period of account will usually coincide with the accounting period and is designed to interfere as little as possible with the freedom of the company to take whatever period of account it likes. If the company has two trades, each

---

[45]   CTA 2009, s 52, ex TA 1988, s 72; *Marshall Hus & Partners Ltd v Bolton* [1981] STC 18, (1981) 55 TC 539.
[46]   CTA 2009, s 52(3), ex FA 1995, s 121.
[47]   *Kelsall v Stipplechoice Ltd* [1995] STC 681, (1995) 67 TC 349, CA.
[48]   TA 1988, s 12(8), not rewritten.
[49]   *Kelsall v Stipplechoice Ltd* [1995] STC 681, 683, (1995) 67 TC 349, 374, *per* Peter Gibson LJ.
[50]   CTA 2009, s 9(1), ex TA 1988, s 12(2).
[51]   CTA 2009, s 9(2), ex TA 1988, s 12(4).
[52]   CTA 2009, s 10, ex TA 1988, s 12(3).

trade has a separate period of account and the company does not make up accounts for the company as a whole, an Officer of the Revenue may determine which accounting date to take for tax purposes, and the profits of the other trade will have to be apportioned.[53] This emphasises the point that the taxable person is the corporation and not the trade.

2.4.2.4 Winding up and Administration

An accounting period ends and a new one begins when the winding up of a company commences or the company goes into administration.[54] Thereafter, the accounting period will end every 12 months until the winding up is complete. A new period begins when the company comes out of administration.[55]

2.4.2.5 Gaps

It is possible for there to be gaps between accounting periods, eg when the company ceases to trade and subsequently starts again. This gives rise to a problem if a capital gain accrues during this period of quiescence. It is therefore provided that an accounting period commences when the chargeable gain or allowable loss accrues to the company.[56] Should the company subsequently begin to trade again, the deemed period will end and a new one will begin.

2.5 Rates: Main Rate, Small Profits Rate and Small Profits Relief[57]

As already seen, the main rate of corporation tax for the financial year 2012 is 24%;[58] a lower rate of corporation tax, now at 20% and designated as the 'small profits rate', applies where the profits do not exceed £300,000.[59] Where the company's profits exceed £300,000, the benefit of the rate is steadily removed by having a higher marginal rate of tax (25% for 2012). Thus, the UK, unlike some other countries, does not have a smoothly progressive corporate tax rate structure. It does give lower rates of corporation tax to companies with low profits, but the benefits of these lower rates are withdrawn successively, resulting in a very odd looking overall marginal rate structure—20%, 25%, 24%.

At one time there was another low rate for profits below £10,000. This was controversial; it complicated the decision whether to incorporate a business; and, in so far as it purported to encourage people to do so, sat oddly with the legislation on personal service companies. When people responded by putting businesses into companies the Government reacted by

---

[53] CTA 2009, s 11, ex TA 1988, s 12(5A) but only if the Officer, on reasonable grounds, thinks the company's own choice inappropriate.

[54] CTA 2009, ss 12 (winding up) and 10(1)(i) (entering administration), ex TA 1988, s 12(7) as amended by FA 2002.

[55] CTA 2009, s 10(1)(j), ex TA 1988, s 12(3)(da).

[56] CTA 2009, s 9(3), ex TA 1988, s 12(6).

[57] CTA 2010, s 3, ex TA 1988, ss 13, 13AA. Capital gains accruing before 17 March 1987 did not qualify for small profits relief and were effectively taxed at 30%; however, the small profits rate was below 30% only for 1986. For pre-1973 rules, see Bolton (chair), *Report on Small Firms*, Cmnd 4811 (1971), ch 13.

[58] FA 2011, s 5(2)(a) modified by rate reduction announced at Budget 2012.

[59] CTA 2010, ss 3, 18, ex TA 1988, s 13; rate and fraction set for 2011 by FA 2011, s 6.

withdrawing the benefit of the 0% rate for profits which were distributed to people other than companies; this was called the non-corporate distribution rate.

These days, the rates of corporation tax are usually known by the start of the financial year. This was not so in the early days and so there was formerly an express provision allowing the use of the previous year's rate if a company was fully wound up before the rate was known.[60] A similar provision (now repealed) was introduced for companies in administration in 2003.[61]

2.5.1 Small Profits Relief

Small profits relief (formerly small companies' relief) has been part of the corporation tax structure for a long time. (The former title is a complete misnomer since the relief is available wherever there are small profits, ie regardless of the size of the company and regardless of the size of profits retained in previous years.) It applies where the company's profits do not exceed a specified limit, currently £300,000; the limit was last increased in 1994.[62] For many years the lower corporation tax rate was tied to the basic or savings rate,[63] but it was changed to 19% for the financial year 2002. It was then increased to 20% for 2007 and to 21% for 2008, before falling to 20% in 2011, the same level as the basic rate.[64] Thanks to the rules for tax credits and the taxation of dividends, there is usually full imputation of the corporate tax for the shareholder (but with no right to repayment). The scheme can also be seen as an element of fiscal neutrality, because the total tax payable was the same whether a company with profits below the specified limit retained those profits or distributed them to any but higher-rate taxpayers (or trusts).

2.5.2 Which Companies?

The rates apply to companies resident in the UK (other than close investment-holding companies—see below at §10.5)[65] but not to non-resident companies with a UK branch.[66] The Revenue interpret the non-discrimination clause in an applicable double tax agreement as entitling the non-resident company to this rate. The *Commerzbank* decision of the ECJ seems to give branches of companies of another Member State a right to use that rate.[67] Perhaps oddly, FA 2000 did not make any amendment here and the provision remains unchanged (see further §2.9.2 below).

2.5.3 Marginal Rates: Phasing Out the Benefits

It is at the £300,000 profit figure that the small profits rate becomes a small profits relief. Phasing out of the benefit of the 20% rate arises when the profits exceed £300,000 but not £1.5 million. The corporation tax due at the full rate of 24% is calculated and then reduced

---

[60] Former TA 1988, s 342.
[61] Former TA 1988, s 342A.
[62] CTA 2010, s 24(2)(a), ex TA 1988, s 13(3), amended by FA 1994, s 86(2).
[63] This was not the formal position; it was just that the two rates moved together.
[64] FA 2002, s 31, FA 2007, s 3, FA 2008, s 7.
[65] CTA 2010, s 18, ex TA 1988, s 13.
[66] However, a non-resident company may be an associated company (see below at §2.5.4).
[67] Case C-330/91 *R v IRC, ex parte Commerzbank AG* [1993] STC 605.

by a sum determined by a complex formula. The reduction declines until the figure reaches £1.5 million, at which point it vanishes, providing a smooth graduation of liability from the lower rate to the full rate of corporation tax. This gives a marginal tax rate higher than the full rate (25% for 2012). The figures of £300,000 and £1.5 million[68] are not index-linked and were last increased in 1994.[69]

The deduction is calculated[70] by subtracting the 'augmented profits' of the company, A, from the upper limit qualifying for relief, U (£1.5 million), then multiplying that sum by a fraction the denominator of which is A again but the numerator of which is N, the amount of taxable total profits,[71] and then multiplying the resulting figure by another fraction, fixed by Parliament—for 2012, 1/100.[72] Taxable total profits (N) are as determined under CTA 2010, section 4, ie both income and capital gains. Augmented profits (A) are the total taxable profits plus franked investment income other than franked investment income from a group company.[73]

Example

For the financial year 2012, Acme Ltd has trading income of £372,000 and capital gains of £28,000. Normal corporation tax at 24% would be £96,000 (24% of £400,000). Both A and N are £400,000. The reduction is: 1/100ths of (£1.5m – £400,000), or £11,000, making corporation tax of £85,000.

If the accountancy period straddles the end of the financial year and rates change, a new period is treated as starting on the first day of the New Year. The new rates and bands apply only to the profits (appropriately calculated) of the New Year.[74] The limits of £300,000 and £1.5 million are proportionately reduced (by days) for periods of less than 12 months.[75]

2.5.4 Associated Companies and Lower Rate

But for express provision, it would be easy to exploit the relief by dividing a business between many companies. It is therefore provided that when the company has one or more associated companies in the accounting period, the figures of £300,000 and £1.5 million shall be divided by the total number of companies which are associated with each other.[76] This technique of crude division by the number of companies, rather than division according to the size of profits, has the effect that two associated companies, each with a profit of

---

[68] The 'lower limit' and 'upper limit', respectively: CTA 2009, s 24.

[69] FA 1994, s 86(2), amending TA 1988, s 13(3); when the company's accounting period straddles the financial year, apportionments must be made.

[70] CTA 2010, s 19, ex TA 1988, s 13(2).

[71] TA 1988 formerly used the term 'basic profits', which was defined in TA 1988, s 13(8); previously, the relief applied only to 'income'. Capital gains were not included for periods ending before 17 March 1987.

[72] FA 2011, s 6(2)(a), modified by FA 2012.

[73] CTA 2010, s 32, ex TA 1988, ss 13(7)–(8AB) and 13ZA. Rules excluding franked investment income from a 51% subsidiary rewritten by FA 2001, s 86 to take account of the need to abolish UK residence as the basis of entitlement to the exception (§2.9.2).

[74] This is a consequence of the rates and fraction being fixed separately for each financial year.

[75] CTA 2010, s 24(4), ex TA 1988, s 13(6).

[76] CTA 2010, s 24(3), ex TA 1988, s 13(3). On associated status generally, see above at §2.3. However, the Revenue treat only a husband, wife or minor child as a relative for the purpose of small companies' rate (now small profits rate); see ESC C9.

£300,000, will together pay less tax than if one had profits of £599,000 and the other had profits of £1,000.[77] It arises, however, because company A may be associated with companies B and C, without B being associated with C. For this purpose, non-resident companies under common control are treated as 'associated companies', even if the non-resident company has no liability to UK tax.

The lower and upper limits for relief are reduced on account of associated companies even though the other company was associated for only part of the accounting period or it was not resident. However, it will be disregarded if it was not carrying on any trade or business at any time during the period of association or the accounting period, whichever is the shorter.[78] In one case it was held that a company which simply had money at a bank was not carrying on a business and therefore did not reduce the limits for small profits relief;[79] the same result was reached where the company simply held a particular property in France.[80]

Particular problems may arise where a person with substantial interests in one company joins in a new venture under the EIS (see below at §22.5). If the two companies are associated, the limits for the relief must be divided between the two companies, something the other members of the new venture may not have expected.

2.5.5 Ring Fence Trades—Supplementary Charge

There is a supplementary levy of 32% on certain profits from oil and gas activities in the UK and its related Continental Shelf.[81] The definition of profits is taken from corporation tax but with exclusion for financing costs. Very carefully, the legislation states that this is a sum charged on the company as if it were corporation tax, and so is not corporation tax itself. The company may claim enhanced capital allowances and use them against profits for general corporation tax liability as well as the supplementary charge.[82]

2.6 Administration

2.6.1 Quarterly Instalments in Advance

The UK has a system of payment of corporation tax in instalments.[83] The regime applies to tax due in respect of profits of companies, including sums in respect of loans to participators (taxable under CTA 2010, section 455, ex TA 1988, section 419) and the controlled foreign companies legislation.[84] The system was phased in just as ACT payments ceased. Most companies which formerly paid ACT on a quarterly basis will now instead pay

---

[77] *Hallamshire Estates Ltd v Walford* [2004] STC (SCD) 330.

[78] CTA 2010, s 25(3), ex TA 1988, s 13(4); *Land Management Ltd v Fox* [2002] STC (SCD) 151. On Revenue practice in relation to holding companies, see Statement of Practice SP 5/94.

[79] *O'Neill and Brennan Construction Ltd v Jowitt* [1998] STC 482.

[80] *John M Harris (Design) Ltd v Lee* [1997] STC (SCD) 249.

[81] CTA 2010, Pt 8, Ch 6, s 330, ex TA 1988, s 501A added by FA 2002, s 91.

[82] FA 2002, s 63 and Sch 21.

[83] Corporation Tax (Instalment Payments) Regulations 1998 (SI 1998/3175), (hereafter 'IP Regs'), made under TMA 1970, s 59E, added by FA 1998, s 30. See also <http://www.hmrc.gov.uk/ct/managing/pay-repay/instalment.htm>.

[84] IP Regs, reg 2(3).

corporation tax by instalments, also on a quarterly basis. The key difference is that payments must be made under the new system regardless of whether there has been a qualifying distribution.

Instalment payments are due electronically and only from 'large' companies. A company is large if its profits exceed the upper limit for small profits relief (£1.5 million).[85] A *de minimis* exception applies if the total corporation tax liability for the accounting period does not exceed £10,000.[86] To protect growing companies, a company is not large if its profits did not exceed £1.5 million last year and do not exceed £10 million this year.[87] Groups of companies may pay on a group-wide basis.[88] The Regulations also contain rules on the surrender of excessive instalment payments within groups.[89]

Tax is due in four instalments, the first instalment being due six months and 13 days after the start of the accounting period, and the last three months and 13 days after the end of that period;[90] the gap between instalments must not exceed three months.[91] For a 12-month accounting period this makes the payments fall 13 days into months 7, 10, 13 and 16. In a nine-month period the sums would fall due 13 days into months 7, 10 and 13. The Regulations provide for the apportionment of profits to the different periods.[92] Underpayments attract an interest charge;[93] deliberate or reckless underpayments attract a penalty of twice the interest charge.[94]

If a company has overestimated its potential liability to corporation tax, it may simply pay less in a later quarter, with consequent risks of an interest charge.[95] These rules are different from the general corporation tax interest provisions; they provide that interest in respect of an underpayment, called 'debit interest' by the Revenue, is to be paid at the 'reference rate' plus 1%,[96] which is lower than the normal interest rate of 2.5% over that rate.[97] If, however, the company has paid more than it should, and this is due to a change in the circumstances of the company since the payments were made, it may seek a repayment from the Revenue[98]—with interest.[99] The rules also differ from normal rules in allowing a company that has paid excessive instalments to make a repayment claim. This is known as 'credit interest' and is based on the reference rate minus 0.25%,[100] in contrast to the normal repayment supplement rate of the reference rate minus 1%.[101] Interest may also be paid if the company has not been a large company in the accounting period concerned.[102]

---

[85] IP Regs, reg 3(1); see also reg 3(4) and (5).

[86] IP Regs, reg 3(2).

[87] IP Regs, reg 3(3); on meaning of last year for new companies, see reg 3(6).

[88] Arrangements are made under FA 1998, s 36; for details, see *Inland Revenue Guide to Self Assessment* (1999), ch 13.

[89] IP Regs, reg 9.

[90] IP Regs, reg 5(3).

[91] IP Regs, reg 5(3).

[92] IP Regs, reg 5(5)–(9).

[93] IP Regs, reg 7.

[94] IP Regs, reg 13.

[95] IP Regs, reg 7.

[96] Taxes (Interest Rates) Regulations 1989 (SI 1989/1297), reg 3ZA.

[97] *Ibid*, reg 3ZB.

[98] IP Regs, reg 6.

[99] IP Regs, reg 8.

[100] Taxes (Interest Rates) Regulations 1989, reg 3BA.

[101] *Ibid*, regs 3B and 3BB.

[102] IP Regs, reg 8(1)(b).

This inflexible obligation is grossly unjust to companies. Many factors can make an honest profit estimate completely wrong, eg a shift in the exchange rate. Moreover, it may cause distortions; thus, a company considering a major disposal of a capital asset in month 12 may be well advised to wait until month 1 of the next year. It seems odd that the company cannot rely on the previous year's figures, as the Revenue happily insist upon under the self-assessment regime for individuals.

For current and historical interest rates, see <http://www.hmrc.gov.uk/rates/interest-ctsa.htm>.

2.6.2 *Self-assessment*

Corporation tax has had a full self-assessment system since 1998.[103] Responsibility for making the assessment rests on the company.[104] The figures in the return are conclusive[105] until amended, whether by the company[106] or by the Revenue.[107] The Revenue may determine the amount of tax payable if the company fails to file a return at all.[108] Where claims are made they must be quantified.[109] Only since 2004 has there been an obligation on a company coming within the scope of corporation tax, whether for the first time or after a dormant period, to notify the Revenue.[110] The company must include any sums due under CTA 2010, section 455 (loans to participators: see below at §10.4) and the controlled foreign company legislation (see chapter seventeen below).[111] The company must also take account of various anti-avoidance rules; other rules require a Revenue notice before the assessed company must take account of them.[112]

Interest paid in respect of late tax is not deductible;[113] the system also provides for credit interest in respect of corporation tax paid early (such interest received by the company being taxable).[114] Like the income tax self-assessment regime, the corporation tax system is based on 'process now—check later'; once the enquiry window of 12 months has passed, the corporation tax return becomes final.[115]

Corporation tax self-assessment is not the same as income tax self-assessment in several ways. Most noticeably, at least for authors and advisers, the legislation on corporation tax self-assessment is laid out in coherent form and modern language (in FA 1998, Schedule 18) and not scattered around that jigsaw known as TMA 1970 (as amended *ad infinitum*).

---

[103] FA 1994, s 199; Finance Act 1999, Section 199 (Appointed Day) Order 1998 (SI 1998/3173), [1991] *Simon's Weekly Tax Intelligence* 97. The Revenue have published a useful *Guide to Corporation Tax Self-Assessment* (hereafter '*CTSA Guide*').

[104] FA 1998, Sch 18, para 7.

[105] FA 1998, Sch 18, para 88.

[106] For example under FA 1998, Sch 18, para 15 or 30.

[107] For example under FA 1998, Sch 18, paras 16 (correction of obvious errors) or 34.

[108] FA 1998, Sch 18, para 36; on which see *CTSA Guide*, ch 9.

[109] FA 1998, Sch 18, paras 54 *et seq*.

[110] FA 2004, s 55.

[111] FA 1998, Sch 18, para 1.

[112] Eg FA 2005, s 88.

[113] TMA 1970, s 90, as amended by FA 1998, s 33.

[114] TA 1988, s 826, as amended by FA 1998, s 34.

[115] On which, see *CTSA Guide*, ch 6.

2.6.3 Liability for Another Company's Tax

A company is usually liable only for its own corporation tax.[116] In 1993 schemes appeared under which companies were sold in circumstances intended to ensure that their corporation tax liabilities arising prior to the date of sale could not be collected.[117] Dicta had already suggested a distinction between tax avoidance and a scheme to prevent the recovery of tax,[118] making the latter a situation for possible penalties. In any event, new rules were introduced by FA 1994 and strengthened in 1997.[119] There are also rules for collecting tax from other group companies.[120]

2.6.4 Senior Accounting Officer Responsibilities

FA 2009, section 93 and Schedule 46 imposed new duties on senior accounting officers (SAOs) of qualifying companies to take reasonable steps to ensure that the company establishes and maintains appropriate tax and accounting arrangements in relation to relevant tax liabilities.[121] The SAO must also take reasonable steps to monitor the accounting arrangements and identify any respect in which the arrangements are not appropriate tax accounting arrangements.[122] A company qualifies if its balance sheet exceeds £2 billion or its turnover exceeds £200 million.[123] FA 2009, section 94 authorises HMRC to publish details of deliberate tax defaulters where the potential lost revenue and penalties exceed £25,000.

2.7   Incorporation of a Business

The consequences of incorporation are varied.[124] The first and obvious difference from being taxed as an unincorporated business is that the profits of the business or other income source, including capital gains, will now be subject to corporation tax instead of income tax, National Insurance Contributions (NICs) and CGT. In this connection, the widening differences between the tax bases are significant. The rate of corporation tax will depend on the level of profits. Directors' remuneration is deductible,[125] so that although

---

[116] There are certain exceptions, eg where someone other than the company realising the gain may be accountable: see TCGA 1992, ss 189 (shareholder following capital distribution of gain), 190 (recovery from another group member), 139(7), (8) (tax on transfer of assets following reconstruction or amalgamation), 179(11), (13) (crystallisation of deferred tax on intra-group transfer of assets, and 137(4) (share-for-share exchange outside protection of bona fide commercial reasons zone); and FA 1990, s 86(8) (unpaid tax from company to which loss transferred by group relief).

[117] See Inland Revenue Press Release, 30 November 1993, [1993] *Simon's Tax Intelligence* 1533.

[118] *Roome v Edwards* [1979] STC 546, 561-65.

[119] CTA 2010, Pt 14, Ch 6 and particularly s 710, ex TA 1988, s 767A, 767B, added by FA 1994, s 135; see also TA 1988, ss 767AA, 767C, added by FA 1998, ss 114–116. For Revenue practice on 1993 rules, see Revenue Interpretation RI 90.

[120] CTA 2010, Pt 22, Ch 7, ex FA 2000, Sch 28 (non-resident group members).

[121] FA 2009, Sch 46, paras 1–15.

[122] For details on the information that must be provided by certificate by the SAO, see FA 2009, Sch 46, para 2.

[123] FA 2009, Sch 46, para 15.

[124] A good starting points is Rayney in *Tolley's Tax Planning*, ch 28.

[125] Subject to ITTOIA 2005, s 34/CTA 2009, s 54, which may prevent the deduction of such part of it as is unreasonable.

the company is not entitled to personal allowances, enough may be paid out to ensure that the personal allowances of the incorporators and their bands of income liable to basic rate income tax are all used up, or to pay out the much smaller sum needed to ensure that the employee had a full year of contributions for National Insurance.

Assuming that the company's profit was substantial and that the director's marginal rate of income tax exceeds the corporation tax rate of 24%, the company appears to be a tax shelter. This seems to be a significant advantage over an unincorporated business if the business is looking to internal sources of finance for growth, and the advantage become more marked as the general rate of corporation tax has dropped from its 1982 rate of 52%. However, taxpayers will, presumably, eventually wish to get their capital out of the company, which means selling shares and so incurring CGT, or taking dividends, which means paying income tax (a dividend is a dividend even if it is a capital dividend) though not NICs. Today the use of the rules relating to demergers or to the purchase by the company of its own shares for its own trading purposes is a way of avoiding dividend treatment.

From the directors' point of view there are advantages and disadvantages to incorporating a business. First, directors become liable to tax under ITEPA 2003 and so to the PAYE system and, of ever greater importance, to NICs payable by both the directors and the company. Secondly, they become liable to the stringent rules surrounding benefits derived from the company (see *Revenue Law*, chapter sixteen). Against this, they may find that the benefit rules are not as strict as might appear at first sight. Further, they will be substantially better off as far as pensions are concerned. As directors, they may have either a defined benefit plan or a defined contribution scheme; as self-employed persons, they fund their own pension and only under a defined contribution scheme. Unless the taxpayers start young and have taken maximum advantage of this entitlement throughout their working lives, they cannot hope to build up so large a fund. Income distributed as salary to the employee/director is fully deductible by the company; income distributed as dividend is not deductible.

Since the company is a separate legal person, its trading or capital losses cannot be set off against the shareholder's income or gains—or vice versa. Other relevant issues are that:

(1) gains made by the company are, in effect, subject to double taxation (see below at §4.3);
(2) a company may need Treasury consent for some of its international transactions (see below at §13.7); and
(3) ITA 2007, section 684 (ex TA 1988, section 703—below §12.5) hangs over the problem of extracting reserves from the company otherwise than by dividend or straightforward liquidation.

Once a company is established, it is possible to use the annual £3,000 exemption for inheritance tax (IHT) to make gifts of shares to trusts for children or others. More generally, it is easier to pass a share in an incorporated business to a child than a portion of an unincorporated business.[126] The present exemption of many business assets and shareholdings from IHT mitigates this difference to some extent (see *Revenue Law* §54.2). On the other hand, individuals exporting a business to a non-resident may run into ITA 2007, section 720 (ex TA 1988, section 739—see below at §15.6) and, as self-employed persons, they must pay Class 2 and Class 4 NICs.

---

[126] On passing on the family business, see Maas, in *Tolley's Tax Planning*, ch 45.

When the business is incorporated, the shift from ITTOIA 2005, Part 2 income tax to corporation tax is made by discontinuing the trade for income tax with an assessment for a long period, perhaps with only a little overlap profit relief. However, loss relief may be preserved and rollover relief is granted for CGT provided all the business assets are transferred to the company in return for shares. All these issues apply whether the business being incorporated is run by a sole person or by a partnership.[127]

The above list has concentrated on the tax aspects of incorporation. However, the non-tax aspects are of great importance and include:

(1)   the costs of running the paperwork of a company;
(2)   the fact of limited liability, although this is likely to be qualified by the bank's insistence on collateral personal liability at least in the early stages; and
(3)   the significant change in status (where more than one person is involved) when moving from equal partner to minority shareholder.

Further, company law requirements seem to be becoming more stringent, and some professions discourage incorporation.

This list has concentrated on problems—because they need to be considered. However, there are also advantages in being able to raise finance through equity as well as debt, and through devices such as a floating charge which an individual cannot create.[128]

2.8   Disincorporation

In 1987 the Inland Revenue and the Department of Trade and Industry produced a discussion document on the problems of removing tax obstacles to disincorporation. They decided that any new legislation would have to be aimed at small, private trading companies, because it was essentially these companies (small, owner-managed, essentially incorporated sole traders or partnerships, with a relatively narrow range of secured and unsecured creditors) that would be interested. Investment companies, groups of companies and non-resident companies would all be excluded. The legislation would have to contain protections to ensure that there was continuity of ownership, trade and management in the new unincorporated form.

Among the problems to be resolved was the treatment of trading losses. To refuse to allow these to be carried forward would be to leave an obstacle, yet to give a rollover on analogy with TCGA 1992, section 162 would ignore the fact that the losses would be reflected in the value of the shares in the company and would make the legislation complicated. To provide relief would be all the more complex when, as in 1987, there were substantial differences in tax rates between the incorporated and the unincorporated sectors. Some elements in determining the loss might have to be removed (eg directors' remuneration). There would also be problems identifying the particular entities to which the losses should be attributed after disincorporation, ie whether they should be set against the business itself and, if the

---

[127]   On LLPs see below §2.13.
[128]   On tax considerations in raising finance generally, see Ball, *Tolley's Tax Planning*, ch 9. For a comparison of companies with partnerships, see *Simon's Direct Tax Service*, para D2.114.

business was run by a partnership, whether losses should be apportioned by reference to profit-sharing ratios or equity interests. Following the analogy of section 162, the document suggested that losses should be allocated to the shareholders in the company, to be set against later income derived from the business.

Other relatively minor difficulties highlighted in the 1987 report included the correct treatment of post-cessation trading income and expenditure of the company, the valuation of trading stock, provision for the continuation of capital allowances and the treatment of bad debts that had been allowed as deductions by the company but which were subsequently paid to the new owners. The report concluded it might be necessary to remove the application of the golden handshake provisions but to retain the relief for interest paid on loans to acquire shares in the enterprise while it was incorporated, provided the shareholder retained an interest in the business. There would also have to be legislation to prevent taxpayers disincorporating and then reincorporating simply for the tax advantages. Special rules would be needed for IHT, eg to treat the old and new ownership as one for the purpose of business relief.

Another significant problem raised in the 1987 report was the correct treatment of capital gains. This stems from the double charge to tax on gains in the corporate sector as contrasted with the single layer for the unincorporated sector. One instance in which the dual charge arises is on liquidation. A disposal occurs at corporate level and a deemed disposal to the shareholders under TCGA 1992, section 122. Parity of reasoning suggests a similar dual charge on disincorporation, and yet this would deter the process. To provide relief, the document discusses, but finds fault with, the idea of eliminating one of the two tiers of charge.

This area raises deep questions about the nature of capital gains taxation, particularly in the corporate sector:

(1)   The value of the shares will not generally equate with that of the company's assets but will take into account the general prospects of the company, whether good or bad. Moreover, to the extent that the shares are related to the company's assets, it must be remembered that not all those assets are relevant to capital gains taxation. Thus, cash, whether from trading profits, a new issue of share capital or the disposal of a capital asset, is not relevant to CGT and, in the case of the first or the third sources, will already have been taxed.
(2)   To grant exemption would make disincorporation more advantageous than other forms of corporate reorganisation which simply granted deferrals.
(3)   The situation in which the disincorporated company is treated more favourably than the continuing company must be avoided.

These considerations led to the idea that the correct solution would be deferral at both shareholder and asset level, and various practical solutions were suggested. Thus, the assets would be transferred on a no gain, no loss basis—but only for trade assets. Problems on the deferral of the share tier charge are concerned principally with the question of what events should trigger the charge. An alternative idea, put forward by the Institute of Taxation, is that the share tier should be exempt, but that shareholders who receive a share of undistributed income accruing with the previous six years should pay income tax on those receipts. The assimilation of tax rates on income and capital gains has done much to reduce the importance of the applicable tax rate, but not the figure to which the rate is to be applied. The Institute also suggested that investors not participating in the business after disincorporation should be taxed under the present system.

In February 2012, the OTS sought to revive interest in this issue, releasing a report recommending the introduction of disincorporation relief for 'micro' companies, which would allow the business of a trading company (including goodwill and possibly property, plant and machinery used wholly in the trade) to pass to an unincorporated business without attracting an immediate tax charge. On current law, see *Tolley's Tax Planning*, chapter 5.

2.9   Non-resident Companies

The rules on the taxation of non-resident companies were modernised in 2003. Under the present rules, such companies are subject to corporation tax only if they are carrying on a trade through a permanent establishment (PE) in the UK and are taxable on all the chargeable profits attributable to the PE.[129] Chargeable profits are then defined[130] as:

(1)   trading income arising directly or indirectly through or from the PE;
(2)   income from property or rights held by the PE, eg royalties on a patent held by the branch and profits on the realisation of assets held on a short-term basis and funded by an insurance company's surpluses;[131] and
(3)   chargeable gains arising—
    (a)   as a result of assets being used in or for the purposes of the trade carried on by the company through the PE, or
    (b)   as a result of assets being used or held for the purpose of the PE, or
    (c)   as a result of assets being acquired for use by or for the purposes of the PE.

Gains under head (3) must also come with TCGA 1992, section 10B, another new provision unique to non-resident companies with a PE. That makes it clear that it applies only to companies carrying on a trade in the UK at the relevant time through the PE.[132]

Example

X Ltd, a non-resident company, carries on a trade in the UK through a PE. The PE has UK trading income of £1,750,000 and sells UK property from its trade, realising a capital gain of £60,000; it also sells overseas property realising a gain of £75,000. UK corporation tax is due on the first two items, but not on the third. This makes chargeable profits of £1,810,000, on which corporation tax is due at 24% (£434,400).

The purpose behind the 2003 changes was to treat the UK branch of a foreign company as if it were a subsidiary with its own capital and to talk in terms of 'permanent

---

[129]   CTA 2009, s 5, ex TA 1988, ss 11 and 11AA; on mode of assessment, see TMA 1970, ss 85, 78, 79. On place of trade, see below at §16.2; for an example, see *IRC v Brackett* [1986] STC 521, (1986) 60 TC 134.
[130]   CTA 2009, s 19(3), ex TA 1988, s 11(2).
[131]   *General Reinsurance Co Ltd v Tomlinson* (1970) 48 TC 81.
[132]   TCGA 1992, s 10B(3) (see below at §18.1).

establishment', not 'branch or agency' as is still done for income tax.[133] The concept of the PE is well known in double tax treaties and is considered below at §20.6.2.[134] The main assumption on which the income arising under these rules is to be calculated is that the PE is a distinct and separate enterprise engaged in the same or similar activities under the same or similar conditions and dealing wholly independently with the non-resident company.[135] The PE is assumed to have the same credit rating as the non-resident company. It is also assumed to have the amount of equity or loan capital that might reasonably be expected under the basic assumption. There is an express provision on allowable expenses, ie expenses of a kind which would be allowable under UK corporation tax. These are deductible if incurred for the purpose of the PE, including executive and general administration expenses incurred for that purpose, whether incurred in the UK or elsewhere.[136]

Further rules include an assumption of arm's length dealing for transactions between the PE and any other part of the non-resident company, and prohibitions on deductions for payments in respect of intangible assets and for interest and other financing costs.[137] Where goods or services are provided by the non-resident company to the PE, an arm's length rules applies if the goods or services are of the kind which the company provides to third parties as part of its business; otherwise the matter is dealt with as an expense incurred by the non-resident company for the purposes of the PE.[138] There are also rules for banks.[139]

Income outside CTA 2009, section 19 and accruing to a non-resident company is charged not to corporation tax but to income tax. There is a limit to liability in respect of certain types of investment and other income; this mirrors the income tax provision discussed in §16.6.3. Lastly, there is a general regulation-making power in section 156 to enable the Treasury to adapt these various changes to overseas life insurance companies.

2.9.1 Change of Status

If a resident company ceases to be resident or ceases to be liable to UK tax, there is a deemed disposal of its capital assets.[140] However, there is no deemed disposal of assets which remain in a PE in the UK and so within the charge to corporation tax.[141] If the company fails to pay the tax within six months from its becoming payable, the tax may be collected from others.[142] Those 'others' are any other group company and the controlling director of that or any other group company at the relevant time.[143] Schemes to avoid this charge by leaving the assets within a branch in the UK at the time of migration but then leasing them to another UK resident company were stopped by the creation of another

---

[133] Inland Revenue Budget Note 25/02, [2002] *Simon's Tax Intelligence* 586. The change was expected to increase the profits taxed in the UK, and to affect foreign banks and insurance companies in particular.

[134] See Arnold, de Sasseville and Zolt (2002) 50 *Canadian Tax J* 1979–2024.

[135] CTA 2009, s 21, ex TA 1988, s 11AA(2).

[136] CTA 2009, s 29, ex TA 1988, s 11AA(4), Sch A1, para 3.

[137] CTA 2009, ss 22, 31, 32, ex TA 1988, Sch A1, added by FA 2003, Sch 25, paras 2–5.

[138] CTA 2009, s 23, ex TA 1988, Sch A1, para 6.

[139] CTA 2009, ss 25–28, ex TA 1988, Sch A1, paras 7–10.

[140] TCGA 1992, s 185; see also below at §13.6.

[141] TCGA 1992, s 185(4).

[142] TCGA 1992, s 191(1).

[143] TCGA 1992, s 191(4)–(7). On special capital gains rules for dual resident investment companies, see below at §13.6.4.

deemed disposal.[144] Where the change of residence arises from the 1994 statutory rule for companies treated as not resident for Treaty purposes, there is no immediate charge.[145] Where the change of residence is to another EU Member State, the provision may violate the fundamental freedoms.[146]

2.9.2 FA 2000: From Residence to Chargeability

Many UK tax rules used to apply only to companies resident in the UK.[147] These rules came under review following the decisions of the ECJ, particularly *ICI v Colmer*.[148] As a result, FA 2000 made major changes to the status of non-resident companies which are subject to UK tax by reason of the rules set out above. These changes are mentioned at various parts of the book, but some may be noted now:

(1)   A non-resident may claim capital allowances (FA 2000, section 74).
(2)   A non-resident company can be a member of a group of companies for purposes of group relief and chargeable gains deferrals (FA 2000, sections 96 and 101; see chapters seven and eight below).
(3)   The UK branch of a non-resident company may claim double tax relief (see §19.4.1 below).

In all these instances the non-resident company is relevant because it is chargeable to UK tax and the rules are recast in those terms. Yet the list is not comprehensive; among provisions remaining unaffected are CTA 2010, sections 18 (small profits rate) and 1049 (stock dividends).

2.10   Beneficial Ownership[149]

Many corporation tax rules refer to shares being in a person's beneficial ownership.[150] These rules may contain further detailed rules of their own, but there is a background of general case law concerning two issues:

(1)   what rights A must have to qualify to be beneficial owner; and
(2)   the effect on those rights of an impending or possible transfer of those shares by A to someone else.

On (1), A is taken as owning shares beneficially if entitled to the dividends. The fact that A is entitled only to the dividends—and not entitled to any share of the assets on a winding

---

[144] Now in TCGA 1992, s 25(3); see below at §18.1.
[145] FA 1994, s 250(3)–(6); see below at §13.6.
[146] See eg Case C-371/10 *National Grid Indus BV v Inspecteur van de Belastingdienst Rijnmond/kantoor Rotterdam* [2012] STC 114 and Case C-9/02 *Lasteyrie du Saillant v Ministere de l'Economie* [2005] STC 1722.
[147] See eg the list in Shipwright and Keeling [1995] EL Rev 580, 596–97.
[148] Case C-264/96 [1998] All ER (EC) 585; [1998] STC 874.
[149] See Rowland [1997] BTR 178.
[150] Eg CTA 2010, s 1154(6), ex TA 1988, s 838(3), to which TCGA 1992, s 170 refers.

up—is irrelevant. On (2), the general approach of the courts has been that a company owns shares beneficially if it is free to dispose of them as it wishes; it is irrelevant that the shares may not be owned for a long period.[151] If a contract for sale has been made, beneficial ownership may at some point shift to the purchaser, but this depends on the contract.[152] It is possible that the ownership may leave the vendor before it reaches the purchaser, ie be in suspense, but this is not favoured these days. So A was treated as still being the beneficial owner of the shares even though B had an option to acquire them, and the terms of the option were such that B was likely to exercise it.[153]

The postponement rules in TCGA 1992, section 171 do not apply to transfers between subsidiary and a parent in liquidation since, once liquidation of the parent has begun, the shares in the subsidiary are not held by the parent beneficially but on trust for its own members.[154] The effect of a voluntary winding up is less clear.[155]

The meaning of the term 'beneficial ownership' also arises in the international context, where it may carry a different sense.[156] There is no reason why the trustee, whether of a pension fund or of a private trust, should not be treated as having beneficial ownership in the international context.

2.11 Subsidiaries, Control, etc

Subsidiary status is a matter of frequent concern in tax law. Section 1154 of CTA 2010 (ex TA 1988, section 838) defines subsidiaries in terms of ownership of ordinary share capital,[157] and refers to 51%, 75% and 90% subsidiaries. The rules allow for direct and indirect holdings to be taken into account and provide calculation rules. If A owns shares in C, A's holding is direct; if A holds share in B which holds shares in C, A's holding in B is direct, but A's holding in C is indirect.

The tax legislation has several tests for determining whether one company has control over another and whether both are under the control of a third party.

The simplest test is that set out in CTA 2010, section 1124 (ex TA 1988, section 840), which refers to the power of a person (P) (ie whether or not a company)

> to secure (a) by means of the holding of shares or the possession of voting power in relation to that or any other body corporate; or (b) as a result of any powers conferred by the articles of association or other document regulating that or any other body corporate, that the affairs of [the] company ... are conducted in accordance with P's wishes.

---

[151] *Burman v Hedges and Butler* [1979] STC 136, (1979) 52 TC 501.

[152] *Wood Preservation Ltd v Prior* (1969) 45 TC 112.

[153] *J Sainsbury plc v O'Connor* [1991] STC 318, (1991) 64 TC 208 CA.

[154] *Ayerst v C & K (Construction) Ltd* [1975] STC 345, [1975] 2 All ER 537, (1975) 50 TC 651. The House of Lords decided only that the company ceased to be beneficial owner of its assets The Court of Appeal had held that the ownership was in suspense; [1975] STC 1, [1975] 1 All ER 162.

[155] *Wadsworth Morton Ltd v Jenkinson* [1966] 3 All ER 702, (1966) 43 TC 479.

[156] See OECD discussion draft 'Clarification of the Meaning of "Beneficial Owner" in the OECD Model Tax Convention' (2011) at <http://www.oecd.org/dataoecd/49/35/47643872.pdf> and also Collier [2011] BTR 684.

[157] Defined in CTA 2010, s 1118, ex TA 1988, s 832(1); founder members' deposits with a mutual society were not such capital in *South Shore Mutual Insurance v Blair* [1999] STC (SCD) 296.

In relation to a partnership, it means the right to a share of more than one half of the assets, or of more than one half of the income, of the partnership. Thus, CTA 2010, section 1124 is satisfied by 51% control. On whether control means (a) the power to carry a resolution at a general meeting, including the power to elect the board of directors; or (b) more narrowly, the power to run the company's affairs, that is power at the director level, the point being that the general meeting cannot usually tell its directors how to manage the day-to-day affairs of the company, see *Steele v EVC International NV*[158] (above at §2.3). A second test is that used in CTA 2010, section 450 (ex TA 1988, section 416) to determine whether a company is a close company. This is a wider test, in that it looks at more factors than CTA 2010, section 1124, but still requires a 51% result (see further below at §10.2.2).

Individual rules may impose further tests and different percentages for their own purposes, especially where groups are concerned. Thus, group relief for losses[159] uses the concept of a 75% subsidiary and imposes further tests by asking whether: (a) the parent company is beneficially entitled to not less than 75% of any profits available for distribution to equity holders of the subsidiary company; and (b) the parent company would be beneficially entitled to not less than 75% of any assets of the subsidiary company available for distribution to its equity holders on a winding up. The question whether these percentages are satisfied by equity holders is then subject to further conditions set out in CTA 2010, sections 158 *et seq* (ex TA 1988, Schedule 18).

2.12   Reorganisations and Acquisitions[160]

2.12.1 Introduction

In this short section we touch on some practical issues, the details of which will arise later in these chapters, especially those on groups. The purpose of this section is to alert the reader to the significance of some of the things which follow and so to make them more interesting—or, at least, less intimidating; this section provides cross-references to the text rather than repeating what will be said later on.

The tax effects of the incorporation—and disincorporation—of a business have been outlined above at §§2.7 and 2.8, but many of the same issues arise when one is looking at one company buying a business. Thus, how does one decide upon ownership of the new business; what does one do about claims for trading losses, capital allowances, unsold trading stock, capital gains and losses in respect of the business being taken over? In so far as the new business is going to be fitted into a group structure alongside the existing businesses, how will the rules discussed in this and the preceding chapter affect things? In so far as the tax system likes to avoid unnecessary dislocation, how might one take advantage of the various reliefs, especially the CGT rules about shareholdings and corporate reorganisations in TCGA 1992, sections 127 *et seq*? How far are the interests of the seller of the business

---

[158] [1996] STC 785, (1996) 69 TC 88.

[159] CTA 2010, s 151, ex TA 1988, s 413(7).

[160] For some assessments of the worth of mergers and takeovers, see papers collected in Fairburn and Kay (eds), *Mergers and Merger Policy* (OUP, 1989), Hughes and Singh (1987) 6 *Contributions to Political Economy* 73 and Singh, 'Corporate Takeovers' in *The New Palgrave Dictionary of Money and Finance* (Palgrave Macmillan, 1992).

compatible with what the buyer wants? A good but still daunting starting point is provided by the chapters in the annual *Tolley's Tax Planning*. The best account of the technical legal material is to be found in the latest edition of *Bramwell's Taxation of Companies and Company Reconstructions*.

Naturally the reconstruction of some types of company receives special attention. One important example is provided by companies with a business of leasing plant and machinery, such as that in the famous *Barclays BMBF* case.[161] The problem for the Revenue was that these contracts usually generate losses in the early years and profits later on. On a solution by CTA 2010, Part 9 (ex FA 2006, Schedule 10), see further §4.5.6 below.

2.12.2 Scenario: Questions

H Ltd, a holding company, owns a business currently held in a subsidiary, G Ltd, and X Ltd, an unconnected company, wants to buy it.

A list of some common questions:

(1) What is to be sold; assets or shares in G?
(2) When is the sale to take place? Effect on time limits for loss relief/CGT loss carry-back rules, etc.
(3) Who should make the sale? Should the business be 'hived down' by G to a separate subsidiary company (GS)?
(4) What should be the form of the consideration provided by X?
(5) How much of the consideration should be left outstanding?
(6) Should there be a pre-sale dividend by G to H to extract cash from the company?
(7) A further set of problems arises if, as is not the case here, the seller wants to have some interest in the company after the sale.

2.12.3 Hive Down

If X wants to buy an incorporated business, X may wish either to buy G Ltd or to buy a separate company (GS) to which G transfers the business. The latter is known as a hive down, ie hiving down the business to a subsidiary, which is a more precise expression than 'hiving off'.

When G transfers the business and its assets to GS, there is a change of ownership but also a 100% parent-subsidiary group relationship. Trading losses will pass to GS on the basis that there is no discontinuance and commencement assuming that the requirements of CTA 2010, sections 940A–953 (ex TA 1988, section 343) (see below at §4.5.2) are met. The trade carried on by GS must be the same as that carried on by G. The transfer does not count as a release of debt so no charge arises under CTA 2009, section 94 (ex TA 1988, section 94). Capital allowances are treated the same as trading losses—CTA 2010, section 948 (ex TA 1988, section 343(2)); this excludes any CAA 2001 rules. Assets subject to capital gains taxation pass on a 'no gain, no loss' basis, thanks to TCGA 1992, section 171 (see below at §8.2.1). However, there is now a potential extra tier of CGT.

---

[161] *Barclays Mercantile Business Finance Ltd v Mawson* [2005] STC 1 (HL); and see *Revenue Law* §5.6.

2.12.4 Pros and Cons of Assets Versus Shares in the Trading Company

The key difference lies in the differing tax treatments of assets and shares. If X takes assets there is no risk of accidentally inheriting some liability incurred by G. However, it is usual for X to buy the business and make G provide all sorts of warranties as to the tax history of the company being sold. GS will now be ignored.

2.12.4.1 Capital Allowances

There are no capital allowances for shares in G bought by X from H; however, G will, subject to conditions, continue to be able to claim the allowances for assets used in the business. If X buys the assets and not the shares, capital allowances may be available to X as a purchaser of machinery or plant to whom the machinery and plant belong or, for the industrial buildings allowance, as purchaser of the relevant interest. There may also be balancing allowances or charges for G.

2.12.4.2 Trading Losses

If X buys the assets, any trading loss will cease to be available to G (unless terminal loss relief applies). X cannot use the losses. If X buys the shares in G, G may also continue to claim the benefit of loss relief—subject to the usual conditions about changes in the conduct of the trade. There may also be problems with surplus property business losses[162] (see below at §4.5.2).

2.12.4.3 Capital Gains

If shares in G are sold by H to X, there is a disposal of those shares by H. As H is a company, we are concerned with indexation. If the assets are sold by G, after leaving H and joining X, there will be a CGT liability on G; the (net of tax) gain will be reflected in the value of the shares to be taxed again should the shares be sold—the dual CGT liability. X may therefore wish to reduce the value of shares before the sale by getting cash out of the company; hence hive downs, pre-transfer distributions, etc.

2.12.4.4 Trading Stock

Proceeds are taxable if G sells these assets pursuant to CTA 2009, section 162 (ex TA 1988, section 100(1)(a)). There is also the very important question of liability for the existing contracts made by G. If X buys only the assets, the contracts remain with G; if X buys the shares in G, X also buys the continuing contracting party. If X buys shares, G will be joining a group with X. Pre-entry capital losses are governed by TCGA 1992, section 177A and Schedule 7A (reversing *Shepherd v Lyntress*[163]) and pre-entry capital gains by TCGA 1992, section 184A *et seq* (especially section 184B), added by FA 2006 and repealing Schedule 7AA (see below at §8.2). If the company forms part of X's group, it will leave H's group so that there may be an exit charge under TCGA 1992, section 179.

---

[162] CTA 2010, ss 683–684 (ex Schedule A loss, TA 1988, s 768D)
[163] [1989] STC 617.

2.12.5 Warranties

If X buys the shares it will want to know all the tax risk inherent in G. For this reason it is customary for the buyer to ask for—and the seller to give—warranties as to the tax history of the company. The list of warranties in the standard books, eg *Tolley's Tax Planning*, provides a checklist for a revision course in corporation tax law.

2.12.6 How Will X, the Buyer, Pay for It?

If X is paying cash, it may need to borrow money; it will therefore have to observe all the loan relationship rules to ensure that interest is deductible. If X is going to issue H with shares, it may need to observe TCGA 1992, section 135. If X issues H with loan stock, H may be able to choose when to realise them and so determine its CGT liability.

2.12.6.1 Deferred Consideration

Consideration may be tied to profitability of business in the hands of new owners. Depending on the form of the consideration, there may be problems in so far as interest may be treated as a distribution under CTA 2010, sections 1000(1)F and 1015(4) (ex TA 1988, section 209(2)(e)(iii))—and so not be deductible by B—or it may be a separate asset with its own potential CGT liability thanks to *Marren v Ingles* (see *Revenue Law* §43.1.1).

2.12.6.2 Annuity—the Other *Ramsay*[164]

X may choose to pay H an annuity. The annuity is deductible as a charge on income. The downside is that X must pay tax on the whole amount received as income under ITTOIA 2005, Part 5, Chapter 7, ex Schedule D, Case III. A stream of payments may have to be analysed to see whether it is an annuity or a loan relationship (see *Revenue Law* §27.4.5).

2.12.7 International

All these problems become more interesting when one or more of the parties is resident outside the UK. Where the other country involved is a Member State of the EU, the EU dimension (see chapter twenty-one below) must be noted, especially the EU's Mergers Directive and its consequent UK legislation (see §4.3.6 below).

2.13 Limited Liability Partnerships

Limited liability partnerships (LLPs) established under the Limited Liability Partnership Act 2000 (LLPA 2000) are a new form of legal entity. An LLP is a body corporate with legal personality separate from that of its members and has unlimited capacity (as distinct from liability).[165] The tax rules in LLPA 2000 (as amended) provide that, despite having independent legal personality, the LLP is taxed on the basis that its partnership activities

---

[164] *Ramsay v IRC* (1935) 20 TC 97.
[165] LLPA 2000, ss 1–4.

are carried on by the members and not by the LLP itself; so gains and profits are taxed as accruing to the partner and will be subject to income tax and CGT, and will attract corporation tax only in the case of a corporate partner.[166]

There are also anti-avoidance rules. These were introduced at a late stage in the passage of the Finance Bill 2001, and apply to prevent pension funds and similar bodies and friendly societies, etc from claiming their normal exemptions from tax where they have interests in a property investment LLP.[167] Lastly, interest relief under ITA 2007, sections 398–399 (ex TA 1988, section 362(2)) is not available for a loan to buy an interest in an investment LLP.

2.14   European Company

The *Societas Europeae* (SE) or European Company was created by EC Council Regulation in 2001. It receives special tax treatment as part of the revised Mergers Directive, and as a result UK tax rules are modified so that a UK company's decision to merge with an SE in another Member State obtains tax neutral treatment in the same way that a company merging with a company in another Member State gets such treatment under the existing Mergers Directive-based rules. They are rules of last resort and so apply only when the ordinary rules do not.

The first set of rules concern capital gains treatment of assets transferred on the merger. TCGA 1992, section 140E applies to the assets remaining within UK tax charge, while section 140F applies if they do not. Section 140G applies to securities issued on merger. None of these rules applies if section 139 does (see below §§4.3.4–4.3.5). Similar rules are provided for the separate code applicable to intangible fixed assets.[168] Similar treatment for loan relationships is provided in CTA 2009, Part 5, Chapter 14, and for derivatives in CTA 2009, section 683. Capital allowance treatment is provided by CAA 2001, section 561A. Continuity of group identity is provided by TCGA 1992, section 171(10A) and, for intangible fixed assets, by CTA 2009, section 770. Further rules provide for held-over gains on such a merger.[169] Lastly, there are special rules on corporate residence (see §13.6). Where the SE transfers its registered office to the UK, CTA 2009, section 16 makes it resident in the UK, and a later move of its registered office out of the UK will not alter that resident status. The rule in CTA 2009, section 18, which says that a company treated as not resident in the UK for tax treaty purposes is non-resident for all UK tax purposes, applies to an SE.

---

[166] CTA 2009, s 1273 (ex TA 1988, s 118ZA) and TCGA 1992, s 59A added by FA 2001, s 75.

[167] ITA 2007, s 399(6), 1004(1), (2), and CTA 2010, s 1135(1), (2), ex TA 1988, s 842B. The restrictions were contained in TA 1988, s 659D. These rules were introduced by FA 2001, Sch 25.

[168] CTA 2009, s 821, ex FA 2002, Sch 29, paras 85A and 87A: see §5.3.

[169] Including TCGA 1992, ss 179(1B) and (1C) (see §8.6) and 154(2A) and (2B). F(No 2)A 2005, s 65 dealt with whether the merger is a relevant event for calculating losses on pre-entry assets for Sch 7A (see §8.2.3).

3

Distributions

3.1   Introduction

Income tax is charged on dividends and other distributions of a UK resident company.[1] Distributions are classified either as 'qualifying' or 'non-qualifying' distributions. Qualifying distributions carry tax credits, non-qualifying do not.[2] Distributions, whether or not qualifying, are not deductible in computing the profits of the company.[3]

While TA 1988 formerly used the expression 'Schedule F income', the rewritten rules in ITTOIA 2005, Part 4, Chapter 3 instead simply refer to 'dividend income'. In addition, while

---

[1] ITTOIA 2005, Pt 4, Ch 3, s 383. Under the schedular system set out in TA 1988, where a distribution is made by a company resident in the UK, the recipient was assessable to income tax under Sch F: TA 1988, s 20. On 'Unit Trusts and Open-ended Investment Companies', see §23.3 below. On shares in approved share investment plans, see ITTOIA 2005, ss 392–396.

[2] For the meaning of 'qualifying distribution', see CTA 2010, s 1136(1), (2), referring to distributions within s 1000(1)C or D; ex TA 1988, s 14(2).

[3] CTA 2009, s 1305, ex TA 1988, ss 6(4) and 337A(1).

TA 1988 dealt with payments by companies not resident in the UK under Schedule D, Case V, such 'foreign dividend income' is now taxed under ITTOIA 2005, Part 4, Chapter 4.[4] It is vital for the reader to understand that the income tax treatment of foreign dividend income is quite different from that of UK dividend income in terms of what receipts are taxable and how they are taxed.[5] For corporation tax purposes, on the other hand, most dividends received by a UK resident company will be exempt from corporation tax, whether paid by a UK or a non-UK resident company.[6]

Under UK company law, money may be returned to shareholders in three main ways:

(1)   dividend;
(2)   return of capital on liquidation; and
(3)   authorised reduction in capital.

Tax law mirrors company law by treating the first as giving rise to income, but the second and third as matters of capital gains. Special tax rules apply to stock dividends, where the tax system imposes tax even though no cash comes out of the company (see below at §3.4). Special rules also apply to purchases by a company of its own shares (see below at §3.5) and demergers (see below at chapter 9), where the tax system grants capital gains treatment rather than income treatment on the assumption that this will be advantageous. Distributions in respect of share capital in a winding up,[7] including surplus assets distributed, are not distributions within ITTOIA 2005, Part 4, Chapter 3, or within any other Schedule.[8] They are simply treated as the return of capital, and perhaps as giving rise to chargeable capital gains or allowable losses.[9] This is so even if the payments represent arrears of undeclared cumulative preference dividends.[10] However, where a payment is treated as a distribution for income tax, it does not matter that it is treated as capital for other purposes, eg trust law.[11]

3.1.1 ITTOIA 2005, Part 4, Chapter 3

If the distribution fell within former Schedule F it was taxed under that Schedule and was not, subject to exceptions, chargeable under any other provision of the Income Tax Acts.[12] ITTOIA 2005 has similar priority rules.[13] Where the income accrues to a person dealing in

---

[4]   In this book foreign dividend income is considered in ch 15.

[5]   On the taxation of shareholders, see below at §3.3.

[6]   CTA 2009, Pt 9A, applicable on or after 1 July 2009.

[7]   This includes dissolution under the Companies Act 2006, s 1000 or s 1003 (ex Companies Act 1985, s 652 or s 652A), where the Registrar strikes off a defunct company—provided certain assurances are given to the inspector in time (ESC C16).

[8]   TA 1988, s 209(1); *IRC v Burrell* [1924] 2 KB 52, (1924) 9 TC 27. This exclusion applies, by concession, to the winding up of social or recreational unincorporated associations, provided the distributions are not large (ESC C15).

[9]   TCGA 1992, s 122; see *Revenue Law*, §41.3.

[10]   *Re Dominion Tar and Chemical Co Ltd* [1929] 2 Ch 387.

[11]   ITTOIA 2005, s 383(3).

[12]   Ex TA 1988, s 20(2).

[13]   ITTOIA 2005, s 366.

securities, the trading income rules in Part 2 apply instead. The dealer is not entitled to the tax credit and the sum received is not grossed up.[14]

Income charged under ITTOIA 2005, Part 4, Chapter 3 cannot be relevant income—and so cannot be used to calculate pensionable earnings.[15]

3.1.2 Definitions: Qualifying and Non-qualifying Distributions

Qualifying distributions are defined by exclusion—all distributions but two are qualifying distributions. The two exceptions are:

(1)   the issue of bonus redeemable shares and bonus securities; and
(2)   the issue of any share capital or security which the company making the distribution has directly or indirectly received from another company in the form of bonus redeemable shares or securities (see below at §3.2.3).[16]

Broadly, distributions resulting in immediate distribution of reserves are qualifying distributions, whereas those causing only a potential claim on profits are non-qualifying distributions.

Today, the main difference is that the tax credit is available only in respect of qualifying distributions. Before 1999 only qualifying distributions gave rise to ACT liability;[17] the distinction remains important, therefore, for the repayment of surplus ACT after that year.

3.2   Distributions

3.2.1 Meaning of 'Distribution'

The definition of 'distribution' for corporation tax purposes formerly in TA 1988, sections 209 *et seq* was rewritten into CTA 2010, sections 1000 *et seq*. According to section 1000(1)A, a distribution, in relation to any company, includes any dividend paid by the company, including a capital dividend. A dividend is regarded as paid when it becomes due and payable,[18] ie when it becomes an enforceable debt, not necessarily at the date of the resolution. A final dividend is, in the absence of any other date in the resolution, prima facie due when declared and so creates an immediate debt; directors have power to stipulate the date and, if this power is exercised, the debt arises only when that date is reached. An interim dividend resolved upon by the directors may be reviewed by them and so does not create an immediate debt.[19] The waiver of a dividend in advance of payment is effective to prevent the income from accruing to the shareholder.[20]

---

[14] ITTOIA 2005, s 366, ex TA 1988, s 95, as amended by F(No 2)A 1997, s 24.
[15] See *Revenue Law*, §7.8.
[16] CTA 2010, s 1136(1), (2), referring to distributions within s 1000(1)C or D; ex TA 1988, s 14(2).
[17] TA 1988, s 14(1) (repealed).
[18] CTA 2010, s 1168, ex TA 1988, s 834(3).
[19] *Potel v IRC* [1971] 2 All ER 504, (1971) 46 TC 658.
[20] For IHT consequences, see *Revenue Law*.

The reference to a 'capital dividend' has caused some confusion. In the 6th edition of *Revenue Law*, it was noted that a dividend paid out of capital is still a dividend, but the matter had given rise to problems before 1965.[21] This issue re-emerged with the introduction of Part 9A of CTA 2009, which extended the scope of exemption for corporation tax purposes for distributions received by UK companies, but specifically excluded from the exemption distributions 'of a capital nature'.[22] In an apparently successful attempt to clarify the situation, new section 1027A was introduced in F(No 3)A 2010, to provide that a dividend arising from a reduction of share capital is to be treated as if it were made out of profits available for distribution. In addition, the exclusion for capital dividends from the exemption in CTA 2009, section 931A(2) was removed. As a result, it should no longer be necessary to consider whether a dividend is income or capital for purposes of the exemption.[23]

3.2.2 Other Distribution out of Assets but in Respect of Shares

CTA 2010, section 1000(1)B covers any other distribution out of the assets of the company, in cash or otherwise, made in respect of shares,[24] eg a distribution by A Ltd to its shareholders of shares held by A Ltd in X Ltd.

A payment is excluded from section 1000(1)B if it represents a repayment of capital on the share or if, and to the extent that, new consideration is received by the company for the distribution.[25] Consideration is new if it is external to the company, ie it is not provided directly or indirectly by the company itself.[26] Thus, a bonus issue is not a distribution since there is no cost to the company; neither is a rights issue, since the consideration is new. The issue of a bonus issue of redeemable shares may give rise to other consequences.

The purchase by a company of its own shares from its shareholders will give rise to distribution treatment under section 1000(1)B unless special rules direct otherwise (see below at §3.5). The amount of the distribution must allow for the deduction of the consideration originally paid for them; since this is an income tax charge, there is neither indexation nor tapering relief. The section applies only to a distribution out of the assets in respect of the shares; a purchase by the company from the shareholder direct is such a purchase, but a purchase in the open market is not. A market purchase is how many large companies buy back shares today; they thus avoid section 1000(1)B problems.

3.2.3 Issue of Redeemable Share Capital or Securities

Under CTA 2010, section 1000(1)C and D, the issue of any redeemable share capital or any security issued by the company in respect of shares or securities is a distribution unless it is

---

[21] Wilson, *Tax-efficient Extraction of Cash from Companies* (Key Haven, 1989), §2.31.

[22] CTA 2009, s 931A(2). See Tank, Weston and Melia [2011] BTR 47. As the authors note in this and a previous article ([2010] BTR 119), HMRC added to the confusion by apparently altering their longstanding position on this issue in arguments made in *First Nationwide v HMRC* [2010] UKFTT 24 (TC).

[23] Tank, Weston and Melia [2011] BTR 47, 48.

[24] Ex TA 1988, s 209(2)(b). On timing, see *John Paterson (Motors) Ltd v IRC* [1978] STC 59, (1978) 52 TC 39 (decision of Special Commissioners that date of approval of balance sheet was correct date upheld).

[25] Ex TA 1988, s 209(2)(b), but note s 1002(1) (ex s 209(6)) excluding transfers between independent companies.

[26] CTA 2010, Pt 23, Ch 8 and especially s 1113 'in respect of shares' and s 1115 'new consideration'; ex TA 1988, s 254(1).

wholly or in part for new consideration.[27] Where part of the amount issued is referable to the old consideration, the excess is treated as a distribution.[28] Thus, the issue of bonus redeemable preference shares, or debentures or loan stock in A Ltd by A Ltd are all treated as distributions. This definition does not cover non-redeemable bonus shares. The mere prospect of an eventual return of capital on a winding up or, since 1981, repurchase probably does not make an ordinary share redeemable, but this is unclear. Bonus securities, on the other hand, are in their nature redeemable and can therefore fall within the term 'distribution'.

The issue of bonus securities or bonus redeemable share capital is not a qualifying distribution. It is provided elsewhere that the redemption of such securities is a qualifying distribution.[29]

3.2.4 Excessive Interest Payments

Under CTA 2010, section 1000(1)E, interest above a certain threshold may be treated as a distribution.[30] More specifically, any interest (or other distribution out of the assets of the company in respect of its securities) will be a distribution if the consideration given by the company represents more than a reasonable commercial return. This rule applies only to the amount of interest which exceeds that reasonable commercial return. CTA 2010 refers to such securities as 'non-commercial securities', which are defined in section 1005.

3.2.5 Thin Capitalisation

TA 1988, section 209(2)(da) formerly treated interest as a distribution to the extent that it was attributable to the tax planning device known as 'thin capitalisation'.[31] This device is now countered by the transfer pricing rules (see below §4.6).

3.2.6 Other Interest Payments

Under CTA 2010, section 1000(1)F, other interest payments are treated as distributions *in full* and not just in part.[32] Although interest payments on debentures are not within the term 'distribution', and therefore are deductible in computing profits, there are rules designed to equate debenture interest payments with dividends where the debenture is more like a share than a genuine debenture. CTA 2010 refers to such securities as 'special securities', which are defined in section 1015. Thus, if the debentures had themselves been distributions, any interest payments or other distribution of assets in respect of those securities are treated as distributions. In addition, payments of interest on securities which are convertible directly or indirectly into shares of the company are distributions, unless the securities are quoted on a recognised stock exchange or are on terms comparable with those of quoted securities.[33]

---

[27] Ex TA 1988, s 209(2)(c).
[28] CTA 2010, s 1003 and s 1004, plus definition of 'new consideration' in CTA 2010, s 1115, ex TA 1988, s 254(1).
[29] TA 1988, ss 210, 211; see below at §§3.2.8 and 3.2.9.
[30] Ex TA 1988, s 209(2)(d).
[31] Introduced by FA 1995; see Oliver [1995] BTR 224.
[32] Ex TA 1988, s 209(2)(e).
[33] CTA 2010, s 1015(3).

CTA 2010 also treats certain payments of interest by a company as distributions if the consideration given by the company for the use of the money is to any extent dependent on the results of the company's business.[34] This was exploited by certain company borrowers whose tax position was such that they would receive no immediate benefit from being able to deduct the interest for corporation tax purposes, but for whom the credit attached to a dividend was, under the prevailing law, most useful. A small part of the consideration for the loan was made dependent on the results of the company's business (so coming within then TA 1988, section 209(2)(e)(iii)); the interest would become a distribution and the lender received the interest as franked investment income instead of as profits liable to corporation tax: the benefit of this was then shared with the borrower by charging a lower rate of interest.

To counter such schemes, CTA 2010, section 1032 directs that the interest paid on such a loan which is paid to a company within the charge to corporation tax is no longer treated as a distribution, save where the recipient would in any case be exempt from tax thereon.[35] Since 1996 the interest (non-distribution) element of the payment enters into the loan relationship calculations. Where the consideration for the loan exceeds a reasonable commercial return for the use of the principal sum, the interest is treated as a distribution to the extent only of the excess.[36] Interest payments on ratchet loans are removed from distribution treatment. Ratchet loans are those where the interest rate falls as business results improve or vice versa, ie are inversely related to the results of the business. Such interest will also therefore fall within the loan relationship rules (see below at §5.1) and will be deductible.[37] Lastly, interest on certain securities 'connected with' shares of the company is caught.[38]

3.2.7 Transfer of Asset at Undervalue

Where a company transfers an asset (or liability) to a member[39] for less than market value, the difference between any new consideration given and that market value is a distribution.[40] Consideration is new if it is external to the company, ie it is not provided directly or indirectly by the company.[41] Exemptions apply to transfers by subsidiary companies to parents or between truly independent companies.[42]

3.2.8 Perpetual Debt/Equity Notes

The boundary between distribution and debt has been further highlighted by the phenomenon of the perpetual debt instrument under which a loan is not repaid, commonly

---

[34] CTA 2010, s 1015(4) and s 1017, ex TA 1988, s 209(2)(e)(iii).

[35] Ex TA 1988, s 212. Note that s 212(4), added by FA 1995, s 87(4) and dealing with charity, was repealed by FA 2004.

[36] CTA 2010, s 1000(1)F(b), ex TA 1988, s 209(2)(d).

[37] CTA 2010, s 1017(1). FA 2000, s 86 added ex TA 1988, s 209(3B) for the purpose of s 209(e)(iii).

[38] CTA 2010, s 1015(5) and s 1017(2); ex TA 1988, s 209(2)(e)(vi).

[39] On the definition of 'member of company', see Companies Act 2006, s 112 (ex Companies Act 1985, s 22).

[40] CTA 2010, s 1020, ex TA 1988, s 209(4).

[41] CTA 2010, s 1115, ex TA 1988, s 254(1).

[42] CTA 2010, ss 1002(2), (3) and 1021(1), ex TA 1988, s 209(5).

known as equity notes.[43] A decision of the Special Commissioners held that payments of interest under such instruments were interest rather than dividends for the purpose of the relevant double tax treaty, and that they were not distributions under the present definition. This led to a tax asymmetry between the United States and the UK. Money would be borrowed in the United States where interest would be deductible; the money would then be transferred to an associated company in the UK as a debt; the repatriation of that money to the United States as interest meant that no tax was charged or withheld by the UK tax authorities.[44] In consequence, payments will be distributions if the equity notes are issued by one company and held by a company which is associated with the issuing company or is a funded company.[45] An equity note is elaborately defined, but broadly means a security which is not redeemable within 50 years from the date of issue; redeemability is defined in terms of the real world.[46]

3.2.9 *Non-qualifying Distribution Followed by Qualifying Distribution in Respect of Capital Issued*

The rule that a distribution out of the assets of the company in respect of shares is a qualifying distribution expressly excludes a repayment of capital (see above at §3.2.2). CTA 2010 goes on to provide two important qualifications of this rule. The first is section 1026, which applies where a company has issued (or paid up) any share capital otherwise than for new consideration, and the amount so paid up was not a qualifying distribution at that time. In such circumstances a subsequent distribution in respect of the capital is not treated as a repayment of capital; it will therefore be treated as a qualifying distribution, with the usual consequences for the dividend status of the receipt.

Since neither a bonus issue of paid-up irredeemable shares nor the repayment of share capital is a distribution, avoidance would be rife but for this rule. If a company had £10,000 to distribute, it would be unwise for the Revenue—from their point of view—to allow the company to capitalise the reserve and distribute it by way of bonus shares and then repay the bonus capital without at any stage falling foul of ITTOIA 2005, Part 4, Chapter 3. The effect of section 1026 is that if a company has made a bonus issue which was not treated as a qualifying distribution, repayments of such share capital are so treated to the extent to which those repayments of capital exceed the amount paid up on the share.[47] Thus, if the company had an issued share capital of 20,000 £1 shares, and distributed by way of bonus 10,000 fully paid-up £1 shares, subsequently making a reduction of capital of 50p per share on all 30,000 issued shares, the payments to shareholders would amount to £15,000, of which £10,000 would be treated as distribution and £5,000 as repayment of capital. To the extent that money has been distributed by way of non-distributions, subsequent

---

[43] For examples of devices exploiting the debt-equity distinction, see Wood (1999) 47 *Can Tax Jo* 49; see also Harlton (1994) 49 *Tax Law Review* 499.

[44] HC Official Report, Standing Committee B, cols 439, 440, 30 June 1992.

[45] CTA 2010, s 2015(6), ex TA 1988, s 209(2)(e)(vii) added by F(No 2)A 1992, s 31; see also Inland Revenue Press Release, 15 May 1992, [1992] *Simon's Tax Intelligence* 519. For history from the Revenue standpoint, see Inland Revenue, *International Tax Manual*, para 1249. On double taxation provision, see below at §20.6.

[46] CTA 2010, s 1016, ex TA 1988, s 209(9) added by F(No 2)A 1992, s 31; on scope, see also ICAEW, Guidance Note Tax 5/93, 19 March 1993.

[47] CTA 2010, ss 1024–1127, ex TA 1988, s 211.

repayments of capital will be treated as distributions. In applying this rule any previous repayments are brought into account.[48]

• Special rules apply to premiums. A premium paid on redemption is not treated as a return of capital.[49] If the share was issued at a premium which represented new consideration, the amount of the premium is treated as part of the share capital and so the repayment of the premium will fall outside section 1026.[50] This exception does not apply where the premium has been applied in paying up share capital.[51] Importantly, section 1026 is subject to a time limit. A distribution in respect of a share originally issued as a bonus which is made more than 10 years after the issue will escape section 1026 provided the company is not closely controlled.[52]

Where a reduction in capital is followed by or concurrent with the distribution of bonus shares, it is provided that although the reduction in capital will not be treated as a distribution, the issue of the bonus shares will be so treated to the extent of the earlier payments.[53]

3.2.10 Bonus Issue Following Repayment of Capital

Where the repayment of share capital is followed by a bonus issue, CTA 2010, section 1022 treats as a distribution the amount paid up on the new shares or the amount repaid on the old shares, whichever is the lower.[54]

Example

A Ltd repaid 50p per £ on its £20,000 ordinary stock; the nominal value of the stock is reduced to £10,000. This stock was originally issued wholly for new consideration, so no distribution arose on the repayment. Two years later A Ltd capitalises its reserves and makes a distribution of stock on the basis of 1 for every £5 stock held. The amount paid up is £2,000. As this is less than the amount repaid (£10,000), the whole £2,000 will be a qualifying distribution.

This rule is modified in two important ways. First, as with section 1026, there is a time limit. Where the new shares are irredeemable bonus shares issued more than 10 years after the reduction in share capital, section 1022 applies only where the company is closely controlled.[55] Secondly, there is an exception for preference shares issued before 6 April 1965, or issued after that time but for new consideration not derived from ordinary shares.[56]

---

[48] CTA 2010, s 1027(3), ex TA 1988, s 211(3).

[49] CTA 2010, s 1024, ex TA 1988, s 211(7).

[50] CTA 2010, s 1025(1), (2), ex TA 1988, s 211(5).

[51] CTA 2010, s 1025(3), ex TA 1988, s 211(6); the share capital may have been paid up under Companies Act 2006, s 610 (ex Companies Act 1985, s 130).

[52] CTA 2010, s 1026(3), referring to a 'relevant company' for purposes of s 739, which includes a company under the control of not more than 5 persons; ex TA 1988, s 211(2). Control is defined by reference to CTA 2010, s 450, ex TA 1988, s 416 (see below at §8.1.1).

[53] CTA 2010, ss 1022–1023, ex TA 1988, s 210.

[54] *Ibid.*

[55] CTA 2010, s 1023(1), (2), ex TA 1988, s 210(3).

[56] CTA 2010, s 1023(3), ex TA 1988, s 210(2).

3.3 Taxation of Shareholders—ITTOIA 2005, Part 4, Chapter 3

3.3.1 UK Resident Individuals and Others Entitled to the Tax Credit

3.3.1.1 Overview

The amount charged to tax under ITTOIA 2005, Part 4, Chapter 3 is the amount of the qualifying distribution plus the amount of the credit.[57] Individuals may set the credit against their income tax liability in respect of the dividend. This income is treated for upper rate purposes as the highest part of the person's income. Repayments to pension funds, authorised unit trusts and open-ended investment companies were stopped for distributions on or after 2 July 1997.[58] Repayments in respect of PEPs and ISAs have now ceased (see further below at §22.3). Special transitional relief rules for charities progressively reduced the value of the credit from 21% in 1999–2000 to 4% in 2003–04, and nil thereafter.[59] These reliefs take the form of payments by the Revenue out of special parliamentary grants—not repayments of the credit.

3.3.1.2 History

From 1996–99, dividends were taxed either at the lower rate (20%) or the higher rate (40%). This meant that a basic rate taxpayer paid at 20% not at the then basic rate (always more than 20%), but as the credit was restricted to 20% this did not make much practical difference. From 1973–96, dividends were taxed at whatever might be the individual's appropriate rate as the lower rate had not been introduced; a zero-rate individual taxpayer could recover the tax represented by the credit—but from the Revenue, not the company.

3.3.1.3 The Tax Credit—Entitlement

The tax credit is available to residents and certain eligible non-residents;[60] a non-resident is eligible if entitled to personal reliefs.[61] A right to the credit may also arise under the terms of a double tax treaty. The question whether EU law gives a resident of a Member State a right to a credit even when the relevant double tax treaty does not provide one (eg UK–Germany) was pre-empted by a change in the UK legislation on personal reliefs to include all EEA nationals (and thus also all UK nationals).

Under UK law before 2008 there was no tax credit in respect of a distribution by a non-resident company because the payment is not within this head of charge (and is discussed in chapter sixteen below). However, FA 2008 began the statutory process of granting the credit in these circumstances.[62]

---

[57] ITTOIA 2005, ss 384 and 394(3), ex TA 1988, ss 20(2), 231(3A).

[58] Ex TA 1988, s 231A, added by F(No 2)A 1997, s 19; the list of funds is contained in s 231A(5).

[59] F(No 2)A 1997, s 35.

[60] ITTOIA 2005, s 397, ex TA 1988, s 231.

[61] Pursuant to ITTOIA 2005, s 397(4), 'eligible non-UK resident' has the meaning it has for ITA 2007, s 56(3); see *Revenue Law*, §11.1. Ex TA 1988, s 232(1) referring to s 278.

[62] ITTOIA 2005, ss 397A and 397AA. There might be a credit under a double tax agreement, but that was a quite different sort of credit.

3.3.1.4 The Tax Credit—Amounts

Since 1999 the value of the credit has been one-ninth of the qualifying distribution,[63] which makes for a rate of 10% on the sum of the dividend and the credit. Thus, if X, a person entitled to the credit, receives a dividend of £90 there will be a credit of £10 and X's income will be £100. The 10% rate was called the 'Schedule F ordinary rate' and now the 'dividend ordinary rate'.

If X is a basic rate taxpayer there is no further tax to pay, because X is liable to tax at the dividend ordinary rate of 10%. If X is a higher-rate taxpayer, X must pay tax at the dividend upper rate of 32.5%, making a liability of £32.50, against which X must set the credit of £10, so leaving X with £67.50.[64] If X is an additional rate taxpayer, further tax (at 42.5%) also will be due. If X has no tax liability at all there is no more tax to pay but, since 1997, there is no right to a repayment of the credit.

There are also special rules for estates in administration.

3.3.1.5 Anti-avoidance Rules: Arrangements to Pass Credits and 'Repos'

The withdrawal of the rights of repayment of credits meant that pension funds could have sold their shares to people who were entitled to the credit themselves but arrange that the benefit of the credits should be passed back to a pension fund in whole or in part. This was counteracted by TA 1988, section 231B, which remains in force and has not yet been rewritten. The section applies where A is entitled to a tax credit in respect of a qualifying distribution and arrangements exist such that B obtains, whether directly or indirectly, a payment representing any of the value of the tax credit[65] and certain arrangements exist. The arrangements must have been entered into for an 'unallowable' purpose; purposes are unallowable if at least one of the parties has a non-commercial purpose.[66] However, this is then softened by a rule ignoring the purpose of gaining a tax advantage[67] if it is not a main purpose of that person.[68] The consequences of such arrangements are that no claim may be made for repayment of the tax. Other anti-avoidance provisions include CTA 2010, sections 805–812 (ex TA 1988, sections 231AA and 231AB) and ITA 2007, sections 592–594 (no credit for borrower or original owner under stock lending and repurchase agreement ('repo')).

3.3.2 *No Entitlement to Credits: Non-qualifying Distributions*

As seen above (at §3.1.2), two types of distribution are not qualifying distributions. These are the *issue* of bonus redeemable shares and securities, and the *issue* of any share capital or security which the company making the distribution has received from another company

---

[63] ITTOIA 2005, s 397(1), ex TA 1988, s 231(1A), added by F(No 2)A 1997, s 30(3).

[64] The reason behind the 32.5% rate was to ensure that X's liability did not increase as a result of the 1999 changes. In 1998–99 the fraction used to calculate the credit was one-quarter, so the credit on a distribution of £90 would have been £22.50, making Sch F income of £112.5; tax at 40% would be £45, also leaving X with £67.50 after payment of the tax.

[65] TA 1988, s 231B(9).

[66] Defined in TA 1988, s 231B(5)–(7).

[67] Defined by reference to CTA 2010, s 1139, ex TA 1988, s 709.

[68] TA 1988, s 231B(7).

in such form.[69] The tax treatment of non-qualifying distributions differs from that of qualifying distributions in that no tax credit is available.

Tax on the recipient of a non-qualifying distribution is determined in the same way as for any other recipient of a distribution in respect of which there is no entitlement to a tax credit.[70] However, the non-qualifying distribution *is* dividend income and therefore will be taxed at the appropriate rate (10%, 32.5% or 42.5% dropping to 37.5% from April 2013 for individuals), but with no tax at 10% and credit for that 10% against the 32.5%/42.5%/37.5% rate. Tax is due on the nominal value of the distribution plus any premium stated to be due on redemption. There is no grossing up of the amount received.[71]

The payment of sums on the *redemption* of such stock or securities is a qualifying distribution. There will then be a qualifying distribution with accompanying tax credit and further liability under ITTOIA 2005, Part 4, Chapter 3. To avoid a double charge, tax paid on the issue of the securities[72] may be set off against any excess liability on redemption.[73] Anyone who paid at the upper rate or additional rate on issue but who now pays at the dividend ordinary rate may use the tax paid on issue as a credit on redemption but cannot recover the tax paid on issue.

Example

X Ltd makes a bonus issue of redeemable preference shares. Stan receives shares the redemption value of which is £250; assume that he pays £17.50 income tax. On redemption of the shares there is deemed to be a qualifying distribution. Assume that Stan is now liable to the dividend upper rate of 32.5%. On redemption the net distribution of £250 is increased by the 1/9 credit (£27.77) to give dividend income of £277.77; tax on £277.77 at 32.5% is £90.27, from which are to be deducted the £27.77 credit now and the £17.50 paid when the shares were issued. This leaves a net tax liability of £45.

3.3.3 *Non-residents*

3.3.3.1 Entitled to Treaty Credit

It is in connection with the treatment of non-residents that the purpose of some features of the 1999 scheme becomes clearer. Where the non-resident is a resident in another country which has a treaty with the UK, the first relevant article will be the dividend article.[74] This will usually begin by saying that the UK may tax the dividend but subject to a cap. That cap will usually first be described as 15% of the gross amount of the dividend; the cap on the

---

[69] CTA 2010, s 1136(1), (2), referring to distributions within s 1000(1)C or D; ex TA 1988, s 14(2).

[70] ITTOIA 2005, ss 399 (person not entitled to tax credit) and 400 (non-qualifying distribution), ex TA 1988, s 233, as amended by F(No 2)A 1992, s 19(3) and FA 1993, Sch 6, para 2.

[71] Inference from ITTOIA 2005, s 399(2) and s 400(2). This is simply because no provision directs it; contrast, for a qualifying distribution, the clear words of TA 1988, s 20 and, for stock dividends, s 249(4).

[72] The legislation does not state how this is to be calculated but it is assumed that the tax is the top slice of the person's income; alternatives are to use the average rate or to treat it as the bottom slice.

[73] ITTOIA 2005, s 401, ex TA 1988, s 233(2). The person receiving the sum on redemption must be the same person who paid the tax on the issue. It is not, apparently, necessary that the person should have held the securities throughout the intervening period.

[74] Eg the UK–US Treaty, Art 10(2)(a)(ii). The withholding of this credit in certain circumstances is authorised by TA 1988, s 812 (not rewritten). On settlement with California, see Treasury Press Release 13 May 1993 and [1993] *Simon's Tax Intelligence* 858, 1250.

UK's taxing right is reduced to only 5% if the beneficial owner is a company controlling at least 25% of the company paying the dividend.

There will then usually be a further provision, which applies instead of the one just described, so long as individuals resident in the UK are entitled to tax credits, ie as now. This will say that the UK 15% applies not to 'the gross amount of the dividend' but to the sum of the dividend and the credit. It will also say that the 5% cap begins with a holding of only 10%, not 25%.

The treaty will then say that T is entitled to a tax credit under UK tax law and that the amount of credit is, unless the beneficial owner is a company controlling at least 10% of the company paying the dividend, one half that to which the UK resident would have been entitled. Moreover, T is entitled to repayment of any excess of that tax credit over his liability to UK tax. Thus, where T receives a dividend of £9,000, T will also be entitled to the UK tax credit of £500, but the UK will be entitled to levy tax at 15% on £9,500, ie £1,425; this is charged at source as a withholding tax. Since the withholding tax (£1,425) exceeds the credit (£500), T's repayment claim to the UK Revenue will fail. T may, of course, use the credit of £500 against tax in T's own country of residence. The UK legislation makes it clear that where, as here, the withholding tax exceeds the credit, the effect is to reduce the amount to which T is entitled by way of repayment of the credit to nil.[75]

Where T is a company with a large enough stake in the company paying the dividend, the UK tax is reduced to 5% of the sum of the dividend and half the credit. If the dividend is £90,000 and the credit is £5,000, the UK will be entitled to withhold 5% of £95,000, ie £4,750, so leaving T with a repayment claim for £250 against the UK Revenue.

These examples explain the 1997 selection of the general credit rate of 10% as opposed to the previous 20%. The rate of 10% is designed to reduce to a minimum the rights of non-residents to reclaim tax from the UK. This minimum is preferred to outright abolition, since abolition would invite retaliatory action by treaty partners.[76] The ECJ has held that the 5% withholding tax is not in breach of the Parent–Subsidiary Directive.[77]

3.3.3.2 No Entitlement to Credit

When a UK resident company makes a distribution to a non-resident, Z, who is not entitled to a tax credit, eg because there is no applicable treaty, Z is liable to income tax on the distribution on the same basis as non-qualifying distributions.[78]

Where no credit is available, there is no liability to income tax at the 10% ordinary rate but only at the higher rate. Thus, if Z receives a dividend of £90 but is liable to tax at the upper dividend rate, there will be a liability to tax at 32.5% on £100 (£32.50), but since Z is treated as having already paid £10, the final liability is £22.50. Z is assessed on the amount of the distribution of £90 grossed up to take account of the credit. Whether Z will actually have to pay the tax is another matter since other rules restrict the UK's right to tax to situations in which Z has a UK representative, eg a permanent establishment here (see §16.6.3).[79]

---

[75] F(No 2)A 1997, s 30(10).
[76] Eg UK–US Treaty, Art 10; abolition of the credit would mean that the scheme in Art 10(2) would not apply and the much less advantageous (to the UK) rules in Art 10(1) would apply instead.
[77] *IRC v Océ Van Der Grinten NV* [2003] STC 1248.
[78] ITTOIA 2005, s 399.
[79] FA 1995, s 128.

3.3.4 Companies

Where the recipient is another company resident in the UK, the qualifying distribution plus the credit is income of the recipient, but it is not liable to corporation tax.[80] A non-qualifying distribution does not come with a credit but, again, is not liable to corporation tax. The concept of franked investment income is retained for the category of income which carries a credit; however, its related concept of 'franked payment' is obsolete and has been abolished.[81] The position of non-resident companies is that they are entitled to the benefit of the exemption from corporation tax if the dividend accrues to a permanent establishment in the UK. The position under treaties was explored at §3.3.3.[82]

3.4 Stock Dividend Income

Where a person has an option to receive either a dividend or additional share capital, special rules treat the share capital so issued as giving rise to a charge to tax on the recipient under ITTOIA 2005, section 410.[83] The payment, however, is not a distribution as such. There is no liability to rates of tax below the dividend upper rate; if there is such a liability, credit is given for the dividend ordinary rate even though not actually paid. Payments to other companies are not income of the recipient.[84]

These rules also apply where: (a) the shareholder has shares which carry the right to receive bonus share capital;[85] and (b) that right is conferred by the terms on which the shares were issued (or later varied if bonus share capital is then issued).[86] It is inherent in every share that it carries the right to any scrip issue, the right arising from the articles of association, but the provision has not been given so wide a scope.[87] These rules apply only to stock dividends paid by companies resident in the UK.

Under ITTOIA 2005, liability is based on 'the cash equivalent of the share capital'.[88] The market value of the shares is substituted where the dividend is substantially greater or smaller than that, or the number of shares issued is not related to any cash dividend. ITTOIA 2005 enacts the Revenue statement of practice that 'substantial' means 15% or more.[89] Liability to the upper/additional (32.5%/42.5% becoming 37.5%) rate of tax may

---

[80] CTA 2009, s 931A *et seq*, ex CTA 2009, s 1285, ex TA 1988, s 208.

[81] TA 1988, s 238, repealed by FA 1998, Sch 3, para 11.

[82] For example the UK-US Treaty, Art 10(2)(a)(i). On interpretation, see FA 1989, s 115, comprehensively and retrospectively, reversing *Union Texas International Corpn v Critchley* [1990] STC 305, (1990) 63 TC 224, CA; see Inland Revenue Press Release, 25 October 1988, [1988] *Simon's Tax Intelligence* 784; see also *Getty Oil Co v Steele* [1990] STC 434. (1990) 63 TC 376.

[83] ITTOIA 2005, s 410, defined in CTA 2010, s 1051(3), ex TA 1988, s 251(l)(c). The failure to exercise a right is taken to be the exercise of the option: s 1051(4).

[84] CTA 2010, ss 1049–1051, ex TA 1988, ss 249–251.

[85] Ie share capital issued otherwise than wholly for new consideration: CTA 2010, s 1051(1), ex TA 1988, s 251(l)(a).

[86] CTA 2010, s 1049(2), ex TA 1988, s 249(2).

[87] Nor, it seems, was it meant to be: see HC Official Report, vol 895, col 1881, 18 July 1975.

[88] Ex TA 1988, s 251(2). On trusts and estates, see ex s 249(5), (6).

[89] ITTOIA 2005, s 412(2) and Statement of Practice A8. On tax treatment where an enhanced stock dividend is received by a trust, see Statement of Practice SP 4/94; *Simon's Direct Tax Service*, Division 113, now ITTOIA 2005, s 414(1).

arise, but the ordinary (10%) rate tax is treated as having been paid.[90] As already seen, ordinary rate tax cannot be recovered.[91]

The incentive for the company to grant a stock dividend rather than a simple cash dividend is that the company's cash position is not affected. Before 1999, ie during the days of ACT, there were also tax advantages for the company in that ACT was not due on a stock dividend but was due on an ordinary dividend; such issues have now been removed.[92] The tax position of the shareholder was also changed in 1999, in that a non-taxable shareholder has now lost the right to repayment of the tax credit. The credit had been repayable on an ordinary dividend but not on a stock dividend; now it is repayable on neither.

3.5 Purchase by Company of Own Shares[93]

3.5.1 *Orthodox Distribution and CGT Treatment*

These rules are not directly affected by ITTOIA 2005. Company law[94] allows a company to issue redeemable equity shares and to purchase its own shares, subject to authorisation in the company's memorandum and articles of association and to various conditions imposed by the Companies Act. For tax purposes, any amount by which the redemption proceeds or purchase consideration exceeds the amount subscribed for the shares is a qualifying distribution within CTA 2010, section 1000(1)B and so is treated as dividend income complete with tax credit. There is also a disposal of the shares for capital gains purposes. At one time a company had actually to cancel shares bought in this way, but this was changed in 2003[95] when it was allowed to keep them in its treasury—hence the term 'treasury shares'. The tax rules are amended to treat the shares bought in as if they had been cancelled and then issued as brand new shares when actually reissued.[96] They are treated as not being acquired by the company or as existing in any other way while resting in the treasury.[97] There are further rules to govern the interaction with the reorganisation rules in TCGA 1992, section 126 where the company holding the shares in its treasury makes a bonus issue.[98] There is also a rule excluding all these rules on the tax treatment of the price paid by the company if the price would be relevant in computing trading income.[99] Reissued treasury shares do not qualify for venture capital trusts (below §22.6).

3.5.2 *Pure CGT Treatment for Unquoted Trading Companies*

The orthodox treatment was thought to be an obstacle to the new power of companies to buy back their own shares; special legislation was therefore passed directing that there should be no qualifying distribution but only CGT.[100] Either the purchaser must have

---

[90] ITTOIA 2005, s 414.
[91] ITTOIA 2005, s 414, ex TA 1988, s 249(4), as amended by FA 1993, s 77(3).
[92] Hutton, *Tolley's Tax Planning*, ch 58.
[93] For history of and critical comment on the legislation, see Tiley [1992] BTR 21.
[94] Companies Act 2006, ss 684–708 (ex Companies Act 1985, ss 159–162).
[95] Companies (Acquisition of Own Shares) Regulations 2003 (SI 2003/1116).
[96] FA 2003, s 195(4) and (8); these rules also apply for IHT; see Hardwick [2003] BTR 417–19.
[97] FA 2003, s 195(2) and (3).
[98] FA 2003, s 195(5) and (6).
[99] FA 2003, s 195(9).
[100] FA 1982, s 53.

the purpose of benefiting the trade, or the proceeds must be used to meet certain IHT liabilities.[101] There are elaborate anti-avoidance rules.

3.5.2.1 Conditions

(1) *Unquoted.* A company buying its own shares must be an unquoted company; this is because there is a ready market for shares in quoted companies, ie companies quoted on an official stock exchange, or the 51% subsidiary of such a company.[102]

(2) *Trading.* The company must be a trading company or a holding company of a trading group. For these purposes a holding company is one whose main business (apart from any trading activities of its own) is to hold shares in one or more 75% subsidiaries.[103] Trades of dealing in shares, securities, land or futures do not qualify.[104]

(3) *Purpose—benefit to trade.* The purchase, etc of shares must be made wholly or mainly to benefit the trade of the company concerned or of any of its 75% subsidiaries.[105] A benefit to the selling shareholder is not the same as a benefit to the trade. It is necessary also to distinguish a benefit to the trade from both (a) some wider commercial purpose to which the seller may put the payment received, and (b) a business purpose of the company which is not itself a trade, eg an investment activity it may carry on.[106] One reason which might qualify as benefiting the trade would be resolving a disagreement at boardroom level. However, in the Revenue view, disagreements as to whether or not to cease trading and become an investment company, where the shareholder being bought out wants the trade to continue, would not qualify. Other qualifying reasons might be allowing an outside shareholder who has provided equity finance to withdraw, enabling a proprietor to retire to make way for new management, or on the death of a shareholder, allowing beneficiaries of the estate to sell the shares. There must not be an avoidance purpose.

(4) *Residence.* The vendor must meet certain residence requirements.[107]

(5) *Minimum holding periods.* The vendor must have owned the shares for at least five years at the time they are purchased by the company.[108] Special rules allow the aggregation of periods when the shares were held by a spouse or civil partner, provided the transferor was then living with the vendor and was then the vendor's spouse or civil partner.[109] Further rules apply where shares were acquired on death, whether as PR or as successor, in which case the overall period is reduced from five years to three.[110] A rule directs a first in, first out system where shares are bought and sold,[111] while another treats bonus shares and other shares acquired on a company reconstruction,

---

[101] CTA 2010, s 1033(2), (3), cx TA 1988, s 219(1)(a), (b).

[102] CTA 2010, s 1048(1), ex TA 1988, s 229.

[103] *Ibid.* A trading group will consist of a holding company or one or more 75% subsidiaries where the main business of the members taken together is the carrying on of the trade or trades.

[104] CTA 2010, s 1048(1), ex TA 1988, s 229.

[105] CTA 2010, s 1033(2), ex TA 1988, s 219(1)(a). The purpose of benefiting the trade will not, of itself, make legal and other expenses associated with the purchase deductible (Revenue Interpretation RI 4).

[106] See Statement of Practice SP 2/82, para 2.

[107] CTA 2010, s 1034, ex TA 1988, s 220. The residence status of a PR is taken to be that of the deceased immediately before his death. The residence and ordinary residence of trustees is determined as for CGT (TCGA 1992, s 69).

[108] CTA 2010, s 1035(1), ex TA 1988, s 220(5).

[109] CTA 2010, s 1036(1), (2), ex TA 1988, s 220(6). It follows that the period may not be added if they are separated, or no longer married or civil partners at the date of the purchase.

[110] CTA 2010, s 1036(3), ex TA 1988, s 220(7).

[111] CTA 2010, s 1035(2), ex TA 1988, s 220(8).

reorganisation or amalgamation as acquired at the same time as the original holding in respect of which they are issued—a treatment which is not extended to rights issues or stock dividends.[112]

(6) *Extent of disposal—severing or substantially reducing the link.* The vendor's interest in the company must either be completely eliminated or substantially reduced as a result of the purchase of the shares by the company.[113] A reduction is substantial only if it is 25% or more.[114] For these purposes, the holdings of associates may be taken into account,[115] and the combined holdings of vendor and associate must be reduced by at least 25%.[116] It is also necessary that there should be a corresponding reduction in shareholders' entitlement to profits.[117] These rules are of great importance where the vendor retains shares of another class.

Where the vendor's holding is not eliminated, there may be difficulty in meeting requirement (3) above—that the purchase is for the sole or main purpose of benefiting the company's trade. Where the vendor's continuing presence is regarded as a danger to the trade the interest ought to be eliminated completely.[118] It is unclear whether a series of purchases by the company can be linked together so as to achieve the 25% reduction where no individual purchase meets that condition; such a linkage is allowed in the United States under the step transaction doctrine, but the doctrine has also had this effect where the taxpayer sells some shares and gives others away, provided it is all part of the one plan; at this stage it is thought unlikely that the UK courts would accede to such an argument, but the Revenue seem prepared to accept it.[119]

(7) *No avoidance.* The purchase must not be part of a scheme or an arrangement which is designed or likely to result in the vendor or any associate having an interest in the company such that if he had that interest immediately after the purchase, any of the previous conditions would not be satisfied.[120] Transactions within one year of each other are presumed to be part of such a scheme.[121]

(8) *No continuing connection.* The vendor must not, immediately after the purchase, be connected with the company or any other member of the group.[122]

---

[112] CTA 2010, s 1035(3), ex TA 1988, s 220(9).

[113] CTA 2010, s 1037(1), ex TA 1988, s 221.

[114] CTA 2010, s 1037(3)–(5), ex TA 1988, s 221(4). If the company is a member of a 51% group, it is the shareholder's interest in the group that must be reduced by at least 25% (CTA 2010, s 1038(1), (2), ex TA 1988, s 221(6)).

[115] CTA 2010, s 1037(2), ex TA 1988, s 221(2); for the definition of 'associate', see ss 1059–1061, ex s 227.

[116] CTA 2010, s 1039(1), (4), (5), ex TA 1988, s 222(3), which extend the rule in s 1040(3) (ex s 222(2)) to the situation in which groups are involved, and s 1043(1), (2) (ex s 224), which provide that where the conditions are satisfied as to the combined holdings of the vendor and the associate and the vendor joined in to help the associate meet those conditions, all the conditions in ss 1037–1042 (ex ss 221–223) are to be treated as satisfied for both of them.

[117] CTA 2010, s 1038, ex TA 1988, s 221(5)–(8).

[118] There is some evidence that a more lenient attitude is adopted where the shares were acquired under an approved share option scheme, since here the Revenue do not insist that the vendor should cease to be an employee (*Simon's Direct Tax Service*, D2.508).

[119] Statement of Practice SP 2/82, para 5.

[120] CTA 2010, s 1042(2), (3), (5), ex TA 1988, s 223(2).

[121] CTA 2010, s 1042(4). However, succession to property on death is not regarded as a 'transaction' for this purpose (see Statement of Practice SP 2/82, para 8).

[122] CTA 2010, s 1042(1), (5), ex TA 1988, s 223(1); on the definition of 'connected', see ss 1062–1063, ex s 228.

3.5.3 Sales to Pay IHT

Special treatment is also available if the purchase is not for the benefit of the trade but the vendor needs the funds to discharge a liability to IHT arising on death. In these circumstances it is only necessary for conditions (1) and (2) above to be met; as such, (3)–(8) do not apply. The whole or substantially the whole—a phrase taken by the Revenue to mean almost all[123]—of the payment must be paid in respect of the liability to IHT falling on the shareholder as a result of a death; this rule is applied after taking out the funds needed to pay any CGT liability consequent upon the purchase. The IHT payment must be made within two years of death and it must be shown that the liability could not have been met without undue hardship otherwise than through the purchase.[124]

3.5.4 Consequences: Choices

If the conditions outlined above are complied with, the transaction will be treated as a disposal by the shareholder for CGT purposes and not as a distribution. If the shareholder is a dealer in securities, the transaction will be treated as a trading transaction and not as a distribution.[125] The company may apply to the Revenue for advance clearance as to the treatment of any payment made by it for the purchase of shares.[126]

The story of this area of law illustrates the way in which the policy of the law may be affected by changes elsewhere in the system. The policy was to remove a fiscal obstacle to a corporate practice. The rule was absolute rather than a matter of election; the assumption behind the policy was that CGT treatment would be advantageous and therefore available only for virtuous cases. This assumption was undermined by the 1988 changes assimilating the rates of tax on income and capital gains. For many shareholders thinking of selling shares back to their companies, the 1988 change did not make matters neutral but actually made income treatment preferable. This was because of the availability of the tax credit alongside the qualifying distribution. Thus, an individual receiving £80 purchase price and paying income tax at 40% only had to find at that time an extra £20, ie 40% of (£80 + £20) less £20 already paid, as opposed to £32 (40% of £80) if CGT treatment were directed. For corporate shareholders there were further advantages, in that the company was treated as receiving 'franked investment income' which was not only exempt from corporation tax but could also be used to frank its own distributions, or sometimes to secure a repayment of the tax credit.

There were still further issues concerning the calculation of the consideration received for the shares and whether or not it included the qualifying distribution received. On one view the sum should not have been included since it was a qualifying distribution; the other view was that it should have been included because it was not subject to corporation tax under TA 1988, section 208. If the former view was right, not only could the company have used the tax credit in the various ways indicated, but it could also have ended up

---

[123] Statement of Practice SP 2/82, para 6.
[124] CTA 2010, s 1033(4), ex TA 1988, s 219(2).
[125] CTA 2009, s 130, ex TA 1988, s 95.
[126] CTA 2010, s 1044–1045, ex TA 1988, s 225.

with a capital loss.[127] The Revenue rejected this view and their position was eventually upheld.[128]

Today the question whether it is advantageous to use these rules so as to receive capital gains treatment is a complex one depending upon individual circumstances.

3.6   The ACT System: Historical Outline

3.6.1 Overview of ACT

ACT is not payable in respect of qualifying distributions on or after 6 April 1999. Previously, ACT was paid by a company when it made a qualifying distribution.[129] The ACT could be set off against its liability to corporation tax; at first this was restricted to tax on income, but after 1987 it was set off against corporation tax payable in respect of all profits including, therefore, capital gains.[130] If the company had no liability to corporation tax that year it could carry the ACT back a number of years (originally two years, but eventually six), and could carry it forward indefinitely.

A restriction on ACT set off was that it could not exceed a sum equal to the ACT which would have been paid if the company had made the maximum possible distribution out of the profits of that year.[131] Suppose that a company had £2 million profits and that the ACT rate was one-quarter of the dividend.[132] If the company distributed £1.6 million, it would have to pay £400,000 of ACT. This would be the maximum set off allowed for that year. The company would have a corporation tax liability of £2 million charged at the relevant rate for that year, eg £700,000 at 35%. The company could set off a maximum of £400,000 against that £700,000. The company would have to find the money to pay the ACT and the £300,000 mainstream corporation tax, as well as the dividend, no doubt using past profits to do so.

ACT was a tax due from the company and so had to be paid whenever the company made a qualifying distribution payment. It made no difference whether the company had any liability to corporation tax that year (eg because it made a loss), or whether the recipient shareholders were rich individuals taxable at the top rate of income tax (which varied between 98% and 40%) or charities or pension funds and so exempt from tax.

A common way in which surplus ACT arose was from the credit system of double taxation relief. A UK multinational company would receive income from foreign subsidiaries and branches. The foreign tax paid would often completely offset any UK corporation tax liability. However, this did not prevent the company from being liable to pay ACT to the Inland Revenue whenever it made a qualifying distribution. To solve the surplus ACT problem the Government did two things. The first was to reduce the rate of ACT and so the rate of tax credit, with consequent reductions in the repayment claims of zero-rate

---

[127] Especially when, after FA 1985, the indexation rules could have been used to create a loss.
[128] *Strand Option and Futures Ltd v Vojak* [2003] EWCA Civ 1457; [2004] STC 64 (CA), upholding Statement of Practice SP 4/89. This outcome has now been legislated—see CTA 2009, s 931A.
[129] Ex TA 1988, s 14(1).
[130] Ex TA 1988, s 239.
[131] Ex TA 1988, s 239(2).
[132] As was the case in 1998–99.

or exempt taxpayers. The second was to introduce the foreign income dividend (FID) scheme.[133] If the company could show that it paid no UK tax on a foreign income stream because of the foreign tax credit, it could recover the ACT it had paid. It will be noted that the ACT had to be paid in the first place and then recovered, although there was an exception for certain headquarters companies. This was often burdensome in administrative terms; it was also unpopular with exempt funds, because the corollary of the absence of ACT was that there was no tax credit and so, in those days, no tax repayment. During the two-year period from 1997–99 when the foreign dividend scheme was in place, but the pension funds had lost their right to repayment, there was a sharp increase in FID payments.

3.6.2 Franked Investment Income and Franked Payments

Under TA 1988, section 208, qualifying distributions received by a company resident in the UK were not subject to corporation tax. One purpose of this rule was to secure tax neutrality between distributions to individual shareholders and distributions to corporate shareholders. It also meant that, provided money stayed within the UK resident corporate sector, only one charge to ACT was made. The recipient company received franked investment income; when it made qualifying distribution payments of its own, it could use the credit element on what it had received to 'frank', ie remove its own liability to pay, ACT.

3.6.3 Pre-1999 Surplus ACT and Post-1999 Shadow ACT: The 1999 Rules

ACT is not payable in respect of qualifying distributions on or after 6 April 1999. Regulations govern the treatment of any remaining unrelieved surplus ACT which had not, by then, been set off against a company's corporation tax liability.[134] This is not of exclusively historical interest—for details see *Revenue Law*, 4th edition.

---

[133] Ex TA 1988, ss 246A *et seq*. See Harris [1997] BTR 82.
[134] Corporation Tax (Treatment of Unrelieved Surplus ACT) Regulations 1999 (SI 1999/573), [1999] *Simon's Weekly Tax Intelligence* 573.

4

Computation (1): General Rules

4.1   General

A consultation document issued in 2002 suggested that tax profits and accounting profit should be aligned more closely.[1] The consultation would have permitted, at least as a starting point, full depreciation in place of capital allowances, but would have required, under fair value accounting, that accrued but unrealised gains on capital assets would have been brought into the tax net. This proposal eventually petered out. However, the common consolidated corporate tax base (CCCTB) towards which the European Commission is

---

[1] HM Treasury, *Reform of Corporation Tax*, August 2002. Later documents include *Corporation Tax Reform*, 2003, which should be read with the background notes, and *Corporation Tax Reform: The Next Steps*, December 2003 and November 2004.

working is very much alive, even if it is unlikely that the UK will be involved as a partner in the outcome.

The 'profits' of a company subject to corporation tax means both income and chargeable gains, and profits are computed according to the principles used for income tax and CGT.[2] Profits accruing for the benefit of the company arising by virtue of its being a partner in a partnership are chargeable to corporation tax as if they had accrued directly to the company.[3] Profits accruing for the benefit of the company arising under a trust are also chargeable to corporation tax as if they had accrued directly to the company.[4] The company is also chargeable on profits accruing during winding up.[5] This could be made to suggest that both corporation tax and income tax could be chargeable on income arising to the company as trustee during the winding up. Income arising to a company as trustee is chargeable to income tax even though the beneficiary is a company.

4.2 Profits of a Company—Income

4.2.1 Income

The amount of income is computed according to income tax principles, except where statute otherwise provides.[6] Where those principles change from one fiscal year to the next and the accounting period spans the two fiscal years, it is the principles in force for the second fiscal year that are applied.[7] It follows that income should be computed under the applicable, rewritten Schedules and Cases. It also follows that a company whose business is to let real property or to make investments is not regarded as trading for tax purposes,[8] and so its income will be assessed under the rules in CTA 2009, Part 4 (ex Schedule A), and Parts 5–10 (depending on the type of investment), rather than CTA 2009, Part 3 (ex Schedule D, Case I). The Capital Allowances Act (CAA) 2001 and ITEPA 2003 have effect for both corporation tax and income tax.

4.2.2 Distinguishing Corporation Tax from Income Tax and CGT

There has been a trend, beginning in the 1990s, to define income and capital gains separately for corporation tax. It was even proposed that a general anti-avoidance rule (GAAR) be applied for corporation tax only, though more recent GAAR proposals, including the Aaronson Report proposal presently under consideration, have not done so.[9] Such a

---

[2] CTA 2009, s 2(2), ex TA 1988, ss 8, 6(1)–(3).

[3] CTA 2009, s 6, ex TA 1988, s 8(2).

[4] CTA 2009, s 7, ex TA 1988, s 8(2).

[5] CTA 2009, s 6(1), (2), ex TA 1988, s 8(2); on the liability of the liquidator, see *Re Mesco Properties Ltd* [1979] STC 788, (1979) 54 TC 238.

[6] CTA 2009, s 2, and see the charging sections of each specific forms of income, eg s 35 for trading income; ex TA 1988, s 9(1); any exemption from income tax applies to corporation tax (CTA 2009, ss 2(4), 969(4), 979(2), ex TA 1988, s 9(4)).

[7] Broadly incorporated in the charging sections of each specific forms of income, eg s 35 for trading income; ex TA 1988, s 9(2).

[8] *Webb v Conelee Properties Ltd* [1982] STC 913, (1982) 56 TC 149.

[9] Eg the 2011 Aaronson GAAR study, available at <http://www.hm-treasury.gov.uk/tax_avoidance_gaar.htm>.

limitation is objectionable in theory and causes much difficulty when, for example, there are mixed partnerships with corporate and non-corporate members. Thus, there have been separate rules for Schedule A (1994–98), and still are for, say, interest from a UK or non-UK source. Among the present differences between corporation tax and income tax are the following:

(1)   A company cannot use any relief (eg personal reliefs) or be subject to any burden (eg higher rate tax) which is expressed to apply to individuals as opposed to persons.[10]

(2)   The special basis of period rules in ITTOIA 2005, sections 196 *et seq* do not apply for corporation tax.[11]

(3)   The special rules for loan relationships and derivatives (discussed in chapter five below) do not apply for income tax.

(4)   The remittance basis of taxation does not apply for corporation tax.[12]

(5)   Dividend income generally is not subject to corporation tax.[13]

(6)   The controlled foreign company legislation which attributes the gains of foreign companies to UK participators applies only to those participators subject to UK corporation tax.

4.2.3 Debts

As part of the changing world of accounting standards, FA 2005, Schedule 4 rewrote the UK tax rules on debts for corporation tax. The very long-standing TA 1988, section 74(1)(j) was repealed and replaced by TA 1988, section 88D, now CTA 2009, sections 55 and 970. Other changes refer to 'statutory insolvency arrangements' instead of arrangement or compromises. The rules on the release of debts, formerly TA 1988, section 89 and now CTA 2009, section 55, were widened to cover impairment losses and debts to be settled otherwise than in money. Thes corporation tax rules on impairment losses and debt are discussed in more detail below beginning at §5.1.1.2. Similar changes were made for income tax by ITTOIA 2005.

4.2.4 Transactions Between a Dealing and an Associated Non-dealing Company

The rule that an expense may be a revenue expense of the payer but a capital receipt of the payee, with consequent leakage of tax, is modified where one company is a dealing company and the other is an associated[14] non-dealing company. A dealing company is one dealing in securities, land or buildings. Section 774 of Taxes Act 1988 (not rewritten) applies if the dealing company becomes entitled to a deduction on account of the depreciation of any right against the other company or makes any deductible payment to the other, and the depreciation or payment is not brought into account in computing the profits or gains of the other; section 774 makes the latter company chargeable to corporation tax on

---

[10]   Broadly incorporated in the charging sections of each specific forms of income, eg s 35 for trading income, and made clear in the specific reliefs, eg in ITA 2007, Pt 3; ex TA 1988, s 9(2).

[11]   Ex TA 1988, s 9(6).

[12]   CTA 2009, s 180(1), ex TA 1988, s 70; and see below at §15.4. Neither did the reduced income basis (TA 1988, s 65(3)), a matter relevant to losses.

[13]   CTA 2009, Pt 9A, ex TA 1988, s 208.

[14]   See *IRC v Lithgows Ltd* (1960) 39 TC 270.

an amount equal to the deduction.[15] If it carries on a trade, the company may elect to have the amount deemed as a trading receipt of such of its trades as it selects. A purchaser of the non-dealing company may thus find an unexpected liability.

An example[16] of a device at which section 774 is aimed is where dealing company A waives a loan which it has made to non-dealing company B; A might get relief for the loan, and but for section 774, B would keep the money tax free; section 774 makes B liable to tax on the amount waived.

4.2.5 Enhanced Expenditure

4.2.5.1 Research Expenditure

FA 2000 introduced enhanced tax relief for expenditure on research and development (R&D)[17] which is incurred by companies;[18] this was widened by FA 2002 and rewritten as CTA 2009, Part 13. The enhanced relief is available only if the company spends at least £10,000 in its 12-month accounting period (or its equivalent over a shorter period).[19] If the condition is met, the relief applies to the whole sum spent, including the first £10,000. Rules are designed to prevent relief if the payments have been artificially inflated.[20]

The relief was at first confined to small or medium-sized enterprises (SMEs),[21] the EU definition being used rather than that in the UK companies legislation. It was extended to larger companies, but in a slightly modified form, in 2002.[22] That year also saw a separate credit for vaccine research.[23] As from 2008, claims by SMEs for R&D relief and by a company of any size for vaccine research relief are barred if the company is not a going concern (and see also the Government announcement on vaccine research relief, below).[24] In order to satisfy the EU state aid rules, the same Act required large companies to declare that the availability of the relief had resulted in an increase in the amount of research and work, or increased the amount of R&D expenditure.[25] For similar reasons, FA 2008 introduced a cap on the total amount of R&D aid that may be claimed—the limit is €7.5 million.[26]

---

[15] Section 774(3) excludes s 774 if the non-dealing company has incurred a non-allowable capital loss as a result of the loan or payment being used as abortive expenditure.

[16] See also *Alherma Investments Ltd v Tomlinson* [1970] 2 All ER 436, (1970) 48 TC 81.

[17] For policy see Dilnot, Emmerson and Simpson (eds), *Green Budget 2002* (Institute for Fiscal Studies, 2002), §6.1; and Chote, Emmerson and Simpson (eds), *Green Budget 2003* (Institute for Fiscal Studies, 2003), §6.5 and symposium (2001) 22 *Fiscal Studies* 271–399 (before changes of 2002 and later years). On 2002 and 2003 changes, see Inland Revenue Budget Note BN 16/02, [2002] *Simon's Tax Intelligence* 577. See Christian [2002] BTR 277–81 and Inland Revenue Budget Note Rev BN 17, [2003] *Simon's Tax Intelligence* 722.

[18] CTA 2010, Pt 13, ss 1039–1142, ex FA 2000, Sch 20.

[19] CTA 2010, s 1050, ex FA 2000, Sch 20, para 1(1)–(3A). The £10,000 minimum threshold replaced £25,000 in 2003.

[20] CTA 2009, s 1084, ex FA 2000, Sch 20, para 21.

[21] FA 2000, Sch 20, para 2; ie Commission Recommendation 96/280/EC of 3 April 1996; for detail see §4.6. The rules for SMEs are now in CTA 2009, Pt 13, Chs 2–4.

[22] FA 2002, Sch 12, Pt 1. The rules for large companies are now in CTA 2009, Pt 13, Ch 5.

[23] The FA 2002, Sch 13 rules for vaccine research are now in CTA 2009, Pt 13, Ch 5. For history, see Inland Revenue Budget Note 14/02, [2002] *Simon's Tax Intelligence* 575; widened by FA 2006, s 28 and Sch 2 to include payments to clinical trial volunteers.

[24] CTA 2009, ss 1046, 1057, 1094, ex FA 2000, Sch 20, para 18A and FA 2002, Sch 13, added by FA 2008, s 28 and Sch 9.

[25] FA 2008, s 30 adding F(No 2)A 2002, Sch 13, para 3A.

[26] CTA 2010, s 1113, ex FA 2008, s 29 and Sch 10, adding, for SMEs, FA 2000, Sch 20, para 1(5) and, for vaccine research, FA 2002, Sch 13, para 1(3).

If the SME relief limit is passed, the company may still claim relief at the rate for large companies.[27]

For R&D expenditure to qualify it must be:[28]

(1) not of a capital nature;
(2) attributable to 'relevant research and development'[29] directly undertaken by the company or on its behalf;
(3) incurred on staffing costs or on software or other consumable stores, or be 'qualifying expenditure' on externally-provided workers or payments to the subjects of a clinical trial;
(4) not incurred by the company in carrying on activities the carrying on of which is contracted out to the company by any person; and
(5) not subsidised.[30]

Subcontractors. Special rules[31] apply if the company uses a subcontractor which is a connected person. The subcontractor payment must have been brought into account in determining the subcontractor's profit or loss for a relevant period along with all of the subcontractor's expenditure, and this must have been in accordance with normal accounting practice. In such circumstances the payment is qualifying expenditure on subcontracted R&D—up to the amount of the subcontractor's relevant expenditure. This treatment is compulsory for connected parties and may be opted into by others. It provides a form of 'see through'. If these rules do not apply, the company may take 65% of the subcontractor payment as its qualifying expenditure.

Tax treatment. For SMEs the payment is to be increased by 125% and taken as a deductible expense[32] or by 225% as a pre-trading expenditure (without having to wait for the trade to begin).[33] It may also be used as a tax credit and used to generate a cash payment by being set against a 'surrenderable' loss, in which case there are consequential restrictions on the carry forward of the loss.[34] The cash payment, which is expressly declared not to be income, works out at 11% of the loss;[35] there are caps on the amount of loss that may be surrendered in this way.[36]

Large companies. For large companies there is simply an additional relief of 30%.[37] Large companies may also claim relief for work subcontracted to SMEs.[38] In turn SMEs may claim the relief—but only at the larger company 30% rate—for subsidised work which

---

[27] CTA 2009, ss 1068 and 1073, ex FA 2002, Sch 12, para 10C.
[28] CTA 2009, ss 1052–1053, ex FA 2000, Sch 20, para 3; the various terms are defined in ss 1123–1140, ex paras 4–9.
[29] See CTA 2009, ss 1041–1042.
[30] CTA 2009, s 1138, ex FA 2000, Sch 20, para 8, is framed in terms of 'notified state aids' but adds that R&D tax credits themselves are not 'notified state aids'; on the effect of the subsidy rule, note also FA 2002, Sch 12, paras 10A and 10B below.
[31] CTA 2009, s 1133–1136, ex FA 2000, Sch 20, paras 10, 11, 12 (as amended).
[32] CTA 2009, s 1044, ex FA 2000, Sch 20, para 13.
[33] CTA 2009, s 1045, ex FA 2000, Sch 20, paras 14.
[34] CTA 2009, ss 1054–1062, ex FA 2000, Sch 20, paras 15, 19.
[35] CTA 2009, s 1058. FA 2011 reduced the rate from 14%; prior to 1 April 2008 the rate had been 16%.
[36] CTA 2009, ss 1058–1061, ex FA 2000, Sch 20, paras 16–18, 20.
[37] CTA 2009, s 1074, ex FA 2002, Sch 12, para 11. The large companies rate was increased from 25% to 30% from 1 April 2008.
[38] CTA 2009, ss 1063–1067, ex FA 2002, Sch 12, paras 7–10.

would meet the conditions for relief but for being subsidised. The expenditure is known as 'qualifying additional SME expenditure'. The reason for this formula is that the tax credit is a state aid for the purposes of EU law. Where the SME receives a subsidy, this reduces the amount of the qualifying expenditure, something which would not happen if the company were a large company; these rules allow the SME to claim the credit (but only at the large companies rate of 30%).[39]

Vaccine research. This relief is modelled on the general regime. SME relief was abolished in Finance Act 2012. Formerly, the SME rate at which relief was given was 20% of qualifying expenditure as a deductible expense[40] or a pre-trading expenditure.[41] A tax credit option was available at 16%.[42] The relief for large companies remains, and is 40%.[43]

Above the line (ATL) credit. At the time of writing the Government is consulting on proposals for a new ATL credit for non-SME R&D, with a view to implementation from April 2013. Presently, relief for large company R&D expenditure is given the form of a 'superdeduction' which reduces taxable profits (as described above). The ATL credit would be calculated instead as a percentage of a company's spending on R&D, with the credit recorded in companies' accounts as a reduction in the cost of R&D (ie above the tax line in the accounts). The current proposed minimum rate for the credit is 9.1% before tax, and the ATL credit will be payable to loss-making companies.

4.2.5.2 Contaminated or Derelict Land

Under CTA 2009, Part 14, enhanced relief is available for company expenditure (including capital expenditure) on remediation of contaminated land.[44] The scope of relief was widened by FA 2009 to provide incentives to bring long-term derelict land—commonly known as brownfield land—into use and to include costs of removing Japanese Knotweed.[45] The company may not claim the relief if it or anyone connected with the company is responsible for the contamination or dereliction, or if the polluter has an interest in the land.[46] The company may not claim the relief if the expenditure qualified for an allowance under CAA 2001.[47]

The relief may be claimed if the land is acquired for the purposes of the company's trade or property business.[48] The conditions for the relief are that the land was in a contaminated or derelict state when the major interest[49] in it was acquired, that the expenditure was

---

[39] CTA 2009, ss 1068–1072, ex FA 2002, Sch 12, paras 10A and 10B, added FA 2003.

[40] Formerly CTA 2009, Pt 13, Ch 7. The rate was in s 1089. It was reduced from 50% to 40% by FA 2008, s 26 and Sch 8, para 3, and from 40% to 20% by FA 2011, before being abolished by FA 2012, ss 16–32.

[41] Formerly CTA 2009, s 1092, ex FA 2002, Sch 13, paras 15 and 15A. If the company was not entitled to a deduction for the qualifying expenditure in computing its trading profits for corporation tax purposes the rate was 140%.

[42] Formerly CTA 2009, ss 1103–1112, ex FA 2002, Sch 13, paras 16–24.

[43] CTA 2009, s 1091, ex FA 2002, Sch 13, para 21(1)–(4). If the company is not entitled to relief under Ch 2 the rate is 120%.

[44] CTA 2009, Pt 14, ss 1143–1179, ex FA 2001, Sch 22, para 1; on contamination see s 1145 (ex para 3).

[45] FA 2009, s 26 and Sch 7. See especially CTA 2009, ss 1145A and 1146A.

[46] CTA 2009, ss 1150 and 1163, ex FA 2001, Sch 22, paras 2(5) and 7; on relevant connection, see s 1178 (ex para 31(3)).

[47] CTA 2009, ss 1147(8) and 1149(8), ex FA 2001, Sch 22, para 1(4).

[48] CTA 2009, ss 1147(2) and 1149(2), ex FA 2001, Sch 22, para 1(1) and Sch 23, para 1.

[49] Defined in CTA 2009, s 1178A. For derelict land, the relevant time is the earlier of 1 April 2008 and date of acquisition.

incurred on relevant land remediation, that the expenditure was incurred on employees, materials or allowable subcontracting costs, that the expenditure would not have been incurred but for the land being contaminated and that the costs are not subsidised.[50] The relief does not extend to the acquisition costs of the land.

If the conditions of the relief are satisfied and the company makes the appropriate election, it may take a deduction for the qualifying capital expenditure and an additional 50% of the qualifying non-capital remediation expenditure (on top of the deduction already allowed in computing profits for corporation tax purposes).[51] If this creates or increases a loss, the loss may be treated as a loss for group relief purposes. A second option, modelled on the R&D tax credit (§4.2.5.1), is to give the company a tax credit equal to 16% of the expenditure.[52] The credit is not taxable income and there are consequential provisions to deal with matters such as loss relief and capital gains computations, so preventing double relief.[53]

4.2.5.3 Capital Allowance First Year Credits for Green Technologies

This applies where a company has incurred expenditure qualifying for first year capital allowance for certain 'green' technologies (below at §6.2.5.2) but is unable to use the allowance because of having a surrenderable loss, ie having a loss arising from the activity which is the qualifying activity for the green capital first year allowance.[54] The company must not be an excluded company.[55] The amount is the lesser of (a) the relevant first year allowance and (b) the unrelieved loss.[56] The credit is 19% of the loss, but this must not exceed an upper limit or cap. The cap is the greater of (a) £250,0000 and (b) the amount of the company's total PAYE and NICs liabilities for the period.[57] Artificially inflated claims are disregarded.[58]

The payment is not income but may carry interest.[59] Where the company surrenders the loss in this way, there are restrictions on other ways in which it may carry the loss forward.[60]

If the item on which the expenditure was incurred is disposed of within four years after the end of the chargeable period for which the credit is paid, there may be a clawback.[61] If this happens the amount of the original loss is restored.[62]

4.2.5.4 Relief for Film Production Companies

CTA 2009, Part 15 (sections 1180–1216) contains the rules formerly in FA 2006, Part 2, Chapter 3, providing a new form of relief for film production companies[63] and withdrawing

---

[50] CTA 2009, ss 1147 (capital expenditure) and 1149 (remediation expenditure), ex FA 2001, Sch 22, para 2; the terms are elaborated on in ex paras 3–11.

[51] CTA 2009, ss 1147(6) (capital expenditure) and 1149(7), (8), ex FA 2001, Sch 22, Pts 2 and 3 (paras 12–19).

[52] CTA 2009, ss 1154, ex FA 2001, Sch 22, para 14.

[53] CTA 2009, ss 1155–1158, ex FA 2001, Sch 22, paras 15–19.

[54] CAA 2001, s 262A and Sch A1, added by FA 2008, s 79 and Sch 25; the first-year allowance s are listed in Sch A1, para 3. The procedure is set out in para 18.

[55] Listed in CAA 2001, Sch A1, para 1(4).

[56] first-year allowance s are listed in CAA 2001, Sch A1, para 3, losses in paras 4–9 and unrelieved losses in para 10–16.

[57] CAA 2001, Sch A1, para 2; for (b) see para 17.

[58] CAA 2001, Sch A1, para 28.

[59] CAA 2001, Sch A1, para 23; see amendments to TA 1988, s 826 (not rewritten).

[60] CAA 2001, Sch A1, paras 19–22.

[61] CAA 2001, Sch A1, paras 24 and 25(10); on administration, see para 27.

[62] CAA 2001, Sch A1, para 26.

[63] Defined in CTA 2009, s 1182, ex FA 2006, s 32.

older reliefs.[64] As with the similarly-structured R&D and remediation regimes just discussed, this scheme provides for additional deductions in calculating profits[65] or a payment in the form of a tax credit,[66] if the relevant conditions are satisfied.[67] This regime was developed after much discussion.[68]

4.2.5.5 Relief for Video Game and Television Production

At Budget 2012, the Government finally announced its long-debated plans to introduce corporation tax reliefs, of some description, for the production of video games, television animation programmes and high–end television productions, with a view to making the UK 'the technology hub of Europe'. Consultation on the design will take place in 2012, with a view to legislating in Finance Act 2013. The Government intends the new tax reliefs to take effect from 1 April 2013, subject to EU state aid approval.

4.2.6 Purchasing Annual Payments and 'Settlement' Income

FA 2007, Schedule 5, paragraphs 1 and 2 introduced new rules designed to stop schemes involving purchasing annual payments and settlement income. HMRC do not admit that these schemes work but have produced pre-emptive legislation anyway. TA 1988, section 347A(1)(b) directed that certain types of annual payment were not within the charge to corporation tax. Companies have purchased such rights and argued that as financial traders they are entitled to deduct their expenses, eg the price, while not being liable to tax on the proceeds. Similarly, companies have tried to enter into arrangements which are settlements in ITTOIA 2005, Part 5, Chapter 5 (ex TA 1988, sections 660A–660G); the company then uses the settlor's (lower) tax rate rather than ordinary corporation tax rate. To prevent such schemes, the words in TA 1988, sections 347A and 660C removing any liability to corporation tax were repealed.

4.3   Capital Gains

Corporation tax is levied on the 'profits' of companies, and 'profits' include chargeable gains.[69] Corporations are not subject to CGT but only to corporation tax. The acts of a liquidator are treated as the acts of the company so as to bring them on to the corporation tax side of the line and to ignore disposals between company and liquidator. Although shareholders are taxed separately from the company, they may be made liable for corporation tax on gains accruing to the company if they are connected with the company and receive a capital distribution arising from a reduction in the capital of the company.[70]

---

[64] See §6.2.14 below.
[65] CTA 2009, ss 1199–1200, ex FA 2006, Sch 5, paras 1–5.
[66] CTA 2009, ss 1201–1203, ex FA 2006, Sch 5, paras 6–14.
[67] CTA 2009, ss 1196–1198, ex FA 2006, Sch 5, paras 39–41.
[68] See FA 2006 note by Shipwright [2006] BTR 517.
[69] CTA 2009, s 2(2), ex TA 1988, s 8.
[70] TCGA 1992, s 189.

4.3.1 Distinctions

Gains are treated differently from income. Since 1987, the importance of the distinction between capital gains and ordinary income for companies has been reduced since the same rate of tax is charged on both types of profit.

Despite these changes, the distinction from CGT still remains of importance:

(1) Indexation relief still applies in full for corporation tax.
(2) If a company ceases to be resident or subject to tax in the UK, there is a deemed disposal of assets. A similar rule applies to trustees but not to individuals; the corporation tax rule arguably violates EU principles.[71]
(3) The share identification rules are different for the two taxes.

There are also some important distinctions between income and capital gains in the corporation tax area:

(1) Where a trading loss is carried forward to a later accounting period under CTA 2010, section 45, it may only be set off against trading income—and not capital gains—of that trade of that period.
(2) A capital loss cannot be set off against ordinary income—even income of the same accounting period.

4.3.2 The Company and the Shareholder—General

A double charge to tax may arise if the company realises a gain but for some reason does not distribute those profits to the shareholders. In such circumstances there will have been a full charge to tax on the gain in the hands of the company and a further charge on the shareholder when the shares are sold. This leads to double taxation where there is a profit, and to double relief where there is a loss. In principle double relief for losses should follow the double charge on gains.

Two major avoidance techniques have been used, particularly when small companies are concerned. The first is to ensure that any appreciating assets are held by the individual shareholder rather than the company.[72] The second is to transfer the asset at full value to a wholly-owned subsidiary which makes the disposal. This transfer will not give rise to a chargeable gain,[73] provided the disposal of the shares in the subsidiary occurs more than six years after the section 171 disposal;[74] the liability in respect of the gain accruing before the transfer to the subsidiary will have been avoided.

---

[71] See eg Case C-371/10 *National Grid Indus BV v Inspecteur van de Belastingdienst Rijnmond/kantoor Rotterdam* [2012] STC 114 and Case C-9/02 *Lasteyrie du Saillant v Ministere de l'Economie* [2005] STC 1722. Whether the trust rule breaks such principles depends on finding the appropriate freedom for it to break.

[72] This may, however, risk the loss of rollover relief under TCGA 1992, s 152; on the obsolete retirement relief see *Plumbly v Spencer* [1999] STC 677.

[73] TCGA 1992, s 171; see below at §8.2.

[74] The transfer must be later than six years after the acquisition to avoid TCGA 1992, s 179; see below at §8.6.

4.3.3 *Substantial Shareholding Exemption*[75]

TCGA 1992, Schedule 7AC exempts gains arising from the disposal of substantial shareholdings. Whether deferral or exemption is the better policy option is a matter for debate. The practical effect of the exemption is very great and removes a major obstacle to corporate restructuring. The effect of the exemption is also to disallow any losses. The exemption applies only where certain conditions are met.

4.3.3.1 Terms

Using the terminology of Schedule 7AC, the regime includes one 'main exemption' and two 'subsidiary exemptions'. The company realising the gain, V (vendor), is called the investing company and the company whose shares are being disposed of is called the 'company invested in', here T (target). The company acquiring the shares will be referred to as P (purchaser). V must have a sufficient shareholding in T to be 'substantial'.[76] The period for which this condition must be satisfied is a continuous 12 months in the two years before the disposal. The calculations involved where a fluctuating holding is concerned may be complex. V's holding must be not less than 10% of the ordinary share capital of T. The shareholding must entitle V to the appropriate rights with regard to profits available for distribution or assets on a winding up; for this purpose the rules in CTA 2010, Part 5, Chapter 6 (group relief) are adopted with slight modifications. Shares held by other group companies are taken into account to reach the 10%.

In ascertaining the two-year period one can look past any earlier no gain/no loss transfers, and conversely not look past any deemed disposals and reacquisition.[77] The period also ceases to run if there has been a sale and repurchase agreement and the shares have come back to the original owner (or other group company); a similar rule applies to stock lending arrangements. The legislation directs one to look through any earlier company reconstructions or demergers.[78] A company is not treated as ceasing to be the beneficial owner just because it is put into liquidation; there are separate rules for insurance companies.[79]

4.3.3.2 Conditions

Various conditions must be satisfied by both V and T.[80] In broad terms, V must be a sole trading company or member of a qualifying group, which is defined as a trading group with an extension for certain not-for-profit activities. Express provision is made to cover the situation in which V is a sole trading company for part of the period and a member of a group for the other. Broadly similar but simpler conditions have to be satisfied by T. The legislation goes on to define the key concepts of 'trading company', 'member of a trading group' and 'member of a trading subgroup', and to make provision for joint ventures, for demergers and reconstructions, etc for T. Various other definitions follow.[81]

---

[75] TCGA 1992, Sch 7AC, added by FA 2002, Sch 8; among much writing, see Haskew [2003] *Private Client Business* 11, comparing this relief with the (then available) taper relief for CGT.

[76] TCGA 1992, Sch 7AC, paras 7–9.

[77] TCGA 1992, Sch 7AC, paras 10–13.

[78] TCGA 1992, Sch 7AC, paras 14–17.

[79] TCGA 1992, Sch 7AC, para 18.

[80] TCGA 1992, Sch 7AC, paras 18–26.

[81] TCGA 1992, Sch 7AC, paras 27–31.

4.3.3.3 The Exemptions[82]

There are three exemptions:

(1)   Under the main exemption, where these various conditions are met, capital gains and
      losses arising on the disposal of the shares in T will be disregarded for corporation
      tax.
(2)   The second (or first subsidiary) exemption applies where the disposal is not of shares
      but of rights related to the shares, such as options, convertible securities and options
      to acquire convertible securities.
(3)   The third (or second subsidiary) exemption extends relief under the main or the first
      subsidiary exemption to situations in which the conditions were met previously but
      are not met at the time of the disposal; in very broad terms, this relatively complicated
      provision allows V and T to look back a further two years.

These exemptions are regarded as so important that they override three rules which would
otherwise apply.[83] The three are all deferral rules which maintain the old cost base for the
assets, so the effect of excluding them is that P acquires the assets at the current market
value rather than at some out-of-date and usually lower figure. These are the reconstruction provisions in TCGA 1992, sections 127, 135 and 136,[84] the exchange of shares for
qualifying corporate bonds under section 116(10) and a demerger section 192(2)(a).

There is a detailed anti-avoidance rule.[85] The exemptions are excluded if, as a result of
relevant arrangements:

(1)   an untaxed gain arises, ie profits which have not been brought into account for UK
      tax purposes;
(2)   the disposal takes place either—
      (a)   after the company has acquired control, or
      (b)   after a significant change in trading activities.

Arrangements are relevant if having as their sole or main benefit the realisation of a gain
which would have been exempt under these rules.

The exemptions do not apply if the relevant disposal is a no gain/no loss disposal.[86] So an
intra-group transfer of a substantial shareholding is given its normal effect.

4.3.3.4 Special Rules

Just to underline the complexities of the capital gains regime, there are a number of
consequential rules. So it is expressly provided that the exempt shares remain 'chargeable'
for the purposes of the corporate venturing scheme.[87] Further, if the new rules would
prevent the loss from being an allowable loss, the taxpayer cannot use the negligible value
relief in TCGA 1992, section 24(2) to back-date the disposal and so create an allowable loss

---

[82]   TCGA 1992, Sch 7AC, paras 1–3.
[83]   TCGA 1992, Sch 7AC, para 4.
[84]   On which there is an interesting Revenue Guidance Note of 21 June 2002.
[85]   TCGA 1992, Sch 7AC, para 5.
[86]   TCGA 1992, Sch 7AC, para 6.
[87]   TCGA 1992, Sch 7AC, para 32.

after all.[88] This rule is followed by other rules designed to ensure that other special gains or losses are dealt with appropriately. So if a substantial shareholding is appropriated as trading stock and now held as trading stock, and this would give rise to an exemption under Schedule 7AC, the shares are still treated for general capital gains purposes as having been acquired for their market value at the time of the appropriation.[89] This rule is beneficial to the taxpayer, but the next protects the Revenue. Where CGT has been deferred under a claim for gift relief, a later disposal of the asset triggers the deferred charge even though it meets the terms of Schedule 7AC.[90] Other rules referred to are reorganisations under section 116(10), the deferred charge under section 140(4), the degrouping charge under TCGA 1992, section 179 and the Forex matching rules.[91]

4.3.4 *Transfer of Business on Company Reconstruction*

Under TCGA 1992, section 139, where a company's business is transferred to another company,[92] the transfer will normally involve the transfer, and so the disposal, of chargeable assets. This result will be mitigated for assets other than trading stock[93] in that neither gain nor loss accrues to the company making the disposal, provided:

(1)   the scheme involves the transfer of the business in whole or in part, as opposed simply to the transfer of assets;[94]
(2)   both companies are UK resident or, for disposals after 31 March 2000, the assets are chargeable assets, ie liable to tax under TCGA 1992, section 10(3);[95] and
(3)   the transferor receives no consideration other than the transferee taking over any liabilities from the transferor.

This provision is mandatory, not a matter of election. It is similar in intent to those which apply on the incorporation or takeover of a business; where the rule applies, the disponee takes over the base cost of the disponor.

   If the main purpose, or one of the main purposes, is the avoidance of liability to corporation tax, CGT or income tax, TCGA 1992, section 139 does not apply and the normal rules applicable to a disposal will apply[96]; any corporation tax due may be recovered from the disponee if the disponor has not paid within six months of the tax becoming payable.[97]

---

[88] TCGA 1992, Sch 7AC, para 33.
[89] TCGA 1992, Sch 7AC, para 36.
[90] TCGA 1992, Sch 7AC, paras 37.
[91] TCGA 1992, Sch 7AC, paras 34, 35, 38 and 39.
[92] But not to a unit trust or an investment trust (TCGA 1992, s 139(4)).
[93] TCGA 1992, s 139(2). Trading stock of the transferor will be valued under CTA 2009, ss 162–170 (ex TA 1988, s 100) for computing income, and so is excluded.
[94] Cf *McGregor v Adcock* [1977] STC 206, (1977) 51 TC 692 and similar cases (see *Revenue Law*, §42.5.1).
[95] Section 140(1A) added by FA 2000, Sch 21, para 9. On transfer to a non-resident, TCTA 1992, s 140 may apply; there are also rules for EU transfers (s 140A) and the risk of challenge under the non-discrimination rules in the TFEU.
[96] TCGA 1992, s 139(5).
[97] TCGA 1992, s 139(7); tax may also be recovered from certain subsequent holders. On clearance procedure, see s 139(5) referring to s 138 (see *Revenue Law*, §41.5.3).

The term 'reconstruction' has been construed by the courts to require a degree of continuity of common ownership.[98] On this view, section 139 would not apply where a business is split between two different groups of shareholders, but the Revenue take a more generous position.[99]

4.3.5 Transfer of Overseas Business to Non-resident Company

Under TCGA 1992, section 140, the charge arising on the disposal of an overseas trade plus its assets[100] to a non-resident company in return for shares may be deferred, provided the transferor company ends up with at least 25% of the ordinary share capital of the transferee company.[101] The charge is postponed until:

(1)   the transferor company disposes of all or any of the shares; or
(2)   the transferee company disposes of all or some of the assets.

However, the charge under (2) arises only if the disposal is within six years.[102] Where only part of the consideration received is in the form of shares or loan stock, then only a proportionate part of the charge is postponed. The purpose of the rule is to acknowledge that the gain is primarily a paper gain, and to give the company time to find the cash; the technique used is a form of rollover. This is a matter of taxpayer election; it has the effect of deferring losses as well as gains, and so the alternative of electing for TCGA 1992, section 152 rollover should be considered. The fact that foreign tax may have been paid and so is available for credit relief may make these elections superfluous or inadvisable. FA 2010 altered the mechanics of section 140(4) with the effect that UK tax is not lost where the consideration received consists of qualifying corporate bonds (QCBs). As QCBs are exempt from tax, the postponed gains previously escaped tax.[103]

4.3.6 The European Union—Tax-free Transfers and the Mergers Directive

The Mergers Directive, which took effect on 1 January 1992[104] and was amended in February 2005,[105] is concerned with allowing companies to merge or demerge their business operations[106] without triggering immediate charges on capital gains.[107] The 2005 amendments were implemented by statutory instrument in 2007 and futher regulations were

---

[98]   *Brooklands Selangor Holdings Ltd v IRC* [1970] 2 All ER 76.

[99]   Statement of Practice SP 5/85.

[100]   But not if the assets consist wholly of cash.

[101]   TCGA 1992, s 140; a claim under s 140C excludes a claim under s 140, and vice versa (see ss 140(6A), 140C(4)). Ordinary share capital is defined in CTA 2010, s 1118 (ex TA 1988, s 832(1)).

[102]   Other than by a group transfer within TCGA 1992, s 171; the non-residence bars in s 170 are ignored for (2). The definitions are modified by FA 2000 to take account of the changed definition of 'groups' to include non-resident companies.

[103]   See Ministerial Statement of 6 January 2010 and Notes to Finance Act.

[104]   Directive 90/434/EEC, [1990]OJ L225/1, on the common system of taxation applicable to mergers, divisions, transfers of assets and exchanges of shares concerning companies of different Member States (hereafter 'Mergers Directive').

[105]   Council Directive 2005/19/EC of 17 February 2005 amending Directive 90/434/EEC 1990.

[106]   For an explanation of why the UK legislation speaks in terms of 'trade' and the Directive in terms of 'business', see HC Official Report, Standing Committee B, col 296, 24 June 1992.

[107]   Inland Revenue, EC Direct Measures—a consultative document (1991), para 2.1.

passed in 2009.[108] The amendments take account of changes in accounting rules of direct effect for tax purposes, and of the emergence of the European Company (§2.14 above).

The normal corporation tax rules are modified in a number of situations involving a qualifying company,[109] company A, making a transfer to another qualifying company, company B, resident in another Member State. A company is resident in a Member State if it is subject to a charge to tax under the law of that state because it is regarded as resident there for the purposes of the charge; this is subject to any overrule by a double taxation agreement giving a different residence for treaty purposes.[110] These rules are not straightforward. Thus, suppose that two banks, one German and one French, have branches in London; if they wish to merge their branches the legislation will apply; if, however, the two branches are both branches of French banks, it will not.

4.3.6.1 Transfers of a UK Trade by A to B

First, where there is a transfer of the whole or part of a trade carried on by A in the UK to B, that transfer is wholly in exchange for shares or debentures and, where both A and B so elect,[111] the two companies, subject to further conditions, are treated so that the assets are transferred at such figure that neither gain nor loss accrues.[112] Although the transfer must be 'wholly' in exchange for shares or debentures, the fact that the buyer takes over liabilities does not disqualify it.[113] It is not necessary that A should be resident in the UK; it is sufficient that A is carrying on the trade in the UK. However, as seen above, if A and B are resident in the same EU country, this provision does not apply.

A condition relates to B's residence. If immediately after the transfer B is not resident in the UK, the condition is that any disposal of the asset would give rise to a charge to corporation tax.[114] If B is resident in the UK, the condition is that the company is not able to escape a charge to UK corporation tax in relation to any of the assets by reference to a double taxation agreement.[115] The effect is to allow deferral only when B will be fully exposed to UK tax in due course.

There is also an anti-avoidance rule. Section 140A does not apply unless the transfer of the business is effected for bona fide commercial reasons and does not form part of a scheme or arrangements of which the main purpose, or one of the main purposes, is the avoidance of liability to income tax, corporation tax or CGT.[116] There is a clearance procedure on an application by A and B.[117] In *Leur-Bloem v Inspecteur der Belastingsdienst*,[118] the European Court considered the application of the Directive to the creation of a holding company and an exchange of shares of the holding company for shares in two trading companies. It held that although the Directive allowed a Member State to prevent its use by

---

[108] The Corporation Tax (Implementation of European Mergers Directive) Regulations 2007 (SI 2007/3186) and the Corporation Tax (Implementation of European Mergers Directive) Regulations 2009 (SI 2009/2797).

[109] Defined as a body incorporated under the law of a Member State; see TCGA 1992, ss 140A(7), 140C(9).

[110] TCGA 1992, ss 140A(5), (6), 140C(6), (7).

[111] TCGA 1992, s 140A, added by F(No 2)A 1992, s 44.

[112] TCGA 1992, s 140A(4); the legislation excludes the deemed disposal otherwise arising under *ibid*, s 25(3) where the owner of an asset ceases to carry on a trade in the UK through a branch or agency here (s 140A(4)(b)).

[113] HMRC *Capital Gains Manual*, para CG 45709.

[114] Ie under TCGA 1992, s 10B (s 140A(2)).

[115] TCGA 1992, s 140A(3).

[116] TCGA 1992, s 140B.

[117] TCGA 1992, s 140B(2); s 138(2)–(5) also apply (s 140B(3)).

[118] Case C-28/59 [1997] STC 1205. See also Case C-436/00 *XY v Rikskatteverkel* [2004] STC 1271.

taxpayers for avoidance purposes, this did not permit the Member State to prohibit whole categories of transactions whether or not there was actual tax avoidance or evasion. The court also held that the Directive could apply even if:

(1)   the acquiring company did not carry on a business itself;
(2)   there was no merger of two companies into a single unit from the financial or economic viewpoint; or
(3)   the same person was sole shareholder and director of both companies.

4.3.6.2 A, Resident in the UK, Transfers a Non-UK Trade to B[119]

Here, A, resident in the UK, makes a transfer of a business in whole or in part to B and, immediately before the transfer, the business is carried on by A in a Member State other than the UK through a permanent establishment. No gain, no loss treatment of the aggregate of gains and losses arising is directed, provided:

(1)   the transfer includes the whole of the assets of company A used for the purposes of the business (although cash, a term which is not defined, may be excluded);
(2)   the transfer is wholly or partly in exchange for shares or debentures issued by B to A; and
(3)   the aggregate of the chargeable gains exceeds the aggregate of allowable losses.[120]

A claim need be made only by A (not A and B).[121] A special double taxation relief rule (see above at §4.3.4) applies.[122]

There is an anti-avoidance provision similar to that for TCGA 1992, section 140A, although here only A applies for clearance.[123] Relief under this rule is excluded if the more general deferral for the transfer by a UK company of a trade to a non-UK resident company (section 140) applies.[124]

This leads to the double taxation relief rule.[125] Double taxation relief, whether unilateral or under a treaty, applies as if the amount of the tax that would have been payable in the other Member State had actually been paid as tax—and so is available on a subsequent disposal of the asset. The effect of this is that the UK gives relief for the tax not paid in the state where the permanent establishment is situated, but is not required to give relief for any other foreign tax.

4.3.6.3 Capital Allowances

Where there is a no gain, no loss rollover on the transfer of a UK trade in circumstances satisfying TCGA 1992, section 140A, the transfer is not to be treated as giving rise to

---

[119] TCGA 1992, s 140C; and TA 1988, s 815A, added by F(No 2)A 1992, s 50.
[120] TCGA 1992, s 140C(1), (3), added by F(No 2)A 1992, s 45; in relation to insurance companies, see TCGA 1992, s 140C(8).
[121] TCGA 1992, s 140C(1)(e).
[122] Ie TA 1988, s 815A; TCGA 1992, s 140C(5).
[123] TCGA 1992, s 140D(2); again s 138(2)–(5) apply.
[124] TCGA 1992, s 140C(4).
[125] TIOPA 2010, ss 122–123, ex TA 1988, s 815A.

any allowances or charges, and everything done by company A is treated as done by company B.[126] Whether this was required by the Directive is uncertain.[127] There is no provision requiring capital allowance rollover on a transfer within section 140C—presumably because this is now a matter for the law of the other Member State. However, this means that a balancing charge or allowance may have to be calculated.

4.3.6.4 Other Merger Directive Matters

Under TCGA 1992, section 135, taxes on an exchange of shares may be deferred.[128] The conditions in section 135(1)(c) were relaxed both to meet the terms of the Directive and for purely domestic matters. It is unclear whether the relief is available for shares obtained in excess of an existing majority, or how a majority is determined where the target company has different classes of shares.[129]

4.3.7 *Capital Losses; Restrictions on Allowable Capital Losses*[130]

FA 2006 introduced major changes to limit tax avoidance through the creation of capital losses. One provision was a wide-ranging anti-avoidance rule, but this was confined to corporation tax. This has been superseded by TCGA 1992, section 16A, which applies both to corporation tax and to CGT. The 2006 rules on groups are considered below at §8.2.5.

Two further 2006 rules on capital losses are considered here. First, TCGA 1992, section 184G involves schemes for converting income into capital. Broadly, the relevant company must have a receipt arising from the disposal of an asset, there are relevant 'arrangements' and the company has a gain arising from that disposal but it also has losses arising from the disposal of another asset.

The next condition is that, but for the arrangements, an amount would have fallen to be taken into account wholly or partly instead of the receipt in calculating the income chargeable to corporation tax of either the relevant company or a group member as set out in section 170. The final condition is that the main purpose, or one of the main purposes, of the arrangements is to secure a tax advantage involving the deduction of any of the losses from the relevant gain.

The Board may then give the relevant company a notice covering the matter set out in the legislation in the form specified. The effect is to forbid the deduction of the loss from the relevant gain. Section 184I contains rules as to notices.

The other rule, section 184H, is aimed at schemes securing deductions. The structure of the provision is similar to that in section 184G, but aimed at any expenditure which is allowable as a deduction in calculating a company's total profits chargeable to corporation tax but which is not allowable as a deduction in computing its gains under section 38.

---

[126] CAA 2001, s 561, originally added by F(No 2)A 1992, s 67; on just and reasonable apportionment of expenditure between assets included in the transfer and other assets, see s 561(3).

[127] Inland Revenue, Guidance Note, 21 June 2002, para 2.5.

[128] EC Council Directive, 23 July 1990, Art 8; on definition, see Art 2(d) and Inland Revenue, *op cit*, para 2.9.

[129] See Lurie, *Tolley's International Tax Planning*, 4th edn (Tolley, 1999), ch 9.

[130] See Williams [2006] BTR 23 and 550.

4.4 Charities and Charges on Profits (Income and Capital)

4.4.1 Charges

For many years charges on profits (ie income and capital) formed a distinct category of deductible items; the origins of the system go back to the 1803 legislation introducing deduction at source for many types of income (see *Revenue Law*, chapter six). Before FA 1996 the list of charges included many types of interest, annuities, and annual payments and royalties; it also included certain gifts to charity, manufactured overseas dividends, the income element of a deep discount security and the discount on a bill of exchange.[131] By March 2005 the list of charges had been reduced to (a) annuities and annual payments payable otherwise than in respect of any of the company's loan relationships, and (b) qualifying donations to charities.[132]

In November 2004 the review of corporation tax had proposed the abolition of the charges on income, for reasons of simplification. After November 2004 the Revenue discovered that tax avoidance schemes had been devised using annuities and annual payments; these schemes relied on the fact that, unlike almost all other deduction rules, there was no unallowable purpose test. FA 2005 therefore removed the category of annual payments leaving just the charitable donation.[133] Annuities and other annual payments for trading purposes are treated as deductible expenses, while others are moved to the category of allowable management expenses of a company with investment business (§23.2 below). The charitable donation relief rules were rewritten as CTA 2010, Part 6. The following explanation is primarily historical.

4.4.2 Deduction of Charges from Profits

The company may deduct charges on income (now restricted to qualifying charitable donations) against its total profits for the period.[134] This applies only to payments actually made—not payments due.

Example

In financial year 2012, X Ltd has trading profit of £165,000, chargeable gains of £166,667 and received rent of £25,000, a total of £356,667. Assume that X Ltd makes annual payments to charity of £75,000 (gross).

X Ltd has overall profits of £356,667. This figure is then reduced by the £75,000 to leave the profits subject to corporation tax at £281,667.

---

[131] Ex TA 1988, s 338.

[132] Ex TA 1988, s 339, amended by FA 2000, s 40.

[133] FA 2005, s 132.

[134] CTA 2010, s 189, ex TA 1988, s 338(1), as reduced by any relief other than group relief; on use of excess charges as trading losses, see below at §4.5.1. Double tax treaty relief by way of credit is not available since it does not 'reduce profits' (*Shaw v Commercial Union* [1999] STC 109).

4.4.3 *Eight Conditions for Charges in ex TA 1988, Section 338 (Now Historical)*

(1) The sum must actually have been paid and the payment must have been made in the accounting period. The courts have held that interest charged on a bank account has been paid.[135] Whether a payment followed by a loan back counts as payment depends on the facts; if the payment is real it will be treated as such, despite the loan back.[136]

(2) The payment must not have been a distribution, whether or not qualifying.[137]

(3) The payment must not have been deductible in computing income or gains; if it was, it must have been treated as such and not as a charge. The line between a charge on profits and a deductible expense was important, first, because some items, eg patent royalties, could be treated only as charges and, secondly, because charges were deducted when made and not on an accruals basis[138] (this means that a charge may be paid at the due date, or early or late with consequent effect) and, thirdly, because an expense deductible in computing trading income affects trading income and so trading losses, whereas a charge could be set off against all types of profit, whether income or capital gain. It followed from the third point that by 2005, annuities and other annual payments for trading purposes were treated as deductions; FA 2005 therefore removes them to the category of allowable management expenses of a company with investment business (§23.2 below).

(4) The payment must ultimately have been borne by the company, so no deduction was allowed if the company was ultimately reimbursed, presumably whether or not there was a legal right to reimbursement.

(5) The payment must not have been charged to capital;[139] if the payment was made out of the proceeds arising on the realisation of a capital asset, the payment was not 'charged to capital' but was payable 'out of' profits and so satisfied rule (5).

(6) The payments will have been deductible only if made under a liability incurred for valuable and sufficient consideration.[140] Value and sufficiency were determined when the liability was incurred; 'incurred' meant 'in return for' rather than 'with a view to', so that an expected business advantage was not sufficient.[141] The consideration must have represented a fair equivalent of the company's liability.

(7) If the payer was a non-resident company, the liability must also have been incurred wholly and exclusively for the purposes of the trade carried on through the permanent establishment in the UK.

---

[135] *Macarthur v Greycoat Estates Mayfair Ltd* [1996] STC 1, 67 TC 598.

[136] *Nightingale Ltd v Price* [1996] STC (SCD) 116. The Special Commissioner rejected an attempt by the Revenue to argue that, following *WT Ramsay Ltd v IRC* [1982] AC 300, the payment under the deed of covenant could not be regarded as having been made since the repayment effectively cancelled the payment. The decision in *Ramsay* gave rise to the composite transactions doctrine under which intermediate steps inserted into a transaction entirely for tax purposes could be ignored; for a detailed discussion of the evolution of the *Ramsay* doctrine see *Revenue Law*, §5.6.4.

[137] Ex TA 1988, s 338(2).

[138] Ex TA 1988, s 338(1). The mere entry of the sum in a book of accounts does not always amount to a payment (*Minsham Properties Ltd v Price* [1990] STC 718, (1990) 63 TC 570).

[139] Ex TA 1988, s 338(5)(a).

[140] Ex TA 1988, s 338(5)(b). On the position where a company assumes a liability to pay an existing annuity, see Revenue Interpretation RI 76.

[141] *Ball v National and Grindlay's Bank Ltd* [1971] 3 All ER 485, (1971) 47 TC 287. The case turns on a provision reversed by ex TA 1988, s 338(2). Today the payment might be deductible as a business expense.

(8)   The deduction of payments to a person not resident in the UK was permitted only
      if the payer company was resident in the UK[142] and the payment satisfied either of
      two tests:
      (a) the payer deducted[143] income tax under the machinery laid down in ex TA 1988,
           section 349; or
      (b) the payment was one payable out of income brought into charge under ex
           Schedule D, Case V, ie wholly overseas income.

It was common for the borrower to insist on payment gross. This frequently occurred on
the Eurobond Market and led to the introduction of TA 1988, section 124, which enabled
interest on Eurobonds to be paid gross. This rule was repealed as part of the general widening
of the rules allowing payments gross.[144]

4.4.4 Special Rules for Payments to Charities

Until April 2000 the UK legislation provided two sets of rules for payments by companies
to charities. The first, the covenanted donation to charity, relaxed some of conditions
(1)–(8) above if a payment to charity was to qualify as a charge. The second, the qualifying
donation to charity, was a separate category of charge as gift aid. These rules were recast in
2000[145] and rewritten as CTA 2010, Part 6, sections 189–217. All references to covenanted
donation to charities were removed in 2000.

The general rule in CTA 2010, section 189 is that qualifying charitable donations made
by a company are allowed as deductions from the company's total profits chargeable to
corporation tax. The donation may be treated as made in an earlier accounting period
than that in which it is actually paid, but the company cannot carry it back more than
nine months.[146] Dividends and other distributions cannot be a qualifying donation (unless
the payment falls within CTA 2010, section 1020 (transfer of assets or liabilities)).[147]
A payment by a company which is itself a charity cannot be a qualifying donation.[148] The
rules extending charitable relief to gifts of shares and land apply to gifts by companies.[149]

As with the rules for individuals:

(1)   there is no obligation to deduct tax from the payment;
(2)   there is no need for a gift aid certificate;
(3)   the rules as to permissible benefits where the gift is by a close company were rewritten;
(4)   any gift of money is treated as a net sum, so enabling the charity to claim repayment.

---

[142] Ex TA 1988, s 338(4). However, a branch of a non-resident company may be able to invoke a non-discrimination
clause in the applicable double tax treaty.

[143] Or was absolved by the Revenue; see SI 1970/488, reg 6. Tax may also be eliminated or reduced by double
tax treaty, eg the UK–US Treaty, Art 11(2). On the importance of a claim, see Revenue Interpretation RI 79.

[144] FA 2000, ss 111 and 112.

[145] FA 2000, s 40; see further at ch 25.

[146] CTA 2010, s 199, ex TA 1988, s 339(7AA). This provision was originally enacted following a submission by
the DTI Deregulation Unit and is deemed to avoid the necessity to estimate profits on insufficient information
and then deliberately to overpay the covenanted sum, creating a loan of the excess.

[147] CTA 2010, s 194, ex TA 1988, s 339(1)(a).

[148] CTA 2010, s 191(4), ex TA 1988, s 339(3G).

[149] CTA 2010, ss 203–216, ex TA 1988, s 587B, added FA 2000, land added FA 2002, s 97.

4.4.5 *Payer's Duty to Deduct Income Tax*

The obligation to deduct income tax at source arises in a number of contexts. These were set out in TA 1988, section 349(1) and (2),[150] rewritten primarily into ITA 2007, sections 874 *et seq*, and cover annuities and other annual payments, royalties and certain type of interest.

For many years companies had to deduct income tax at the 'applicable rate', ie currently the lower rate of 20%,[151] when making the payment, and account to the Revenue on a quarterly basis for the sums deducted.[152] The scope of the obligations was reduced in 2001, in line with Government policy in its negotiations with other EU Member States that the right way to make sure that tax is paid is by exchange of information rather than a general withholding tax.[153]

Under the 2001 rules there is no obligation to deduct—and so no right to deduct either—if the payment is made by a company,[154] and at that time the company reasonably believes that either of two conditions specified in ITA 2007, sections 933–937 (ex TA 1988, section 349B) is satisfied. The first condition is that the person beneficially entitled to the income in respect of which the payment is made is (a) a company resident in the UK, or (b) a partnership each member of which is a company resident in the UK. The second condition is similar but international: (a) that the person beneficially entitled to the income in respect of which the payment is made is a company not resident in the UK ('the non-resident company'), (b) the non-resident company carries on a trade in the UK through a branch or agency, and (c) the payment falls to be brought into account in computing the chargeable profits of the non-resident company. The effect of this condition is that the payee must be within the UK corporation tax net, and so the Revenue will get their money anyway unless the 2003 Savings Directive applies. Where the payment is made gross, the payer may deduct the payment in computing profits.

Penalties may be charged where the belief is non-existent or unreasonable.[155] Where the belief is reasonable but incorrect, the Revenue may still collect tax,[156] leaving the company to such restitution or other claims as it may have. This point apart, it will be recognised that the reason for making the test one of reasonable belief rather than the actual state of the payee company is that the question whether the payee company meets one or other condition is often not easy for the paying company to determine, and may be much more easily answered by the payee. The Board may issue a notice directing that tax is to be withheld after all if the Board has reasonable grounds for believing, as respects each payment to which the direction relates, that it is likely that neither of the specified conditions will be satisfied in relation to the payment at the time the payment is made.[157]

---

[150] See *Revenue Law*, §27.5; on changes in 2001 and 2002 see Hardwick [2001] BTR 339–43 and [2002] BTR 321–25.

[151] TA 1988, s 4(1), (1A).

[152] For details, see TA 1988, Sch 16, paras 2, 9.

[153] See §7.4.2 on the EU's Interest and Royalties Directive of 2003, which exempts payments of interest, etc where the source is a UK company and the recipient is an associate company in another Member State.

[154] ITA 2007, s 930, ex TA 1988, s 349A(5), (6).

[155] TMA 1970, s 98 (4A)–(4C).

[156] ITA 2007, s 932 and 938, ex TA 1988, s 349D.

[157] ITA 2007, s 931, ex TA 1988, s 349C.

The duty to withhold was removed from payments by local authorities in 2002. At the time the duty was removed from payment by companies to various specified tax-exempt bodies, or to partnerships consisting of companies or such tax-exempt bodies.[158]

In 2002 the right to make royalty payments without withholding tax was extended to royalties paid by a company in the UK where it reasonably believes that the recipient company is entitled to relief under a double tax arrangement.[159] This was extended by FA 2004 to payments of royalties between associated companies under the Interest and Royalties Directive[160] (see §7.4.1).

Where the duty to account survives, it applies quarterly and extends to all payments within ex TA 1988, section 349, now ITA 2007,[161] including yearly interest. This obligation is therefore not affected by the introduction of the FA 1996 rules for loan relationships (see below at §5.1).

4.5 Losses[162]

4.5.1 Trading Loss

4.5.1.1 Set-off Against Future Trading Income from the Trade

Where a company incurs a trading loss, it may roll the loss forward and set it off against the trading income of the trade of succeeding accounting periods under CTA 2010, section 45 (ex TA 1988, section 393(1)), provided the company remains within the charge to corporation tax, the loss being set off against the earliest available profits.[163] The boundary between trading income and other income may be a fine one.

4.5.1.2 Interest or Dividends as Trading Income

Alternatively, where there are not enough trading profits for a period to absorb all or even some of the loss, the loss may be set against 'any interest or dividends' which would have been taken into account as trading receipts in computing that income but for the fact that they have been subjected to tax under other provisions.[164] In applying this test the courts look to the nature of the business and the purpose for which the fund is held, and ask whether the investment is in some way integral to the trade.[165] A bank or an insurance business would meet this test, but it is not clear how many others will. In *Nuclear Energy*

---

[158] FA 2002 s 94.

[159] ITA 2007, ss 911–913, ex TA 1988, s 349E, added by FA 2002 s 96.

[160] Directive 2003/49/EC.

[161] ITA 2007, ss 946 and 961(1), (6), ex TA 1988, s 350(4); on payment of interest to the UK branch of a non-resident company, see Revenue Interpretation RI 49.

[162] For some dated comparative material, see *Taxing Profits in a Global Economy* (OECD, 1991), ch 3, Table 3.8; for an invaluable analysis of tax losses from a primarily Canadian policy perspective, see Donnelly and Young (2002) 50 *Canadian Tax J* 429 and [2005] BTR 432. See also the Tucker Committee Report, Cmd 8189 (1951), paras 77–83 and Royal Commission on the Taxation of Profits and Income, *Final Report*, Cmd 9474 (1955), paras 480–88.

[163] CTA 2010, ss 45 and 36(3), ex TA 1988, s 393(1), (10). The general rules for claim under self-assessment are in FA 1998, Sch 18, Pt VII, ie paras 54–77.

[164] CTA 2010, s 46, ex TA 1988, s 393(8).

[165] *Nuclear Electric plc v Bradley* [1996] STC 405, 68 TC 670, HL.

plc v Bradley,[166] the House of Lords held that in the particular circumstances of that case, interest received on long loans taken out to fund expenses on the eventual decommissioning of nuclear power stations could not be regarded as trading income against which brought forward losses could be put. The case concerned large sums of money over long periods; short-term deposits by a trader to meet current or short-term liabilities would be treated differently.[167]

The other element is 'interest or dividends'. Profits from loan relationships arising out of trading transactions now enter into the trading profit calculation. Profits from non-trading relationships will usually fail to satisfy the first element anyway. It will be noted that the test used is 'dividends' and not 'distributions'. The effect of these rules is to break down the boundaries of the schedular system, but only where the investment income would have been trading income but for that system.

4.5.1.3 Set-off Against General Profits of the Same Accounting Period and the Preceding Year (Three Years for Terminal Losses)

The rules on carrying across and back losses in TA 1988, section 393A and now in CTA 2010, section 37 were recast in 1991 to allow greater carry-back of losses[168]—felt to be necessary in time of recession. The flexibility was largely withdrawn in 1997.[169] The whole loss eligible for relief must be used; partial claims are not allowed.[170] Whether a company should cut short an accounting period straddling the year end in order to accelerate the loss relief is a matter of judgement. Any unused capital allowances which have not been given effect as deductions in computing profits, and so in calculating the loss, are to be treated similarly.[171]

(1) The company may set the loss against its profits of whatever description, ie covering both non-trading income and capital gains, of the same accounting period.[172]

(2) The company may carry the loss back and set it against its profits of whatever description of preceding accounting periods falling wholly or partly within the period of one year immediately preceding the period in which the loss occurs; to qualify for this carry-back the company must have been carrying on the trade and been within the charge to corporation tax in that prior accounting period.[173] Where there is an accounting period straddling the anniversary, the loss may be set only against that part of the profits attributable to the period falling within the year.

(3) The period of one year is extended to three years in the case of a terminal loss, ie any loss incurred in the trade in the last 12 months of trading, apportioning the profits of any period straddling that anniversary.[174] This preserves one effect of the 1991 change, in that the loss may be set against profits of whatever description and not just trading income.

---

[166] *Ibid*; see also *Bank Line Ltd v IRC* [1974] STC 342, 49 TC 307 (fund to pay for replacement of company's fixed assets—interest not available for loss relief).

[167] [1996] STC 405, 412, 68 TC 670, 717, *per* Lord Jauncey.

[168] FA 1991, s 73.

[169] F(No 2)A 1997, s 39; on transition, note *Camcrown Ltd v Mcdonald* [1999] STC (SCD) 255.

[170] CTA 2010, s 37(1)–(8), ex TA 1988, s 393A(l) refers to 'the amount of the loss'.

[171] Ex TA 1988, s 393A(5), repealed.

[172] CTA 2010, s 37, ex TA 1988, s 393A(1).

[173] CTA 2010, ss 35–37 , ex TA 1988, s 393A(l)(b), (2), (9).

[174] CTA 2010, s 39, ex TA 1988, s 393A(7A).

The general rule is that losses must be set against profits of later periods first.[175] Any repayment supplement due in respect of a repayment of tax already paid will be calculated by reference to the year in which the loss arises.[176] Relief under (2) above must not interfere with any relief given for a charge on income.[177]

FA 2009, section 23 and Schedule 6, paragraph 3 allowed a company to carry a trading loss back three years instead of just one; this period already applies to terminal losses but was made general, subject to a £50,000 limit each year. The years are determined by reference to accounting periods specified in paragraph 3(3). This was to help businesses through the recession. FA 2009, section 62, dealing with cessations of trade on or after 21 May 2009, provided that terminal loss relief is not available if, when the company ceases to carry on a trade, any of the activities are taken over by a person who is not (or by persons any or all of whom are not) within the charge to corporation tax. The section applies only if the main purpose or one of the main purposes of the company's cessation is to secure the terminal loss relief. The purpose of section 62 is to counter an avoidance scheme.[178]

4.5.1.4 Non-allowable Trading Losses

The privilege of loss relief under CTA 2010, section 37 does not apply to trades carried on wholly outside the UK,[179] nor to dealings in commodity futures.[180] The income tax restrictions on loss relief applied to persons in respect of farming and market gardening also apply here.[181] Further, as with income tax, the trade, whether or not connected with farming, must either have been carried on (a) under some enactment, or (b) on a commercial basis and with a view to the realisation of gain, whether in itself or as part of a larger undertaking of which the trade formed part.[182] A reasonable expectation of gain at the end of the period will satisfy this test.[183]

4.5.1.5 Charges Incurred for Trading Purposes as Losses

The scope of this rule will be greatly reduced by F(No 2)A 2005, which removes annual payments from the scope of charges (see above §4.4.1). However, the rule remains in place. Annual payments paid before 16 March 2005 remain 'charges'.

Where charges on income consisting of payments made wholly and exclusively for the purposes of a trade carried on by the company, and those and other charges on income, exceed the profits of that period against which they are deductible then, whichever is the smaller of those payments or the excess, is treated as a trading expense[184] and so becomes entitled to loss relief. If the company has charges of £500 and profits of £600, the profits will be reduced to £100; if, however, the profits are only £410, the excess charges of £90 will

---

[175] CTA 2010, s 37(8), ex TA 1988, s 393A(l).

[176] This was by analogy to the rules for the carry-back of surplus ACT (HC Official Report, Standing Committee B, col 358, 18 June 1991).

[177] Ex TA 1988, s 393A(8).

[178] See HMRC Notes on Clauses, Finance Bill 2009, new clause 8.

[179] CTA 2010, s 37(5), ex TA 1988, s 393A(3).

[180] CTA 2010, s 52, ex TA 1988, s 399(2)–(4).

[181] CTA 2010, ss 48–51, ex TA 1988, s 397; see *Revenue Law*, §20.10.5.

[182] CTA 2010, ss 37(5),(6) and 44(1),(2),(4), ex TA 1988, s 393A(3).

[183] CTA 2010, s 44(1), (3), ex TA 1988, s 393A(4).

[184] Ex TA 1988, s 393(9); on management expenses of an investment company, see CTA 2010, ss 1219(3) and 1221(1), ex TA 1988, s 75(3).

available as loss relief. Where the company carries on two trades, the excess charge which falls to be treated as an allowable loss may only be set off against future income of the trade for which the charge was raised; the fact that there are individual (beneficial) side-effects for the other trade is irrelevant.[185]

4.5.2 Carry Forward for Use by Another Company—Company Reconstruction Without Change of Ownership

Where a company:

(1) transfers a trade or part of a trade to another company; and
(2) there is no change of ownership,

the change is ignored so as to allow any trading loss to be rolled forward to be set off against the subsequent trading income under CTA 2010, section 45, subject only to the first company's right to set the loss against other profits under section 37.[186] This treatment is given only where the conditions in CTA 2010, Part 22, Chapter 1, sections 940A–953 (ex TA 1988, section 343) are satisfied. Where a company ceases to trade or to carry on a part of a trade, restrictions apply if the transferring company is insolvent;[187] in these circumstances, the amount of the loss that may be taken over is reduced by the amount by which the transferor company's 'relevant liabilities' exceed its 'relevant assets'.

These are the only purposes for which the change is ignored. Therefore the successor company cannot use any miscellaneous losses under CTA 2010, section 91 (ex Schedule D, Case VI) or capital losses of its predecessor.[188] This is scarcely unreasonable since, for this rule to apply, it is only necessary that the predecessor company cease to trade. It is not necessary that the company should cease to exist; such losses will be relieved by being set against subsequent miscellaneous gains or capital gains of the predecessor company.

4.5.2.1 Conditions

There must be no change of ownership. This will be satisfied if on, or at any time within two years of, the ending of the trade by the predecessor, the trade or an interest amounting to not less than a three-quarter share in it should belong to the same persons as the trade or such interest belonged to within one year before the event.[189] It is also necessary that the trade should be carried on by companies which are within the charge to corporation tax.[190]

---

[185] *Olin Energy Systems Ltd v Scorer* [1982] STC 800, (1982) 58 TC 592.

[186] CTA 2010, s 944(3), (4), ex TA 1988, s 343(3). The change is also ignored for capital allowances in so far as they have not been given relief as trading expenses. Assets qualifying for capital allowances will be transferred at the written-down value (CAA 2001, ss 557 and 559 (general) and 265 *et seq* (machinery and plant)); there will therefore be no balancing charges (or allowances), or any first-year allowance .

[187] CTA 2010, s 945(1), (4), (5), ex TA 1988, s 343(4); on relevant assets and liabilities, see ex TA 1988, ss 344(5) *et seq*. A liability assumed by the transferee company cannot be a relevant liability (s 344(6)).

[188] See below at §4.5.7.

[189] CTA 2010, s 944(1), ex TA 1988, s 343(1)(a).

[190] CTA 2010, s 944(1), ex TA 1988, s 343(1)(b).

Provision is also made for the situation in which the successor company transfers its trade to a new owner,[191] and for that in which the successor company treats the trade as part of its trade.[192] Where the first successor company does not satisfy the common control test, but the second one does (in comparison with the original transferor), the losses may be used by the second successor—provided this is within the three-year period.

4.5.2.2 Hive-downs

If a company wishes to separate a particular business and place it in a subsidiary (often called a hive-down), CTA 2010, section 944 on accrued trading losses will often be invoked (see further above at §2.12.3). TCGA 1992, section 171 (see below at §8.2.1) will be used for assets with potential capital gains liability. Capital assets qualifying for capital allowances which take effect in taxing the trade will be transferred to the new owner but will usually be transferred at the written-down value;[193] there will therefore be no balancing charges (or allowances), nor any first year allowance. The Revenue have indicated that where a receiver intending to sell off a company, trade or part of it affects a hive-down, the *Ramsay*[194] composite-transactions doctrine under which intermediate steps inserted into a transaction entirely for tax purposes could be ignored,will not normally be considered relevant, provided the entire trade (or part) and its assets are transferred with a view to its being carried on in other hands.[195]

4.5.2.3 Beneficial Ownership[196]

In determining whether the trade belongs to the same persons, the law pierces not only the veil of any company but also any trust, identifying shareholders and beneficiaries as the people with the interest in each case.[197] Persons who are relatives or who are entitled to the income of the trust are treated as one person.[198] If shares in company A Ltd are held on trust for L, M, N and P, and the company transfers the trade to a company whose shares are held on trust for L, M, N, P and Q, it would appear that there has been a change in ownership since, although less than 75% of the interest has been changed, each body of beneficiaries is treated as a single person. In determining the extent of a person's interest in a trade, it is necessary to look to the extent of his entitlement to share in the profits.[199]

4.5.2.4 Companies Leasing Plant and Machinery

CTA 2010, section 950 (ex TA 1988, section 343A) applies in place of section 944 where there is what the legislation calls a qualifying change of ownership of such a company (or partner company).[200]

---

[191] CTA 2010, s 953, ex TA 1988, s 343(7).

[192] CTA 2010, ss 951(1)–(4), 952(1), ex TA 1988, s 343(8), (9); as to whether enough trading activities have been taken over, see *Falmer Jeans Ltd v Rodin* [1990] STC 270, (1990) 63 TC 65; and *Revenue Law*, §20.8.3.

[193] Under CAA 2001, ss 265 *et seq* (machinery and plant), 557 and 559.

[194] *WT Ramsay Ltd v IRC* [1982] AC 300 and, see in particular, *Furniss v Dawson* [1984] AC 474. The evolution of the *Ramsay* doctrine is discussed in detail in *Revenue Law*, §5.6.4.

[195] See a letter sent by the Revenue to the ICAEW, [1985] *Simon's Tax Intelligence* 568; but the Revenue would not give an assurance that the new approach would never be relevant.

[196] CTA 2010, s 942(2), (3), (6), (8), ex TA 1988, s 344(3)(a); on beneficial ownership, see above at §2.10.

[197] CTA 2010, s 941(6), ex TA 1988, s 344(1).

[198] CTA 2010, s 941(7), (8), ex TA 1988, s 344(4).

[199] CTA 2010, s 941(5), ex TA 1988, s 344(1).

[200] Added FA 2007, s 31.

4.5.2.5 Historical Note

Section 343 read (and CTA 2010, Part 22, Chapter 1 still does read) oddly and more like an anti-avoidance provision than a permissive one—hence its restrictions as to time and the fact that it is not an election. This is probably precisely because the structure was originally used as an anti-avoidance provision.[201]

4.5.3 Restriction on Carryforward—Change of Ownership of Company and Change in Trade

The converse case arises where the control of the trade passes to other people but the identity of the person trading remains the same. The right to roll losses forward under CTA 2010, section 45 is excluded under sections 673–675 (ex TA 1988, section 768) if either:

(1)   within any period of three years there is both a change in the ownership of the company *and* (either earlier, or later or simultaneously) a major change in the nature or conduct of a trade carried on by the company; or

(2)   there is a change in the ownership of the company at any time—and not just within a three-year period—after the scale of the activities in a trade carried on by a company has become small or negligible, and before any considerable revival of the trade.

Where these conditions are satisfied, losses accruing up to the date of the change in ownership are not carried forward. These provisions were introduced in 1969 to stop the sale of companies simply for their tax losses. The going rate was then the equivalent of 10p for £1 of loss. Some companies were kept in existence only for their losses—hence (2) above. This provision does not apply to capital losses, which have their own rules.

A similar rule applies to prevent the carry back of losses to accounting periods beginning before the change in ownership.[202] There are also further rules about investment companies[203] for surplus UK property business losses,[204] and a category added by F(No 2)A 2005 for non-trading loan relationship deficits.[205]

4.5.3.1 Change of Ownership[206]

Two rules apply to changes of ownership. First, a change of ownership is to be disregarded if, before and after the change, the company is a 75% subsidiary of another company. This provision is aimed at the situation in which the company ceases to be the directly-owned 75% subsidiary of another company but remains within the same ultimate ownership.[207] Secondly, and conversely, where a company, P, owns a 75% subsidiary, S, directly or indirectly, a change of ownership of P also brings about a change in the ownership of S (save where the first rule applies). There may also be a deemed change of ownership where a

---

[201] FA 1954, s 17.

[202] CTA 2010, s 673–674, ex TA 1988, s 768A; s 768(2)–(4), (8)–(9) were applied by s 768A(2).

[203] CTA 2010, ss 677–682 and 692–702, ex TA 1988, ss 768B, 768C.

[204] CTA 2010, ss 677–705, ex TA 1988, s 768D.

[205] CTA 2010, ss 680(2), (3) and 697(3), (4), ex TA 1988, Sch 28A paras 9A and 10A, added by F(No 2)A 2005, Sch 7, para 3.

[206] CTA 2010, ss 677–682 and 692–702, ex TA 1988, ss 768B, 768C.

[207] CTA 2010, s 724. On wide test of ownership, see CTA 2010, ss 719–726, ex TA 1988, s 769(6C).

subsidiary is a 60% subsidiary of one company within a group and the 40% subsidiary of another such company (or the 50% subsidiary of each); the sale of the 60% holding and of the 40% holding to the same purchaser brings about a change in the ownership of the subsidiary for this purpose.[208]

4.5.3.2 Major Change in Trade

The concept of a major change in the trade is amplified by 'including' a major change in the property dealt in, services or facilities provided, or in the customers, outlets or markets.[209] Moreover, where the change has been a gradual process, it may be treated as a change even though it took more than three years. In *Purchase v Tesco Stores Ltd*,[210] it was said that the word 'major' imported something more than significant but less than fundamental; the effects of the change should be considered. In *Willis v Peeters Picture Frames Ltd*,[211] it was emphasised that these are essentially matters of fact. There, the taxpayer company was taken over by a group, and its sales to its former customers were divided among distribution companies in the same group; this reorganisation was held by the Commissioners not to be a major change and the court declined to interfere with that decision. Since it is almost inevitable that a person taking over a loss-making business will want to make some changes, the courts may have some nice questions to decide; Revenue practice is not to treat a change as major if a company rationalises its product range by withdrawing unprofitable items and, possibly, replacing them with new items of a kind already being produced, or if the company makes changes to increase its efficiency or to keep pace with changing technology or management techniques.[212]

Technical provisions treat a company reconstruction without a change in ownership as concerning only one company[213] and for allowing for intra-group transfers to take place without triggering CTA 2010, section 674.[214] Where the loss is due to an unused capital allowance, provisions ensure that no balancing charge applies to the extent that the charge reflects the unallowable loss.[215]

4.5.3.3 Further Restriction on Loss Carryovers

Two minor rules require mention. First, CTA 2010, section 53 (ex TA 1988, section 395) excludes sections 45 and 37 where a company has incurred expenditure on machinery and plant which it leases to another person, and there are arrangements[216] whereby a successor company will be able to carry on any part of that company's trade which includes that lease. But for this special provision, the first company would be able to create a loss to set off against its profits while giving the successor company profits to set off against its losses,

---

[208] CTA 2010, s 723, ex TA 1988, s 769 as amended by FA 1989, s 100.

[209] CTA 2010, 673(4), ex TA 1988, s 768(4). Of course, if the change in trade was sufficiently great, losses could not be carried forward, whether the trader was an individual or a company, by virtue of the rules as to discontinuance of a trade (see *Revenue Law*, §20.7).

[210] [1984] STC 304 (1984) 58 TC 46; see also *Pobjoy Mint Ltd v Lane* [1985] STC 314, (1985) 58 TC 421, CA (both cases on stock relief under FA 1976, Sch 5, para 23).

[211] [1983] STC 453, (1983) 56 TC 436.

[212] Statement of Practice SP 10/91, amended 1996.

[213] CTA 2010, s 676, ex TA 1988, s 768(5).

[214] CTA 2010, ss 675(1)–(3) and 687(4), (5), ex TA 1988, s 768(6).

[215] CTA 2010, ss 675(4) and 687(6), ex TA 1988, s 768(7).

[216] Arrangements may be of any kind, whether or not in writing (CTA 2010, s 53(5), ex TA 1988, s 395(5)); see also *Pilkington Bros Ltd v IRC* [1982] STC 103, (1982) 55 TC 705.

thus, in effect, permitting the assignment of the generous capital allowances provided for machinery and plant.

Another rule bars the transfer of relief where the company is a member of a partnership and arrangements exist for adjusting the company's share of profits or losses in return for consideration in money or money's worth.[217]

4.5.4 Other Income Losses

UK property business (ex Schedule A) losses may be set against total profits for the period of the loss[218] and then rolled forward to be set against total profits of a later period, provided the UK property business is carried on.[219] It will be noted that the word used is 'profits'—not 'income'—and it is indeed true that UK property business losses, like trading losses, may be set off against capital gains from that business realised in later years. Losses from an overseas property business (ex Schedule D, Case V losses) may only be set against profits of that business for later years.[220] Miscellaneous losses (ex Schedule D, Case VI losses) may be set off against other miscellaneous losses for that or any subsequent accounting period.[221]

A problem arises with post-trading expenses where a company has ceased trading and, in the process of selling up its assets, receives investment income on its funds. Reliefs for the incidental expenses will not be available since it is no longer a trading company and was not set up as an investment company. Unrelieved trading losses from its trading days cannot be used since the company is no longer trading.

4.5.5 Loss Relief and Partnership Schemes

FA 2004 includes rules countering schemes where a company is in a partnership and receives capital from the partnership.[222] Where the company receives an amount greater than the amounts the company has put into the partnership, a charge on the excess may be charged under miscellaneous losses (ex Schedule D, Case VI). The charge does not arise if the excess results from a sharing of profits in accordance with the partnership capital shares.

4.5.6 Leasing Plant and Machinery

Companies with a business of leasing plant and machinery, such as that in the famous *Barclays BMBF* case,[223] caused problems for the Revenue. The main problem was that these contracts usually generate losses in the early years and profits later on. Hence these companies were often sold as they moved into profit, to buyers who then used the losses

---

[217] CTA 2010, ss 958–962, ex TA 1988, s 116.
[218] CTA 2010, s 62(1),(3), ex TA 1988, s 392A(1).
[219] CTA 2010, s 62(4), (5), ex TA 1988, s 392A(2).
[220] CTA 2010, ss 66(1)–(3) and 67, ex TA 1988, s 392B.
[221] CTA 2010, s 91, ex TA 1988, s 396.
[222] FA 2004, ss 131 and 132; s 133 deals with the interaction with capital gains taxation; see Shipwright [2004] BTR 510–19.
[223] *Barclays Mercantile Business Finance Ltd v Mawson* [2005] STC 1 (HL) and see *Revenue Law*, §5.6.

against their own profits. This practice is countered by the rules in FA 2006, Schedule 10. These were widened in 2008 to counter sales to a single company.[224] The rules in FA 2006, Schedule 10 were amended by FA 2009, section 63 and Schedule 31, to make changes to help industry during the recession. FA 2010, section 29 amends the rules on when a company is owned by a consortium. An indirect 75% subsidiary of a company owned by a consortium will now be treated as a company owned by a consortium, so that any change in the consortium member's interest will now generate a proportionate charge.

4.5.7 Capital Losses

Allowable capital losses may be set off against chargeable gains of that or any later accounting period,[225] but not against income. Such losses are not affected by CTA 2010, sections 673–675. Group relief does not extend to capital losses. These rules are not affected by the changes made by FA 2005. It should be noted that while CTA 2010, section 37 allows relief for trading losses against capital gains of the relevant accounting periods, section 45 does not provide the same relief.

4.6 Transfer Pricing and Thin Capitalisation

The current rules on transfer pricing and thin capitalisation were introduced by FA 2004 and applied as from 1 April 2004, with the consequent splitting of many accounting periods that did not end on 31 March 2004. The 2004 changes took the form of (a) a substantial rewriting of the rules on transfer pricing,[226] and (b) making the rule on thin capitalisation part of the transfer pricing rules.[227]

Transfer pricing refers to the problem of how the tax system should deal with transfers of assets or services between companies or other traders who are not at arm's length. Unfettered taxpayer freedom here would allow the taxpayers to allocate profits or losses to different parts of their enterprise. In the international context this would allow the profits to appear in low tax areas and the losses in high tax areas. In the purely domestic context, the profits and losses might find their way to tax-advantaged areas. For many years the UK tax system worried about only the international problem. However, ECJ case law declared such rules to be discriminatory and so void. In reaction, the UK rules were extended to purely domestic situations. The rules contained in TIOPA 2010, Parts 4 and 5 (ex TA 1988, section 770A and Schedule 28AA), as amended, substitute an arm's length price for any price agreed between the parties.

Thin capitalisation refers to a technique whereby one company (P) set up another company (S) on terms which provide a thin amount of share capital and a thick amount of debt. In this way P can in due course make S pass profits back to it as tax-deductible interest rather than non-deductible dividends. While it is perfectly normal for companies to set up subsidiaries with a mixture of equity and debt, the tax issue arises when the

---

[224] Changes made by FA 2008, s 56.
[225] TCGA 1992, s 8(1).
[226] FA 2004, ss 30–33, see Van der Wolk [2004] BTR 465–68.
[227] Ex TA 1988, Sch 28AA, paras 1A, 1B, 6C–6E, added by FA 2004, ss 34–36.

balance is not such as could be obtained in a normal commercial transaction. Before 2004 this was addressed by a rule in TA 1988, section 209 treating the excess interest element as a dividend. Since 2004 the loan is treated as a provision of services (money) and so within the transfer pricing regime.[228]

Although it was thought that the 2004 rules applied to corporation tax and not to income tax—and so they are discussed in this book in their corporation tax setting— TIOPA 2010, section 146 now clearly states that the transfer pricing regime applies for income tax purposes as well. The (now somewhat moot) argument that the transfer pricing regime applied only to corporation tax was that the rules can apply only where there is the relevant degree of control, and that the test for control seemed to apply where companies were involved but not where individuals or trusts were parties.[229]

Control is defined in a particular way for the transfer pricing rules; a 40% interest can be treated as giving control.[230] Under the control test, one of the affected persons must be directly or indirectly involved in the management, control or capital of the other; or the same person must be directly or indirectly involved in the management, control or capital of each of the affected persons. FA 2005 adds a further twist by applying the transfer pricing rules if persons have been 'acting together' in relation to financing arrangements.[231]

The rules do not apply to dormant companies. More importantly, they do not usually apply to SMEs,[232] though such enterprises may elect irrevocably to be subject to these rules and the Revenue may direct that a medium-sized enterprise apply them.[233] To be small an enterprise must, at the time of writing, have fewer than 50 employees, and either its turnover or its assets (or both) must be no more than €10 million. The enterprise is not just the individual company but any other companies with certain joint consolidated accounts and any 'linked' enterprises.[234] To be medium-sized an enterprise must, at the time of writing, have fewer than 500 employees, its turnover must be less than €100 million and its assets must be less than €86 million. It is clear that decisions to increase or reduce staff, or turnover or assets may have significant effects—as may the exchange rate.

The exemption does not apply if the other affected person or some other party is a resident of a non-qualifying territory. 'Qualifying'—and so 'non-qualifying'—territories are defined. A territory qualifies if it is one with which the UK has a double tax treaty containing a non-discrimination clause. A dual-resident company with residence in a qualifying territory and a non-qualifying territory is excluded from the exemption.[235]

The transfer pricing rules apply to each transaction (or 'provision') separately rather than having the broad sweep of the US code (IRC §482). They compare the actual

---

[228] TIOPA 2010, ss 152–154, ex TA 1988, Sch 28AA, para 1A. On claims, see TIOPA 2010, ss 181–184, 191 (ex TA 1988, Sch 28AA, para 6C); on guarantees see ss 153–154 (ex para 1B) and ss 201–204 (ex para 7D). See also the EU law aspects discussed in ch 21 below.

[229] See *Simon's Direct Tax Service*, B.3.1815; also the FA 2004 rules appear in the statute under the heading 'Corporation tax'. Despite this, competent figures in the Revenue had been heard to say that the rules could apply to income tax.

[230] TIOPA 2010, ss 157–163 , ex TA 1988, Sch 28AA, para 4.

[231] TIOPA 2010, ss 148, 149, 158, 161, 162, ex TA 1988, Sch 28AA, para 4A, added by F(No2) A 2005, s 40 and Sch 8; see Green Taxation, 28 April 2005 106–108. On transition, see F(No 2)A 205, Sch 8, para 4.

[232] TIOPA 2010, s 166, ex TA 1988, Sch 28AA, paras 5B–5E; referring to the European Commission recommendation 263/2003/EC, 6 May 2003.

[233] TIOPA 2010, s 167(2), ex TA 1988, Sch 28AA, paras 5B and 5C.

[234] TIOPA 2010, s 172, ex TA 1988, Sch 28AA, para 5D.

[235] TIOPA 2010, ss 166, 167 and 173, ex TA 1988, Sch 28AA, para 5B esp (4) and 5E.

provision with the provision that would have been made between independent enterprises (the arm's-length provision) and then ask whether the actual provision confers a potential advantage in relation to UK taxation on one of the affected persons or (whether or not the same advantage) on each of them. The legislation will apply only if the arm's-length principle means a potential tax advantage for UK taxpayers, ie it will apply only to reduce a loss or increase a profit.[236] The legislation enables the parties to make tax-free balancing payments to each other to bring their cash position into line with the tax result.[237]

Further rules in TIOPA 2010, Part 4 eliminate double counting, make provision for trading stock on closing the business, allow a compensating adjustment where the advantaged person is a controlled foreign company, for guarantees, for double taxation relief, for securities, for foreign exchange transactions and derivatives—and for oil. The rules are not to affect the computation of capital allowances or charges or capital gains.[238]

These rules are considered further in their international context—see below §16.4.

4.7 Avoidance Involving Tax Arbitrage

Tax arbitrage refers to transactions or arrangements which exploit differences in tax rules; the differences may arise in a purely domestic situation or between the tax codes of different countries. Part 6 of TIOPA 2010 provides rules, which apply only to companies, to enable the Revenue to issue notices counteracting the effects of such arbitrage; this may be seen as part of a worldwide movement by tax authorities.[239] Examples of such rules include the double dip—under which a company obtains a deduction of the same expense in two countries (the deduction problem), or has obtained a deduction but the equivalent receipt has escaped tax (the receipts problem). The UK legislation has a rule for each problem. However, they apply only where the Revenue issue a notice, and Revenue guidance notes show that they are not overly concerned with simple schemes such as the double dip. Thus, although the Revenue have gone for wide words in the legislation, they apply them narrowly. This does not raise quite the same issue as the legality of extra statutory concessions because of the requirement of a notice. Practitioner reaction suggests that HMRC are applying the rules sensibly.[240]

The arbitrage rules apply to certain types of hybrid entityand instruments having hybrid effect The rules apply to deny or reduce a deduction (sections 232–48), or to impose a chargeable receipt (sections 249–54). Sections 255–57 deal with administrative matters and interpretation.

The deduction rule applies where there is a qualifying scheme, there will be a tax deduction or other set off, and the purpose or one of the main purposes of the scheme is

---

[236] The expression 'tax advantage' is defined in TIOPA 2010, s 155, ex TA 1988, Sch 28AA, para 5.

[237] TIOPA 2010, ss 195–204, ex TA 1988, Sch 28AA, paras 6–7.

[238] TIOPA 2010, s 213, 214, ex TA 1988, Sch 28AA, para 13.

[239] TIOPA 2010, Pt 6, ss 232–259, ex F(No 2)A 2005, ss 24–31 and Sch 3; detailed Revenue guidance on the rule is available on their website. On policy, see Edgar (2003) 51 *Canadian Tax Jo* 1082–1158.

[240] Luder, *Tax Journal* (24 October 2005), 9; Collins and Bird, *Tax Journal* (22 May 2006), 13, though the unannounced withdrawal of HMRC's FAQs in relation to the anti-arbitrage rules came under some criticism in 2011—see Mehta, *Tax Journal* (7 October 2011), 9.

to obtain a UK tax advantage, unless it is minimal.[241] The deduction is disallowed if the same expense is allowed for the purpose of any other tax, which means UK or foreign tax.[242] The effect may be to disallow the expense in both countries, so the lesson is not to claim it twice. A second rule applies where a transaction or series of transactions involves a payment which creates a deduction or an allowance for the payer but the recipient is not subject to tax unless because of specified exemptions.[243] The receipts rule applies when five conditions are satisfied:

(1) there must be a scheme, a company on whom the notice is served and a person making the payment to the company;
(2) there is a qualifying payment—one which increases the capital of the company;
(3) the person making the payment is entitled to certain types of deduction, whether in the UK or elsewhere;
(4) the amount received has not been taken into account for its own tax assessment; and
(5) a benefit arises from (4).[244]

The correct amount treated as arising under this rule must be brought into the company's self-assessment, whether by making or amending its self-assessment.[245]

4.8 The Patent Box

As part of its move towards a more competitive, territorial-focused and business-friendly UK corporate tax regime, the Government announced in its November 2010 Corporate Tax Roadmap plans to attract and encourage innovation in the UK by introducing a preferential rate of corporation tax of 10% for profits attributable to patents and other similar types of intellectual property (IP). The so-called 'patent box' regime was introduced by Finance Act 2012, Schedule 2 as CTA 2010, Part 8A. The patent box is to be phased in over five years from 1 April 2013, and applies to existing IP as well as newly-commercialised IP. The regime is intended to apply to a proportion of profits derived from the sale or licensing of patent rights, or from the sale of patented inventions or products incorporating the patented invention.[246]

The main operative provision is section 357A of CTA 2010, which provides that a company may elect that any 'relevant IP profits' of a trade of the company for an accounting period for which it is a 'qualifying company' are chargeable at a special IP rate of corporation tax of 10%. Part 8A, Chapter 2 sets out the conditions for a 'qualifying company'. Pursuant to section 357B, the company must satisfy either condition A or B: condition A is that the company holds qualifying IP rights, or an exclusive licence in respect of qualifying IP rights;

---

[241] 'Scheme' or 'arrangement' and 'UK tax advantage' are defined in TIOPA 2010, ss 258(1)–(5) and 234(1)–(3), ex F(No 2)A 2005, s 30.
[242] TIOPA 2010, ss 244(1)–(5), ex F(No 2)A 2005, s 25(3)–(5).
[243] TIOPA 2010, ss 239–242, 259, ex F(No 2)A 2005, Sch 3, paras (7)–(11).
[244] TIOPA 2010, ss 249–252, ex F(No 2)A 2005, s 26.
[245] TIOPA 2010, ss 254(1)–(3) and 250(4), ex F(No 2)A 2005, s 27.
[246] As described in the HMRC Technical Note and Guide to the Draft Legislation, dated 6 December 2011.

condition B is that the company held such rights in the past and has received income in respect of those rights. Section 357BB defines qualifying IP rights as, principally, UK or European Patent Office patents. A company that is a member of a group must satisfy an additional condition C, requiring active ownership and management of the IP rights. All companies must satisfy a further 'development condition' in section 357BC, which basically requires that they:

(1)   create or significantly contribute to the creation of items protected by the patent; or
(2)   perform a significant amount of activity for the purposes of developing items protected by the patent or any item incorporating protected items.

A company's 'relevant IP profits' are determined in accordance with a complex formulaic approach set out in Part 8A, Chapter 3. There are five broad types of profits that may qualify:

(1)   profits from the sale of the patented item, or an item incorporating it;
(2)   licence fees and royalties from rights the company grants others;
(3)   income from the sale or disposal of the patent;
(4)   infringement receipts; and
(5)   a notional arm's-length royalty for the use of the patent in other parts of the company.[247]

Section 357CJ provides a simpler 'small claims treatment' for qualifying profits of a company (and any associated companies) below £1 million—the company is able to allocate 75% of its qualifying profits to the patent box.

Chapter 4 provides an alternative method of determining relevant IP profits, known as 'streaming': see sections 357D *et seq*. Chapter 5 outlines rules in respect of relevant IP losses of a trade. Basically, patent box losses must be offset against current year patent box profits of other companies in the group, or be carried forward against the company's own future patent box profits. The obligatory anti-avoidance rules are found in Chapter 6 and attempt to prevent companies from seeking to obtain an artificial tax advantage by inflating their patent box profits.

---

[247] *Ibid.*

5

Computation (2): Accounting-based Rules for Specific Transactions

In this chapter we look at four sets of tax rules which draw heavily on accounting concepts. These are those dealing with loan relationships (including foreign exchange transactions) (see §5.1), derivatives (previously called financial instruments) (see §5.2), fixed asset intangibles or intellectual property (see §5.3) and certain rules about the currency to be used in calculating profits (see §5.4). They are treated together because they raise similar problems and because they were for a time the leading edge area of tax law as the UK moved from the ideas of 1803 towards the world of accounting principles—but only for corporation tax.

The modern financial world offers products which fragment a transaction into different elements and then reconstitute them in a different way with different tax results; other products enable the risk inherent in a transaction to be removed and sold (shifted) to someone else. Matters began to get out of hand (from a tax point of view) when corporate finance theory developed in the 1960s. A typical example was the put-call parity theorem.[1]

---

[1] See, generally, Warren (1993) 107 *HLR* 460; and Colloquium on Financial Instruments (1995) 50 *Tax L Rev* 487.

Using the language of options, where 'put' means sell and 'call' means buy, this theorem stated that if one holds shares but takes out an option to sell shares (a put option), one is in exactly the same economic position as having debt and an option to buy shares (a call option). Thus one is able to turn any pure equity position into a pure debt position (or vice versa) by taking out the appropriate option. An option is one example of a category called derivative instruments, so called because they derive their values from something else.

Faced with this fragmented world, the tax system could do any one or more of five things:[2]

(1)   move away from its traditional basis of taxing income when realised and a capital gain only when the asset was disposed of, in favour of a new accounting basis such as mark-to-market or amortised cost fair value, or even whatever practices the accountants manage to devise;
(2)   integrate the financial products by treating them as one and taxing the unit according to its economic substance;
(3)   bifurcate products into separate parts and tax each according to economic substance;
(4)   develop specific formulae for specific products; or
(5)   limit the deduction of expenses associated with the product unless the income is taxed currently.

UK corporation tax has opted for (1) in the areas considered in this chapter, but has developed as accounting practice has developed. Income tax and CGT, by contrast, have been left to struggle with the traditional concepts, subject only to ITTOIA 2005, section 25 for income tax.

5.1   Loan Relationships

5.1.1 Introduction—History, Purpose and Structure

The modern legislation has developed in four principal stages—1996, 2002, 2004 and 2009. Confusingly, the second and third stages both took the form of amending the original 1996 legislation; the fourth is the rewrite of the previous three into CTA 2009, Parts 5–7. Since 1 April 1996, corporate and government debt have been subject to a single regime called 'loan relationships'.[3] Since 2002 this regime has incorporated the previously separate rules relating to foreign exchange (FOREX) transactions.[4] The scheme brings together both interest arising on debt and the gain or loss arising from the holding of a financial

---

[2]   Schenk (1995) 50 *Tax L Rev* 571, summarising Warren, *op cit*.
[3]   CTA 2009, Pts 5–7, ex FA 1996, ss 80–105, Schs 8–11, all as much amended. The ideas are explained in Revenue Consultative Document, *Taxation of Gilts and Bonds* (May 1995). See Hole [1995] BTR 511 and [1996] BTR 347. For the likely source of inspiration, see New Zealand Treasury Consultative Document (October 1986); for a review of New Zealand legislation, see Smith (1998) 46 *Can Tax Jo* 819 and Glazebrook *et al*, *The New Zealand Accruals Regime: A practical guide* (CCH New Zealand, 1999). There is very useful guidance in the HMRC *Corporate Finance Manual* at <http://www.hmrc.gov.uk/manuals/cfmmanual/cfm30000.htm>.
[4]   CTA 2009, s 328, ex FA 1996, s 84A, added by FA 2002, s 79; see Lindsay [2002] BTR 292–96.

instrument. The profits and gains were taxed under Schedule D, Case III, even if there was a foreign element.

FA 2002 made two major sets of changes with different timescales. The first[5] consisted of a series of changes designed to prevent avoidance and was generally dated back to their announcement to the House of Commons. The second[6] was a major rewriting of the loan relationship rules to take account of experience since 1996 and to incorporate into the loan relationship rules most of the provisions relating to FOREX transactions. This rewriting took the form of a newly-enacted version of the relevant parts of FA 1996 and the repeal of the FOREX material in FA 1993.[7] The FA 2002 changes generally took effect for accounting periods beginning on or after 1 October 2002, with transitional provisions in Schedule 28.[8]

FA 2004 introduced changes to the 2002 scheme to incorporate the general move to generally-accepted accounting practice (GAAP), whether UK or under International Accounting Standards (IASs). These changes are outlined below. All three schemes represented a significant rationalisation of the scope of the charge, with more consistent rules for both receipts and expenditure. The rules apply to premiums and discounts, to yearly interest and short interest, to loans and to bonds. The intricacies flowing from having one set of rules for capital gains and another (but chaotic) set for income were swept away. In addition, many special statutory provisions introduced over a number of years to deal with special situations were abolished for corporation tax; these are the accrued income scheme and the statutory provisions for deep discounted securities. The reforms affected not only income received under loan relationships but also expenditure incurred, eg sums paid out. There are special rules for partnerships involving companies.[9] F(No 2)A 2005 added anti-avoidance rules.

However, this is not to say that everything has moved to a Haig-Simons world of comprehensive income taxation. While the distinction between capital and income is abandoned, that between trading and non-trading is not. Relief for trade interest is obtained by bringing the expense into the calculation of trading profit subject to tax under CTA 2009, Part 3;[10] non-trade interest is dealt with in CTA 2009, section 301.[11] Although the rules do not usually turn on the actual time when payments are made, that issue remains important for other reasons.[12] While the distinction between yearly interest and short interest is not important in the scheme, it remains important for withholding tax.

CTA 2009, Part 6 (relationships treated as loan relationships) was amended by FA 2009, which added two mains sets of rules. First sections 486A–486E were added as Chapter 2A to deal with disguised interest payments. Secondly, sections 521A–521F were added as Chapter 6A to deal with shares accounted as liabilities. F(No 2)A 2010, Schedule 5 extended the anti-avoidance rules governing amounts not fully recognised for accounting purposes in sections 311, 312 and 599A of CTA 2009 to close certain avoidance schemes of which the

---

[5] FA 2002, ss 71–78.
[6] FA 2002, Sch 25.
[7] Previously FA 1993, ss 125 *et seq.*
[8] On the review, see Inland Revenue Press Release, 18 December 2001, [2002] *Simon's Tax Intelligence* 9.
[9] CTA 2009, ss 380–385, ex FA 1996, Sch 9, paras 19 and 20; FA 2004, Sch 8, para 7 modified the test of 'major interest' in para 20 to prevent avoidance.
[10] CTA 2009, s 297, ex FA 1996, s 82(2).
[11] Ex FA 1996, s 82(3).
[12] Eg CTA 2009, s 464 and 465, ex FA 1996, Sch 9, para 2 (interest due between connected parties).

Revenue became aware. In a further attempt by the Revenue to counter avoidance transactions that seek to exploit asymmetries in the accounting treatment of loan relationship and derivative contract transactions, FA 2011, sections 28–30 amended the loan relationships and derivative contracts rules relating to cases where amounts are not fully recognised for accounting purposes, for loan relationships involving connected debtor and creditor, and for group mismatch schemes.[13] FA 2012, section 23 added additional rules governing debts becoming held by connected companies.

5.1.1.1 Practical Issues[14]

Borrowers and their advisers want to know the answers to the following questions:

- Are the sums paid in respect of loans deductible and, if so, when?
- Will the interest payment be subject to withholding tax?
- Is the benefit received from a premium or a discount taxable—whether on redemption or earlier?
- How is the lender/investor taxed, and does he get any tax benefit which could be shared with the other party?

The lenders/investors want to know the answers to the equivalent questions in reverse:

- Are the sums paid in respect of loans taxable and, if so, when?
- Will the sums paid be subject to withholding tax?
- Will the premium or discount on redemption be taxable and, if so, when?
- Will any special tax benefit be obtained which could be shared with the other party?

5.1.1.2 History—1996 and 2004

The essence of the 1996 scheme was that the company's accounting treatment was followed for tax purposes, subject to the accounting treatment being one of two authorised accounting methods: (a) accruals, and (b) mark-to-market. The accruals method was primarily relevant to issues such as when interest becomes taxable and how a single series of payments should be split between interest and repayment of capital. The mark-to-market method was primarily relevant to the treatment of debt instruments such as bonds and similar securities. (See further below, §5.1.5.)

In 2004 the essence of the scheme was modernised in line with the rapid developments in accounting practice. Gains and losses must be recognised either—in line with UK GAAP—in the company's profit or loss account, or in the statement of recognised gains or losses (STRGL), or in line with the IAS equivalent (the statement of changes in equity).[15] The accruals basis and mark-to-market method are no longer mentioned, but the legislation does from to time refer specifically to two similar bases—the amortised cost basis and the fair value basis. These bases are defined in CTA 2009.[16] In essence, fair value

---

[13] See Lindsay [2011] BTR 391 for the details.
[14] This list adapted gratefully from Murphy, 'Interest and Currency Management', in *Tolley's Tax Planning 1999–2000*, 865.
[15] CTA 2009, ss 308 and 310, ex FA 1996, s 85B, as inserted by FA 2004, Sch 10, para 3.
[16] CTA 2009, s 313(4), (5), ex FA 1996, s 103(1)—added by FA 2004. See IAS 39.

accounting takes note not only of interest payments but also of changes in the value of the underlying rights and liabilities. 'Amortised cost basis' means a basis under which an asset or a liability representing the loan is shown in the company's accounts at cost, adjusted for cumulative amortisation and any impairment, repayment or release; 'impairment' includes uncollectability. To illustrate the new language, the legislation no longer talks of 'bad debts' but of 'impairment relief'.[17]

5.1.2 Loan Relationship—Definition

A loan relationship[18] occurs whenever:

(1)   a company is a debtor or a creditor in respect of a money debt which arose as a result of a transaction for the lending of money; or

(2)   an instrument is issued for the purpose of representing security for, or the rights of a creditor in respect of, a money debt.[19]

The precise role of accounting practice with regard to this issue has yet to be determined; a transaction which was not treated as a loan in the accounts of a finance company has been held not to be within these rules.[20]

5.1.2.1 Phrase (1)

The insistence on a transaction for the lending of money means that finance leases and hire-purchase contracts are not loan relationships.[21] A guarantee is not within (1) because, in order for a loan relationship to exist, the company must be a creditor or a debtor, and a guarantor is not, itself, in that relationship.[22] This does not stop relief as a trading expense for a loss on a guarantee being given if the company carries on a trade of providing guarantees.

5.1.2.2 Phrase (2)

In (2) the critical words are 'instrument' and 'security'. The issue of an insurance policy is not the issue of a security, neither is the issue of a share.[23] Loan notes and promissory notes are instruments; if no instrument is issued, the debt cannot come within (2).[24]

---

[17] See also FA 2005, Sch 5 and CTA 2009, ss 55(2) and 970(2), ex TA 1988, s 88D, replacing TA 1988, s 74(1) (i). It was found that the 2005 changes did not interact correctly with the general trade rules. If a trade debt was released by a creditor connected with the debtor company, the creditor was denied relief under the loan relationship rules but the debtor was charged to tax under TA 1988, s 94 unless the release was part of a statutory insolvency arrangement. A change made by FA 2009, s 42 applies the loan relationship rules to both parties and removes the anomaly. The Notes to Clauses point out that if the parties are not connected and carry on a property business, the effect of the change will convert the profit from property income to a non-trading loan relationship credit—which may be disadvantageous.

[18] CTA 2009, ss 302 and 303, ex FA 1996, s 81(1).

[19] CTA 2009, s 303(3), ex FA 1996, s 81; a money debt is one which falls to be settled by the payment of money or the transfer of a right to settlement, such as by the issue of a security or 'by the issue or transfer of any share in any company' (s 303(1)(a), ex s 81(2), the words quoted added by FA 2008, Sch 4, para 10—to prevent avoidance).

[20] *HSBC Life (UK) Ltd v Stubbs* [2002] STC (SCD) 9; this case also considers the meaning of 'advance of money' in s 103.

[21] HMRC *Corporate Finance Manual*, CFM31040.

[22] HMRC *Corporate Finance Manual*, CFM31100.

[23] CTA 2009, s 303(4), ex FA 1996, s 81(4). See also HMRC *Corporate Finance Manual*, CFM31070.

[24] Statement by the Economic Secretary to the Treasury, HC Official Report, col 613, 28 February 1996. See also HMRC *Corporate Finance Manual*, CFM31060.

5.1.2.3 Effect of There Being no Loan Relationship

Gains and losses on annual valuations of debts, or on other events such as the purchase or sale of securities, which are called 'related transactions', are brought into the CTA 2009, Part 5 scheme only if there is a loan relationship.[25] However, interest comes within the rules whether or not there is a loan relationship. Thus, interest arising from a trade creditor is aggregated with other interest, as is interest computed under judgment debts, transfer pricing legislation, dividends on building society shares, interest on building society accounts, and dividends on industrial and provident society shares. Profits from the disposal of interest and from all discounts are also included.[26] All these are taxed on an accruals basis.

5.1.3 Debits, Credits and Timing

Computations under the loan relationship rules must be in accordance with GAAP.[27] Income and expenditure come within the scheme if they fairly represent the company's profits, gains and losses arising from its loan relationships and its related transactions.[28] The section specifically includes gains of a capital nature. Where interest paid is capitalised by the payer, the interest is, nevertheless, brought into the calculation for tax purposes and relief is obtained; the relief is granted on an accruals basis.[29] Also to be brought into account are interest, charges and expenses.[30]

5.1.3.1 Expenses

Expenses for which relief is available are restricted to:

(1)   those incurred in bringing the loan relationship into existence, making payments under that relationship and ensuring that payments are received; and
(2)   expenses in relation to a 'related transaction',[31] defined as any disposal or acquisition of rights and liabilities under a loan relationship.[32] This concept is important, because all profits or gains or losses arising from such transactions have to be brought into account; it covers not only sale or gift, but also the surrender, redemption or release of a debt.[33]

Abortive expenditure is specifically allowed, provided it falls within the categories of expenditure that are permitted where a project is taken to its anticipated conclusion.[34]

---

[25] CTA 2009, ss 479–481, ex FA 1996, s 100(1), (2).
[26] CTA 2009, s 480, ex FA 1996, s 100(1A) and related changes made by F(No 2)A 2005, Sch 7, para 12 and by FA 2006, Sch 6, para 17—to prevent avoidance; see relevant HMRC Notes on Clauses.
[27] CTA 2009, s 307(2), ex FA 1996, ss 85A and 85B.
[28] CTA 2009, s 307(3), ex FA 1996, s 84(1).
[29] CTA 2009, s 320, ex FA 1996, Sch 9, para 14. Relief is also given for the capitalised costs of obtaining loan finance written off over the life of the loan, as required by FRS 4.
[30] CTA 2009, s 307(2), ex FA 1996, s 84(1).
[31] CTA 2009, s 307(4), ex FA 1996, s 84(3).
[32] CTA 2009, s 304(1), (2), ex FA 1996, s 84(5), (6).
[33] CTA 2009, s 304(2) and HMRC *Corporate Finance Manual*, CFM31130; on 'repos' and stock lending, see CTA 2009, s 332, ex FA 1996, Sch 9, para 15, and HMRC *Corporate Finance Manual*, CFM45000.
[34] CTA 2009, s 329(1), (2), ex FA 1996, s 84(4).

5.1.3.2 Sums

Sums included are interest payable, interest receivable, any discount, premiums, gains and losses arising from the disposal of the instrument, any reimbursement required to a lender, the costs of obtaining loan finance such as bank fees, abortive expenditure in respect of loan finance which is not drawn down, early redemption penalties and any costs in pursuing debtors.[35]

5.1.4 Anti-avoidance

There are a number of anti-avoidance rules. One deals with the importing of a loan relationship where a loss arose at a time when the relationship was not subject to UK tax, and excludes such losses unless fair value accounting is used.[36] Another imposes special valuation rules where the transaction is not made at arm's length.[37]

A more wide-ranging rule bars relief for debits where or to the extent that the loan relationship was incurred for an unallowable purpose;[38] this bar extends not just to the loan relationship rules but for any other rule of corporation tax.[39] This tainting purpose may arise from the loan relationship itself, or from a related transaction. Although a business or commercial purpose is normally an allowable purpose, this will not be so if the purpose relates to an activity not within the charge to corporation tax, eg the purposes of an overseas subsidiary (as opposed to an overseas branch, even though none of its profits are charged to corporation tax because any UK tax liability is wiped out by the overseas tax credit). A tax avoidance purpose is not a business purpose unless it is not the main or one of the main purposes—the concept of tax avoidance takes its familiar meaning in terms of a tax advantage under CTA 2010, section 732 (ex TA 1988, section 709). The Revenue will not give advice on the meaning of the term beyond the recitation of a ministerial mantra.[40]

Other rules give tax-neutral continuity of treatment for loan relationship transactions on a group basis, with intra-group transactions generally ignored.[41] These rules were refined by FA 2003, 2005 and 2006 to prevent avoidance.[42]

5.1.5 GAAP

CTA 2009, section 307(2) directs that the amounts to be brought into account are those which, in accordance with GAAP, are recognised in determining the profit or loss for the period. Where the company's accounts do not confirm to GAAP, the correct GAAP principles are to be applied.[43] If the company uses correct accounts for the period but has used

---

[35] HMRC *Corporate Finance Manual*, CFM31040.

[36] CTA 2009, s 327, ex FA 1996, Sch 9, para 10.

[37] CTA 2009, ss 444–452, ex FA 1996, Sch 9, paras 11 and 11A (exchange transactions).

[38] CTA 2009, s 441–442, ex FA 1996, Sch 9, para 13; note [1997] *Simon's Weekly Tax Intelligence* 544.

[39] CTA 2009, s 441(4),(5), ex FA 1996, Sch 9, para 13(1A) added by FA 2002.

[40] For terms of mantra, see Hansard, Finance Bill Report Stage, cols 1192–93, 28 March 1996; reprinted in HMRC *Corporate Finance Manual*, CFM38170. The section is not to be applied without reference to CD(SIS 1); see *Corporation Tax Manual*, para 12681.

[41] CTA 2009, Pt 5, Ch 4, ex FA 1996, Sch 9, para 12 (see ch 7 below).

[42] Eg CTA 2009, ss 340(8), 341(1)–(4), ex FA 1996, Sch 9, para 12(2A), added by FA 2006, Sch 6, para 19.

[43] CTA 2009, s 309, ex FA 1996, s 85A(2).

incorrect accounts for an earlier period, the correct treatment is applied to that earlier period if this is relevant.[44] Two particular methods of accounting are mentioned from time to time—fair value accounting and amortised cost basis. These terms are defined.[45] In essence fair value accounting takes note not only on interest payments but also of changes in the value of the underlying rights and liabilities. Amortised cost basis means a basis under which an asset or liability representing the loan is shown in the company's accounts at cost, adjusted for cumulative amortisation and any impairment, repayment or release; impairment includes uncollectability.

Section 308 provides more guidance on the basic accounting recognition rule in section 307(2). It refers to the company's profit and loss account, or the STRGL in UK GAAP and the statement of changes in equity under IAS. Where the IAS rule leads to a recognition of a 'fundamental error', the company is not allowed just to recognise it in that year; the Revenue may go back and insist on recalculating the earlier years—with interest and penalties.[46] This is backed up by further regulation-making powers.[47] Sections 311 and 312 are needed if assets and liabilities are 'matched', but GAAP has the effect that some of the income is still not recognised. These provisions approve the official view that such non-recognition for GAAP has no effect for tax purposes—and so the income is still taxable.[48]

With the new accounting approach there is no need for a general provision on changes of accounting method, as there was in the original FA 1996, section 90. However, there is a need for a particular power to prevent assets or liabilities which have previously been dealt with on an amortised basis being moved over to a fair value accounting, and this is achieved by giving the Treasury a power to make regulations to that effect. [49]

At one time there was a separate rule giving relief for bad debts.[50] As the new concept of amortisation includes relief for 'impairment', there is no need for this separate rule and the term 'bad debt' is replaced by 'impairment losses'. There is still a need for a rule governing releases, and this removes the taxable credit that would otherwise arise in the circumstances stated.[51] There are also rules on the relationship between consortium group relief and impairment losses,[52] impairment losses where the parties are connected,[53] insolvency[54] and where companies become connected or cease to be so.[55] Where there is a release of a liability concerning the writing off a government investment, the sum is credited in the period of the release.[56]

Sometimes the legislation insists on fair value accounting being used. One such rule deals with bonds, the terms of which are changed if there is also a tax advantage purpose. The change may be in the rate of interest, the amount payable to pay off the debt or the date

---

[44] CTA 2009, s 309(2), ex FA 1996, s 85A(3).
[45] CTA 2009, s 313(4), (5), ex FA 1996, s 103; terms added by FA 2004. See IAS 39.
[46] CTA 2009, s 308(2), (3), ex FA 1996, s 85B(2).
[47] CTA 2009, s 310, ex FA 1996, s 85B(3)–(6).
[48] Ex FA 1996, s 85C added by FA 2006, Sch 6, para 12; see HMRC Notes on Clauses, FA 2006.
[49] CTA 2009, s 314, ex FA 1996, s 90A.
[50] FA 1996, Sch 9, para 5 (original version).
[51] CTA 2009, ss 322(1), (2), 358(1), (2) and 359(1), (2), ex FA 1996, Sch 9, para 5(3).
[52] CTA 2009, ss 364–371, ex FA 1996, Sch 9, para 5A.
[53] CTA 2009, ss 352, 354, 356, and 360, ex FA 1996, Sch 9, para 6.
[54] CTA 2009, ss 353 and 355, ex FA 1996, Sch 9, paras 6B and 6C.
[55] CTA 2009, ss 350–351, ex FA 1996, Sch 9, paras 6, 6A and 6B.
[56] CTA 2009, s 326, ex FA 1996, Sch 9, para 7.

of the maturity of the obligation.[57] In such a case the asset must be brought into account on the basis of fair value accounting. Equally the legislature may insist on an amortised cost basis where the parties have a connection.[58]

5.1.6 Deficits on Loan Relationships (Net Losses)

5.1.6.1 Trade

In this context the legislation distinguishes 'trade interest' from 'non-trade interest'. Trade interest covers a relationship to which the company is a party for the purposes of a trade carried on by it,[59] including, therefore, interest payable on a loan to purchase a trading asset. A stricter test applies where the company is the creditor rather than the debtor; here, the loan must be an integral part of the trade.[60] Trade interest is brought into the CTA 2009, Part 3 profit calculation.[61] Where a deficit arises from such loan relationships, relief is given by the rules applying to Part 3.[62] It is convenient to follow the statute and use 'deficit' rather than 'loss' to avoid confusion with other types of loss.

5.1.6.2 Non-trade Interest

This is brought into the calculation of the sum subject to income tax under CTA 2009, section 301.[63] A company with a non-trading deficit on its loan relationships may claim for the whole or part of the deficit to be set against any of its profits of the deficit period unless it has been surrendered for group relief,[64] to be carried back against profits of earlier accounting periods;[65] or, if not surrendered for group relief, to be carried forward as a deficit to be set against non-trading profits of the next accounting period.[66] Provisions have been needed here to prevent abuse where distributions (as opposed to interest) have been used to obtain a tax advantage.[67]

5.1.6.3 Carry-back of Deficits

Priority is given for relief against profits of the current accounting period.[68] Subject to this, a deficit may be carried back whether it is a deficit on a trading relationship or on a non-trading relationship. The mechanism, however, differs. The carry-back of a non-trading deficit is against any profits of the preceding 12 months, with relief being applied in a later year before an earlier year.[69]

---

[57] CTA 2009, s 454, ex FA 1996, s 88A, added by FA 2002, s 71; see Amin [2002] BTR 286.

[58] CTA 2009, s 349–51, ex FA 1996, s 87(2)–(2C).

[59] CTA 2009, s 297, ex FA 1996, s 82(2).

[60] CTA 2009, s 298, ex FA 1996, s 103(2); and HMRC *Corporate Finance Manual*, CFM32020; see also *Nuclear Electricity plc Ltd v Bradley* [1996] STC 405, 68 TC 670, HL, above at §4.5.1.2.

[61] CTA 2009, s 297, ex FA 1996, s 82(2).

[62] CTA 2009, s 297, ex FA 1996, ss 80(2), 82(2); and see below chapter 5.

[63] CTA 2009, s 301(2), (4), (6), ex FA 1996, s 82(3). Interest incurred on pre-trading loans is the subject of a special provision (TA 1988, s 401(1AC)).

[64] CTA 2009, s 459(1)(a), ex FA 1996, s 83(2)(a). On making the claim, see also s 461.

[65] CTA 2009, s 459(1)(b), ex FA 1996, s 83(2)(c). On making the claim, see also s 462.

[66] CTA 2009, s 457, ex FA 1996, s 83(3A)(a). On making the claim, see also s 458.

[67] CTA 2009, s 465, ex FA 2008, Sch 22, para 3.

[68] CTA 2009, ss 461(5), (6) and 462(5), ex FA 1996, Sch 8, para 3(2).

[69] CTA 2009, s 459(1)(b), ex FA 1996, s 83(2)(c), Sch 8, para 3.

Certain other current year reliefs must be used before carry-back relief is allowed.[70] These include CTA 2010, section 37 trading losses, CTA 2009, section 459(1)(a) deficit set-offs, and charitable donations relief under CTA 2010, Part 6. There are further rules specific to investment companies.[71]

5.1.7 Connected Party Transactions

The following rules apply to connected party transactions:

(1) Any loan relationship with a connected person must be dealt with on an amortised cost basis and not under fair value rules.[72]

(2) Where the interest is not paid within 12 months of the end of the accounting period in which it accrued, the debits for the interest due are allowed only if the corresponding credits are brought into account.[73] There is relief from this rule for debt-equity swaps.[74] FA 2003 widened the definition of 'participators' in order to catch the transaction where loan relationships are transferred within a group.[75]

(3) There is an equivalent provision in respect of relief for a discount.[76] For a close company, an even stricter rule applies, and no relief is available on a discount held by a participator or his associate until the discounted security is redeemed.[77]

(4) Deficits (losses) suffered on a connected party debt do not normally attract relief, even when they arise on the sale of the debt to an unconnected third party.[78] The rules about bad debts are relaxed so that relief is allowed if—
   (a) the creditor is insolvent and an administration order has been made; or
   (b) the debt arose before the connection; or
   (c) the debt became bad during a period of connection but there is now no connection.[79]

(5) Further rules apply if the loan relationship is treated differently by debtor and creditor, and they are in the same group.[80]

In 2009, the rules in CTA 2009, sections 374–376 were amended for the same reasons as for the changes to dividends (chapter three above). These rules allow a deduction for interest between connected parties only where the interest is paid. This ban on the deduction for interest due but not paid applied where the creditor company was not taxable under the

---

[70] CTA 2009, s 463(5), ex FA 1996, Sch 8, para 3(6).

[71] CTA 2009, s 463(5)(e), ex FA 1996, para 3(6)(c).

[72] CTA 2009, s 349(2), ex FA 1996, s 87(2); see, generally, HMRC *Corporate Finance Manual*, CFM35000 *et seq*.

[73] CTA 2009, s 373, ex FA 1996, Sch 9, para 2. On relief for close companies with limited partnerships where collective investment scheme (venture capital) involved, see ss 374–375 (ex para 2(1B) added by FA 2004).

[74] Concessionary relief was replaced by legislation in 2002: see CTA 2009, s 322(4) (ex ESC C17–18 and C28).

[75] CTA 2009, ss 373(5), 376(2)–(5), 472(1) and 476(1), ex FA 1996, Sch 9, para 2(5A) and (6) added and amended by FA 2003, Sch 37.

[76] CTA 2009, ss 406–408, 412 and 472–473, ex FA 1996, Sch 9, para 17—amended FA 2003, Sch 37, para 4; Inland Revenue 2003 Press Release BN 13, [2003] *Simon's Tax Intelligence* 718.

[77] CTA 2009, ss 409–412, 474 and 476, ex FA 1996, Sch 9, para 18, also amended by FA 2003.

[78] CTA 2009, ss 352, 354, 356 and 360, ex FA 1996, Sch 9, para 6; see also RI 172.

[79] CTA 2009, ss 323, 355 and 357, ex FA 1996, Sch 9, paras 6A, 6B and 6C, all added by FA 2002.

[80] CTA 2009, ss 418–419, ex FA 1996, s 94B, added by FA 2008, Sch 22, para 14.

loan relationship rules, eg where it was not resident. This ban is now removed as long as the company is resident in a qualifying territory (and only so resident). As in chapter three above, a territory is a qualifying territory if it is one with which the UK has a double taxation agreement containing a non-discrimination clause. A similar widening change is made in the rules on postponement of relief until redemption for discounts—see CTA 2009, sections 407, 409 and 410. In 2010, the CTA 2009, section 322 exemption for certain rescue situations was narrowed to cases of genuine corporate rescue, or where a group engages in self-rescue by issuing new debts or shares in exchange for old. Thus the exemption is no longer available where a company buys publicly-issued debt which has been traded at a discount.[81]

Two companies are treated as connected for this purpose if, at any time in either the accounting period or in the preceding 24 months, one company had control of the other or the two companies were under common control.[82] Instead of relying on other parts of the legislation for a definition of 'control', rule (1) above has its own definition, which refers to a power to secure that the affairs of the company are conducted in accordance with the person's wishes; this power may arise from shares or from voting power, or from any power in the company's article of association or other documents.[83] Shares held as trading stock— and any related voting power—are, as usual, excluded.[84]

5.1.8 Special Types of Securities

The loan relationships regime is meant to provide rules for loans, not for shares, and so the rules do not apply to 'excluded securities'.[85] The effect of exclusion is to provide CGT treatment instead.

There are also special rules for loan relationships with embedded derivatives,[86] which remain subject to these rules and not the separate rules for derivatives;[87] these rules supersede a number of earlier categories.[88] These are concerned with hybrid instruments which receive split or, as the jargon has it, 'bifurcated' accounting treatment under IAS 32 and 39. Under these rules the bifurcation applies for tax purposes too; one part receives loan relationship treatment and the other derivative treatment. Regulations will ensure that the changes in value will be treated as chargeable gains or allowable losses—or exempt.[89] As a result of a late amendment to the Finance Bill 2004, this bifurcated treatment applies also to the issuer of convertible securities; this was achieved by repealing the old rule for convertible securities and widening the scope of the provision giving bifurcated treatment to include equity instruments.[90]

---

[81] See relevant HMRC Notes on Clauses.

[82] CTA 2009, s 466(2), ex FA 1996, s 87(3)(a), (b). There are, however, exceptions to this general rule: ss 468–471 (ex s 88).

[83] CTA 2009, ss 466(6), 472 and 476(1), ex FA 1996, s 87A, added by FA 2002.

[84] CTA 2009, s 472(3), (4), ex FA 1996, s 87A(2).

[85] For deemed disposal on change of status, see former FA 1996, s 92(7)–(11), added by FA 1999, s 68.

[86] CTA 2009, ss 415 and 585, ex FA 1996, s 94A added by FA 2004.

[87] CTA 2009, s 700(3), ex FA 1996, s 101(1A) added by FA 2004.

[88] Repealed provisions are ss 92 (convertible securities) 93, 93A and 93B (asset-linked securities) and 94 (index-linked gilts).

[89] Revenue Notes to Clause 52, para 46.

[90] Report Stage Amendments 80 and 81; s 92 which was originally to be amended is simply repealed.

Two specified gilts are subject to these rules only so far as interest is concerned, so ignoring changes in the underlying values—unless held as trading stock by the company.[91] There are also express rules for gilt strips.[92]

A further provision was added by the 2006 rule to counter exploitation of these boundaries.[93] This is concerned with a situation in which the company (L1) lends money but part of the profit accrues to another company (LC) which is connected to the lender. LC's argument that it is not taxable since it is not party to the loan relationship is ended by the statutory provision.

F(No 2)A 2005 added certain categories of shares which are treated as loan relationships, eg shares subject to outstanding third party obligations, all of which are highly unusual types of investment. The effect of moving these into the loan relationships category is to ensure that any distribution is not removed from tax by CTA 2009, Part 9A, and that fair value accounting is applied, not capital gains.[94] Provisions were needed here to prevent abuse; changes were needed to prevent the use of shares subject to third party obligations and to deal with the application of the rules to non-qualifying shares.[95]

The rules were widened in 2008 to apply to all types of distribution and not just two.[96] They were also needed to prevent abuse of the fair value rules through depreciatory transactions and other devices,[97] through artificial fluctuations in value, through foreign exchange transactions[98] and through exit arrangements taking undue advantage of the concept of redeemability[99] schemes to reproduce interest-like returns.[100] Other provisos have dealt with partnerships and the commercial rate of interest.[101]

5.1.9 Miscellaneous Rules

The loan relationship scheme contains a number of other rules. One rule directs tax-neutral continuity of treatment of related transactions between the members of the same group.[102] Another applies where a sum is treated under the relevant GAAP as part of the capital expenditure; the GAAP is overruled.[103] Other rules apply to capital redemption policies, repo transactions and stock lending, imputed interest, discounted securities where companies are connected, discounted securities of close companies and partnerships involving companies.[104] There are also rules on manufactured interest.[105] Separate regimes deal with

---

[91] CTA 2009, Sch 2, para 69(1), (2) , ex FA 1996, s 96 (3.5% funding 1999–2004 and 5.5% Treasury 2008–2012).
[92] CTA 2009, ss 401–403, ex FA 1996, s 95.
[93] CTA 2009, ss 453(1)–(5) and 1316(1), ex FA 1996, s 93C, added by FA 2006, Sch 6, para 16.
[94] CTA 2009, ss 522–535, ex FA 1996, ss 91A–91G added by F(No 2)A 2005, Sch 7, para 10; para 9 makes a consequential changes to TCGA 1992, s 171.
[95] Changes to FA 1996, ss 91A and 91B made by FA 2006, Sch 6, paras 11 and 12.
[96] Ex FA 2008, Sch 22, para 4.
[97] Ex FA 2008, Sch 22, paras 5–7.
[98] Ex FA 2008, Sch 22, paras 8–10.
[99] Ex FA 2008, Sch 22, para 11.
[100] Ex FA 2008, Sch 22, para 12.
[101] CTA 2009, ss 536–538, ex FA 1996, ss 91H and 91I, added by FA 2008, Sch 22, para 14; and changes to s103(3A) made by para 14.
[102] CTA 2009, Pt 5, Ch 4, ex FA 1996, Sch 9, para 12, amended by F(No 2)A 2005, Sch 7, paras 17 and 18.
[103] CTA 2009, s 320, ex FA 1996, Sch 9, para 14.
[104] CTA 2009, ss 315–318, 319, 332, 380–385, 406–412, 441–442, 446, and 472–476, ex FA 1996, Sch 9, paras 1A, 13, 15–20, amended by F(No 2)A 2005, Sch 7, paras 14 and 19.
[105] CTA 2009, ss 539–541, ex FA 1996, s 97 and F(No 2)A 2005, Sch 7, para 11.

collective investment schemes and insurers.[106] Where a loan giving rise to a charge under CTA 2010, section 455 is written off in favour of a participator (see further §10.4.5), no debit arises under the loan relationship rules.[107]

5.1.10 Foreign Exchange

As has been indicated in the text above, the rule on FOREX is now part of the loan relationships regime, the operative proviso being CTA 2009, section 338. The area is of historic interest as it was the first one to be modernised—by FA 1993—which was brought into force in 1996 at the same time as the loan relationship and financial instrument (now derivative) rules. The FOREX rules were modernised again by FA 2004. The exchange gains may arise from an asset or a liability, or where a branch profit is translated. It must be recognised in the STRGL or the IAS equivalent (the statement of changes in equity). The Treasury may, by regulation, prescribe gains which are to be disregarded. The notes to the Finance Bill, clause 52 say that this power is to be used to exclude gains and losses on liabilities to finance share acquisitions and where the company uses IASs. This is because the IAS rules contain nothing similar to the 'cover' method in UK SSAP 20, paragraph 51. The same will happen where the company uses sterling in presenting its accounts but another currency for its actual business. Here, too, patching-up legislation has been needed.[108]

Section 328 allows for the disregard of certain matching FOREX transactions. This was based on the assumption that this would lead to the disregard of a loss as often as the non-taxing of a gain. However, some schemes used 'one-way' exchange effects, and these are now stopped by CTA 2009, sections 328A–328H.[109]

5.2 Derivatives

5.2.1 Introduction

As with loan relationships, so here FA 2004 made major changes to the derivative legislation for accounting periods beginning on or after 1 January 2005.[110] Like the loan relationship changes, these build on the IP rule precedents (§5.3) and give GAAP direct, as opposed to indirect, effect. For accounting periods not under FA 2004 but beginning on or after 1 October 2002, the rules were to be found in FA 2002, section 83 and Schedules 26–28; these were a complete rewrite of the 'financial instruments' regime enacted by FA 1994 and not, as with loans relationships, a change to the original rules. The 2002 change to 'derivative' was deliberate; the previous term was thought to be too wide as it covered debt and some equity instruments as well as derivatives in the narrow sense. The 2002 changes made the rules for derivatives closer to those for loan relationships. The 2004 rules prepare the way for the use of GAAP, whether UK or IAS.

---

[106] CTA 2009, Pt 5, Chs 10–11, ex FA 1996, Schs 10 and 11.
[107] CTA 2009, s 321A, added by FA 2010, s 43, for releases, etc on or after 24 March 2010.
[108] See eg FA 2006, Sch 6, paras 18–20.
[109] These rules are wider than those introduced as regulations in 2006, which were repealed.
[110] Lindsay [2004] BTR 468.

The 2002 and 2004 rules, now rewritten as CTA 2009, Part 7, apply to all profits arising to a company from its derivative contracts and treat the profits as income.[111] There is no deduction at source. Both the 2002 and 2004 rules were drafted in the new narrative style. So, to take but one example, the legislation refers to a relevant contract 'of' a person. In turn, therefore, this requires a rule referring to a relevant contract entered into or acquired by a person and then other rules which tell us when a person acquires a contract (when that person becomes entitled to the rights, and subject to the liabilities, under the relevant contract whether by assignment or otherwise).[112] In turn, provision has to be made for a company ceasing to be a party to a relevant contract and, more subtly, bringing into account certain debits and credits arising or treated as arising to the company in a post-cessation period.[113] This drafting style continues in CTA 2009.

5.2.2 Derivative Contracts: Definitions

The model for many of these definitions is the Regulated Activities Order 2001 (SI 2001/544), articles 83–85. A derivative contract is (a) an option, (b) a future, or (c) a contract for differences (CfD).[114] These terms are defined in CTA 2009, sections 580–582. An option includes a warrant.[115] A future is a contract to sell property with delivery at a later date but agreed at the time of the contract and at a price agreed then too. A contract which includes a term not for the delivery of property but for the payment of a cash sum is not within (a) or (b)[116] but may come within (c). The term 'contract for differences' is defined at some length.[117] It is a contract the purpose or pretended purpose of which is to make a profit or avoid a loss by reference to fluctuations in (a) the value or price of property described in the contract, or (b) an index or other factor designated in the contract.[118] For the purposes of sub-paragraph (b), an index or other factor may be determined by reference to any matter and, for those purposes, a numerical value may be attributed to any variation in a matter.

Certain matters are excluded from being a CfD.[119] These are: (a) an option; (b) a future; (c) a contract of insurance; (d) a capital redemption policy; (e) a contract of indemnity; (f) a guarantee; (g) a warranty; (h) a loan relationship. As already noted, a 'future' is a contract for the sale of property under which delivery is to be made at a future date agreed when the contract is made, and at a price so agreed; but this is followed by further language glossing the notion of a price being agreed when the contract is made where the price relates to a market or can be adjusted by reference to a certain level of quality or quantity. An 'option' is stated to include a warrant, which is then defined as an instrument which entitles the holder to subscribe for shares in a company or assets representing a loan

---

[111] CTA 2009, s 571(1), ex FA 2002, Sch 26, para 1—based on FA 1996, s 80(1); see Ball [2002] BTR 296.

[112] CTA 2009, s 578, ex FA 2002, Sch 26, para 53(1), (2) and (6).

[113] CTA 2009, s 608, ex FA 2002, Sch 26, para 53(3)–(5).

[114] CTA 2009, s 576 and 577, ex FA 2002, Sch 26, para 2.

[115] CTA 2009, s 580(1), ex FA 2002, Sch 26, para 12(8).

[116] CTA 2009, s 581, ex FA 2002, Sch 26, para 12(10).

[117] For an example of when it matters whether a contract is a CfD or some other type of derivative, see ex FA 2002, Sch 26, para 46, allowing apportionment for futures and options but not for CfDs.

[118] CTA 2009, s 582(1), ex FA 2002, Sch 26, para 12(3) and (4).

[119] CTA 2009, s 582(2), ex FA 2002, Sch 26, para 12(5).

relationship of a company; for these purposes it is immaterial whether the shares or assets to which the warrant relates exist or are identifiable.

A contract cannot be a future or option for these purposes if the contract does not provide for the delivery of property but for a settlement by cash payments—such a contract is treated as a CfD and so may still be a derivative but of a different sort.[120] However, a future or option the underlying subject matter of which is currency is included as a future or option.

5.2.3 Subject Matter Narrowed

The contract must meet one of three tests to be a relevant contract for these rules:

(1) The contract must be treated as a derivative financial instrument for accounting purposes.[121]

(2) It must be treated as a financial asset for accounting purposes, though this applies only to certain types of such contract.[122]

(3) The third test is satisfied where the underlying subject matter[123] of the contract is either commodities, or a CfD where the underlying subject matter is intangible fixed assets, weather conditions or creditworthiness.[124]

The presence of certain underlying subject matters, in whole or in part, will often prevent Part 7 from applying; the list includes real assets such as land, shares and loan relationships, as well as tangible movable property, intangible fixed assets and rights as unit holder in a unit trust scheme.[125] There is also a *de minimis* rule.[126] The Treasury may amend any of these rules by order.[127] Further rules were added in 2006, designed to treat contracts like derivatives as derivatives.[128]

5.2.4 Tax Treatment

The new rules are close to those in force for loan relationships. To the extent that the contract is one to which the company is party for the purposes of a trade, the relevant credits and debits are treated as receipts or expenses of the trade.[129] Non-trading credits and debits are treated as if they arise under the loan relationship rules.[130] Which debits and credits are to be brought into account when and at what value is determined by reference to

---

[120] This may matter from time to time, eg ex FA 2002, Sch 26, para 46 applied only to futures and options.
[121] CTA 2009, s 579(1)(a), ex FA 2002, Sch 26, para 3(1)(a).
[122] CTA 2009, s 579(1)(b), ex FA 2002, Sch 26, para 3(1)(b).
[123] Defined in CTA 2009, s 583, ex FA 2002, Sch 26, para 11.
[124] CTA 2009, s 579(2), ex FA 2002, Sch 26, para 3(2).
[125] CTA 2009, s 589(2), ex FA 2002, Sch 26, para 4.
[126] CTA 2009, s 590, ex FA 2002, Sch 26, para 9.
[127] CTA 2009, s 701, ex FA 2002, Sch 26, para 13.
[128] Ex FA 2002, Sch 26, para 16.
[129] CTA 2009, s 573, ex FA 2002, Sch 26, para 14(2) and (4).
[130] CTA 2009, s 574, ex FA 2002, Sch 26, para 14(3).

GAAP.[131] The discharge of the contract by performance is a related transaction.[132] Where the profits and losses arise from a FOREX derivative contract, the words of CTA 2009, section 328 dealing with FOREX contracts are reproduced and adapted.[133]

As with loan relationships, the amounts to be brought into account are those recognised in the company's accounts in determining the company's profit or loss for the period, provided these are in accordance with GAAP—and subject to the general statutory rules.[134] To assist this transition there are extensive regulation-making powers; late changes widened these powers to allow amounts arising as a result of the transition to IAS to be excluded and to allow a different accounting treatment for certain derivative contracts when IAS treatment is disregarded.[135] The recognition may be in the company's profit and loss account, the statement of recognised gains or losses or statement of changes in equity, or in some other statement for the period.[136] It is still necessary that the figures should fairly represent the profit or loss of the period.[137] Accounts not in accordance with GAAP—incorrect accounts—must be made correct for tax purposes; periods for which no accounts are prepared at all are treated as periods with incorrect accounts.[138] Incorrect figures from previous periods which impact on this period's figures must be corrected for this period. Amounts in the accounts to correct a fundamental error are treated for tax purposes as not relevant for the year in which the corrections is made;[139] this enables the Revenue to go back to correct the figures for the original year, and to collect tax for that year—with interest and penalties.

5.2.5 *Other Rules*

(1) *Release of liability.* The rules on releases of debts are the same as for loan relationships.[140]
(2) *Migration.* The company is treated as assigning its rights for fair value and immediately reacquiring them.[141]
(3) *Groups.* When one group company replaces another as party to the contract, the matter is treated as simply that and so as giving rise to no relevant event.[142] There are special rules excluding this neutral approach if one of the main purposes of the arrangement is to secure a tax advantage.[143] There are also rules on leaving groups.[144]

---

[131] CTA 2009, s 595, ex FA 2002, Sch 26, para 15.
[132] CTA 2009, s 596, ex FA 2002, Sch 26, para 15(7) and (8).
[133] CTA 2009, ss 606–606H, ex FA 2002, Sch 26, para 16.
[134] CTA 2009, s 595(3), ex FA 2002, Sch 26, para 17A, added by FA 2004.
[135] Report Stage Amendments 82 and 83.
[136] CTA 2009, s 597(1), ex FA 2002, Sch 26, para 17B(1).
[137] CTA 2009, s 595(3), ex FA 2002, Sch 26, para 15(1).
[138] CTA 2009, s 599, ex FA 2002, Sch 26, para 17A(2) and (4); see also changes to para 17A by FA 2007, Sch 5, para 17.
[139] CTA 2009, s 597(2), (3), ex FA 2002, Sch 26, para 17B(2).
[140] CTA 2009, s 611, ex FA 2002, Sch 26, para 22 derived from FA 1996, Sch 9, para 5. There is, however, no rule analogous to Sch 9, para 6 concerning connected parties—IR Notes to Finance Bill 2002, para 111.
[141] CTA 2009, s 609, ex FA 2002, Sch 26, para 22A; added by FA 2004—based on FA 2002, para 108.
[142] CTA 2009, s 625, ex FA 2002, Sch 26, para 28; however, note refinements by FA 2003, s 179 dealing with novation and by F(No 2)A 2005, Sch 7, para 22 to prevent avoidance.
[143] CTA 2009, s 629, ex FA 2002, Sch 26, para 28(3ZB)–(3ZD).
[144] CTA 2009, ss 630–632, ex FA 2002, Sch 26, para 30A, added by F(No 2)A 2005, Sch 7, para 24.

Other rules deal with groups and transactions under which fair value accounting gives an inappropriate result.[145]

(4)   *Capitalisation.* Where debits and credits are capitalised as allowed under a GAAP, they are treated as giving rise to debits and credits at the time of capitalisation.[146]

5.2.6 Anti-avoidance

CTA 2009, Part 7, Chapter 11, entitled 'Tax Avoidance', begins with rules about derivative contracts which have an unallowable purpose.[147] A purpose is unallowable if it is not amongst the business or other commercial purposes of the company; a tax avoidance purpose is a business or other commercial purpose only where it is not a main purpose for entering into a transaction.[148] Where the company has activities outside the charge to UK corporation tax, the purposes relating to those activities are not business and other commercial purposes; so transactions for those purposes are unallowable.[149] The effects of an unallowable purpose depend on whether there is an exchange credit or gain.[150] One first hives off any exchange credit.[151] The amount by which the debits for unallowable purposes exceed the exchange credits just hived off is treated as net loss.[152] A net loss may be set off against credits. There is a concept of a credit for an unallowable purpose.

Specific rules apply where the derivative is entered into by the qualifying company with a person who is not resident in the UK, whether they are parties from the outset or become parties to the contract later. These rules replaced the original proposal that there should be a withholding tax. Where debits and credits arise, eg payments under an interest or currency rate swap, any 'relevant debits' are excluded. Relevant debits arise if the contract makes provision for notional interest payments. This exclusion is limited to the amounts arising while they are both parties to the contract.[153] Notional interest payments arise when the amount of a payment falls to be determined by applying to a notional principal amount specified in a derivative contract, for a period so specified, a rate the value of which at all times is the same as that of a rate of interest so specified.[154]

This exclusion does not apply in three sets of circumstances. The first is where the qualifying company is a bank, building society or financial trader and it holds the qualifying contract solely for the purposes of a trade or part of a trade carried on by it in the UK, provided it is not party to the contract as agent or nominee of another person.[155] The second is where the non-resident holds the qualifying contract solely for the purposes of a trade or part of a trade carried on by him in the UK through a branch or an agency; again, he must not be an agent or nominee of another person.[156] The third is where the

---

[145] CTA 2009, s 628, ex FA 2002, Sch 26, para 28 as amended by FA 2006, Sch 6, paras 22 and 23.
[146] CTA 2009, ss 604–605, ex FA 2002, Sch 26, para 25.
[147] CTA 2009, ss 690–692, ex FA 2002, Sch 26, paras 23 and 24.
[148] CTA 2009, s 691, ex FA 2002, Sch 26, para 24(1) and (3)–(5).
[149] CTA 2009, s 691(2), ex FA 2002, Sch 26, para 24(2).
[150] CTA 2009, s 690, ex FA 2002, Sch 26, para 23.
[151] CTA 2009, s 690(2), ex FA 2002, Sch 26, para 23(2).
[152] CTA 2009, s 690(2), ex FA 2002, Sch 26, para 23(3)–(5).
[153] CTA 2009, s 696, ex FA 2002, Sch 26, para 31(1)–(3).
[154] CTA 2009, s 696(4), ex FA 2002, Sch 26, para 31(4).
[155] CTA 2009, s 697(1), ex FA 2002, Sch 26, para 31(5).
[156] CTA 2009, s 697(2), ex FA 2002, Sch 26, para 31(5).

non-resident is resident in a territory with which the UK has a double tax treaty which makes provision, whether for relief or otherwise, in relation to interest (as defined in the arrangements). In this situation the non-resident may be an agent or a nominee of another person, but the rule has effect as if the reference to the territory in which the non-resident is resident were a reference to the territory in which the real beneficiary is resident.[157]

5.2.7 *Special Situations*

5.2.7.1 Special Savings Vehicles

The Part 7 rules make special provision for various savings vehicles. For example, contracts relating to holdings in unit trusts, open-ended investment companies (OEICs) and off-shore funds start by not being derivative contracts, but the rules treat them as if they were and require them to use an authorised mark-to-market.[158] Further provisions set out how the transition to the derivative regime applies to an existing contract which changes its character so as to become subject to the rules.[159] Other rules apply to VCTs and investment trusts; for example, carrying debts and credits to reserve does not give rise to a debit or credit.[160] Yet further rules apply to insurance and mutual trading companies.[161]

5.2.7.2 Apportionments

The next rules apply only to contract and futures and not to CfD. Where the contract would be excluded as relating to a prohibited underlying subject matter of an excluded type, an apportionment can be made between the part qualifying for derivative treatment, eg debt, and the non-qualifying part.[162] The apportionment is on a just and reasonable basis.

5.2.7.3 Partnerships Involving Companies

Following the loan relationship rules, each partner's share is calculated separately, including the share of the corporate partner.[163] A normal GAAP basis must be used, save where the company does not account for the partnership assets separately, in which case a fair value accounting basis must be used.[164] Rules govern the adjustments to be made where the company changes to IAS.[165]

5.2.7.4 Hedged Index-linked Gilt-edged Securities

Where a company holds indexed-linked gilts (ILGs) the normal rule is that gains are exempt. Where the company is not exposed to the inflationary aspect of holding the ILG because of a hedging arrangement, the exemption is reduced.[166]

---

[157] CTA 2009, s 697(3)–(5), ex FA 2002, Sch 26, para 31(6) and (7).

[158] CTA 2009, s 587, ex FA 2002, Sch 26, para 36.

[159] CTA 2009, s 602, ex FA 2002, Sch 26, para 37.

[160] CTA 2009, ss 637–638, ex FA 2002, Sch 26, para 38.

[161] CTA 2009, ss 633 and 634, ex FA 2002, Sch 26, paras 41–43.

[162] CTA 2009, s 593, ex FA 2002, Sch 26, para 46.

[163] CTA 2009, s 619–620, ex FA 2002, Sch 26, para 49 following FA 1996, Sch 9, para 19.

[164] CTA 2009, s 621, ex FA 2002, Sch 26, para 50.

[165] CTA 2009, ss 613–615 , ex FA 2002, Sch 26, para 50A.

[166] CTA 2009, ss 400A–400C, introduced by FA 2010, s 41 and Sch 14.

5.3   Intangible Fixed Assets (Capital Intellectual Property)

5.3.1 Introduction

The rules governing intangibles introduced by FA 2002 and rewritten as CTA 2009, Part 8 are important for a number of reasons. First, they have provided a coherent and relatively satisfactory way of dealing with the tax problems presented by the ever-growing field of IP. Those problems arose, as had those for loan relationships and derivatives, from the unsatisfactory nature of the traditional income tax and capital gains tax rules. The success of the 2002 rules paved the way for the 2004 adoption of GAAP and IAS elsewhere. This is, however, an area in which the ASB rule (SSAP 13) and the IASB rule (IAS 38) conflicted, and so new rules were required to resolve the matter.[167]

Secondly, these rules attempt to solve these problems by bringing the tax treatment closer to the treatment in the accounts by reference to accounting principles and practice. Accounting concepts are deeply embedded.[168] These will determine not only the measure of a liability, but also the occasion on which a liability may arise.

Thirdly, they provide a self-standing code for rules dealing with the income and capital gains consequences of holding IP as a fixed asset. They therefore present a model for a possible future general corporation tax code.

5.3.2 Outline

FA 2002, Schedule 29 introduced radically new rules for expenditure on and receipts from fixed intangible assets on or after 1 April 2002.[169] The scope of the new rules—now in CTA 2009, Part 8 (sections 711–906)—is wide since they apply to all IP, goodwill[170] and other intangible assets held as fixed assets or, as the statute puts it, acquired or created by the company for use on a continuing basis in the course of the company's activities.[171] The paradigm case of fixedness is found where the asset has been capitalised in the balance sheet of the company. The rules are confined to companies subject to corporation tax.

Where assets were acquired before 1 April 2002 they remain subject to the old rules until there is a disposal and acquisition, the disposal being treated under the old rules and the acquisition under the new rules. This rather broad statement needs to be taken in conjunction with the detailed interpretation rules in Chapter 16 (ex Part 14). Rules were found to be needed where assets were derived from pre-2002 assets to prevent unintended relief.[172]

To paraphrase the Revenue's explanation,[173] the tax treatment is to follow the accounting treatment, and so will in most cases be based on the amortisation reflected in their accounts. Amortisation is a term used in relation to intangible assets when depreciation

---

[167] FA 2004, s 53.

[168] See SSAP 13, IAS 38 and Fairpo (2004) 748 *The Tax Journal* (5 July 2004), 13.

[169] See Shipwright [2002] BTR 301.

[170] CTA 2009, s 715, ex FA 2002, Sch 29, para 4. FA 2009, s 70 enacted the view held widely, but not apparently universally, that goodwill created in the course of carrying on the business is subject to these rules. CTA 2009, s 712(2) was amended to confirm that an intangible asset includes an internally-generated asset. We shall have to see whether the alternative (minority) view is upheld by the courts.

[171] CTA 2009, s 713, ex FA 2002, Sch 29, para 3.

[172] CTA 2009, Ch 16, ss 880–900, ex FA 2002, Sch 29, paras 14A, 127A and 127B, added by FA 2006, s 77.

[173] Inland Revenue Press Release BN10 23 April 2002, [2002] *Simon's Tax Intelligence* 571.

is used for tangibles. The fall-back allowance is at a fixed rate of 4% per annum,[174] but accounting principles will normally provide a more rapid rate of write off so that the 4% rate is for indefinite or longer-life assets.

The regime applies to all expenditure, whether capital or revenue, incurred on the creation, acquisition and enhancement of intangible assets (including abortive expenditure), as well as expenditure on their preservation and maintenance. Relief under the new regime will therefore be available for the cost of internal development, as well as acquisition, of intangible assets.

Payments made for the use of intangibles, eg royalties, also come within the new regime and so are treated in line with accounting principles, as do royalty receipts. Disposals of intangible assets are taxed on an income basis; however, a roll-over relief applies where disposal proceeds are reinvested in new intangible assets within the regime.

There is a wide-ranging anti-avoidance rule, which directs that certain tax avoidance arrangements are to be disregarded in determining whether a debit or credit is to be brought into account under Part 8, or the amount of such debit or credit.[175] The term 'arrangements' is widely defined; arrangements are tax avoidance arrangements if their main object or one of their main objects is to enable a company to obtain debits or increased debit, or to avoid having to bring any credit into account at all or only a reduced amount.

Another major provision excludes an intangible fixed asset from Part 8 to the extent that it is held (a) for a purpose that is not a business or other commercial purpose of the company, or (b) for the purpose of activities in respect of which the company is not within the charge to corporation tax.[176] Although section 803 contains the words 'to the extent that', section 802 indicates that an apportionment may be made in the case of dual purposes, with the apportioned part treated as a separate asset.

Lastly, CTA 2009, Part 9 provides special rules in respect of dispositions of know-how (sections 908–910), sales of patent rights (sections 911–923) and relief from corporation tax on patent income (sections 924–925), as well as supplementary provisions (sections 926–931).

5.3.3 Basic Rules: Credits and Debits Generally

The new rules are concerned with IP and any other intangible fixed assets[177]—so not with tangible fixed assets, nor with intangible assets held as trading stock. Thus, they cover patents, copyrights, trademarks and know-how, as well as design rights. Not just ownership but also the rights to use these types of property will be subject to Part 8 if they are fixed assets. Also covered is any information or technique not protected by a right but having industrial, commercial or other economic value. There are also many exclusions in Chapter 10; there are many definitions and boundaries too. There is an express rule governing the adjustments to be made on a change of accounting policy.[178]

---

[174] CTA 2009, s 731, ex FA 2002, Sch 29, para 10.
[175] CTA 2009, s 864, ex FA 2002, Sch 29, para 111—words were added by FA 2003 to make sure that debits and credits arising under all parts of Sch 29 were caught.
[176] CTA 2009, s 803, ex FA 2002, Sch 29, para 77.
[177] CTA 2009, ss 712–713, ex FA 2002, Sch 29, para 2.
[178] CTA 2009, Ch 15, ss 871–879, ex FA 2002, Sch 29, para 116A added by FA 2004.

The assets must be acquired or created by the company for use on a continuing basis in the course of the company's activities.[179] The paradigm case of fixedness is found where the asset has been capitalised in the balance sheet of the company—which means that rules have to be provided for assets which have not yet been capitalised, or which having lost all value are no longer so capitalised or which cease to be capitalised. Special rules apply if the company uses incorrect accounts—the bedrock rule being to make them use accounting rules anyway.[180] Another special rule applies if the consolidated group accounting rule is different from this company's.[181]

The rules are framed in terms of gains and losses.[182] The rules have to be framed in terms of the schedular system and so cover assets held for trades, for property business, for businesses which the tax legislation treats as trades and then non-trading situations.

We start with trades and assume that the asset is held for the purposes of the trade. To determine gains and losses one has to have regard to debits (or accounting losses), which are sums which may be deducted as trading expenses, and credits (or accounting gains), which are to be brought in as trading receipts.[183]

5.3.3.1 Debits (Expenditures)

Sums recognised in the company's profit and loss account are debits and are recognised as incurred, eg a royalty for using the fixed asset[184] (royalties remain subject to deduction of tax at source). So the rules recognise all expenditure of an income nature but leave the treatment entirely in the hands of the accountants. The accounting treatment determines both its deductibility and the timing, and so, in the absence of any other rule, the value of that deductibility.

A debit may also arise as a result of writing down. This may be either for amortisation, or for a loss recognised following an impairment review if it is recognised in the profit and loss account.[185] Amortisation is a term used in place of depreciation when talking of intangibles. The general rule recognising debits when and if they are recognised in the accounts leaves everything to accounting principles—whether there can be a claim at all and the extent of the claim. As an alternative, the legislation grants amortisation at the fixed rate of 4% of the written-down value on a straight-line basis.[186]

Thus, the deduction will be an appropriate portion, whether as recognised in the accounts or 4%, of the written-down value. The statute refers to the amount of loss recognised for accounting purposes applied to a fraction the numerator of which is the tax written-down value of the expenditure and the denominator the value of the asset recognised for accounting purposes.[187] Where the company elects for the 4% fixed rate basis, this is applied to the cost of the asset or, if less, the tax written-down value.[188] So if the asset

---

[179] CTA 2009, s 713, ex FA 2002, Sch 29, para 3.
[180] CTA 2009, ss 716–718, ex FA 2002, Sch 29, para 5.
[181] CTA 2009, s 719, ex FA 2002, Sch 29, para 6.
[182] CTA 2009, s 711, ex FA 2002, Sch 29, para 1.
[183] CTA 2009, s 747, ex FA 2002, Sch 29, para 31.
[184] CTA 2009, s 728, ex FA 2002, Sch 29, para 8.
[185] CTA 2009, s 729, ex FA 2002, Sch 29, para 9.
[186] CTA 2009, ss 730–731, ex FA 2002, Sch 29, paras 10 and 11.
[187] CTA 2009, s 729(5), ex FA 2002, Sch 29, para 9.
[188] CTA 2009, s 731, ex FA 2002, Sch 29, para 11(1); 'tax written-down value' is explained in ss 742–743 (ex para 28).

costs £100,000, the fixed rate allowance is £4,000 pa. If the company elects for the 4% rule, the company will avoid any revaluation charge.[189]

A loss also arises if there is a reversal of a previous accounting gain and this is recognised in the profit and loss account.[190]

5.3.3.2 Credits (Receipts)

Mirroring the rule for expenses, the first rule for credits is that sums recognised in the company's profit and loss account as receipts in respect of intangible fixed asset are credits; again, this accounting treatment determines both its liability to tax in this way and its timing, and so, in the absence of any other rule, the extent of that liability.[191] The principal example of such receipts will be the royalty, but the rule applies to any receipt recognised in the account as being in respect of the intangible fixed asset.

A credit will also arise on a revaluation in the very limited circumstances envisaged by FRS 10.[192] The credit arising on the sale or other disposal of an asset is not within this part of the Act but within Chapter 4—the key difference being that only sums falling within Chapter 4 qualify for reinvestment relief. A credit may also arise if a gain is recognised in the profit and loss account in respect of negative goodwill.[193] A credit may further arise if a previous accounting loss is reversed and, again, is recognised in the profit and loss account.[194]

5.3.4 Realisations, Tax Written-down Values, Taxing the Net Sums

CTA 2009, Part 8, Chapter 4 (sections 733–741) concerns the treatment of debits and credits arising when an intangible fixed assets is realised.[195] Realisation means an event as a result of which the asset is no longer recognised in the balance sheet, eg a sale. It also means an event which gives rise to a reduction in accounting value.[196] If the asset has no balance sheet value, it is treated as if it had one.[197]

The net debit or credit is calculated by reference to the difference between the proceeds of realisation and the tax written-down value.[198] If the net sum is positive, it is treated as a credit (like the old balancing charge); if it is negative, it is treated as a debit (like the old balancing allowance). If the asset has not yet been written down when it is sold, eg sold soon after acquisition, the relevant cost is the capital expenditure as adjusted.[199] This is all very much like the old CAA rules, not the capital gains rules—there is no indexation relief. There is a part realisation provision, the apportionment rules of which resemble

---

[189] This arises under CTA 2009, s 723, ex FA 2002, Sch 29, para 15; the exclusion is in 723(6), ex para 15(6).
[190] CTA 2009, s 732, ex FA 2002, Sch 29, para 12.
[191] CTA 2009, ss 720–722, ex FA 2002, Sch 29, paras 13–14A, but subject to any rules in Ch 4 and TIOPA 2010, Pt 4 (transfer pricing).
[192] CTA 2009, s 723, ex FA 2002, Sch 29, para 15.
[193] CTA 2009, s 724, ex FA 2002, Sch 29, para 16 and FRS 7.
[194] CTA 2009, s 725, ex FA 2002, Sch 29, para 17.
[195] CTA 2009, s 733, ex FA 2002, Sch 29, para 18(1).
[196] Defined in CTA 2009, s 734, ex FA 2002, Sch 29, para 19; on part realisation, see s 734(4), ex para 19(3).
[197] CTA 2009, s 734(3), ex FA 2002, Sch 29, para 19(2).
[198] CTA 2009, s 735, ex FA 2002, Sch 29, para 20.
[199] CTA 2009, s 736, ex FA 2002, Sch 29, paras 21 and 135.

TCGA 1992, section 42, but it uses accounting values.[200] If the assets are not shown in the balance sheet and so have no balance sheet value, the proceeds of realisation are brought in in full.[201]

The meaning of 'proceeds of realisation' is, once more, defined by reference to accounting principles. There is also a deduction for incidental cost—if recognised for accounting purposes.[202] Where expenditure is incurred on a transaction that would have been a realisation but which is not completed, the abortive expenditure is recognised as a debit.[203]

Further rules govern the calculation of any tax written-down value. Normally this will be the tax cost less the debits recognised under section 729, but plus any credits recognised under the revaluation rules.[204] The situation is simpler if the company has opted for the rate of 4% in section 731, as there are no revaluation complications[205] and one looks simply at the tax cost less any debits made under section 731. There is a separate rule for part realisation.[206]

5.3.4.1 Recognising Debits and Credits

The way in which these debits and credits are recognised is set out in Chapter 6. Debits and credits arising from an asset held for trade purposes are treated as expenses or receipts of the trade.[207] Assets held for the purposes of a property business are treated as credits and debits of that business.[208] Mines and transport undertakings also have their own basis.[209] Other gains and losses, called non-trading gains and losses, are netted out. Net non-trading gains are chargeable to corporation tax,[210] while non-trading losses may be offset against total profits on a claim being made.[211] This offset may be surrendered to other group companies; any non-trading loss balance may be carried forward as a non-trading debit.[212]

5.3.5 *Rollover Relief*

Part 8, Chapter 7 provides relief if a company realises an intangible fixed asset and incurs expenditure on other intangible fixed assets. The asset being disposed of must fall within the requirements necessary for a realisation to have taken place.[213] The intention of the statute here is to differentiate between those intangibles that are basically of a revenue nature, and thus dealt with by the credits and debits outlined above, and those that are really capital by nature for which rollover relief is available.

---

[200] CTA 2009, s 737, ex FA 2002, Sch 29, para 22.
[201] CTA 2009, s 738, ex FA 2002, Sch 29, para 23.
[202] CTA 2009, s 739, ex FA 2002, Sch 29, para 25.
[203] CTA 2009, s 740, ex FA 2002, Sch 29, para 26.
[204] CTA 2009, s 742, ex FA 2002, Sch 29, para 27.
[205] CTA 2009, s 743, ex FA 2002, Sch 29, para 28.
[206] CTA 2009, s 744, ex FA 2002, Sch 29, para 29.
[207] CTA 2009, s 747, ex FA 2002, Sch 29, para 31.
[208] CTA 2009, s 748, ex FA 2002, Sch 29, para 32.
[209] CTA 2009, s 749, ex FA 2002, Sch 29, para 33 and TA 1988, s 55.
[210] CTA 2009, s 751–52, ex FA 2002, Sch 29, para 34.
[211] CTA 2009, s 753, ex FA 2002, Sch 29, para 35.
[212] CTA 2009, s 753(3), ex FA 2002, Sch 29, para 35(3).
[213] CTA 2009, s 734, ex FA 2002, Sch 29, para 19.

Rollover relief may be claimed[214] where the proceeds from a chargeable intangible asset,[215] including those from a partial realisation,[216] are reinvested in chargeable intangible assets. These assets must be capitalised in the accounts and the reinvestment must take place within 12 months before or three years after the date of realisation.[217] The effect of the claim is to reduce the realisation proceeds of the old asset and the cost of the new asset by the same amount.[218] It is possible to make a declaration of provisional entitlement to relief before formally making the claim.[219] Partial relief is available where part only of the proceeds is reinvested.[220] Generally, deemed acquisition and disposals are disregarded for this rollover relief, with the exception of the charge arising on degrouping (see §5.3.6 below).[221] Capital gains arising on the disposal of IP acquired or created before 1 April 2002, and so under the old regime, are also eligible for this rollover relief.[222] This also includes circumstances when there is a degrouping charge on an old-regime intangible asset.[223] It should be noted that this rollover relief may not be particularly beneficial, because the amortisation subsequently allowed each year will be based on a lower cost figure.

5.3.6 Groups

Part 8, Chapter 8 defines groups and is modelled on the definition in TCGA 1992, section 170, expanded by the approach adopted by the Tax Law Rewrite project. Chapter 9 contains the group rules for transfers of chargeable intangible assets. So these may be transferred at book value on a tax-neutral basis in a similar way to chargeable assets covered by the capital gains rules.[224] The rollover relief has its own rules which, if satisfied, allow two group companies to be treated as one;[225] while another rule extends the reinvestment relief to the acquisition of shares in certain companies, with the acquisition of the group companies being treated as equivalent to the acquisition of the underlying assets.[226]

Part 8 also has to have its own degrouping charge for use when a company leaves the group within six years of a transfer.[227] Special rules apply if the degrouping comes about by reason of an exempt distribution or a merger carried out for bona fide commercial reasons.[228]

There is a rollover relief for the degrouping charge, while other rules allow the companies to reallocate the charge within the group, and so there is a rule governing reinvestment

---

[214] CTA 2009, s 757, ex FA 2002, Sch 29, para 40.
[215] CTA 2009, s 755, ex FA 2002, Sch 29, paras 38 and 136.
[216] CTA 2009, s 755(2)(b), ex FA 2002, Sch 29, para 38.
[217] CTA 2009, s 756, ex FA 2002, Sch 29, paras 38, 39 and 40.
[218] CTA 2009, s 758, ex FA 2002, Sch 29, para 41.
[219] CTA 2009, s 761, ex FA 2002, Sch 29, para 43.
[220] CTA 2009, s 759, ex FA 2002, Sch 29, paras 41 and 42.
[221] CTA 2009, s 763, ex FA 2002, Sch 29, para 35 referring to paras 65, 67 and 45.
[222] CTA 2009, s 898, ex FA 2002, Sch 29, para 129.
[223] CTA 2009, s 899, ex FA 2002, Sch 29, paras 130–136, as amended by F(No 2)A, s 41(4).
[224] CTA 2009, ss 775–776, ex FA 2002, Sch 29, para 55—a rule which overrides the more general rules.
[225] CTA 2009, s 777, ex FA 2002, Sch 29, para 56.
[226] CTA 2009, ss 778–779, ex FA 2002, Sch 29, para 57.
[227] CTA 2009, ss 780–788, ex FA 2002, Sch 29, paras 58–60.
[228] CTA 2009, ss 789–790, ex FA 2002, Sch 29, paras 61 (referring to TA 1988, s 213(2)) and 62.

relief where the charge is reallocated.[229] The charge, whether as originally arising or reallocated, may be recovered from a director or a controlling director.[230]

Lastly, payments between group members for reinvestment relief or the reallocation of a degrouping charge may be tax free.[231]

5.3.7 Excluded Assets

Some assets are excluded for all purposes of Part 8 by the rules in Chapter 10; others are brought into Part 8 so far as royalties are concerned but excluded for all other purposes, while there is also a third miscellaneous category of intermediate exclusion.[232]

The first group of complete exclusions is for rights over assets which are not intangibles. So there is a complete exclusion for rights over land or tangible movable property, oil licences, film production, financial assets and shares/rights/interests in companies, trusts and partnerships.[233] FA 2004 adds to this list an asset in respect of which capital allowances were previously made as plant and machinery because it was a tangible asset, but which is now an intangible asset.[234] Section 803 is rather different—it excludes assets held for non-business purposes or for purposes outside the scope of UK corporation tax. More formally, it excludes an intangible fixed assets held (a) for a purpose that is not a business or other commercial purpose of the company, or (b) for the purpose of activities in respect of which the company is not within the charge to corporation tax. Although these are described as entirely excluded, this is only half true. The exclusions apply to the extent that there are such rights or purposes, and section 802 makes it clear that there is to be an apportionment where the exclusion relates to part of an asset; here the untainted part of the asset is treated as a separate asset.

The second group of exclusions in sections 810–813 allows Part 8 to apply so far as royalties are concerned. The new accounting-based rules, especially for timing, are thought to be so superior to the old that they must apply even though it is not appropriate to apply rules like reinvestment relief. There are exclusions for mutual trade or business, film and sound recordings, and for computer software to the extent that it is treated as part of the related hardware.[235]

The third group in sections 814–815 concerns two situations. First, Chapters 2 and 3 of Part 8 do not apply to expenditure on R&D; here, presumably, the R&D tax credit (see §4.2.5 above) is more appropriate. However, Chapter 4, realisations, does apply—on the basis that any expense on R&D is excluded.[236] The other rule concerns computer software and allows that company to elect (irrevocably) for first-year allowances.[237] Again, Chapter 4 may apply on a realisation of the software.

---

[229] CTA 2009, ss 791–794, ex FA 2002, Sch 29, para 65–67.
[230] CTA 2009, ss 795–798, ex FA 2002, Sch 29, paras 68–70.
[231] CTA 2009, s 799, ex FA 2002, Sch 29, para 71.
[232] CTA 2009, s 800, ex FA 2002, Sch 29, para 72.
[233] CTA 2009, ss 805–809, ex FA 2002, Sch 29, paras 73–26.
[234] CTA 2009, s 804, ex FA 2002, Sch 29, para 73A.
[235] CTA 2009, ss 810–813, ex FA 2002, Sch 29, paras 79 and 80.
[236] CTA 2009, s 814, ex FA 2002, Sch 29, paras 81 and 82.
[237] CTA 2009, s 815, ex FA 2002, Sch 29, para 83.

5.3.8 *Remaining Rules*

5.3.8.1 Chapter 11—Transfer of Business or Trade

Since Part 8 is free-standing, it has to have its own version of a number of CGT rules. So where one has a scheme of reconstruction or amalgamation involving the transfer of the whole or part of a business from one company to another, a special rule provides a deferral.[238] This is subject to the intra-group transfer rules. Other rules concern:

(1) the transfer of a UK trade between companies resident in different EU Member States;
(2) the transfer of intangible fixed assets to certain non-resident companies; and
(3) the transfer of a non-UK trade from a EU company resident in another EU state or when a company makes a qualifying merger with the new European Company.[239]

There is a statutory clearance procedure.[240]

Other deferrals concern transfers from a building society to a company and amalgamation of certain societies, eg building or provident societies (or the transfer of engagements from one society to another).[241]

5.3.8.2 Chapters 12–13—Related Parties

Transfers of chargeable intangible assets between related parties are treated as taking place at market value;[242] however, this is subject to TIOPA 2010, Part 4—the transfer pricing rules—and other exceptions. There is also a rule denying rollover relief under Chapter 7 for part realisations involving related parties;[243] while another rule deals with the delayed payment of royalties, denying any deduction until the sum is paid.[244] Further provisions define related parties in terms of control and, in the case of a close company, participators and their associates.[245] Curiously, the original definition of a 'related party' in section 95 did not cover the situation in which the two companies were simply companies in the same group, but that this was remedied by FA 2003. Another change was needed to ensure that a person (other than an individual) remained a related party even though going into insolvency or similar arrangements.[246]

5.3.8.3 Chapters 14–18—Supplementary

Chapter 14 contains a number of rules of varying degrees of interest which show further the need to legislate carefully when creating a self-contained area of law. Thus, there are rules dealing with grants and contributions which require them to be taken into account

---

[238] CTA 2009, s 818, ex FA 2002, Sch 29, para 84 echoing TCGA 1992, s 139.
[239] CTA 2009, ss 819–823 and 827, ex FA 2002, Sch 29, paras 85A–87A.
[240] CTA 2009, ss 831–833, ex FA 2002, Sch 29, para 88.
[241] CTA 2009, ss 824–830, ex FA 2002, Sch 29, paras 89–91.
[242] CTA 2009, ss 845–849, ex FA 2002, Sch 29, para 92, exception added by F(No 2)A 2005, s 41(2).
[243] CTA 2009, s 850, ex FA 2002, Sch 29, para 93.
[244] CTA 2009, s 851, ex FA 2002, Sch 29, para 94.
[245] CTA 2009, ss 834–843, ex FA 2002, Sch 29, paras 95–101 as amended by F(No 2)A 2005, s 41(3).
[246] CTA 2009, s 835(7)–(9), ex FA 2002, Sch 29, para 95A, added by FA 2008, s 65.

unless exempt,[247] and a rule that empowers the Treasury to bring finance lessors within the scope of Part 8 by statutory instrument.[248]

There are apportioning powers for situations in which assets are acquired or realised together,[249] while another rule deals with the situation in which the legislation directs a disposal at market value but the assets have no accounting value in the hands of the transferee; the assets are treated as acquired at market value anyway.[250] Fungible assets, ie those of a nature to be dealt in without identifying the particular assets involved, are taken as forming one single asset.[251]

There are deemed realisations at market value when an intangible ceases to be a 'chargeable intangible asset'.[252] This occurs where:

(1)   the company ceases to be resident in the UK;
(2)   the asset is held by a company not resident in the UK and the company stops using it for the UK permanent establishment's trade; or
(3)   the asset begins to be used for the purposes of a mutual business.

It may be possible to postpone the gain arising. The question whether (1) and (2) will be acceptable under EU law may need to be considered in light of ECJ rulings on exit charges.[253] There is a converse deemed acquisition at market value when the asset becomes a chargeable intangible asset.[254]

Chapter 15 contains express rules governing the adjustments to be made on a change of accounting policy.[255]

There is a wide-ranging anti-avoidance rule. Tax avoidance arrangements are to be disregarded in determining whether debits are to be brought into account under Chapter 3 (writing down on accounting basis) or the amount of such debits. Likewise, they are disregarded in considering whether a credit is to be brought into account under Chapter 2 or the amount of any such credit. Arrangements are widely defined as including any scheme, agreement or understanding, whether or not legally enforceable; arrangements are tax avoidance arrangements if their main object or one of their main objects is to enable a company to obtain the debits or increased debit, or to avoid having to bring the credit into account at all or only a reduced amount.

Since Part 8 operates outside the normal structure, there are rules about deductibility of payments.[256] Thus, debits may not be brought into account if in respect of expenditure that is generally not deductible for tax purposes. This leads to a reference to a number of rules elsewhere in CTA 2009, including sections 1298 (business entertainment or gifts), 1304 (crime-related expenditure) and 56 (expensive hired cars), and FA 2004,

---

[247]   CTA 2009, ss 852–853, ex FA 2002, Sch 29, paras 102 and 103.
[248]   CTA 2009, ss 854–855, ex FA 2002, Sch 29, para 104.
[249]   CTA 2009, s 856, ex FA 2002, Sch 29, para 105.
[250]   CTA 2009, s 857, ex FA 2002, Sch 29, para 106.
[251]   CTA 2009, s 858, ex FA 2002, Sch 29, para 107.
[252]   CTA 2009, ss 859–862, ex FA 2002, Sch 29, paras 108 and 109.
[253]   See eg Case C-371/10 *National Grid Indus BV v Inspecteur van de Belastingdienst Rijnmond/kantoor Rotterdam* [2012] STC 114 and Case C-9/02 *Lasteyrie du Saillant v Ministère de l'Economie* [2005] STC 1722.
[254]   CTA 2009, s 863, ex FA 2002, Sch 29, para 110.
[255]   CTA 2009, ss 871–879, ex FA 2002, Sch 29, para 116A added by FA 2004.
[256]   CTA 2009, s 865, ex FA 2002, Sch 29, paras 112–114.

section 246(2) (benefits under employer-financed retirement benefits schemes). Sections 866–867 apply if there is a delayed payment of employees' remuneration where such employees are associated with the intangible asset. An example might be staff employed in promoting the company's brand names. Section 869 governs the treatment of bad debts.

Lastly, Chapter 17 deals with insurance companies, and Chapter 18 sets out priority rules for corporation tax purposes.

5.4   International Trade—Trading Currency

5.4.1 Introduction

One must distinguish the currency in which the company's profits are computed for fiscal purposes and expressed from that used to determine the profits and losses of the business which are to be 'computed' and 'expressed'. The first task must be carried out in sterling;[257] for the second one usually looks to use either the currency in which the company reports its earnings (also called the 'accounts currency') or its functional currency.[258] The company's functional currency is defined as the currency of the primary economic environment in which the company operates.[259]

The original rules were introduced by FA 1993, and they were rewritten by FA 2000 in an attempt to make them more friendly to business. They were rewritten again in 2004 as a result of the use of GAAP. The 2004 rules, rewritten once more and now found in CTA 2010, Part 1, Chapter 4, apply to periods of account beginning on or after 1 January 2005.[260] Part of their interest is as one more historical example of tax law moving closer to accounting practice. Before FA 2000 the use of the foreign currency was a matter of taxpayer election.[261] The rules still apply only for corporation tax and not for income tax.

5.4.2 Detail

The premise is that for corporation tax, the income and chargeable gains of a company for an accounting period should be calculated and expressed in sterling.[262] However, the determination of the profits or losses to be reported is a separate matter, and the choice of currency depends on the situation to be covered. Profits and losses are not defined further; before FA 2004 capital gains and allowable losses were excluded, but this is no longer needed.[263] A number of short rules are set out. These rules apply only where profits and losses fall to be computed in accordance with GAAP.[264] They are, therefore, irrelevant both

---

[257] CTA 2010, s 5(1), ex FA 1993, s 92(1); previous version introduced by FA 2004, Sch 10, Pt 4.
[258] CTA 2010, s 5(2), ex FA 1993, s 93(1).
[259] CTA 2010, s 17(4), ex FA 1993, s 92E(3).
[260] FA 2004, s 52(3); the original Bill was oddly arranged and a revised version was introduced at the Report stage—Report Stage Amendment 84.
[261] Ex FA 1993, s 93(1)(b) original version. The original rules were in FA 1993 and SI 1994/3230; see Inland Revenue *Corporation Tax Manual*, paras 13620 *et seq*.
[262] CTA 2010, s 5(1), ex FA 1993, s 92 (2004 version).
[263] Ex FA 1993, s 93(5).
[264] CTA 2010, s 5(2), ex FA 1993, s 93(2).

to capital gains and to capital allowances. Under CTA 2009, section 46 they are relevant to trading profits and, under section 210(2) referring to section 46, to profits from land. They are also relevant to matters dealt with elsewhere in this chapter—loan relationships, derivatives, intangible fixed assets—and also to management expenses. These are the principal GAAP-related tax rules—but not the only ones.

The first rule, which, it is thought, will be rare, arises where the functional currency is sterling but the accounts are prepared in a foreign currency. Here the sterling figures are used.[265]

The second rule[266] applies where the company is resident in the UK but, in order to fit in with a GAAP such as IAS (IAS 21), the company prepares the accounts in one currency but in those accounts identifies another currency as being the currency of the primary economic environment and that currency is not sterling. The company is to calculate its profits using the functional currency and then taking the sterling equivalent of those profits or losses.[267] IAS 21, paragraph 53 requires a company to disclose its functional currency if this is not the accounts currency.

The third rule[268] has two strands. The first is where the company prepares its accounts not in sterling but in some other currency and neither of the first two rules applies.[269] Here the accounts currency is taken and that figure is translated into sterling. The second strand of the third rule arises where the company is not resident in the UK but prepares its accounts in a non-sterling currency.[270] Here too, the accounts currency is taken and that figure is translated into sterling.

The legislation contains its own rules for translating results from one currency to another. This may be needed to translate an amount in a foreign currency into sterling, or an amount into its foreign currency equivalent or the accounts currency.[271] In either event, one uses either the average exchange rate of the current accounting period or the spot rate for the transaction in question.[272] A special proviso overrides one of the self-assessment rules which would otherwise upset this scheme.[273]

FA 2009 amended now CTA 2010, section 11 and inserted sections 12–17 (ex TA 1988, sections 92DA–92DE) in reaction to uncertainty in the currency markets. The old rules required unused losses to remain converted into sterling when they accrued. Sections 12–13 allows them to be computed in the currency in which they were originally computed; so, as the Notes on Clauses explain, losses incurred in a foreign currency will be set against the same measure of profits. Sections 14–15 deal with losses computed in sterling which are used in a different period and the profits are computed in that other period in a currency other than sterling. Sections 16–17 contain definitions.

---

[265] CTA 2010, s 6, ex FA 1993, s 92A; the view on rarity is in Revenue Notes to the Report Stage Amendment 84, para 6; the other currency is likely to be used only in the consolidated accounts which are not relevant to UK tax.

[266] CTA 2010, s 7, ex FA 1993, s 92B; and see Revenue Notes to the Report Stage Amendment 84, paras 10 *et seq.*

[267] CTA 2010, s 7(2), ex FA 1993, s 92B(2).

[268] CTA 2010, s 8, ex FA 1993, s 92C; Revenue Notes to the Report Stage Amendment 84, paras 16 *et seq.*

[269] CTA 2010, s 8(1)(b), ex FA 1993, s 92C(1).

[270] CTA 2010, s 9, ex FA 1993, s 92C(2).

[271] CTA 2010, s 11(1), ex FA 1993, s 92D(1).

[272] CTA 2010, s 11(2), ex FA 1993, s 92D(2).

[273] CTA 2010, s 9(4), ex FA 1993, s 92E(2) overrides FA 1988, Sch 18, para 88.

5.5   Repos

The rules applicable to the sale and repurchase of securities (repos), formerly in FA 2007, Schedule 13, have been (mostly) rewritten as CTA 2009, Part 6, Chapter 10. The Chapter 10 repo rules reflect the influence of the Australian draft legislation by starting in section 542 with a purpose clause—the purpose being that arrangements involving the sale and subsequent purchase of securities which equate in substance to the lending of money by or to a company (with securities in substance acting as collateral) are to be subject to a charge for corporation tax that reflects that substance.

The legislation distinguishes 'debtor repos', which are usually executed under normal market documentation,[274] from 'debtor quasi repos', which are economically similar but on non-standard terms.[275] The elements of debtor repos are similar to the structured finance arrangements rules introduced in 2006 (see §5.6 below). One condition is that the subsequent buying of the securities extinguishes the financial liability recorded in the accounts. Section 550[276] introduces an anti-avoidance rule for 'relevant arrangements'. FA 2010 added section 550(5A) and Schedule 13, paragraph 4(aa) to ensure that where manufactured payments are received by companies in the course of a repo transaction, they are to be brought into account whether or not they are recognised on the companies' balance sheets. As the HMRC notes have it, the GAAP result is respected even if the accounts take in manufactured payments instead of real income. Interestingly, this change is treated as 'always having had effect', ie back to 1 October 2007.

Subject to that, section 551 (ex paragraph 5) then directs that the borrower is to obtain relief for any finance charge shown in the accounts and which represents the cost of borrowing. FA 2007, Schedule 13, paragraph 6 (not rewritten) replaces TCGA 1992, section 263A for corporation tax purposes—but not for CGT. Section 543 (ex paragraph 7) introduces 'creditor repos', which are the reverse of debtor repos, and section 544 (ex paragraph 8) creditor quasi-repos. Section 545 (ex paragraph 9) is the anti-avoidance analogue of section 550. Section 546 (ex paragraph 10) contain the basic rule analogous to section 551.

For a useful explanation of repos, an attack on the disgraceful form of the legislation and a decision not to the Revenue's liking, see *DCC Holdings v Revenue & Customs Commissioners*.[277] HMRC's appeal in *DCC Holdings* was successful before the Court of Appeal[278] and, for slightly different reasons, the Supreme Court, where Lord Walker invoked a principle of symmetry.[279]

5.6   Structured Finance Arrangements; Factoring of Income Receipts; Abusing Finance Transaction Treatment

The structured finance arrangements (SFA) rules in CTA 2010, Part 16, Chapter 2 apply to corporation tax; the counterparts for income tax are in ITA 2007, Part 13, Chapters 5B

---

[274] CTA 2009, s 548, ex FA 2007, Sch 13, para 2.
[275] CTA 2009, s 549, ex FA 2007, Sch 13, para 3.
[276] Ex FA 2007, Sch 13, para 4, only partially repealed.
[277] [2009] STC 77, [2008] EWHC 2429 (Civ), *per* Norris J, [1] and [22], and generally.
[278] [2009] EWCA Civ 1165.
[279] [2010] UKSC 58, [2011] STC 326.

and 5C (not discussed here).[280] The Part 16, Chapter 2 rules supersede the rent factoring rules, as the rules on rent factoring now apply to a wider range of assets and not just land. It cannot be pretended that this material is at all easy either to understand or to digest; Gething and Gething's Finance Act Note devotes 26 pages to it.[281]

HMRC's *Corporate Finance Manual* has useful material at paragraphs 6752 *et seq*, and it provides the following example at paragraph 6758. Suppose a company obtains a loan of £100 million at interest from a finance provider. It would typically have to give security for the loan. Over the five-year period it might pay, say, £2.5 million interest pa, giving total repayments of £112.5 million. For tax purposes, relief would be available for each annual payment of £2.5 million interest, but not for repayment of the £100 million principal. No one in their right mind would think this treatment in any way inappropriate.

However, consider this alternative, which uses a structured finance-income alienation scheme. Company A holds an asset on which income of £22.5 million a year will arise. It transfers this asset to the finance provider, a bank, for a lump sum of £100 million for a period of five years, at the end of which it can reacquire the asset for nothing. During the five years, income of total £112.5 million is paid to the bank. The income stream acquired by the bank will be enough to repay both the lump sum and the interest. There are likely to be arrangements such as options under which the asset and income reverts to the company at the end of five years. The transfer of the asset is in substance by way of security only. As the company has retained substantially all the risks and rewards of ownership of that asset, and is in effect simply applying the income that arises from it to repaying the loan, under GAAP it will continue to recognise the asset and will record the lump sum as a financial liability, that is, as a loan. Income from the asset will continue to be shown in the accounts, and over five years a finance charge equal to the difference between the gross receipts and the lump sum will be debited to profit and loss account.

The substance of the second example is exactly the same as the first example. In both cases the lender has had the benefit of the income that is paid to the lender, but in the second has applied it directly in repaying the lump sum. However, under the second method the company claims in effect to escape tax on the £112.5 million of income which would arise to it during the period of the arrangement.

CTA 2010, sections 758–762 (ex TA 1988, sections 774A and 774B) counter the income alienation scheme, referred to in the legislation as a 'type 1 finance arrangement'. Section 758 begins by describing the scheme as one where, first, a borrower (B) sells a right to income (or an income-bearing asset) to a third party, the lender (L), and B either avoids being assessed to tax on such income or becomes entitled to a deduction. Secondly, the transaction is treated (correctly) under GAAP as a financing transaction in the relevant accounts. Thirdly, the arrangement is structured so that either (a) the asset or right to income ceases to exist after a given period, or (b) the asset or income right is transferred back to B, so that in either event it disappears from the books of L. The legislation counteracts the scheme by directing (sections 759–762) that B is taxable after all or cannot obtain the deduction. The transaction is still treated as a financing transaction but for B and not L—any finance charges are treated as payments of interest to L only.[282] There are

---

[280] The corporation tax rules were formerly TA 1988, ss 774A–774G, introduced by FA 2006. The income tax rules in ss 809BZA *et seq* were introduced by TIOPA 2010, Sch 5.

[281] [2006] BTR 561.

[282] On interaction with capital gains rules, see TCGA 1992, s 263E.

some exceptions in sections 771–773—these are usually because the income is brought into account for tax purposes by some other mechanism.

Sections 763–769 (ex TA 1988, sections 774C and 774D) concern more complex schemes involving partnerships, referred to in the legislation as 'type 2' and 'type 3' finance arrangements. HMRC's *Corporate Finance Manual* has an example at paragraph 6796. Once more, the company wishes to borrow £100 million and has an asset on which income of £112.5 million will arise over the next five years. But instead of selling the asset to the lender, the borrower transfers it to a partnership of which it is a member. The lender then joins the partnership for a capital contribution of, say, £100 million, in return for the right to receive partnership profits amounting to £112.5 million over the next five years. The partnership will then lend the £100 million to the company. After five years, all of the rights to receive partnership profits will revert to the borrower (who may be able to buy out the lender's interest for a nominal consideration or have the right to expel the lender). In substance, the lender has made a loan of £100 million for the benefit of the borrower which is repaid with interest by the borrower.

Again, it is claimed that the borrower is not taxable on the income of £112.5 million, which flows to the partnership and is allocated to the lender. In these types of arrangements, the lender's 'loan' is made in the form of a contribution to the partnership, and its profit share is such that payments are made to it which repay that contribution together with interest. Once the repayment with interest has been made, the lender will cease to be a member of the partnership or to share in its profits.

These arrangements would not be caught by section 758 (ex TA 198, section 774A(3)); that provision deals with cases where it is the partnership itself that borrows by transferring to the lender an income-producing asset of the partnership. However, in this case the borrower is a member of a partnership who transfers to that partnership an income-producing asset, with the bulk of that income then appropriated to another partner who supplies the amount that equates to a loan. The schemes are now caught by sections 765–766 and 768–769.

The rules as enacted were found not to be completely fireproof. As a result, FA 2007 added three further sets of rules. The first brought into the scheme arrangements under which existing liabilities are refinanced using an structured finance arrangement. The second brought into the scheme assets which are not income-producing at the time of transfer but later produce income which equates in substance to a repayment. The third dealt with assets which have been used as collateral, and makes the charge continue to apply even though the assets have been changed.

5.7   Risk Transfer Schemes

FA 2010, section 46 and Schedule 16 added CTA 2010, sections 937A to 937O on risk transfer schemes. These rules deal with over- and under-hedging arrangements. The effect is that any losses are ring-fenced and may be relieved only against profits from the same risk transfer scheme.

The details of the risk transfer scheme rules are beyond the scope of this book.

6

Capital Allowances

The legislation on this subject is contained within the Capital Allowances Act (CAA) 2001, as later amended.[1] The 2001 Act was the first major product of the Tax Law Rewrite Project. FA 2008, Part 3 (sections 68–86) made many changes to the legislation, the outcome of a long but useful period of consultation. Many of the changes were changes of rates, and details of the transitional rates are outlined below. Two allowances—Industrial Buildings and Agricultural Buildings—were withdrawn entirely after April 2011. Where the taxpayer's basis period was the same as the tax year the changes were easy to make. If the rate for

---

[1] See Pearce [2001] BTR 359.

2007–08 was 25% and that for 2008–09 was 20%, those rates applied respectively for each period. If, however, the days in the period fell to 3/5ths in 2007–08 and 2/5ths in 2008–09, the 25% rate was applied to 3/5ths of the profits and the 2008–09 rate to 2/5ths. This makes an effective rate of 23% for the period.[2]

The 2001 Act sensibly begins with general provisions affecting all allowances, before passing on to the individual allowances. Allowances for Plant and Machinery (Part 2 of the Act, sections 10–270) are followed by those for Industrial Buildings (Part 3, sections 271–360); Converting Unused Business Premises in Disadvantaged Areas (Part 3A, sections 360A–360Z4); Agricultural Buildings (Part 4, sections 361–393); Flat Conversions (Part 4A, sections 393A–393W); Mineral Extraction (Part 5, sections 394–436); Research and Development (Part 6, sections 437–451); Know-How (Part 7, sections 452–463); Patents (Part 8, sections 464–483); Dredging (Part 9, sections 484–489); and Assured Tenancy Allowances (Part 10, sections 490–531). Part 10 has expired, in that claims cannot be made for new expenditure but existing allowances still run; hence CAA 2001, section 570A, the anti-avoidance rule introduced by FA 2003 and explained at §6.3.6.2, applies here too. This statutory order of Parts 2 and 3 is a reversal of previous practice in legislation on capital allowances and reflects, at last, the change in the economic importance of the different allowances since 1945. The present chapter follows the new scheme, save that assured tenancies are dealt with under 'Industrial Buildings' instead of as a separate head.

6.1   Introduction

6.1.1 The Problem

Expenses incurred in the acquisition of a capital asset are not deductible in computing the profits of a trade.[3] If the asset has a limited life, its value to the business will decline. The causes of this decline may be physical, such as wear and tear on plant and machinery, or economic, such as obsolescence or a change in trading policy. The decline causes the cost of the asset to become an expense to the company for accounting purposes; the capital has been consumed. Accounting principles recognise this cost by allowing a deduction for depreciation for accounting purposes, but no provision was originally made for tax purposes, perhaps because income tax was thought to be only temporary.

The UK tax system has relaxed this strict approach by making allowances for certain capital expenditure, including the capital allowance system. When claimed, capital allowances displace the deductibility of expenditure on renewals.[4] The structure of the present system goes back to the Income Tax Act 1945, which defined certain types of capital expenditure qualifying for allowances and specified different rates of allowance. Broadly speaking, the list is the same today, although there have been changes in the way in which the allowances are made. The legislation was consolidated in the Capital Allowances Acts of 1968 and 1990, now superseded by CAA 2001.

---

[2] Eg, FA 2008, ss 80(10), 83(2) and 85(5), (6).
[3] See *Revenue Law*, §22.4 and *Coltness Iron Co v Black* (1881) 6 App Cas 315, 1 TC 311.
[4] See *Revenue Law*, §22.4.3.9.

6.1.2 History[5]

The first statutory allowance was granted in 1878, 'as representing the diminished value by reason of wear and tear during the year' of plant and machinery used in a trade. This allowance was held not to extend to obsolescence, a matter changed by concession in 1897 and by statute in 1918. Also in 1918, special depreciation allowances were made to mills, factories and other similar premises,[6] on the basis that the vibrations from the machinery might weaken the building. The Royal Commission of 1920 considered, but rejected, any general scheme of capital allowances.

The Income Tax Act 1945 took a wider view; its basic structure remains in place today even though the material was substantially rearranged, as well as being rewritten, by CAA 2001. It defined those types of capital expenditure which qualified for allowances; many did not—and still do not—qualify. Apart from allowances for plant and machinery, all allowances were confined to trading income taxable under old Schedule D, Case I (some clearly to particular trades) and did not extend to professions (old Schedule D, Case II) or employment income (old Schedule E). A few allowances applied to property income (old Schedule A); these were widened and brought closer to trading income by FA 1997.[7]

6.1.3 Accelerated Allowances

For many years the tax system enshrined the belief that tax allowances encouraged investment. Hence, elaborate allowances were given to allow the writing off of capital expenditure far ahead of any real depreciation or obsolescence—either by first-year allowances or by generous writing-down allowances. However, legislation in 1984 and 1985 reduced the rates of allowances, making them closer to actual depreciation, and compensated for this by reducing the rate of corporation tax. This has not prevented Parliament from reviving specially enhanced allowances from time to time. Since 1997 we have got used to a battery of much-targeted allowances for plant and machinery of particular types and particular taxpayers. Those who believe that adjusting allowance affects the overall level of investment point to the fact that capital investment by UK businesses is a lower percentage of GNP than spending by either consumers or governments; it is also much more volatile.[8]

Although the idea of using real depreciation as measured by accounting standards was mentioned as part of the Review of Corporation Tax in August 2002, there was never any chance of its being adopted. The use of accounting principles for tax depreciation is frequently to be found in Continental European tax systems. Such systems had previously had very conservative accounting principles—in marked contrast to the present accounting principles, with their increased emphasis on relevance and fair value accounting.

---

[5] On the history, see Royal Commission on the Taxation of Profits and Income, *Final Report*, Cmd 9474 (1955), paras 308–26; Richardson Committee on Turnover Taxation, Cmnd 2300 (1964), ch 6; and Edwards [1976] BTR 300 and below at §6.12.2.

[6] To be found in CAA 1990, s 18(1)(a), now superseded by CAA 2001, s 274.

[7] CAA 2001, s 248; see also ss 249 (furnished holiday lettings) and 250 (overseas property business).

[8] See below at §6.12.2.

6.1.4 *Types of Allowance*

The UK system uses three principal types of allowance, with another two types added in 2008:[9]

(1)   an initial or first-year allowance[10] of a substantial percentage of the capital expenditure, only a few of which are currently available;
(2)   a writing-down allowance during the life of the asset, which clearly does not apply if a 100% initial allowance has been used;
(3)   a balancing adjustment, which may take the form of either an allowance or a charge on the occurrence of an appropriate event, such as the end of the trade or the disposal of the asset;
(4)   a tax credit or enhanced tax allowance (added in 2008). As this is available only for companies which have spent money on green technologies qualifying for first-year allowances but also have a loss (and so no profits against which to set the allowance), it is discussed in §4.2.5 of this book;
(5)   an Annual Investment Allowance of £25,000 (from April 2012) for business investment in most types of plant and machinery (added in 2008 and originally £50,000). Where the business spends more than £25,000, the excess is governed by the normal allowance rules; it is therefore best seen as a form of initial 100% allowance tied to the amount spent.

Of these, the first is self-explanatory. However, the second and third are not. Writing-down allowances may be given on a straight-line basis, so that the same amount is written off each year and all the expenditure will be written off after a certain number of years—so the assured tenancy allowance of 4% writes off expenditure of £100,000 (if incurred before 1 April 1992) at the rate of £4,000 a year and will have written off the whole sum after 25 years.

Writing-down allowances may also be given on a reducing balance basis, so that the same percentage, eg 20%, is given each year but applied to a reducing balance of expenditure. So £100,000 of expenditure attracting an allowance at 20% will give rise to an allowance of £20,000 (20% of £100,000) the first year, leaving £80,000 as the balance of expenditure not yet written off. The allowance for the second year will be £16,000 (ie 20% of £80,000), leaving a balance of £64,000. For the third year, the allowance is 20% of £64,000 or £12,800, and so on. The reducing balance achieves total write off only after an infinite number of years. The choice between straight-line and reducing balance bases is made by CAA 2001. There is no accounting option.

The balancing allowance or charge is designed to bring the allowances into line with actual expense. If the amount so far allowed is less than the amount spent, an extra or 'balancing' allowance is permitted. If, however, the allowance exceeds the expense, a sum is imposed by way of 'balancing charge' to recapture that part of the allowance which

---

[9]   In 1954 an investment allowance was introduced, which was, in effect, a tax-free subsidy. It did not reduce the depreciable cost of the asset for other allowances, neither was it taken into account for the purpose of any balancing allowance or charge. See, further, Cmnd 9667. It was abolished in 1966 (FA 1966, s 35).

[10]   The difference is that an initial allowance and a writing-down allowance may be claimed in the first year; but a first-year allowance and a writing-down allowance cannot both be claimed in the first year.

was not needed. The charge recovers only the amount that has been allowed, any excess being a matter for CGT. There is no provision whereby the balancing charge may be spread over the number of years for which the allowance was claimed, so the tax charged might, in extreme circumstances, exceed the tax saved through the allowance. Today, a balancing charge is treated as a receipt of the trade or other type of qualifying activity or business.[11]

A balancing allowance may be denied where the sale proceeds have been reduced by a tax avoidance scheme;[12] this rule applies to the allowance for industrial buildings in Part 3 of the Act but also to those for Building Renovation and Assured Tenancies (§6.3.7.2), Agricultural Land (§6.5), Flat Conversions (§6.6), Mining (§6.7).

Example

A buys an asset for £100,000 and has claimed £50,000 allowances A sells it for (a) £60,000; (b) £45,000; (c) £120,000. In (a) there is a balancing charge of £10,000; in (b) there is a balancing allowance of £5,000; and in (c) there is a balancing charge of £50,000, the remaining £20,000 being left to CGT.

6.1.5 Incurring Capital Expenditure

Perhaps oddly, capital expenditure is defined by exclusion, and is any sum spent on the acquisition of the asset, etc, provided the sum is not allowable as a deduction in computing the profits or gains of the qualifying activity carried on, which may be a trade, profession or vocation, property business or employment carried on by the person incurring the expense.[13] Sums falling within ITA 2007, Part 15, Chapter 6 are also excluded.[14]

As the material in *Revenue Law*, chapter twenty-two (on the distinction between capital and revenue) shows, these boundaries are not precise.[15] In general, allowances cannot be claimed for sums met directly or indirectly by others; however, an allowance may be claimed if the other person is not a public body and is not eligible for tax relief in respect of the payment.[16] In relation to public bodies, there is special exemption for certain grants for Northern Ireland under the Industrial Development Act 1982.[17] Provision is made, however, for allowances for contributions to the capital expenditure of others.[18]

Further rules exclude double relief claims.[19]

---

[11] Eg for plant and machinery, CAA 2001, ss 55(3) and 247–252. For other types of allowance, see ss 352, 391, 432, 450, 463, 478 and 489. In *IRC v Wood Bros (Birkenhead) Ltd* [1959] AC 487, 38 TC 275, the House of Lords held that the balancing charge was not income of the company for the purpose of the surtax direction. This was reversed for the apportionment of the income of close companies under the 1965 scheme.

[12] CAA 2001, s 570A, added by FA 2003, s 164.

[13] CAA 2001, s 4(2).

[14] CAA 2001, s 4(4).

[15] Eg *Rose & Co (Wallpaper and Paints) v Campbell* [1968] 1 All ER 405, 44 TC 500 (pattern books of current wallpaper stock not capital expenditure).

[16] CAA 2001, ss 532 *et seq.*

[17] CAA 2001, s 534; and see *Birmingham Corpn v Barnes* [1935] AC 292, 19 TC 195. See also ESC B49 for allowances where the grant to the taxpayer is revoked.

[18] CAA 2001, ss 537–541; see also s 155.

[19] CAA 2001, ss 7–10.

6.1.5.1 Not for Finance

The capital expenditure must have been incurred on the provision of the plant and machinery or the construction of the building;[20] it follows that sums spent merely on the provision of finance do not qualify. In *Ben-Odeco Ltd v Powlson*,[21] the taxpayer was going to carry on a trade of hiring out an oil rig. In order to finance the construction of the rig, it had to borrow money, and for this had to pay commitment fees (£59,002) and interest (£435,988). These sums were charged to capital (correctly) in the company's accounts. However, the House of Lords held that the sums did not qualify for capital allowance treatment; they had been spent not on the provision of plant and machinery but on the provision of money. This case was distinguished in *Van Arkadie v Sterling Coated Materials Ltd*,[22] where the extra (sterling) cost of a price to be paid by instalments but in foreign currency was treated as allowable expenditure. It was critical in this case that the contract provided for payment to be made by instalments; a different conclusion would have been reached if the contract had provided for a single payment made with the aid of a loan from a bank which the purchaser then paid off in instalments.

The question whether expenditure incurred for tax avoidance purposes comes within the Act is considered below and in relation to the *Barclays BMBF* case.[23]

6.1.5.2 When Incurred?

CAA 2001, section 5 provides two rules, but these do not apply to plant and machinery. The first looks at the date on which there is an unconditional obligation to pay, ie in the case of a conditional obligation, the moment when the obligation to pay becomes unconditional.[24] Where the purchaser acquires title before the obligation becomes unconditional, the expenditure will be treated as incurred in the period in which title passed, provided the obligation becomes unconditional not more than one month after the end of that period.[25] The second rule applies to the date on which the expenditure became payable.[26] It applies where the due date for payment is more than four months after the obligation to pay has become unconditional.

Originally, only the second rule applied. The reason behind this change adding the first rule was to bring the capital allowance rules into line with accountancy practice (which takes this date as the one on which title normally passes). The difference is that an obligation to pay may have become unconditional even though the sum does not have to be paid until a later date;[27] here the due date for payment is taken. The rules on timing also include an anti-avoidance rule which applies where the obligation to pay becomes unconditional on a date earlier than that which accords with normal commercial usage and the sole or main benefit to be derived is the obtaining of the allowance.[28]

---

[20] CAA 2001, s 11(4).
[21] [1978] STC 460, [1978] 2 All ER 1111.
[22] [1983] STC 95.
[23] *Barclays Mercantile Business Finance Ltd v Mawson* [2005] STC 1 (HL) and see *Revenue Law*, §5.6.
[24] CAA 2001, s 5(1); see also Inland Revenue interpretation RI 54.
[25] CAA 2001, s 5(4).
[26] CAA 2001, s 5(5).
[27] CAA 2001, s 5(5).
[28] CAA 2001, s 5(6).

6.1.5.3 A Special Case—Non-recourse Finance

Under a non-recourse finance arrangement the lender does not seek repayment from the borrower personally but is content with some other source, eg the stream of income from the asset. Such loans are common in extraction industries, where the bank is content to be repaid from the stream of money flowing from the ore extracted. However, such arrangements have also been used in tax avoidance schemes. The status of expenditure financed by non-recourse loans was unclear following the opaque speech of Lord Templeman in *Ensign Tankers (Leasing) Ltd v Stokes*.[29] In principle, as Millett J had held at first instance, the fact that a borrower who obtains a non-recourse loan incurs no personal liability to repay the lender ought to be irrelevant; the capital allowance legislation is concerned with the taxpayer's ability to spend capital in acquiring the asset, not with the taxpayer's liability to repay the lender.[30] In the House of Lords, Lord Goff explained that the non-recourse nature of the loan was only one of the elements which enabled him to conclude that this expenditure had not been incurred by the taxpayer: other factors included the fact that the lender (L) was also the (US) company producing the film; that the money was paid into a special bank account opened at a bank nominated by L; and that when the money was paid in by L, an identical sum was repaid by the taxpayer to L out of the same account on the same day. On such facts Lord Goff found it impossible to conclude that the money paid into the account by L was in any meaningful sense a loan; the payment was simply money paid in as the first step in a tax avoidance scheme.[31] Lord Templeman, however, with whom all the other judges agreed, stated:[32]

> By reason of the non-recourse provision of the loan agreement the loan was not repayable by [the taxpayer] or anyone else. A creditor who receives a participation in profits in addition to the repayment of his loan is of course a creditor. But a creditor who receives a participation in profits instead of the repayment of his loan is not a creditor. The language of the document in the latter case does not accurately describe the true legal effect of the transaction which is a capital investment by the 'creditor' in return for a participation in profits.

After mentioning the views of Millett J, Lord Templeman went on to set out the type of facts which Lord Goff had stressed. The result was that it was unclear whether non-recourse finance never works, or whether it fails only in circumstances such as those in *Ensign Tankers*.[33] This issue arose again when *Ensign Tankers* was applied in the 2011 case of *Tower MCashback LLP 1 and another v Revenue & Customs Commissioners*.[34] It now appears that judges will take into consideration the non-recourse nature of financing as one factor in interpreting the facts before them 'realistically' (under Ribeiro PJ's much-cited, modern formulation of the *Ramsay*[35] principle in *Arrowtown*[36]) in arriving at a conclusion as to

---

[29] [1992] STC 226, 64 TC 617, HL (see *Revenue Law* §5.6.4); on US experience, see Shaviro (1989) 43 *Tax Law Review* 401.

[30] [1989] STC 705, 769, 64 TC 617, 705.

[31] [1992] STC 226, 246, 64 TC 617, 747-8.

[32] *Ibid*, 233, 733.

[33] For Revenue treatment of 'security' arrangements in relation to the special allowances for films, see Statement of Practice SP 1/98, paras 66-68.

[34] [2011] UKSC 19, [2011] STC 1143.

[35] *WT Ramsay Ltd v IRC* [1982] AC 300, giving rise to the composite transactions doctrine under which intermediate steps inserted into a transaction entirely for tax purposes could be ignored. For a detailed discussion of the evolution of the *Ramsay* doctrine see *Revenue Law*, §5.6.4.

[36] *Collector of Stamp Revenue v Arrowtown Assets Ltd* [2003] HKCFA 26.

the amount of qualifying expenditure incurred for capital allowances purposes. In *Tower MCashback*, the Supreme Court held that the taxpayer LLPs were not entitled to their full claim for 100% first-year capital allowances in respect of certain software licences partly purchased with investor funds (25%) and partly financed through uncommercial, non-recourse loans (75%), because the LLPs had not 'incurred', in any meaningful sense, qualifying expenditure of the amount claimed. The claim instead was restricted to 25% of the consideration payable under the software licence agreement as that, in the Court's view, was the amount actually incurred on acquiring the rights under the agreement. Lord Walker, giving the lead judgment, also addressed arguments as to the 'uncertain' application of the CAA 2001 provisions, and the relationship between *Ensign Tankers* and the more recent, and apparently conflicting, result in favour of the taxpayer in *Barclays Mercantile Business Finance Ltd v Mawson (Inspector of Taxes)*,[37] stating (at para 80):

> The composite transactions in this case, like that in *Ensign* (and unlike that in *BMBF*) did not, on a realistic appraisal of the facts, meet the test laid down by the CAA, which requires real expenditure for the real purpose of acquiring plant for use in a trade. Any uncertainty that there may be will arise from the unremitting ingenuity of tax consultants and investment bankers determined to test the limits of the capital allowances legislation.

6.1.6 Giving Effect to Allowances

The rules as to giving effect to capital allowances are set out in relation to each allowance. They are normally given effect in taxing the trade or other qualifying activity,[38] and so are claimed in the return of income from that source. Sometimes, where there is no relevant source, the allowance must be claimed in another way.[39]

6.1.6.1 The Qualifying Activity: ITTOIA 2005, Parts 2 and 3/Trade, Property Business, etc

Where the allowance is given effect in taxing the trade or other qualifying activity, it is treated as a deductible expense for the period of account to which it relates; similarly, a balancing charge is treated as a trading receipt.[40] Therefore, the correct profits figure will be profit less capital allowances, and any excess allowances will automatically generate a trading loss. Claims for allowances are normally made in the tax return.[41]

The widest allowance, for plant and machinery, is given for any qualifying activity, of which trade is the first example. Other activities include any ordinary UK property business, furnished holiday lettings, overseas property business, profession or vocation, mining, etc concerns listed in ITTOIA 2005, section 12/CTA 2009, section 39(4), the management of an investment company, special leasing of plant or machinery, and an employment or office. Each such source treats the capital allowance in the same way.[42]

---

[37] [2004] UKHL 51, [2005] STC 1; Tiley [2005] BTR 273. See also *Revenue Law*, §5.6.

[38] See, for plant and machinery, CAA 2001, ss 15 and 247; and for other allowances, ss 352, 360Z, 391, 392, 393T, 432, 450, 463, 478, 489 and 529.

[39] CAA 2001, s 3(4) and (5); on partnership returns, see ss 3(6) and 258.

[40] CAA 2001, s 247(b); the list of ss is the same as in n 38.

[41] CAA 2001, s 3(2); a very few are made under TMA 1970, s 42—see s 3(4). For treatment under self-assessment under corporation tax, see FA 1998, Sch 18, Pt IX.

[42] CAA 2001, ss 248–262.

The allowance is 'treated as' an expense rather than being an expense. Hence, a taxpayer is under no obligation to take allowances available but has discretion whether to take them or not.[43] In relation to non-resident companies, rules direct the separation of sources subject to income tax from those subject to corporation tax.[44] Allowances are computed by reference to qualifying expenditure and disposals in each chargeable period.[45] Since allowances are given on an annual basis, they will be increased or reduced if the chargeable period is greater or less than 12 months. The concept of the chargeable period replaced the old concept of the basis period in 1994.[46]

The 'chargeable period' is the accounting period of a company or the period of account of someone liable to income tax.[47] Where the allowance is made in taxing the trade, profession or vocation, the period of account is usually any period for which accounts are made up for the purposes of the trade.[48] Where, as in the opening two years, two periods of account overlap, the period common to both is deemed to fall in the first period of account only. If there is an interval between two periods of account, the interval is deemed to be part of the first period of account.[49] In this way the allowance—or charge—is given only once. Any period of account greater than 18 months is subdivided; the first subdivision begins with the commencement date of the original period, and later subdivisions are set at 12-month intervals.[50] Any net loss is, in the case of a trade, given effect for income tax as an ordinary trading loss and so set off against general income under ITA 2007, section 64 or 72, or rolled forward against future profits under section 83.

For sources other than trades professions or vocations, eg a property business, the period taken is the tax year.[51] For UK and overseas property businesses, see *Revenue Law*, §10.3.2.

6.1.6.2 Other Allowances Given by Repayment

Other allowances where there is no available trade must be claimed and are given effect by discharge or repayment of tax on the appropriate income.[52] Examples are allowances for investment and insurance companies.[53] Any excess is carried forward to the income of the same class in succeeding years. The period of account is the year of assessment.[54]

6.1.7 Amounts: Price or Market Value?

6.1.7.1 Sales Between Connected Persons

The amount of a charge or an allowance due on a sale clearly depends upon the amount received. Normally, the actual sale price is taken. However, CAA 2001 contains a number of rules directing that market value is taken instead. The first, the 'control' test, is an elective

[43] CAA 2001, s 3(1), confirming *Elliss v BP Oil Northern Ireland Refinery Ltd* [1987] STC 52, 59 TC 474, CA.
[44] CAA 2001, s 566.
[45] Defined in CAA 2001, s 6.
[46] See CAA 1990, s 160 for the original version.
[47] CAA 2001, s 161(2), as amended by FA 1994.
[48] CAA 2001, s 6(4), s 160(2), substituted by FA 1994, s 212.
[49] CAA 2001, s 6(5).
[50] CAA 2001, s 6(6).
[51] CAA 2001, s 6(2)(b).
[52] CAA 2001, s 3 and, for leasing businesses, ss 258–261.
[53] See CAA 2001, ss 253–257, referring to CTA 2009, s 1233 and TA 1988, s 76 (not rewritten).
[54] CAA 2001, s 6(2).

rule designed at least in part to help business.[55] For allowances under Parts 3 (industrial buildings), 4 (agricultural buildings), 5 (mining), 6 (research and development) and 10 (assured tenancies), market value is taken in two situations. The first situation uses the control test and applies where (a) the buyer is a body of persons[56] over whom the seller has control,[57] or (b) vice versa, or (c) both buyer and seller are under the control of some other person,[58] or (d) they are connected persons. The sale will be treated as being at market value unless the parties elect for it to be at the alternative amount of the written-down value of the assets. The purpose behind the main rule may be to prevent avoidance, at least for those situations in which the alternative test does not apply; the purpose behind the alternative is to allow the transfer of the property between such persons in such a way that no balancing adjustment is necessary. Hence this election is available only when capital allowances and charges can be made on both parties.[59] The election must be made within two years of the sale.[60] The election is not open to a dual resident investment company.[61]

The second situation, the 'tax advantage' test, in which market value is taken, is whenever it appears that the sole or main benefit which might have been expected to accrue was the obtaining of a tax advantage, ie any allowance under CAA 2001 other than plant and machinery, which once more has its own rules.[62] No election is possible here.[63] A separate rule applies to the transfer of a UK trade carried on by a company resident in another EU Member State.[64] The transfer is treated as giving rise to neither allowances nor charges, provided the transferee is within the charge to UK tax.[65]

This tax advantage test is quite distinct from the rule denying a balancing allowance where sale proceeds have been reduced by tax avoidance scheme.[66]

As already indicated, plant and machinery has its own, more complex, regime.[67] Know-how also its own provision.[68]

6.1.7.2 Apportionment of Proceeds When Sold Together

Special rules apply when the sale involves both an asset in respect of which allowances have been claimed and another asset.[69] The net proceeds of sale must be apportioned on a just and reasonable basis; the Commissioners are not bound by any apportionment made by the parties.[70]

---

[55] CAA 2001, s 567. Plant and machinery have their own rules, *ibid*, s 214.

[56] Defined in TA 1988, s 832(1), ITA 2007, s 995.

[57] Defined in CAA 2001, s 574.

[58] Defined in CAA 2001, ss 574 and 575, modelled on ex TA 1988, s 839. Allowances under CAA 2001, Pts 3A, 4 or 4A are excluded (s 570(1)).

[59] CAA 2001, s 570(2)(a).

[60] CAA 2001, s 570(5).

[61] CAA 2001, s 570(2)(b). See below at §13.6.

[62] CAA 2001, s 567(4); see *Barclays Mercantile Industrial Finance Ltd v Melluish* [1990] STC 314, 63 TC 95.

[63] CAA 2001, s 569(1)(b).

[64] CAA 2001, s 567(5) excludes ss 568–570; s 561(2) applies instead.

[65] CAA 2001, s 561, esp s 561(1)(c).

[66] CAA 2001, s 570A, added by FA 2003, s 164. This rules applies to the allowance for industrial buildings in Pt 3 of the Act but also to those for agricultural land (§6.5), flat conversions (§6.6), mining (§6.7) and assured tenancies (§6.3.7.2).

[67] CAA 2001, ss 214 *et seq* (see below at §6.4.7); and for successions, etc see s 567(1).

[68] CAA 2001, s 455; this has the 'control' test without an election but has no 'avoidance' test.

[69] CAA 2001, ss 562 and 572(1)–(3).

[70] CAA 2001, s 562; eg *Fitton v Gilders and Heaton* (1955) 36 TC 233; *A Wood & Co Ltd v Provan* (1968) 44 TC 701.

6.1.7.3 Discontinuance and Deferrals: Succession to Trades

In general, where a person carrying on an activity which qualifies for capital allowances, eg a trader (T1), discontinues a trade, a balancing charge or allowance is made. Any capital allowances still unused cannot be carried forward if one trade ends and another one begins.[71] If property—as opposed to the trade—is acquired by another person (T2), T2 may be able to claim allowances in respect of its own capital expenditure, including that in respect of items bought from T1; that expenditure may in turn give rise to balancing charges or allowances to T1.

A special rule applies where there is the transfer of a UK trade to a company resident in another EU Member State and TCGA 1992, section 140A applies to capital assets. Since the effect of section 140A is to apply a no gain, no loss rule to the capital asset for capital gains purposes, the same result is achieved for capital allowance purposes, provided the transferee is within the charge to UK tax.[72] The effect is that the transfer itself does not give rise to any allowances or charges, and that the new owner's allowances are calculated on the same basis as the old owner's allowances. The same tax-neutral effect applies when an asset is transferred under a merger within TCGA 1992, section 140E—the formation of a European Company where the asset remains within the UK tax charge (see §2.14).[73]

Where the trade is acquired by T2 so that there is succession to the trade, market value is used. The new traders are entitled to allowances as if they had acquired the assets at market price,[74] although they are not entitled to initial, as opposed to writing-down and first-year, allowances. Market value is also used when companies cease to trade under section 337(1).[75] Curiously, perhaps, these rules do not apply to allowances under Part 2 (plant and machinery has its own rules), Part 6 (research and development) or Part 10 (assured tenancy).[76]

6.1.8 Choice of Allowances

A capital expense may fall within more than one category of allowance. In the absence of any express provision the taxpayer may choose the most favourable category, subject to general rules designed to prevent double allowances.[77]

6.1.9 Capital Allowance and Revenue Expense Compared

It is worth setting out the ways in which a capital allowance differs from a deductible expense, as follows:

(1)   The allowance must be an item of capital expenditure as distinct from revenue.
(2)   Whereas a revenue expense is deductible unless statute directs otherwise, a capital allowance is made only if the statute so permits.

---

[71] See *Revenue Law*, §20.8 and above at §4.2.
[72] CAA 2001, s 561, esp s 561(1)(c).
[73] CAA 2001, s 561A added by F(No 2)A 2005, s 56.
[74] CAA 2001, s 559.
[75] CAA 2001, s 558; see FA 2001, Sch 21, para 4, correcting CAA 2001, s 558.
[76] CAA 2001, s 557.
[77] CAA 2001, s 7(1).

(3)   Whereas an allowance may be claimed in respect of expenditure incurred before a trade or other qualifying activity commences (although only when the activity begins),[78] an expense so incurred is deductible only if it is incurred within seven years of the trade beginning.

(4)   A revenue expense incurred partly for trade and partly for other purposes is not deductible, whereas such duality results in an apportionment of capital expenditure.[79]

(5)   A revenue expense is deductible at once and in full, whereas allowances are made only at specified rates and often over several years.

(6)   A revenue expense must be taken into account at the proper time, whereas there is no obligation to claim a capital allowance.

6.2   Plant and Machinery

6.2.1 *Elements*

6.2.1.1 First-year Allowances and Writing-down Allowances

The present scheme of capital allowances for plant and machinery was first enacted by FA 1971; the scheme has been much amended. The basic structure consists of first-year allowances[80] and annual writing-down allowances.[81] For some time up to 1984, first-year allowances were given at a rate of 100%. These were abolished by FA 1984 but were revived for particular purposes subsequently, such as the lower rate temporary allowance because the economy was in recession (1992–93),[82] or out of a wish to help SMEs (each year since 1997)[83] or to encourage investment by small enterprises in plant or machinery which is either to do with information and communication technology (ICT)[84] or (by an enterprise of any size) energy saving.[85] The rate—and scope—of these revived first-year allowances has varied. First-year allowances were at one time also available under transitional relief for certain regional projects in development areas.[86] FA 2008 repealed some provisions which are spent (CAA 2001, sections 40–43 and 45).

As from April 2012, writing-down allowances are given at a rate of 18% on the value of qualifying expenditure; expenditure on (and receipts on the disposal of) different items of plant and machinery is usually pooled. Special rules apply to certain assets. The pooling rules were simplified as from April 2008.

---

[78]   CAA 2001, s 6(2).

[79]   Eg *GH Chambers (Northiam Farms) Ltd v Watmough* [1956] 3 All ER 485, 36 TC 711, where an extravagant choice of motor car for personal reasons led to a reduction in the allowance. ITTOIA 2005, s 34(2) and CTA 2009, s 54(2) now provide for apportionment where dual purpose expenses can be dissected into permissible and impermissible portions.

[80]   CAA 2001, ss 39–52. It was not possible to claim both the first-year allowance and the writing-down allowance for the same period—which is why the allowance is called a first-year allowance rather than an initial allowance.

[81]   CAA 2001, ss 52 and 56.

[82]   CAA 2001, ss 47–49.

[83]   On the current scope of first-year allowances, see CAA 2001, ss 39–51 and §6.3.5 below.

[84]   CAA 2001, s 45, repealed in 2008 and replaced by the AIA.

[85]   CAA 2001, s 45A.

[86]   CAA 1990, s 22(2); for history and avoiding Hybrid Bill status, see Lawson, *The View from No 11: Memoirs of a Tory Radical* (Bantam Press, 1992) 354.

The plant and machinery must be used for a qualifying activity (see further §6.1.6.1).[87] Where the asset is provided or used only partly for a qualifying activity, any first-year allowance must be reduced and any writing-down allowance must be calculated on the basis that the asset is the subject of a single asset pool.[88] These rules represent a sharp contrast to the rules for deductible revenue expenditure, where of course there is no deduction for expenditure which is incurred for dual purposes.[89] Expenditure on a share in plant or machinery qualifies for an allowance.[90] Further rules restrict both first-year and writing-down allowances if there is what CAA 2001 calls a 'partial depreciation subsidy', ie a contribution.[91]

6.2.1.2 Successions

The plant and machinery provisions in CAA 2001 include special rules allowing the transfer of assets without balancing adjustments on successions to businesses, so that the result is tax neutral.[92] However, acquisitions by sales and other relevant transactions between connected persons may also attract certain anti-avoidance rules, some of which insist on market value being used (below §6.2.15).[93]

6.2.1.3 Unusual Acquisitions: Change of Use and Gifts—Market Value?

The amount of expenditure for which the taxpayer, T, is entitled to claim is not usually a problem where the asset is bought outright. If T brings plant or machinery into use in the trade and had originally bought the asset for other purposes, or if the asset is acquired by way of gift, it used to be the market value of the asset when it was brought into the use of the trade which was taken as the amount of expenditure incurred.[94]

However, the allowance will be based on the lower of that market value and the (unindexed) original cost.[95] So if a world-class violinist buys a Stradivarius for his collection and later decides to use it for public performance, the allowance will be given by reference to the original cost; of course the term 'cost' has to be taken in its CAA 2001 context, so that if the violinist inherited the violin, the market value at the time of the inheritance would be used rather than cost.

The precise treatment of non-residents with taxable activities in the UK through a permanent establishment has been clarified.[96] Entitlement to the allowance depends on liability to UK tax. So where only a part of the trade is subject to UK tax, only an equivalent part of the allowance may be claimed; to achieve this, the UK part of the trade is treated as a separate trade. Consequential rules have to apply to changes in the amount of UK trade, so that there is a reduction in the allowance if the portion of the trade attributable to the UK part declines.[97]

---

[87] CAA 2001, ss 15–20.
[88] CAA 2001, ss 205–208.
[89] CAA 2001, ss 11(4), 205–207.
[90] CAA 2001, s 270.
[91] CAA 2001, ss 209–212.
[92] CAA 2001, s 265.
[93] CAA 2001, ss 213 *et seq.*
[94] CAA 1990, s 81; the gift is treated as a purchase from the donor for this amount for the purposes of s 75.
[95] CAA 2001, ss 13 (change of purpose) and 14 (acquisition as gift); original versions added by FA 2000, s 75.
[96] CAA 2001, s 15(1), originally added by FA 2000, s 75; naturally this does not apply to those parts of the CAA 2001 which already refer to activities outside the UK.
[97] CAA 2001, s 208, original version added by FA 2000, s 75.

6.2.1.4 Similar Reliefs

Equivalent but distinct relief is given under CAA 2001 for expenditure on thermal insulation (section 28), safety at sports grounds (sections 30–32) and on personal security measures (section 33).[98] While these expenditures attract capital allowances, they do not give rise to balancing charges. At one time there was an allowance for fire safety matters, but this was repealed in 2008; most of the expenditure incurred was revenue in nature and the people who benefited from the allowance were those in default of their responsibilities; subsidising the non-compliant was not sensible.[99]

6.2.1.5 Partners

Where the plant is used by a partnership for a trade carried on by the partnership, allowances will be given to the partners in the usual way. Special provision is made where a partner owns the asset but allows the partnership to use it for its trade. Here, the allowance will be given to the partnership, and any sale or gift by the partner to the partners will be ignored. This provision does not apply where the plant is leased to the partnership for payment.[100]

6.2.1.6 Qualifying Activities: General

Plant and machinery allowances can apply only if the taxpayer is carrying on a qualifying activity.[101] Such activities cover not only trades, professions and vocations,[102] but also UK property businesses,[103] furnished holiday lettings,[104] overseas property businesses,[105] mines and similar concerns listed in ITTOIA 2005, section 12/CTA 2009, section 39(4),[106] the management of investment companies[107] and special leasing arrangements.[108] These activities all have their own rules for giving effect to the allowances. These activities qualify only to the extent that any profits or gains would be chargeable to UK tax.[109]

6.2.1.7 Qualifying Activities: Employment

An employment or office is also a qualifying activity, and so an employee or office holder may obtain capital allowances to set against employment income in respect of 'plant and machinery necessarily provided by the employee for use in his employment'.[110] The term 'necessarily' means that a finding that another holder of the office could have performed the duties without incurring the expense is fatal to the claim.[111] For most employments, it is not possible for E, the employee, to claim a capital allowance for a computer/word

---

[98] CAA 2001, ss 28 and 30–33; s 28 widened to all qualifying activities by FA 2008, s 71.
[99] CAA 2001, s 29 repealed by FA 2008, cl 72.
[100] CAA 1990, s 65.
[101] CAA 2001, s 15.
[102] CAA 2001, ss 15 and 247.
[103] CAA 2001, ss 16 and 248.
[104] CAA 2001, ss 17 and 249.
[105] CAA 2001, ss 15 and 250.
[106] CAA 2001, ss 15 and 251.
[107] CAA 2001, ss 18 and 253; on life assurance businesses, see ss 254–257.
[108] CAA 2001, ss 19 and 258–261.
[109] CAA 2001, s 15(1).
[110] CAA 2001, ss 15 and 36; see also ss 20 (excluding certain offices, etc) and 262.
[111] *White v Higginbotham* [1983] STC 143, 57 TC 2839 (no allowance for audio visual aids for clergyman).

processor purchased by E for use in E's employment, since it is usually possible to perform the duties of that employment equally by pen, paper and brain.[112] Moreover, the Revenue often argue that the very fact that E rather than his employer purchases the equipment is proof that the purchase is not 'necessary' for the employment.

However, an employee may not claim any allowances for purchases of motor vehicles or bicycles. Instead the employee must claim under the Revenue's fixed-profit car scheme, which includes an allowance for the capital cost of the vehicle (see *Revenue Law*, §18.2.6).[113]

6.2.2 'Belong to' / 'Owned by'

6.2.2.1 Overview

Under CAA 1990, the asset had to 'belong to' the person incurring the expense in consequence of the payment. This was changed by CA 2001 to the possibly more understandable rule that the asset must be 'owned by' that person; the change is meant to be simply stylistic.[114] In *Stokes v Costain Property Investments Ltd*,[115] a tenant had installed a lift in a leased building. Since the lifts immediately became the property of the landlord under general land law principles, they could not be said to 'belong to' the tenant, and so it was held that the tenant was not entitled to the allowance.[116] Further, in *Melluish v BMI (No 3)*,[117] the House of Lords held that a lessee has no right to an allowance if he has a right to remove the fixture at some future time, eg at the end of the lease, but which fixture has become the property of the landlord in the meantime. This is because the concept of a fixture which remains personal property is a contradiction in terms and an impossibility in law;[118] and because the argument would make it uncertain whether an asset belonged to—or ceased to belong to—the lessee according to whether he had or had not got a right to remove the asset (eg where the landlord committed a breach of the lease which the tenant then forgave). It follows that a contractual right to remove the fixture cannot prevent its becoming part of the land and so ceasing to belong to the installer.

In *Melluish*, the words 'in consequence of' in the 1990 Act were held to be satisfied where a payment was made by the taxpayer to induce the holder of an option to reacquire the property to release that option.[119] These words form no part of CAA 2001, which refers simply to capital expenditure incurred on the provision of plant of machinery.[120]

In *Melluish*, the taxpayer leased central heating, boilers, lifts and similar equipment to local authorities. The items were installed in buildings owned by the local authorities. In so far as *Melluish* decided that equipment-lessors could obtain allowances under the

---

[112] On the now-repealed absence of a tax charge where a computer was provided by the employer, see *Revenue Law*, §16.3.3.2.

[113] FA 2001, s 59 amending CAA 2001, s 36; on ministerial statement, see Standing Committee A, 1 May 2001.

[114] CAA 2001, ss 11(4)(b) and 52(1)(b); for earlier rules, see CAA 1990, ss 22(1)(b), 24(1)(b).

[115] [1984] STC 204, [1984] 1 All ER 849, CA; see Scott [1985] BTR 46. Contrast the 'relevant interest' rules for industrial buildings (below at §6.3.3). See also *Melluish v BMI (No 3) Ltd* [1995] STC 964, 68 TC 1.

[116] The landlord (to whom the lifts did belong) could not claim an allowance because it had not incurred the expenditure.

[117] [1995] STC 964, 68 TC 1.

[118] *Ibid*, 971, 974, 71–72, 75, *per* Lord Browne-Wilkinson.

[119] *Bolton v International Drilling Ltd* [1983] STC 70, 56 TC 449.

[120] CAA 2001, s 11(4)(a).

special rules introduced to reverse *Costain* where plant was leased to non-taxpayers such as charities or local authorities, the decision was reversed—save where the *lessor* had an interest in the land.[121]

6.2.2.2 Reversing *Costain*: The Fixtures Rules

The situation resulting from *Stokes v Costain* was unjust, and a new scheme was introduced for expenditure incurred in 1984.[122] A fixture is treated as owned by the lessee (L) (or similar person) who incurred the expenditure in providing the plant or machinery for the purposes of a trade carried on by L (or for leasing otherwise than in the course of a trade) if (a) the plant or machinery becomes in law a part of the land, and (b) at that time L has an interest in the relevant land.[123] The rules also apply where the plant becomes a fixture before the capital expenditure is incurred. The lessee's allowance excludes the lessor's allowance, but a lessor who contributes to the expenditure is not excluded.[124] Naturally, (a) and (b) above turn on land law principles. Tax courts have had to consider whether automatic public conveniences (APCs) and bus shelters were part of the land (they were), and whether a right to enter to clean, maintain and repair was enough to satisfy (b) (it was not).[125]

FA 2000 widened the definition for qualifying expenditure by an equipment lessor to cover leased assets under the Affordable Warmth Programme.[126] The same Act amended the definition of 'fixture' so as to include boilers and radiators, even though these are (relatively) easy to remove; as this was always thought to be the law, the change had retroactive effect.[127] A later Act governs fixtures supplied by energy service providers.[128] The effect is to treat the equipment lessor or provider as being the owner, but only for CAA 2001 purposes.

Special provisions govern disputes over whether the item is a fixture,[129] expenditure (and disposals) by equipment lessors[130] and the transfer to a lessee of the right to an allowance.[131] Rules also apply where an interest in the land is sold and the price is referable to the fixture,[132] and when the fixture ceases to belong to a particular person.[133] These rules are to be taken at face value; the allowances are not confined to cases where the user is liable to tax.[134] Other rules limit the amount qualifying for allowances to the original cost of the fixtures and prevent multiple claims.[135] Rules also prevent the acceleration of allowances.[136]

---

[121] CAA 1990, s 53(1A)–(1C) added by FA 1997, Sch 16, para 3, now superseded by CAA 2001, ss 177(3).

[122] Now CAA 2001, ss 172–204. Before 1984 matters were dealt with by concession; the taxpayers in *Stokes v Costain* were apparently not willing to agree to one of the conditions in that concession.

[123] Defined in CAA 2001, ss 173–175 and 202.

[124] Under CAA 2001, ss 172(5) and 537.

[125] *Decaux v Francis* [1996] STC (SCD) 281.

[126] CAA 2001, ss 180 and 203, original amendments made by FA 2000, s 79.

[127] CAA 2001, ss 172(1) and 173(1) and (2), original amendments made by FA 2000, s 78.

[128] CAA 2001, s 180A added by FA 2001 s 66.

[129] CAA 2001, s 204.

[130] CAA 2001, ss 177–180 and 192–196.

[131] CAA 2001, s 183; and where the lessee would be entitled to the allowance, but the lessor would not (s 184).

[132] CAA 2001, s 181.

[133] CAA 2001, ss 188–191.

[134] *Melluish v BMI (No 3) Ltd* [1995] STC 964, 980b, 68 TC 1, 82I, HL, *per* Lord Browne-Wilkinson.

[135] CAA 2001, ss 9 and 182–184, original version added by FA 1997, Sch 16, para 4.

[136] CAA 2001, s 197, original version added by FA 1997, Sch 16, para 5.

The 1997 legislation allowed the vendor and purchaser of property to allocate part of the purchase price to fixtures.[137]

There are also rules imposing obligations on taxpayers to amend their returns to report relevant changes of circumstances in relation to these rules.[138]

6.2.3 What is Plant and Machinery?

6.2.3.1 General

Neither 'plant' nor 'machinery' is defined in CAA 2001, and the question whether an item is plant or machinery depends on the facts of the case. Where an item qualified both for plant and machinery allowance and industrial buildings allowance (withdrawn from April 2011),[139] it was likely that the former, usually more generous, relief was claimed.[140] In 1994 Parliament provided some clarification on the boundary between plant and its setting, but difficult cases still appear (see below at §6.2.4).

Different definitions have been suggested for specific instances. In *Yarmouth v France*, a claim was brought by a workman under the Employers' Liability Act 1880 for damages for injuries sustained due to a defect in his employer's plant, in that case a vicious horse. Lindley LJ stated:[141]

> ...[I]n its ordinary sense [plant] includes whatever apparatus is used by a business man for carrying on his   business—not his stock-in-trade which he buys or makes for sale; but all goods and chattels, fixed or moveable, live or dead, which he keeps for permanent employment in his business....

This test has been helpful but not exclusive[142] in capital allowance cases. The test clearly covers fixtures and fittings of a durable nature. Therefore, railway locomotives and carriages[143] and tramway rails[144] have been held to be plant, as have knives and lasts used in the manufacture of shoes,[145] but not the bed of a harbour,[146] nor stallions for stud purposes.[147]

It is now clear that plant and machinery is not confined to things used physically[148] but extends to the intellectual storehouse of the trade or profession, eg the purchase of law books by a barrister.[149] However, rights to exploit plant are not 'plant'—a matter of great

---

[137] CAA 2001, s 198, original version added by FA 1997, Sch 16, para 6.

[138] CAA 2001, s 203.

[139] *IRC v Barclay Curle & Co Ltd* [1969] 1 All ER 732, 45 TC 221 (see below at §6.2.4); the area of overlap has been reduced by statutory rules on when setting is plant.

[140] Double allowances are excluded by CAA 2001, s 7.

[141] (1887) 19 QBD 647 at 658.

[142] Lord Donovan in *IRC v Barclay Curle & Co Ltd* [1969] 1 All ER 732, 751, 45 TC 221, 249.

[143] *Caledonian Rly Co v Banks* (1880) 1 TC 487.

[144] *LCC v Edwards* (1909) 5 TC 383.

[145] *Hinton v Maden and Ireland Ltd* [1959] 3 All ER 356, 38 TC 391 (expected to last only three years); noted at [1959] BTR 454.

[146] *Dumbarton Harbour Board v Cox* (1918) 7 TC 147.

[147] *Earl of Derby v Aylmer* [1915] 3 KB 374, 6 TC 665.

[148] *McVeigh v Arthur Sanderson & Sons Ltd* [1969] 2 All ER 771, 775, *per* Cross J; noted at [1969] BTR 130.

[149] *Munby v Furlong* [1977] STC 232, [1977] 2 All ER 953.

concern in the area of IP.[150] It is not necessary that the object be active, although a passive object may be less obviously plant.[151]

It has been suggested, eg by the Revenue, that a thing which lacks physical manifestation cannot be 'plant'. If this is true, it leads to a substantial and regrettable lack of clarity with regard to many items of IP. The piecemeal income tax provisions for copyright, know-how and certain types of scientific research are no substitute for modern and coherent law. Special legislation now applies to computer software.

6.2.3.2 Computer Software

Where capital expenditure is incurred on the outright acquisition of computer software, the normal plant and machinery allowance is available.[152] However, problems arise where a capital sum is paid for a licence to use the software or for the provision of software by electronic means. In the first instance, it cannot be said that the software is owned by the taxpayer, while in the second, it may lack the degree of tangibility necessary for plant to exist.[153] Today, software acquired under a licence is treated as owned by the person carrying on the qualifying activity (T) as long as T is entitled to the right, while computer software is treated as being plant or machinery.[154] The disposal values depend on the circumstances of the grant of the licence.[155]

6.2.4 Plant or Setting

6.2.4.1 Statutory Prescription of Settings[156]

Since 1994, statute has in part governed the boundary between plant and machinery and settings; originally CAA 1990, Schedule AA1, now CAA 2001, sections 21–25. Section 21 provides List A, which are assets which must be treated as *buildings* and not as plant, while section 22 provides List B, which are certain *structures* which must be treated in the same way. Section 23 gives us List C, which is a long list of exceptions to Lists A and B where established case law doctrine is still to apply. This elaboration does not affect a number of special provisions which treat specified expenditure as if it were on plant or machinery—eg thermal insulation, sports grounds and security.[157] Section 23(3) states, somewhat cryptically, that whether expenditure on List C is expenditure on the provision of plant or machinery is not affected by sections 21 and 22. The implication is that the question must be answered by the courts on the particular facts, but bearing in mind that the assets on List C are ones that had previously satisfied the test of plant.[158] List C includes not only expenditure on the provision of a dry dock but also any glasshouse which is constructed so that the required environment (ie air, heat, light, irrigation and temperature) for

---

[150] *Barclays Mercantile Industrial Finance Ltd v Melluish* [1990] STC 314, 63 TC 93, 122.
[151] *Jarrold v John Good & Sons Ltd* [1963] 1 All ER 141, 40 TC 681.
[152] On boundary between capital and revenue, note Inland Revenue interpretation RI 56.
[153] *Barclays Mercantile Industrial Finance Ltd v Melluish* [1990] STC 314, 63 TC 93, 122.
[154] CAA 2001, s 71, predecessor originally added by F(No 2)A 1992, s 68.
[155] CAA 2001, s 72; on limits, see s 73.
[156] Originally added by FA 1994, s 117.
[157] CAA 2001, ss 27–33; on application of thermal insulation on industrial buildings to overseas property business, see FA 2001, Sch 21, para 1, amending CAA 2001, s 28.
[158] CAA 2001, s 23, List C, paras 23 and 17.

growing plants is provided automatically by means of devices which are an integral part of its structure. Lastly, to give taxpayers some comfort in these rules, section 25 provides that expenditure on building alterations connected with the installation of plant and machinery is to be treated as being incurred on the plant and machinery.

The premise behind the post-1994 statutory framework is that buildings and structures cannot qualify as plant (although it is also stated that the broad aim is that expenditure on buildings and structures which already qualify as plant should continue to do so).[159] However, for the most part the lists reflect what the courts have achieved. The effect of the change is partly to provide detailed guidance and partly to prevent judges from changing the law themselves.

(a) *Buildings.* CAA 2001, section 21 begins with buildings, and excludes from the category of 'plant or machinery' any expenditure on the provision of a building. It defines 'building' as including any asset in the building which is incorporated into the building, or which, by reason of being movable or otherwise, is not so incorporated but is of a kind normally incorporated into buildings.[160] This abstract statement is supplemented by Lists A (section 21) and C (section 23). List A sets out six categories of assets which *cannot* be plant or machinery,[161] including walls, floors, ceilings, doors, gates, shutters, windows and stairs, mains services, waste disposal, sewerage and drainage, shafts, etc for lifts, and moving walkways and fire safety systems; examples of the 33 items in List C, and so which *may* be 'plant' under case law principles, are electrical, cold water, gas and sewerage systems provided mainly to meet the particular requirements of the trade, or provided mainly to serve particular plant or machinery used for the purposes of the trade. Cold stores, caravans provided mainly for holiday lettings and any movable building intended to be moved in the course of the trade are also in List C and so may also be plant. The legislation leaves it to the taxpayer to establish that these items are plant under existing case law. To make things clearer, it is provided that an asset cannot come within any of the first 16 items in List C if its principal purpose is to insulate or enclose the interior of the building, or to provide an interior wall, a floor or a ceiling which (in each case) is intended to remain permanently in place.[162] FA 2008 adds to List C expenditure on the installation or replacement of specified 'integral features'; these will therefore qualify for writing-down allowance of 8%. The features are electrical and cold-water systems, heating and air-conditioning systems, escalators and moving walkways, and external solar shading (being thought to be environmentally beneficial).[163]

(b) *Structures, assets and works.* Again, the legislation (CAA 2001, section 22) begins with a prohibition—expenditure on the provision of plant or machinery does not include any expenditure on the provision of structures or other specified assets in List B, or any works involving the alteration of land.[164] Section 22 defines a 'structure' as a fixed structure of any kind, other than a building. List B contains seven categories

---

[159] Inland Revenue Press Release, 30 November 1993, [1993] *Simon's Tax Intelligence* 1539.
[160] CAA 2001, s 21(3).
[161] CAA 2001, s 23 List C, para 2.
[162] CAA 2001, s 23(4).
[163] CAA 2001, ss 33A and 33B added by FA 2008, s 73; the list is in s 33A(5).
[164] On which, see *Family Golf Centres Ltd v Thorne* [1998] STC (SCD) 106.

which cannot qualify. It includes not only tunnels, bridges, railways and airstrips, but also any dam, reservoir or barrage (including any sluices, gates, generators and other equipment associated with it), any dock and any dike, sea wall, weir or drainage ditch; the list ends ominously with any structure not within any other item in this list (a statement that is then qualified with a few exceptions, including telecommunication and gas structures).

List C includes expenditure on the provision of towers used to support floodlights, of any reservoir incorporated into a water treatment works, of silos used for temporary storage or on the provision of storage tanks, of swimming pools, including diving boards, slides and any structure supporting them and of fish tanks or fish ponds. List C was substantially widened in the course of the Parliamentary debate.[165]

(c)	*Land.* Lastly, CAA 2001, section 24 provides that expenditure on the acquisition of any interest in land cannot qualify as expenditure on plant. This bar also extends to any asset which is so installed or otherwise fixed in or to any description of land as to become, in law, part of that land.[166]

6.2.4.2 Plant or Setting: Case Law Principles

Plant does not include the place where the business is carried on; 'plant' is that *with which* the trade is carried on as opposed to the 'setting or premises' *in which* it is carried on.[167] Plant carries with it a connotation of equipment or apparatus, either fixed or unfixed. It does not convey a meaning wide enough to cover buildings in general. It may cover equipment of any size. Equipment does not cease to be plant merely because it discharges an additional function, such as providing the place in which the business is carried on, eg a dry dock,[168] but these categories are not necessarily mutually exclusive and the different scope of the allowances makes correct classification of great practical importance. It has been held that special partitioning used by shipping agents to subdivide floor space to accommodate fluctuating office accommodation requirements was plant, some stress being laid on the fact that office flexibility was needed.[169] Something which becomes part of the premises, as opposed to merely embellishing them, is not plant, save where the premises are themselves plant,[170] as in *IRC v Barclay, Curle & Co Ltd* (see §6.2.4.3 below).

6.2.4.3 Defining the Unit

It is often a crucial question whether various items are taken separately or treated as one installation. This is a question of fact and so for the Tribunals (formerly Commissioners) to decide, subject only to the tests in *Edwards v Bairstow and Harrison*, namely where the appellant judge concludes that the only true and reasonable conclusion contradicts the

---

[165] See Inland Revenue Press Release, 9 March 1994, [1994] *Simon's Tax Intelligence* 339.

[166] CAA 2001, s 24; rule added to CAA 1990 by FA 1994, s 117; the definition of 'land' in the Interpretation Act 1978 is modified, CAA 2001, s 24(2).

[167] *Jarrold v John Good & Sons Ltd* [1963] 1 All ER 141, 40 TC 681, 696, *per* Pearson LJ.

[168] See Sir Donald Nicholls V-C in *Carr v Sayer* [1992] STC 396, 402, 65 TC 15, 22.

[169] *Jarrold v John Good & Sons Ltd* [1963] 1 All ER 141, 40 TC 681. The decision of the Commissioners was left intact.

[170] *Wimpy International Ltd v Warland* [1989] STC 273, 279e, 61 TC 51, 96, CA, *per* Fox LJ.

Tribunal's determination.[171] In *Cole Brothers Ltd v Phillips*,[172] the taxpayer, T, had spent money on electrical installations in a large department store (John Lewis at the Brent Cross shopping centre, London). One argument advanced by T was that the whole electrical installation was one item. This was rejected by the Commissioners; the appellate courts treated the issue as a matter of fact for the Commissioners, but the discomfort shown by the speeches in the House of Lords is marked.[173] The issue arose later in *Attwood v Anduff Carwash Ltd*,[174] where the question was whether a car-wash site was a single plant. The Commissioners held that it was, but the appellate courts held that neither the whole site nor the wash hall alone could be treated as a single unit.

(a)   *Dry dock—IRC v Barclay, Curle & Co Ltd.* While there is a clear distinction between the shell of a building and the machinery currently used in it, there are considerable difficulties where a large and durable structure is created for a specific purpose. This occurred in the leading case of *IRC v Barclay, Curle & Co Ltd*.[175] The taxpayer had constructed a dry dock, a process requiring the excavation of the site and the construction of a concrete lining. The Revenue agreed that such expenditure incurred on the dock gate and operating gear, the cast-iron keel blocks and the electrical and pumping installations related to plant, but argued that, while the expenses of excavation and concreting might relate to industrial building, they did not relate to plant and machinery. The Revenue lost.

It will be noted that while a dock is now classified as a structure, and so not capable of qualifying for allowances as plant, a dry dock is classified differently. The expenditure on the concrete lining was held to be in respect of plant, because it could not be regarded as the mere setting in which the trade was carried on but was an integral part of the means required for the trading operation. Lord Reid said that a structure which fulfils the function of plant was, prima facie, plant.[176] However, later cases show that this 'business' or 'function' test must yield to the 'premises' test (see (b) below). CAA 2001 expressly provides that where capital expenditure is incurred on alterations to an existing building incidental to the installation of plant or machinery for the purposes of trade, allowances may be claimed in respect of such expenditure just as if the works formed part of the plant or machinery.[177]

(b)   *Fast food restaurant—Wimpy v Warland.* The fact that an item has a business use (the business test) is not enough to make it plant; an item cannot be plant if its use is as the premises or place on which the business is conducted (the premises test).[178] In *Wimpy v Warland*,[179] the taxpayer sought (unsuccessfully) to claim allowances for expenditure on shop fronts, wall panels, suspended ceilings, mezzanine floor, decorative brickwork, wall finishes, a trapdoor and ladder. As Fox LJ stated:

---

[171] [1955] 3 All ER 48. See *Revenue Law* at §4.4.4.
[172] [1982] STC 307 HL; [1981] STC 671, 55 TC 188, CA.
[173] See [1982] STC 307, 312–13, *per* Lord Hailsham, 314f, *per* Lord Wilberforce, and 316a, *per* Lord Edmund-Davies
[174] [1997] STC 1167, CA.
[175] [1969] 1 All ER 732, 45 TC 221.
[176] *Ibid*, 740, 239.
[177] CAA 2001, s 25.
[178] *Wimpy International v Warland* [1988] STC 149, 171b; 61 TC 51, 82d, *per* Hoffmann J.
[179] [1989] STC 273, 279; 61 TC 51, 96, CA.

There is a well established distinction, in general terms, between the premises in which the business is carried on and the plant with which the business is carried on. The premises are not plant. In its simplest form that is illustrated by [the] example of the creation of atmosphere in a hotel by beautiful buildings and gardens on the one hand and fine china, glass and other tableware on the other. The latter are plant; the former are not. The former are simply the premises in which the business is conducted.

(c)   *Planteria—Gray v Seymour's.* The case of *Gray v Seymour's*[180] involved what might loosely be called a high-tech glasshouse used in a garden centre. As Nourse LJ stated:

> While the cold frames which formerly provided a similar function to that of the planteria might well have been plant, the same cannot be said of the planteria itself. It is a structure to which plants are brought already in a saleable condition, albeit that some of them tend to be in there for quite considerable periods and others require special treatment … The fact that the planteria provides the function of nurturing and preserving the plants while they are there cannot transform it into something other than part of the premises in which the business is carried on. The highest it can be put is that it functions as a purpose-built structure. But … that is not enough to make the structure plant.

6.2.4.4 Defining Setting

The distinction between setting and plant depends in part upon the degree of sophistication to be employed in the concept of a setting.[181] The problem is acute when electrical apparatus and wiring are concerned.[182] The matter must be resolved by the use of the functional test, so that, for example, while lighting will not usually be plant, it will become so if it is of a specialised nature, as where it is designed to provide a particular atmosphere in a hotel; this must be judged by reference to the intended market.[183] The Revenue have consistently refused to treat wiring leading to such apparatus as plant. Under section 21, List A places mains services and systems of electricity generally in the category of assets which cannot qualify as plant, while List C *allows* electrical systems to be plant if provided mainly to meet the particular requirements of the trade, or to serve particular plant or machinery used for the purposes of the trade.[184]

---

[180] [1995] STC 706, 711b; 67 TC 401, 413. For a general Revenue view on glasshouses, see Inland Revenue interpretation RI 33, updated by RI 185.

[181] *Imperial Chemical Industries of Australia and New Zealand v Taxation Commr of the Commonwealth of Australia* (1970) 120 CLR 396.

[182] In *Cole Brothers v Phillips* [1982] STC 307, HL; [1981] STC 671, 55 TC 188, CA, the Revenue agreed that wiring to certain items such as alarms and clocks was plant, but said that (a) transformers, switchgear and the main switchboard, and (b) specially designed lighting fittings were not plant. The Commissioners held that the transformers were plant, but not the other items under (a) or any of (b). The Court of Appeal held that the switchboard was plant because of the fact that some of the wiring had been agreed to be plant. The House of Lords agreed with the Court of Appeal in treating the remaining items as matters for the Commissioners' decision as matters of fact.

[183] *Cole Bros Ltd v Phillips* [1982] STC 307, 55 TC 188, HL; *Hunt v Henry Quick Ltd* [1992] STC 633, 65 TC 108; *IRC v Scottish and Newcastle Breweries Ltd* [1982] STC 296, 55 TC 252 (note that the light fitting was allowed in *Wimpy International Ltd v Warland* [1988] STC 149, 176; 61 TC 51, 88). On the 1982 House of Lords decisions, see [1983] BTR 54.

[184] The Revenue rely strongly on *J Lyons & Co Ltd v A-G* [1944] Ch 281, [1944] 1 All ER 477.

6.2.4.5 Case Law Survey

The case law distinction between buildings and apparatus is, perhaps inevitably, indistinct. The cases have shown that items which cannot be plant under the case law test include a prefabricated building at a school used to accommodate a chemical laboratory,[185] a canopy over a petrol station[186] (although this has since been doubted),[187] an inflatable cover over a tennis court[188] and a floating ship used as a restaurant.[189] These failed the business test since they performed no function in the trade. Many of these cases now appear in the statutory list of assets which cannot qualify as plant. Permanent quarantine kennels,[190] putting greens at a nine-hole golf course,[191] a car-washing facility operated on a conveyor belt system[192] and an all-weather race track for horse racing[193] probably met the business test, but certainly failed the premises test. On the other hand, it has been held that a silo used in the trade of grain importing was not simply part of the setting and had to be considered together with the machinery and other equipment within it.[194] Similarly, a swimming pool at a caravan site was held to be plant since it was part of the apparatus of the business.[195] Also held to be plant were decorative screens placed in the windows of a building society's offices (since the screens were not the structure within which the business was carried on)[196] and, perhaps surprisingly, mezzanine platforms installed by a wholesale merchant to increase storage space.[197] In the celebrated House of Lords case of *IRC v Scottish and Newcastle Breweries Ltd*,[198] murals designed to attract customers were held to be plant, as was a metal seagull sculpture and other items designed to create 'ambience'.

These cases prove the old adage that an ounce of evidence (before the Commissioners) is worth a ton of law. Of the 13 High Court cases reported between 1975 and 2004, eight were cases in which the Revenue successfully appealed against a Commissioner's determination that the items were plant, one was a successful appeal by a taxpayer against a Commissioner's decision in favour of the Revenue, in two the court agreed with the Commissioners that the items were plant, and in two the Commissioners had originally decided that *some* items were plant, but the court subsequently decided that *more* items were plant. Of the items which the courts have decided are plant, one or two have now been set out in the non-plant category by the statutory list.[199]

---

[185] *St John's School v Ward* [1975] STC 7, 49 TC 524 (note the astonishingly harsh refusal by Templeman J to allow an apportionment between the building and the equipment).

[186] *Dixon v Fitch's Garage Ltd* [1975] STC 480, [1975] 3 All ER 455, 50 TC 509.

[187] *Cole Bros Ltd v Phillips* [1982] STC 307, 311; 55 TC, 223, *per* Lord Hailsham; but see the pointed comment of Walton J in *Thomas v Reynolds* [1987] STC 135, 140; 59 TC 502, 508.

[188] *Thomas v Reynolds* [1987] STC 135, 59 TC 502.

[189] *Benson v Yard Arm Club Ltd* [1979] STC 266, [1979] 2 All ER 336, 53 TC 607.

[190] *Carr v Sayer* [1992] STC 396, 65 TC 15.

[191] *Family Golf Centres Ltd v Thorne* [1998] STC (SCD) 106.

[192] *Attwood v Anduff Car Wash Ltd* [1997] STC 1167, CA.

[193] *Shove v Lingfield Park (1991) Ltd* [2004] EWCA Civ 391; [2004] STC 805; in a similar vein the Special Commissioners refused to treat a five-a-side football pitch as plant in *Anchor International v IRC* [2003] STC (SCD) 115.

[194] *Schofield v R and H Hall Ltd* [1975] STC 353, 49 TC 538.

[195] *Cooke v Beach Station Caravans Ltd* [1974] STC 402, [1974] 3 All ER 159, 49 TC 514.

[196] *Leeds Permanent Building Society v Procter* [1982] STC 821, 56 TC 293.

[197] *Hunt v Henry Quick Ltd* [1992] STC 633, 643–44; 65 TC 108, 124 (note the doubts of Vinelott J).

[198] [1982] STC 296, 55 TC 252, HL.

[199] Eg the windows in *Leeds Permanent Building Society v Procter* [1982] STC 821.

6.2.5 *First-year Allowances and the Annual Investment Allowance*

6.2.5.1 General

The expenditure on plant and machinery qualifying for first-year allowances is set out in CAA 2001, Part 2, Chapter 4 (sections 39–51); the rules for calculating the allowances are in section 52, which includes a helpful table.

Although general first-year allowances were abolished by FA 1984, as part of Nigel Lawson's corporation tax reform, Chancellors have been unable to resist bringing them back for specific purposes, but there are fewer after the changes of 2008.[200]

To help businesses through the recession where new expenditure exceeds the annual investment allowance (AIA), a first-year allowance of 40% was given by FA 2009, section 24, amending CAA 2001, sections 39 and 52(3). For timing and conditions, see section 52(2)–(6). The allowance was increased from 20%—for one year. Among the exclusions are special rate expenditures.

6.2.5.2 Current First-year Allowances

(1) First-year allowances of 100% are available for expenditure on plant and machinery which is energy-saving.[201] The plant must be new or, if secondhand, unused. The definition of plant which is energy-saving is to be found in a Treasury regulation.[202] The regulations may require certification that the particular item of plant is energy-efficient, and may also impose limits in situations in which the energy-efficient plant is part of a larger item.[203] The allowance is available to all companies regardless of size. The allowance is simply part of the scheme in Part 2 of the Act, and so general rules apply excluding first-year allowances in certain situations, but this is spelt out.[204]

(2) There are 100% allowances, added by FA 2002, to cover cars with low carbon dioxide emissions and electric cars,[205] and for expenditure on gas refuelling stations[206] (the gas may be natural gas or hydrogen).[207] These provisions have their own sunset rule and were to expire on 31 March 2013, but the date was extended by an announcement at Budget 2012 to 31 March 2015.[208] The normal rule barring first-year allowances where such assets are leased does not apply[209] and was removed by FA 2002, section 62, but leased business cars do not qualify.

---

[200] CAA 1990, s 22(2); for history and avoiding hybrid Bill status, see Lawson, *op cit*, 354. It was not possible to claim both the first-year allowance and the writing-down allowance for the same period, which is why the allowance is called a first-year allowance rather than an initial allowance.

[201] CAA 2001, ss 39 and 52(3), amended by FA 2001, Sch 17 and adding ss 45A–45C; on timing of expenditure, see Sch 17, para 6.

[202] CAA 2001, s 45A(3) and Capital Allowances (Energy-saving Plant and Machinery) Order SI 2000/2541 and Amendments in SI 2003/1744, SI 2004/2093, SI 2005/2424, SI 2006/2233, SI 2007/2165, SI 2008/1919 and SI 2009/1863; see also Revenue Briefing Note BN 10, 7 March 2001.

[203] CAA 2001, ss 45B and 45C.

[204] CAA 2001, s 46, as amended by FA 2001, Sch 17.

[205] See CAA 2001, ss 39 and 45D, as amended by FA 2002, s 59.

[206] CAA 2001, ss 39 and 45E, as amended by FA 2002, s 61.

[207] CAA 2001, s 45E.

[208] Amendments were also made by FA 2008, ss 77 and 78.

[209] CAA 2001, ss 46(4) and (5) added by FA 2002, s 62.

(3) Water-efficient plant and machinery, etc. FA 2003 continued the trend by creating 100% first-year allowances for expenditure on plant or machinery that is regarded as environmentally beneficial.[210] The Treasury are given regulation-making powers to describe the various types of plant or machinery that will qualify.[211] The relevant Press Release, Rev BN 26, refers to expenditure reducing water use or improving water quality, and states that the relevant list is available from <www.eca.gov.uk>. The rules apply to expenditure on or after 1 April 2003. The machinery must be unused and not secondhand, not be a long-life asset and not be excluded by the general rules in section 46. At Budget 2012, the Government announced that this list and the list of designated energy-saving technology will be updated.

The matters covered in (1)–(3) above are compendiously called 'green technologies'. These are the first-year allowances which can give rise to a tax credit or enhanced allowance where a company is concerned and the company has a loss (and so is unable to make good use of the allowance straight away).[212]

(4) The table in CAA 2001, section 52 also lists a first-year plant and machinery mineral extraction allowance for special ring-fenced businesses—mostly to do with North Sea Oil.[213] The rate is 100%, but this is reduced to 24% if the asset is a long-life asset.

(5) Plant and machinery investment in enterprise zones.[214] From 1 April 2012, 100% allowances are available if the investment is made in one of the zones listed on the Treasury website, including London Royal Docks.

6.2.5.3 Repealed First-year Allowances

Allowances for expenditure on machinery and plant by SMEs have been repealed to make way for the AIA of £25,000.[215] Also repealed in 2008 is the legislation on the special 100% rate used to apply for expenditure on assets to be used wholly (and not just partly) in Northern Ireland.[216] This was because the allowances no longer applied. The rate applied only to small or medium-sized businesses for expenditure from 12 May 1998 to 11 May 2002, and had to be modified to meet EC rules on state aids. Another 'spent' allowance repealed in 2008 is the 100% allowance for ICT expenditure incurred by small enterprises (see §6.2.1.1 above).

6.2.5.4 The Annual Investment Allowance

The AIA is, in effect, a 100% first-year allowance. The AIA is £25,000 from April 2012 but was temporarily increased to £250,000 from January 2013 for two years. The principal legislation is in CAA 2001, Part 2, Chapter 3A (sections 38A and 38, and sections 51A–51N), all added by FA 2008, section 74 and Schedule 24.

---

[210] CAA 2001, s 45H added by FA 2003, s 167 and Sch 30.

[211] CAA 2001, s 45H(3) and (4) and Capital Allowances (Environmentally Beneficial Plant and Machinery) Order SI 2003/2076 and Amendments in SI 2005/2423, SI 2006/2235, SI 2007/2166, SI 2008/1917 and SI 2009/1864.

[212] FA 2008, s 79 and Sch 25.

[213] CAA 2001, ss 45F and 45G added by FA 2002, Sch 21, para 10.

[214] CAA 2001, s 45K, added by FA 2012, Sch 11, para 3.

[215] Ex CAA 2001, s 44.

[216] CAA 2001, ss 40 and 41.

AIA is available if the expenditure is incurred by a qualifying person and is not excluded by the list in section 38B.[217] That list refers to the period during which permanent discontinuance takes place (no AIA), cars, ring-fence trades, transfer of assets to another business which has not used up its AIA entitlement and certain deemed expenditures—real expenditures are needed. As with the other allowances, T must incur the expenditure in the chargeable period and own the asset at some point during that period.[218] The maximum allowance for a 12-month period increased from £50,000 to £100,000 by FA 2010, section 5 for expenditure incurred from April 2010, but dropped to £25,000 from April 2012. T may choose part only of the allowance. If the chargeable period is less than 12 months the allowance is reduced proportionately. The figure may be altered by statutory instrument. The legislation lists provisions restricting allowances which restrict the AIA as well. These apply where the asset is used only partly for the qualifying activity, there is a partial subsidy and where the asset is acquired in certain listed circumstances, eg from a connected person; further, no allowance may be claimed for an additional VAT liability.[219] FA 2008 added section 218A to deal expressly with the AIA; thus the allowance is not available if there is an arrangement entered into wholly and/or mainly to enable a person to obtain an AIA to which that person would not otherwise be entitled.

As it is a single capped allowance, the AIA rules contain many restrictions to prevent people getting too much relief. So a company can only have one AIA, no matter how many qualifying activities it carries on. If the company forms part of a group, there is only one AIA per group—though the group may allocate the AIA to any company with right amount of qualifying expenditure. There are further rules on companies under common control though not technically part of a group (section 51E). Section 51D covers two or more groups under common control. Terms such as 'control' and 'related' are defined in sections 51F and 51G. Companies are related if they share premises or have similar activities, ie more than 50% of turnover is derived from qualifying activities of the same type—an EU classification system is used.

With sections 51H–51K we move beyond the corporation tax sector to individuals and partnerships consisting only of individuals. We find rules analogous to the company rules. A restriction applies where there are two or more qualifying activities carried on by a qualifying person and they are both (a) controlled by the same person and (b) related to each other. The restriction is that only AIA may be used—though it may be allocated as the taxpayer wishes. For some reason the legislation does not include any provisions on how the AIA may be used by trusts.

There are special rules for short periods (section 51L). Each chargeable period must be looked at separately. The problem of periods longer than 12 months is taken care of for companies by the corporation tax rule that an accounting period cannot exceed 12 months (§2.4.2). For other businesses, equivalent rules are provided by section 51M. Section 51N modifies the rule in section 51M to deal with the situation in which a person controls two or more related activities in a tax year and more than one of the related activities has a chargeable period of more than one year. The HMRC Notes on the Finance Bill include worked examples for section 51N.

---

[217] CAA 2001, s 38A; the amount is given by s 51A.
[218] CAA 2001, s 51A(1)(2).
[219] CAA 2001, ss 205, 210, 214–217 and 241.

There is a bar on double allowances where the expenditure also qualifies for a first-year allowance. The taxpayer has a free choice but must choose.[220] The concept of pooling has no part to play in the treatment of AIA or first-year allowances.[221]

6.2.6 *Writing-down Allowances, Balances and the Pool*

The 'main' writing-down allowance, which is now given on a 18% reducing balance basis, applies where the taxpayer, T, incurs capital expenditure on the provision of plant and machinery wholly or partly for the purposes of the trade.[222] In addition, as we have seen, the asset must be owned by T.[223] For many years the percentage was 25% then 20%, but this is changed to 18% as from 1 April 2012 for corporation tax and 6 April for income tax.[224] The 25% figure remains for 'ring-fence' trades.[225]

It is not necessary that the asset should have been brought into use in the trade. If the chargeable period is greater or less than 12 months, the figure of 18% is increased or reduced accordingly.[226]

Whether T is entitled to writing-down allowance, a balancing allowance or a balancing charge depends on the amount of available qualifying expenditure (AQE), the total value of any disposal receipts (TDR) and what has happened. If the AQE exceeds the TDR, T is entitled to the writing-down allowance; this becomes a balancing allowance only for the final chargeable period of the qualifying activity.[227] Where the AQE is less than the TDR, there is no writing-down allowance but there is a balancing charge—even though the qualifying activity continues.

6.2.6.1 Pooling

Although practitioners had talked for years of pools and pooling, these terms did not become part of the statutory language until CAA 2001. Today there are three main pools to talk about; in addition, some assets form pools on their own—single asset pools.

The main pool Generally, all plant and machinery used in the trade is placed in one pool—the main pool—and the 18% main writing-down allowance is applied to the value of that pool as a whole.[228]

The special rate pool[229] Here the rate of writing-down allowance is 8% or 10%.[230] Expenditure in this pool is that on:

(a)   thermal insulation;
(b)   integral features (see §6.2.4.1 above at *(a)*);

---

[220] CAA 2001, s 52A.
[221] CAA 2001, s 53.
[222] CAA 2001, s 11(4)(a).
[223] CAA 2001, s 11 (4)(b).
[224] CAA 2001, s 56, as amended by FA 2008, s 80.
[225] CAA 2001, s 56(1A), added by FA 2008.
[226] CAA 2001, s 56(2).
[227] CAA 2001, s 54(4).
[228] CAA 2001, s 54.
[229] CAA 2001, Ch 10A (ss 104A–104E).
[230] CAA 2001, s 104D.

(c)   long-life assets acquired on or after 1 or 6 April 2008;
(d)   long-life assets acquired before those dates and now transferred to the pool. For (d) the transfer means an increase in the rate from 6% to 10%;[231]
(e)   cars acquired after April 2009 with high carbon dioxide emissions (see §6.2.10.2 below); and
(f)   expenditure incurred on or after 1 April 2010 on the provision of cushion gas.

The small pool.[232] This rule applies only to the main pool and special rate pool. Where the unrelieved expenditure is £1,000 or less, the whole balance may be written off at once (a 100% writing-down allowance). This writing off applies where the unrelieved expenditure is in the main pool or the special pool, or both. The taxpayer does not have to do this and may elect to take part only. The thinking behind the pool is that with the introduction of the AIA (for new expenditure—see §6.2.5.4), businesses are likely to have small pockets of pre-2008 expenditures which are unlikely to grow. Businesses should not be made to keep track of these.

Separate pooling. Certain items *must* be pooled separately. The first group forms single asset pools, which naturally means that only expenditure on the particular asset is relevant.[233] The rate of 18% applies as from April 2012. The relevant assets are:

(1)   'expensive' road vehicles;[234]
(2)   short-life assets;[235]
(3)   ships[236] (here the law allows deferments of writing-down allowances at will);
(4)   assets used partly for non-qualifying purposes;[237]
(5)   assets the wear and tear on which is subsidised.[238]

Other separate pooling rules. One group of assets attracts a 10% rate of write off and must be pooled on its own, ie overseas leasing.[239]

   Separate pooling used to come about under the 1990 Act if the statute deemed a separate trade to be carried on, eg each lease otherwise than in the course of the trade of leasing.[240] As we have seen, CAA 2001 rejects the paradigm case of trading in favour of the abstract phrase 'qualifying activity', so this particular example is redesignated as the qualifying activity of special leasing of plant and machinery.[241]
   Certain short-life assets *may* be pooled separately if the taxpayer so elects.[242] As we have seen (§6.1.7.3), no writing-down allowance may be claimed for the period during which

---

[231] On long-life assets, see CAA 2001, ss 54(4) and (5), referring to s 101.
[232] CAA 2001, s 56A, added by FA 2008, s 81.
[233] CAA 2001, s 54(6).
[234] CAA 2001, s 74; see also §6.2.10.2 below.
[235] CAA 2001, s 86.
[236] CAA 2001, s 127.
[237] CAA 2001, s 206.
[238] CAA 2001, ss 211 and 538.
[239] CAA 2001, s 54(4) and (5), referring to s 107.
[240] CAA 1990, s 61(1), not needed as part of CAA 2001 and so not re-enacted.
[241] CAA 2001, s 15(1), 19 and 258–261.
[242] CAA 2001, s 86, below §6.3.3.

permanent discontinuance takes place; only a balancing allowance (or charge) is made.[243] A balancing adjustment may be made where a non-resident trades through a permanent establishment in the UK and the proportion of the total trade represented by the UK branch or agency changes—downwards (ie is reduced).[244]

Examples

(1) If an asset cost £1,000 and it was the only asset in the pool, the AQE is £1,000 and the TDR is zero; the writing-down allowance for that year would be £180 (18% of £1,000), but 18% of £820, ie £148, in the second year.

(2) Suppose that an asset was bought in the first year for £1,000 so that a £180 allowance was claimed in the first year, and that a second asset was bought in the second year for £9,200. There are still no disposals. The pool of AQE for the second year is £820 left unrelieved from the first year, plus £9,200 for the new asset, making a total of £10,020 and so a maximum writing-down allowance of £1,804.

(3) Continuing on from (2), suppose that the first asset was sold in the third year for £1,000. Assuming that all allowances have been claimed, the AQE at the start of the year would be £8,216. This must now be reduced by the £1,000 TDR, so that in the third year the allowance will be 18% of £7,216, or £1,299.

6.2.7 Disposal Value[245]

Disposal value is relevant when a disposal event occurs.[246] In the account that follows, T is the person who has incurred the qualifying expenditure.[247] Disposal events arise when:

(1) the asset ceases to belong to T, eg it is sold;
(2) T loses possession of the asset in circumstances in which it is reasonable to assume that the loss is permanent;
(3) the asset has been used in mineral exploration and access, and has been abandoned on site;
(4) the asset ceases to exist as such (as a result of destruction, dismantling or otherwise);
(5) the asset begins to be used wholly or partly for purposes other than those of the trade;[248] or
(6) the trade is permanently discontinued.

When a disposal event occurs, the relevant disposal value must be brought into account.[249]

In the final chargeable period of the activity there may be a balancing charge—if the cumulative allowances exceed the expenditure. Alternatively, there may be a balancing

---

[243] CAA 2001, ss 55(4) and (5), and 65.
[244] CAA 2001, s 208.
[245] Defined in CAA 2001, s 61(1) (see above at §6.2.4). See also s 66 helpfully listing provisions about disposal values in other parts of the Act.
[246] See CAA 2001, s 61(2) and, in relation to computer software, ss 72, 281A, s 55(4).
[247] On hire purchase, note CAA 2001, s 67(4).
[248] On assets used partly for qualifying activity, see CAA 2001, ss 11(4) and 205–207.
[249] CAA 2001, s 60.

allowance if the allowances are less than the[250] expenditure. There cannot be writing-down allowance in this final period.[251]

6.2.7.1 Amounts

The disposal value to be brought into account depends upon the event by reason of which it is taken into account,[252] but it cannot exceed the capital expenditure incurred on that item, any excess being subject to capital gains legislation. The disposal value to be deducted from the pool must not exceed the cost of the plant to the person disposing of it.

Market value. Where the plant was acquired as a result of a transaction or series of transactions between connected persons, the greatest acquisition expenditure incurred in any of the transactions concerned is the maximum disposal value.[253] This rule not only applies on a disposal to a connected person or to an acquisition from a connected person, but also extends to an acquisition as a result of a transaction between connected persons with whom the disposer need not be connected.[254] If the asset has been sold,[255] the proceeds of sale are taken; and if that sale has been affected by some event, for example if the asset has been damaged, account is also taken of any insurance or compensation money received.

Where the market value is greater than the proceeds of sale, market value will be taken unless there is a charge to tax under ITEPA 2003 or the buyer can, in turn, claim a capital allowance in respect of plant or machinery or an R&D allowance.[256] The reason for this is presumably because the low sale price will give rise, in turn, to low allowances. There is also a bar on taking an undervalue if the buyer is a dual resident investment company connected with the seller—introduced as part of the general drive against such companies.[257]

End of asset. If the event is the demolition or destruction of the asset, the disposal value is the sum received for the remains, together with any insurance or compensation. In other instances of permanent loss, eg theft, the disposal value is simply any insurance or compensation. In all other cases, market value is taken.[258]

End of trade—and successions. If the event is the permanent discontinuance of the trade, which is followed by the sale, demolition, destruction or permanent loss of the asset, the disposal value on discontinuance is that specified for the event.[259] A special election may apply if there is a succession to a trade by a connected person,[260] in which case the predecessor's written-down value will override other provisions referring to market value.[261] These rules apply

---

[250] For general rules, see CAA 2001, ss 55–56.
[251] CAA 2001, s 55(4) and (5).
[252] CAA 2001, s 61(2).
[253] CAA 2001, s 62(2) and (3).
[254] *Ibid.*
[255] See *IRC v West* (1950) 31 TC 402.
[256] CAA 2001, s 61(2) and (4)(a).
[257] CAA 2001, s 61(2) and (4)(b).
[258] CAA 2001, s 61(2), items 3 and 4.
[259] CAA 2001, s 61(2), item 6.
[260] CAA 2001, s 266.
[261] CAA 2001, ss 266 and 267. The provisions overridden are ss 104 (long life assets), 108 (overseas leasing pool) and 265 (normal succession rule).

for the writing-down allowances; first-year allowances—and the AIAs—are not available where one person succeeds to a qualifying activity carried on by another person.[262]

No election may be made if the buyer is a dual resident investment company.[263] The right to elect is restricted to cases where both parties are within the charge to UK tax on the profits of the trade, and is subject to a time limit of two years starting with the date of the transaction.[264] The election may be made by a partnership.[265] In all other cases market value is taken.[266] For the period in which permanent discontinuance occurs, neither a first-year nor a writing-down allowance is given, everything being settled by the balancing allowance or charge.

Where two items are sold together, as will often be the case when the trade ends, the disposal proceeds will be apportioned on a just and reasonable basis.[267]

Where the disposal comprises certain qualifying gifts, eg to an educational establishment within ITTOIA 2005, section 108/CTA 2009, section 105, there is a nil disposal value.[268]

6.2.8 *Short-life Assets—The Non-pooling Option*

The effect of the 18% writing-down allowance is that, thanks to its reducing balance basis, approximately 90% of the cost will be written off over 12 years. Because some assets have a shorter life expectancy, rules allow such assets to be kept out of the general pool.[269] If the asset is disposed of, any balancing allowance is given immediately instead of waiting for the overall effect on a pool—but only if it is disposed of within, approximately, five years.

The asset will be kept in a pool of its own and the normal 18% writing-down allowance applied on a reducing basis.[270] The (irrevocable) election to treat the asset as a short-life asset must be made within two years of the year of acquisition.[271] The election is not available in relation to assets which seem to have in common the fact that they are required to be pooled separately in any case.[272]

In practice, assets which have an expected useful life of less than two years are depreciated over the life span, and are not pooled.[273] Further rules apply where short-life assets are provided for leasing, there is a sale at an under value or a disposal to connected persons.[274]

FA 2011 extended the specified cut-off period for short-life assets from four years from the end of the chargeable period in which the expenditure is incurred to eight years on expenditure incurred after April 2011.

---

[262] CAA 2001, s 265, as amended by FA 2008, Sch 24, para 14.
[263] CAA 2001, s 266(1)(c).
[264] CAA 2001, s 266(1)(b); see FA 2001, Sch 21, para 4, amending CAA 2001, s 266.
[265] CAA 2001, s 574.
[266] CAA 2001, s 265; on succession on death, note s 268(5)–(7), added by FA 1990.
[267] CAA 2001, ss 562—on procedure, see s 563.
[268] CAA 2001, s 63.
[269] CAA 2001, ss 83–89. On practice, see Statement of Practice SP 1/86.
[270] CAA 2001, s 86(1).
[271] CAA 2001, s 85(1)–(4).
[272] The list is in CAA 2001, s 84.
[273] *Tax Bulletin* (November 1993).
[274] CAA 2001, ss 87–89.

6.2.9 Long-life Assets

Before 2008 the writing-down allowance for plant and machinery was set at 6% per annum, calculated on a reducing balance, where it was reasonable to expect that the plant and machinery would have an economic life of at least 25 years.[275] FA 2008 moved long-life assets to the special rate pool and the 10% writing-down allowance. The original rate of 6% was set because of the substantial disparity between the rapid rate at which capital allowances are given and the slow rate at which plant, such as reservoirs and power stations, is written down in the financial accounts of newly-privatised companies. Assets excluded from this rule include fixtures in a dwelling house, retail shop, showroom, hotel or office, ships, railways assets and any mechanically-propelled road vehicle.[276] This reduced rate of allowance is not meant to hurt small businesses and so does not apply where the total expenditure is £100,000 or less; an individual or partnership must satisfy further conditions about active involvement in the business.[277] Where this treatment is applied, the long-life asset is treated as creating a pool separate from other assets. Other provisions apportion composite expenditure between a long-life asset and an asset with a shorter life.[278]

An anti-avoidance rule applies where a claim has been made on a long-life asset and a later claim (by that claimant or another person) in respect of any qualifying expenditure incurred on the same asset is made—here the long-life rules are to continue to apply even though, eg the new owner otherwise might be within the £100,000 exemption.[279]

6.2.10 Motor Vehicles

The capital allowance treatment of cars depends on whether the car was acquired before 6 April 2009 or after. The 'new' regime is discussed below at §6.2.10.2 and the 'old' regime at §6.2.10.3.

6.2.10.1 Full Allowances

Expenditure on certain types of road vehicle may be treated as ordinary expenditure on plant and machinery. The favoured vehicles are:[280]

(1) goods vehicles of a construction primarily suited to the carriage of goods or burdens of any description;
(2) vehicles of a type not commonly used as private vehicles and unsuitable to be so used, eg works buses and minivans;[281] and
(3) qualifying hire cars, ie vehicles provided wholly or mainly for hire to, or for carriage of, members of the public in the ordinary course of a trade.[282] Rules distinguish the

---

[275] CAA 2001, ss 90–104; on definition, see s 91, added by FA 1997; on problems of definition, see Gammie [1997] BTR 241. The 6% limit is applied by s 102.
[276] CAA 2001, ss 93–96, added by FA 1997.
[277] CAA 2001, ss 97–100.
[278] CAA 2001, s 92(1).
[279] CAA 2001, s 103.
[280] CAA 2001, s 81.
[281] *Roberts v Granada TV Rental Ltd* [1970] 2 All ER 764, 46 TC 295.
[282] CAA 2001, s 82.

ordinary car rental business from the increasingly common leasing arrangement whereby a (new) car is leased to a person for two or three years; however, cars leased to persons receiving mobility allowance are treated favourably.[283]

6.2.10.2 The Post-April 2009 Regime for Cars

Under the 'new' regime, capital allowances in respect of expenditure on a car are determined according to the car's carbon dioxide emissions.[284] Under this regime, cars with CO_2 emissions of between 110g and 160g per kilometre qualify for the main rate of WDAs.[285] Cars with higher CO_2 emissions are allocated to the special pool and qualify for 10% WDAs.[286] Electric cars and cars with CO_2 emissions below 110g per kilometre qualify for 100% FYAs.[287]

6.2.10.3 The Pre-April 2009 Regime—Restricted Allowances on 'Expensive' Motor Cars

The 'old' regime applicable to 'expensive cars' described herein relates to expenditure incurred before April 2009 and applies only until April 2014, when any balance not yet written off will be transferred to the main pool.[288] Under this regime, expenditure on cars outside the above categories and costing more than £12,000 is pooled separately from other assets but forms one single pool.[289] These restrictions do not apply to cars with low carbon dioxide emissions and electric cars.[290] Other changes exclude the restrictions on the hire costs of cars in ITTOIA 2005, section 48/CTA 2009, section 56 for such vehicles. Where the capital expenditure on a car exceeds £12,000, each car is treated as a separate asset and the allowance is limited to a maximum of £3,000 (ie 25% of £12,000). The effect of the £3,000 limit is to defer the benefit of the relief. The figures of £3,000 and £12,000 are reduced or increased proportionately if the chargeable period is less or greater than 12 months.[291] Further rules apply where a part of the expenditure is met by another person, the car is used partly for a non-qualifying activity or there is a partial deprecation subsidy.[292] There are also further rules where what the Act calls the anti-avoidance rules in the sections on finance leases, etc apply.[293]

When a car costing more than £12,000 is *leased*, further special rules apply to restrict the relief normally given in computing profit for hiring charges;[294] this meant a new rule then in TA 1988 and not, as previously, in CAA 2001. These special rules do not apply where the car is subject to a hire-purchase agreement under which the hirer has an option to buy the

---

[283] A category defined by CAA 2001, s 82(4).

[284] FA 2009, Sch 11. Para 26.

[285] CAA 2001, s 104AA, added by FA 2009, Sch 11. Para 8.

[286] CAA 2001, s 104A, amended by FA 2009, Sch 11. Para 7.

[287] CAA 2001, s 45D.

[288] FA 2009, Sch 11, paras 29 *et seq*.

[289] CAA 2001, s 74(1).

[290] CAA 2001, s 74(2)(c), added by FA 2002, Sch 19, para 6.

[291] CAA 2001, s 75.

[292] CAA 2001, ss 76–78.

[293] CAA 2001, s 79, referring to ss 213–233.

[294] Ex TA 1988, s 578A; on effect of rebate of hire charge, see ex ESC B28. The current rules are in ITTOIA 2005, ss 48–50 and CTA 2009, ss 56–58, 1231,1251,

car for an amount equivalent to 1% (or less) of the retail price of the car when new.[295] The amount paid by way of rent is reduced in the proportion which the £12,000, plus half the amount by which the retail price of the vehicle when new exceeds £12,000, bears to that retail price. Thus, if a car cost £18,000 new and the rent is £5,600, the amount claimable for tax is (£12,000 + (£18,000 − 12,000)/2)/£18,000 or 5/6 × £5,600 = £4,666. The missing 1/6 will never qualify for relief. The restrictions on the hire costs of cars in ex TA 1988, section 587A do not apply to cars with low carbon dioxide emissions and electric cars.[296]

6.2.11 Hire Purchase

Where plant or machinery is purchased by the taxpayer, T, on hire purchase or conditional sale contracts, first-year and writing-down allowances may be claimed in respect of the capital element.[297] The plant or machinery is treated as belonging to T and to no one else, provided T is entitled to the benefit of the contract. Capital expenditure to be incurred by T under the contract after the plant or machinery has been brought into use in the trade is treated as incurred at that time. T is thus treated as incurring the full capital cost at that time. Special provisions apply where the option under the contract is not exercised.[298] The actual words of this provision go wider than merely hire purchase. The Revenue have pointed out that the words of the provision are apt to cover situations in which capital expenditure is incurred on goods which are never owned, eg a deposit paid for goods which are then not supplied.[299]

Where this rule deems the asset to belong to X but the special rules for fixtures deemed it to belong to Y, the fixtures rule prevails;[300] although this was introduced by FA 2000, it is deemed always to have had effect. Where the hire-purchase rule deems the asset to be X's and it then becomes a fixture and so is deemed as belonging to Y, X is treated as selling the asset to Y.

6.2.12 Leasing—Special Rules

6.2.12.1 Trade of Leasing Qualifies

If T leases out an asset—ie is the lessor—in the course of a trade, capital allowances will be available in the usual way.[301] The use to which the lessee puts the asset is not relevant in determining the lessor's rights. T is entitled, as owner of the goods leased, to the allowances, whether these are first-year or writing-down allowances. There may be difficulties in showing that the asset 'is owned by' T if the lessee has been given an option to purchase the

[295] Ex TA 1988, s 578B(2), added by FA 1991, s 61, CAA 2001, s 67(1)–(3). A hirer under such an agreement is very different from a mere lessee; see Inland Revenue Press Release, 27 October 1986, [1986] *Simon's Tax Intelligence* 680.
[296] Ex TA 1988, s 578(2A), added by FA 2002, s 60.
[297] A hirer under such an agreement is very different from a mere lessee; see Inland Revenue Press Release, 27 October 1986, [1986] *Simon's Tax Intelligence* 680.
[298] CAA 2001, s 67(4); on disposal value, see s 68.
[299] Inland Revenue interpretation RI 10.
[300] CAA 2001, s 69, added by FA 2000, s 80.
[301] *Barclay Mercantile Business Finance Ltd v Mawson* [2004] UKHL 51, [2005] STC 1; and *Revenue Law*, §5.6.

asset, but this issue remains unexplored.[302] The particular trade of finance leasing attracts special rules (see §6.2.15 below).

6.2.12.2 Not in Course of Trade—Separate Qualifying Activity

Where T leases out an asset otherwise than in the course of trade, CAA 2001 directs that it is to be treated as the separate qualifying activity of special leasing.[303] Any charge is treated as arising for corporation tax in accordance with section 259.[304] Capital allowances may still be available but cannot be set against general income of the lessor—only against other income from special leasing.[305] However, if the asset is not used for the purpose of a qualifying activity carried on by the lessee, the lessor may only set the allowance off against other income from that particular special leasing activity.[306] Unused allowances may be rolled forward indefinitely.[307] There are separate rules for corporation tax.[308] The effect of this is to make equipment leasing an unattractive proposition, except when it is a full-time business. The right to allowances does not apply where the plant or machinery is let for use in a domestic house.[309] The 1992 restriction on first-year allowances, which applied where the lessor carried on a trade of leasing, also applies here.[310]

6.2.12.3 Overseas Leasing

A number of special rules apply to overseas leasing. First, it may attract rates of 18%, 10% or 0%. Overseas leasing is defined as meaning a lease under which the lessee is not resident in the UK and does not use the asset exclusively for earning profits chargeable to tax.[311] So, if a person is resident in the UK and the asset is exclusively for the purposes of earning profits which are chargeable to tax in the UK, the normal 18% rate will apply. However, 'profits or gains chargeable to UK tax' do not include those arising to a person who can claim relief under a double taxation agreement, eg the UK branch of a foreign company.[312] The full rate of 18% may also be claimed if the asset comes within what the Act calls 'protected leasing', a term which covers both short-term leasing of plant or machinery and certain arrangements for ships, aircraft or transport containers.[313]

If the overseas leasing does not come within the notion of protected leasing, the rate of writing-down allowance is restricted to 10%, unless the long-life asset rate of 6% would apply anyway.[314] The restriction to 10% is to apply only for the designated period, which means broadly 10 years from the time the person brought the asset into use.[315] However,

---

[302] The effect of an option needs close attention; in practice, the lessee can be given much the same economic benefit by reducing the leasing charge or extending the period of the lease. This is all subject to the post-2006 rules on long-funded leases: see below at §6.2.12.6.

[303] CAA 2001, ss 15 and 19 and superseding CAA 1990, s 65; s 19 contains rules on the cessation of leasing.

[304] The income tax charge arises under s 258.

[305] CAA 2001, s 258.

[306] CAA 2001, s 258(3).

[307] CAA 2001, s 258(5).

[308] CAA 2001, ss 259 and 260; group relief is excluded by s 260(7). On life assurance companies, see s 261.

[309] CAA 2001, s 15(3), referring to s 35.

[310] CAA 2001, Sch 3, para 47(5).

[311] CAA 2001, s 105.

[312] CAA 2001, s 110.

[313] CAA 2001, s 105(5) and ss 121, 123 and 124.

[314] CAA 2001, s 109.

[315] CAA 2001, ss 109(2)(a) and 106.

even that reduced rate of allowance is not available if the asset is used for a non-qualifying purpose and certain other conditions are satisfied, eg the lease is for more than 13 years.[316]

In applying the 10% rate a separate overseas leasing pool must be established; a long-life asset must be the subject of a separate asset pool, as must any other asset required to be placed in a separate pool by other rules.[317] A disposal from the overseas pool to a connected person may attract a restriction, in that allowances on the disposal and the new acquisition must be calculated by reference to disposal value if that is lower than the market value.[318]

6.2.12.4 Administration, Qualifying Purpose, Partnerships

CAA 2001 includes rules on the recovery of excess allowance and of allowances which should not have been claimed at all, for joint lessees and on duties to supply information.[319]

The concept of 'qualifying purpose' is relevant to whether or not the taxpayer's allowance is reduced from 10% to 0%; some of the concepts are also used in the definition of a protected transaction. The qualifying situations are those in which:

(1)   the buyer uses the asset for short-term leasing;
(2)   the lessee uses the asset for short-term leasing and either is resident in the UK or uses it in a trade carried on here; or
(3)   the buyer uses the asset for the purposes of a trade other than leasing.[320]

The purpose of these rules is to exclude the situation in which the lessee uses the asset for personal consumption. The other qualifying purpose rules relate to ships and aircraft transport; these rules all require that the asset is leased to lessees who use it for purposes other than leasing, and the lessees would have been entitled to capital allowances in respect of the asset if they had incurred the expenditure themselves[321]—this provides a fiscal connection between the lessee and the UK.

Restrictions apply to leasing partnerships. For example, X, Y and Z Ltd are partners who buy plant and claim allowances. X and Y then withdraw from the partnership, leaving Z to face the balancing charge, but Z is a non-resident company. Relief under TA 1988, sections 380 and 381 is denied where the scheme has been entered into with a company partner in prospect.[322]

6.2.12.5 Lessee's Expenditure

Where the lessee (L) incurs capital expenditure on the provision of plant or machinery for the purposes of L's trade under the terms of L's lease, the asset is treated as belonging to L

---

[316] CAA 2001, s 110.
[317] CAA 2001, s 107.
[318] CAA 2001, s 108.
[319] CAA 2001, ss 111–120.
[320] CAA 2001, ss 121 and 122. Interpreted by the Court of Appeal in *BMBF (No 24) v IRC* [2004] STC 97.
[321] CAA 2001, ss 123–125.
[322] TA 1988, s 384A moved out of the CAA by Sch 2, para 30—previously CAA 1990, s 142.

provided the trade continues.[323] The asset in fact belongs to the owner-lessor (O). When the lease ends the rules as to disposal value and balancing charges are applied as if the original expenditure had been incurred by O. Thus, the allowance is given to L, but any balancing charge may be levied on O. As a result of the rules reversing *Stokes v Costain Property Investments Ltd*,[324] this does not now apply to plant and machinery which becomes part of a building on other land.

6.2.12.6 Long Funding Leases

Reversing the *Barclays* case,[325] under CAA 2001, sections 70A *et seq*,[326] expenditure incurred on provision of plant or machinery for leasing under a long funding lease is not allowable expenditure for the lessor. The lessee may claim allowances under the rules in sections 70A–70E; these provide different amounts according to whether the lease is a long funding operating lease or a long funding finance lease.[327] A lease is a long lease only if it exceeds five years; further rules exclude it if it does not exceed seven years.[328]

A funding lease is defined as a plant or machinery lease which meets one or of more of three tests: the finance lease test, the lease payments test (section 70O) and the useful economic life test (section 70P).[329] The lessee's right to claim an allowance may be excluded if the lessor may claim it.[330] There are also exclusions for certain allowances relating to buildings where the lessor may still claim.[331] There is an anti-avoidance rule (section 70V) and many rules on transfer variations, etc.[332]

There are also related CGT rules on a deemed disposal by the lessor, with special values, when plant or machinery is used under a long funding lease, and on the relationship between capital allowances and CGT.[333]

FA 2009, section 64 and Schedule 32 introduced a number of changes to the taxation of long funding leases in response to taxpayers' disclosure of schemes to avoid tax. The first change was to the value to be brought into account where a long funding lease commences;[334] it is now the greater of (a) the market value of the plant and (b) the qualifying lease payments.[335] The second change makes sure that the definition of 'disposal receipts' in section 60 includes a disposal on the determination of a long funding lease under section 70E. The third is favourable to taxpayers and makes sure that an initial payment brought in as a disposal value is not also taxed as income.[336] Lastly, the rules make it clear that the AIA is not available to the lessee under (a) a transfer and long funding leaseback arrangement, or (b) a hire-purchase and long funding leaseback arrangement.[337]

---

[323] TA 1988, s 61(4).
[324] [1984] STC 204, [1984] 1 All ER 849, CA; CAA 1990, s 61(4)(b) (see above at §6.2.2.1).
[325] *Barclays Mercantile Business Finance Ltd v Mawson* [2005] STC 1 (HL).
[326] Added by FA 2006, s 81 and Sch 8; note CAA 2001, ss 70YE–70YJ for definitions.
[327] CAA 2001, ss 70B and 70C.
[328] CAA 2001, s 70I; note modification by FA 2008 as a result of other changes.
[329] CAA 2001, ss 70K, and 70N–70P.
[330] CAA 2001, s 70Q.
[331] CAA 2001, ss 70G and 70R–70U.
[332] CAA 2001, ss 70V–70YD.
[333] TCGA 1992, ss 26A and 41A.
[334] CAA 2001, s 61, Table 1, item 5A.
[335] Defined in CAA 2001, s 61(5A).
[336] CTA 2010, s 890, ex TA 1988, s 785B.
[337] Amended CAA 2001, s 51A (10)).

FA 2011, section 33 closed down a scheme involving long funding leases that sought to benefit more than once from the tax relief for the residual value payment.

FA 2010, section 28 added special rules for expenditure on cushion gas in a gas storage facility. As from 1 April 2010, these are treated as funding leases and so qualify for writing-down allowances at 10%.[338] The second rule changed CAA 2001, section 70J to make these leases funding leases. The effect, as explained in the HMRC explanatory notes, is that any such lease for five years or more will be taxed by reference to its commercial substance rather than legal form. The important fact is that cushion gas, unlike other items of plant and machinery, does not wear out, and so without this change, companies could have created long operating leases without ever triggering the long funding lease rules.

6.2.13 Ships

For many years, ships have been treated specially for capital allowance purposes. In effect, free depreciation is allowed.[339] Expenditure on ships is not pooled. There is no statutory definition of a 'ship', but there have been many decisions on its meaning under the Merchant Shipping Acts. A hopper barge without engine or sail was held to be a ship,[340] but a floating gas container without power and not fitted for navigation was not.[341] A statutory definition of qualifying ships is, however, provided for the purpose of the 1995 rules on deferment of balancing charges.[342]

Balancing charges arising on the disposal of qualifying ships[343] may be rolled over for a period of up to three years to be set off against subsequent expenditure[344] on new ships within that period. The ship may have been owned by the taxpayer previously, but there must be a six-year gap between ownerships.[345]

FA 2000 introduced an alternative basis of taxation of shipping under which corporation tax would be based, in part, on tonnage.[346]

6.2.14 Films and Sound Recordings; Master Versions

The story of the tax treatment of the film and sound recording industries is convoluted and highly political.[347] For present purposes only a few brief points need be made. When a film is made, many of the production costs will be deductible as ordinary revenue expenditure. Some items will be capital and so open to relief through the capital allowance system. These capital items would include the costs of acquisition of a film tape or disk. In the days of

---

[338] Amended CAA 2001, s 104A.

[339] CAA 2001, ss 127–158.

[340] *The Mac* (1882) 7 PD 126, CA.

[341] *Wells v Gas Float Whitton No 2 (Owners)* [1897] AC 337, HL; see also *Wirth Ltd v SS Acadia Forest* [1974] 2 Lloyd's Rep 563.

[342] This limit does not apply if the ship is lost at sea or is irreparably damaged: CAA 2001, s 151.

[343] Defined by CAA 2001, ss 151–154, added by FA 1995. See Inland Revenue Press Release, 20 July 1994, [1994] *Simon's Tax Intelligence* 882.

[344] Defined by CAA 2001, ss 146–150.

[345] CAA 2001, s 147.

[346] FA 2000, s 82 and Sch 22. There is much useful background in HM Treasury, *Independent Inquiry into a Tonnage Tax* (12 August 1999).

[347] Those wanting to follow the twists and turn of the last several years should read the excellent notes by Shipwright in the various Finance Act issues of the BTR.

100% first-year capital allowances, much less turned on the distinction than previously. CAA 1990, section 68 allowed taxpayers to take such expenditures as revenue expenditure. Revenue treatment was required unless the taxpayers elected for capital allowance treatment. More detailed rules followed, eg F(No 2)A 1992, sections 40A *et seq*. After this, the Revenue became worried about 'abuse' of the allowances they had so carefully created. Special legislation was therefore passed in F(No 2)A 2002, section 99, which restricted the 1992 reliefs. For example, these were to be withheld unless the film was 'genuinely intended for theatrical release', as defined in section 99.[348]

Since then further rules followed. As far as income tax was concerned, these were gathered together in ITTOIA 2005, Part 2, Chapter 9 (sections 130–144, mostly now repealed). However, they were immediately strengthened—from a Revenue perspective—by FA 2005.[349] FA 2006 produced a completely new system of rules for films, but left the ITTOIA 2005 rules, in a very reduced form, to apply to sound recordings.

A quite different set of rules has been concerned with ensuring that if the various qualifying expenditures gave rise to losses, only the right sort of losses accruing to the right sorts of people would qualify, a matter of particular moment to partnerships (see *Revenue Law*, §20.10 and below §6.2.14.2).

6.2.14.1 Basic Rules

As far as sound recordings are concerned, expenditure incurred on the production or acquisition of the original master version of a sound recording is revenue in nature.[350] There are also rules for the allocation of that expenditure.[351] However, the option to elect back into the capital allowance system was removed. ITTOIA 2005 applies only for income tax; there are separate rules for corporation tax.[352]

FA 2006 removed films from the ambit of ITTOIA 2005, and in section 42 and Schedule 5 gave a tax credit to film production companies instead (see above §4.2.5.4). Special loss rules are contained in FA 2006, sections 43–45.

6.2.14.2 Avoidance

The tax treatment of films shows the UK tax system at its most typical. Reliefs are given to humour a particularly vociferous or influential group. The reliefs are limited so as to benefit only that group. The group or their advisers then seek to undermine the spirit of reliefs and the Government retaliates by restricting the relief. For example, FA 2002 introduced rules to restrict the 1992 reliefs unless the film was genuinely intended for release, and to deal with successive acquisitions of the same film. It did so by limiting the relief to sums paid for the first acquisition from the producer.[353] In turn, these rules were superseded by wider rules in FA 2005.

---

[348] Later ITTOIA 2005, s 144.
[349] ITTOIA 2005, ss 140A–140E, repealed by FA 2006, s 178 and Sch 26 Pt 3(4).
[350] ITTOIA 2005, s 134.
[351] ITTOIA 2005, s 135.
[352] FA 2006, ss 48–50.
[353] ITTOIA 2005, s 140(2), FA 2002, s 101.

FA 2004[354] was directed at schemes which had, in the Government's view, exploited these film reliefs. The purpose behind the original rules was to grant accelerated recognition of costs, so giving rise to loss relief. When or, more often, if the film proved to be profitable, the loss relief would be recaptured by a charge to tax. Schemes had been devised which turned the intended deferral relief into a permanent relief, so that no charge arose when later profits accrued from the film. The 2004 rules (now ITA 2007, sections 797 *et seq*) were designed to ensure that a charge would arise after all. The charge applies where there is a disposal of the individual's right to profits from the trade. FA 2005 added rules specific to film reliefs in connection with partnership losses and the at-risk rules were amended.[355] These are now ITA 2007, sections 790 *et seq*.

Lastly, FA 2009, section 65 and Schedule 33 introduced yet more anti-avoidance rules in response to taxpayers' disclosures, this time concerning long funding leases of films.[356] The schemes disclosed involved partnerships ending existing leases and replacing them with new leases intended to qualify as long funding leases for plant. The blocking legislation is not confined to partnerships.

6.2.15 Anti-avoidance: Relevant Transactions, Finance Leases and Leasebacks

The provisions on plant and machinery contain rules to deal with certain avoidance situations. The rules generally remove any right to any AIA or first-year allowance and restrict the right to writing-down allowances.[357]

The first restrictions are aimed at 'relevant transactions', broadly sales, hire purchase and assignments of right under contracts.[358] The restrictions apply if there is a relevant transaction:

(1) between connected persons;
(2) that has an "avoidance purpose", ie where the main purpose, or one of the main purposes, of a party entering into the transaction was to obtain a tax advantage; or
(3) which falls within the description of sale and leaseback, ie if the asset which has been used in the seller's business continues to be so used despite the sale.[359]

The next restrictions are aimed at situations in which the asset is used by a connected person or there is no continuity in the seller's business. The restrictions are that the buyer cannot obtain an AIA or first-year allowance[360] and writing-down allowances are given to the buyer by reference to the disposal value brought into account by the seller.[361] These restrictions do not apply if the plant and machinery is the subject of a sale and finance leaseback.[362]

---

[354] FA 2004, ss 119–123. See also Inland Revenue Press Release 10 December 2003, [2003] *Simon's Tax Intelligence* 2321; and Revenue examples 10 February 2004, [2004] *Simon's Tax Intelligence* 332.
[355] FA 2005, s 79.
[356] CTA 2010, s 376, ex TA 1988, s 502GD. See also ITTOIA 2005, s 148FD.
[357] CAA 2001, ss 213–230.
[358] CAA 2001, s 213.
[359] CAA 2001, ss 214–216. On predecessor of s 215, see *Barclays Mercantile Industrial Finance Ltd v Melluish* [1990] STC 314, 63 TC 95. See also s 218ZA governing restrictions on writing-down allowances under s 215.
[360] CAA 2001, s 217.
[361] CAA 2001, s 218.
[362] CAA 2001, ss 217 and 218, as amended by FA 2008, Sch 20.

In relation to the AIA, there is a further restriction which denies the allowance where there are arrangements designed to obtain the allowance to which the person would not otherwise be entitled.[363] This is a free-standing provision and not confined to related transactions.

Further and similar restrictions apply if the transaction is a finance lease.[364] A finance lease is a lease which is treated in the accounts of the lessor (or a person connected with the lessor) as a finance lease or loan under properly drawn-up accounts. No writing-down allowance is to be given for that part of the chargeable period which falls before the expenditure was incurred; the effect of this is to delay, not prohibit, the entitlement to the allowance for the expenditure incurred.[365] The rule does not apply if there is also a disposal of the asset in the same period.[366]

Where there is a sale and finance leaseback, meaning a sale and leaseback where a finance lease is involved, several provisions in this part of the Act used to apply, but these were greatly reduced in 2008 and in 2004. CAA 2001, section 225 then removes any entitlement to any allowances if the lessor does not bear the greater part of the risk of non-payment;[367] for this purpose, guarantees by the persons connected with the lessee are ignored.

Finance leasebacks received further legislative attention in 2004.[368] The 2004 rules apply only where the disposal value has already been restricted under the preceding rules, and are designed to prevent taxpayers from obtaining not only the benefit of the capital allowances but also deductions for lease rentals. The amount of rental that may be deducted is restricted to a 'permitted maximum', ie the total of the finance charge shown in the accounts and depreciation, but using the value after applying the restriction.[369] Other provisions deal with early terminations of leases and other events that 'crystallise' the future benefits. These increase the profits of the lessee and are to prevent the taxpayer from 'sidestepping' the new rule.[370] There are consequential adjustments to the rules for lessors; some of these rules no longer apply to lease and finance leasebacks but only to sale and leasebacks.[371] These rules are subject to some degree of mitigation. There is a special election for both sale and leaseback and sale and finance leaseback where the transaction involves assets which are both new and unused.[372] There is a provision to explain how these rules apply to hire-purchase contracts; this does not involve new and unused assets.[373] Lastly, there is an exception, once more involving new and used assets, sold by manufacturer or suppliers in the ordinary course of their business.[374]

Schemes involving leasing of plant and machinery are the subject of many rules in this part. FA 2010, section 27 and Schedule 5 dealt with two more schemes, restricting qualifying expenditure to the present value of the lessor's income from the asset plus the present

---

[363] CAA 2001, s 218A.

[364] CAA 2001, ss 219–220.

[365] CAA 2001, ss 219 and 220.

[366] CAA 2001, s 220(3).

[367] CAA 2001, s 225.

[368] CAA 2001, ss 228A–228J added by FA 2004, s 134 and Sch 23, providing transitional rules. Sections amended by FA 2007, Sch 5, para 16 to prevent avoidance; s 228A amended by FA 2008.

[369] CAA 2001, s 228B.

[370] CAA 2001, s 228C; 'sidestepping' comes from para 91 of the Revenue Note on the clause.

[371] CAA 2001, s 228D, as amended by FA 2007, Sch 5, and s 228E.

[372] CAA 2001, ss 227 and 228.

[373] CAA 2001, s 229.

[374] CAA 2001, s 230.

value of the asset after any rental rebate.[375] The Schedule also restricts the deduction for the rental rebate.[376] A disallowed loss may still be allowable for chargeable gains purposes (paragraph 2(6)). Additional rules, applicable only for corporation tax, are designed to counter avoidance arising from the transfer of entitlement to benefit from a capital allowance on plant and machinery used for the purpose of a trade.[377] The problem arises where tax written-down value is greater than its balance sheet value. The Revenue have seen transactions where companies with large pools of unclaimed capital allowances have been sold into a new group principally to enable the new group to get at the allowances through group relief.[378] The legislation uses an 'unallowable purpose rule'.[379]

6.3   Industrial Buildings

6.3.1   General

CAA 2001, Part 3 (sections 271–360) governs allowances for industrial buildings. The availability and amount of industrial building allowances was greatly reduced in recent years, until they were withdrawn completely after 1 April 2011 (for corporation tax) or 6 April 2011 (for income tax).[380] The discussion that follows relates now only to pre-2011 allowances. These rules permit capital allowances to be claimed where capital expenditure has been incurred on the construction of an industrial building or structure which is to be occupied, principally, for the purposes of a trade.[381] If the building is to be occupied by a qualifying lessee or licensee it is the occupier's trade that generally is relevant.[382] Highway undertakings receive special attention.[383]

  Where the business year is the same as the tax year, the writing-down allowance was 4% for 2007–08, 3% for 2008–09, then 2%, 1% and now 0%.[384] Where the business year is not the same, an apportionment is carried out on the basis of days in the relevant tax year.[385] For this the person must be entitled to an interest in the building or structure, that interest must be a 'relevant' interest and the building is an industrial building at the end of the relevant period (see further §6.3.5 below).[386] Secondly, there is an initial allowance, but this is relevant only to certain expenditure in enterprise zones (see §6.3.4 below). Lastly, there are balancing adjustments, sometimes a balancing allowance and sometimes a balancing charge (§6.3.6 below).

  Allowances are confined to the expenses of construction; the cost of the land is excluded.[387] The costs of certain preliminary works, such as cutting, levelling and tunnelling, may be claimed only if the works are carried out in order to prepare the land for the installation of

---

[375] CAA 2001, s 228MA and see definitions in s 228MC.
[376] See CTA 2009, s 60A and ITTOIA 2005, s 55B.
[377] CAA 2001, ss 212A–212S, added by FA 2010, s 26 and Sch 4.
[378] HMRC Explanatory Notes on FA 2010, para 76.
[379] CAA 2001, s 212M.
[380] FA 2008, s 81 and Sch 27.
[381] CAA 2001, s 305.
[382] CAA 2001, s 305(4) and see Statement of Practice SP 4/80 (separate lettings of workshops for small businesses).
[383] CAA 2001, ss 341–344.
[384] FA 2008, s 82(3).
[385] FA 2008, s 82 (4) and (5).
[386] CAA 2001, s 309.
[387] CAA 2001, ss 271–272; a private road built on industrial estate may qualify, s 284.

plant or machinery.[388] The costs of repairs are allowed as if they were construction costs, unless they are deductible as revenue expenses. So, if a building is improved or altered, the costs of that work are treated as a separate subject for allowances.[389]

6.3.2 Definition of Industrial Building

To qualify, the building must be an industrial building or structure, which is elaborately defined in CAA 2001, section 274, Tables A and B. This area has been much litigated. It is fair to say that the courts, taking their lead from some narrow legislation, have taken a consistently restrictive view of what can come within this category. The general effect of the definition is to confine allowances to productive, as opposed to distributive, industries. It is not necessary that the building be constructed in this country, and foreign plantations are expressly mentioned and defined (Table A, paragraph 5); however, the profits or gains of the foreign trade must be assessable to UK corporation tax under CTA 2009, Part 3 or ITTOIA 2005, Part 2 for income tax.[390]

6.3.2.1 Qualifying Trades

CAA 2001 rewrites the definition: it includes sewerage, transport, highways, tunnels, bridges, inland navigation and docks—which qualify only if carried on by way of trade.

Manufacturing and processing. Table A's first qualifying trade section has the byword 'manufacturing' and is defined as one consisting of manufacturing goods or materials. The second has the byword 'processing' and is defined as a trade consisting of subjecting goods or materials to a process, a phrase which is to include maintaining or repairing goods or materials.[391]

The older language used in CAA 1990, section 18(1)(e) put these two together and referred to buildings used for the manufacturing or processing of materials or subjecting goods or material to any process. 'Goods' was held to mean—and so probably still means—merchandise rather than simply chattels—so that a human corpse is not goods.[392] In *Buckingham v Securitas Properties Ltd*,[393] a security firm constructed a special area in which bulk coins and notes were broken down into individual wage packets. The court held that the notes and coins were not 'goods'; if they had been goods, the court would have held that they were not being 'subjected to any process'. A similar approach was adopted in *Girobank plc v Clarke*,[394] where a document- or data-processing centre did not qualify. In *Bestway Holdings Ltd v Luff*,[395] the court held that goods were not subjected to a process where they were checked and packaged as part of a cash-and-carry warehouse operation. A

---

[388] CAA 2001, s 273. 'Cutting' received a narrow construction in *McIntosh v Manchester Corpn* [1952] 2 All ER 444, 33 TC 428.

[389] CAA 1990, s 272(2).

[390] CAA 2001, s 282.

[391] CAA 2001, s 274.

[392] *Bourne v Norwich Crematorium Ltd* [1967] 2 All ER 576, 44 TC 164; it is a nice question whether this expenditure would seem now to qualify as plant in the light of *IRC v Barclay, Curle & Co Ltd* [1969] 1 All ER 732, 45 TC 221 (see above at §6.2.4).

[393] [1980] STC 166, 53 TC 292.

[394] [1998] STC 182, CA. It is unclear whether the Court of Appeal thought that the assets were 'subjected to a process'; Nourse LJ expressed no opinion.

[395] [1998] STC 357; see Salter [1999] BTR 189; see also *Revenue Bulletin*, December 1999..

building used for the maintenance or repair of goods will qualify if the goods or materials are employed in a trade or undertaking which itself qualifies.[396]

Storage. The next head of Table A refers to 'storage', ie a trade consisting of: (a) storing[397] goods or materials which are to be used in the manufacture of other goods or materials, (b) which are to be subject to a process or (c) which have been manufactured or processed and are awaiting delivery to a customer. The trade will also qualify if (d) it is for the storage of goods or materials on arrival in the UK from a place outside the UK. The word 'storage' has been held to indicate that the category was confined to buildings in the vicinity of an airport or seaport and to facilities needed in the ordinary process of physically transporting goods (so not extending to quarantine kennels).[398] The test is whether the building is used for the purposes of a trade which consists in the storage of qualifying goods, and not whether the building is used for the storage of such goods.[399] An allowance may therefore be claimed for a building even though it is also used in part for the storage of other goods.[400] So, while a warehouse used for the storage of tyres before being remoulded qualified as an industrial building,[401] a cash-and-carry warehouse did not; in the first case the storage was part of the trade, while in the second it was simply a necessary and transitory incident of the conduct of the supermarket.[402] Another case where the allowance was not available arose where the taxpayer imported goods (doors and window fittings) from its Austrian parent company. Large batches of these would arrive and have to be stored in the taxpayer's warehouse. On a successful HMRC appeal, the court held that no allowance could be claimed where, although the storage was carried out in a separate building and was in that sense physically separate from the selling of the goods, it was not a separate part of a composite business because it was not a commercial activity in its own right.[403]

Others. There is now no mention of mills, factory or other similar premises. Under the old law a building was a factory only if something was made there, and so it followed that a repair depot could not normally qualify.[404] Today the same decision would be reached, since the court went on to hold that the building could not be treated as one in which goods were subject to a process since a process connoted a substantial degree of uniformity or system of treatment and not the individual treatment of each item as it came in.

---

[396] CAA 2001, s 276(3).

[397] See *Dale v Johnson Bros* (1951) 32 TC 487.

[398] *Copol Clothing Co Ltd v Hindmarch* [1984] STC 33, [1984] 1 WLR 411, CA; see Marsh [1984] BTR 124; and *Carr v Sayer* [1992] STC 396, where the provision was confined to facilities needed in the ordinary process of physically transporting goods and so did not extend to quarantine kennels.

[399] *Bestway Holdings v Luff* [1998] STC 357; see also *IR Tax Bulletin*, December 1999.

[400] *Saxone Lilley and Skinner (Holdings) Ltd v IRC* [1967] 1 All ER 756, 44 TC 122 (HL).

[401] See *Bestway Holdings v Luff* [1998] STC 357.

[402] *Crusabridge Investments Ltd v Casings International Ltd* (1979) 54 TC 246, as explained in *Bestway Holdings*.

[403] *Maco Door and Window Hardware (UK) Ltd v HMRC* [2006] EWHC 1832 (Ch), [2007] STC 721, confirmed by the House of Lords, see [2008] UKHL 54. This case overruled *Crusabridge Investments Ltd v Casings International Ltd* (1979) 54 TC 246 in so far as it was decided under what was then CAA 1990, s 18(1), now s 274, Table A. On the 1979 case, see Inland Revenue Press Release, 26 March 1982, [1982] *Simon's Tax Intelligence* 145.

[404] *Vibroplant Ltd v Holland* [1982] STC 164, 54 TC 658. CAA 2001, s 276(3) would not have helped in the *Vibroplant* case since the trade of plant hire would not qualify under CAA 2001, s 274(1), Table A.

The trade consisting of catching or taking fish or shellfish is still in the approved list.[405] The other trades mentioned in Table A are agricultural contracting, working foreign plantations and mineral extraction.

6.3.2.2 Exclusions

Section 277 specifically excludes any building used as, or as part of, a dwelling house, retail shop, showroom, hotel or office, and of any building ancillary to the purposes of those excluded.[406] In determining what an office is, the courts have not been blinded by terminology. Thus, a drawing office is no more an office than a machine shop is a shop.[407] The question whether a storage area is a warehouse in its own right or merely ancillary to a shop is one of the fact and degree; a Commissioner's finding that a document- and data-processing centre was not an office was held by the Court of Appeal to be one which he was entitled to reach.[408] 'Ancillary' means 'subservient' or 'subordinate', so buildings which are warehouses used exclusively to receive and store goods and then distribute those goods for retail sales in a group's retail shops clearly come within that subordinate role and so cannot attract allowances.[409] However, the result may be different if the building is used to serve not only the taxpayers' retail shops, but also a wholesale business for other customers.[410]

6.3.2.3 Extensions Beyond Qualifying Trades

A commercial building built in a designated enterprise zone qualifies for special 100% initial allowances, together with 25% writing-down allowances as appropriate.[411] Also, the allowance is extended to the provision of qualifying sports pavilions,[412] whether or not the trade falls within the qualifying list. Expenditure on safety at sports grounds may qualify for the more generous machinery and plant allowance.[413]

Qualifying hotels may also obtain the benefit of this allowance (below §6.3.7.1).[414]

6.3.2.4 Parts of Buildings

If only part of a building qualifies for an allowance, an apportionment is made. However, the whole cost is allowed where the cost of the qualifying part is 75% or more of the total cost.[415] This raises the difficult problem of defining a building. If a building includes an office, the cost of which is less than 25%, an allowance is made in respect of the whole cost.

---

[405] CAA 2001, s 274.

[406] CAA 2001, s 277.

[407] *IRC v Lambhill Ironworks Ltd* (1950) 31 TC 393 (where the office qualified because of its essentially industrial character).

[408] *Girobank plc v Clarke* [1998] STC 182; see Morgan [1998] BTR 517.

[409] *Sarsfield v Dixons Group plc* [1998] STC 938; mysteriously this case does not even discuss the decision of the House of Lords in *Saxone Lilley and Skinner (Holdings) Ltd v IRC* [1967] 1 All ER 756, 44 TC 122.

[410] *Kilmarnock Equitable Cooperate Society Ltd v IRC* (1966) 42 TC 675; distinguished in the *Dixon* case. See Hughes [1980] BTR 459.

[411] CAA 2001, ss 271, 305, and 310(1)(a); on qualifying expenditure see *ibid*, ss 280–304; on enterprise zones in general, see Watson, *Tolleys Tax Planning 2003–2004*, ch 20.

[412] CAA 2001, s 280.

[413] See CAA 2001, ss 27, 30–33.

[414] CAA 2001, s 279.

[415] CAA 2001, s 283; this raises nice questions if the building contains machinery which is affixed to the floor.

If, however, the office is a separate building, no allowance can be made even though its cost is 25% or less of the total cost of the building. Separate blocks which are not physically integrated do not form one building.[416]

Example

30% of the area of a factory building is used as a showroom, and the capital expenditure on the showroom area is 20% of the total. The expenditure on the showroom is less than 25% of the total cost, so no apportionment is necessary.

6.3.3 The Relevant Interest—Who can Claim the Writing-down Allowances?

The concept of 'relevant interest' is central to almost all aspects of the industrial buildings allowance. Although not relevant to the initial allowance—which is claimed by the person who incurs the cost of the building—it is vital to the other allowances, since writing-down and balancing allowances may be claimed only by the person with the relevant interest.[417] On a sale of the relevant interest, the buyer may be entitled to further allowances and the seller to a balancing charge.[418]

The 'relevant interest' in relation to any qualifying expenditure is the interest in the building to which the person, O, who incurred the expenditure on the construction of the building was entitled when the expenditure was incurred.[419] So, if a lessee, L, spends money improving property, L can claim the allowance but L's landlord cannot. If O, the owner of the freehold, incurs the expense and later leases the building to someone else, O may use the allowances as part of his property business;[420] it is, however, essential that the lessee use the building for qualifying purposes.[421] A person entitled to a highway concession in respect of a toll road is treated as having an interest in the road, and that interest can be a relevant interest.[422]

6.3.3.1 Election for Long Lease

The rigid insistence on tying the right to the allowance to the relevant interest would be inefficient in circumstances where, for example, a pension fund (which pays no tax and which therefore cannot make use of the allowances) wishes to finance the construction of a building which would then be used by a tenant under a long lease. Therefore, where a long lease is granted, and both lessor and lessee so elect, the lessee may claim the allowances even though the expenditure was incurred by the lessor. The mechanism for this change is that the newly-created lease is designated the relevant interest in place of the reversionary interest.[423] The same applies where a long sub-lease is created out of a lease. Any capital sum paid by the lessee (or sub-lessee) becomes the sum in respect of

---

[416] *Abbott Laboratories Ltd v Carmody* [1968] 2 All ER 879, 44 TC 569.
[417] CAA 2001, s 309(1)(b). On the situation where the expense is shared, see *ibid*, ss 537 and 539.
[418] CAA 2001, s 314.
[419] CAA 2001, s 286.
[420] Under CAA 2001, s 353.
[421] CAA 2001, s 271(b)(i); or come with the extensions listed above and set out in the rest of s 271(b).
[422] CAA 2001, s 342; the rules on highways are gathered together at ss 341–344, but see FA 2001, Sch 21, para 6, amending CAA 2001, s 341.
[423] CAA 2001, ss 290, 11. Claims must be made within two years of the date the lease takes effect (s 291(4)).

which the allowance may be claimed. It follows that the grant of such a lease may cause a balancing allowance or charge to accrue to the lessor. A long lease is defined as one exceeding 50 years.[424]

6.3.3.2 No Election

The election may generally not be made where lessor and lessee are connected persons.[425] The election is also excluded if it appears that the sole or main benefit which might be expected to accrue is the obtaining of a balancing *allowance*.[426] It appears that the sole object of obtaining a balancing *charge*, perhaps to soak up other reliefs, does not prevent the election rule from operating.

6.3.3.3 Initial Allowance for Lessee

If the building has not been used before the lease is granted, the lessee may claim not only the writing-down allowance but also, in the very limited circumstances now prevailing in relation to enterprise zones, any initial allowance. This is of particular importance where the lessor is an exempt person, such as a local authority or charity, since it is only the lessee who will have taxable income against which to set the allowance.

6.3.3.4 Lease Ends: Allowances Continue

If the relevant interest is a lease, the holder of that interest may still claim the allowance even after the lease has ended if there is a holding over with the consent of the landlord, or if a new lease is taken in pursuance of an option in the first lease.[427] Where the lease is surrendered and so becomes merged in another interest, that other interest becomes the relevant interest so that the right to the allowance is not lost[428]—similarly if the lessee acquires the reversionary interest. This scheme does not apply where the new lease is granted to the original lessee otherwise than under a right in the original lease. In such circumstances a balancing allowance or charge cannot be avoided.

If the relevant interest is a lease and the lease ends but the landlord pays the lessee a sum, eg for improvements carried out by the lessee, the lease is treated as if it had been surrendered.[429] If the landlord grants a new lease to a different person and the new lessee pays a sum to the first lessee, the leases are treated as one and the same so that the new lessee now has the 'relevant interest'.[430]

6.3.3.5 Initial Allowance: Licence as Good as Lease

A licence is particularly useful for those starting up small workshops and businesses, since the obligations of a licensee are normally less onerous than those of a lessee—an important consideration if cash problems are an issue. Previously, where industrial property

---

[424] CAA 2001, s 291(3) refers to the rules in CTA 2009, ss 243 and 244, ex TA 1988, s 34 (see *Revenue Law*, §25.5.1); CAA 2001, s 359(3) is ignored (s 291(3)).

[425] CAA 2001, s 291(1); there is an exception for bodies exercising statutory functions, *ibid*; on connected person status, see *ibid*, s 575, modelled on ex TA 1988, s 839.

[426] CAA 2001, ss 291(2), 11(6)(b), ex TA 1988, s 839. See *Barclays Mercantile Industrial Finance Ltd v Melluish* [1990] STC 314.

[427] CAA 2001, s 359(2)(3).

[428] CAA 2001, s 289.

[429] CAA 2001, s 359(4).

[430] CAA 2001, s 359(5).

was occupied by someone (S) for the purposes of S's trade only under a licence, S had no property interest and could not therefore claim any industrial buildings allowances. The legislation was therefore extended to cover licensees. Today, where an owner, O, or a lessee, L, grants a licence to S, S's interest is treated as if it is subject to a lease, thus allowing S to claim any initial allowances.[431]

Claims for allowances may also be made where the premises are occupied by more than one licensee, provided all the licensees are carrying on industrial businesses.[432]

6.3.4 *Initial Allowances: Enterprise Zones*

Like the general industrial buildings allowances, these allowances were abolished as from 2011; this entailed a time apportionment where the business's chargeable period strad-dled the abolition date.[433] However, later events may give rise to balancing charges for a maximum of seven years from the first use of the building.[434]

CAA 2001 deals only with initial allowances in relation to enterprise zones.[435] This is presumably because initial allowances are not otherwise available, having been repealed at the behest of Nigel Lawson in the 1980s. Expenditure qualifies for the initial allowance only if incurred where the site of the building is in an enterprise zone and the expenditure was incurred not more than 10 years after the site was first included, or up to 20 years if the contract was entered into in those first 10 years.[436]

The rate of allowance was 100%; at one time this was reduced to 75% for certain regional development expenditure, but this is now obsolete.[437] Allowances are available not only for industrial buildings and hotels, but also for all other commercial buildings used for trading or professional purposes—other than dwelling houses.[438]

Further provisions are designed to ensure that the purchaser of a building buying it after the expiry of the 10-year period but before the building is brought into use is entitled to the initial allowance.[439] Similarly, where buildings are sold once within two years of being brought into use, there is a balancing charge or allowance on the seller.[440] These allowances are available only for expenditure incurred within the first 10-year period,[441] or contracted for within that 10-year period but only if actually incurred within 20 years after the site first became part of an enterprise zone.[442]

There was a temporary reintroduction of initial allowances for capital expenditure on any industrial buildings for a period of one year beginning 1 November 1992. CAA 1990, section 1, the general provision for initial allowances, was modified by a new CAA 1990, section 2A.[443] The rate of allowance was 20%.

---

[431] CAA 2001, s 305.
[432] CAA 2001, s 278.
[433] FA 2008, ss 81 (abolition) and 83 (apportionment).
[434] FA 2008, Sch 27, para 31.
[435] CAA 2001, ss 305–308.
[436] CAA 2001, s 298(1); note FA 2001, Sch 21, para 5 correcting CAA 2001, s 298(3).
[437] CAA 2001, s 306(1).
[438] CAA 2001, s 281.
[439] CAA 2001, s 302 referring to ss 295 and 296; originally added by F(No 2)A 1992, on which see Inland Revenue Press Release, 16 December 1991, [1992] *Simon's Tax Intelligence* 5.
[440] CAA 2001, s 303 also added by F(No 2)A 1992.
[441] CAA 2001, ss 302 and 298(1).
[442] CAA 2001, s 298(1) also added by F(No 2)A 1992.
[443] Added by FA 1993, s 113.

6.3.5 *The Writing-down Allowance*

Writing-down allowances were available to the person entitled to the relevant interest in the building, provided the building was used as 'an industrial building' at the end of the chargeable period.[444] Unless the building is in an enterprise zone, the allowance was, as seen above, 4% for 2007–08, 3% for 2008–09, 2% for 2009–10 and 1% for 2010–11, this to be reduced or increased if the chargeable period was less or more than 12 months.[445] If the building is in an enterprise zone the rate is 25%.[446] Allowances are available during periods of temporary disuse.[447] In a straightforward case the expense will have been written off after 25 years.

6.3.6 *Balancing Adjustments: Allowances and Charges*

The writing-down allowances are exhausted after 25 years. It follows that no balancing adjustment is made if the balancing event occurred more than 25 years after the building was first used.[448] Within that 25-year period too—for events on or after 1 April (for corporation tax) or 6 April (for income tax) 2008—the buyer simply steps into the shoes of the seller and is entitled to the writing-down allowances (at 4%,3%, 2% or 1%)) down to, at the latest, 2011. The pre-2008 rules were most unusual and required a willing suspension of disbelief, especially on the part of those familiar with other systems. They are explained in *Revenue Law*, 5th edition, at §24.3.6.

A balancing adjustment, whether by allowance or charge, arises if, within 25 years of the building being first used, the relevant interest is sold, or the building is demolished, destroyed or ceases to be used altogether.[449] No adjustment is made merely because the building ceases to be used for the purpose of a qualifying trade, although an adjustment will be made on a subsequent sale or demolition, etc.[450] In the meantime, the writing-down allowance ceases unless the cessation of use is purely temporary.[451]

A balance is also struck if, within 25 years of the building being first used, the relevant interest ends and is not deemed to continue[452]—as where the interest merges in the reversionary interest—or where the relevant interest depends upon a foreign concession which ends.

6.3.6.1 The Residue of Qualifying Expenditure

The amount and nature of the adjustment depend on the 'residue of qualifying expenditure', which is the qualifying expenditure not yet written off[453] or, more fully, what CAA 2001 calls the 'starting expenditure' (ie the original cost) minus the allowances made (whether initial or writing-down). This residue is set against the proceeds from the

---

[444] CAA 2001, s 309.
[445] CAA 2001, s 310.
[446] CAA 2001, s 310(1)(a).
[447] CAA 2001, s 285.
[448] CAA 2001, s 314(4).
[449] CAA 2001, ss 314 and 315.
[450] CAA 2001, s 319.
[451] CAA 2001, s 336.
[452] CAA 2001, s 315.
[453] CAA 2001, s 313, ie written off in accordance with the rules in ss 332–340; on starting cost, see s 322.

balancing event, ie any sale, insurance compensation or salvage monies.[454] Where the residue is greater than those sums, the difference is the subject of the balancing allowance; where it is less, the difference is the subject of the balancing charge, subject to the rule that the charge may not exceed the allowances made.[455] In making these calculations, any periods during which the relevant interest was held by the Crown or by someone outside the charge to UK tax are treated as if any allowances that could have been claimed by an ordinary taxpayer had been claimed.[456] The calculations are straightforward when the building has been used as an industrial building—or for R&D—throughout the period.[457] More precisely, the period is described as the relevant period of ownership, which is defined as running from the date the building was first used or the date of any later sale down to the date of the balancing event.[458]

Example 1

S's building cost £1,000,000 in the first year, but is destroyed in the thirteenth year. The total allowances will be £520,000 (13 years at 4%), making a residue of expenditure of £480,000. If compensation amounts to £400,000, there will be a balancing allowance of £80,000 to bring the total allowances in line with total expenditure. If the compensation is £600,000, there will be a balancing charge of £120,000.

If the building was not used for a qualifying trade throughout the period, the balancing adjustment must reflect this fact. Allowances or charges are made by reference to what one might call the 'adjusted net cost' of the building, which is the excess of capital expenditure over the proceeds, reduced in the proportion that the period of qualifying use bears to the whole period.[459] The concept of starting expenditure has to be used here too, but is defined differently from the situation covered in Example 1.[460]

Example 2

An industrial building was constructed for £250,000. It was used for a qualifying purpose for two years, then as an office (a non-qualifying purpose) for one year and then reverted to a qualifying use for the fourth year. The building is sold at the end of the fifth year for £170,000. The balancing adjustment is calculated as follows:

(1) calculate the net cost of the building to the taxpayer (£80,000) and then the proportion of that figure which is attributable to qualifying use (£64,000, ie 4/5 × £80,000);

(2) calculate the allowances given (£50,000, or 5 years at £10,000 a year) and deduct the net cost applicable to the qualifying use (£64,000).

This gives a balancing allowance of £14,000 (ie £64,000 − £50,000).

---

[454] Defined in CAA 2001, s 316.
[455] CAA 2001, s 320.
[456] CAA 2001, ss 358 and 359.
[457] CAA 2001, s 318.
[458] CAA 2001, s 321.
[459] CAA 2001, s 319.
[460] CAA 2001, s 322(3).

6.3.6.2 The Buyer

The buyer, B, is entitled to an allowance provided the building is used by B for a qualifying purpose. B is entitled to writing-down allowance based on the residue of expenditure, ie the remaining unrelieved expenditure of B's seller (S), *plus* any balancing charge (or minus a balancing allowance).[461] This sum is spread evenly over the remaining 25-year period, and is in no way tied to a 4% figure. Therefore, if, in Example 1 above, the building had been sold for £400,000, S would have been given a balancing allowance of £80,000. B could then have spread the £400,000 over the 12 years remaining of the 25 years. This means that B's £40,000 would be written off at the rate of £33,333 pa, as opposed to S's £40,000. If the building had been sold for £1,000,000, S would have had a balancing charge of £520,000 and B would have written off the £1,000,000 over 12 years, making it £83,333 a year. It also follows that if the sale took place after 25 years had expired, S would get no balancing charge and B would get no allowance at all. The sharp contrasts for both parties—between a disposal after 24 years and 364 days and a disposal one day later—are striking; whether they are sensible is a very different matter.[462]

An anti-avoidance rule was added in 2003.[463] The rule bars any balancing allowance where, as a result of a tax avoidance scheme, the amount to be brought into account as the proceeds of the event are less that it would otherwise have been (CAA 2001, s 570A(2)). Moreover, to make matters worse for the avoider or, more immediately, the person buying from the avoider, the residue of any qualifying expenditure immediately after the balancing event is calculated as if the allowance had actually been made (CAA 2001, s 570A(4)). The scheme is a tax avoidance scheme if the main purpose or one of the main purposes is the obtaining of a tax advantage by the taxpayer (CAA 2001, s 570A(3)). This provision applies not only to the allowance for industrial buildings in Part 3 of the Act, but also to those for agricultural land (§6.5), flat conversions (§6.6), mineral extraction (§6.7) and assured tenancies (§6.3.7.2).

6.3.6.3 Minor Matters

The residue of expenditure is calculated by taking account of any reliefs that could have been claimed but were not because the relevant interest was held by the Crown or by an exempt person.[464]

On a sale between connected persons who elect for the building to be transferred at its written-down value, the residue of expenditure is carried through to the purchaser, save where there is a tax avoidance motive, in which case market value is taken.[465]

6.3.6.4 Building not Land: Artificial Arrangements

Special rules clarify the sum paid on the sale of a relevant interest if there are arrangements artificially to enhance the value of the relevant interest.[466] Since the allowance is

---

[461] CAA 2001, s 3(3). On relief when vendor's expense was on revenue account, see s 10(4) and (5).

[462] Thus, if the parties try to avoid a sale within the period by the device of a lease plus an option to buy after the 25-year period has expired, they run the risk of any premium for the lease being treated in part as income.

[463] CAA 2001, s 570A added by FA 2003 s 164; see generally Inland Revenue Press Release Rev BN 14, 9 April 2003, [2003] *Simon's Tax Intelligence* 719.

[464] CAA 2001, s 339.

[465] CAA 2001, ss 569, 570.

[466] CAA 2001, s 357 added by FA 1995, s 100; see Inland Revenue Press Release, 29 November 1994, [1994] *Simon's Tax Intelligence* 1482.

intended to cover the element of the price paid for the building, the value of the land must be deducted, and any value attributable to elements over and above those which would feature in a normal commercial lease must be negotiated in the open market. This is achieved by describing any of the elements as arrangements which have an artificial effect on pricing, and then directing that the amount of the price paid which is attributable to such arrangements be not allowed.

6.3.7 *Other Buildings*

6.3.7.1 Qualifying Hotel Buildings and Extensions

As with industrial building allowances, the special regime applicable to hotels was repealed with effect from April 2011. The discussion that follows relates now only to pre- April 2011 allowances. Hotels do not qualify for the general industrial buildings allowances since they do not come within the list of trades permitted. However, an annual writing-down allowance of 4% is available, calculated on a straight-line basis.[467] Subsequent holders of the relevant interest may write off the residue of the expenditure over the balance of the 25-year period.[468] A person buying a qualifying hotel unused is treated as having incurred expenditure on its construction when the purchase price becomes payable.[469] The hotel must be a 'qualifying hotel', a concept which is elaborately defined.[470] The hotel may be outside the UK but the profit from its trade must be taxed in full. The allowance does not extend to the costs of dwelling accommodation for the owner, but accommodation for staff is treated as part of the hotel.[471] It follows that accommodation which would be disqualified as being for the owner may qualify if the trade were incorporated and so the accommodation was for a director or an employee. There are special rules for calculating the balancing adjustments if the hotel has ceased to be a qualifying hotel for more than two years before the balancing event occurs.[472]

6.3.7.2 Dwelling Houses—Assured Tenancies

Allowances may also be given for the cost incurred before 1 April 1992 in the construction of 'qualifying dwelling houses', which, broadly speaking, must be let on assured tenancies within the meaning of the Housing Act 1980, section 56, or its successor in Part I of the Housing Act 1988.[473] Although it is not necessary for the landlord to be a company for the purposes of the assured tenancy scheme, the landlord must be a company if capital allowances are claimed under these provisions. This is now contained in Part 10 of CAA 2001; a writing-down allowance of 4% per annum and balancing allowances and charges apply as appropriate.[474] Expenditure for which capital allowances have been given under these

---

[467] CAA 2001, ss 279 and 309.
[468] Under CAA 2001, s 311, ex CAA 1990, s 3(3).
[469] CAA 2001, ss 295–297.
[470] CAA 2001, s 279(1); on the requirement to offer breakfast and dinner, see Statement of Practice SP 9/87.
[471] CAA 2001, ss 279(6) and (7).
[472] CAA 2001, s 317.
[473] CAA 2001, ss 490–491 and 504. An initial allowance had been phased out by 1986.
[474] CAA 2001, ss 507–510 (writing–down allowance) and 513–522 (balancing adjustments).

provisions is not deductible when computing any allowable loss for CGT purposes on the disposal of the building.[475]

6.4 Renovation or Conversion of Unused Business Premises in Disadvantaged Area

CAA 2001, Part 3A (sections 360A–360Z4)[476] concerns qualifying expenditure incurred after 10 April 2007 and before April 2017 on converting a qualifying building into qualifying business premises, or renovating a qualifying building which is or will be qualifying business premises.[477] This regime is unaffected by the withdrawal of industrial building allowances from April 2011. Expenditure does not qualify if it is the cost of the land itself, of extending a qualifying building, of developing adjacent land and most machinery and plant. The building must be in a designated disadvantaged area. The premises must not be available for use as a dwelling house—or be so used. The person claiming the allowance must have a relevant interest in the building. The building must not have been used for a year or more.

The initial allowance is 100%; there is also a 25% writing-down allowance.[478] There are rules on the effect of grants, on balancing allowances and charges adjustments, on how expenditure is to be written off and on VAT liabilities and rebates.[479] Further supplementary rules include important provisions on how the allowances and charges are to be given effect for trades, lessors and licensees.[480]

6.5 Agricultural Buildings

Part 4 (sections 361–393) governs the allowances for expenditure on agricultural land. An allowance may be claimed by a person with a relevant interest in agricultural land who incurs capital expenditure on the construction of a building such as a farmhouse, farm building or cottage, fences and other works, eg drainage.[481] Before 2008 the allowance was a writing-down allowance over 25 years, ie 4% pa.[482] As with the industrial buildings allowance, this allowance is abolished as from April 2011 after a period of phasing out.[483] The discussion that follows relates now only to pre-2011 allowances.

---

[475] TCGA 1992, s 41(4).

[476] Added by FA 2005, s 92 and Sch 6, para 1 with effect for expenditure on or after 11 April 2007.

[477] CAA 2001, ss 360B–360D.

[478] CAA 2001, ss 360G–360K.

[479] CAA 2001, ss 360L–360S.

[480] CAA 2001, ss 360T–360Z4.

[481] CAA 2001, s 361. A person with a 'relevant interest' is defined in s 364 and includes an owner in fee simple, a lessee and the Scottish equivalents; allowances for forestry land were abolished for chargeable periods beginning on or after 20 June 1989 (FA 1989, s 120).

[482] CAA 2001, ss 364–368, with further definitions, eg in relation to Scotland, in s 393s; the mortgagor holds the relevant interest rather than the mortgagee: s 366.

[483] FA 2008, s 82; the formula in s 82(6) for calculating the allowances where the business year is not the same as the tax year is slightly different from that for the industrial buildings allowance but with the same effect.

The 'relevant interest' means the freehold or leasehold interest of the person incurring the expenditure. Further rules ignore the creation of a sub-lease, the merger of a leasehold interest with a superior interest and the ending of one lease if it is followed by a new one for the same lessee.[484] For expenditure incurred before 1 April 1987 under a contract entered into before 14 March 1984, the allowances comprised an initial allowance of 20%, followed by a straight-line writing-down allowance of the remaining 80% over the next eight years. The 20% initial allowance was revived for expenditure incurred between 1 November 1992 and 31 October 1993,[485] but not since. The allowance is set primarily against the taxpayer's ITTOIA 2005, Parts 2 or 3 trading or UK property business income, as appropriate.[486] The separate industrial buildings allowance may sometimes be available, but of course the taxpayer cannot claim both.

The expenditure must have been incurred by the person with the relevant interest for the purposes of husbandry[487] on that agricultural land, but an apportionment is made where the expenditure is only partly for that purpose.[488] Where the expenditure is on a farmhouse, only one-third is allowable, and a smaller proportion is taken if the accommodation and amenities of the farmhouse are 'out of due relation to the nature and extent of the farm'.[489] A farmhouse is a building used by the person running the farm as a farmhouse.[490] In *Lindsay v IRC*,[491] the only house on a sheep farm was occupied by a shepherd and the owner resided in the United States, but the house was held to be a farmhouse. In *IRC v John M Whiteford & Son*,[492] the fact that the occupier was one of the partners running the farm did not mean that his house was necessarily a farmhouse; rather, it could be an agricultural cottage and so entitled to the full allowance. The proper criterion is not the status of the occupant but the purpose of the occupation of the premises.[493] In that case there was evidence that the farm was run from the house of the other partner. In both cases the decision of the Commissioners was upheld. If the farmhouse is of a scale extravagantly large for the purpose for which it is being used, it may be entitled to no allowance whatsoever.[494]

The details of the allowance are similar to those for industrial buildings. The expenditure must be qualifying expenditure, which means capital expenditure on the construction of the building incurred for the purposes of husbandry. The relevant interest must not have been sold, although this rule is waived if the sale was only after the first use of the building. Where there is a purchase of the relevant interest before the first use of the building, the allowance is given by reference to whichever is the lower of the construction cost and the purchase price.

There are also rules for balancing allowances or charges on the happening of a 'balancing event', which is defined as arising when the relevant interest is transferred and where

---

484 *Ibid.*
485 CAA 1990, s 124, added by FA 1993, Sch 12.
486 CAA 2001, ss 391 and 392.
487 CAA 2001, s 361(1)(b); 'husbandry' is defined in s 362 to include intensive rearing of livestock or fish.
488 CAA 2001, s 124.
489 CAA 2001, s 369(3).
490 *Lindsay v IRC* (1952) 34 TC 289, 292, *per* Lord Carmont.
491 *Ibid.*
492 (1962) 40 TC 379.
493 *Ibid*, 384, *per* Lord Clyde.
494 *Ibid.*

the building is demolished, destroyed or otherwise ceases to be used.[495] This is a matter of election if the relevant interest is sold; both seller and buyer must elect.[496] Under the pre-1986 system, balances were not struck, so there were neither balancing allowances nor balancing charges. Where one party has control over the other, the parties are under common control or are connected persons, or the object of the disposal is to obtain a deduction or allowance, the anti-avoidance provisions with regard to sales are adopted for this allowance, but without the right to elect to substitute market value for the price agreed by the parties.[497] A separate rule directs the adjustment of the proceeds of sale where the relevant interest is disposed of subject to a subordinate interest; the value of the subordinate interest may not be ignored.[498]

CAA 2001, section 570A, the anti-avoidance rule explained at §6.3.6.2, applies here too.

6.6 A Conversion of Parts of Business Premises into Residential Flats

Part 4A (sections 393A–393W) was added by FA 2001 to give capital allowances for expenditure on converting or renovating qualifying business premises into flats. The scheme must be seen in the context of other fiscal incentives to assist urban regeneration— brown land. This regime applies in respect of expenditure incurred prior to April 2013.

Unlike the allowances for hotels, this is not fitted into the structure of the industrial buildings allowance but is free-standing. However, the industrial buildings allowance is clearly the model for this, as is shown by the use of the concept of the relevant interest.[499] The writing-down allowance is 25% of the relevant expenditure, but there is an initial (not first-year) allowance of 100%.[500] There are also rules for calculating balancing adjustments.[501] The allowance is given in calculating the profits of the claimant's property business relating to the flat; if there is no such business, one is deemed to exist.[502]

The relief is meant to be precisely targeted, so no allowance may be claimed for expenditure on acquiring the land, extending the building, developing adjacent land or providing furniture or chattels.[503] The construction of the building being converted must have been completed before 1980. The legislation is silent on the effect of building works since then, but one could say that such a building would not qualify since it had not been 'completed'. The building must have the ground floor authorised for business use; it must have not more than four storeys above the ground floor (ignoring attics) and it must appear that the storeys above the ground floor were originally intended for use as a dwelling.[504] There are also detailed rules about which flats qualify. So the flat must be suitable for letting as a

---

[495] CAA 2001, ss 380 and 381.
[496] CAA 2001, s 381; the election also applies to certain accidents (see s 129(1)(b)).
[497] CAA 2001, s 573.
[498] CAA 2001, s 389.
[499] CAA 2001, ss 393A(2), 393F and 393G.
[500] CAA 2001, ss 393H and 393J.
[501] CAA 2001, ss 393M–393P.
[502] CAA 2001, s 393T.
[503] CAA 2001, s 393B.
[504] CAA 2001, s 393C.

dwelling, held for short-term letting (not more than five years), have not more than four rooms (as defined) and not be a high-value flat.[505]

CAA 2001, section 570A, the anti-avoidance rule explained at §6.3.6.2, applies here too.

6.7   Mineral Extraction

Part 5 (sections 394–436) governs mineral extraction allowances. UK companies operating abroad or in the North Sea usually derive their money from mining metals and/or oil and gas. Companies operating within the UK mine mostly building materials, notably sand and gravel, china clay and slate. The history of capital allowances has been erratic to say the least, and different rules applied according to the place being mined. The current rules were introduced by FA 1986.[506] They apply where the taxpayer carries on a mineral extraction trade, ie working of a source of mineral deposits, the last phrase being extended to cover geothermal energy.[507]

'Qualifying expenditure' is defined by both inclusion[508] and exclusion.[509] Thus, the expense incurred in an abortive application for planning permission is allowed,[510] but expense incurred on the acquisition of a site on which further expense will be incurred which will qualify for relief is not.[511] Expenditure on plant and machinery is usually left to the plant and machinery system of allowances (see §6.2 above), but this will not apply where the expense is a pre-trading expense and the asset is disposed of before the trade begins; such expense may, therefore, be qualifying expenditure.[512] A similar rule applies to pre-trading exploration expenditure.[513] Also included are certain payments by mining concerns for site comfort and development outside the UK.[514] Expenditure on restoring a site at the end of the operation also qualifies.[515]

When qualifying expenditure is incurred for the purposes of mineral extraction, writing-down allowance is given by reference to the amount by which the qualifying expenditure exceeds any disposal proceeds received during the period. The scheme is a simple reducing balance, so that previous allowances reduce the qualifying expenditure. For pre-trading expenditure on plant and machinery disposed of before the trade begins, and pre-trading exploration expenditure, the figure is 10%; for other qualifying expenditure, the figure is 25%.[516] The allowance is given in taxing the mineral extraction trade.[517] The cost of the land is not qualifying expenditure; a valuation is carried out by assuming that there is no

---

[505] CAA 2001, ss 393D and 393E.
[506] On transition, see CAA 1990, s 119.
[507] CAA 2001, s 394.
[508] CAA 2001, s 395.
[509] CAA 2001, s 399.
[510] CAA 2001, s 396(2).
[511] CAA 2001, s 414(2).
[512] CAA 2001, s 402; otherwise the plant and machinery rules apply (s 399(1)).
[513] CAA 2001, s 401.
[514] CAA 2001, s 415; where the building is in the UK the industrial buildings allowance may apply (eg s 277(2), (3)).
[515] CAA 2001, s 416 (but only if the work is carried out within three years of the termination; the cost is treated as incurred when the trade ends).
[516] CAA 2001, s 418.
[517] CAA 2001, s 432.

source of mineral deposits and that only existing or authorised use is allowed.[518] Further rules apply to qualifying expenditure on secondhand assets.[519] CAA 2001, section 570A, the anti-avoidance rule explained at §6.3.6.2, applies here too.

FA 2002 imposed a corporation tax surcharge on certain ring-fenced trades. As if in compensation, it added a first-year allowance to the mineral extraction allowance.[520] The allowance is 100% of the expenditure, and there is an express provision to deal with artificially-inflated claims for first-year allowances.

6.8   Research and Development Allowances

Part 6 (sections 437–451) governs R&D allowances. FA 2000 made two important changes in this area. First, it provided some new definitions and procedures for the long-established scientific research allowance, now renamed 'research and development allowances'. Secondly, it provided a new tax credit for expenditure on R&D by companies; the credit is not available if the expenditure is capital in nature and so is not considered here,[521] but see above at §§4.2.2 and 4.2.5.

Research and development allowances are available for capital expenditure on R&D, provided it is related to the trade carried on (or to be carried on).[522] The research may be carried on by someone other than the trader, provided it is on behalf of the trader, an expression which requires something close to agency.[523] Whether activities are R&D is now decided by reference to accounting concepts.[524] Costs in acquiring rights in scientific research are not allowed.[525] There are also exclusions for expenditure on dwellings and on land, but with exceptions and qualifications.[526] Apportionment of expenditure is permitted.[527]

The allowance is 100% of the cost, less any sums received for disposal values. Disposal values arise if the taxpayer ceases to own the asset, or it is demolished or destroyed while in his ownership.[528] Allowances are given as receipts of the trade and charges as expenses.[529] The relevant chargeable period is that in which the expenditure was incurred, save that

---

[518]   CAA 2001, s 404; a similar valuation is used for calculating the disposal proceeds (s 400(2)).

[519]   CAA 2001, ss 407–413.

[520]   CAA 2001, ss 416A–416E, added by FA 2002, Sch 21, paras 8–13. The surcharge was added by TA 1988, s 501A, inserted by FA 2002 s 91.

[521]   FA 2000, Sch 21, para 3(2); appeals on whether expenditure was on R&D were brought within the ordinary tax appeal structure and not, as previously, decided by the Secretary of State for Trade and Industry; CAA 1990, s 82A as added by FA 2000, Sch 19.

[522]   CAA 2001, ss 437 and 439. On 'relating to', see *Salt v Young* [1999] STC (SCD) 213, where the Special Commissioner said that one should not trace causality back too far. T's trade was in publishing books, but that did not mean that expenditure on a computer used in carrying out research in writing the book was deductible under this head. On meaning of 'research and development', see ITA 2007, s 1006(1)–(5) and CTA 2010, s 1138(1)–(5), ex TA 1988, s 837A (referred to by CAA 2001, s 437(2)).

[523]   CAA 2001, s 439(1); *Gaspet Ltd v Elliss* [1985] STC 572.

[524]   ITA 2007, s 1006(1)–(5) and CTA 2010, s 1138(1)–(5), ex TA 1988, s 837A(2)–(5); this brings in SSAP 13.

[525]   CAA 2001, s 438(2).

[526]   CAA 2001, ss 438 and 440.

[527]   CAA 2001, s 439(4).

[528]   CAA 2001, s 443.

[529]   CAA 2001, s 450.

for pre-trading expenditure the chargeable period beginning with the commencement is taken.[530]

The taxpayer may reduce the amount of the allowance claimed in any one period; unclaimed allowances are taken into account in calculating balancing charges.[531] Sums paid to approved research associations, universities and institutions may be deductible as if they were revenue expenditure.[532]

6.9 Know-how

Part 7 (sections 452–463) governs know how. Know–how means any industrial information or techniques likely to assist in the manufacture or processing of goods or materials.[533] The phrase is then widened to cover working mineral deposits and operations in agriculture, fishery or forestry.

Qualifying expenditure is then given relief if the person acquiring the know–how uses it in his trade, or subsequently uses it in a trade set up later. There are also rules allowing relief when goodwill has been acquired, or the trade was acquired and was previously carried on wholly outside the UK, ie outside the charge to UK tax.[534] Certain expenditure is excluded, ie where the know-how is acquired in circumstances where there is control, or if the expenditure would be given relief under some other rule.[535]

The form of relief follows the familiar pattern of a separate pooling and asking whether the AQE exceeds the TDV.[536] Unlike expenditure on patents (below), the allowance is given only for 25% of the excess of AQE over TDV.[537]

6.10 Patents

Part 8 (sections 464–483) governs patents. CAA 2001 introduces a new regime for patents. Allowances are now given when a person incurs qualifying expenditure on 'the purchase of patent rights', a phrase which extends to the acquisition of a licence.[538] Expenditure is subdivided into trading and non-trading; such expenditure 'qualifies' if the trade is within the charge to UK tax or the non-trading income is liable to UK tax.[539]

The expenditure is then pooled, each trade being a separate pool and all the non-trading expenditure a separate pool.[540] One then calculates the AQE, ie expenditure for the current

---

[530] CAA 2001, s 441(2).

[531] CAA 2001, ss 442–443; on timing see s 444, and on costs of demolition s 445.

[532] Under ITTOIA 2005, s 88, CTA 2009, s 88 (ex TA1988, s 82B), very correctly relocating CAA 1990, s 136. On accounting treatment, see SSAP 13.

[533] CAA 2001, s 452.

[534] CAA 2001, s 454.

[535] CAA 2001, s 455 also referring to CTA 2009, s 178(1)–(3), ex TA 1988, s 531(2).

[536] CAA 2001, ss 456–463.

[537] CAA 2001, ss 400D, 458(1).

[538] CAA 2001, ss 464–466.

[539] CAA 2001, ss 467–469.

[540] CAA 2001, s 470.

period plus any unrelieved from a previous period.[541] Where the AQE exceeds the TDR, a 25% writing-down allowance is given;[542] if TDR exceeds the AQE, the whole excess is charged to tax. There are rules for allocated expenditure to pools[543] and for calculating the TDR; it is provided that the TDR may not exceed the original capital expenditure,[544] showing once more that the purpose of the balance is to recapture the allowance, not to charge any gain.

The allowance or charge is given effect in taxing the trade. If there is no trade, the allowance is set off against patent income[545] and a charge is made; there is a separate rule for corporation tax.[546]

There is the usual anti-avoidance rule where buyer and seller are connected or the sole or main benefit for the sale or other transaction is to obtain an allowance under this part of the Act (Part 8).[547]

Capital payments received for the disposal of patent rights are taxed as income and spread over six years.[548] If the individual dies before the six-year period ends, any remaining instalments may be spread back; similar rules apply on discontinuance or on the winding up of a company.[549]

The rule allowing certain receipts from royalties to be spread over several years remains in force.[550]

6.11 Dredging

Part 9 (sections 484–489) deals with dredging. Allowances are given for capital expenditure incurred in dredging. The trade must consist of maintaining or improving the navigation of a harbour, estuary or waterway; alternatively, the dredging must be for the benefit of vessels using a dock occupied for the purpose of the trade, as where a trader incurs its own expense for its own dock.[551] Dredging refers only to acts done in the interests of navigation.[552] In general, the allowance is similar to that for industrial buildings. The straight-line writing-down allowance is 4%.[553] If the trade is permanently discontinued before the expenditure has been written off, there is an immediate write off of the balance.[554] There is no balancing charge. This allowance is not affected by any of the changes made in 2008.

---

[541] CAA 2001, ss 473–475.
[542] CAA 2001, ss 471–472.
[543] CAA 2001, s 474.
[544] CAA 2001, s 476.
[545] Defined CAA 2001, s 483.
[546] CAA 2001, ss 479 and 480.
[547] CAA 2001, s 481.
[548] CTA 2009, ss 912–920, ex TA 1988, s 524.
[549] CTA 2009, ss 918 and 1272, ex TA 1988, s 525.
[550] CTA 2009, ss 924–925, ex TA 1988, s 528.
[551] CAA 2001, s 484, undoing *Dumbarton Harbour Board v Cox* (1918) 7 TC 147.
[552] CAA 2001, s 484(3).
[553] CAA 2001, s 487.
[554] CAA 2001, s 488.

6.12   Commentary: Policy and History

6.12.1 Policy

The need for tax rules for capital allowance arises from the initial decision to deny any deduction for capital expenditure. As was seen at the beginning of this chapter, the background problem arises from the need to recognise that there is a cost to the business because of the decline in the value of the assets due to physical deterioration or obsolescence. The declining value could be recognised by annual valuations, but it was thought that this would be too subjective and/or expensive in practice. Accountants often used a simple cost recovery or writing-off system.[555]

6.12.2 Grander Theories

Depreciation rules would also be needed under a comprehensive income tax, unless an accounting definition of income was adopted so that full depreciation was made over an appropriate period. Such rules would not be needed under an expenditure tax since all investment would be deductible immediately.

A price is paid if such alternatives are rejected. Theorists complain that systems such as the UK's begin by discriminating against capital spending and in favour of employment costs; these systems then adjust by giving allowances, and overcompensate by also allowing a deduction for interest on the money used to buy the asset. Theorists have further enjoyment with the idea of an economic rent which would take capital expenditure into account.[556] The big question whether allowances can affect investment decisions must be seen as part of a wider view of the effects of taxes on business behaviour.[557] Those who believe that adjusting allowances affects the overall level of investment, point to the fact that capital investment by businesses is a lower percentage of GNP than spending by either consumers or governments; also, it is much more volatile.[558]

6.12.3 The UK System—Scope and Rates[559]

As has been seen, the UK tax system of allowances is as haphazard and history-driven as other parts of the system. The UK system is unusually strict (ie mean) in relation to assets for which it allows deductions, notably by the exclusion for many years of non-industrial buildings, from 2008–2011 the phasing out of allowances entirely even for industrial

---

[555] See FRS15 and Thomas, *Introduction to Financial Accounting*, 4th edn (McGraw Hill, 2002) ch 11.

[556] The idea of rent is associated particularly with the great economist Ricardo; see Sraffa (ed), *The Works and Correspondence of David Ricardo* (CUP, 1981). A rent resource tax for oil and gas is discussed by Garnaut and Ross, (1975) 85 *Economic Journal* 272; on North Sea Oil taxation, see Devereux and Morris, *IFS Report Series No 6* (Institute for Fiscal Studies,1983).

[557] See Mintz (1996) 16(4) *Fiscal Studies* 23, 46–49.

[558] Eg, Ford and Poret, *OECD Economic Studies No 16* (OECD, 1990).

[559] HM Treasury, *Corporation Tax*, Cmnd 8456 (1982), ch 15. For comparative material, see *Taxing Profits in a Global Economy* (OECD, 1991), ch 3, Tables 3.5, 3.9–3.12.

buildings and, at least until 2000, the shamefully slow refusal to do much more than the minimum to adapt the system to take account of the development of IP rights.

The UK's policy on the actual rate of depreciation has shifted dramatically over the years. This is because, although the current view is that the tax system should recognise the need to write off the cost of depreciating assets, another view would argue that the stimulation of investment demands tax incentives (which view dominated in the period before 1984).[560] This older idea may be traced back to 1932—the middle of the Depression— when allowances were first made available at a rate faster than the commercial rate of depreciation. The decision to revive, even if on a temporary basis, the first-year allowance, in 1992,[561] was also attributable to the need to give relief for the recession.[562] In 1954 investment allowances were added to the rights under the writing-off process. The weakening of the depreciation basis was also seen in the rules for plant and machinery, which, apart from the first-year allowance, applied a single rate of depreciation (25%) whatever the life of the asset, to any remaining expenditure and to a general pool of such expenditure. Today, special rules for short- or long-life assets modify this criticism in part. However, the palliatives for SMEs may be seen as some crude offset for other regulatory burdens imposed upon them. Meanwhile, the combination of the rules on rates and scope means that very different rates of return may be made from different investments. Those who like the present system argue that there is little evidence of underinvestment. There is a significant need for helpful empirical work here.

It was perhaps ironic that the tax system abandoned depreciation as the rational basis of its allowances system just as such evidence as there was suggested that the incentive effects of the allowances were limited and related more to the timing of investment than to its volume. When 100% allowances were given, the question could be asked what further incentives remained, other than outright cash grants,[563] and where it would all stop. Was the effect of the system simply to maintain marginally profitable businesses and to exempt manufacturing industries from liability to corporation tax?

In 2008, as in 1984, the taxpayers paid for reduced corporation tax rates by having reduced capital allowances; the overall result in 1984 was to reduce the incentives to invest but with very marked, short-term opportunities as the new rates came in.[564] This was coupled with the further irony of a rapidly contracting manufacturing base, the very area of the economy most favoured by the 1970s' approach.[565]

---

[560] See Prest and Barr, *Public Finance in Theory and Practice* (Weidenfeld & Nicolson, 1985), 16.4; and Hendershott and Cheng, *How Taxes Affect Economic Behaviour* (Brookings Institute, 1981), 85, both stressing other factors affecting investment decisions such as interest rates and inflation. See also the review of older literature by Sumner, *IFS Lecture Series No 4* (Institute for Fiscal Studies, 1976).

[561] Accountancy depreciation can consider the individual asset; a tax system must accommodate many kinds of assets in one rate, unless it opts for free depreciation.

[562] On effects, see Bond, Denney and Devereux (1993) 14(2) *Fiscal Studies* 1. Other alleviating rules, eg extending relief for corporate losses, were introduced at the same time by FA 1992.

[563] Allowances are also given in the form of relief for interest payments. Grants were introduced between 1966 and 1970; see, *inter alia*, Lazar [1966] BTR 179; White Paper, *Investment Incentives*, Cmnd 4516 (HMSO, 1970), §2; and, in a wider context, Sharpe (1979) 95 *LQR* 206. On discretionary element, see *British Oxygen Co Ltd v Minister of Technology* [1971] AC 610, [1970] 3 All ER 165.

[564] Devereux (1988) 9(1) *Fiscal Studies* 62.

[565] Feldstein and Summers (1979) 32 *National Tax Jo* 4.

6.12.4 Further Problems

Other issues remain.[566] Why should the allowances be on an historic cost basis with no allowance for inflation?[567] In a period without inflation there is no problem, since the replacement cost will equal the allowed cost—for an exactly equivalent asset. The issue is whether the purpose is to find the correct balance if the trade were to cease that day, or is to tackle the problem of financing a continuing trade. However, such a rise in cost base would also require adjustments to the balancing charges,[568] which is at present levied on purely paper gains. Again, why should the balancing charge be limited to recapturing the allowance already made? Why not extend it to the capital gain arising on disposal? Why should there be such different allowances for such different assets? At present, pooling is confined to plant and machinery, and its effect is close to permitting rollover relief, as in CGT. Why should there be no allowance for the depreciation of what, for many, is their most important capital asset—their own earning power?[569] Why should one not be able to write off the costs of one's training for a profession?[570] Again, why should the system take the form of a deferral of tax? In such form it is a long-term credit and therefore has no effect on reported profits; an immediate tax credit might be preferable.[571] To all these proposals there is one short reply, namely, that they make the mistake of supposing that the system has something to do with justice, equity and depreciation; it has not. Such proposals are best seen as (possibly expensive) tools of economic planning.

---

[566] See ideas discussed in HM Treasury, *Corporation Tax, op cit*, chs 11, 15.

[567] For a comparison of accelerated depreciation with inflation adjustments, see Feldstein (1981) 34 *National Tax Jo* 29.

[568] See Tucker Committee Report, Cmd 8189 (1951) §§102–115; Royal Commission on the Taxation of Profits and Income, *Final Report*, Cmd 9474 (1955), paras 350–62, and Morley, *Fiscal Implications of Inflation Accounting* (Institute for Fiscal Studies, 1974), ch 1.

[569] In 1915 excess profits duty was applied to trades but not to professions. McKenna, the Chancellor of the Exchequer, justified this on the ground that it would be impossible to devise a satisfactory datum line in the case of members of a profession who made their profits by the excessive expenditure of their capital, that is their energy, brain power and health.

[570] On human capital, see Beer [1987] BTR 392; and other articles cited in *Revenue Law*, §7.1.1.

[571] See discussions by Lindholm (1951) 4 *National Tax Jo* 180; Wiseman (1963) 16 *National Tax Jo* 36; and Bird (1963) 16 *National Tax Jo* 41.

7

Groups and Consortium Companies: General

7.1 Introduction

The UK tax system starts from the premise that each company is a separate taxpayer.[1] The effects of this premise are then modified by a number of special rules which apply either to groups or to consortia.

7.1.1 Groups

A group consists of a parent company and its subsidiaries which may, in turn, have their own subsidiaries. Broadly, a company is a subsidiary if the other company owns the relevant percentage of its ordinary share capital[2]—more than 50% (commonly called a 51% subsidiary), 75% or more, 90% or more and even 100%. A parent must be a company and not an individual. If P, an individual, owns all the shares in X Ltd and in Y Ltd, X and Y

---

[1] For an example of the basic principle of UK tax law that the tax system respects the separate existence of members of a corporate group, see *Gripple Ltd v Revenue and Customs Commissioners* [2010] EWHC 1609 (Ch), [2010] STC 2283, where staffing costs incurred in one company could not be used in another company for purposes of the R&D credit.

[2] CTA 2010, s 1154, ex TA 1988, s 838(1). On the meaning of ordinary share capital, see HMRC Brief 54/2007, 6 August 2007.

may be associated companies but they do not form a group. A group can exist only if there is more than one company; thus, if all but one of the members of a group leaves that group, the group ceases to exist and the survivor is no longer a member of a group.[3]

7.1.1.1 Ordinary Share Capital

Ordinary share capital is defined by excluding share capital the holders of which have a right to a dividend at a fixed rate and no other right to share in the profits of the company.[4] Thus, loan stock and non-participating preference shares are not treated as ordinary share capital unless convertible into, or giving an option to acquire, shares or securities carrying a right greater than that of a dividend at a fixed rate. Conversely, however, shares may be ordinary share capital even if they carry no voting rights.

Ownership of such capital must be beneficial,[5] but may be direct or indirect.[6] Indirect ownership is determined by multiplication. If A Ltd owns 80% of the ordinary share capital of B Ltd and B Ltd owns 70% of such share capital of C Ltd, A Ltd is taken to own 56% of C and so C has '51% subsidiary' status vis-à-vis A. If B Ltd had owned only 60% of C Ltd, A Ltd would have had a 48% share in C, and C would not have been a 51% subsidiary. If P Ltd owns 70% of Q Ltd and Q Ltd owns 30% of M Ltd, but P Ltd also owns 35% of M Ltd, P Ltd's ownership of M Ltd is a mixture of direct (35%) and indirect (21%), making M Ltd a 51% subsidiary of P Ltd.

In particular instances[7] the statute may provide that only share capital held as an investment and not as a trading asset may be included.[8] It may also be necessary to satisfy[9] these percentages not just in terms of the beneficial ownership of share capital, but also in terms of the economic reality, ie an entitlement to similar percentages of profits available for distribution and the division of assets available on winding up.

It is unclear how companies without share capital, eg a company incorporated by Royal Charter or limited by guarantee, can fit some of these rules.[10]

7.1.1.2 Residence

Statute might provide that a company must be resident in the UK, eg in the old rule that a company was to be regarded as a holding company of a trading group only if the majority of the subsidiaries were UK-resident trading companies.[11] In *ICI v Colmer*,[12] the taxpayer company claimed consortium relief by reference to an investment company which had

---

[3] *Dunlop International AG v Pardoe* [1999] STC 909 CA.

[4] CTA 2010, s 1118, ex TA 1988, s 832(1); a preference share with a fixed rate of dividend but a right to share in surplus assets on a winding up is ordinary share capital since the surplus assets are from profits of the company (*Tilcon Ltd v Holland* [1981] STC 365, (1981) 54 TC 464).

[5] See above §2.10 and CTA 1154(6), ex TA 1988, s 838(3). See also Statement of Practice SP 3/93.

[6] CTA 2010, s 1154(5), ex TA 1988, s 838(2).

[7] Eg CTA 151(3), ex TA 1988, s 413(5)(a).

[8] On which, see *Cooper v C & J Clark Ltd* [1982] STC 335, (1982) 54 TC 670.

[9] Other rules involving groups include CTA 2010, s 271(1), ex TA 1988, s 502(3), and see also TCGA 1992, s 140, Sch 2 (assets held on 6 April 1965).

[10] *Simon's Direct Tax Service*, para D2.621 and *Southshore Mutual Insurance Co v Blair* [1999] SRC (SCD) 296, where a company limited by guarantee was held not to have ordinary share capital for the purpose of being a 75% subsidiary. Some later statutes have attempted to address this issue—eg FA 2002, rewriting TCGA 1992, s 135(5).

[11] Ex TA 1988, s 413(5).

[12] Case C-264/96 [1998] All ER (EC) 585; [1998] STC 874; restriction ruled unlawful in so far as it did not take account of companies with seats in other Member States (answers implemented by the House of Lords at [1999] STC 1089).

23 trading subsidiaries. Both sides agreed that the claim would fail if only UK-resident companies could be counted for this purpose. The ECJ held that the restriction to UK-resident companies was in breach of EC Treaty law on freedom of establishment, and that companies with seats in other Member States should also be taken into account.[13]

In response to the decision in *Colmer*, FA 2000 changed radically the treatment of non-resident companies. So group relief (below at §7.6) may be claimed by a non-resident company which is a member of a group whether the company is resident or is carrying on a trade in the UK through a permanent establishment (PE).[14] In addition, two UK companies with a common non-resident parent may now form a group, whether or not the non-resident company has a branch trading in the UK. In consequence, any rules using the group relief definition of 'group' will also extend to take account of non-resident companies. There are also many changes to the rules for capital gains (see chapter eight below). There are also rules for recovering tax payable by a non-resident company from other group companies. The company paying the tax may not claim any relief in computing profits; however, it is given a right of indemnity against the defaulting company. These changes are noted in the text, and apply whether the non-resident is resident in the EU or elsewhere. The treatment of losses was not addressed in FA 2000; for new rules introduced in 2006, see below at §7.6.7.

However, it is also worth recalling now those rules which have not been widened to assist the non-resident PE. See also §2.9.2 above.

7.1.2 Consortia

Some—but not all[15]—of the group rules also apply to consortia of companies. These are to encourage and facilitate the ad hoc merger of a number of different corporate interests in a single common enterprise.[16] The different corporate interests (the consortium members) come together to finance a project which is developed through a company (the consortium company). Allowing the consortium company to pay interest or charges gross, or to pass the benefit of losses through to the members, is designed to help the members to pool resources and risks. The definition of a consortium varies, as will be seen in §7.6.4 below.

7.1.3 EU Law Associate Status

Two EU Directives use the term 'associate status'. The Parent–Subsidiary Directive of 1990[17] originally used a 25% test to determine such status, but this was reduced to 20% in 2003, to 15% from 1 January 2007 and to 10% from 1 January 2009.[18] The original version did not apparently require much change to UK law.[19]

---

[13] It is probably not enough simply to show that a majority of the companies had seats in the Member States—the courts may have regard to matters such as turnover (see Lord Nolan at *ICI v Colmer* [1996] STC 352, 361h) or some other measure to be determined.

[14] CTA 2010, ss 130–134, ex TA 1988, s 402(3A) and (3B), added by FA 2000, Sch 27, para 1.

[15] Eg the CGT rules discussed in ch 8 do not apply to consortia.

[16] *ICI v Colmer* [1996] STC 352, 358e, *per* Lord Nolan.

[17] EC Parent-Subsidiary Directive, 90/435/EEC of 23 July 1990.

[18] New para 1 substituted by Council Directive 2003/1123/EC, Art 1(3).

[19] F(No 2)A 1992, s 30 amended the collecting agent rules; on whether the UK was right to be so complacent, see Wijnen, *Survey of the Implementation of the EC Corporate Tax Directives* (IBFD, 1995), ch 28.

The second, the Interest and Royalties Directive of 2003, deals with payments of interest and royalties.[20] There are express provisions exempting interest and royalties from tax in the UK where the companies are 25% associates and the recipient is a company of another Member State.[21]

7.2   Choice of Structure—One Company or a Group?

If a company's trading activities are divided up between different companies, the premise of UK tax law is that each company is a separate entity with separate profits and therefore separate corporation tax liability. There is no simple charging of the group as a whole on its group profits—as there is in other countries which allow 'group reporting'. However, this premise is relaxed by the following rules. Special rules apply, say, to continuity treatment of loan relationships within groups, the ability of groups to pay corporation tax under self-assessment and the quarterly instalments on a group basis.

The decision whether to run a business through one company or through a group of companies depends upon many factors, not all concerned with taxation. It appears that, in practice, the activities of a single company will be regarded as one trade unless they are widely different. This has tax advantages, in that expenditure incurred for dual purposes is non-deductible unless those purposes are regarded as one trade;[22] the problem of the non-deductibility of pre-commencement and post-cessation expenses may also be avoided. Further, trade sales within the group will give rise to immediate profits, whereas in a single company profits will not accrue until the sale is made to an outsider. By concession the existence of separate companies is ignored for certain rules concerning directors.[23]

7.3   Intra-group Dividends—Group Income

A subsidiary, S, may wish to pass profit to its parent, P, by way of dividend. In the ACT era, ACT would be due unless the companies made a 'group income' election.[24] Today, intra-group dividends are treated in the same way as any other qualifying distributions and so are not subject to corporation tax in the hands of the recipient.[25] Even the term 'group income' has disappeared from the tax lexicon.[26]

---

[20] EC Interest and Royalties Directive, 2003/48/EC of 3 June 2003, implemented by FA 2004, ss 97–106.
[21] Terms defined FA 2004, ss 98(3), (4) and 103.
[22] See *Revenue Law*, §22.2.
[23] See ESC A4.
[24] TA 1988, s 247.
[25] CTA 2009, ss 931A *et seq*, ex TA 1988, s 208.
[26] TA 1988, s 13(7) was amended by FA 1998 to read 'franked investment income'. However, there are echoes in the shadow ACT regulations—Corporation Tax (Treatment of Unrelieved Surplus ACT) Regulations 1999 (SI 1999/358), reg 11(2)–(4).

7.3.1 The Parent–Subsidiary Directive

If S is resident in one country and P in another, S's state may require a withholding tax[27] to be charged on the dividend. The 1990 EC Parent–Subsidiary Directive[28] was designed to enable dividends to flow free of such taxes within groups where the groups straddle national boundaries within the European Community (now European Union or EU). The Directive bars a withholding tax where S, resident in one Member State, pays a dividend to P, a company resident in another Member State, provided P has the relevant minimum holding.

While normal UK tax law (prior to 2009) did not allow a non-resident to have a tax credit on a dividend, many treaties allow a partial credit subject to abatement (or withholding). A question arises whether this abatement is a withholding tax, and therefore prohibited by the Directive if paid between subsidiary and parent. The UK view that this practice is permitted under another part of the Directive[29] has been upheld by the ECJ.[30]

Under the Directive, P must have a minimum percentage of the capital, 15% on 1 January 2007 and 10% from 1 January 2009.[31] Member States may withhold this treatment unless the company maintains that holding for an uninterrupted period of at least two years. The ECJ has held that this allows the Member State to refuse P the benefit of the Directive during those two years, but that it is not permissible to refuse to repay the tax in respect of those two years once the period has expired.[32]

7.3.2 The Parent–Subsidiary Directive—Specific Issues

The Directive raises many other issues, including the following[33]:

(1) *Company residence*—the conditions for applicability include a requirement that each company should be a resident and subject to corporation tax in that State. Certain Luxembourg holding companies are not subject to (Luxembourg) corporation tax and therefore cannot use the Directive. Certain dual resident companies similarly fail to qualify if the country of second residence is outside the EU.
(2) *Percentage condition*—the percentage condition raises a further issue, ie whether the shares must be owned beneficially. Is the percentage condition simply a reference to 10% of issued share capital—in which case the issue of abnormal share capital might enable a company to use the Directive?[34]

---

[27] ACT was not—in UK eyes—a withholding tax on the dividend since it was a tax on the company. The reduction in the value of the tax credit to 10% as from 1999 weakened but did not destroy the UK argument: Gammie (1997) 25 *Intertax* 333, 339.

[28] Council Directive of 23 July 1990 90/435/EEC, EC L225/6, [1990] *Simon's Tax Intelligence* 749; see de Hosson (1990) 10 *Intertax* 414. Directive implemented in the UK by F(No 2)A 1992; on which, see McGregor [1992] BTR 131.

[29] Art 7(2); see also Inland Revenue, *EC Direct Tax Measures: a Consultative Document* (December 1991), 21.

[30] *IRC v Océ Van Der Grinten NV* [2003] STC 1248. The court separated the tax on the dividend from the treaty credit arrangement and held that the credit was not affected by Art 5(1) of the Directive at all as it was a fiscal instrument to prevent double taxation. The tax on the dividend *was* covered by Art 5(1) but was saved by Art 7(2).

[31] Para 1 as substituted by Council Directive 2003/1123/EC, Art 1(3).

[32] *Denkavit International BV v Bundesamt für Finanzen* [1996] STC 1445 (see ch 21 below).

[33] See Lurie, *Tolley's International Tax Planning*, 4th edn (Tolleys, 1999), ch 9.

[34] See also the invaluable IBFD survey by Wijnen, *op cit.*

7.4   Transfer Payments—Interest Payments
and Other Charges on Income

At one time TA 1988, sections 247 and 248 gave group companies the right to opt out of the normal rules requiring companies to withhold income tax (at 20%) when making payments of interest or other charges on income to another group company. As these rules were framed in terms of companies resident in the UK they were contrary to EU law.[35] The general rules requiring withholding were repealed in 2001 for payment where both companies were resident in the UK,[36] and so these special group rules were repealed from the same date.[37]

7.4.1   *Interest and Royalties Directive—25% Associates*

ITTOIA 2005 exempts from UK tax certain payments arising in the UK but made to a company of another Member State.[38] The company must be beneficially entitled to the income, and the payer and the payee must be 25% associates.[39] The person beneficially entitled must be an EU company, or its PE (other than a UK PE or PE outside the EU).[40] Where the payment is one of interest, as opposed to royalties, HMRC must have issued an exemption notice.[41] Where the payment is of royalties, the payer may make the payment without deducting tax so long as the payer has a reasonable belief that the recipient is entitled to the exemption. There are restrictions on the exemptions where there are special relationships, and there is a purpose-based anti-avoidance rule.[42]

The rule just discussed affects payments going from the UK to another EU Member State. Although the broad effect of the Interest and Royalties Directive is to exempt these types of income from tax—and so remove any duty or right to withhold tax—some Member States were given a transitional period during which they could continue to levy withholding tax. A second set of rules provides relief against UK tax by way of credit for the tax charged in the other Member States.[43]

7.5   Special Rules for Distributions: Assets at Undervalue

The transfer of an asset at undervalue is normally to be treated as a distribution. However, this does not apply when both transferor and recipient are resident in the UK and one is a 51% subsidiary of the other, or both are 51% subsidiaries of another resident company.[44]

---

[35] By extension from *ICI v Colmer* [1998] STC 874.
[36] Ex TA 1988, s 349B(1).
[37] FA 2001, s 85(5).
[38] For terms see Arts 1.2 and 3(a) of the EC Interest and Royalties Directive, 2003/48/EC.
[39] ITTOIA 2005, s 758(1)–(4), ex FA 2004, ss 98(3), 98(4) and 103.
[40] ITTOIA 2005, s 758(3), ex FA 2004, s 98(3).
[41] ITTOIA 2005, s 758(5), ex FA 2004, ss 98(4) and 95.
[42] ITTOIA 2005, ss 764 and 765 , ex FA 2004, ss 103 and 104.
[43] TIOPA 2010, Pt 3, ex FA 2004, ss 107–115.
[44] CTA 2010, s 1021(1), ex TA 1988, s 209(5).

In determining whether one company is a 51% subsidiary of the other, holdings, whether direct or indirect, do not qualify if a profit on the sale would be a trading receipt or if the company is non-resident.[45]

In other respects the definition of distribution is unchanged, save that a distribution made by one company out of its assets but in respect of shares or securities of another company in the same 90% group is treated as a distribution if all other conditions are satisfied.[46] This is primarily concerned to extend to groups another provision dealing with distribution by two or more companies to each other's members under an arrangement made between them.[47]

7.6   Group and Consortium Relief for Losses, etc

7.6.1 Basics

Group relief enables current trading losses, capital allowances, non-trading deficit on loan relationships, excess management expenses of investment companies and excess charges on income to be surrendered by one company (the surrendering company) to another (the claimant company), enabling the latter to put the other company's loss, etc, against its total profits.[48] Both companies must satisfy the group or consortium tests throughout their respective accounting period; however, they need not be members of the same group or consortium when the claim is made.[49] Relief is not available to a company which is a 'dual resident investing company'.[50] The self-assessment legislation contains rules for claiming this relief.[51] It often comes as a surprise to those from civil law backgrounds that a company can assign a loss to another group member in this way without the assignee company becoming liable for the debts of the assignor—but it is so. Under UK company law, groups of companies have the right to arrange affairs so as to isolate risk in subsidiaries.[52]

If company A makes a loss and surrenders that relief to company B, company A may insist upon receiving some payment. This will be particularly so if it is not a wholly-owned subsidiary so that there will be different minority interests as well as different creditors. If the amount paid is due under a legally enforceable agreement[53] and does not exceed the amount surrendered, the payment is ignored in computing the profits and losses of either company, and is treated neither as a distribution nor as a charge on income. This device is of particular use when, for example, a company with foreign income is already relieved from corporation tax by the foreign tax credit, or where the surrendering company is entitled to the reduced rate of 20% and the claimant is not.

---

[45] CTA 2010, s 1021(1)–(3), ex TA 1988, s 209(7).
[46] CTA 2010, s 1072(1),(2), ex TA 1988, s 254(3).
[47] CTA 2010, s 1112(1)–(3), ex TA 1988, s 254(8).
[48] CTA 2010, Pt 5, esp ss 99–109, ex TA 1988, s 402.
[49] *AW Chapman Ltd v Hennessey* [1982] STC 214, (1982) 55 TC 516.
[50] CTA 2010, s 109, ex TA 1988, s 404(1).
[51] FA 1998, Sch 18, paras 67–77. For modification to take account of non-resident companies, see FA 2000, Sch 27, para 11.
[52] *Adams v Cape Industries plc* [1990] Ch 433.
[53] *Haddock v Wilmot Breeden Ltd* [1975] STC 255, (1975) 50 TC 132.

7.6.2 The Group[54]

7.6.2.1 Basic Rule: Residence

Two companies are members of the same group for group relief purposes if one is a 75% subsidiary of the other or both are 75% subsidiaries of a third company. Today group relief may now be claimed or surrendered by a company which is a member of a group and either resident in the UK or carrying on a trade in the UK through a PE.[55] For periods not affected by FA 2000 the rules on group membership stated that only a body corporate resident in the UK qualified;[56] the status of this rule in the light of the EU's non-discrimination principles was not directly in issue in *ICI v Colmer*,[57] which was concerned with consortium relief, but it was clearly vulnerable. If *Colmer* applies, two UK-resident companies with a French parent should be able to pass losses to each other; whether they could pass losses to the French parent to set against some of the parent's UK income is a separate question.

The rules restricting group relief where a member of the group is a resident of a non-EU state were challenged in *FCE Bank plc v Revenue and Customs Commissioners*.[58] In this case, a loss-making UK-resident subsidiary (FL) of a US company (FM) sought to surrender losses to a profitable sister company (FC) also resident in the UK. HMRC rejected FC's claim for group relief on the grounds that the parent company was resident in the US. The First-Tier Tribunal allowed the appeal on the basis that the effect of the non-discrimination article in the 1975 UK/USA double taxation agreement was that group relief should be available between two UK-resident directly-held 75% subsidiaries of a US parent company in circumstances where it would be available if the parent company were UK-resident.

Trading. Any share capital owned directly or indirectly in a non-resident company and any share capital owned directly or indirectly must be ignored if a profit on sale would be a trading receipt of the direct owners.[59]

7.6.2.2 Anti-avoidance—Unreal Holdings, Arrangements and Options

Three sets of rules apply here:

(1) *Real holdings.* The parent must be entitled to not less than 75% of any profits available for distribution to equity holders of the subsidiary company, and to not less than 75% of any of its assets available for distribution to its equity holders on a winding up.[60] In determining this percentage, certain loans of a non-commercial nature are treated as equity,[61] and the court must have regard to any 'arrangements' which might affect those rights.[62] Rules determine the notional profit distribution and the assets

---

[54] CTA 2010, ss 150–153, ex TA 1988, s 413 and Sch 18.

[55] CTA 2010, s 112 and 136, ex TA 1988, s 402(3A) and (3B) added by FA 2000, Sch 27.

[56] Ex TA 1988, s 413(5).

[57] Case C-264/96 [1998] All ER (EC) 585; [1998] STC 874.

[58] [2010] UKFTT 136 (TC).

[59] CTA 2010, s 151(3), ex TA 1988, s 413(5)(a)–(c).

[60] CTA 2010, s 151(4), ex TA 1988, s 413(7).

[61] CTA 2010, ss 157 and 158, ex TA 1988, Sch 18, para 1. Sections 162 *et seq*, ex paras 1(5) *et seq*, define 'normal commercial loan' and treat certain non-recourse loans as commercial loans and not as equity. Interest payments on ratchet loans are treated as normal commercial loans; these are loans where the interest rate falls as business results improve or vice versa, ie are inversely related to the results of the business: CTA 2010, s 163(1), (2), ex TA 1988, Sch 18, para 1(5E) amended by FA 2000.

[62] CTA 2010, s 169–72, ex TA 1988, Sch 18, para 5.

available on a winding up.[63] Any limitation on the rights of equity holders is to be given effect if this would yield a lower percentage.[64] These provisions have received a narrow but purposive construction.[65] The purpose of these rules is to confine the passing of the reliefs, especially capital allowance, to parents which were such in commercial as well as legal terms at some time during the accounting period in which the loss arises.

(2) *Transfer arrangements—no temporary holdings.* It is also necessary, for similar reasons, to show that there are no arrangements in existence for transfer of control of the surrendering company without also transferring control of the claimant company.[66] Here, the term 'arrangements' is broadly construed.[67] However, the arrangement must be one by which control is or might be obtained. An arrangement subject to the consent of X is not in existence until X consents.[68] Without such a rule an outside company could buy participation preference shares to establish 75% control, and later the shares would be redeemed or sold back to the parent; in this way the loss might be sold to an outsider. Where arrangements are in force, the effect of these provisions is to bar relief for those losses attributable to the period during which the arrangements subsisted.[69] The Revenue do not view the offer of 'first refusal' as sufficient to trigger these rules.[70]

(3) *Options.* As originally enacted, these provisions were held not to reach the alteration of rights which might follow from the exercise of an option to acquire or dispose of shares, since the option did not affect the nature of the rights attached to the shares but only the ownership of those shares.[71] This decision is now reversed by statute. The essence of the new rules is that in order to calculate the extent of the equity holder's entitlement to profits or assets, the entitlements must be recalculated on the basis that the option has been exercised. The equity holder is then treated as being entitled only to the lowest percentage.[72]

The legislation makes it clear that each of the tests is to be applied to the original sets of rights (ie percentage of profits or assets on winding up) independently and cumulatively, with only the lowest percentages used.[73] This is then applied to situations in which there are both fixed-element rights and variable rights.[74] All 'relevant preference shares'

---

[63] CTA 2010, ss 165, 166, ex TA 1988, Sch 18, paras 2, 3.

[64] CTA 2010, ss 169–170, ex TA 1988, Sch 18, para 4.

[65] *J Sainsbury plc v O'Connor* [1991] STC 318, (1991) 64 TC 208 CA.

[66] CTA 2010, ss 154–156, ex TA 1988, s 410(1)–(6). For this purpose, members of a consortium are not held to be 'acting together' to control a company (s 410(5) as amended by FA 1997, s 68); and see Revenue Interpretation RI 160).

[67] *Pilkington Bros Ltd v IRC* [1982] STC 103; see notes by Wyatt [1982] BTR 244 and [1981] BTR 241. See also *Irving v Tesco Stores (Holdings) Ltd* [1982] STC 881.

[68] *Scottish and Universal Newspapers Ltd v Fisher* [1996] STC (SCD) 311.

[69] *Shepherd v Law Land plc* [1990] STC 795, (1990) 63 TC 692, rejecting the Revenue view that relief was barred for all the losses arising in the accounting period during part of which the arrangements subsisted.

[70] On scope of arrangements, see Statement of Practice SP 3/93.

[71] *J Sainsbury plc v O'Connor* [1991] STC 318, (1991) 64 TC 208 CA.

[72] CTA 2010, ss 173, 174, ex TA 1988, Sch 18, para 5B, added by F(No 2)A 1992; Inland Revenue Press Release, 29 January 1992, [1992] *Simon's Tax Intelligence* 90, and Inland Revenue Press Release, 15 November 1991, [1991] *Simon's Tax Intelligence* 1042.

[73] CTA 2010, s 174(1), ex TA 1988, Sch 18, para 5B(9), added by F(No 2)A 1992, Sch 6, para 6.

[74] CTA 2010, s 175, ex TA 1988, Sch 18, para 5A, replacing the old para 5(5).

will be ignored. If the relevant shares carry a right to a dividend they must meet various conditions, including one relating to a reasonable commercial return.

7.6.2.3 Overlapping Accounting Periods

The relief allows one company to use the losses sustained by the other in the overlapping accounting period.[75] If both companies have the same accounting period, the whole loss is available for offset, assuming, of course, that they fulfil all the other conditions for group membership at that time.[76] Conversely, when the company joins or leaves the group, the profits of the relevant accounting periods must be apportioned to ensure that only losses of post-entry or pre-departure periods are used. To carry out this process the legislation creates the concepts of the 'surrenderable amount' of the loss and the 'unrelieved part of the profits'. The amount of the loss which may be set off against the profits of the claimant is the lesser of two sums—one is the unused part of the surrenderable amount for the overlapping period, and the other is the unrelieved part of the claimant's profits for the period. The balance of the loss may either be set off against profits of other group companies, or be rolled forward under the rule set out below.[77] In computing the first of these sums, account must be taken of any previous surrenders which have already been made during that period; in computing the second sum, account must be taken of any previous group relief claims.

A time basis is used to allocate these amounts to different parts of an accounting period unless that would be unjust or unreasonable in relation to any person, in which case a just and reasonable basis is used, but only to the extent necessary to avoid injustice and unreasonableness.[78] This last formulation is a considerable tightening in comparison with the old law and creates its own problems, eg if what would be required to be just to one party would create injustice for another; presumably the time apportionment applies.

7.6.3 *Groups and Consortia: Link Companies*

Where a consortium member is itself a member of a group, it is known as a 'link' company.[79] The consortium relief may flow through the link company to the member's own group.[80] The usual rules on group membership for the appropriate accounting periods apply:[81] the link may not increase the amount of relief.[82] It is also possible to surrender part of the available relief to a group company and part to a consortium company, subject to restrictions on the amount available for relief.[83]

---

[75] CTA 2010, ss 138–42, ex TA 1988, s 403A, added by F(No 2)A 1997, Sch 7 and replacing older rules; see Inland Revenue Press Release, 2 July 1997, para 6, [1997] *Simon's Tax Intelligence* 912.
[76] CTA 2010, s 99–106, 137, ex TA 1988, s 403(1), (8)–(10).
[77] CTA 2010, ss 99–105, 147, ex TA 1988, s 403(2), 403ZA–403ZE.
[78] CTA 2010, ss 139–141, ex TA 1988, s 403B, replacing s 408.
[79] CTA 2010, s 133(1),(2), ex TA 1988, s 406(1).
[80] CTA 2010, ss 133, 142, 145–49 , ex TA 1988, s 406.
[81] CTA 2010, ss 133(1), (3), (4), 145(2), 147(2), 148(2), 149(2), ex TA 1988, s 406(2), (9).
[82] CTA 2010, ss 146(2), (3), (8) and 146(5)–(8), ex TA 1988, s 406(4), (8).
[83] CTA 2010, ss 148, 149, ex TA 1988, ss 405, 411(9).

7.6.4 *Consortium Relief*

Relief may also be claimed by members of a consortium for losses incurred by companies owned by the consortium.[84] However, a member's right to use the loss sustained by the consortium company is limited to that proportion of the loss which corresponds to the member's interest.[85] This was expanded in the new form of the relief introduced in 2000. The maximum amount available for consortium relief depends on the 'relevant fraction'. This relates to the interest which the member has in the consortium, and is the lowest of ordinary share capital, profits available for distribution and on any distribution of assets. Fluctuating percentages are dealt with by averaging. Where the claimant company is a member of the consortium this fraction is applied to the company's surrenderable amount for the overlapping period.[86] A similar fraction is applied where the surrendering company is a member of the consortium.[87]

A consortium owns a company if 75% of the ordinary share capital of that company is directly and beneficially owned between the consortium members, each owning at least 5%.[88] FA 2000 amended the definition of 'consortium' so that a non-resident company with a UK PE can be a member.[89] For periods unaffected by FA 2000 and subject to the requirements of EU law as stated in *ICI v Colmer*,[90] all the companies had to be resident in the UK.[91] Like group relief, consortium relief is strictly controlled in the case of overlapping accounting periods.[92]

Group relief may be claimed by members of a consortium in three situations:[93]

(1) the surrendering company is owned by the consortium and is not a 75% subsidiary of any company but is a trading company;
(2) the surrendering company is a 90% subsidiary of a holding company which is owned by the consortium and is not a 75% subsidiary of any other company but is a trading company; and
(3) the surrendering company is a holding company which is owned by the consortium and is not a 75% subsidiary of any company.

The relief is claimed by the member of the consortium, not by the holding company. At one time the claim was barred if the member company's share in the consortium company in that company's accounting period was nil.[94] Since a company is only a consortium

---

[84] CTA 2010, ss 132, 133, 153, ex TA 1988, s 402(3).

[85] CTA 2010, s 144, ex TA 1988, s 403C(3) replacing s 403(9).

[86] CTA 2010, ss 143, 144, ex TA 1988, s 403C(2) added by FA 2000, s 100 which also repeals s 413(8), (9).

[87] CTA 2010, s 144, ex TA 1988, s 403C(3) added by FA 2000, s 100.

[88] CTA 2010, s 153(1)–(3), ex TA 1988, s 413(6).

[89] FA 2000, Sch 27, para 32, repealing TA 1988, s 413(5).

[90] Case C-264/96 [1998] All ER (EC) 585; [1998] STC 874.

[91] Thus, before FA 2000 the membership of one non-resident company was fatal to group relief for the other members. In such circumstances assets are commonly owned by the non-resident company and leased by the company owned by the consortium—of which, of course, the non-resident was not a member. Whereas a group of resident companies within a larger group may form a group on its own, this is not open to a consortium.

[92] CTA 2010, ss 143–144, ex TA 1988, s 403C.

[93] CTA 2010, s 153, ex TA 1988, s 402(3); the terms are defined in s 185 (ex s 413(3)(b), (c)).

[94] CTA 2010, ss 132(4), (5) and 133(3), (4), ex TA 1988, s 402(4) and FA 2000, s 100(3)(a).

company if the members have at least a 5% holding, it was not clear how this provision was meant to operate, and it was repealed with retroactive effect by FA 2000.[95]

Relief within a consortium may pass in either direction,[96] but not between the members of the consortium themselves. As already seen, each member may claim only that part of the loss which is proportionate to its share in the consortium.[97] Where a member surrenders downwards to a trading company, that amount may be set only against a similar proportion of the trading company's profits. There is no surrender to the intermediate holding company, but that company may claim group relief proper. There is no objection to finding a group within a group or a group within a consortium.

In response to *Philips Electronics UK Ltd v HMRC*,[98] F(No 3)A 2010, Schedule 6 replaced the requirement to be UK resident for consortium relief with the requirement that the link company be UK resident or established in the EEA. New section 134A of CTA 2010 describes when a company is established in the EEA. Where the link company is not UK resident, it must be a member of the same group of companies as the other group company without the involvement of a company that is not established in the EEA. CTA 2010, sections 143 and 144—which provide for limitation of the relief by reference to the extent of the claimant company's interest in the surrendering company (and vice versa)—are amended. Schedule 6 also inserted new sections 146A and 146B into CTA 2010, which provide additional rules as to when a trading company is owned by a consortium so that consortium relief may be available.

7.6.5 The Sums Qualifying for Relief [99]

The following may be surrendered to the claimant company and set against total profits of the claimant company for its overlapping accounting period:

(1) trading losses[100]—the trading losses of a consortium-owned company must, as far as possible, be set off against the company's other profits of the same accounting period, and only the balance is available for set off against the profits of consortium member companies;[101]

(2) minor capital allowances[102]—these allowances attract relief through the discharge of tax rather than being treated as a trading expense (see above at §6.1);

(3) any non-trading deficit on loan relationships;[103]

(4) non-trading losses on intangible fixed assets;[104]

---

[95] CTA 2010, s 153(1), ex TA 1988, s 413(6)(a); presumably the remaining member companies can meet the consortium conditions on their own, but this still leaves the problem of a company with, say, a 3% stake.

[96] CTA 2010, ss 132(2), (3), 133(1), (2), 153(1), (3), ex TA 1988, s 402(3); a surrender downwards may affect that company's ability to surrender further losses within its group.

[97] CTA 2010, s 144(2)–(4), ex TA 1988, s 403C(3).

[98] [2009] UKFTT 226 (TC).

[99] This formulation is used because of the words of Lord Hoffmann in *Taylor v MEPC Holdings* [2004] STC 123, para 19.

[100] CTA 2010, s 100, ex TA 1988, s 403(1), as amended by FA 1988, Sch 5, para 29.

[101] CTA 2010, ss 143–144, ex TA 1988, s 403C.

[102] CTA 2010, s 101, ex TA 1988, s 403(1)(a), 403ZB.

[103] CTA 2010, s 99, ex TA 1988, ss 83(2), 403ZC.

[104] CTA 2010, s 104.

(5)   UK property business (ex Schedule A) losses;[105]
(6)   excess management expenses;[106]
(7)   qualifying charitable donations.[107]

Reliefs (1)–(3) may be surrendered even if the surrendering company has other profits for that period against which it might set them.[108] Items (4)–(6) may be surrendered only to the extent that they exceed the surrendering company's gross profits for the period, and are to be taken in the order (4), (5) and (6).[109] This means, for example, that if charges are carried forward from a previous period, they cannot be used to free current reliefs for grouping; such charges may therefore become locked into the company. A problem has arisen over these charges, since the Revenue sometimes argue that excess charges may be surrendered only if incurred wholly and exclusively for the purpose of the trade of the surrendering company. On this reasoning, no relief could be given where a loan is raised to finance the acquisition of a subsidiary; there seems to be nothing in the group relief rules to justify this approach. Relief for items (4)–(6) may be permanently lost if the company's income bears only foreign, as opposed to UK, tax since none may be rolled forward.

The relief, if claimed, is taken as first exhausting profits of the accounting period in which it is claimed in priority to other reliefs that may be brought back into that period from future periods.[110]

7.6.6 International Aspects

Further rules govern the group relief rules applicable to the UK PE of a non-resident company and the overseas PE of a UK company. These apply to accounting periods ending on or after 1 April 2000.[111]

The non-resident company with the UK PE may only surrender amounts which:

(1)   are attributable to activities within the charge to the UK corporation tax;
(2)   are not exempt from corporation tax by virtue of any double taxation arrangement; and
(3)   are not relievable, in any period, against non-UK profits of any person for the purposes of any foreign tax.[112]

'Non-UK profits' are amounts on which a person is charged to foreign tax but which are not chargeable to UK corporation tax. The purpose behind rule (3), which is supplemented

---

[105] CTA 2010, s 102, ex TA 1988, s 403(1)(b).
[106] CTA 2010, s 103. See below at §23.2.
[107] CTA 2010, Pt 6.
[108] CTA 2010, s 99(3), ex TA 1988, s 403(2).
[109] CTA 2010, s 99(4), 105(1)–(4), ex TA 1988, s 403(3).
[110] CTA 2010, s 137(4)–(6), ex TA 1988, s 407. Terminal loss relief may be given only against trading income, whereas group relief may be given against total profits—hence, group relief should be claimed against non-trading income and chargeable gains if terminal loss relief is foreseen.
[111] For more precise transitional rules, see FA 2000, Sch 27, para 6.
[112] CTA 2010, ss 108(1)–(3), 140(8), ex TA 1988, s 403D(2), (3).

by a number of detailed rules,[113] is to make losses relievable against profits arising in the place where the company is resident rather than in the UK.

In the converse case of the foreign branch of the UK-resident company, restrictive rules apply to the amounts available for surrender by a UK-resident company where the loss is attributable to an overseas PE and any part of it is relievable, in any period, against non-UK profits of another person for the purposes of any foreign tax.[114] A loss attributable to an overseas PE is the amount which would be available for surrender by the company if that amount were computed only by reference to the overseas PE.[115]

Where deductibility under the foreign law depends on deductibility in the UK, it is treated as deductible if and only if the company resident in the UK is also treated as resident in the relevant foreign territory.[116] The result of this is that the country of residence (the UK) has the primary responsibility for relieving the loss except in the case of dual residence.

7.6.7 Legislation on EEA Losses Post-Marks & Spencer

In the latest development in the decade-long *Marks & Spencer* group relief litigation (see §21.3.4 below), the Court of Appeal has upheld the decision of the Upper Tribunal in favour of the taxpayer on the issue of availability of group relief in respect of losses of its German and Belgium subsidiaries, and also on the method of quantifying such relief.[117] HMRC are likely to appeal to the Supreme Court.

In addition, in response to the decision of the ECJ in *Marks & Spencer*,[118] FA 2006 inserted new rules for relief where the surrendering company is not resident in the UK.[119] The conditions to be satisfied by such losses are contained in CTA 2010, sections 112 and 113 (ex TA 1988, section 403F and Schedule 18A). These rules have effect as from 1 April 2006 and allow a claim if the company is resident in an EEA territory, or not so resident but carries on a trade there through a PE. Claims are made under the new FA 1998, Schedule 18, paragraph 77A. This is backed up by an anti-avoidance rule in CTA 2010, section 127 (ex TA 1988, section 403G), which has effect from 20 February 2006 and bans losses claimed as a result of relevant arrangements, ie arrangements where the main purpose—or one of the main purposes—was to secure that the amount would qualify for group relief. On commencement, see also FA 2006, Schedule 1, paragraph 9.

The loss must meet four conditions:

(1)   an equivalence condition—the loss must be equivalent to one for which relief is given to companies resident in the UK (CTA 2010, section 114);

(2)   an EEA tax loss condition—where the company is resident in an EEA territory, section 115 provides that there must be a loss in the overseas territory which must

---

[113] CTA 2010, ss 107(7)–(9), 108(3), ex TA 1988, s 403D(4)–(6).

[114] CTA 2010, s 106(1), (2), (5), ex TA 1988, s 403E(1), (2).

[115] CTA 2010, s 106(3), (4); this is determined using the same rules as those in ss 107–108 (ex 403D) when finding the loss of a UK branch of a non-resident company, ex s 403E(4), (5).

[116] CTA 2010, s 106(6), (7), ex TA 1988, s 403E(8).

[117] [2011] EWCA Civ 1156.

[118] Case C-446/03 *Marks & Spencer v Halsey* [2006] STC 237.

[119] CTA 2010, ss 112, 113,127, and Sch 2, ex TA 1988, ss 403F, 403G and Sch 18A, inserted by FA 2006, s 27 and Sch 1; for analysis, see Cussons [2006] BTR 497.

not be attributable to a UK PE of the company. Where the company is not so resident, section 116 applies; the loss must arise in the overseas territory and the loss must not relate to activities outside the UK tax net by reason of a double tax treaty;

(3)   qualifying loss condition—under section 117, the loss is limited to an amount which cannot be given relief in the EEA and for which relief has not been given in any territory outside the UK; these rules are amplified in sections 11–120;

(4)   lastly, there is a precedence condition—relief may be given under these rules only if it cannot be given in a qualifying territory (section 121).

CTA 2010, sections 122–126 contain rules on the assumptions to be made when the UK rules are applied to the non-resident company and how the 'EEA amount' of the loss is determined.

Cussons has pointed out that this legislation concentrates on the fact situation in *Marks & Spencer* and does not go as far as it might. Thus it does not deal with 'sideways' cross-border relief claimed by a profitable subsidiary of an EU non-UK parent with a loss-making EU (non-UK) sister subsidiary of a non-UK parent.[120]

7.7   Transfer of Company Tax Refund under Self-assessment

The rate of interest charged on unpaid tax is distinct from that used for repayment supplement. Where one company in a group, A, has a duty to pay unpaid tax and another, B, has a right to a tax repayment, the companies may merge the duty and the right, and so avoid letting the Revenue get the benefit of the difference in interest rates.[121] A and B must share the same accounting period for the period in respect of which the repayment claim is being surrendered, and must be members of the same group from the start of the accounting period for which the claim is made until the date of the surrender notice.[122] Any sums paid in exchange for the surrender are ignored, provided they do not exceed the amount of the refund in question—they are neither taxable receipts of the surrendering company nor deductible items for the claimant company.[123] The definition of 'group' is the same as 'group' relief (see above at §7.6.2).[124] The rules apply not only to normal corporation tax liabilities but also to over—and under—payments under the quarterly instalment payments regime. A company entitled to a refund[125] may prefer to transfer the benefit of that overpayment to another group company.[126]

---

[120] Cussons [2006] BTR 497.

[121] CTA 2010, ss 963–966, ex FA 1989, s 102.

[122] CTA 2010, ss 963(1)–(5), ex FA 1989, s 102(1)–(2), (4). Provisions ensure that the interest rules apply equally to companies in the group as they apply to single companies (ex s 102(4A), added by FA 1993, Sch 14, para 11).

[123] CTA 2010, s 966(1), (2), ex FA 1989, s 102(7); this is similar to payments for group relief under CTA 2010, s 183(1), (2), ex TA 1988, s 402(6).

[124] CTA 2010, s 963(5), ex FA 1989, s 102(8).

[125] Corporation Tax (Instalment Payments) Regulations 1998 (SI 1998/3175), reg 6.

[126] *Ibid*, reg 9.

7.8   Transfer of Loans

Where a loan is transferred between companies in a 75% group, the basic provision is that the transfer is not treated as giving rise to any charge or allowance on either the transferor or the transferee.[127] The transferee company, following the transfer, becomes entitled to any debits and credits arising thereafter which are not related to the transfer. This treatment extends to a 'related transaction'[128] between two group companies and to any series of transactions, where two companies were members of the same group at some time during the course of the series of transactions. The treatment applies where there is an effective transfer by novation. Thus, the release of the former borrower does not cause a taxable receipt in the hands of that company.

7.9   Group Financing Costs—The Worldwide Debt Cap

The worldwide debt cap applies to accounting periods beginning on or after 1 January 2010, and the rules are found in TIOPA 2010, Part 7, sections 260 *et seq*. The legislation introducing the cap—FA 2009, section 35 and Schedule 15—was altered considerably during the passage of the Finance Bill; the changes are explained in HMRC Technical Note, 8 April 2009.[129]

The purpose of the worldwide debt cap is to restrict the tax deduction in the UK of finance expenses of groups of companies. TIOPA 2010, section 261 directs that the rules apply if the UK net debt (see sections 262–263) exceeds 75% of the worldwide gross debt (section 264); the figure of 75% may be changed by statutory instrument. Subject to this 75% threshold, the system limits the aggregate UK tax deduction for the UK members of a group of companies that have net finance expenses to the consolidated group's finance expense. The disallowance is laid down by section 274. The restriction is calculated by comparing the UK measure of net finance expenses with the worldwide measure of the groups finance expense. More technically, section 274 asks whether (a) the tested expense amount, defined in Chapter 8 (sections 329–331), exceeds (b) the available amount, defined in Chapter 9 (sections 332–336). If so, the excess is disallowed. Sections 275–285 set out the procedure for making a report detailing the allocation of the disallowed amount to one or more UK group companies.

Chapter 4 deals with the group's financing income amounts. These give rise to exemption from corporation tax if the group has had finance expenses which have been disallowed; further rules deal with the allocation of the exemptions among the companies. Chapter 5 deals with various EEA matters where financing income is received from certain EEA countries. Chapter 6 contains various anti-avoidance rules. Chapter 7 contains the key definitions of the financing expenses of a company, the financing income amounts of

---

[127] CTA 2009, ss 335–347, ex FA 1996, Sch 9, para 12, as much amended.
[128] CTA 2009, ss 293, 304, 307, 329, ex FA 1996, s 84.
[129] The detail of the rules are beyond the scope of this book; interested readers are referred to Richards [2009] BTR 541.

a company, and Group Treasury companies. There follow special rules granting conditional exclusions for Real Estate Investment Trusts, companies with oil extraction activities, intra-group short-term finance, short-term loan relationships, stranded deficits and stranded management expenses; there are exemptions for amounts paid to charities and other bodies. The exclusion for financial services is in Chapter 2.

Further changes have been made to the operation of the worldwide debt cap since its introduction.[130]

---

[130] See Sch 5 to F(No 3)A 2010 for the details, and analysis by Ball [2011] BTR 51. See also FA 2012, Sch 5.

8

Control, Groups and Consortium Companies: Capital Gains

8.1   The Group

8.1.1 General: 75% Test

TCGA 1992 contains a number of provisions for groups. A group comprises a principal company and all its 75% subsidiaries, including 75% subsidiaries of those subsidiaries and so on.[1] The 75% test is applied simply to the beneficial ownership[2] of shares; unlike group income reliefs, this test ignores the presence of shares held as trading stock.

This is one more of those areas in which, in response to the decision in *Colmer* (see §7.1.1.2), FA 2000 changed radically the treatment of non-resident companies. For disposals before 1 April 2000, the definition of a 'group' meant that the group could consist only of companies resident in the UK.[3] For disposals on or after that date the definition of

---

[1] TCGA 1992, s 170(2).
[2] See above at §2.10.
[3] TCGA 1992, s 170(2).

group is changed,[4] so that a non-resident company may be a group member; in addition, a number of detailed rule changes mean that transfer by or to a non-resident company may qualify for special tax-neutral treatment, provided the transfer concerns a UK PE. The key to tax-neutral treatment is no longer residence but chargeability to UK tax. Merger with one of the new SEs resident in another Member State may get similar treatment.[5]

It is expressly provided that the winding up of a company in the group does not result in either that company or any other company in the group being treated as ceasing to be a member of the group.[6] The mere passing of a winding-up resolution or order is not sufficient to end group membership.[7] Further, the group remains the same group provided the same company remains the principal company. If the principal company becomes a 75% subsidiary of another company, the group is regarded as expanded rather than ended and refounded.

8.1.2 *Bridge Companies and the 51% Effective Subsidiary Test*

A subsidiary which is a 75% subsidiary on the first test may be a member of a group only if it is also an 'effective' 51% subsidiary.[8] A company is an effective 51% subsidiary only if the parent is beneficially entitled to more than 50% of any profits available for distribution or of any assets on a winding up.[9] Further, a company is a 'principal company' only if it is at the head of the corporate chain. Thus, a company cannot be a principal company if it is a 75% subsidiary of another company;[10] however, a company prevented from being part of a group because it is not an effective 51% subsidiary (but is a 75% subsidiary) may be a principal company.[11]

To reinforce this policy it is provided that a company may not be a member of more than one group. To carry this policy through, the legislation contains a descending order of tests.[12] To prevent a charge from arising unexpectedly as a result of this change where a principal company subsequently becomes a 75% subsidiary of another company, thereby bringing two groups together, the two are regarded as being the same group for the purposes of determining whether there has been a transfer of an asset within the group (TCGA 1992, section 171) and whether a company has ceased to be a member of another group (section 179).[13] Thus, a charge under section 179 is not triggered simply by such an event.

The 51% test was designed to counter the use of 'bridge' companies.[14] These were companies with special classes of share which enabled the commercial control of companies to pass to a company outside the group, while allowing the company to remain within

---

[4] TCGA 1992, s 170, as amended by FA 2000, Sch 29, para 1; for transitional provision, see Sch 29, para 46.
[5] TCGA 1992, s 170(10A) added by F(No 2)A 2005, s 61.
[6] TCGA 1992, s 170(12).
[7] TCGA 1992, s 170(11).
[8] TCGA 1992, s 170(3).
[9] TCGA 1992, s 170(7); CTA 2010, Pt 5, Ch 6 (ex TA 1988, Sch 18, etc) applies here (s 170(8)).
[10] TCGA 1992, s 170(4).
[11] TCGA 1992, s 170(5).
[12] TCGA 1992, s 170(6).
[13] TCGA 1992, s 170(11).
[14] There is also a consequential change for IHT under IHTA 1984, s 97. These rules are further backed up by a cross-reference to CTA 2010, Pt 5, Ch 6 (ex TA 1988, Sch 18).

the group structure for TCGA 1992 purposes and so avoiding the triggering of charges that would otherwise arise on the company ceasing to be a member of the group.[15]

8.1.3 Control

It has become common for rules, sometimes of an anti-avoidance character, to be enacted which apply (a) when a company joins a group of companies, (b) when it ceases to be a member of the group, or (c) when the company becomes subject to different control. Rules introduced in 2006 are typical.[16] A company becomes subject to different control in three situations. The first is where a person (P) has control of the company (C) at that time (whether alone or together with one or more others) and P did not previously have control of C. The second is where P has control of the company at that time together with one or more others and P previously had control of the company alone. The third is where P ceases to have control of the company at that time (whether having control alone or together with one or more others).

The general rule is subject to the following exceptions:

(1)   A company does not become subject to different control in any case where it joins a group of companies and the case is the excepted case mentioned at §8.1.2 above.
(2)   A company ('the subsidiary') does not become subject to different control at any time in any case where:
    (a)   immediately before that time the subsidiary is the 75% subsidiary of another company; and
    (b)   (although there is a change in the direct ownership of the subsidiary) that other company continues immediately after that time to own it as a 75% subsidiary.

8.2   Intra-group Transfers of Capital Assets

8.2.1 Tax Neutrality: TCGA 1992, Section 171

The transfer of a chargeable asset between two members of a group takes place at such figure as ensures that there is neither a chargeable gain nor an allowable loss.[17] The effect is to postpone any capital gains liability until the asset is disposed of outside the group. This is a matter of law, not of election, and overrides the normal rule that bargains otherwise than at arm's length are to be treated as taking place at market value.[18] A nice question arises if one company surrenders a lease of land to another group member, since it may be argued that the lease ends and the landlord company acquires no asset at all.[19]

---

[15] [1989] *Simon's Tax Intelligence* 222; HC Official Report, Standing Committee G (1989), col 597.
[16] TCGA 1992, s 184C(6)–(9), added by FA 2006, s 70.
[17] TCGA 1992, s 171.
[18] TCGA 1992, s 17; s 171 applies 'notwithstanding any provision in CGTA fixing the amount of the considera-tion deemed to be received'. It might be argued that if a sale takes place at market value, s 171 should not apply as there is nothing 'deemed' about the consideration; however, this seems unlikely to succeed.
[19] See Law Society, *Revenue Law Reform Proposals* (1991) *Simon's Tax Intelligence* 1069.

The companies must be members of the same group, and either both must be resident in the UK or, if either or both are non-resident, the asset must be subject to charge to corporation tax, ie within TCGA 1992, section 10.[20]

8.2.1.1 Exceptions

The general rule in TCGA 1992, section 171(1) is excluded in certain situations by further rules in section 171; what these have in common is that value is being received by one company but the capital gains system, for reasons of its own, treats the receipt as being in exchange for an asset. The first situation is where a debt is disposed of by one group member to another and the debt is disposed of by being satisfied in whole or in part.

The second is where redeemable shares are disposed of on redemption. Thus, a gain on redemption will be taxable notwithstanding that there is a disposal of the shares in exchange for the consideration received on redemption.

The third is a disposal by or to an investment trust, venture capital trust, qualifying friendly society, dual resident investing company, a company which is, or is a member of, a UK REIT,[21] or to a group company which is or will become exempt from tax on its gains, such as an investment trust or venture capital trust.[22]

The fourth is the deemed disposal of shares in a company on receipt of a capital distribution within TCGA 1992, section 122; there will still be a disposal by the company making the capital distribution and this may fall within section 171.[23]

Where the asset is disposed of by destruction and compensation is payable, the disposal is deemed to be to the person who ultimately bears the burden of paying the compensation money, eg an insurance company.[24]

Fifthly, tax-neutral treatment does not apply to a disposal by a compay in fulfillment of its obligations under an option granted to another company at a time when the two companies were not members of the same group.[25]

8.2.1.2 Deemed Disposals and No Disposals

Section 171 applies whether there is an actual disposal or a deemed disposal and acquisition. However, it is now provided that the principle does not apply where the statute directs that there is neither a disposal nor an acquisition, as on a corporate reorganisation.[26]

8.2.1.3 Liquidation, etc

Section 171's postponement rules do not apply to transfers between a subsidiary and a parent in liquidation since, once liquidation of the parent has begun, the shares in the

---

[20] TCGA 1992, s 171(1A), added by FA 2000, Sch 29, para 2; on commencement, see Sch 29, para 6.
[21] TCGA 1992, s 171(2)(c)-(d)(a).
[22] TCGA 1992, s 101A-101C, inserted by FA 1998, ss 131–133.
[23] *Innocent v Whaddon Estates Ltd* [1982] STC 115, (1982) 55 TC 476, dicussed in the Revenue CGT manual CGT45320.
[24] TCGA 1992, s 171(4).
[25] TCGA 1992, s 171(2)(db), added by FA 2007, Sch 5, para 10.
[26] TCGA 1992, s 171(3): the corporate reorganisation provisions are ss 127, 135 (see *Revenue Law*, §41.5). This provision reverses *Westcott v Woolcombers Ltd* [1986] STC 182, 60 TC 575; on which, see London [1986] BTR 117; see also *NAP Holdings UK Ltd v Whittles* [1994] STC 979, 67 TC 166, HL.

subsidiary are not held by the parent beneficially but on trust for its own members.[27] The effect of a voluntary winding up is less clear.[28] Distributions by a subsidiary in liquidation are similarly taxed immediately. These problems may be overcome by arranging for transfers and distributions by or to the parent before liquidation.

8.2.2 Sink Companies and Capital Losses

Since there was no group relief for capital losses until 2000, it was common to use one company, known as a 'sink' company because of the number of assets put into it, to make all disposals of all chargeable assets outside the group. This ensured that allowable losses and chargeable gains arose in the same company and so were available for set off. Legislation was passed to counter bringing pre-entry losses into the group, ie by acquiring companies which had assets with unrealised losses (TCGA 1992, Schedule 7A; see below at §8.2.3) and a related scheme concerning post-entry gains (Schedule 7AA, now superseded by other provisions; see below at §8.2.4). The Revenue view was that it was unlikely that the new approach in *Ramsay*[29] could have been used to counter this use of sink companies 'where losses were a relatively insubstantial element in the acquisition, as evidenced by the circumstances in which they were utilised and the commerciality of the circumstances surrounding the acquisition'.[30] This cautious view of the applicability of the new approach to intra-group transfers was confirmed by the decision of Vinelott J in *Shepherd v Lyntress Ltd*.[31]

The legislature finally realised the futility of its refusal to allow relief for capital losses in 2000, when TCGA 1992, section 171A was introduced. Under this rule, whenever A, one company in a group, disposes of an asset to C, a person who is not a member of the group, the disposal may be treated as made by another group member, B.[32] C may use the incidental costs incurred by A.[33] Under the sink practice, A would have transferred the asset to B, which would have transferred it to C. The same result is achieved by a simple election instead of an actual transfer; the election may be made if an actual transfer between A and B would have been within section 171.[34]

The election must be made by notice in writing to an officer of the Board, and must be made jointly by A and B; it must also be made before the second anniversary of the end of the accounting period of A in which the disposal to C was made.[35]

TCGA 1992, section 171A was further simplified and completely rewritten by FA 2009, section 31 and Schedule 12; it is now sections 171A–171C. Where a gain or loss would arise on a transfer to another group member, the companies may simply elect that the gain

---

[27] *Ayerst v C & K (Construction) Ltd* [1975] STC 345, [1975] 2 All ER 537, 50 TC 651. The House of Lords decided only that the company ceased to be beneficial owner of its assets. The Court of Appeal had held that the ownership was in suspense ([1975] STC 1, [1975] 1 All ER 162).

[28] *Wadsworth Morton Ltd v Jenkinson* [1966] 3 All ER 702, (1966) 43 TC 479.

[29] *WT Ramsay Ltd v IRC* [1982] AC 300, giving rise to the composite transactions doctrine under which intermediate steps inserted into a transaction entirely for tax purposes could be ignored; for a detailed discussion of the evolution of the *Ramsay* doctrine see *Revenue Law*, §5.6.4.

[30] [1985] *Simon's Tax Intelligence* 568, 570.

[31] [1989] STC 617, (1989) 62 TC 495.

[32] TCGA 1992, s 171A, added by FA 2000, s 101.

[33] TCGA 1992, s 171A(2)(d), added by FA 2001.

[34] TCGA 1992, s 171A(3).

[35] TCGA 1992, s 171A(2), (4).

or loss be transferred—in whole or in part—from the disposing company to any other member of the group. This allows full and immediate matching of gains and losses within the group without having to wait for there to be a disposal outside the group. The effects of the election are spelt out in section 171B; there is a special rule for insurance companies in section 171C. An amendment ensures that the new rule applies where the group wishes to reallocate a gain or loss to a non-resident group member carrying on a trade in the UK through a PE.

8.2.3 Statutory Restriction on Use of Pre-entry Losses[36]

Whatever the vulnerability under the new approach of schemes to use losses incurred before the company entered the group, matters are now governed by legislation restricting the use of such losses. TCGA 1992, Schedule 7A ring-fences the capital losses available to a company at the time it joins the group. Such losses will, in future, enjoy unrestricted rights of set off only against gains arising in respect of assets held by the company at the date of its entry into the group, or acquired by that company from outside the new group and used in a trade carried on by the company before it joined the new group.[37] Although FA 2006 added many new rules to restrict the rights of companies to buy losses and gains, Schedule 7A remains in place.[38] These rules were simplified and eased by FA 2011. In particular, the use of losses that arise after a company joins a group are no longer restricted under the amended regime.

The key concept of pre-entry loss is defined as covering any allowable loss that accrued to that company at a time before it became a member of the relevant group.[39] Pre-entry losses may be set against certain specified gains only.[40] These are later defined as those accruing from:

(1)   disposals made before the company joined the group;
(2)   assets held at the time of joining; and
(3)   assets acquired from persons outside the group after joining and which have been used only for the purposes of a trade which had been carried on before the company joined the group.[41]

FA 2011 expanded the scope for the use of restricted pre-entry losses by allowing them to be used against gains arising on assets used in the same *business* that the company conducted before joining the group; previously this was restricted to assets used in the same *trade*.[42] Further rules apply if the initial company was a member of another group when it joined the group and other companies joined at the same time.[43]

---

[36]   TCGA 1992, s 177A and Sch 7A, added by FA 1993; on timing, see TCGA 1992, Sch 7A, para 6(2)(a); FA 1993, s 88(3)(b)(i). On effect of change of law on contract for sale of such losses, see *Bromarin v IMD Investments* [1999] STC 301; and Virgo [1999] *CLJ* 273.
[37]   Inland Revenue Press Release, 16 March 1993, [1993] *Simon's Tax Intelligence* 474.
[38]   On overlap see Williams [2006] BTR 27.
[39]   TCGA 1992, Sch 7A, para 1(2).
[40]   TCGA 1992, Sch 7A, para 6.
[41]   TCGA 1992, Sch 7A, para 7(1).
[42]   HMRC Explanatory Notes to cl 46 and Sch 11.
[43]   TCGA 1992, Sch 7A, para 7(3).

These rules were adapted by FA 2000 to meet the new worldwide definition of groups. New events, called 'relevant events', can trigger Schedule 7A. Thus losses are restricted by Schedule 7A whenever a company joins the worldwide group and it is either resident in the UK, or brings assets within the UK tax net. Schedule 7A also applies if the non-resident company being already a member of the worldwide group transfers assets so that they become chargeable to UK corporation tax, either because they are transferred to a UK PE or because the company itself becomes UK resident. Schedule 7A excludes that part of the loss referable to the period prior to these events.[44] Naturally, the legislation contains rules for the order in which the reliefs are to be given. Broadly, where pre-entry losses can be set against a gain, those of the current or a previous accounting period are offset before other losses of such periods,[45] and pre-entry losses of the current period are used before those brought forward from an earlier period. Where there is more than one pre-entry loss, the company may elect the order in which they are to be set off, but must do so within two years of the end of the accounting period in which the gain offset accrues; in the absence of an election, older losses are used first.

Further restrictions apply where, within a three-year period, there is both a major change in the nature of the company's trade or business and the company joins the group.[46] Rules also cover the situation in which the company belongs to more than one group, and to determine which the relevant group is and how the loss should be apportioned.[47] Rules apply to appropriations of trading stock[48] and various changes of company form.[49]

8.2.4 Statutory Restriction on Use of Pre-entry Gains (Superseded 2006)

While TCGA 1992, Schedule 7A prevented the import of companies with accrued capital losses into groups with gains, it failed to deal with the opposite case—where a company with realised gains, G, was imported into a group with unrealised losses. Once in the new group, G would transfer the assets to the company with the potential loss, L; this transfer would be tax free under section 171, and L would then realise those losses and set them off against the gains. This was first dealt with by Schedule 7AA, introduced by FA 1998.[50] Where two companies left one group and joined a second group together, the two companies were treated as one so that pre-entry gains of one might be set against pre-entry losses of the other. FA 2006 added many new rules to restrict the rights of companies to buy losses and gains, and Schedule 7AA is superseded.

8.2.5 Pre-change Assets and Losses (FA 2006)

TCGA 1992, section 184A imposes restrictions on buying losses where there has been at any time a 'qualifying change of ownership'.[51] It restricts losses arising to a 'relevant

---

[44] TCGA 1992, Sch 7A, para 1(3A), added by FA 2000, Sch 29, para 7. For example, see Inland Revenue Notes to Finance Bill 2000, paras 79–82.
[45] TCGA 1992, Sch 7A, para 6(1).
[46] TCGA 1992, Sch 7A, para 8.
[47] TCGA 1992, Sch 7A, para 9; strengthened by FA 1998.
[48] TCGA 1992, Sch 7A, para 10.
[49] TCGA 1992, Sch 7A, paras 11, 12.
[50] FA 1998, s 135(5) and TCGA 1992, Sch 7AA, para 1 (removing companies joining a group before that date).
[51] Defined in TCGA 1992, s 184C.

company' (RC) on the disposal of a pre-change asset. A pre-change asset is, in broad terms, an asset held by the RC before the relevant change of ownership. The restriction applies if the change of ownership is tainted with a tax advantage purpose.[52] All these terms are elaborately defined. The effect of the restriction is that the loss may be set off only against gains arising to the company on a disposal of pre-change assets. This is so whether the loss precedes or follows the change of ownership, and whether the advantage accrues to the company or any other company.[53]

Various events do not trigger the restriction. These include the insertion of a new holding company.[54] Similarly, if a company, Y, is the 75% subsidiary of X—and remains so—then Y does not undergo a change of ownership even though there is a change in the ownership of X.[55] Further provisions deal with the interaction of the identification of pre-change assets with the various deferral rules.[56]

Another problem arises where the asset has been disposed of under these rules but then goes outside the group on a disposal which is normal disposal and not one within the no-gain, no-loss rule in section 171. If the asset loses its pre-change status, does it resume it if comes back in? The answer seems to be that it does not.

The technicalities of these rules is emphasised by the fact that the contributor to the *British Tax Review* takes many pages to discuss the original proposals, and still more to discuss the Act.[57]

Even this provision proved vulnerable to the planners and was amended a year later. As just seen, there was a limited set of reliefs for losses accruing on the disposal of assets held before the change of ownership. HMRC became aware of schemes which involved arranging for the company incurring a qualifying loss or gain to be sold with one or more subsidiary companies (S) whose shares would be pre-change assets. Once under the new ownership, S would acquire other assets on which a gain—or loss—might be expected to arise. When these assets come to be sold, the sale would be carried out by a sale of the shares of S. Under the FA 2007 changes this offset is no longer available. However, an exception is still made.[58] As the HMRC notes put it:

> Qualifying losses can be set against gains on pre-change assets held by a company that was a member of the group that the relevant company left so long as the company seeking to use the loss is still controlled by the parent company of the group.

8.3 Intra-group Transfers and Trading Stock

Where one company transfers a capital asset to another company in the group, and the recipient company appropriates the asset to trading stock, the rule that the disposal should be at such a figure that neither gain nor loss accrues collides with the principle that the

---

[52] Defined in TCGA 1992, s 184D.
[53] TCGA 1992, s 184A(5).
[54] TCGA 1992, s 184C.
[55] TCGA 1992, s 184C(7).
[56] TCGA 1992, s 184E(9).
[57] DF Williams [2006] BTR 26 and 550.
[58] FA 2006, s 70(12), added by FA 2007.

asset should enter the trading stock at market value. The legislation therefore provides that the recipient company should receive the asset as a capital asset and then transfer the asset to trading stock at market value.[59] This gives the recipient the right to choose between an immediate chargeable gain and a later trading profit. Where the asset transferred was trading stock of the transferring company, but is received as a capital asset by the recipient, it is treated as having ceased to be trading stock before the transfer; the consequence is that for capital gains purposes the transferor is treated as having disposed of the asset to itself at whatever figure is entered in the books of the trade in respect of the asset.[60] For a company to appropriate an asset as trading stock there must be a genuine intention to trade and not simply a wish to gain a tax advantage.[61] The asset must not only be of a kind sold in the ordinary course of the trade, it must have been acquired with a view to resale at a profit.[62]

This provision was rewritten by FA 2000 to extend its rules to transfers between companies within the new worldwide group.[63]

8.4   Disposal Outside the Group

Once the asset is disposed of to a person outside the group, the normal liability to corporation tax in respect of the capital gain will follow.[64] If an asset has been acquired under an intra-group transfer or on the transfer of an asset from the PE of a non-resident company to a UK company, and is later disposed of outside the group, provision must be made to reflect the group's ownership of the asset. Thus, the disposing company is treated as having acquired the asset when it was originally acquired by a group member.[65] Provision is made for recognising the previous ownership by another group member both for pre-1965 acquisitions[66] and for capital allowances, so account must be taken of any capital allowances made to previous group owners.[67] The tax may be recovered from the principal member at the time the gain accrues and from any previous owner.[68]

8.5   Business Assets: Rollover Relief

Another way in which the group is recognised as the relevant owner concerns the rollover provisions for business assets.

---

[59] TCGA 1992, s 173, referring to s 161; see *Revenue Law*, §42.3.

[60] TCGA 1992, s 173(2), referring to s 161 which treats the disposal as being at such figure as is entered in the computation of trading profit; this will usually be current market value following *Sharkey v Wernher* [1956] AC 58.

[61] *Coates v Arndale Properties Ltd* [1984] STC 637, (1984) 59 TC 516, HL; *Reed v Nova Securities Ltd* [1985] STC 124, (1985) 59 TC 516 HL. See also *Re Loquitur* [2003] STC 1394 and *New Angel Court v Adam* [2004] STC 779; and *Revenue Law*, §42.3.

[62] *Reed v Nova Securities Ltd* [1985] STC 124, 130, (1985) 59 TC 516, 563 HL, *per* Lord Templeman.

[63] FA 2000, Sch 29, para 11.

[64] TCGA 1992, s 8.

[65] TCGA 1992, s 174(1)–(3), referring to ss 171, 172; however, this does not apply to a disposal to or by an investment trust (see s 174(5)).

[66] TCGA 1992, s 174(4).

[67] TCGA 1992, s 174(1), applying s 41.

[68] TCGA 1992, s 190.

8.5.1 All One Trade

First, all the trades of the member companies are treated as being one trade, so that if X Co sells an asset and buys another for use by Y Co (its subsidiary), rollover relief may be claimed.[69] As a result of FA 2000, the trade may be carried on either by a company resident in the UK or by a company resident elsewhere but trading in the UK through a PE. However, the relief is still not available if the investment in the new asset is made by a dual resident investment company.[70] It is also excluded where the company acquiring the asset does so on an occasion which is a no gain, no loss disposal;[71] here, the no gain, no loss rule prevails, and the gain made cannot be rolled into the acquisition.[72]

8.5.2 Timing of Group Status

Rollover relief also applies where the disposal is by a company which, at the time of the disposal, is a member of a group of companies and the acquisition is by another company which, at the time of the acquisition by the first company, is a member of the same group. It is not necessary for the acquiring company to satisfy the group requirements when the other company made the disposal.[73]

8.5.3 Non-trading Member

Rollover relief applies where a non-trading member of the group disposes of assets (or an interest in assets) used, and used only, for the purposes of the trade deemed to be carried on by the other trading members of the group.[74] The same applies to acquisitions by the non-trading member.

For the purposes of the rule restricting rollover relief where the replacement asset is a depreciating asset, not only are all the trades treated as one, but that trade is deemed to be carried on by one person.[75] Where an event occurs giving rise to a chargeable gain, that gain accrues to the member holding the replacement asset at that time.

8.6 Company Leaving Group After Section 171 Acquisition: Degrouping Charge

The privilege given by TCGA 1992, section 171 of postponing tax liability on transfers within the group was in addition to the basic rule that there could be no charge without a disposal of the asset. An asset would therefore be transferred to another company within

---

[69] TCGA 1992, s 175(1).

[70] TCGA 1992, s 175(2), as amended by FA 1994, s 251(8) (unless the asset was acquired before 29 November 1994). On dual resident investment companies, see below at §13.6.4.

[71] TCGA 1992, s 175(2C), added by FA 1995.

[72] TCGA 1992, s 175(2C), inserted by FA 1995, s 48(1).

[73] TCGA 1992, s 175(2A), enacting Revenue view set out in Statement of Practice SP 8/81 and so deemed always to have had effect (FA 1995, s 48(3)). The claim must be made by both companies.

[74] TCGA 1992, s 175(2B), enacting ex ESC D30 and added by FA 1995, s 48. On the position of a non-trading member, see [1971] BTR 268.

[75] TCGA 1992, s 175(3).

the group in exchange for shares, which would then be sold to a stranger company without giving rise to a chargeable gain.

This situation is regulated by section 179. Perhaps surprisingly, this does not prescribe a deemed disposal when the company ceases to be a member of the group, but instead directs that if a company (the departing company) leaves a group[76] and it then holds a chargeable asset which it has acquired from another member of the group within the previous six years, the departing member is treated as having disposed of the asset and reacquired it at its market value at the time of that intra-group *acquisition*.[77]

Section 179A allows the degrouping charge to be reallocated among different group members.[78] Section 179B has the effect of allowing the degrouping charge to be rolled over under the reinvestment in business asset rules in sections 152 or 153, if the relevant company (company A) incurs relevant qualifying expenditure.[79]

Before FA 2000 a company was treated as leaving a group for this purpose when it ceased to be resident in the UK[80] as, in defining 'the group', a company not resident in the UK was ignored.[81] FA 2000 amended these rules to reflect its then new worldwide group possibilities; so the charge applies to the worldwide group and not just to the UK group.[82] It follows that there will be a charge under section 179 only if the company leaves the group and the asset has throughout the period been held by a UK-resident company or by the UK PE of a UK non-resident company.[83] On merger with a European Company, see §2.14.

The gain or loss accruing to the company is treated as arising immediately after the beginning (or end) of the accounting period in which the company ceases to be a member of the group or, if later, when it acquired the asset from the other member of the group, although the calculation of the gain is based on the transfer taking place at the time of the intra-group transfer.[84] The effect of this is to remove retrospectively the immunity enjoyed by the intra-group acquisition, but to impose the charge primarily on the company then acquiring the asset. There is power to recover the unpaid tax from the principal member of the group and from the company which formerly owned the asset—and from a controlling director.[85] Those assessed have the right to recover tax from the chargeable company— including the right to recover any interest they have to pay.[86]

FA 2011, section 45 and Schedule 10 significantly changed the operation of the degrouping provisions, such that where a transferee company ceases to be a member of the group as a consequence of one or more disposals of shares made by another group member, the chargeable gain or allowable loss that would arise under the degrouping provisions may

---

[76] TCGA 1992, s 170(10).
[77] TCGA 1992, s 179(1), (3). On extension of time limit for election in respect of pre-1965 assets, see Statement of Practice SP D21. Where a company becomes non-resident as a result of the new rule for companies which are non-resident for treaty purposes, no charge arises under s 179 (FA 1994, s 250(2)).
[78] Added by FA 2002 s 42.
[79] Added by FA 2002, s 43.
[80] See *Dunlop International AG v Pardoe* [1999] STC 909; originally *Lion Ltd v Inspector of Taxes* [1997] STC (SCD) 133.
[81] TCGA 1992, s 170(2)(a), (3)(a), (7).
[82] For gains accruing on or after 1 April 2000, FA 2000, Sch 29, para 4(7).
[83] TCGA 1992, s 179, as amended by FA 2000, Sch 29, para 4. For examples see IR Notes to Finance Bill 2000, paras 76–78.
[84] TCGA 1992, s 179(4), as amended by FA 1993, s 89.
[85] TCGA 1992, s 190, as revised by FA 2000 and superseding s 179(11).
[86] *Ibid.*

be treated as increasing or reducing the gain on the disposal of those shares and not as accruing to the transferee company. The substantial shareholding exemption then may apply to exempt the gain (or disallow the loss). If the specified conditions are not satisfied, the original provisions under which the gain is treated as accruing to the transferee company will apply. FA 2011, section 31 also amended TCGA 1992, section 179(2A) by adding an additional circumstance in which the degrouping charge arises—where there ceases to be a connection between the first group of companies and the second group of companies, before the transferee company has ceased to be a member of the second group of companies. Also, for section 179(2A) to apply, the new rules make it clear that the transferee company must become a member of the second group of companies on leaving the first group.[87]

8.6.1 Scope

Section 179 will apply where an asset is transferred to a subsidiary and the subsidiary later leaves the group through the parent's selling its shares. Logically, but probably not in practice, section 179 applies equally clearly where the asset is transferred by the subsidiary to the parent and the parent leaves the group through the sale of its shares in the subsidiary.[88]

8.6.2 Combining Groups

Where a principal company subsequently becomes a 75% subsidiary of another company, thereby bringing two groups together, the two are regarded as being the same group so that this event will not, of itself, cause a company to cease to be a member of the group;[89] the winding up of a company will not have such an effect either.[90]

Where these rules would be triggered in respect of a company deemed to leave the group but only by reason of the principal company becoming a member of another group, a sale of assets previously transferred under section 171 to the company leaving the group will be deemed to occur if, within six years of the company leaving the group, the company ceases to satisfy certain conditions.[91] Those conditions are[92] that it should remain a 75% subsidiary and an effective 51% subsidiary of one of the members of the group. The chargeable gain or allowable loss arises at the time the conditions cease to be satisfied.[93] In calculating the gain or loss the tax-free benefit rule in TCGA 1992, section 30 applies.[94]

---

[87] See Ball [2011] BTR 395 and 406 for an analysis of the detail, including the new rules applicable to sub-groups addressing the issues raised in *Johnston Publishing (North) Limited v HMRC* [2008] EWCA Civ 858; [2008] STC 3116 and *Dunlop International AG v Pardoe (Inspector of Taxes)* [1999] STC 909 (CA).

[88] It is understood that the Revenue do not currently view this as falling within s 179.

[89] TCGA 1992, s 179(3).

[90] TCGA 1992, s 179(1).

[91] TCGA 1992, s 179(6).

[92] TCGA 1992, s 179(7).

[93] TCGA 1992, s 179(8).

[94] TCGA 1992, s 179(9); see *Revenue Law*, §35.5.

8.6.3 *Deferral and Rollover*

Section 179 applies whether the company, on leaving the group, owns the original asset or another in respect of which replacement rollover relief has been obtained under TCGA 1992, sections 152–158.[95] Rollover relief cannot be claimed when the new company leaves the group, since it applies only when a new asset is acquired. An asset owned by the chargeable company when it leaves the group is also treated as being the same as the asset acquired from the other group member if it derives its value in whole or in part from the first asset.[96] This rather Delphic rule is stated to apply specifically where the first asset was a leasehold interest and the second asset is the freehold—the lessee having, in the meantime, acquired the reversionary interest.[97]

8.6.4 *Extension: Sub-group Departs*

Where two or more companies leave the group at the same time and together they form a group, section 179 does not apply to acquisitions which had taken place between companies within the newly independent group.[98] As originally drafted this meant that the two companies concerned with the transfer of the asset could then leave the new group without incurring the charge under section 179(1). There was no degrouping charge on the break-up of the first group because of section 179(1), while there was no charge on the second group since the asset was acquired before the second group was established. Restrictions, however, now apply where the company ceases to be a member of the second group,[99] but only if there has been (what the legislation calls) a connection between the two groups; 'connection' is elaborately defined, but basically means that the companies must have been under common control.[100] In these circumstances the charge in section 179(1) applies after all; the section has effect as if it had been the second group of which both companies had been members at the time of the acquisition. These changes are not the end of the story because they made the deferred charge arise only where the common control was exercised by a company. A charge will now arise where the company leaves the second of the two groups, whether the common control is by any person or persons (ie companies) or other bodies.[101]

8.6.5 *Other Exclusions*

Also outside the rules are certain types of merger, provided they do not have the avoidance of tax as one of their main objects.[102] The relevant provision on mergers was enacted to assist with the long-ago Dunlop–Pirelli merger. The essence is that cross-holdings of

---

[95] TCGA 1992, s 179(10).
[96] TCGA 1992, s 179(10)(b).
[97] TCGA 1992, s 179(10)(c).
[98] TCGA 1992, s 179(2).
[99] TCGA 1992, s 179(2A), added by FA 1995, s 49; see Inland Revenue Press Release, 29 November 1994, [1994] *Simon's Tax Intelligence* 1485.
[100] Defined in TCGA 1992, s 179(2B); on control, see TA 1988, s 416.
[101] FA 1998, s 137, amending TCGA 1992, s 179(2B)(b), (c); Inland Revenue Press Release, 17 March 1998, [1998] *Simon's Weekly Tax Intelligence* 455, para 9. For exception for investments trusts, see TCGA 1992, s 179(2C).
[102] TCGA 1992, s 181.

at least 25% are established for full value. Demergers are outside section 179,[103] which section is also excluded if the company ceases to be a member of the group by being wound up or dissolved, or in consequence of another member of the group ceasing to exist.[104] The reference to the other company 'ceasing to exist' is a new formulation which applies to companies ceasing to be members of groups, eg on simultaneous liquidation.[105] The intention is to ensure that the charge under section 179 will be lost to the Revenue only if the company ceases to exist, ie it leaves the group on the final act of liquidation, and not just in the course of liquidation.[106]

Example

A has a subsidiary, B. In 2004 A transferred to B an asset with a base cost of £10,000 but with a current value of £15,000. Section 171 ensures that the base cost to B is £10,000 and that no chargeable gain arises in 2004.

If, in September 2007, A sells its shareholding in B, B will be treated as receiving a chargeable gain of £5,000. This will be calculated by reference to values in 2004, but taxed as profit arising in 2007.

If, in 2006, B had sold the asset to an independent purchaser for £18,000 and replaced it with another asset which cost £18,000, the rollover relief in section 152 will then have treated the disposal as being for £10,000. When section 179 is applied in 2006, B will be treated as notionally disposing of the replacement asset at £15,000 with consequent adjustment to its cost base. If rollover relief had not been claimed, section 179 will not apply— because the capital gains liability would have been discharged in 2006.

8.7   Losses Attributable to Depreciatory Transactions Within a Group and Dividend Stripping

8.7.1 Depreciatory Transactions Within a Group

If there is a disposal[107] by one group member to another of an asset at a nominal figure, neither gain nor loss arises (section 171). This may cause a decline in the value of the former company. Losses resulting from such depreciatory transactions[108] which are realised on a subsequent disposal of the shares or securities within six years of the depreciatory transaction are disallowed by section 176. The disallowance is limited to the undervalue of the transaction.[109] If there is a later disposal of the shares in the acquiring company, the

---

[103] F(No 2)A 1992, s 25(2); below §9.3.

[104] TCGA 1992, s 179(1) as amended by F(No 2)A 1992, s 25(1).

[105] TCGA 1992, s 25(2).

[106] See Inland Revenue Press Release, 29 January 1992, [1992] *Simon's Tax Intelligence* 90; and Inland Revenue Press Release, 15 November 1991, [1991] *Simon's Tax Intelligence* 1042.

[107] TCGA 1992, s 176(8) includes a claim under s 24(2) that the value of shares or securities has become negligible. However, s 29 (value shifting) (see *Revenue Law*, §36.6), does not apply to intra-group transfers.

[108] Defined by TCGA 1992, s 176(3) as including the cancellation of securities under Companies Act 2006, s 641 (ex Companies Act 1985, s 135).

[109] On effect of indexation allowance, see *X plc v Roe* [1996] STC (SCD) 139 and *Whitehall Electric Investments v Owen* [2002] STC (SCD) 228.

previously disallowed loss may reduce the gain.[110] Section 176 restricts losses; it does not create or increase gains.[111]

8.7.2 Dividend Stripping

Under TCGA 1992, section 177, payment of accumulated profits by means of an intra-group dividend may be treated as giving rise to a depreciatory transaction, and any resulting capital loss is therefore disallowed by section 176. This was introduced in 1969 as a companion to ex TA 1988, section 736 (see below at §12.4), which deals with share-dealing companies.

Example

X buys the share capital of Y for £100,000. A dividend of £60,000 is then declared by Y which is then liquidated. The distribution to X on the liquidation of Y is £40,000. Although X has a capital loss of £60,000 on its investment in Y, section 177 enables the inspector to disallow that loss to the extent of the dividend received (£60,000).

Section 177 deals only with the disallowance of losses; it does not apply to the reduction of gains. It follows that the common practice of a subsidiary making a distribution shortly before it is sold—so reducing the gain on the sale of those shares—is not caught by this provision. TCGA 1992, sections 178 and 180, which also applied to depreciating transactions, have been repealed.[112]

8.8　Value-shifting Transactions

By 1989 the practice of reducing the value of subsidiary companies prior to disposal of those companies outside the group had become a standard feature of UK tax practice. The purpose was to reduce the capital gains liability of the owners, and to reduce the exposure to double taxation. The Revenue distinguished two situations: in the first the value was reduced by extracting profits from a subsidiary before sale by an ordinary intra-group dividend payment where the profits supporting that dividend had borne tax; in the second the gains were extracted by the payment of a dividend from artificially-created profits that had not borne tax.[113] The Revenue were not concerned about the first situation, but became very concerned about the second. TCGA 1992, section 30 (see *Revenue Law*, §35.5) was not able to prevent this since, in its original version, it specifically excluded the shifting of value arising from the payment of dividends between members of a group of companies within the meaning of section 170 and the disposal of assets between them.

FA 2011, section 44 and Schedule 9 replaced the long, complex value-shifting rules in TCGA 1992, sections 30–33, which allowed the Revenue to adjust the consideration received on certain disposals to take account of material reductions in value, thereby

---

[110]　TCGA 1992, s 176(6).

[111]　Defined by TCGA 1992, s 176(7).

[112]　Repealed by FA 2000, Sch 29, paras 26, 27 (spent); TCGA 1992, s 177 is amended by para 25.

[113]　HC Official Report, Standing Committee G, col 598 (Mr Lamont). One example was where a group lent money to one subsidiary to buy an asset from another.

reducing a loss realised on the disposal, increasing a gain realised on the disposal, or converting a loss into a gain.[114] The amended section 30 provides that it does not have effect for the purposes of corporation tax if the disposal of the asset is a disposal by a company of shares in, or securities of, another company. This is subject to a targeted anti-avoidance rule in new section 31, which sets out three conditions:

(1) arrangements have been made whereby the value of those shares or securities, or of a relevant asset, is materially reduced;

(2) the main purpose, or one of the main purposes, of the arrangements is to obtain a tax advantage; and

(3) the arrangements do not consist solely of making an exempt distribution.

If these three conditions are satisfied, any allowable loss or chargeable gain accruing on the disposal is to be calculated as if the consideration were to be increased by such amount as is just and reasonable, having regard to the arrangements and any charge to, or relief from, corporation tax that, in the absence of section 31, would arise in consequence of the disposal or the arrangements.

---

[114] See Ball [2011] BTR 403 for background and more detail.

9

Exempt Distributions: Demergers

9.1 Introduction

Until 1980 it was difficult—but not impossible—to split a group. The difficulty was that the transfer of the piece being split off would cause the value received by the shareholder to be treated as a qualifying distribution and so give rise to dividend income (see above at §3.2.1). In addition, capital gains, development land tax (DLT) (now long repealed) and stamp duty problems arose when a company or assets left the group. As part of a campaign to free British industry from unnecessary constraints, Parliament included certain provisions—now CTA 2010, sections 1073–1099 (ex TA 1988, sections 213–218)—to encourage the process of 'demerging' by removing some of the obstacles.[1]

The three types of demerger allowed are explained below at §9.3. These rules do not apply where the company has a trade which it wishes to transfer to its shareholders directly, ie by transferring ownership of the trade itself (section 1076). It should also be noted that the scheme is not designed to assist intra-group demergers; when dealing with a chain of companies, the group must be demerged from the bottom up. If these rules apply, the distribution is an 'exempt distribution' (section 1075).

To assist the process in some respects, it is possible to apply to the Revenue for clearance and thus obtain their binding agreement that the proposed distribution is indeed within these rules.

9.2 Conditions

(1)　There must be a transaction which would otherwise be a distribution of income under CTA 2010, sections 1000 *et seq* (ex TA 1988, section 209). This means, inter alia, that these reliefs cannot apply to a demerger in the course of liquidation. In addition,

---

[1] See [1980] *Simon's Tax Intelligence* 171, 418; and Statement of Practice SP 13/80.

a distribution other than a dividend, eg a distribution of shares, is not a distribution if it represents a repayment of capital.[2]

(2) The company making the distribution must, at the time of the distribution, be a trading company[3] (or a member of a trading group—a phrase which will not be repeated); certain trades, notably those dealing in shares, land and commodity futures, are excluded.[4]

(3) The transaction must be wholly or mainly to benefit some or all of the trading activities involved in the demerger.[5] This test is narrow. A demerger will not qualify simply because there are bona fide commercial reasons for it. It is probably sufficient that the benefit should be either to the retained or to the transferred trade and not to both, but this is not absolutely clear. The combination of conditions (2) and (3) means that relief is available only where trade is being demerged from trade and so not, for example, to the demerger of trade from investment. In many instances the exact status of the secondary business of an unlisted company may be in doubt; such doubts need to be resolved before a demerger is embarked upon.

(4) The newly-demerged trade should be left free to operate under its new independent management—separate from the former parent. To this end it is provided that where the company distributes shares in its subsidiary to its members (see below at §9.3.1), those shares must not be redeemable and must represent the whole or substantially the whole of the distributing company's interest.[6] If the transfer is of a trade to another company (see below at §9.3.2), the distributing company must not retain anything more than a minor interest in the trade;[7] while if the transfer is of shares in a subsidiary (see below at §9.3.3), the shares must not be redeemable and must represent the whole or substantially the whole of the distributing company's interest.[8]

(5) All the companies involved must be resident in an EU Member State at the time of the distribution.[9]

(6) The transfer must not fall foul of the elaborate anti-avoidance provisions. Thus, the demerger must not be part of a scheme or an arrangement for the avoidance of tax, for the making of a chargeable payment,[10] for the acquisition of control of any company involved by a third person, or for the cessation of a trade or its sale after demerger. The purpose of the demerger provisions is to encourage the hiving-off of active businesses so that they may thrive on their own. As such, the provisions are designed to ensure that assets remain within the corporate sector and are not used to obtain tax advantages on what is really the sale of a business. Hence, a passing of control to another company in return for shares which flow back to the shareholders in the previous owners is essential. Intra-group transfers cannot qualify for this treatment.

---

[2] See above at §3.1.
[3] CTA 2010, s 1081(2), ex TA 1988, s 213(5); the terms are defined in s 1099 (ex s 218).
[4] CTA 2010, s 1099, ex TA 1988, s 218(1)—'trading'.
[5] CTA 2010, s 1081(3), ex TA 1988, s 213(10).
[6] CTA 2010, s 1082(1)–(2), ex TA 1988, s 213(6).
[7] CTA 2010, s 1083(1), ex TA 1988, s 213(8)(a).
[8] CTA 2010, s 1083(2), ex TA 1988, s 213(8)(b).
[9] CTA 2010, s 1081(1), ex TA 1988, s 213(4), which formerly required UK residence.
[10] CTA 2010, s 1081(4)–(7), ex TA 1988, s 213(11).

9.3 The Three Situations

9.3.1 Demerger of Existing Subsidiaries

Demerger of an existing subsidiary occurs where one company, C, transfers to all or any of its members, ie ordinary shareholders,[11] shares in a directly-owned 75% subsidiary, S.[12] This allows a simple spinning-off of the distinct business run by S which is already a separate entity, and takes the form of a simple distribution in specie. The insistence on a 75% holding in S is to be noted. The transfer must be to C's shareholders and not simply to another conglomerate.

A transfer of shares by C of this sort would normally cause a number of tax consequences; some of these are modified. First, the distribution is to be exempt;[13] it follows that there will be no dividend income tax, neither will there be a capital distribution to the shareholders which might otherwise cause capital gains consequences under TCGA 1992, section 122[14] (capital gains liability is thus deferred until the shares are disposed of). Further, as S is leaving the group, there may be a deferred charge under TCGA 1992, section 179 on assets acquired from other members of the group within the last six years.[15] However, the receipt of a chargeable payment within five years will revive such a charge (below §9.4).[16]

Some tax consequences, however, remain. First, since S ceases to be a member of the group it will not in future be entitled to group privileges such as, for example, group loss relief. Secondly, the change in control of S will mean that the restrictions on loss relief in TA 1988, section 768 and the potential liability for unpaid corporation tax under section 767AA may have to be noted should a change in S's trade be contemplated. However the Revenue have indicated sympathetic treatment in such circumstances by treating the underlying ownership as remaining unchanged. Thirdly, where close companies are involved there may be IHT implications.

Another very important tax consequence is that C will be disposing of its holding in S, a disposal that may give rise to substantial liability on the gains involved, save where the substantial shareholding exemption applies. This cost may be reduced either if the gains are minimal or if C has unrelieved capital losses. Where this is not so, it may be possible to reduce the value of the shares in S by paying a dividend. However, the more unusual the steps taken, the greater the risk that the scheme will fall into the anti-avoidance provisions on the ground that it forms part of a scheme one of the main purposes of which is the avoidance of tax. This very high tax cost used to inhibit many schemes of demerger under these rules.

---

[11] CTA 2010, s 1099, ex TA 1988, s 218(1).
[12] CTA 2010, s 1076, ex TA 1988, s 213(3)(a).
[13] CTA 2010, ss 1075–1077, ex TA 1988, s 213(2).
[14] TCGA 1992, s 192.
[15] TCGA 1992, s 192(3).
[16] TCGA 1992, s 192(4).

9.3.2 Three-Part Demergers

Here C disposes of a trade to Y and, in exchange, Y issues shares not to C but to the ordinary shareholders of C. In this way the trade is hived-off from the rest of C's activities and thus demerged, and C's ordinary shareholders receive shares in Y.[17]

Normally, such a distribution by C of its assets would be treated as a distribution, but as with the first type of demerger, it is provided that the distribution is exempt and so does not give rise to dividend income.[18] In addition, TCGA 1992, section 179 is excluded.[19] The legislature has not thought it necessary to exclude any charge as a capital distribution under TCGA 1992, section 122 in these circumstances, presumably because Y rather than C is making the distribution to C's shareholders. However, the rules make no provision for other consequences. Thus, C is disposing of the trade, one of its capital assets, and its shareholders are receiving an amount with capital gains implications; these consequences may be avoided by ensuring that the scheme is a company reconstruction and so making use of the deferral provisions such as TCGA 1992, sections 136 and 139. In addition, the fact that C ceases to carry on this trade and Y carries it on will give rise to all the usual problems of discontinuance and commencement, with restrictions on losses, unused capital allowances and possible changes of accounting date.

9.3.3 Indirect Demerger to Shareholders

This is a mixture of the first two types of demerger. Here, C transfers shares in its 75% subsidiary, S, to Y, and Y, in turn, issues shares in S to the ordinary shareholders of C.

The tax consequences are a similar mixture of the first and the second type of demerger. As with the first type, the distribution of the shares in Y is to be an exempt distribution,[20] with the result that there is no dividend income tax liability. S leaves the group controlled by C and there is exemption from TCGA 1992, section 179.[21] C's disposal of the shares in S may give rise to chargeable gains, but those may be avoided by using a reconstruction; the same device will save the shareholders in C from liability. Since the control of S passes from C, matters of losses and loss of group benefits will be raised as already set out under the first type. Where this type of demerger scores over the first is in the matter of the tax cost arising from the realisation of any gains on the disposal of the shares in S; that tax cost is avoided.

9.4 Anti-avoidance: Subsequent Chargeable Payments as Income, etc

Although a demerger under these rules may have been successfully carried through, a subsequent 'chargeable payment'[22] during any of the next five years may have serious consequences. A chargeable payment is any payment which is not itself a distribution (or an

---

[17] CTA 2010, s 1077, ex TA 1988, s 213(3)(b). On consequences where trusts are involved, see Law Society Press Release, 22 July 1992, [1992] *Simon's Tax Intelligence* 762.

[18] CTA 2010, ss 1075–1077, ex TA 1988, s 213(2).

[19] TCGA 1992, s 192(3); however, the receipt of a chargeable payment within five years will revive the liability under these rules (s 192(4)).

[20] CTA 2010, ss 1075–1077, ex TA 1988, s 213(2).

[21] TCGA 1992, s 192(3); this is subject to the receipt of a chargeable payment in the next five years (s 192(4)).

[22] Defined in CTA 2010, s 1088, ex TA 1988, s 214(2), (3).

exempt distribution) made otherwise than for a bona fide commercial reason, or forming part of a scheme or an arrangement for the avoidance of tax and made between companies or between a company and a shareholder in a company involved in the demerger. The payment must have been made in connection with the shares of the company.[23] Only intragroup payments are saved from the ambit of this definition,[24] which is widened yet further when in relation to unquoted companies.[25] Such a payment within the five-year period is treated as income of the recipient and chargeable to tax.[26] No deduction for the payment can be made in computing profits chargeable to corporation tax.[27]

An example of a situation in which this will arise is where a company demerges a subsidiary by transferring shares to its members and then buys them back. The repurchase price would normally be a capital receipt, but is instead taxed as income of the shareholder. Parliament has preferred this device to the alternative of retrospectively withdrawing exemption from the distribution.

---

[23] CTA 2010, s 1088(3), ex TA 1988, s 214(2).
[24] CTA 2010, s 1088(5), ex TA 1988, s 214(2)(c).
[25] CTA 2010, s 1089, ex TA 1988, s 214(3).
[26] CTA 2010, s 1086, ex TA 1988, s 214(1)(a); the reference to s 349(1) is removed by ITA 2007.
[27] CTA 2010, s 1087, ex TA 1988, s 214(1)(c); neither is it a repayment of capital within ss 210, 211; see TA 1988, s 214(1)(d).

10

Close Companies

10.1 Introduction: Importance of Close Companies

10.1.1 Overview

This chapter deals with certain rules which apply only to close companies or to a subset called 'close investment holding companies'. However, the definition of a 'close company' is of importance in many other areas of the tax system, including not only corporation tax, but also income tax and IHT.[1]

The present taxation of close companies differs from that of other companies in three major respects. First, the law takes a wider view of what amounts to a distribution, with the result that not only are such payments not deductible in computing profits of the close company, but they are also taxable as ITTOIA 2005, Part 4, Chapter 6 income in the hands of the recipients. Secondly, a payment equivalent to corporation tax at a special rate of 25% must be made to the Revenue where the company makes a loan to a participator. Thirdly, a close company which is a close investment holding company must pay corporation tax at the full rate (24% in 2012) on all its profits and cannot use the small profits rate of 20%. The close companies rules formerly in TA 1988, sections 414–422 were rewritten as CTA 2010, sections 438–465 and 1064–1069.

In so far as the shareholders envisage an eventual sale of the company, they may find that their expected CGT liability is turned into an income tax liability by ITA 2007, Part 13, Chapter 1,[2] a provision which applies particularly to small companies, although it is not so confined. The 1988 assimilation of CGT and income tax rates undermined this point

---

[1] For further examples, see *Revenue Law*, §44.3.1.5 on IHT on transfer of value by a close company, and see §8.2.2 above.

[2] Ex TA 1988, s 703. See also ITA 2007, s 689, ex TA 1988, s 704D; see below at §12.6.

in part, but the exemption of pre-1982 gains remained. The 1998 introduction of tapering relief restored the point that income tax treatment may be different from that under CGT, as does the present dual CGT rate band of 18%/28% as compared to the 20%/40%/50% rates of income tax.

10.1.2 History[3]

For earlier accounting periods, some very different principles have applied. From 1965–89, the law specified a certain amount of profit which might be distributed.[4] The sum by which actual distributions fell short of that amount was notionally apportioned among the participators; the income tax due on these notional distributions was collected from the company. The purpose of this rule was to prevent the use of companies as incorporated piggy-banks in which profits might be taxed at company rates instead of individual rates, the latter sometimes reaching 98%; the retained profits might then be realised as capital gains and so, before 1965, free of further tax. With the reduction in 1979 in top rates of tax on earned income to 60%, there was no tax advantage in retaining profits in the company, and so the power to apportion trading income of trading companies was abolished; however, it remained for non-trading income of such companies and for all income of non-trading companies. This power to apportion undistributed profit was repealed in 1989 following the further reduction of the top rate of income tax to 40%.

Between 1965 and 1973 the classical system of taxation meant that the participator could not claim credit for basic rate income tax paid by the company. Hence, participators were liable to basic rate tax as well as excess liability when an apportionment was made. The same fact led to special rules for restrictive covenants;[5] these rules were repealed on the introduction of the imputation system in 1973.

Before the introduction of corporation tax in 1965, companies paid income tax and other taxes on their profits. Even then, rules treated the income of the company as income of the participators; these rules empowered the Revenue to make 'surtax directions' on companies which were known, however inaccurately, as 'one-man companies'.

Today, a deduction for excessive remuneration paid by the company to a director, whether or not the company is close, may be disallowed under the rules for computing trading profits or CTA 2009, Part 16, ex TA 1988, section 75 (companies with investment business). The payment is, however, valid in that the director is perfectly entitled to retain the excess. For tax purposes the excess is treated as a distribution—unless it is refunded.[6] Between 1965 and 1969 there were special restrictions on the level of director's remuneration for close companies;[7] however, these were abolished because they were too complicated. Retention might have pre-empted *Jones v Garnett (Inspector of Taxes)*.[8]

---

[3] For older history, see Royal Commission on the Income Tax, *Final Report*, Cmd 615 (1920), §575; Royal Commission on the Taxation of Profits and Income, *Final Report*, Cmd 9474 (1955), paras 1021, 1036; for 1965 regime, see Talbot, *Corporation Tax and Income Tax upon Company Distributions* (Sweet & Maxwell, 1968), chs 15–17.

[4] For detail, see *Butterworths UK Tax Guide 1989–1990* (Butterworths, 1989), §27:13.

[5] TA 1970, s 288.

[6] On which, see Statement of Practice SP C4. On policy, see Oliver and Harris in Avery Jones, Harris & Oliver (eds), *Comparative Perspectives on Revenue Law* (CUP, 2008), ch 11.

[7] FA 1965, s 74.

[8] [2007] UKHL 35, [2007] STC 1536.

10.2 Definition of a Close Company

10.2.1 The Tests

A company will be designated a close company if it satisfies any of three tests. There are exceptions discussed below. The tests are:

(1) that it is controlled by five or fewer participators;[9] or
(2) that it is controlled by its directors; or
(3) if there are five or fewer participators, or participators who are directors, together they possess or are entitled to acquire such rights as would, in the event of the winding up of the company, entitle them to receive the greater part of the assets of the relevant company which would then be available for distribution among the participators.[10]

For test (3) above, the company will also be a close company if these persons could obtain such rights as would in that event entitle them to that greater part if the rights of all loan creditors were disregarded.[11] Elaborate rules set out the basis upon which the hypothetical winding up is to be carried out.[12] Rules also provide for the possible winding up of any other company which is a participator in the close company.[13] In the application of this rule to the notional winding up of the other company and to any further notional winding up required by CTA 2010, section 439(3)(b) (or by any further application of that paragraph), references to 'the relevant company' have effect as references to the company concerned. In applying these rules the rights of a participator which is a company are not taken into account unless it holds the rights in a fiduciary or representative capacity.[14]

Examples

(1) The share capital of X Ltd (a private company) is owned as to 25% by three directors and the 75% balance by 10 individuals, no five of which own over 50%. X Ltd is not a close company.
(2) The directors of X Ltd, numbering 12, own 51% of the ordinary share capital. X Ltd is a close company.
(3) The directors of Z Ltd, numbering three, own 45% of the ordinary share capital. Two other unconnected individuals own 8%. Since five persons own 53% of the share capital of Z Ltd, it is a close company.

The Revenue have extensive information-gathering powers.[15]

---

[9] CTA 2010, s 439(2), ex TA 1988, s 414(1).
[10] CTA 2010, s 439(3)(a), ex TA 1988, s 414(2)(a).
[11] CTA 2010, s 439(3)(b), ex TA 1988, s 414(2)(b), as amended by FA 1989, s 104.
[12] CTA 2010, s 440, ex TA 1988, s 414(2A), added by FA 1989, s 104.
[13] CTA 2010, s 440, ex TA 1988, s 414(2B), added by FA 1989, s 104. Section 441(2) (ex 414(2C)) provides that a person is to be treated as a participator in or as a director of the relevant company if he is a participator in or director of any other company which would be entitled to receive assets in the notional winding up of the relevant company on the basis set out in s 440 (ex s 414(2A), (2B)). CTA 2009, s 451 (ex TA 1988, s 416(4)–(6)) also applies, by the operation of s 439(5), ex s 414(2D).
[14] CTA 2010, s 441(3), ex TA 1988, s 414(2C); however, s 439(3) (ex s 414(2)(a)) is an exception to this.
[15] CTA 2010, s 465, ex FA 1989, Sch 12, paras 1–4.

10.2.2 Control

10.2.2.1 What Is It?

This element is central to the first two tests set out in §10.2.1 above, but it may be satisfied in many, sometimes overlapping, ways. A person is taken to control a company if he exercises or is able to exercise now or as of right in the future, or is entitled to acquire (now or as of right in the future) control over the company's affairs.[16] 'Control over the company's affairs' is not defined and may mean control at a general meeting or control of those matters which are within the discretion of the directors. Precise analysis is unnecessary since the statute gives the following instances, which are additional to and therefore do not detract from the generality of the principle.[17] A person will have control where he holds:

(1)   the greater part of the share capital or of the issued share capital; or
(2)   the greater part of the voting power of the company; or
(3)   so much of the issued share capital as would entitle him to receive the greater part of the income of the company if, ignoring the rights of loan creditors, it was all distributed among the participators; or
(4)   such rights as would enable him to receive the greater part of the assets of the company in the event of a winding up or in any other circumstances.

10.2.2.2 Who Has It?

If two or more persons together satisfy the test of control they are taken together to have control.[18] In assessing the extent of a person's control, all rights and powers held by him or by nominees are, of course, included.[19]

Less obviously, but equally crucial in establishing the extent of a person's control, is the attribution to a person of all the rights and powers held by an associate.[20] An associate means[21] any relative—which means spouse or civil partner, direct ancestor or issue, or brother or sister[22]—or partner, and any trustee of a settlement of which he, or any relative, as previously defined, is the settlor.[23] If the Revenue form the view that those other persons are indeed associates, they have a duty to attribute those rights to the other persons;

---

[16] CTA 2010, s 450–451, ex TA 1988, s 416(2); see also above at §2.11.

[17] *R v IRC, ex parte Newfield Developments Ltd* [2001] STC 901 (HL); case concerns TA 1988, s 13, but is applicable here too. Dicta by Lord Hoffmann cited by Lightman J in *Gascoine's Group Ltd v Inspector of Taxes* [2004] EWHC ChD 640; [2004] STC 844.

[18] CTA 2010, s 451(5), ex TA 1988, s 416(3).

[19] CTA 2010, s 451(3), ex TA 1988, s 416(5). The Revenue have no really effective means of discovering whether a shareholder is a nominee. TMA 1970, s 26 is, in practice, insufficient.

[20] CTA 2010, s 451(4)–(6), ex TA 1988, s 416(6). On the (non) relationship between TA 1988, s 416(6) and the definition of control in TA 1988, s 13(4), see *R v IRC, ex parte Newfield Developments Ltd* (HL), *op cit*, at para 32.

[21] CTA 2010, s 448, ex TA 1988, s 417(3). For a nice example of section 417(3)(a) operating see Revenue Note to Finance Bill 2004, cl 48, para 15.

[22] CTA 2010, s 448(2), ex TA 1988, s 417(4). But in practice relatives other than spouse or civil partner and minor children are usually ignored; see Statement of Practice SP C4, para 2.

[23] The definition of 'settlor' is now by reference to ITA 2007, ss 467 *et seq* for both income tax and corporation tax. A will is not a settlement (*Willingale v Islington Green Investment Co* [1972] 1 All ER 199, (1972) 48 TC 547); see Goldberg [1971] BTR 380.

they have no discretion in the matter.[24] Where the participator is interested in any shares or obligations of a company which are subject to any trust, the trustees of the settlement concerned are associates.[25] Similarly, if the participator is a company and is interested in shares held on trust, any other company interested in those shares or obligations is an associate.[26] These rules also apply where shares are held as part of the estate of a deceased person. The effect is to make the trustees associates rather than the beneficiaries, save where the beneficiary is another company.[27] The term 'interested' is not defined; it is unclear whether being an object of a discretion is sufficient to make one 'interested'.

If a participator has control of another company, the powers of that company and of any other he may control are attributed to him, as are powers of companies controlled by him and his associates.[28] While the powers of nominees of associates are attributed to the participator, those of associates of associates are not, so the rights of a sister-in-law would be ignored.

10.2.2.3 Control by Directors[29]

A company controlled by its directors is a close company no matter how many directors there are. Persons listed as directors are any persons occupying the position of director by whatever name called, and any person in accordance with whose wishes the directors are accustomed to act. Also qualifying as a director is any person who is a manager or otherwise concerned with the management of the company's trade or business, and who controls (or is able to control) 20% of the ordinary share capital of the company. There is the customary attribution of the control of associates and intermediate companies even if the manager himself has no shares at all.

10.2.2.4 Control by Participators[30]

If control does not rest in the directors, the company will still be close if control rests in five or fewer participators. A participator is defined as any person with a share or interest in the capital or income of the company and, in particular:

(1)   one with—or who is entitled to acquire—share capital or voting rights; or
(2)   one who is entitled to secure that income or assets (present or future) will be applied directly or indirectly for his benefit; or
(3)   one who is entitled to receive or participate in distributions of the company, or entitled to any amounts payable by the company in cash or in kind by way of premium on redemption; or

---

[24]   Lord Hoffmann in *R v IRC, ex parte Newfield Developments Ltd* [2001] STC 901 at para 18.
[25]   CTA 2010, s 448(1)(d), ex TA 1988, s 417(3)(c)(i), modified by FA 2006.
[26]   CTA 2010, s 448(1)(e), ex TA 1988, s 417(3)(c)(ii).
[27]   For previous law, see TA 1970, s 303(3)(c); it was then held that an executor was interested in shares held as part of an incompletely administered estate (*Willingale v Islington Green Investment Co* [1972] 1 All ER 199, (1972) 48 TC 547).
[28]   CTA 2010, s 451(4)–(6), ex TA 1988, s 416(6).
[29]   CTA 2010, s 452, ex TA 1988, s 417(5).
[30]   CTA 2010, s 454, ex TA 1988, s 417(1).

(4)   certain loan creditors,[31] a term defined to include one who has a beneficial interest in the debt. A creditor of a nearly insolvent company may be entitled to the greater part of the company's assets and thus could be a participator, with the result that the company would be a close company. To avoid such complications, bona fide commercial loans, salvage operations and business loans made by a person carrying on a banking business are ignored.

A person may be a director even though not a participator.

10.2.2.5 Exceptions

Certain companies cannot be close companies even though they satisfy one or other of the above tests, eg non-resident companies[32] or those controlled by the Crown.[33] Further, a company is not a close company if it is controlled by one or more open companies and it cannot be treated as close except by taking an open company as one of its five or fewer participators.[34] Thus the subsidiary of a non-close company is not close any more than a company set up by two or three such companies. However, if another test of control would result in its being a close company, the company would be close.

Also excluded is a company which is close only because it has one or more open companies as loan creditors with control,[35] under the rule which gives control to one entitled to the greater share of the assets on a winding up.

In looking at these cases of control by non-close companies, a non-resident company which would be a close company if it were resident is treated as if it were close.[36]

10.2.2.6 Quoted Companies—the 35% Rule

A quoted company is not a close company if shares carrying 35% or more of the voting power[37] of the company have been allotted unconditionally to, or acquired unconditionally by, and are at the time beneficially held by, members of the public.[38] Shares entitled to a fixed rate of dividend do not count towards the 35%, but they do count towards the 100%, even though they carry voting rights and participate in profits.

Shares are not treated as held by the public if they are owned by:

(1)   a principal member (ie the top five[39] of those with more than 5% of the voting power, other than an approved pension scheme or a non-close company);
(2)   any director or his associate;
(3)   any company controlled by (2);

---

[31]   Defined in CTA 2010, s 453, ex TA 1988, s 417(7)–(9). This is omitted for IHT (see *Revenue Law*). Recognised money brokers lending to stock jobbers formerly were excluded by concession (ex ESC C8).

[32]   CTA 2010, s 442, ex TA 1988, s 414(1).

[33]   CTA 2010, s 443, ex TA 1988, s 414(4).

[34]   CTA 2010, s 444(2), ex TA 1988, s 414(5)(a).

[35]   CTA 2010, s 444(3), ex TA 1988, ss 414(5)(b), 416(2)(c).

[36]   CTA 2010, s 444(4), ex TA 1988, s 416(2)(c).

[37]   Thus, the surrender of voting shares for non-voting shares may enable a company to come within this rule. Where the public own less than 35% only for a short period, which unhappily straddles the end of the accounting period, the Revenue promise 'sympathetic treatment' (Statement of Practice SP C4, para 9).

[38]   CTA 2010, s 446(1), ex TA 1988, s 415.

[39]   CTA 2010, s 446(4), ex TA 1988, s 415(6)(a): if there are two or more with equal percentages, five may be increased to six or more.

(4) any associated company; and

(5) any fund (eg a pension fund) for the benefit of any employee or director of the company or of a company within (3) or (4).

This exception does not apply if the voting power possessed by all the principal members is more than 85%. At first sight, since shares held in a principal member's holding cannot be held by the public, it is hard to see how a company with 35% of its shares held by the public could have 85% of its shares held by principal members. However, shares held by open companies or approved superannuation funds are treated as owned by the public even if the company or fund is a principal member. Therefore, where one of the principal members is an open company with, say, 25% of the voting power, and together the principal members control 80% of the voting power, the company so controlled is an open company under the 35% rule. If, however, the principal members controlled 86%, it would be a close company.

10.3 Wider Definition of Distribution: Incurring Expense on Participators or Their Associates

The definition of 'distribution' is widened in the case of a close company to cover expenses incurred by the company for the benefit of a participator. When a company has incurred expense in providing a participator, including one who is a participator in a controlling company or who is an associate of a participator,[40] with the provision of living or other accommodation, entertainment, domestic or other services, or other benefits or facilities of whatsoever nature, CTA 2010, section 1064 (ex TA 1988, section 418) directs that expense so incurred is to be treated as a distribution.[41] The analogy is with ITEPA 2003, Part 3, Chapter 10; section 1064 is excluded if the participator comes within that head of charge.[42] The rules laid down for valuation in Chapter 10 are incorporated into section 1064.[43] There is no grossing-up of the expense and there is a deduction for sums made good by the participator. The very wide meaning given by the House of Lords to the concept of the 'shadow director' means that the scope of these rules is not as wide as at once thought.[44]

Section 1064 does not apply to expenses incurred in the provision of living accommodation provided by reason of the employment, or of benefits on death or retirement for the participator or his dependants.[45] It is also excluded if the participator is another close company and one is the subsidiary of the other, or both are subsidiaries of a third company, and the benefit arises on the transfer of assets or liabilities by or to the company.[46]

Attempts could be made to avoid section 1064 where there is a participator in one close company but not in another close company, and the companies agree that the other pays or

---

[40] CTA 2010, s 1069, ex TA 1988, s 418(8).
[41] CTA 2010, s 1064, ex TA 1988, s 418(2).
[42] See *Revenue Law*, ch 16.
[43] CTA 2010, s 1064(3), ex TA 1988, s 418(4).
[44] Mullan [2002] BTR 156 commenting on *R v Allen* [2001] UKHL 45, [2001] STC 1537.
[45] CTA 2010, s 1065, ex TA 1988, s 418(3).
[46] CTA 2010, s 1066, ex TA 1988, s 418(5); 'subsidiary' is defined in s 1066(2), ex s 418(6).

should provide the facilities for that person. In such circumstances the payment is treated as coming from the company in which the person is a participator.[47]

The payment is a qualifying distribution; income tax under ITTOIA 2005, Part 4, Chapter 3 is therefore due—complete with a 10% credit.

10.4   Quasi-distributions: Loans to Participators

10.4.1 The 25% Charge

Where a close company makes a loan to a participator, CTA 2010, section 455 (ex TA 1988, section 419) directs that a sum equal to corporation tax at a special rate of 25% is payable by the company. This payment cannot be set off against the company's own liability to corporation tax on its profits; it is a payment 'equal to' corporation tax, not corporation tax itself. (It is, however, part of the company's self-assessment liability and may therefore form part of the liability of a large company to be paid on a quarterly basis.[48]) One reason for this non-deduction is that when (or if) the loan is repaid, the tax is refunded to the company,[49] so the rule operates as requiring the company to pay a special refundable deposit. Without some rule governing loans to participators and their associates, it would be easy for the company to avoid the widened definition of 'distribution' and still enable the participators to enjoy the untaxed capital reserves of the company.[50] Section 455 does not apply if the loan is made in the ordinary course of a business carried on by the company, which includes the lending of money;[51] a company which made eight loans over 14 years was held not to come within this exception.[52] However, section 455 does apply whenever a 'debt' has been incurred (see below at §10.4.3). If the loan is at a low rate of interest, the borrower may also incur liability under ITEPA 2003 (see *Revenue Law*, §16.4.3). Before 1999 the sum paid was not an arbitrary 25% but a sum equal to ACT.[53]

10.4.2 Extension

Section 460 applies when the loan is made neither by the close company, A, nor by another close company which A controls, but by a non-close company which A controls.[54] To catch obvious avoidance devices, loans existing when A acquires control are treated as being made after that control was acquired, thus falling within section 460.

Section 460 is aimed at schemes to avoid section 455, and therefore section 461 provides an exception when it is shown that no person has made any arrangements (otherwise than

---

[47] CTA 2010, s 1067, ex TA 1988, s 418(7).
[48] On self-assessment, see FA 1998, Sch 18, para 8. On payment by instalments, see above at §2.6.1.
[49] CTA 2010, s 458, ex TA 1988, s 419(4).
[50] See *Jacobs v IRC* (1925) 10 TC 1.
[51] CTA 2010, s 456(1), ex TA 1988, s 419(1); and see Revenue Interpretation RI 16.
[52] *Brennan v Deanby Investments Ltd* [2001] STC 536 (CA, NI) reversing Special Commissioner.
[53] TA 1988, s 419(1) (original version).
[54] CTA 2010, s 458, ex TA 1988, s 419(4); when two or more companies control the lender, the company is treated as controlled by each but the loan is apportioned between them: s 459 (ex s 419(5)).

in the ordinary course of a business carried on by the person) as a result of which there is a connection:

(1) between—
    (a) the making of the loan or advance, and
    (b) the acquisition of control; or
(2) between—
    (a) the making of the loan or advance, and
    (b) the provision by the close company of funds for the company making the loan.

Section 461(2) further provides that the close company shall be regarded as providing funds as aforesaid if it directly or indirectly makes any payment or transfers any property to, or realises or satisfies (in whole or in part) a liability of, the company making the loan. The onus of establishing that the loan was in the ordinary course of business or that there was no arrangement is thus placed on the taxpayer.

Interest runs against the company if the payment is not made by the due date. In the case of a company outside the obligation to pay by quarterly instalments, interest runs nine months after the end of the accounting period. A consequence of this provision is that no corporation tax is payable and no interest charge arises if the participator has repaid the loan by that date.[55] If the loan is repaid after this date, relief by way of refund of the tax may not be given until nine months after the end of the accounting period in which the repayment is made.[56]

10.4.3 Loans

The statute gives a wide definition of 'loan'.[57] It has been held that there must be some consensual element, so that money due to a company by way of restitution of sums misappropriated by a director was not within ex TA 1988, section 419 (now CTA 2010, section 456).[58] However, it is also provided that a company is regarded as making a loan when a person 'incurs a debt' to the close company, and this liability to make good the misappropriation was held to be a loan for this purpose.[59] In *Andrew Grant Services Ltd v Watton*,[60] it was held that a debt was incurred for this purpose when the fact of liability was established, even though the payment became due at some future time and was for an indefinite amount. In that case an estate agent ran his business as an unincorporated business but formed a personal service company of which he was a participator; the sums unpaid and due from the business to the company were held to fall within the former TA 1988, section 419.

---

[55] TA 1988, s 826(4)—not rewritten—amended by FA 1996, s 173(5).
[56] CTA 2010, s 458(5), ex TA 1988, s 419(4A), added by FA 1996, s 173(3).
[57] CTA 2010, s 455(4), ex TA 1988, s 419(2).
[58] *Stephens v T Pittas Ltd* [1983] STC 576, (1983) 56 TC 722.
[59] This was held by the Special Commissioners in *Stephens v T Pittas Ltd*, but was not the subject of an appeal to the High Court. The issue raises interesting questions about the meaning of the word 'debt'. CTA 2010, s 455(4), ex TA 1988, s 419(2) also covers the assignment of a debt due from the participator to another person by that person to the close company.
[60] [1999] STC 330.

10.4.4 Exceptions from Charge

10.4.4.1 Full-time Worker

If the borrower is a full-time worker for, and does not have a material interest in, the company or an associated company, section 455 is excluded if the total loan outstanding does not exceed £15,000.[61] In computing the amount of the loan, included are loans made to the spouse or civil partner of the director or employee, but not to other associates. Provision is made for the possibility of acquiring a material interest after the date of the loan by deeming a new loan on that occasion. A participator who is neither a director nor an employee is not entitled to these exceptions.

10.4.4.2 Others

Exceptions are also made for ordinary trade credit (subject to a six-month maximum period) and for certain loans made to certain directors or employees of that or an associated company.[62]

10.4.4.3 Non-resident Company

At one time, TA 1988, section 419 applied to loans made by a non-resident company which was a participator. However, non-resident companies were removed in 1996, at least in part, for fear of challenge under the EU free movement of capital provisions.[63]

10.4.5 Release of Loan as Qualifying Distribution

Where a loan, falling within CTA 2010, section 455, is later released or written off in whole or in part, the person to whom it was made is treated as receiving an amount grossed up by the amount of income tax at 10% which would have been payable had it been a distribution. This part of TA 1988 was rewritten by ITTOIA 2005, Part 4, Chapter 6; unfortunately, and rather confusingly, Chapter 6 comprises sections 415–421A. Since a distribution is a qualifying distribution unless treated as a non-qualifying distribution,[64] it follows that the release carries a tax credit and is taxed at the appropriate dividend tax rate. The grossing up is to achieve parity with distributions proper, but has effect only if the person thereby becomes liable to higher-rate tax.[65] The income cannot form part of modified net income for the purposes of ITA 2007, Part 8, Chapter 4 (deduction of tax from annual payments, etc), ex TA 1988, sections 348 and 349.[66]

The term 'release' is not defined, and is therefore given its plain and ordinary meaning. It is not necessary that the release should be voluntary or for inadequate consideration; the substitution of a new debtor for the original borrower is therefore a release.[67] The only question is whether the taxpayer has been released from his obligation to pay otherwise

---

[61] CTA 2010, s 456. A special rule applied for pre-1971 housing loans under TA 1988, s 420(2).
[62] CTA 2010, s 456, ex TA 1988, s 420(2).
[63] See Brannan [1996] BTR 378, commenting on FA 1996, s 173.
[64] CTA 2010, s 1136(1), (2), referring to distributions within s 1000(1)C or D; ex TA 1988, s 14(2).
[65] ITTOIA 2005, s 421, TA 1988, s 421(1).
[66] ITTOIA 2005, s 421, TA 1988, s 421(1).
[67] *Collins v Addies* [1991] STC 445.

than by performance or satisfaction. A covenant not to sue will, on this broad interpretation, be treated as a release.

If the loan is repaid, so causing a repayment of tax, that repayment is calculated by reference to the amount of corporation tax paid when the loan was made.[68] However, when a loan is released, the amount released is grossed up at the dividend rate prevailing at that time. Therefore, if, in 1995, a company made a loan of £40,000 within then section 419, the company would at that time have had to pay a sum of £13,333 under the relevant rate then of 25/75ths of the loan. If, in July 2007, the loan is repaid as to half, the other half being released, the company will recover tax on £20,000 at 1996 rates, ie £6,666, but the participator's £20,000 will be grossed up at 10% to give a total of £22,222, which will be added to income with a credit of £2,222. For repayment supplement purposes, the repayment is treated as being corporation tax paid in the repayment period[69]—ie the supplement, if any, is not calculated by reference to the date of the original payment to the Revenue under CTA 2010, section 455.

ITTOIA 2005 breaks open TA 1988, section 421 (and part of section 422). It has four general provisions (sections 416–418 and section 421) plus the separate rules on loans to persons who die (section 419) and loans to trusts that have ended (section 420). Under ITTOIA 2005, section 420, tax is due from the person from whom the debt is due when released or written off. The same rule applies under ITTOIA 2005, section 419, unless the debt is due for the borrower's PRs.

10.5   Close Investment-holding Companies

Following FA 1989, profits of close investment-holding companies cannot take advantage of the small profits rate (§2.5 above) and must instead bear the full corporation tax rate.[70] The Act also contained provisions restricting the repayment of credits if the actual pattern of distributions by the company was unusual;[71] however, the virtual abolition of the right of repayment of such credits made these provisions redundant and they were repealed as from 6 April 1999. The 1989 Finance Bill had originally proposed that such companies should be subjected to corporation tax at the top rate of income tax (then 40%).

10.5.1 Defining a Close Investment-holding Company

A company is a close investment-holding company if it is a close company and fails to satisfy the statutory test[72] which allows the company to escape designation. The company will escape such designation if, throughout the relevant accounting period, it exists wholly or mainly for any one or more of six purposes, of which the first two are the most important. In practice, the Revenue accept that a company exists *mainly* for one of these

---

[68] CTA 2010, s 458, ex TA 1988, s 419(4).

[69] TA 1988, s 825.

[70] TA 1988, s 13A, added by FA 1989, s 105.

[71] TA 1988, s 231(3A).

[72] CTA 2010, ss 439–441. FA 1989, s 104, replaced TA 1988, s 414(2) and inserted the now rewritten rules at s 414(2)–(2D).

purposes if more than 50% of its business is for that purpose. The effect of the list is to exclude trading companies and property investment companies that are part of a group the main purpose of which is to support the trading or property investment activities of the group.[73]

The first qualifying purpose is carrying on a trade or trades on a commercial basis.[74] This definition does not extend to professions. The second purpose is the making of investments in land where the land is, or is intended to be, let to unconnected persons.[75]

The remaining qualifying purposes embroider the first two. Thus, a company will escape close investment-holding company status if its purpose is to hold shares in and securities of, or making loans to, a qualifying company[76] or to co-ordinate the administration of two or more qualifying companies.[77] A company may also exist for the purposes either:

(1)   of a trade carried on, on a commercial basis, by a company which controls it or by a qualifying company; or
(2)   of making investments by a company which controls it or by another qualifying company.

There is a special provision for companies in the course of a winding up.[78]

10.5.2 Consequences for the Company

If the company is a close investment-holding company, a matter determined by reference to the company's purpose throughout the accounting period, the reduced rate of corporation tax is not applicable and all profits will be charged at the main corporation tax rate regardless of the overall level of the profits of the company.[79] The profits of the company will be calculated in the usual way, with the normal deduction of expenses and interest payments.

---

[73] HC Official Report, Standing Committee G, col 587, 22 June 1989.
[74] CTA 2010, s 34(2)(a), ex TA 1988, s 13A(2)(a), added by FA 1989, s 105(2).
[75] CTA 2010, s 34(2)(b), ex TA 1988, s 13A(2)(b), added by FA 1989, s 105(2).
[76] CTA 2010, s 34(2)(c), ex TA 1988, s 13A(2)(c), added by FA 1989, s 105(2); on definition of 'qualifying company', see CTA 2010, s 34(2)(6), ex TA 1988, s 13A(3).
[77] CTA 2010, s 34(2)(d), ex TA 1988, s 13A(2)(d), added by FA 1989, s 105(2).
[78] CTA 2010, s 34(5), ex TA 1988, s 13A(4), added by FA 1989, s 105(2); on application to companies in liquidation, see Revenue Interpretation RI 21; *Simon's Direct Tax Service*, Div 115.4.
[79] CTA 2010, s 34(1), ex TA 1988, s 13A(1), added by FA 1989, s 105.

11

Employee Share Schemes

11.1 General Introduction[1]

11.1.1 Legislative History: The Statute Outlined

This chapter deals with Part 7 of ITEPA 2003, which is entitled 'Employment income; income and exemptions relating to securities'.[2] Despite its length and complexity, Part 7 is not all-embracing; it begins (section 418) by warning the reader that these provisions are

---

[1] For a comparison of the Canadian and US rules on stock options but raising wider issues, see Sandler (2001) 49 *Canadian Tax J* 259.

[2] On the FA 2003 changes, see Stratton [2003] BTR 374.

not the only ones that may be relevant, and specifically mentions section 62 and Part 3, Chapter 10.[3]

Part 7 has two main purposes. First, it seeks to restrict the use of securities, interests in securities and options to avoid tax under ITEPA 2003, NICs or PAYE. The use of the term 'securities' is deliberately wider than 'shares'. The tax treatments of options in relation to assets which are not on the list of securities, eg land, remain subject to general principles. Secondly, Part 7 seeks to recognise the use of shares as an acceptable method of remuneration and so provide appropriate tax exemptions. The twin aims make for complicated rules. Part 7 relates to the structure of ITEPA 2003 through section 7(2), which classifies Part 7 income as an amount which 'counts as' employment income. Those chapters of Part 7 (Chapters 6–10) which provide rules for the use of securities (usually shares) as remuneration do not apply to office holders.[4] There are also special rules narrowing the normal international scope of ITEPA 2003.[5] These rules cannot generate a negative amount; such an amount is treated as nil.[6]

FA 2003 was enacted after ITEPA 2003 had come into force and provided a major overhaul of the legislation in this area. One may regret that the overhaul was not done earlier, since the resulting scarring of the statute book is not attractive. There were three principal changes. The first was the overdue extension of the rules to cover all securities and not just shares. The second was a new set of Chapters, 3A–3D, dealing with acquisitions above or below market value and the manipulation of values; this enabled the repeal of a number of other rules in ITEPA 2003, including two entire chapters of the benefits code—Part 3, Chapters 8 and 9.[7] The third was the extension of PAYE and NICs to produce a uniform application across the rules.

The Chapters of Part 7 are structured as follows: Chapter 1 deals with introductory matters; Chapter 2 with restricted securities, which may be seen as a wider version of the previous conditional interests in shares; Chapter 3 with convertible securities; Chapter 4 with post-acquisition benefits from securities; and Chapter 5 with securities options. Into this scheme FA 2003 planted Chapters 3A–3D, all concerned with potential avoidance through the manipulation of values, so Chapter 3A deals with securities with artificially depressed market value; Chapter 3B with securities acquired with artificially enhanced market value; Chapter 3C with securities acquired for less than market value; and Chapter 3D with securities disposed of for more than market value. Chapters 3A to 3D contain their own heads of charge. However they do not radically alter the situations giving rise to charge—rather they have their own rules imposing tax on the acquisition of securities (Chapter 5) or the removal of restrictions on securities (Chapter 2), or on the conversion of convertible securities (Chapter 3) and so on. Sometimes they adjust the value to be used for the other provision; more usually they apply their own head of charge.

As a result of these rules there are many opportunities for the Revenue to tax. It is a welcome feature of these rules that taxpayers may often elect that they do not apply. This usually means that taxpayers are given the chance to pay tax at once by reference to the unmanipulated value rather than in stages. This is presumably in response to points made

---

[3] The old TA 1988, s 154; see further §11.1.4.
[4] ITEPA 2003, s 417(6).
[5] Eg ITEPA 2003, ss 421E and 474.
[6] ITEPA 2003, s 419; for explanation, see ITEPA 2003 Technical Note 43.
[7] Rules repealed included the old growth in value charge (FA 1988, s 77).

in the long period of consultation. Special rules apply to research institution spin-out companies (see §11.10).

ITEPA 2003, Part 7, Chapter 6, originally introduced by FA 2000, applies to all employees and has three distinct elements: free shares (maximum £3,000 pa), partnership shares (bought by the employee up to £1,500 pa) and matching shares (given on a 2-for-1 basis by the employer to match the partnership shares). Chapter 7 (sections 516–520) covers Approved SAYE option schemes, while Chapter 8 (sections 521–526) addresses Approved Company Share Option Schemes. Chapter 9 (sections 527–541) deals with Enterprise Management Incentives, also dating from FA 2000. This is a very generous share option scheme which is available to only relatively few employees. Chapter 10 (sections 542–548) deals with priority share allocations.

Because these rules are often complex and restrictive, it is still common for employers to offer employees (usually only key employees) benefit schemes which fall outside the rules. Unapproved share option schemes became more popular after 1996 when the then approved schemes were limited to £30,000, but suffer from the rules also introduced in 1996 which make them subject not only to income tax but also to NICs and PAYE.[8] Any discount on the grant of non-approved options is subject to NICs. 'Phantom schemes' also exist under which a tax bonus is tied to the company's share price. Neither actual shares nor options are involved here. Other, intermediate schemes may be set up, in which the company buys shares for an employee but holds them in trust.

The ability to earn profits in approved employee share schemes eligible for CGT treatment rather than income tax, and thus subject to the comparatively low 18%/28% rates of tax (plus large allowance) rather than the top rate of income tax of 50% (45% from 6 April 2013), makes these forms of compensation potentially very attractive. The schemes can be somewhat burdensome to operate, however. In 2011 the Office for Tax Simplification (OTS) launched a review of employee share schemes, beginning with the four approved schemes, in order to identify where they are complex and place unnecessary administrative burdens on their users, and to suggest ways in which they might be simplified. In its March 2012 report, the OTS recommended abandoning the cumbersome HMRC approval process and moving to a self-certification process in line with self-assessment principles. The OTS also questioned whether the company share option plan (CSOP) scheme could be phased out or merged with the EMI scheme. Lastly, the OTS made many detailed recommendations related to harmonising definitions, adjusting time limits and modifying scheme conditions. At Budget 2012 the Government responded to the OTS report, stating that it would consider the OTS recommendations and consult on how best to take the proposals forward.

11.1.2 Older Schemes

Various older schemes have either ceased to exist altogether or to be brought into existence. For this reason they do not feature in the pages of ITEPA 2003.

(1) Discretionary schemes for executives (generally known as 'executive' approved share option schemes) are still in existence, but no new schemes could be created after 1996.

---

[8] ITEPA 2003, s 698 rewritten by FA 2003; originally TA 1988, s 203FB.

(2)   Profit-related pay (PRP) (TA 1988, sections 169–184). These rules give tax benefits to a certain level of pay made out of profits. They cannot apply to profit periods beginning after 31 December 1999 (see *Revenue Law*, 4th edition, §16.11).

(3)   Approved profit-sharing schemes (APSSs) (TA 1988, sections 186–187 and Schedules 9 and 10). These schemes do not involve options but the issue or transfer of actual shares to be held for employees. (See *Revenue Law*, 4th edition, §17.8.) Contributions to such schemes are no longer deductible. On phasing out, see FA 2000, section 49.

(4)   Employee share ownership plans (ESOPs) (FA 1989, sections 67–74 and Schedule 5). These plans concern trusts (qualifying employee share trusts (QUESTs)) which may be used to receive money from the employer with which trustees later buy shares for employees. (See *Revenue Law*, 4th edition, §16.9.) Contributions to such schemes are no longer deductible. See FA 2003, section 142.

11.1.3 Tax and Non-tax Factors Affecting Choice of Scheme[9]

In studying the rules the following points must be noted which affect the willingness of the employer and employee to choose a particular benefit, bearing in mind always that their interests may not be the same:

- Does the employer incur an expense—if so, is it deductible in computing profits?
- If the employee receives a benefit, when will it be taxable?
- If the employee receives a benefit, will it be taxable to income tax under ITEPA 2003, or to CGT under TCGA 1992?
- If the employee receives a benefit, will it be subject to PAYE?
- If the employee receives a benefit, will it be subject to NICs?
- Will the employee incur a charge to tax if shares are sold within a certain period?
- What are the risks of unexpected tax charges (usually called 'chargeable events')?

From a wider perspective:

- Must the scheme be available to all employees?
- Is there any limit on the amount that can be put into the scheme?
- What does the scheme do to the share structure of the company? Is there a risk of dilution? Does the company receive any money from the employee?
- Will the scheme give rise to employee participation in the company to a degree which 'management' may find unacceptable?
- How free are employees to sell the shares and thus rid themselves of the links with the company which these schemes are meant to foster?
- How flexible are the schemes? Clearly, approved schemes will be less flexible than unapproved schemes since they have to conform to statutory conditions.
- What financial risks are inherent in the scheme (share values may go down as well as up)?

---

[9] See, generally, Scott and Savage, *Tolley's Tax Planning 1999–2000*, ch 56, 1622–69, esp at 1643–55; and Williams, *Taxation of Employee Share Schemes* (Butterworths, 1995), ch 1. Company law aspects are well covered by Whitewright, McMichael and Lawson, *Tolley's Tax Planning 2003–04*, 56.24 *et seq.*

- From the employee's viewpoint, share options have attractions over other share plans in that no money has to be invested, there is no risk of loss since options do not have to be exercised and success may lead to a very high rate of return owing to the element of gearing involved.

The battery of sets of rules and factors makes this area complicated. In this book it is not appropriate to cover every detail; as such only the principal points will be considered in relation to each scheme. However, some other general points must be grasped.

First, this is a political minefield. Some believe in the value of share schemes as ways of encouraging better performance by executives and general loyalty of the workforce as a whole. A profit-sharer tends to take a longer-term view of company, is less inclined to leave and is probably more sympathetic to the introduction of new machinery or work practices. However, a company does not benefit if it simply uses such schemes as a way of warding off takeovers. Loyalty is important not only for the company itself but also more widely, since a company with a loyal workforce is far more likely to spend money in its training and development, a matter seen as a real problem when the UK is compared with other countries. When the logic of such reward systems became too obvious, as in the case of the newly-privatised companies which made substantial profits in cutting expenses by making staff redundant, the populist streak of Conservatism meant that benefits were restricted (eg the £30,000 limit imposed in 1996). By contrast (Old) Labour governments have traditionally been hostile to schemes attracting tax privileges, and have usually sought to impose tax penalties. Profit-sharing schemes have been anathema both to the hard left (collaborationist) and the right-to-manage right, but one may oppose them on other grounds. Some critics emphasise that options may become valueless due to a change in the general market conditions even though the company itself has been successful in comparison with other companies in the sector in which it competes. Such critics prefer long-term incentive plans using such comparisons.[10] The Liberal Democrats[11] were responsible for the introduction of savings-related option schemes and approved profit-sharing schemes in the period of minority government from 1977–79.

Secondly, much of the practical effect of the different schemes must be assessed against a changing background of the relationship between income tax and CGT. The alignment of the rates of tax in 1988 reduced the advantage of having capital gains rather than income; however, the advantage was widened first by the introduction in 1998 of increasingly generous taper relief, and remained after the move to the 18% flat rate of CGT (combined with the repeal of taper relief) in 2008. The advantage has narrowed somewhat with the 2010 addition of the 28% top rate of CGT, but compared to income tax rates of 40%–50% the advantage clearly remains. The question whether it is better for a particular taxpayer to have capital gain or ordinary income does depend, however, on the taxpayer's circumstances.

Thirdly, it is open to any employer to arrange a mix of these benefits, so taking full advantage of the statutory reliefs while adding unapproved schemes on top.

At Budget 2012, the Government announced that HM Treasury will conduct an internal review to examine the role of employee ownership in supporting growth, and consider options for removing barriers to take-up. This review will also consider the findings of an

---

[10] For example, Goobey, *The Times*, 25 November 1995, Business letters.
[11] Technically, their predecessor parties.

ongoing project on employee ownership led by the Minister for Employment Relations, Consumer and Postal Affairs.

11.1.4 *Emoluments in form of Shares and Share Options—Basic Rules*

ITEPA 2003, section 7(2) introduces a distinct type of income, being an amount which 'counts as' employment income; this type includes[12] income falling with Part 7 of the Act or 'income ... relating to securities'.

11.1.4.1 Remuneration in Shares

If, in return for services, an employee, E, receives shares in the employing company, tax is chargeable on the value of those shares.[13] Since the charge does not arise under any of the special rules in Part 7, this will be ordinary earnings within section 62. If the shares are ordinary shares, the market value on the date of receipt will be taken as the taxable amount since they could be sold at that price. If, however, they are received subject to conditions which reduce their value, that reduction will usually be reflected in a reduction in the taxable amount.[14] This was used as the basis of much planning in share incentive schemes.

11.1.4.2 Priority Allocations and ITEPA 2003, Part 7, Chapter 10

Income may also arise within ITEPA 2003, section 62 if employees are given priority in a public offer and so end up with more shares than they would have got as members of the public—assuming that the values at allocation exceeded the price paid.

Special rules in ITEPA 2003 may exclude the charge in such cases.[15] Chapter 10 first deals with offers to the public and employees, and provides an exemption where there is a genuine offer to the public at a fixed price or tender.[16] The exemption applies even though the employees are given priority, provided:

(1) the number of priority shares is limited and no more than 10% of the shares are offered to the employees in priority;[17]
(2) all persons entitled to the priority allocation receive it on similar terms; and
(3) the offer is not restricted wholly or mainly to directors or employees above a certain level of remuneration.[18]

The exemption does not apply to any discount.[19]

Secondly Chapter 10 provides separate but similar rules granting exemption where there is both an offer to the public and a separate offer to employees at the same time.[20] The rules are aligned so that one looks at both issues together to apply the limits as to the

---

[12] ITEPA 2003, s 7(6). The other (Pt 6) is a ragbag of rules.
[13] *Weight v Salmon* (1935) 19 TC 174.
[14] *Ede v Wilson and Cornwall* [1945] 1 All ER 367, 26 TC 381.
[15] ITEPA 2003, Pt 7, Ch 10, ss 542–548, ex FA 1988, s 68; see [1987] *Simon's Tax Intelligence* 716, 866.
[16] ITEPA 2003, s 542.
[17] ITEPA 2003, s 542(3) and (4). For explanation, see ITEPA 2003 Technical Note 52. Ex FA 1988, s 68(1A) (a), added by FA 1989, s 66 and FA 1991, s 44(4); see [1988] *Simon's Tax Intelligence* 748, and [1989] *Simon's Tax Intelligence* 106.
[18] ITEPA 2003, s 542(5)–(6); on 'similar terms' see s 546.
[19] ITEPA 2003, s 543.
[20] ITEPA 2003, s 544.

number of employee shares.[21] Again the exemption does not extend to discounts, although the enactment of this statutory purpose is more complicated and uses the device of a 'registrant discount'.[22]

In practice, many flotations are made by placement and not by public offer, and so technically fall outside these protective rules.[23] These rules had to be modified to take account of privatisations involving two or more companies.[24]

11.1.4.3 Options to Acquire Shares

Acquisition of option. If E receives an option to buy shares, income arises under section 62 equal to the value of the option, ie the difference between the price payable under the option and the market value of the shares on the date of receipt of the option.[25] If, therefore, the price payable under the option is the market value at the time of the grant, no tax is due under section 62.

Exercise of option. If the shares rise in value before the exercise of the option, a charge to tax will not arise under section 62 when the option is exercised. However, a charge may arise under Part 7 thanks to section 476 (which does not apply, however, to the various favoured schemes). The reason why no charge arises under section 62 was explained by the House of Lords in *Abbott v Philbin*.[26] There, E received an option to buy shares at £3.42 each, the market value at the date of the option, and exercised it in a subsequent tax year when the market value of the shares was £4.10. The House of Lords held that the emolument arose in the year the option was acquired, and at that time E received no benefit from it since he was merely given an option to buy at what was then full market value. The fact that the emolument subsequently increased in value did not mean that that increase in value was an emolument. Although this case has been reversed for options over shares—and now securities—it remains good law for options over other types of property.

Disposal of shares. Disposal will usually trigger a charge to CGT rather than income tax; any income tax could arise only under ITTOIA 2005, Part 2. Since the asset disposed of is the shareholding, CGT will be charged on the gain realised after the acquisition of the shares.

Loans to acquire shares. ITEPA 2003, Part 3, Chapter 7 may apply if the loan is on advantageous terms or is written off (*Revenue Law*, §16.4.3 and §16.4.4).[27]

11.2 FA 2003—Scope and Background

FA 2003 provided a major overhaul of the legislation in this area, the only regret being that the overhaul was not done in time to be taken into account properly in ITEPA 2003. As already seen, there were three principal changes. The first was the extension of the rules

---

[21] ITEPA 2003, s 544(3) and (4).
[22] ITEPA 2003, s 545; the discount is defined further in s 547.
[23] Cohen [1997] *Business Law Review* 131.
[24] ITEPA 2003, s 544, ex FA 1988, s 68 (1ZA), (1ZB), added as from 16 January 1991 by FA 1991, s 44(3).
[25] *Weight v Salmon* (1935) 19 TC 173.
[26] [1961] AC 352, [1960] 2 All ER 763, 39 TC 82.
[27] ITEPA 2003, Pt 3, Ch 8, which created a notional loan in certain situations, and Ch 9, which applied where shares were disposed of for more than market value, were repealed by FA 2003, their scope having been absorbed into the new rules.

to cover all securities and not just shares. The second was a new set of chapters, Chapters 3A–3D, dealing with acquisitions above or below market value, and with the manipulation of values. The third was the extension of PAYE and NICs to produce a uniform application across the rules.

11.2.1 Securities

Securities are defined in section 420 to cover not only shares and debentures but also warrants, certificates, futures rights under certain insurance policies and rights under contracts for differences.[28] FA 2006, section 92 first brought options within the concept of security in section 420(1)(f); it then amended section 420(5)(e) by excluding options to acquire securities (unless they fail a purpose test) from Part 3, Chapters 1–5. These changes were backdated to 2 December 2004. The application of PAYE to such retrospective charges, both in the context of section 92 and generally, is governed by changes made by FA 2006, section 94. The Treasury is given power to amend this Part of the Act by statutory instrument.[29] Market value is defined by reference to the CGT rules and envisages consideration in non-monetary form.[30]

Sections 421B–421L provide some overarching rules for ITEPA 2003, Part 7, Chapters 2–4A (see §11.3), now including Chapters 3A–3D (see §11.4). So the rules apply where the securities are employment-related securities, ie securities acquired by a person by reason of the employment of that (or some other) person;[31] employment includes former or prospective employment. Acquisition is determined by reference to beneficial entitlement.[32] The expression 'by reason of employment' is elaborated upon in the same way as for other provisions of the Act, eg section 201, so a security is not acquired by reason of employment if made available to the person by an individual in the normal course of the individual's domestic, family or personal relationships.[33]

The rules cease to apply in three situations.[34] They cease to apply immediately after the securities are disposed of—unless to an associated person—or immediately before the death of the employee. They also cease to apply seven years from the ending of the employment. However, this rule has to be widened to cover situations in which the person was employed by one company but had shares in another, or obtains employment with a person connected with the employer or company. The start of the seven-year period must be after the acquisition of the securities.

11.2.2 Associated Persons

Section 421C defines associated persons in relation to employment-related securities. This concept is important and potentially misleading. Other parts of the tax legislation use

---

[28] ITEPA 2003, s 420 as amended F(No2)A 2005, Sch 2. For example, see Notes to Finance Bill.
[29] ITEPA 2003, s 420(6).
[30] ITEPA 2003, ss 421 and 421A.
[31] ITEPA 2003, s 421B(1).
[32] ITEPA 2003, s 421B(2).
[33] ITEPA 2003, s 421B(3).
[34] ITEPA 2003, s 421(4)–(7).

expressions such as 'the employee and any associates of the employee'. Section 421C uses a different technique by lumping together the employee and the associates and describing them all as 'associated persons'. So the definition covers both the person acquiring the shares and, if different, the employee. It also includes 'any relevant linked person', ie someone who is a connected person or member of the same household. This too is interesting; the more old-fashioned 'connected person' is defined in terms of legal relationships.[35] The 'household' refers to less formal relationships but is not further defined.

Rules are provided for situations in which shares or other securities are replaced or added to, or where there is a change in the person's interest.[36] These rules give us expressions such as 'additional securities' and 'replacement securities'.

11.2.3 Exclusions

First as to residence. Section 421E(1) makes Chapters 2, 3 and 4 apply only if the employee was resident at the relevant time, which is the time of acquisition. The new Chapters 3A–3D have a slightly wider rule—section 421E(2)—referring to a charge arising under any of the provisions in sections 14–41. Section 421E goes on to make the residence rules apply to former employments. More formally, Chapters 2–4 do not apply to former employments if they would not have applied if the acquisition had taken place in the last year in which the employment was held. Similarly, the rules apply for prospective employments only if they would have applied if the shares had been acquired in the first year in which the employment is held.[37]

Originally, the rules in Chapters 2–4 did not apply to shares acquired under an offer made to the public.[38] However, the scope of this exception was reduced as part of the FA 2004 anti-avoidance drive; it now applies only to Chapters 2, 3 and 3C, but there is an anti-avoidance main purpose test.[39] Previously the rules did not apply to matters within Chapters 6–8, but these exceptions were repealed.[40] There are definitions of employee-controlled companies and associated company, the CTA 2010, section 449 definition being used.[41] Further, since some rules (Chapters 2, 3 and 3A) refer to the acquisition of employment-related securities, rules are needed to determine the consideration given for such acquisitions.[42] These rules take account of options and replacement options, and contain a rule linking certain transactions to form one transaction.[43]

Lastly, there is an elaborate duty to provide information, backed up by a list of reportable events, and of persons obliged to report.[44]

---

[35] ITEPA 2003, s 718 refers to ITA 2007, s 993 (ex TA 1988, s 839).
[36] ITEPA 2003, s 421D.
[37] ITEPA 2003, s 421E(4).
[38] ITEPA 2003, s 421F.
[39] ITEPA 2003, s 421F(1A).
[40] ITEPA 2003, s 421G, repealed by FA 2004, s 88.
[41] ITEPA 2003, s 421H.
[42] ITEPA 2003, s 421I.
[43] ITEPA 2003, s 421I(5)-(7), especially s 421I((7), which takes 'release' of a right to include agreeing to the restriction of its exercise.
[44] ITEPA 2003, ss 421J-421L.

11.3   Securities Schemes

The first type of security scheme relevant here was the share purchase incentive scheme. This was introduced to avoid ITEPA 2003, section 476.[45] Instead of being given an option to buy a share for £1—the current market value of the share which might in due course be worth £3—E would be issued with a share which ordinarily would have had a current market value of £3 but which was subject to restrictions making it worth only £1. At a later date the restrictions would be removed. The increase in value could not be subject to tax under what is now section 476, since the employee did not realise a gain by exercising a right to acquire shares—the shares were already owned. If the company capitalised its profits to pay them up, there would be a charge under the residual charge for the director, etc in section 203 (ex TA 1988, section 154) on the employee on the amount so spent, but this would usually be much less than the gain realised.

Faced with such schemes the legislature provided two sets of rules. Set one (see §11.3.1 and §11.3.2 below) introduced in 1998, clarified the treatment of conditional acquisitions of shares and the conversion of convertible shares. Set two (see §11.3.3), introduced—and amended—much earlier, provided a separate charge on the growth in the value of shares in certain circumstances. FA 2003 rewrote these rules, extending them to securities as opposed to just shares, but also, sometimes, simplifying them. Some of the simplification is achieved by the addition of Chapters 3A–3D (§11.4 below) and the consequent relocation of provisions.

Here we follow the order in the 2003 Act rather than the historical order.

11.3.1   Restricted Securities (Previously Conditional Interest in Shares)[46]

The legislative restrictions on the use of share options (see §11.5 below) led in practice to greater use of long-term share incentive schemes in which benefits accrued only if performance conditions attached to the shares were satisfied. However, the assumption that there was no charge on the grant of such shares, but only when the conditions were satisfied and benefits received, rested, until 1998, on general principle rather than express provision. It could, contrary to the general assumption, be argued, on the basis of *Abbott v Philbin*,[47] that there should be a charge on the grant of the shares based on a prediction, ie a guess, as to the chance that the particular employee would derive a benefit in the fullness of time thanks to the success of the company or the stock market's assessment of the company. If this was correct, the charge based on guesswork at the time of the grant would exclude any charge when the conditions were removed. Therefore, in 1998 the Revenue moved to enact rules validating the general assumption.

The rules to be considered apply to what were at first termed 'conditional acquisitions of shares'; ITEPA 2003 originally changed the heading to Chapter 2, 'Conditional Interest in Shares', but FA 2003 renamed it 'Restricted Securities'. In any event, the securities must be employment-related securities (see §11.2.1 above).[48] FA 2003 made the

---

[45] Ex TA 1988, s 135.
[46] On pre-ITEPA 2003 changes see Richards [1999] BTR 340.
[47] [1961] AC 354, (1961) 39 TC 382.
[48] ITEPA 2003, s 422–432.

whole application of Chapter 2 a matter of election, but usually in the interest of paying the tax up front (see below).

There are elaborate rules as to when securities are restricted.[49] There are also exceptions where the securities are subject to forfeiture for misconduct or for other permitted reasons; these exceptions are subject to a tax-avoidance main purpose test, but redeemable securities are caught anyway.[50] If the condition attached to the securities must be satisfied (or not) within five years, there will be no charge on the acquisition of the securities.[51] The exclusion from charge on acquisition does not prevent any liability arising under Chapters 3 (acquisition by conversion), 3C (the rule on acquisition for less than market value) or 5 (acquisition by exercise of a share option), but the employer and employee may jointly elect irrevocably that the charges under Chapters 3, 3C and 5 do not apply.[52]

There will, however, be a charge on the occurrence of a chargeable event if and when the holding becomes unrestricted, or on any earlier sale of the securities or any interest in them.[53] The charge is on a portion of the market value of the shares (when the holding becomes unconditional or on prior disposal), less allowable deductions[54] and relief for employer's Class 1 NICs paid by the employee.[55] Any liability on the grant of the shares will be taken into account to prevent a double charge.[56] There is an exclusion from this charge if the employment-related securities are shares in a class, the restriction applies to all the shares in the class and the non employment-related shares in that class are also affected by a similar event.[57] This exception was used as the basis for avoidance, and so FA 2004 added a rule that the exception is available only if the avoidance of tax or NICs was not the main purpose, or one of the main purposes, of the arrangements under which the right or opportunity to acquire employment-related securities was made available.[58]

If the market value has been manipulated in the ways envisaged under Chapters 3A–3D, charges may arise under those Chapters. There are consequential rules for CGT and relief from corporation tax for the contributions.[59] FA 2003 provided an election that all outstanding restrictions should be ignored, so enabling the tax to be finalised—on the basis of the full unmanipulated value—instead of having to drag on until another chargeable event just because of some trivial condition.[60]

However section 431 goes even further and makes the application of the rules in Chapter 2 a matter of election. Employer and employee may jointly elect that either all the restrictions or any specified restrictions should not apply.[61] The effect of this is to open up the entire value to possible charges under the general principle in section 62, or under

[49] ITEPA 2003, s 423, ex TA 1988, s 140C; for parallel NIC treatment, see [1998] *Simon's Tax Intelligence* 729, 1358.

[50] ITEPA 2003, s 424 amended by F(No 2)A 2005, Sch 2, ex TA 1988, s 140C(1A), (3A), added by FA 1999, s 43.

[51] ITEPA 2003, s 425, ex TA 1988, s 140A(3) is subject to s 476, ex 135 (charge on exercise of unapproved share options).

[52] ITEPA 2003, s 425(3)–(5); on forms and time limits, see s 425(5).

[53] ITEPA 2003, ss 426 and 427, ex TA 1988, s 140A(4).

[54] ITEPA 2003, s 428, ex TA 1988, s 140A(5); market value is defined in s 421, ex s 145A(6) and allowable deductions in s 428(7), ex ss 140A(7), 140B.

[55] ITEPA 2003, s 428A, added by FA 2004, s 85 and Sch 16, para 1.

[56] ITEPA 2003, s 428, ex TA 1988, s 140A(7).

[57] ITEPA 2003, s 429 test modified by F(No 2)A 2005, Sch 2.

[58] ITEPA 2003, s 429(1A) added by FA 2004, s 86.

[59] See TCGA 1992, ss 119A and 149AA and FA 2003, Sch 23.

[60] ITEPA 2003, s 430.

[61] ITEPA 2003, s 431(1) and (2).

the rule for conversions in section 439(3)(a) or under Chapters 3C, 5 or Part 7A—unless an exception applies. So a full charge arises at once if the right was acquired as part of an avoidance scheme.[62] However, the election is beneficial if the shares are acquired under an approved scheme or research institution spin-out.[63] At one time, if the condition could be satisfied beyond the five-year period there was an immediate charge when the shares were obtained. The charge has now been abolished for shares issued after the relevant date.[64]

11.3.2 Convertible Securities: Charge on Conversion, etc

Rules creating a charge on the conversion of securities were originally introduced—in 1998[65]—to supplement another charge, known as the growth-in-value charge[66] (FA 1988, section 78), which did not apply when one class of shares was converted into another. The charge on conversion survives in Chapter 3 even though the growth-in-value charge does not.

The condition for the charge to arise is that the person has acquired employment-related securities,[67] and the securities carry a right or a possible entitlement to convert them into securities of a different description.[68] The charge no longer arises simply on conversion. Instead it arises first—under section 439(3)(a)—where on the conversion the beneficial entitlement to the new securities accrues to an associated person. Other parts of section 439 apply to the disposal of the securities by an associated person otherwise than to another associated person, the release of the right to convert, or the receipt by an associated person of any benefit in money or money's worth other than the new securities. Remembering the definition of 'associated person' in section 421C, one can see that the charge arises whether the person is the person who acquired the employment-related securities in the first place, the employee or any relevant linked person.[69]

The charge is on the market value of the new securities following conversion, less any deductible amounts[70] and relief for employer's NICs paid by the employee.[71] There is, however, an exception for the entire conversion of shares of one class if the conversion affects any other shares similarly.[72] In order to take advantage of this exception, the company must be employee-controlled by virtue of these shares immediately before the conversion. Alternatively, the majority of the company's shares of the original class must at that time not be employment-related securities.[73] If the market value has been manipulated in the ways envisaged under Chapters 3A–3D, charges may arise under those Chapters. Here too the exception was used as the basis for avoidance, and so FA 2004 added a rule that the exception is available only if the avoidance of tax or NICs was not the main purpose, or

---

[62] ITEPA 2003, s 431B.

[63] ITEPA 2003, ss 431A (added 2004) and 454 (added 2005).

[64] FA 1999, s 42(2).

[65] TA 1988, ss 140D–140F, inserted by FA 1998, s 51.

[66] FA 1988, s 78.

[67] ITEPA 2003, s 435. On employment-related securities, see ITEPA 2003, s 421B(8), ex TA 1988, s 140H.

[68] ITEPA 2003, s 436, ex TA 1988, s 140D(2); definition tightened by F(No 2)A 2005, Sch 2. For parallel NIC treatment, see [1998] *Simon's Tax Intelligence* 729, 1358.

[69] ITEPA 2003, s 421C; the definition was tightened by FA 2004, s 90.

[70] ITEPA 2003, ss 440–442, ex TA 1988, s 140D and 140E.

[71] ITEPA 2003, s 442A added by FA 2004, s 85.

[72] ITEPA 2003, s 443(1)–(3), ex TA 1988, s 140D(8), (9), modified by F(No 2)A 2005, Sch 2.

[73] ITEPA 2003, s 443(3) and (4).

one of the main purposes, of the arrangements under which the right or opportunity to acquire employment-related securities was made available.[74]

Again there are consequential rules for CGT and corporation tax rules on relief for contributions.[75]

11.3.3 Post-acquisition Benefits

ITEPA 2003, Chapter 4 originally stretched from section 447 to section 470; as a result of FA 2003 it now runs from section 447 to section 450. As compared with the rules described in *Revenue Law*, 4th edition, §16.4.3, the major change is the removal of any mention of dependent subsidiaries, which was only made possible by the introduction of Chapters 3A–3D (see §11.4 below).

The charge in section 447 applies where the securities are employment-related securities and a benefit is received by an associated person in connection with the securities. Remembering the definition of 'associated person', one can see that the charge arises whether the person is the person who acquired the employment-related securities in the first place, the employee or any relevant linked person.[76] The charge arises in the year in which the benefit is received and is on the full market value of the benefit. There is the usual exception where the securities are shares of a class, the benefit is received by all the share owners in that class and either the company is employee-controlled by virtue of that holding or the majority of the shares of that class are not employment-related securities.[77] The usual exception was used as the basis for avoidance, and so here too FA 2004 added a rule that the exception is available only if the avoidance of tax or NICs was not the main purpose, or one of the main purposes, of the arrangements under which the right or opportunity to acquire employment-related securities was made available.[78] On research institution spin-out companies, see §11.10.

11.4   Anti-avoidance: Manipulation of Values

Into this legislative scheme FA 2003 planted Chapters 3A–3D, sections 446A–446Z,[79] all concerned with avoidance through the manipulation of values: Chapter 3A deals with securities with artificially depressed market value; Chapter 3B with securities with artificially enhanced market value; Chapter 3C with securities acquired for less than market value; and Chapter 3D with securities disposed of for more than market value.

11.4.1 Securities with Artificially Depressed Market Value

Chapter 3A applies where the market value of employment-related securities is reduced by things done 'otherwise than for genuine commercial purposes', a phrase defined as

---

[74] ITEPA 2003, s 443(1A), added by FA 2004, s 86.
[75] TCGA 1992, ss 119A and 149AA, and FA 2003, Sch 23.
[76] ITEPA 2003, s 421C.
[77] ITEPA 2003, s 449.
[78] ITEPA 2003, s 449(1A), added by FA 2004, s 86, strengthened by F(No 2)A 2005, Sch 2.
[79] IRPR BN 29, April 2003, [2003] *Simon's Tax Intelligence* 741.

including situations where tax avoidance is a main purpose.[80] There is also an arm's-length test for group transactions, but with an exception for a payment for group relief under CTA 2010, section 183(1).[81]

11.4.1.1 Acquisition[82]

There is a charge where the market value of the employment-related securities at the time of acquisition has been reduced by at least 10% by transactions over the previous seven years. The charge is not to affect various other charges—section 62, section 203, Chapters 3, 3C or 5 of Part 7, and Chapter 2 of Part 7A.[83] However, a charge under section 425(2) excludes a charge here.

The amount taxed is usually that by which the fair market value of the securities has been reduced, judging the facts as at the time of acquisition. If that reduction is less than the consideration actually paid for the employment-related securities, the acute consideration is taken instead.[84] Where a charge under Chapter 2 would arise (post-acquisition charges on restricted securities), it is excluded in favour of the charge under Chapter 3A.[85] If the securities are convertible and so come within Chapter 3, the value for Chapter 3A is to be determined as if they were not convertible, so leaving the convertibility increase to be dealt with under Chapter 3.[86]

11.4.1.2 Other Tax Charges

The section 426 charge on restricted securities applies if the market value of the employment-related securities has been reduced by 10% within the period of seven years ending with the chargeable event.[87] It also imposes a charge if the value is artificially low on 5 April of any year.[88]

11.4.1.3 Conditional Interests

The legislative technique used here is different. Where the employee has a conditional interest in the securities and a chargeable event occurs but the market value of the securities has been artificially reduced, the necessary adjustments are made to the post-chargeable event market value. This means that the charge still arises under sections 427 or 428 by reference to the adjusted value.

Convertible securities under Chapter 3 receive similar treatment. The charge under section 439(3)(a) is based on the fair not depressed value;[89] there are consequential changes to the value of the consideration or benefit received.[90] FA 2004 made changes in consequence of its new anti-avoidance rule.[91]

[80] ITEPA 2003, s 446A.
[81] ITEPA 2003, s 446A(2)(b).
[82] ITEPA 2003, s 446B.
[83] ITEPA 2003, s 446B(3) and (4).
[84] ITEPA 2003, s 446C.
[85] ITEPA 2003, s 446D(1).
[86] ITEPA 2003, s 446D(2).
[87] ITEPA 2003, s 446E(1)(a).
[88] ITEPA 2003, s 446E(1)(b).
[89] ITEPA 2003, s 446H.
[90] ITEPA 2003, s 446I.
[91] ITEPA 2003, s 446IA.

11.4.2 Securities with Artificially Enhanced Market Value

Chapter 3B, section 446L imposes a charge on the amount by which the market value of securities has been increased by artificial, ie non-commercial, means, provided the increase is at least 10%.[92] Artificiality is determined using the same tests as for Chapter 3A. Where the securities are 'relevant' restricted securities, the amount charged under section 446L is adjusted.[93] Section 446N deals with the situation in which the securities have been relevant restricted securities during the relevant period, and makes further deductions/adjustments to reflect the earlier charge on the occurrence of the chargeable event under section 428. FA 2004 added an anti-avoidance rule.[94]

11.4.3 Securities Acquired for Less Than Market Value

Chapter 3C deals with employment-related securities acquired either for no payment at all, or for a payment which is less than the market value. The rule is framed in terms of payment as opposed to consideration and expressly states that any obligation to make a payment after the acquisition is to be ignored—only actual payments will do. 'Payment' is not further defined, so the position of consideration in non-monetary form is unclear.[95]

The effect is to create a notional loan of the underpayment by the employer to the employee and then make the relevant parts of the low-interest loan rule in Part 3, Chapter 7 apply.[96] Further rules determine the amount of the loan.[97] A further charge arises if the loan is treated as discharged where the employment-related securities are disposed of to an associated person or there is a release of the obligation to pay.[98] Release is then supplemented by 'transferred or adjusted so as no longer to bind any associated person'. However, the notional loan is also treated as ended if the employee dies or payment of any of the amounts outstanding is made by an associated person. It seems that payments by a person about to become an associated person are not caught. FA 2005 added an anti-avoidance rule.[99]

Chapter 3C is excluded in certain situations.[100] These are where the shares are in one class and all the shares in that class have been acquired at less than market value and either the company is employee controlled by virtue of that class or, going in the opposite direction, less than half the securities are employment-related securities.[101] Here too the exception was used as the basis for avoidance and so FA 2004 added a rule that the exception is available only if the avoidance of tax or national insurance contributions was not the main purpose, or one of the main purposes, of the arrangements under which the right or opportunity to acquire employment-related securities was made available.[102]

---

[92] ITEPA 2003, s 446L.
[93] ITEPA 2003, ss 446M and 446N; relevance determined under s 446M(4).
[94] ITEPA 2003, s 446NA.
[95] There is no cross-reference to s 197(3).
[96] ITEPA 2003, s 446S(3).
[97] ITEPA 2003, s 446T.
[98] ITEPA 2003, s 446U.
[99] ITEPA 2003, s 446UA added by F(No 2)A 2005, Sch 2.
[100] ITEPA 2003, s 446R.
[101] ITEPA 2003, s 446R(1)–(4).
[102] ITEPA 2003, s 446R(1A) added by FA 2004, s 86.

Where Chapter 3C applies, the charge is additional to any other head—section 62, section 203, Chapters 3, 3A and 5 of Part 7, or Chapter 2 of Part 7A.[103]

11.4.4 Securities Disposed of for More Than Market Value

The final anti-avoidance measure is Chapter 3D dealing with securities disposed of for a consideration which exceeds market value. It applies where the employment-related securities are disposed of by an associated person so that no associated person is any longer beneficially entitled to them.[104] The amount of the consideration less the market value of the securities and any allowable expense in connection with the disposal counts as employment income of the employee.[105] The Scottish case *Gray's Timber Products v Revenue & Customs Commissioners*[106] sheds some light on the determination of market value of shares under these rules. At issue was whether rights under a subscription agreement requiring the purchase of the taxpayer's shares along with an extra payment to him in the event that more than 50% of the company's shares were sold, were to be taken into account in determining the market value of his shares for purposes of ITEPA 2003, section 446X(b) when such a sale occurred. The majority (Lord Osbourne dissenting) held that the rights were personal to the taxpayer and were not to be so taken into account; the taxpayer's shares had the same value as the other ordinary shares. The extra payment was subject to income tax under ITEPA 2003, section 446Y. The result, and the majority's reasoning, was confirmed on appeal by a unanimous Supreme Court, with Lord Walker expressing the hope 'that Parliament may find time to review the complex and obscure provisions of Part 7 of ITEPA 2003'.[107]

11.5   Special Tax Rules for Securities Options

11.5.1 Introduction

FA 2003 rewrote the original ITEPA 2003, Chapter 5, with sections 471–484 replacing the original sections 471–487. Securities option schemes cause problems in any tax system. Most tax systems agree that the grant of an option to buy, for example, shares at a figure below the market value is taxable earnings, and that the gain accruing between the time of acquisition of the shares, ie the exercise of the option, and the date of disposal should be charged as a capital gain. Problems arise over how to tax the change in value between the date of the grant of the option and the date of its exercise.

The rules in Chapter 5 of ITEPA 2003 apply where the option has been acquired by reason of employment of that person—or any other person;[108] such an option is called an employment-related securities option. The Chapter has its own definition of associated persons.[109]

---

[103] ITEPA 2003, s 446V.
[104] *Ibid.*
[105] ITEPA 2003, s 446Y(3).
[106] [2009] STC 889, [2009] CSIH 11.
[107] [2010] UKSC 4, at para 45.
[108] ITEPA 2003, s 471.
[109] ITEPA 2003, s 472—it is similar in content to s 421C but framed for options; hence this definition also was tightened by FA 2004, s 90.

11.5.2 Acquisition of Option and Later Chargeable Events

ITEPA 2003, section 473 emphasises that section 475 excludes any liability under s 62 or under Part 3, Chapter 10 where an employment-related securities option is acquired. A slight but necessary qualification is made for the situation in which an approved share option is acquired at a discount.[110] However, it then provides[111] that a charge may arise under section 446B (Chapter 3A) where the market value has been artificially depressed, Chapter 3C where the securities are acquired for less than market value or section 476 where the securities are acquired as the result of the exercise of an option already within Chapter 5. Liability under section 476 may also arise on the assignment or release of the option, and so that liability has to be preserved.[112] Any liability under these rules may be excluded if the option comes within Chapters 7, 8 or 9—ie approved SAYE option schemes, approved CSOP schemes or enterprise management incentives, discussed below at §§11.7–11.9.

It will be seen that section 475 excludes liability whether the option can only be exercised within 10 years or not; the previous law made a valuation distinction here, but that is not part of the final 2003 scheme.[113] ITEPA 2003, section 476 on chargeable events also applies where the option is an employment-related securities option.[114] The list of chargeable events[115] is:

(1) the acquisition of securities 'pursuant to' the option, ie the exercise of the option;
(2) assigning or releasing of the option where the assignment is for consideration and not to another associated person;
(3) the receipt of a benefit in money or money's worth in connection with the option, apart of course from the securities acquired under (1) or the consideration received under (2).

11.5.3 Amount Charged[116]

The taxable amount as determined under the legislation counts as employment income under Part 7 of ITEPA 2003. Normally the amount will be the difference between the price paid under the option (including the price of the option) and the market value of the shares acquired under the option—ie the gain less any deductible amounts.[117] Analogous rules apply to the assignment or release of the option,[118] and in all cases there are further special relief rules, eg for Class 1 NICs or any special social security contributions paid by the employee.[119] Further rules apply where one option is exchanged for another; a form of rollover is applied.[120]

---

[110] ITEPA 2003, s 475(2), referring to s 526.
[111] ITEPA 2003, s 473(2).
[112] ITEPA 2003, s 473(3).
[113] Contrast ITEPA 2003, s 475.
[114] ITEPA 2003, ss 471 and 476, ex TA 1988, s 135.
[115] ITEPA 2003, s 477; the definition was tightened by FA 2004, s 90.
[116] ITEPA 2003, ss 478, 479 (especially subss (1)–(4)) and 480.
[117] ITEPA 2003, s 478.
[118] ITEPA 2003, ss 478, 479(5)–(8) and 480.
[119] ITEPA 2003, ss 481 and 482.
[120] ITEPA 2003, s 483.

These rules do not prevent substantial gains being made when options are given in the run-up to the flotation of a private company, since the value of the share will rise following flotation as there is now a market for the shares.[121] In the light of this, companies often allow employees to have options tied to the post-flotation price.

The predecessor of section 476 (ex TA 1988, section 135) was held to be an independent charging section and therefore applied whether or not the benefit of the option could be converted into cash.[122] It was also applied to the exclusion of what is now section 62.[123] Section 476 does not apply in certain international situations.[124]

The effect of section 476 has been to make share option schemes unattractive in tax terms outside the approved schemes. The company receives money when the option is exercised, but not as much as on a sale to the public at that time. Although E will not normally have to pay tax until the exercise of the option, the gain on exercise is treated as E's employment income. Moreover, E may have to sell some of the shares to raise the money to pay the tax. The scheme also involves some dilution of equity. One variant scheme addresses these issues: on the exercise of the option, the company pays money to a trust, which then buys shares for E and transfers them to E. This does not avoid section 476, but since only the net-of-tax sum is invested, it avoids any need to sell shares and reduces equity dilution. As has already been stressed, the better way of avoiding section 476 is to take advantage of the statutorily-approved exceptions to that section (see ITEPA 2003, Part 7, Chapters 7, 8 and 9).

11.6   Approved Share Incentive Plans

11.6.1 Introduction

FA 2000 introduced yet another scheme, then called an 'all employee share plan' and now, since ITEPA 2003, an 'approved share incentive plan' or SIP (Part 7, Chapter 6). The plan was expected eventually to cost around £400 million a year, with around 625,000 employees owning shares in their companies for the first time.[125] In 2009–10, 860 plans appropriated shares at a tax cost of £130 million and NIC cost of £90 million.[126] If the conditions are observed, all shares in the plan, held for five years, are completely free of income tax and CGT while so held.[127]

The plan may contain three elements, each with its own rules.[128] These are called free shares, partnership shares and matching shares; there is also a fourth category comprising dividend shares. The plan may be on a group basis.[129] It needs to be approved by the Revenue.[130] It must have a purpose, as defined by the legislation, to provide benefits to employees in the

---

[121] Cohen [1997] *Business Law Review* 132, stating that the average discount given for option grants between 6 and 12 months before flotation worked out at 84.4%.

[122] *Ball v Phillips* [1990] STC 675, 63 TC 529.

[123] *Wilcock v Eve* [1995] STC 18, 67 TC 223.

[124] ITEPA 2003, s 474.

[125] See Inland Revenue Press Release, 10 November 1999, [1999] *Simon's Tax Intelligence* 1803.

[126] HMRC Share Scheme Statistics Table, 30 June 2011.

[127] On income tax advantages, see ITEPA 2003, ss 489–499 as amended by FA 2003; on s 499, see ITEPA 2003 Explanatory Notes, Change 127. On CGT, see TCGA 1992, Sch 7D, paras 1–8, added by ITEPA 2003, Sch 6, para 221.

[128] See generally ITEPA 2003, s 488 and Sch 2, and specifically Sch 2, para 2, ex FA 2000, Sch 8, para 1.

[129] ITEPA 2003, Sch 2, para 4, ex FA 2000, Sch 8, para 2.

[130] ITEPA 2003, Sch 2, paras 81 and 82, ex FA 2000, Sch 8, paras 4, 5.

nature of shares which give them a continuing stake in the company; it must not have features which are neither essential nor reasonably incidental to that purpose.[131]

The plan must be available to all employees resident in the UK who meet certain conditions of eligibility.[132] There must be no preferential treatment of directors, no further conditions and no loan arrangements.[133] The employee may not also have any options held under another approved SIP;[134] however, where the employee participates in more than one SIP run by the same company or a connected company, the several plans are treated as one.[135] The employee must not have a 'material interest' in a close company the shares of which may be awarded under the plan, or in a company controlling such a company or in a member of a consortium controlling such a company. Control of more than 25% of the ordinary share capital makes an interest 'material'.[136]

There are also conditions as to equal treatment to ensure that all are eligible to participate and that those who do so participate on similar terms.[137] However, this does not prevent discrimination on the basis of hours worked, remuneration or length of service; neither does it prevent plans from being performance-related (see §11.6.2 below). The shares must be ordinary shares which are fully paid-up and not redeemable.[138] Only certain kinds of restrictions in respect of the shares are allowed: the shares may be non-voting, subject to forfeiture in certain cases and subject to pre-emption rights on the part of the company on the employee ceasing employment.[139] The shares must either be listed or be shares of a company which is not under the control of another company, save where that other company is a listed company.[140]

For a table showing the different features, see below at §11.6.7.

11.6.2 The Free Share Plan

Employers may give up to £3,000 pa of shares to employees.[141] Employers do not have to treat all employees alike but may discriminate among them, eg for reaching performance targets and so rewarding 'personal, team or divisional performance'. These plans resemble APSSs; however, unlike those schemes, the award of free shares may be linked to performance provided the criteria are objective and are fair to all employees, ie the targets set are broadly comparable.[142] Comparable does not mean identical and, under one variant, up to 80% of shares may be awarded on the basis of performance, as long as the highest performance award is not more than four times greater than the highest non-performance

---

[131] ITEPA 2003, Sch 2, para 7, ex FA 2000, Sch 8, para 7.
[132] ITEPA 2003, Sch 2, paras 8, 14–17, ex FA 2000, Sch 8, paras 7, 13–14.
[133] ITEPA 2003, Sch 2, paras 10–12, ex FA 2000, Sch 8, paras 10–12.
[134] ITEPA 2003, Sch 2, para 18, ex FA 2000, Sch 8, para 16.
[135] ITEPA 2003, Sch 2, para 18A added by FA 2003.
[136] ITEPA 2003, Sch 2, paras 19–24; for references to employee benefit trust in para 23, see also ITEPA 2003, ss 550–554, ex FA 2000, Sch 8, paras 15, 17–22.
[137] ITEPA 2003, Sch 2, paras 8 and 9, ex FA 2000, Sch 8, paras 8, 9.
[138] ITEPA 2003, Sch 2, paras 25–28, ex FA 2000, Sch 8, paras 59–62.
[139] ITEPA 2003, Sch 2, paras 30–33 and 99, ex FA 2000, Sch 8, paras 63–66.
[140] ITEPA 2003, Sch 2, para 29, ex FA 2000, Sch 8, para 67.
[141] ITEPA 2003, Sch 2, para 35.
[142] ITEPA 2003, Sch 2, paras 38–42, ex FA 2000, Sch 8, paras 27–30.

award to an employee on similar terms.[143] There are also rules about the information to be given to employees.[144]

Free shares are held by trustees and appropriated to the participant.[145] The shares must remain with the trustee for a period of at least three years and not more than five years.[146] If the shares leave the plan before three years, there is a charge on the market value of the shares on leaving.[147] The shares may be withdrawn tax-free within the three-year period if the employment ends because of redundancy or disability, or for other accepted cause.[148] If the shares are withdrawn between years three and five, there is a charge on the lesser of the value of the shares when awarded and the value of the shares when leaving.[149]

11.6.3 Reinvestment of Cash Dividends (Dividend Shares)

Dividends accruing on the plans shares may either be distributed in the usual (taxable) way, or be reinvested in 'dividend shares'.[150] There is a reinvestment ceiling of £1,500 a year in any tax year.[151] The shares have their own three-year holding period.[152] Once the three years have passed there is no income tax charge on these shares. The share may be left in the plan or transferred, as the employee wishes. If the holding period rules are broken, the dividend used to pay for the shares becomes taxable.[153] Certain amounts which are not reinvested may be retained by the trustees and then paid out if not used.[154]

11.6.4 CGT Liability

A CGT liability may accrue if the employee, having had the shares transferred, then sells them. No liability arises on the appropriation or on withdrawal[155] as the shares are treated as having been disposed of without giving rise to a chargeable gain and immediately reacquired at market value; neither is there any liability on disposal of rights under a rights issue.[156] Since the base cost of the shares will be the value when they are transferred to the employee, little if any liability will arise if the employee sells them immediately. So long as the shares remain in the plan the employee is treated as beneficially entitled to them as against the trustee.[157] Once the shares have been withdrawn by the employee—something required after five years anyway—they become chargeable assets and potentially liable to CGT. The shares are pooled separately.[158]

---

[143] ITEPA 2003, Sch 2, para 41(2)(c), ex FA 2000, Sch 8, para 29(1)(c).

[144] ITEPA 2003, Sch 2, para 40, ex FA 2000, Sch 8, para 28. ITEPA 2003 Explanatory Notes, Change 161. On para 42, see ITEPA 2003 Technical Note 64.

[145] On powers and duties see ITEPA 2003, Sch 2, paras 70–85 ex FA 2000,Sch 8, paras 68–86.

[146] ITEPA 2003, Sch 2, para 36, ex FA 2000, Sch 8, para 31; the participant may direct the trustees to do various things, including accepting certain offers in relation to the shares—see ITEPA 2003, Sch 2, para 37, ex FA 2000, Sch 8, para 32.

[147] ITEPA 2003, s 505(2), ex FA 2000, Sch 8, para 81(2).

[148] ITEPA 2003, s 498, ex FA 2000, Sch 8, para 87.

[149] ITEPA 2003, s 505(3) ex FA 2000, Sch 8, para 81(3).

[150] ITEPA 2003, Sch 2, paras 62–68, ex FA 2000, Sch 8, paras 53–58. See also ITEPA 2003 Technical Note 66.

[151] ITEPA 2003, Sch 2, para 64, ex FA 2000, Sch 8, para 54.

[152] ITEPA 2003, Sch 2, para 67, ex FA 2000, Sch 8, para 57.

[153] ITEPA 2003, Sch 2, para 67, ex FA 2000, Sch 8, para 57.

[154] ITEPA 2003, Sch 2, para 68, ex FA 2000, Sch 8, para 58.

[155] TCGA 1992, Sch 7D, para 5, ex FA 2000, Sch 8, para 101.

[156] TCGA 1992, Sch 7D, para 8, ITEPA 2003, Sch 6, para 55, ex FA 2000, Sch 8, para 104.

[157] TCGA 1992, Sch 7D, para 3, ITEPA 2003, Sch 6, para 55, ch 8, para 99.

[158] TCGA 1992, Sch 7D, para 4, ITEPA 2003, Sch 6, para 55, ex FA 2000, Sch 8, para 100.

CGT holdover reliefs are available not only to trustees where funds are transferred to one of these funds from a qualifying ESOP,[159] but also to existing shareholders wanting to sell their shares to a new plan trust for the benefit of employees.

Gains realised by the trustees are not normally liable to CGT.[160]

11.6.5 The Partnership Share Plan[161]

Employees may buy shares out of their pre-tax monthly salary or weekly wages up to a maximum of £1,500 a year or £125 a month.[162] There is also a maximum limit of 10% of salary.[163] Another rule requires the employee to be informed about the possible effect of these rights on benefit entitlement.[164] The rules give the employee a tax deduction for the sums spent on the purchase of the shares. The payments must be deducted from the employee's salary.[165] The plan may allow for money to be accumulated; if it does not, the sum must be invested within 30 days.[166] Sums may not be accumulated beyond 12 months.

As the employee has paid for the shares, there is no minimum period during which the shares must be retained and the employee will face no charge if the shares are left in the plan for five years. If shares are removed before three years have passed, the employee must pay income tax on the value of the shares when they are removed.[167] There is no deduction for the original price since it was tax free. If shares are removed between years three and five, the employee must pay income tax on the lesser of the sums used to buy the shares and the value when removed.[168] Charges may also arise if share money is paid over to the employee or on cancellation payments to E.[169] Sums set aside by the employee in this way are tax free yet are not deductible from salary in computing relevant earnings for pension's limits.

Dividend shares may arise under a partnership share scheme. The rules are the same as for free shares (see §11.6.2 above).

11.6.6 Matching (Partnership) Shares

Employers may match 'partnership' shares by giving employees up to two free shares for each partnership share they buy. The matching shares must be on the same terms and carry the same rights as the partnership shares; the matching shares must be appropriated at the same time[170] and to all employees on the same basis. There are rules about

---

[159] ITEPA 2003, Sch 2 para 78, ex FA 2000, Sch 8, para 76.

[160] TCGA 1992, Sch 7D, para 2.

[161] ITEPA 2003, Sch 2, paras 43–57, ex FA 2000, Sch 8, paras 33–48.

[162] ITEPA 2003, Sch 2, para 46, ex FA 2000, Sch 8, para 36; there is also a minimum of £10 a month, ITEPA 2003, Sch 2 para 47, ex FA 2000, Sch 8, para 37.

[163] ITEPA 2003, Sch 2, para 46(2), ex FA 2000, Sch 8, para 36(2); on salary, see ITEPA 2003, Sch 2, para 43, ex FA 2000, Sch 8, para 48.

[164] ITEPA 2003, Sch 2, para 48, ex FA 2000, Sch 8, para 38.

[165] ITEPA 2003, Sch 2, para 45(1), ex FA 2000, Sch 8, para 35(1).

[166] ITEPA 2003, Sch 2, para 50, ex FA 2000, Sch 8, para 40; on plans with accumulation powers, see ITEPA 2003, Sch 2, para 52(2), ex FA 2000, Sch 8, para 42(2).

[167] ITEPA 2003, s 506(2), ex FA 2000, Sch 8, para 86(2).

[168] ITEPA 2003, s 506(3), ex FA 2000, Sch 8, para 86(3).

[169] ITEPA 2003, ss 503 and 504, ex FA 2000, Sch 8, paras 84, 86.

[170] ITEPA 2003, Sch 2, paras 58–61, ex FA 2000, Sch 8, paras 49–52.

giving employees information. The holding period rules are the same as for free shares (§11.6.2 above); further rules allow the company to require forfeiture of the matching shares when the employee leaves the employment.[171]

Income tax and CGT rules are the same as for free shares. The rules for dividend shares apply here too (§11.6.3 above).

11.6.7 *Miscellaneous*

Employers may deduct the costs of setting up and running the plan, and the market value of any free and matching shares used in the plan.[172] The trustees are given a power to borrow money to buy the shares or subscribe for rights issues.[173] FA 2010 introduced CTA 2009, section 989(1)(aa), which denies a corporation tax deduction where a payment to a SIP trust is made as part of a tax avoidance scheme, where the main purpose or one of the main purposes of the paying company is to obtain the deduction. The measure has effect from 24 March 2010. HMRC may withdraw approval of a SIP where alterations to share capital or changes in rights attaching to shares materially affect the value of shares that are subject to the plan trust.

Inland Revenue Table: Consultative Document New Employee Share Plan November 1999, p 8 (updated by authors)

	Free Shares	**Partnership Shares**	**Matching Shares**	**Dividend Shares**
Employment before eligibility	Up to 12 months' employment	Up to 12 months' employment	Only awarded to employees who buy partnership shares	Must be acquired with dividends from plan shares
Limits	Up to £3,000 per tax year	Up to £1,500 per tax year, capped at lower of: £125 per month and 10% of monthly salary	Up to 2 matching shares for each partnership share bought	Dividends from shares in the plan reinvested: up to £1,500 per tax year
Minimum Amount if stated[a]		£10 per month		
Performance measures[b]	Yes	No	No	No

(Continued)

---

[171] ITEPA 2003, s 505, ex FA 2000, Sch 8, para 81.
[172] ITEPA 2003, s 515 referring to CTA 2009, Pt 11, Ch 1, ex TA 1988, Sch 4AA, added by ITEPA 2003, Sch 6, original rules in FA 2000, Sch 8, paras 105–113.
[173] ITEPA 2003, Sch 2, para 76, ex FA 2000, Sch 8, para 69.

	Free Shares	Partnership Shares	Matching Shares	Dividend Shares
Holding Period	At least 3 years from award[b]	None	At least 3 years from award[b]	3 years from acquisition
Forfeiture on cessation of employment[a]	Yes	No	Yes	No
Tax on award	None	None—tax relief for salary used to buy shares	None	None
Tax on removal of shares from plan[c]	On market value when taken out within 3 years of award	On market value when taken out of plan	On market value when taken out of plan	Original dividend taxable but in year when shares taken out
Tax on removal between 3 and 5 years of award[c]	On lower of:	On lower of:	On lower of:	None
	Value at award and value on removal	Salary used to buy and value on removal	Value at award and Value on removal	
Tax on removal after 5 years	None	None	None	None
CGT on removal any time	None	None	None	None

[a] These conditions may be included at the option of the company.
[b] The holding period may be up to five years at the option of the company.
[c] PAYE and NICs will be operated in relation to any employment income tax charge where the shares are readily convertible assets.

11.7 Approved SAYE Option Schemes

Since 1980 it has been possible to combine an approved share option scheme with an approved savings scheme so as to take advantage of the tax efficiency of the savings scheme to provide the funds to finance the exercise of the option.[174] HMRC statistics show that, by the end of 2009–10, 720 schemes were live; the initial market value of shares over which options had been granted over that year totalled £3 billion; in that year the average value per employee of the shares over which options had been granted was £4,100; the cost of the tax relief was £110 million and NIC relief was £70 million.

---

[174] TA 1988, s 185, Sch 9, Pts I–III, VI. On amendments relating to the retirement age and to ensure equality of treatment for men and women, see FA 1991, s 38.

11.7.1 Conditions of Approval

11.7.1.1 The Scheme

The ITEPA 2003, Part 7, Chapter 7 savings scheme must be within ITTOIA 2005, section 702 and be approved by the Revenue for this purpose.[175] The contribution must not exceed £250 a month.[176] The option is not normally exercisable for five or seven years (ie the period needed to attract the bonus on maturity of the savings scheme) and the price for the shares must not exceed the proceeds of the contract.

11.7.1.2 Who May Participate?

The participants in the scheme, ie those eligible to participate, must include all UK-resident and ordinarily resident employees (whether full-time or part-time) or full-time directors with, in each case, at least five years' service,[177] but must not include outsiders nor those with a material interest in the company if it is a close company.[178]

11.7.1.3 Shares

The shares must be ordinary share capital and must be quoted, or shares in a company not controlled by another company or shares under the control of a non-close quoted company.[179] It follows from this that if a company is taken over, the existing scheme must be wound up (since approval will be withdrawn) and a new scheme, with its own five- or seven-year period, started in relation to the new head company.[180] The shares must be fully paid up and not redeemable. The only restrictions permitted are those imposed by the company's articles requiring employees to dispose of their shares at the end of their employment.[181] The price at which the shares may be acquired must not be manifestly less than 80% of the market value at the time the option is acquired[182] (oddly the 80% figure was not changed in 1996). Schemes may contain provisions allowing for the transfer of rights following a takeover so as to give rights to acquire shares in the new company.[183] This must be agreed by the new company, and the value of the new option must be the same as that of the old option.

---

[175] ITEPA 2003, s 516 and Sch 3, para 24, ex TA 1988, Sch 9, para 16A.

[176] ITEPA 2003, Sch 3, para 25(3)(a), ex TA 1988, Sch 9, para 24(2)(a).

[177] ITEPA 2003, Sch 3, paras 6–10, ex TA 1988, Sch 9, para 26, as amended by FA 1995, s 137.

[178] ITEPA 2003, Sch 3, paras 11–16, ex TA 1988, Sch 9, paras 8, 26. For traps where a person still has a material interest even though the company is no longer close, see Cohen [1997] *Business Law Review* 131, 132 (neither s 415 nor non-resident status can help them in such circumstances).

[179] ITEPA 2003, Sch 3, para 19, ex TA 1988, Sch 9, para 11.

[180] See also ITEPA 2003, Sch 3, para 3, ex TA 1988, Sch 9, para 1(3), (4); on concessionary relief for jointly-owned companies, see ITEPA 2003, Sch 3, para 46 and Sch 4, para 34, ex ESC B27. So, 51% control will suffice, 50% will not (*IRC v Reed International plc* [1994] STC 396, 67 TC 552).

[181] ITEPA 2003, Sch 3, paras 20 and 21, ex TA 1988, Sch 9, paras 12, 13; ITEPA 2003, Explanatory Notes Change 168.

[182] ITEPA 2003, Sch 3, para 28, ex TA 1988, Sch 9, para 25 as amended by FA 1989, s 62(3); see also cases on Sch 9, para 29. On para 28, see ITEPA 2003, Explanatory Notes Change 169.

[183] ITEPA 2003, Sch 3, paras 38 and 39, ex TA 1988, Sch 9, para 15; on capital gains consequences, see TCGA 1992, s 238.

11.7.2 Tax Treatment

If these conditions are met, no charge arises on the grant of the option.[184] No income tax liability charge arises on the exercise of the option unless it is exercised within three years of the grant.[185] Certain exercises within that period, eg when that scheme ends, are also exempt.[186] Special rules may apply if the company is taken over or some similar event occurs.[187] The employer may deduct the costs of introducing such schemes.[188] FA 2009 moved some functions concerning the administration of SAYE schemes from the Treasury to HMRC, and made other changes, eg removing the requirement that certain notices must be sent by post.

11.8 Approved Company Share Option Plan Schemes

11.8.1 Background

A survey showed that whereas in 1987, 90% of companies had approved schemes compared with 10% that had unapproved schemes, by 1996, 80% of companies had approved schemes compared with 85% unapproved.[189] Explanations included the 1988 equalisation of tax rates for CGT and income tax, and the 1996 reduction in the limit for approved schemes to options over shares with a market value of £30,000. Another explanation was the 1996 rule that schemes had to be open to all employees, which applied as from 1996 and did not affect existing options. Symbolically—and accurately—the 1996 rule changes meant that schemes which had previously been called 'discretionary' schemes were instead called 'company' share schemes. In 1993–94, 70,000 employees received options over shares with an initial value totalling £1,750 million; the average per employee was £25,000 and the cost of the tax relief was £70 million; in 2009–10 the figures were 40,000, £280 million, £7,300 and £30 million (plus NIC relief of another £30 million).[190] There is a decided downward trend in these figures, particularly in recent years. In its March 2012 report on approved share schemes, the OTS questioned whether the CSOP scheme was still relevant and recommended that the Government consider phasing it out or, in the alternative, merging it with the EMI scheme. For now at least, the relevant rules are in ITEPA 2003, Part 7, Chapter 8.

11.8.2 Approved Company Share Option Schemes or CSOPs

11.8.2.1 Benefits of Approval

No charge on exercise; CGT on disposal. Where an option is granted under an approved scheme, no charge arises on the exercise of the option provided it is exercised not less than

---

[184] ITEPA 2003, s 475.
[185] ITEPA 2003, s 519.
[186] ITEPA 2003, s 519(3).
[187] ITEPA 2003, Sch 3, paras 34–38, ex TA 1988, Sch 9, para 21.
[188] CTA 2009, s 1221 referring to s 999, ex TA 1988, s 84A added by FA 1991, s 42.
[189] Cohen [1997] *Business Law Review* 131.
[190] HMRC Share Schemes Statistics Table, 30 June 2011.

three nor more than 10 years after the grant.[191] Instead, a charge to CGT arises on the disposal of the shares on the difference between the full cost of the option shares and the disposal proceeds. This is all subject to the anti-avoidance provision in section 524(2)(c).

Charge on grant at discount. Under ITEPA 2003, section 475, no tax charge arises on the grant of the option. However, section 475 is subject to section 526. Under section 526, where the amount or value of the consideration given for the option and the price payable under it is less than the market value of the shares at that time, the difference is treated as share-related employment income in the year of the grant.[192] The right under an option to acquire shares at a discount of up to 15% of market value was abolished by FA 1996 as part of the reaction against gains being made by certain executives following privatisation.[193] The amount chargeable to income tax is treated as consideration given on the acquisition of the shares when one comes to calculate the gain on the disposal of the shares.[194]

Any capital gain is calculated by reference to the actual consideration received rather than market value;[195] the value of services or past services rendered by the employee is excluded,[196] so that virtually the only consideration to be brought in will be pecuniary.

11.8.2.2 Conditions for Approval

Who may participate? From 1 May 1995, any full-time director or qualifying employee (whether full-time or part-time) of the company establishing the scheme (the grantor company), or of another company covered by the group scheme, is eligible to participate.[197] Anyone with a material interest in a company must be excluded, as must a part-time director.[198]

Value? As from 1996 the value of the shares (at the time the option is granted) over which each participator may hold unexercised options is restricted to £30,000. For earlier schemes the limit was the greater of (a) £100,000, and (b) four times the emoluments (for PAYE purposes, less benefits) in the year of assessment or the preceding year (or the 12 months beginning on the first day in the year of assessment for which there are such emoluments).[199] Within these limits the size of the option is at the company's discretion. FA 2010 responded to so-called 'geared growth' arrangements designed to circumvent the £30,000 maximum limit on the value of CSOP shares. The avoidance schemes involved

---

[191] ITEPA 2003, s 524, ex TA 1988, s 185(3), (5).

[192] ITEPA 2003, s 526, ex TA 1988, s 185(4).

[193] TA 1988, s 185(6B), added by FA 1991, s 39(5), which also amended s 185(6) and added s 185(6A) on interaction with CGT and amendment of TCGA 1992, s 120 to avoid double charge (see FA 1993, s 105). Not in ITEPA 2003 because spent.

[194] TCGA 1992, Sch 7D, para 12, ex TA 1988, s 185(7).

[195] TCGA 1992, Sch 7D, para 13, added by ITEPA 2003, Sch 6, paras 207 and 221.

[196] TCGA 1992, s 149A(3).

[197] ITEPA 2003, Sch 4, paras 7 and 8, ex TA 1988, Sch 9, para 27, as amended by FA 1995, s 137; previously only full-time directors and full-time employees qualified, although they might exercise the rights after the employment ended. HMRC accept that the exercise of a CSOP option can be made subject to the attainment of objective targets (by the company or option-holder): see HMRC Employee Share Schemes User Manual ESSUM44250, based on principles established in *IRC v Burton Group plc* [1990] STC 242, 63 TC 191.

[198] ITEPA 2003, Sch 4, para 8(1) and 9, ex TA 1988, Sch 9, para 8; on definition of material interest, see ITEPA 2003, Sch 4, paras 10–14, ex TA 1988, s 187(3), Sch 9, paras 37–40; ITEPA 2003, Sch 4, para 13, ex TA 1988, Sch 9, para 40, was originally added by FA 1989, s 65 and excludes shares held in an employee benefit trust in the calculation of a person's holding, unless caught by ITEPA 2003, Sch 4, para 15(2), ex TA 1988, Sch 9, para 40(3). See also FA 1989, Sch 12, para 9. On para 11, see ITEPA 2003 Explanatory Notes Change 174.

[199] ITEPA 2003, Sch 4, para 6, ex TA 1988, Sch 9, para 28.

share options granted over shares in companies which were under the control of a listed company. FA 2010, section 39 removed ITEPA 2003, Schedule 4, paragraph 17(1)(c), so that from 24 March 2010 (subject to a six-month transition period to allow plans to be amended) shares in a company which is under the control of a listed company will no longer be shares to which an approved CSOP scheme might apply.

Shares. The shares must be part of the fully paid-up ordinary share capital of the grantor company (or certain controlling companies)[200] and must be (a) quoted on a recognised stock exchange, or (b) shares in a company not under the control of another company unless the controlling company is quoted (and is not a close company).[201] The only special restriction permitted[202] is one imposed by the company's articles requiring the employee or director to dispose of the scheme shares at the end of the employment.[203] Conditions may also be imposed in so far as they require the shares to be pledged as security for a loan to buy them, or to be disposed of in repayment of such a loan.[204] There are further rules relating to the other shareholdings. The majority must be 'employee control' shares or 'open market' shares.[205]

Rights. The rights must be non-transferable. However, the PRs of deceased participants may exercise rights within one year of death (and subject to the 10-year rule—see §11.8.2.1 above).[206]

Approval. The company establishing the scheme must apply for approval in writing. The Revenue may demand a wide range of information, and withdraw approval if the conditions cease to be met. The company may appeal to the Special Commissioners against such a decision.[207] An amendment to a scheme under which the holder of the option obtains new rights, eg reducing the period of time before the option becomes exercisable, cannot be made without Revenue approval.[208]

The company. The company must be, or be controlled by, a single company.[209] The scheme may contain provisions allowing for the exchange of rights following a takeover; rights to acquire shares in the new company may be acquired.[210] This has to be agreed by

---

[200] ITEPA 2003, Sch 4, paras 16–19, ex, TA 1988, Sch 9, paras 10–12. TA 1988, Sch 9, para 10(c)(i), relating to shares in a consortium company, was repealed by FA 1989, s 64. The effect is to reduce the stake to be held by a member company of the consortium from 15 to five, making it easier for the consortium members shares to be used in this way. On paras 18 and 19, see ITEPA 2003, Explanatory Notes Changes 175 and 168 respectively.

[201] ITEPA 2003, Sch 4, para 17(2), ex TA 1988, Sch 9, paras 11, 12.

[202] ITEPA 2003, Sch 4, para 19, ex TA 1988, Sch 9, paras 12, 13. On the effect of directors' discretion to refuse to register a transfer or to compel an employee to sell shares on the termination of employment, see Sch 4, para 19(7); Revenue Press Release, 11 June 1985, [1985] *Simon's Tax Intelligence* 342.

[203] ITEPA 2003, Sch 4, para 19(2)–(4), ex TA 1988, Sch 9, para 12(2)–(4); such conditions are of particular benefit to family-run companies.

[204] ITEPA 2003, Sch 4, para 19(6), ex TA 1988, Sch 9, para 13(3), added by FA 1988, s 66. See [1987] *Simon's Tax Intelligence* 782. This rule does not apply to savings-related share option schemes. The rule is retroactive (FA 1984, Sch 10, para 10(3), added by FA 1988, s 69).

[205] ITEPA 2003, Sch 4, para 20, ex TA 1988, Sch 9, para 14.

[206] ITEPA 2003, Sch 4, paras 23–25, ex TA 1988, Sch 9, para 27(2), (3). On para 26, see ITEPA 2003 Explanatory Notes Change 176.

[207] ITEPA 2003, Sch 4, paras 28–32, ex TA 1988, Sch 9, paras 5, 6. See ITEPA 2003 Explanatory Notes Changes 170 and 171.

[208] *IRC v Eurocopy plc* [1991] STC 707, 64 TC 370; and *IRC v Reed International plc* [1994] STC 396, 67 TC 552.

[209] ITEPA 2003, Sch 4, para 2, ex TA 1988, Sch 9, para 1(3); on relief for jointly-owned companies, see Sch 4, para 34, previously ESC B27. See ITEPA 2003 Explanatory Notes Change 173.

[210] ITEPA 2003, Sch 4, paras 26 and 27, ex TA 1988, Sch 9, para 15(7); on capital gains consequences, see TCGA 1992, s 238.

the new company and the value of the new option must be the same as that of the old option. The employer could deduct the costs of introducing such schemes.[211]

11.9   Enterprise Management Incentives

11.9.1 Definition of an EMI

11.9.1.1 Overview

Enterprise management incentives (EMIs) are share option schemes designed to help small companies attract and retain the key people they need, and to reward employees for taking a risk by investing their time and skills in helping small companies achieve their potential. The rules introduced in 2000 were widened in 2001,[212] EMIs bear testimony to New Labour's striking willingness to grant great favours to small groups of people, and are found in ITEPA 2003, Part 7, Chapter 9. An option qualifies only[213] if granted for commercial reasons in order to recruit or retain an employee (originally, ie in FA 2000, a 'key' employee) to or in a company; it must not be part of a scheme or arrangement the main purpose of which is the avoidance of tax. There is presently a limit of £120,000 per employee and the company may grant up to £3 million (originally £1.5 million) of these EMI share options.[214] Where an employee holds options over £120,000, EMI treatment will apply to the first £120,000. The £120,000 limit applies to a three-year period beginning with the date of the grant; so if an employee is given £120,000 of share options in the first year and exercises them in the third year, no new options may be taken out until year four when the third anniversary of the grant comes round. At Budget 2012, the Government announced it intends to raise the £120,000 grant limit to £250,000, to commence at the earliest opportunity following EU state aid approval. In 2009–10, 2,190 companies had granted these options in favour of 16,900 employees; the average value per employee was £9,000. The annual tax cost was estimated to be £9 million and a NIC cost of £40 million.[215] As with other approved schemes, participation rates, grants and tax cost have declined dramatically in recent years.

This scheme is meant to apply to small, high-risk companies. The company must be a qualifying company,[216] ie one which is an independent[217] trading[218] company with fewer than 250 full-time employees and gross assets not exceeding £30 million.[219] The company may be listed or unlisted, but must meet qualifying conditions and in particular must not be involved in certain prohibited types of trade.[220] The receipt of substantial sums by way of royalty or licence fee will disqualify a company, unless the IP rights were created by the

---

[211]   CTA 2009, s 1221, referring to s 999, ex TA 1988, s 84A, added by FA 1991, s 42.

[212]   FA 2001, ss 61 and 62, See Cohen [2001] BTR 309.

[213]   ITEPA 2003, Sch 5, para 4, ex FA 2000, Sch 14, para 9.

[214]   ITEPA 2003, Sch 5, paras 5–7, ex FA 2000, Sch 14, paras 10, 11. At Budget 2008, the employee limit was raised from £100,000 to £120,000 in respect of options granted on or after 6 April 2008.

[215]   HMRC Share Schemes Statistics Table, 30 June 2011.

[216]   ITEPA 2003, Sch 5, paras 8–23, ex FA 2000, Sch 14, paras 12–17.

[217]   ITEPA 2003, Sch 5, para 9, ex FA 2000, Sch 14, para 13.

[218]   ITEPA 2003, Sch 5, paras 13 and 14, ex FA 2000, Sch 14, para 17.

[219]   ITEPA 2003, Sch 5, paras 12–12A, ex FA 2000, Sch 14, para 16.

[220]   ITEPA 2003, Sch 5, paras 15–23, ex FA 2000, Sch 14, paras 18–26.

company or another group company.[221] To ensure that the EMI scheme complies with EU state aid guidelines, F(No 3)A 2010 removed the need for a company granting EMI options to operate wholly or mainly in the UK. Instead, the company will only need to have a PE in the UK. In the case of a parent company, at least one company in the group that is carrying on a qualifying trade must have a PE in the UK.[222] Only qualifying companies may form a group; only the parent may grant EMI options. Subsidiaries will prevent the parent from granting EMI options unless each subsidiary meets certain control and holding requirements.[223] These requirements were amended by FA 2004, making it easier for a subsidiary to satisfy the tests; for a trading subsidiary the threshold is reduced to 51% subsidiaries. The provisions also permit certain property management subsidiaries to qualify, so long as they meet the higher, 90% subsidiary threshold.[224] The relief also applies to a company carrying on activities of R&D from which it is intended that a qualifying trade will emerge.[225]

There is no provision expressly allowing the company to deduct the costs of setting up these schemes.

11.9.1.2 The Employee[226]

Eligible employees must work for the company for a substantial amount of their time, ie 25 hours per week or, if less, 75% of their working time;[227] they may be inventors, scientists or experts in raising finance. The idea is that company may offer up to £3 million worth of share options to help it recruit and retain the people that they need to make their company successful and grow. There are rules on the relationship between this and other share schemes.[228] The employee must not have a material interest, ie control of 30% or more of the ordinary share capital.[229]

The option must be capable of being exercised within 10 years;[230] a charge arises if it is not exercised within the period.[231] The option may be conditional, provided the condition can occur within the period. The option must be over the ordinary share capital of the company and must be fully paid-up and not redeemable.[232]

The option must be non-assignable[233] and the terms must be agreed in writing.[234] However, there are no rules directing the conditions under which the share may be issued;

---

[221] ITEPA 2003, Sch 5, para 19, ex FA 2000, Sch 14, para 22. Pursuant to Sch 5, para 19, receipt of royalties is an excluded activity except where from 'relevant intangible asset' (RIA). The RIA category was widened by FA 2007, s 61 to allow assets to be transferred to new subsidiaries without losing RIA status.

[222] ITEPA 2003, Sch 5, paras 14A and 15, ex FA 2000, Sch 14, para 18.

[223] ITEPA 2003, Sch 5, paras 10 and 11, ex FA 2000, Sch 14, paras 14, 15.

[224] Amending ITEPA 2003, Sch 5, para 11 and adding paras 11A and 11B.

[225] ITEPA 2003, Sch 5, para 15(2), ex FA 2000, Sch 14, para 18(2).

[226] ITEPA 2003, Sch 5, paras 24–33, ex FA 2000, Sch 14, paras 27–36.

[227] ITEPA 2003, Sch 5, paras 26 and 27, ex FA 2000, Sch 14, para 29.

[228] ITEPA 2003, Sch 5, para 5(4), ex FA 2000, Sch 14, para 10(6). Options under para 5(4) count towards £120,000 limit.

[229] ITEPA 2003, Sch 5, paras 28–33; on employee trust see ITEPA 2003, ss 550–554, ex FA 2000, Sch 14, paras 30–36.

[230] ITEPA 2003, Sch 5, para 36, ex FA 2000, Sch 14, para 39.

[231] ITEPA 2003, s 529(2)(3), ex FA 2000, Sch 14, para 42(2).

[232] ITEPA 2003, Sch 5, para 35, ex FA 2000, Sch 14, para 38(1)(a).

[233] ITEPA 2003, Sch 5, para 38, ex FA 2000, Sch 14, para 41.

[234] ITEPA 2003, Sch 5, para 37, ex FA 2000, Sch 14, para 40.

so the shares may be non-voting or subject to pre-emption rights on the part of the company. This is to allow the company to protect its independence.[235]

11.9.2 Tax Treatment

If the option is granted at current market value, there is no income tax liability on either the grant[236] or the exercise of the option.[237] However, if the option price is below market value, the value of the discount counts as employment income of the year of the grant.[238] The company may grant options at a price above market value if it wishes. The rules giving the company a deduction for corporation tax were widened by FA 2006 where the qualifying EMI option is over restricted shares and is at a discount. Previously the deduction was limited to the amount of the discount; it now extends to the amount that would have been taxable but for the income tax relief under the EMI rules. Another change widens the corporation tax relief where the EMI option is over convertible shares.[239] At Budget 2012, the Government indicated that it plans to extend entrepreneurs' relief (see *Revenue Law*, §32.7) to capital gains in respect of EMI shares from April 2013, subject to EU state aid approval.

11.9.2.1 Disqualifying Events[240]

The precise effect of such an event depends on its nature. The events are:

(1) loss of independence, ie becoming a 51% subsidiary of another company or otherwise coming under the control of another company;[241]
(2) ceasing to meet the correct trading activities requirements;
(3) ceasing to meet the eligible employee requirements, eg the 75% working time conditions;[242]
(4) alterations in the terms of the option, the effect of which is to increase the value of the shares or to break the rules as to qualifying options;[243]
(5) any relevant alteration in the share capital of the company;[244]
(6) any relevant conversion of the shares;[245]
(7) granting the employee an option under another scheme if this would take the employee over the £120,000 maximum level.[246]

---

[235] Inland Revenue Memorandum, 4.7 and 4.9.
[236] ITEPA 2003, s 475, ex ITEPA 2003, s 528.
[237] ITEPA 2003, s 530, ex FA 2000, Sch 14, para 45.
[238] ITEPA 2003, s 531, ex FA 2000, Sch 14, para 45.
[239] The rules for restricted and also convertible shares were rewritten into CTA 2009, s 1012, ex FA 2003, Sch 23, paras 21–22C. See HMRC Notes on clauses for examples.
[240] ITEPA 2003, ss 533–539, ex FA 2000, Sch 14, paras 47–53.
[241] On control, see ITEPA 2003 Technical Note 51.
[242] ITEPA 2003, s 535, ex FA 2000, Sch 14, para 52.
[243] ITEPA 2003, s 536(1)(a).
[244] ITEPA 2003, s 536(1)(b) and (c) and 537, ex FA 2000, Sch 14, para 49.
[245] ITEPA 2003, ss 536(1)(d) and 538, ex FA 2000, Sch 14, para 50.
[246] ITEPA 2003, ss 536(1)(e) and 539.

The shares must be valued at the date of the disqualifying event.[247] Relief on the value down to that event continues to be available, but any later increase in value is subject to a charge under Part 5.[248]

11.9.2.2 Other Employment Income Share Option Rules

ITEPA 2003, Part 7, Chapter 3C, which would otherwise deem a loan if the option price were below market value, is excluded.[249] However, the legislation makes it clear that nothing in the EMI code affects the operation of various provisions in Part 7 which are listed as Chapters 2–4, subject to what has just been said about Chapters 3C and 5 (§11.9.2.1 above). So nothing in the new rules will prevent a charge from arising under section 476 on the release of rights attached to shares acquired under a qualifying option or where conditions on securities are removed and the charge arises under Chapter 2, section 427 (ex TA 1988, section 140A) or, if there is a conversion coming within Chapter 3, section 438 (ex TA 1988, section 140D).[250] There will also be a charge under section 476 (ex TA 1988, section 135) if a sum is received for the release of rights under the option itself.[251]

Capital gains tax[252] will be payable when the shares are sold. Where there is a rights issue in respect of shares acquired under these options, there is no amalgamation of the two holdings for CGT purposes.[253]

Further rules apply to the effect of a company reorganisation, as where the company in which the employee had the relevant options is taken over and new replacement options are given by the new company.[254]

The scheme must be acceptable to the Revenue, but this takes the form of notification and not approval.[255] Of course the company then runs the risk that the Revenue will argue that the qualifying conditions have not been met.

11.10   Research Institution Spin-out Companies

One class of shares—those in research institution spin-out companies—receive specially favourable treatment in ITEPA 2003, Part 7, Chapter 4A.[256] The treatment arises where there is a transfer of IP to or from one or more research institutions to a spin-out company. The shares in the spin-out company must be acquired before the IP transfer agreement or within 183 days afterwards, and the opportunity to acquire the shares must arise

---

[247] ITEPA 2003, s 532, ex FA 2000, Sch 14, para 53; ITEPA 2003 Explanatory Notes Change 130.

[248] ITEPA 2003, s 541, ex FA 2000, Sch 14, para 55.

[249] ITEPA 2003, s 540(1), ex FA 2000, Sch 14, para 54.

[250] ITEPA 2003, s 541(1), ex FA 2000, Sch 14, para 55(1)(b) or (c); note s 541(2) on valuation.

[251] ITEPA 2003, s 541(2), ex FA 2000, Sch 14, para 55(1)(a).

[252] TCGA 1992, Sch 7D, paras 14–15, added by ITEPA 2003, Sch 6, para 221, ex FA 2000, Sch 14, paras 56–57.

[253] TCGA 1992, Sch 7D, para 16, added by ITEPA 2003, Sch 6, para 221. The rules in TCGA 1992, Sch 7D, para 16 disapply the usual reorganisation or reduction of share capital rules in TCGA 1992, ss 127–130.

[254] ITEPA 2003, Sch 5, paras 39–43, ex Sch 14, paras 59–63; note also s 534 para 42(2). On replacement options, see ITEPA 2003 Explanatory Notes Change 177.

[255] ITEPA 2003, Sch 5, paras 44–50, ex FA 2000, Sch 14, paras 2–7; the details required in the notice and the time limit for the notice (92 days) are set out in para 44. See also ITEPA 2003 Explanatory Notes Changes 177 and 178.

[256] Added by FA 2005, s 20. FA 2005 made other consequential changes to various parts of the legislation.

by reason of the employment by the research institutions or company. In addition, the person acquiring the shares must be involved in the research. Tax avoidance must not be a main purpose of the arrangement under which the opportunity to acquire the shares arose.[257]

If the conditions are satisfied, the taxable amount under Chapter 4 (post-acquisition benefit) in respect of the benefits from IP transfer is nil (section 453). In addition, there is a deemed election under section 431 to disapply Chapter 2 (section 454) and Chapter 3B (section 455). The overall effect is to prevent charges from arising at a time when the researcher will have acquired the shares but, being an academic, may not have funds with which to pay the tax.

---

[257] ITEPA 2003, ss 451 and 456–460.

12

Anti-avoidance: Special Provisions

12.1 General

12.2.1 General

This chapter deals with a number of anti-avoidance provisions mostly relating to companies,[1] shares and bonds. More general issues relating to the control of avoidance are considered in *Revenue Law*, chapter five. The provisions were designed in and for an age of Revenue assessment; the advent of self-assessment and surcharges for incorrect returns make these particularly sharp weapons where they apply. The provisions were also devised for the most part against a background of very high rates of income tax for individuals[2] and low, or non-existent, rates of CGT.

12.2.2 Dividend Stripping—The Idea

When a taxpayer transfers shares in a company, the tax system is normally content to accept that income payments made by the company after a sale of shares must be taxed according to the tax circumstances of the new owner of the shares; the fact that the previous owner had a higher marginal tax rate does not entitle the Revenue to tax the new owner at his

---

[1] Or, in the case of ITA 2007, ss 773–785 and 752–766 (ex TA 1988, ss 775, 776), other persons; however, companies are usually used.

[2] Eg 91.25%; see below at §12.6.

predecessor's rates. However, if the new owner is able to extract all the surplus cash in the company without incurring any liability to tax, ie to strip the company of its cash tax free, the Revenue have cause to worry and the legislature to come to their aid.

12.2.3 The Strip

This stripping may be achieved in the following way. A has a controlling interest in company X. A sells those shares to B. B uses the voting power to compel the company to pay a large dividend to B. B then sells the shares back to A or to someone else. At first sight there is nothing inequitable about this. If B's marginal rate is simply lower than that of A, there is a loss of tax. However, this lower rate may be achieved not only if B is simply less well-off than A, but also if B is an exempt person, such as a charity or pension fund. Moreover, if B is a dealer in securities, the dividend paid out may be offset by the trading loss incurred on the sale of shares back to A, even though the loss is due to the payment of the dividend out of the cash reserve of the company. The effect is that the payment will have been drawn out free of tax while A has received a sum which reflects the value of those cash reserves, and that sum will be treated as a capital payment only.

12.2.4 Legislative Reaction

Attempts to obstruct these schemes have proved ineffective unless drastic. Thus, it was not clear whether the courts would hold that the transaction of buying in order to resell at a loss was a trading transaction.[3] If it was not a trading transaction, no relief could be given in respect of the loss and the scheme would fail. The UK courts at first accepted the arguments on behalf of B that it was a trading transaction and so allowed the whole dividend-stripping industry to get underway.

Some legislation was designed to prevent the accumulations from arising in the first place, this being the purpose of much of the early close company legislation (repealed in 1989). In the 1950s the Revenue tried, by a separate avenue, to undo the tax advantages of stripping. Such devices, however, have always been subject to exceptions which exemplify the ambivalent attitudes of government to small, and therefore largely unregulated, businesses. At first, legislation was designed to interfere with the sales to security dealers and exempt persons, but in 1960 the legislature aimed at transactions in securities generally. See below at §12.5.

12.2   Bond Washing

12.2.1 General

Securities, ie stocks and shares, generate income in the form of dividends and interest. These become taxable income only when they are due and payable, or sometimes when

---

[3] This is not a happy area for believers in precedents. Although the final 1970s' view seems to be that this is not a trading transaction—see *FA and AB Ltd v Lupton* [1971] 3 All ER 948, (1971) 47 TC 580—earlier cases, especially *Griffiths v J P Harrison (Watford) Ltd* [1962] 1 All ER 909, (1962) 40 TC 281, were distinguished not overruled (see [1970] BTR 77 and 153) and the issues were still live in cases like *Barclays Mercantile Business Finance Ltd v Mawson* [2005] STC 1 (HL). See *Revenue Law*, §§5.6. and 19.3.2.

paid;[4] for tax purposes the income is not apportioned over the period in respect of which it is declared.[5] Time usually elapses between the announcement of a proposed dividend by the company and its becoming payable. If, during this time, high-rate taxpayers sell securities to others paying tax at a lower rate, the purchase price received, although reflecting the value of the impending payment, cannot be segregated into an amount on account of capital and another amount on account of the dividend so as to tax the latter.[6]

This is still the premise of the law. However, that premise has been reversed by legislative schemes such as the accrued income scheme (*Revenue Law*, §26.4), which splits the payment received, the rules for deeply-discounted securities (*Revenue Law*, §26.6) and the loan relationship rules for companies (see chapter five above), which, more radically, abolish the distinction between income and capital. However, none of these changes affects shares.

Legislation to counter bond-washing schemes is not complete and so 'abuses' remain. One abuse is where a vendor, V, sells shares to a purchaser, P, who collects the dividend taxed at P's lower rate and then sells the shares back to V, all this being planned under the original agreement.[7] In this way the bond or shares[8] are said to be 'washed' of their dividend. It cannot be argued that P, the temporary purchaser, was not beneficially entitled to the dividend, since it is of the essence of the scheme that P is so entitled. It is also hard to apply ITTOIA 2005, Part 5, Chapter 5 (ex TA 1988, section 660A *et seq*) since there is no element of bounty about the scheme.

12.2.2 Legislative Counteraction

In 1937,[9] a more serious attempt was made to counteract one type of tax avoidance involving the sale and repurchase of securities. This applied where a high-rate taxpayer agreed to transfer securities,[10] and either in the same or in a collateral[11] agreement there was an agreement, or an option, to buy back those or similar securities.[12] If the result of such a transaction was that any interest (a term defined to include a dividend) became payable in respect of the securities and was receivable by someone other than the vendor, it was deemed to be the vendor's income. Thus, the legislation was primarily intended to nullify any advantage to the vendor. Section 729 was first reduced in scope and finally repealed in 1996.[13] Its scope has been taken over by the accrued income scheme (*Revenue Law*, §26.4) and by the repo rules in ITA 2007, sections 601–606 (ex TA 1988, section 737A—see §12.3 below).

Section 730 was passed in 1938[14] to cover the situation where the vendor sold not the shares but simply the right to the dividend. In *Paget v IRC*,[15] the taxpayer held Hungarian

---

[4] See *Revenue Law*, §26.1.2, and §3.1 above.
[5] *Wigmore v Thomas Summerson & Sons Ltd* [1926] 1 KB 131, (1926) 9 TC 577; it may be apportioned for other purposes.
[6] *Thompson v Trust and Loan Co of Canada* [1932] 1 KB 517, (1932) 16 TC 394.
[7] TA 1988, s 231B, added by F(No 2)A 1997, s 28, concerns schemes to claim repayment of credits and does not address the situation of different tax rates.
[8] On the treatment of certificates of deposit and of rights to have such certificates issued, see *Revenue Law*, §26.7.
[9] FA 1937, s 12.
[10] TA 1988, s 729.
[11] See *Re Athill; Athill v Athill* (1880) 16 Ch D 211, 222.
[12] Defined in TA 1988, s 729(2)(c).
[13] Except for certain transactions entered into before 6 November 1996.
[14] FA 1938, s 24.
[15] [1938] 2 KB 25, (1938) 21 TC 677; on deduction of tax from interest, see Inland Revenue Tax Bulletin, Issue 20 (December 1995).

bonds which carried the right to interest payable in sterling in London; the right to interest was attached to coupons. She was held not to be taxable on the purchase price received by her when she sold the coupons to a coupon dealer. Section 730 deems the interest to belong to the coupon vendor. It should be noted that in *IRC v McGuckian*[16] the House of Lords treated the payment of a price for the right to dividends as income for the purposes of section 730. While an Australian case suggested that *Paget* may be ripe for re-examination, it is unlikely that UK courts would think so.[17] As the coupon is almost certainly going to arise from a foreign asset, the income tax charge now arises under ITTOIA 2005, Part 4, Chapter 13. Section 730 was repealed in 2009 as part of a streamlining of the statue book.

The rules on the distinction between interest and other payments are refined by section 730A, added in 1995, dealing with price differentials arising from the sale and repurchase of securities (known as 'repo' transactions). This was rewritten into ITA 2007, sections 607–611.[18] Section 730C, added in 1996 and now rewritten as ITTOIA 2005, sections 151–154, deals with the stripping and reconstitution of gilts, which includes a regulation-making power. [19]

Sales of the right to interest payment have now been brought within the deeply-discounted securities rules in ITTOIA 2005, Part 4, Chapter 8. Sales of the right to non-excluded annual payments now have their own rule.

FA 2009 replaced section 730 and two other provisions with a new general rule on the transfer of income streams affecting both income tax (ITA 2007, sections 809AZA–809AZG) and corporation tax (CTA 2009, sections 486F–486G and CTA 2010, sections 752–757).[20] It is an important and welcome essay in a new style of drafting. The new general rule, in its income tax form ITA 2007, section 809AZA, applies where a person makes a transfer of a right to 'relevant receipts'. *McGuckian*[21] would be a classic example. Receipts are 'relevant' if they would, but for the transfer, be income in the hands of the transferor or brought into account in computing profits of the transferor. So the rules catch both a transfer of a right to pure income and the sale of a right to income which forms part of trading profits. Section 809AZA does not apply if the transfer also applies to the asset from which the receipts arose, though there is an express exclusion if the asset is a right to annual payments.[22]

Section 809AZB charges the amount of the consideration or, if that is too low, the market value of the right. These rules do not apply if the receipt is already taxed as income in some other way (section 809AZC). There are also exceptions for life annuities and pension

---

[16] [1997] STC 908, (1997) 69 TC 1; see *Revenue Law*, §5.6.4.

[17] *IRC v John Lewi Properties plc* [2003] STC 117 (CA); the Australian case is *FCT v Myer Emporium Ltd* (1987) 18 ATR 693. At one time s 730 extended to shares, interest and annual payments, but F(No 2)A 2005 restricted it to distributions in respect of shares.

[18] On history, see Henderson J in *Revenue and Customs Commissioners v Bank of Ireland Britain Holdings Ltd* [2008] STC 253, [2007] EWHC 941 (Ch). See also *Revenue Law*, §5.5. Ex TA 1988, ss 731–734 were repealed by FA 2008, s 66, along with ss 735 and 736. The reason why these are no longer needed is that CTA 2009, Pt 3, Ch 9 (ex TA 1988, s 95) makes dealers in securities, etc taxable under the trading rules.

[19] See HMRC Notes to Finance Bill 2008, cl 63, para 10. However, some rule is needed for insurance companies with non-life business as s 95 does not apply to them; the new rule is 95ZA, added by FA 2008, Sch 17, and not rewritten. Care is needed on the commencement provisions.

[20] The additional provisions repealed were TA 1988, ss 775A and 785A, the latter concerning rent factoring of leases of plant and machinery. Among the fascinating points in the Notes on Clauses are the 2006 American case of *Lattera v Lattera* (see para 9) and an explanation of a change to TA 1988 s 785A made by FA 2008 (see para 19).

[21] *IRC v McGuckian* [1997] STC 908, HL.

[22] ITA 2007, s 809AZA(1)(b) and (3).

income (section 809AZCA), and for transfers of two other sorts of annuity (section 809AZD) or by way of security (section 809AZE).

12.3 Manufactured Dividends and Repos

These rules are an updated version of a provision first introduced in 1960, when the scheme was described as something 'which the ordinary layman could fairly describe as a swindle at the expense of the honest taxpayer—not a criminal conspiracy but a racket'.[23] The essence of the scheme is that individuals make 'manufactured' payments but do not suffer any overall economic loss.[24]

Manufactured payments are payments due under a contract or other arrangements for the transfer of shares, and represent dividend or interest. Tax is charged in various sets of circumstances on the amount representing the dividend or interest; the definition of that amount is made according to precise rules in each set of circumstances. The charge arises only if the manufacturer is not itself entitled to the dividend or interest payment. The legislation has been frequently amended and now includes a non-allowable purpose test.[25]

The rules are now mostly to be found in CTA 2010, Part 17 (ex TA 1988, Schedule 23A) for corporation tax and ITA 2007, Part 11 (for income tax). The rules apply to manufactured dividends on UK equities and interest on UK securities.[26] There are further rules for manufactured overseas dividends[27] and irregular manufactured payments.[28] All try to apply to the manufactured payments at least some of the rules which would apply to actual payments of dividend or interest.

The rules in ex TA 1988, section 737A and Schedule 23A, rewritten as CTA 2010, Part 17, Chapter 5 and ITA 2007, sections 596–601, also apply to certain deemed manufactured payments arising from the sale and repurchase of securities, and deemed manufactured payments in the case of stock lending. In all instances there are duties on the person making the payment to supply the appropriate information for tax purposes. A charge under these rules excludes any charge under the accrued income scheme.[29] Further changes were made by FA 2007 (Schedule 5, paragraph 9) and FA 2008, Schedule 23. FA 2012, section 22 added yet further anti-avoidance rules. The detail is way beyond a book such as this, but the topic is interesting.

12.4 Dividend Stripping

TA 1988, section 736 was one of a number of provisions introduced because of dividend stripping. Many of these provisions were repealed following the 1999 changes to corporation tax abolishing the right of an exempt person to reclaim tax on a dividend. However,

---

[23] HC Official Report 1960, Vol 624, col 451 (Sir Edward Boyle).
[24] See further Tiley and Collison, *UK Tax Guide* (LexisNexis, 2012)§§4.18 *et seq.*
[25] CTA 2010, ss 799–801, ex TA 1988, Sch 23A, para 7A added by FA 2004.
[26] CTA 2010, ss 782–789 (on manufactured dividends) and ITA 2007, ss 573–578 (manufactured dividends and interest), ex TA 1988, Sch 23A, paras 2–3.
[27] CTA 2010, ss 790–795 and ITA 2007, s 581, ex TA 1988, Sch 23A, para 4.
[28] CTA 2010, ss 796–798 and ITA 2007, s 583, ex TA 1988, Sch 23A, para 7.
[29] TA 1988, s 715(6), rewritten to ITA 2007, ss 638(2), (3), 647(2)–(4), (6), 663(1)–(3).

section 736 survived until 2008.[30] It applied where a company dealing in securities obtained a holding of more than 10% in another company and there was one or more distributions by that other company, the net effect of which was materially to reduce the value of the holding. Section 736 directed that the reduction in the value of the holding was added to the value of the security.[31] The purpose of this was to counteract the tax advantage obtained in a typical dividend strip by simply wiping out the loss on the shares which the dealing company would hope to put against the distribution. When section 736 applied, the rules for accounting for tax on manufactured dividends and interest were modelled on those for real dividends and interest (ie quarterly accounting).[32] Leading up to its repeal in 2008, the Revenue used ex TA 1988, section 703 (discussed in §12.5.1 below) in preference to section 736, a course which is scarcely surprising. The Revenue also used the (now drastically reduced) CGT value-shifting rules (TCGA 1992, sections 30 *et seq*).

12.5 Cancellation of Tax Advantages: Transactions in Securities

12.5.1 General

ITA 2007, Part 13, Chapter 1, sections 682–713 contain rules originally introduced in 1960; the corporation tax rules are contained in CTA 2010, Part 15, sections 731–751 (ex TA 1988, sections 703–709). The technique used is to allow the Revenue to issue a notice counteracting tax advantages gained in certain circumstances prescribed in language of broad and so often uncertain scope.[33] The effect of the notice is to undo the transaction but only for tax purposes. Briefly, (a) the tax advantage must have been obtained as a result of a transaction in securities, and (b) it must fall within one of three (formerly five) sets of circumstances (described at §12.5.3 below). It is, however, open to the taxpayer to show that the transaction was carried out either for bona fide commercial reasons, or in the ordinary course of making or managing investments and, in either event, not with the obtaining of a tax advantage as its main or one of its main objects.[34] The modern approach of the court is not to restrict the section to contrived transactions carried on away from the open market, but simply to ask whether the particular transaction comes within its scope.[35]

The rewritten income tax legislation in ITA 2007 was rewritten again in 2010, to simplify the rules and limit their scope. The definition of 'tax advantage' in ITA 2007, section 687 was narrowed, and the references to a 'relevant company' were replaced by 'close company'. The sets of circumstances triggering the application of the transaction in securities counteraction were condensed into one section (section 685) with two conditions corresponding to circumstances (D) and (E) that apply for corporation tax (discussed below). In addition, a new exemption was introduced for transactions immediately following a

---

[30] Repealed by FA 2008 s 66(1) with effect in relation to distributions made on or after 1 April 2008.

[31] Cf TCGA 1992, s 177; see above at §8.7.

[32] See ex TA 1988, Sch 23A.

[33] However, the Revenue are under a duty to exercise their power fairly (*R v IRC, ex parte Preston* [1983] STC 257, 59 TC 1).

[34] ITA 2007, s 685 and CTA 2010, s 734, ex TA 1988, s 703(1).

[35] *IRC v Trustees of the Sema Group Pensions Scheme* [2002] EWCA Civ 1857, [2003] STC 95.

fundamental change in the ownership of the close company (new ITA 2007, section 686). The discussion below focuses on the corporation tax formulation in CTA 2010.

The original section 703 was introduced before the new approach in *Ramsay*,[36] and judicial views on the relationship between the two have wavered. However, a sensible way forward, consistent with the *Barclays BMBF* case,[37] is to say that the new approach is simply a way of interpreting the facts to which the legislation applies. In *Bird v IRC*,[38] Lord Keith said that it was open to the Revenue to choose whether to use section 703 or the new approach as a means of applying section 419. Similarly, in *McGuckian v IRC*,[39] some judges felt able to bring the facts within section 703 without having to rely on the new approach at all; this now seems correct. These provisions are among the most difficult in the UK tax law. Thirty years ago they were denounced as being, generally speaking, the most obscure, while the penalties for infringing them were the most severe, and they were barely touched upon by published statements of Revenue practice.[40] Since then we have got used to other wide provisions, and the language of the ITA 2007 and CTA 2010 versions is undoubtedly somewhat easier to disentangle (as opposed to understand), but the other criticisms are still correct. A further difficulty is the absence of any provision governing the interaction with CGT. Where the proceeds of sale of shares fall within these rules, Revenue practice is to allow the tax so charged as a credit against CGT; the concessionary status of this way of avoiding double taxation has been condemned.[41] A clearance procedure applies.[42]

A good example of the operation of these rules is *IRC v Wiggins*.[43] A company restored and sold picture frames. One frame was found to contain a valuable painting, *The Holy Family*, by Poussin.[44] Rather than simply sell the painting and distribute the profits as dividend, the company first sold all its other stock to one company, after which another company bought the shares of the first company for £45,000. The courts held that the £45,000 represented the value of trading stock, so that section 704, paragraph D (now CTA 2010, section 737) applied, and the £45,000 could be treated as income of those who had sold their shares. More recently, in *Grogan v Revenue & Customs Commissioners*, Warren J held that a scheme involving a qualifying employee share trust (QUEST) was caught by these anti-avoidance rules.[45]

---

[36] *WT Ramsay Ltd v IRC* [1982] AC 300; see *Revenue Law*, §5.6.4.

[37] *Barclays Mercantile Business Finance Ltd v Mawson* [2005] STC 1 (HL) and see *Revenue Law*, §5.6.

[38] [1985] STC 584, (1985) 61 TC 238. At first instance Vinelott J said that it was not open to the Revenue to rely on *Furniss v Dawson* [1984] AC 474 and TA 1988, s 704 in the same transaction, while in the same case the Court of Appeal held that the taxpayer could not use the new approach to disregard a step which s 703 said had to be taken into account.

[39] [1997] STC 908, 69 TC 1, HL. See also the interesting but now outdated dicta of Vinelott J in *Bird v IRC* [1985] STC 584, 647; 61 TC 238, 312.

[40] Nolan, IFS Conference (28 June 1974) 25, para 3.

[41] See Lord Wilberforce in *IRC v Garvin* [1981] STC 344, and Lord Bridge, *ibid* at 349, 353; 55 TC 24, 86, 90.

[42] ITA 2007, s 701 and CTA 2010, s 748, ex TA 1988, s 707; see *Balen v IRC* [1978] STC 420, 52 TC 406; and Statement of Practice SP 3/80. Prior to 2009 there was also a special tribunal to hear appeals from the Tribunals, appeal from which was on a point of law only and was still by way of case stated. ITA 2007, ss 706–711, TA 1988, ss 705, 706. On jurisdiction, see *Marwood Homes Ltd v IRC* [1998] STC (SCD) 53.

[43] [1979] STC 244, [1979] 2 All ER 245; see Walters [1979] BTR 183.

[44] The frame was bought in 1955 for £50; the picture was found to be by Poussin 10 years later, valued at £130,000.

[45] [2011] STC 1, [2010] UKUT 416 (TTC).

12.5.2 The Three Elements

12.5.2.1 Tax Advantage

'Tax advantage' is defined for corporation tax as:

(1)   a relief or increased relief from corporation tax;
(2)   a repayment or increased repayment of corporation tax;
(3)   the avoidance or reduction of a charge to or an assessment to corporation tax; or
(4)   the avoidance of a possible assessment to corporation tax.[46]

It does not matter whether the avoidance or reduction is effected by receipts accruing in such a way that the recipient does not pay or bear corporation tax on them, or by a deduction in calculating profits or gains. A similar definition used to apply for income tax, but the definition was narrowed in 2010. ITA 2007, section 687 now provides that a person obtains an income tax advantage if:

(1)   the amount of any income tax which would be payable by the person in respect of the relevant consideration if it constituted a qualifying distribution, exceeds the amount of any CGT payable in respect of it; or
(2)   income tax would be payable by the person in respect of the relevant consideration if it constituted a qualifying distribution and no CGT is payable in respect of it.

Exemption and relief. At one time a relief was distinguished from an exemption. A relief indicated an alleviation of an obligation, whereas an exemption indicated a removal of the obligation altogether. It followed that a person with no obligation to pay tax did not obtain a tax advantage if income accrued to him rather than to someone else in whose hands it would not be exempt from tax. This over-nice distinction, which placed far too much weight on a particular view of the tax structure not always appreciated by a draftsman, has quite rightly been rejected. It follows that where a company issued shares in favour of charitable trustees and other shareholders waived their rights to a dividend, so that all the dividends accrued to the trustees, the trustees were not entitled to a tax repayment and were stopped by section 703.[47]

Advantage. The definition of 'tax advantage' for corporation tax suggests that there must be a contrast of the actual case where there is an accrual in a non-taxable way with a possible accrual in a taxable way.[48] Thus, where a company had issued and later redeemed bonus debentures, there was an avoidance of tax in that, had the money been distributed as dividends, it would have been taxable.[49] However, whether the issue or the redemption constitutes the tax advantage is still unclear.[50]

In *Cleary v IRC*[51] it was argued that the words 'avoidance of a possible assessment thereto' indicated that Parliament had in mind the reduction of profits available for

---

[46]   CTA 2010, s 732, ex TA 1988, s 709.
[47]   *Universities Superannuation Scheme Ltd v IRC* [1997] STC 1; overruling *Sheppard v IRC (No 2)* [1993] STC 240.
[48]   *IRC v Parker* [1966] AC 141, 178–79, (1966) 43 TC 396, 441, *per* Lord Wilberforce.
[49]   *IRC v Parker, ibid; cf Anysz v IRC* [1978] STC 296.
[50]   See *IRC v Parker, op cit.*
[51]   [1967] 2 All ER 48, (1967) 44 TC 399.

dividends and not the reduction of physical assets for that purpose, so that there would be no tax advantage if a company simply used its cash resources to buy shares in another company. However, this view was rejected by the House of Lords. In the case, two sisters owned the shares of two companies and extracted the cash from one company by allowing that company to buy their shares in the other. They thus avoided the possible assessment that would have arisen if the cash had been paid out by way of dividend.[52] The fact that this would have been the worst possible procedure, and so unlikely to happen, did not matter. This case is disturbing since, when the purchasing company in turn made its distribution, no credit could have been claimed for the tax already exacted.[53]

In *Emery v IRC*,[54] where a company had made a large trading profit, the taxpayer was held to have derived a tax advantage when he sold his shares because he could have got the company to declare a dividend or go into liquidation. In *Bird v IRC*,[55] Lord Keith said that the quantum of the advantage was ascertained by contrasting the non-taxable receipt with a similar receipt that might have accrued in some other, taxable way. Further, the House of Lords held that in determining what should be done to counter such an advantage there was an obligation to make an accurate measure of the tax advantage obtained. When the taxpayer has to make good the liability of another person, that should reduce the tax advantage obtained.

In the earlier case of *IRC v Brebner*,[56] Lord Upjohn said that one choice of a method which carried less tax than another did not necessarily mean that one of its main objects was to obtain a tax advantage. In another early case it was said that a charity does not have a tax advantage as one of its main objects simply because, in reaching a decision, it is influenced by its privileged tax status.[57]

12.5.2.2 Transaction in Securities

'Transaction' is defined for both income tax and corporation tax as including transactions of whatever description relating to securities and, in particular:

(1)   the purchase, sale or exchange of securities;
(2)   issuing or securing the issue of new securities;
(3)   applying for or subscribing for new securities; and
(4)   altering or securing the alteration of the rights attached to securities.[58]

---

[52] See *Hague v IRC* [1968] 2 All ER 1252, 44 TC 619. In a judgment not easy to reconcile with *IRC v Parker* or *Cleary v IRC*, the Court of Appeal refused to accept as a 'possible' assessment one which would arise if spouses at that time had opted for separate assessments, a possibility scarcely more fanciful than that envisaged by the House of Lords in *Cleary v IRC*. This was later reversed by TA 1988, s 703(7)—now repealed (FA 1988, Sch 14, Pt VIII).

[53] In the Court of Appeal Lord Denning said that 'the courts are well able to take care of that contingency'. However, there is no legislation analogous to TA 1988, s 419(4) or the now long-repealed TA 1988, s 427(4). It is therefore hard to see what his Lordship had in mind.

[54] [1981] STC 150, 54 TC 607.

[55] [1988] STC 312, 316–17; 61 TC 238, 341–43.

[56] (1968) 43 TC 705, 718.

[57] *IRC v Kleinwort Benson Ltd* [1969] 2 All ER 737, 743; 45 TC 369, 382, *per* Cross J.

[58] ITA 2007, s 684(2) and CTA 2010, s 751, ex TA 1988, s 709(2).

This wide definition is not qualified in any way.[59] Hence, repayment of share capital as a reduction is a transaction,[60] as is the payment of the purchase price for shares by instalments, at least when the instalments were related to dividends,[61] and perhaps even if not so related.[62] The definition is based on the premise that the liquidation of a company is not a transaction in securities.[63] This has now been decided by the House of Lords, their Lordships saying that there was no sound reason to distinguish a payment in the course of a liquidation from the payment of a dividend;[64] however, the combination of a transaction with a liquidation may give rise to a charge.[65] In reliance on various statements in the House of Lords, the rewritten income tax rule makes it clear that the definition is exhaustive.[66]

12.5.2.3 Securities

'Securities' is defined to include shares and stock, and, in relation to a company not limited by shares (whether or not it has a share capital), includes a reference to the interest of a member of the company as such.[67] Thus, debentures and securities are included, and their redemption is a transaction in securities. A loan note, even though unsecured, is a security;[68] similarly, the receipt of a loan from—and repayable to—a controlled company is a transaction in securities.[69]

12.5.3 *The Sets of Circumstances*

12.5.3.1 Abnormally High Dividends to Exploit Relief—Repealed

The first circumstance, formerly TA 1988, section 704 paragraph A and repealed in 2010, concerned abnormally high dividends where, in connection with the distribution of profits of a company or in connection with the sale or purchase of securities followed by the purchase or sale of the same or other securities, the person in question received an abnormal amount by way of dividend, being entitled by reason of:

(1)   any exemption from tax;
(2)   the setting off of losses against profits or income;
(3)   the deduction for interest under ITA 2007, section 383.

---

[59] *IRC v Parker* [1966] AC 141, 172-3, 43 TC 396, 437, per Lord Guest.
[60] *IRC v Brebner* [1967] 1 All ER 779, 43 TC 705.
[61] *Greenberg v IRC* [1972] AC 109, 47 TC 240; see [1971] BTR 319.
[62] See a reluctant Lord Reid in *Greenberg v IRC (ibid)*, 137, 272.
[63] This view was accepted by Lord Dilhorne and Lord Diplock in *IRC v Joiner* [1975] 3 All ER 1050, 1057, 1060, 50 TC 449, 483, 488.
[64] *Laird Group plc v IRC* [2003] UKHL 54; [2003] STC 722.
[65] *IRC v Joiner, op cit.*
[66] See explanatory notes to ex ITA 2007, s 713.
[67] ITA 2007, s 713 and CTA 2010, s 751, ex TA 1988, s 703(2).
[68] *IRC v Joiner* [1975] 3 All ER 1050, 1056, per Lord Wilberforce. What if, in *Cleary v IRC* [1967] 2 All ER 48, 44 TC 399, the assets sold had been personal property, such as a picture, and not shares?
[69] *Williams v IRC* [1980] STC 535, [1980] 3 All ER 321, 54 TC 247, HL.

The rules for corporation tax also referred to:

(4)   the giving of group relief, to recover tax in respect of dividends received by that person;
(5)   the application of franked investment income for the purpose of the shadow ACT regulations;[70]
(6)   the computation of profits or gains out of which are made payments within TA 1988, sections 348 and 349.

There were further rules in the days of ACT.

A dividend is regarded as abnormal[71] if:

(1)   it substantially exceeds a normal return on the consideration provided for securities (the 'excessive return condition'); or
(2)   it is a dividend at a fixed rate and substantially exceeds the amount which the recipient would have received if the dividend had accrued from day to day and he had been entitled only to so much of the dividend as accrued while he held the securities (the 'excessive accrual condition').

Rule (2) applies only if the recipient sells or acquires a right to sell those or similar securities within six months. The word 'profits' is defined to include income, reserves or other assets. This is unfortunate when compared with standard accountancy definitions, but indicated the wide scope of the section.[72] The burden of proof lies with the Revenue to establish that the distribution was of an abnormal amount.[73]

This test of abnormality is exhaustive. In *IRC v Sema Group Pensions Scheme*,[74] dividends were paid to pension fund trustees as part of a buy-back scheme; at that time pension fund trustees were entitled to a tax credit repayment. The Court of Appeal held that the trustees had not received an abnormal amount by way of dividend since it was not abnormal when one looked at the length of time the trustees had held the shares and the total amount of dividends and other distributions made during that time, this being the test set out in the statute.[75] It was not right simply to look at the particular payment and decide that it was large—and so abnormal—when viewed on its own. The Court agreed that the trustees had obtained a tax advantage and had, as one of their objects, the avoidance of tax, but section 703 would apply only if the facts came within paragraph A—and they did not.

12.5.3.2 No Abnormal Dividend: Deduction for Loss Arising from Distributions or Dealings—Repealed

This circumstance, formerly TA 1988, section 704 paragraph B and also now repealed, concerned the drop in the value of securities as a result of the dividend. It was of relevance

---

[70] Corporation Tax (Treatment of Unrelieved Surplus Advance Corporation Tax) Regulations 1999 (SI 1999/358), reg 23.

[71] ITA 2007, ss 692–694, and CTA 2010, 740–742, ex TA 1988, s 709(4). For example, see Inland Revenue Tax Bulletin, Issue 5 (November 1992).

[72] See comments by Lord Upjohn in *Cleary v IRC* [1967] 2 All ER 48, 56; 44 TC 396, 428.

[73] *Universities Superannuation Scheme Ltd v IRC* [1997] STC 1.

[74] [2002] EWCA Civ 1857, [2003] STC 95.

[75] TA 1988, s 709(4)(b) and (6)(b).

when the person involved was tax exempt or a share dealer. Since a dealer in shares is no longer exempt from tax on dividends and since exempt bodies can no longer claim back any tax or tax credits on dividends, this provision was found to be superfluous and was repealed by FA 2008, section 66. The purpose here was to catch the dividend stripper who did not receive an abnormal dividend but who simply claimed a loss, as in *IRC v Kleinwort Benson Ltd*.[76]

12.5.3.3 Receipt of Consideration Representing Company's Assets, Future Receipts or Trading Stock

CTA 2010, section 736 (ex TA 1988, section 704, paragraph C) applies if a company receives consideration which:

(1)   is or represents the value of assets which are available for distribution by a company by way of dividend (or which would have been so available apart from anything done by the company in question);
(2)   is received in respect of future receipts of a company; or
(3)   is or represents the value of trading stock of a company,

and the receipt is 'in consequence of' a transaction whereby another person subsequently receives or has received an abnormal amount by way of dividend and, further, the company receiving the consideration does not pay or bear corporation tax on income in respect of the receipt.

This deals with the opposite side of the transaction from that covered by the circumstances set out in §§12.5.3.1 and 12.5.3.2 above. The definition of 'abnormal dividend' described in (now repealed) TA 1988, section 704, paragraph A (above §12.5.3.1) continues to apply for this purpose. 'Available for distribution by way of dividend' means legally available, not commercially available.[77]

In the ordinary dividend strip or bond-washing operation, it was not to be supposed that all the economic advantage would be confined to the purchaser. Thus, in one instance[78] a company had 15,000 unclassified £1 shares. These were converted into 300,000 1s ordinary shares and a once-for-all dividend of 47s 6d was declared. These shares were sold to superannuation funds and to charities at 67s 6d, which then reclaimed the tax paid on the dividend. After the dividend the shares were worth about 1s 6d each. The funds and charities had paid 67s 6d in effect for a net dividend of 47s 6d, an operation that made sense only on the basis that they collected tax of about 30s per share thanks to their exempt status. Thus the vendor made £1 and the funds 10s per share—free of tax. Hence this circumstance.

Scissors and forward strip. This rule catches two other devices, known as forward stripping and 'scissors', or stock stripping. Forward stripping occurred when a company was

---

[76] [1969] 2 All ER 737, (1969) 45 TC 369.
[77] Ex TA 1988, s 704(3); *IRC v Brown* [1971] 3 All ER 502, even though current liabilities exceed current assets. See now Companies Act 2006, ss 830 and 841.
[78] HC Official Report 1960, vol 624, col 626 (Sir Edward Boyle).

about to make a large profit.[79] Special shares were created carrying a high rate of dividend, and these would be sold to a dealing company for a capital sum. The dealer would then set off the loss on resale against the predicted dividend which had subsequently accrued.

Stock stripping occurs where a company has stock on its books at the correct conservative figure of cost or market value, whichever is the lower. If the stock were realised there would be a considerable income receipt. Enter the finance company which also deals in stock. The company buys both stock and shares at book value. The increased price obtained by sale at market value is offset by the drop in the value of the shares. Thanks to CTA 2010, section 736 the original company, if it is allowed its loss, will be subject to tax as having obtained a tax advantage.

The Revenue must not only establish each element but also show that the transaction and the abnormal dividend (or whatever it may be) are causally linked; this flows from the word 'whereby'.[80] In deciding the scope of the transaction the court may take a broad view and is not limited to the immediate cause of the dividend, but still the causal connection must be shown.[81] Where, as is usually the case, more than one step is involved, this causal connection may be established even though the taxpayer does not take part in each one.[82] It has also been decided that the causal link may be found in the purpose and design of those who, for a fee and instructed by the taxpayers, controlled the operation of the schemes.[83]

12.5.3.4 Relevant Company Distribution and Receipt of Consideration

This circumstance has given the courts the most difficulty. *IRC v Wiggins* (see above at §12.5.1) is an example of this rule. In its TA 1988 version in section 704, paragraph D it contained an outstandingly unhelpful example of legislation by reference.[84] The CTA 2010 version is much improved, and the ITA 2007 version was simplified.

CTA 2010, section 737 refers to a 'relevant company', which is defined in section 739 as under the control[85] of five or fewer persons and all unquoted companies, unless under the control of a quoted company. Like the previous circumstance (§12.5.3.3), this circumstance applies to the vendor rather than the purchaser, but unlike the situation described in §12.5.3.3, there is no requirement that there should be an abnormal payment. These matters give this circumstance its wide ambit. Section 737 refers to assets of the relevant company; assets are ignored if they represent a return of sums paid to subscribers on the issue of such securities.[86]

---

[79] See *Greenberg v IRC* [1972] AC 109, [1971] 3 All ER 136, 47 TC 240, HL.

[80] *Bird v IRC* [1985] STC 584.

[81] *IRC v Garvin* [1981] STC 344.

[82] *Emery v IRC* [1981] STC 150.

[83] *Bird v IRC* [1985] STC 584.

[84] TA 1988, s 704 para D stated 'in connection with the distribution of profits of a company to which this paragraph applies, the person in question so receives as is mentioned in paragraph C (i), (ii) or (iii) such a consideration as is therein mentioned'. When the Finance Bill 1960 was first presented, para D was part of para C; hence, perhaps, the reference.

[85] Defined this by reference to the close company test in CTA 2010, s 450, ex TA 1988, s 416(2)–(6); see above at §10.2.

[86] CTA 2010, s 737(5), ex TA 1988, s 704(C2).

Under section 737, the company must have received consideration in connection with the distribution, transfer or realisation of assets of a relevant company, or the application of such assets in discharge of liabilities. The consideration will be caught if it:

(1)   is or represents the value of assets which are available for distribution by way of dividend by the company, or assets which would have been available but for anything done by the company;
(2)   is or is received in respect of future receipts of the company; or
(3)   is or represents the value of trading stock by the company.

Thus, the capitalisation of undistributed profits, followed by a reduction in capital, is a distribution for this purpose,[87] as are a reduction in capital followed by capitalisation,[88] an issue and redemption of debentures,[89] and even the purchase of one company's shares by another.[90] There may be a distribution of profits without diminution of assets.[91] Control must be shown to exist. This will trigger liability whether it exists at the time the asset is realised or at the time of the subsequent distribution, but it is not enough for the Revenue simply to prove control when the sum is received.[92]

This rule requires that the sum be received 'in connection with' the distribution of profits. This imposes a less definite causal link than the word 'whereby' in the circumstance described in §12.5.3.3.[93] Returning to *IRC v Wiggins* (see above at §12.5.1), we find that the purchase price paid for the shares in the company owning the picture represented the value of that company's trading stock, so that the taxpayer received consideration of the proscribed type; the company was controlled, a tax advantage was obtained and there was a transaction in securities. As the sum was not otherwise chargeable to income tax, these rules made it so.

12.5.3.5 Twin Trouble; Receipt of Assets of Relevant Company

Here again we are concerned with a relevant company as just defined above. This circumstance, formerly TA 1988, section 704 paragraph E now CTA 2010, section 738, was originally added in 1966. It applies where there are two or more relevant companies and where the taxpayer receives non-taxable consideration in the form of share capital or a security issued by a relevant company in connection with the transfer, directly or indirectly, of assets of one such company to another, and the consideration is or represents the value of assets available for distribution by such a company. If the consideration is non-redeemable share capital, the liability arises when the share capital is repaid.[94] If it takes any other form, liability arises upon receipt. It is very unclear whether this adds anything to the other paragraphs. In *Williams v IRC*,[95] the Court of Appeal held that where a transaction falls

---

[87] *Hague v IRC* [1968] 2 All ER 1252, 44 TC 619.
[88] *IRC v Horrocks* [1968] 3 All ER 296, 44 TC 645.
[89] *IRC v Parker* [1966] 1 All ER 399, 43 TC 396.
[90] *Cleary v IRC* [1967] 2 All ER 48, 44 TC 399.
[91] *Ibid.*
[92] *IRC v Garvin* [1981] STC 344, 55 TC 24.
[93] *Emery v IRC* [1981] STC 150, 54 TC 607, referring to TA 1988, s 704 para C.
[94] CTA 2010, s 738(5), ex TA 1988, s 704 para E(2).
[95] [1979] STC 598, 54 TC 257.

within both TA 1988, section 704, paragraph D and paragraph E then paragraph E should apply. This point was not considered in the House of Lords.

12.5.4 Defences

For corporation tax, these rules do not apply if the taxpayer shows that the transaction was carried out for genuine commercial reasons,[96] or in the ordinary course of making or managing investments, and that no transaction had as its main object or one of its main objects to enable tax advantages to be obtained.[97] It is perhaps interesting, in view of the decision of the House of Lords in *FA and AB Ltd v Lupton*,[98] to note that this defence presupposes that a transaction the main object of which was the obtaining of a tax advantage could be in the ordinary course of making investments or have bona fide commercial reasons. This is an area in which appellate courts will not interfere if the Tribunals (previously the Commissioners) have asked the right questions and considered all the evidence.[99] For income tax purposes, the purpose condition is no longer a defence but has been incorporated into the main charging provision; thus the rules apply only if the main purpose, or one of the main purposes, is to obtain an income tax advantage.[100]

Perhaps correctly, this is the only part of the legislation in which the courts have shown any sympathy for the taxpayer. In determining what are bona fide commercial reasons, the word 'commercial' includes non-financial reasons. Hence, a view that to retain family control of a company is important for the future prosperity of the company, whether in the context of company–customer or employer–employee relationships, can be good commercial reasons, so that steps taken to preserve that control will escape these rules.[101] Similarly trustees of a pension fund required by the Occupational Pensions Board to reduce a particular holding were given the protection of this defence when the route they took (purchase of share by the company) was cheaper and simpler and was what any prudent investor would have done.[102]

In *Marwood Homes v IRC*,[103] a Special Commissioner held that the main object of an intra-group transfer of shares followed by the payment of dividends totalling £1,040,000 from subsidiary companies, the payment being outside a group income election, was to enable the reserves in the subsidiaries to be passed through to the taxpayer company in order to strengthen the financial position of the taxpayer company. However, this decision was reversed by the special appeal tribunal, which held that the obtaining of a tax advantage was a main reason, even if it was not *the* main reason for the transaction.[104]

---

[96] TA 1988, s 703(1) used the older form 'bona fide'. On the importance of onus of proof, note *Hasloch v IRC* (1971) 47 TC 50, where the transaction was instituted by a board of directors of which the taxpayer was not a member. The transaction was the redemption of certain preference shares, a move which would improve the capital structure of the company but also confer a tax advantage on the taxpayer, who failed to persuade the Commissioners that the latter was not an object. The case also shows that the transactions in securities provisions apply even though the intention to save tax exists only for some of the time.

[97] CTA 2010, s 734, ex TA 1988, s 703(1).

[98] [1971] 3 All ER 948; see *Revenue Law*, §19.3.2.

[99] Eg *IRC v Sema Group Pensions Scheme* [2002] EWCA Civ 1857; [2003] STC 95, esp para 117.

[100] ITA 2007, s 684(1)(c), ex s 685.

[101] *IRC v Goodwin* [1976] STC 28, HL.

[102] *Lewis v IRC* [1999] STC (SCD) 349.

[103] [1997] STC (SCD) 37.

[104] [1999] *Simon's Weekly Tax Intelligence* 55.

In deciding whether there are commercial reasons it is not necessary for the taxpayer to show that those reasons are connected with the company concerned. Thus, in *Clark v IRC*,[105] the taxpayer, a farmer, decided to sell shares in a controlled company in order to raise money with which to buy another farm; his claim to use this defence was upheld. Most litigants have argued that the obtaining of a tax advantage was not one of the main objects. The test is subjective and the question is one of fact.[106] If a business operation is carried out in two distinct phases, one of which is purely commercial and the other having tax advantages as its main objects, it is a question of fact for the Tribunals (previously the Commissioners) whether there was one transaction or two. The House of Lords has commended a 'broad commonsense view' to the Commissioners.[107]

In *IRC v Brebner*,[108] the respondent and his colleagues were resisting a takeover bid and so made a counter-offer for the shares. This was financed by a loan from a bank on terms requiring early repayment. After two unsuccessful attempts to persuade the minority interests to sell out, the original counter-offer was accepted by a majority of the shareholders. The company then resolved first to increase its capital by £75,000 by capitalising its reserves, and then to reduce them by the same amount, thus causing £75,000 to come out of the company to the new shareholders who used the sum to pay off the loans from the bank. The Commissioners held that the whole was one transaction and that it did not have as one of its main objects the obtaining of a tax advantage. A notice to counteract the advantage therefore failed. The House of Lords held that there was ample evidence to support the findings. Lord Upjohn said that a choice of a method which carried less tax than another did not necessarily mean that one of its main objects was to obtain a tax advantage.[109]

Another defence is that the Revenue notice counteracting the advantage is made out of time (ie more than six years after the chargeable period to which the tax advantage relates).[110]

12.6   Sale of Income Derived from Individual's Personal Activities

ITA 2007, Part 13, Chapter 4 provides a special regime for certain income derived from personal activities. It was introduced in 1969 to prevent taxpayers from converting future taxable income into capital; the income tax escaped would have been 91.25%.[111] The practice was particularly prevalent in the entertainment industry, the members of which were, of course, more likely than others to suffer from the absence of any proper averaging

---

[105] [1978] STC 614, [1979] 1 All ER 385.

[106] *IRC v Brebner* [1967] 2 AC 18, 30 *per* Lord Upjohn; *ibid*, 26, *per* Lord Pearce. In the first five reported cases the Commissioners' decision on fact has (eventually) been upheld (*IRC v Brebner* (*ibid*); *IRC v Hague* [1968] 2 All ER 1252; *Hasloch v IRC* (1971) 47 TC 50; *IRC v Goodwin* [1976] STC 28, HL; and *Clark v IRC* [1978] STC 614, [1979] 1 All ER 385). The sixth is *Marwood Homes v IRC* [1999] *Simon's Weekly Tax Intelligence*, 55, in which the Special Commissioner was reversed by the s 703 tribunal.

[107] Lord Pearce in *IRC v Brebner* [1967] 2 AC 18, 26.

[108] *Ibid*.

[109] *Ibid*, 30, *per* Lord Upjohn.

[110] ITA 2007, s 698(5) and CTA 2010, s 746(5), ex TA 1988, s 703(12); this may be what the taxpayer's adviser was trying to achieve in *IRC v McGuckian* [1997] STC 908, HL with his tactics of non co-operation.

[111] The provision began life as FA 1969, s 31, Sch 16.

clause in the UK tax system at a time of very high marginal rates of tax. This provision is quite distinct for that applying a duty to deduct tax from certain payments to non-resident entertainers and sportsmen (see below at §16.6.4).

Suppose that a film was about to be made and that £1 million was available for the star's services. A company would acquire the star's services in return for an option to take shares in the company. It would pay £50,000 by way of living allowance to cover expenses, these being taxable to the individual under what is now ITEPA 2003, but deductible by the company. The company would sell the star's services to the film company in return for £1 million, would receive that sum and would suffer corporation tax, so that some tax would be paid but significantly less than the 91.5% which might (then) apply for income tax.

The scope of these rules as drafted is much wider than the covering of these devices in the entertainment industry. It applies where:

(1) arrangements are made to exploit the earning capacity of an individual by putting some other person (eg the company) into a position to receive the income from his activities; and

(2) as part of the arrangement the individual or any other receives a capital amount; provided

(3) that the main object or one of the main objects was the avoidance of tax.[112]

Since the purpose of the provision appears to be to stop rather than to regulate this kind of contract, the whole capital sum is taxable under Part 13 of ITA 2007; there is no provision for top-slicing or any other form of relief, and it does not appear to be treated as relevant earnings for pension purposes since the capital sum is charged under ITA 2007, Part 13 and not ITTOIA 2005, Part 2.[113] Further, the section applies to all persons regardless of their residence, provided the occupation is carried on in whole or in part in the UK,[114] and to any indirect methods of enhancing the value of property.[115]

The section does not apply to a capital amount obtained in respect of the disposal of assets (including any goodwill) of a profession or vocation, or shares in a company so far as the value is attributable to the value of the business as a going concern.[116] However, an exception is made where the value of the business as a going concern is derived to a material extent from the individual's activities and for which he does not get full consideration. A capital amount means any amount in money or money's worth which would not otherwise fall to be included in any computation of income for the purpose of the Tax Acts.[117]

The position with regard to losses is the same as for §12.7 below—loss relief is available under ITA 2007, section 152 because this head of charge is listed in section 1016(2) of Part 2 of that Act.

---

[112] Presumably, this has a subjective meaning; cf the transaction in securities rules above at §12.5.1.
[113] On 'relevant earnings', see FA 2004, s 189 (not rewritten).
[114] ITA 2007, s 777, ex TA 1988, s 775(9).
[115] ITA 2007, s 780 and CTA 2010, s 823(1), ex TA 1988, s 777(2).
[116] ITA 2007, s 784, ex TA 1988 , s 775(4).
[117] ITA 2007, s 777(7) and CTA 2010, ss 829–830, ex TA 1988, s 777(13). Consider unremitted partnership profits when the remittance basis applies. Is there a charge at once under this rule and again when the profits are remitted? Presumably not, as the remittance basis has to be claimed (ITTOIA 2005, s 833).

12.7   Transactions in Land[118]

TA 1988, section 776 for corporation tax was also introduced in 1969 to charge to income tax certain gains of a capital nature arising from the disposal of land. The purpose was to charge profits that escaped being trading income and to charge the prime mover in schemes such as *Ransom v Higgs*[119] rather than the person making the trading profit.[120] The section is not confined to 'artificial transactions' in land, ie to transactions entered into for the purpose of tax avoidance.[121] It is no wonder that some regard the section as being concerned not with artificial transactions in land so much as with artificial taxation of natural transactions in land. They were no doubt pleased that the word 'artificial' does not appear in the title in the rewritten income tax version in ITA 2007, Part 13, Chapter 3, or the rewritten corporation tax version in CTA 2010, Part 18.

CTA 2010, section 819(1) (ex TA 1988, section 776(2)) states that the section applies to a gain if any of the conditions in section 819(2) is met in respect of land, the gain is a capital gain from the disposal of all or part of the land, the land is situated in the UK and a person within section 820(1)(a), (b) or (c) obtains the gain. The conditions are:

(1)   that the land, or any property deriving its value from the land, is acquired with the sole or main object of realising a gain from disposing of the land; or
(2)   the land is held as trading stock; or
(3)   the land is developed with the sole or main object of realising a gain from disposing of the land when developed, and any gain of a capital nature is obtained from the disposal of all or part of the land when developed.

The person described in section 820(1) is:

(a)   the person acquiring, holding or developing the land, or
(b)   a connected person, or
(c)   a person who is a party to, or concerned in, the arrangement or scheme that is effected as respects the land which enables a gain to be realised by any indirect method, or by any series of transactions.

The same words are to be found in ITA 2007, sections 756 and 757.

Thus, the section applies only to the gain arising on an actual disposal of the land which had been so acquired, held or developed. The rule that the gain must be derived from the disposal of land is taken more widely where (c) is involved. In *Page v Lowther*,[122] X

---

[118] The heading in TA 1988 was 'Artificial transactions in land', but the word 'artificial' is not in ITA 2007 or CTA 2010.

[119] [1974] 3 All ER 949 and see *Revenue Law*, §19.1.2.

[120] FA 1969, s 32. On validity of alternative assessments, see *Lord Advocate v McKenna* [1989] STC 485; and on whether assessments are cumulative or alternative, see *IRC v Wilkinson* [1992] STC 454, CA. On these provisions see also Holroyd Pearce [1980] BTR 382 and Avery Jones [1980] BTR 465.

[121] *Page v Lowther* [1983] STC 799 (CA). The taxpayer argued unsuccessfully that the heading of TA 1988, Pt XVII (in which s 776 occurs) 'Tax avoidance', and the side heading of s 776, 'Artificial transactions in land', restricted the scope of the section.

[122] [1983] STC 799 (CA).

granted a lease of land to Y and, in accordance with an arrangement between X and Y, Y arranged for payments due on the grants of sub-leases to be made to X by the sub-lessee. Y having developed the land, the court held that X was liable under section 776(2)(c), as X had arranged for a gain to be realised by X by an indirect method, getting Y to make the sub-lessee make the payments to X.

The charge arises under CTA 2010, section 818 for corporation tax and under ITA 2007, section 755 for income tax, and is generally made on the person realising the gain.[123] However, when A provides B with an opportunity of realising a gain, the gain which B makes may be taxed as the income of A: A is given an indemnity against B.[124] The charge is on the whole of the gain and is made for the year in which the gain is obtained, but an amount in money or money's worth will not be regarded as receivable by some person until that person is able effectively to enjoy or dispose of it.[125] Thus, A's liability does not arise until B effectively enjoys or disposes of the gain. The income is investment income, not earned income.

The charge arises regardless of the residence of the taxpayer if all or any part of the land is situated in the UK.[126] This is of crucial importance since CGT does not apply to non-residents. The extent to which taxpayers can get round this charge by invoking double tax treaties is a matter of great interest—and difficulty.

12.7.1 Disposal of Land with the Object of Realising a Gain

12.7.1.1 Land or Property

'Land' includes references to all or any part of the land, and includes buildings and any estate or interest in land or buildings.[127] A disposal of the benefit of a contract to buy land or the grant of a lease is covered. The interest may be legal or equitable.[128] Property deriving its value from land includes a shareholding in a company deriving its value directly or indirectly from land. A right to insist that a sale should take place only with A's consent may give A the necessary property deriving its value from the land.

12.7.1.2 Disposal

The property is disposed of if the property in the land or the property deriving its value from the land, or control over the land is effectually disposed of.[129] The words are widened still further[130] by taking account of any method, however indirect, by which any property or right is transferred or transmitted, or the value of any property or right is enhanced or diminished. A number of transactions may be treated as one disposal.[131]

---

[123] See ITA 2007, s 759 and CTA 2010, s 820–821, ex TA 1988, s 776(3)(b).

[124] ITA 2007, s 768 and CTA 2010, s 821, ex TA 1988, s 776(8). The indemnity is in ITA 2007, s 768–769 and CTA 2010, s 821, 829, ex TA 1988, s 777(8). B is treated as having paid income tax for the purposes of CGT.

[125] ITA 2007, s 768(2) and CTA 2010, s 829(2), ex TA 1988, s 777(13).

[126] ITA 2007, ss 756(1), 759(8) and CTA 2010, s 819(1)(c), ex TA 1988, s 776(14); in the case of a non-resident the Board may direct the deduction of income tax at basic rate under ITA 2007, s 944.

[127] ITA 2007, s 756, and CTA 2010, s 819, and explicitly so defined in ex TA 1988, ss 776(13), 777(5).

[128] *Winterton v Edwards* [1980] STC 206, [1980] 2 All ER 56, 52 TC 655.

[129] ITA 2007, s 757 and CTA 2010, s 820, ex TA 1988, s 776(4).

[130] By ITA 2007, s 761(1) and CTA 2010, s 823(1), ex TA 1988, s 777(2).

[131] ITA 2007, s 757(3) and CTA 2010, s 820(3), ex TA 1988, s 776(5).

12.7.1.3 Object

The sole or main object must be the realising of a gain from disposing of the land; this should be the object at the time of acquisition.[132] The object of gain must relate to the property acquired and not some other land. If two objects are equal, it would appear to follow that the charge cannot apply. If land is acquired with this object, a subsequent change of mind is irrelevant. On similar Australian legislation the section applies to property acquired under a testamentary gift;[133] however, buying the land from executors in satisfaction of a pecuniary legacy is clearly distinguishable.

Objects other than making a gain include deriving income from land, the preservation of visual or other amenity value of existing land, the provision of accommodation for a relative and in the case of company retention of family control.

12.7.2 Trading Stock

When land held as a trading stock is disposed of, the profits would normally enter a computation under ITTOIA 2005, Part 2 and, as such, would be outside this charge. The purpose of ITA 2007, section 756(3)(c) and CTA 2010, section 819(2)(c) is to catch the indirect disposals which might otherwise give rise to income accruing to others. This charge does not extend to property deriving its value from land.

12.7.3 Later Development

If land is acquired without the object of realising a gain from disposing of the land, the first situation (§12.7.1) is not established. Where, however, land is later developed with that object, a charge arises. 'Development' is not defined. The object of realising a gain on disposal must presumably exist at the moment of development, but it is unclear whether it is necessary that the object should be to dispose of the land immediately the land is developed. The fact that it is envisaged that the land should be used as a source of, say, rental income for a few years before its final effectual disposal, should be only one factor in deciding whether the sole or main object of the development is to realise the gain.

Conversely, if the object is to use the property developed as a source of rental income but, after development, a change of mind occurs, no charge under these rules can arise. What happens when the change of mind occurs during the development is less clear, since the rule states simply that the land is to be developed with the object of realising a gain. Such words would appear apt to cover any development in the course of which there was at any time such a sole or main object.

The rule does not catch a gain attributable to the period before the intention to develop is formed.[134] ITA 2007 expressly notes that the reader must not overlook the ITTOIA 2005, Part 2 rules on appropriation of property as trading stock.

HMRC have an information-gathering power specific to these rules.[135]

---

[132] For example *Sugarwhite v Budd* [1988] STC 533, CA.

[133] *McCelland v Taxation Comr of Australian Commonwealth* [1971] 1 All ER 969.

[134] ITA 2007, s 765 and CTA 2010, s 827, ex TA 1988, s 776(7). This slice is chargeable to CGT. Presumably the existing use value is taken as the figure at which the change for capital gain to taxable income occurs.

[135] ITA 2007, s 771 and CTA 2010, s 832, ex TA 1988, s 778.

12.7.4 Exceptions

12.7.4.1 Residence

The charge does not apply to a gain accruing on the disposal of the taxpayer's principal private residence, as defined for CGT purposes. However, such a residence which was bought partly with a view to gain, while not exempt from CGT, is not liable to a charge under ITA 2007, section 755.[136]

12.7.4.2 Companies

The charge does not apply where there is a disposal of shares in a company which holds land as trading stock, or in a company which is a dealing company, not an investment company, and which owns directly or indirectly 90% or more of the ordinary share capital of another company which holds land as trading stock, provided all the land so held is disposed of in the normal course of trade, and so that all opportunity of profit accrues to the company.[137] This exclusion applies to the straightforward disposition of the shares, but does not apply to a scheme or an arrangement enabling a gain to be achieved by indirect means.

When the land is held by a company, it may be in the company's interest to escape this charge since, as well as tax being paid at a lower rate, the company may also be able to use rollover relief. Apparently some companies avoid the charge by revaluing the property and then distributing a capital profit dividend.

12.7.5 Computation, Clearance and Losses

The computation of the gain is defined in very broad terms, the statute merely directing that there shall be used such method as is just and reasonable in the circumstances, taking into account the value obtained for the land, but allowing only such expenses as are attributable to the land disposed of.[138] This broadness may assist the taxpayer. If T submits a computation based on ITTOIA 2005, Part 2 principles, it appears that in practice it will be for the Revenue to show that the computation is not just and reasonable—it is not enough for the Revenue to show that another method is also just and reasonable.

Because of the vague and broad nature of the charge there is a clearance procedure.[139] However, taxpayers seldom apply for clearance and, when they do, are usually refused. Income arising under ITA 2007, Chapter 13, Part 3 is expressly listed in section 1016(2) of Part 2, so is available for the set-off of losses under ITA 2007, section 152. So losses under Chapter 3 may be set against profits in that list—and vice versa. There is no such clear-cut provision for corporation tax, but the result is the same under the miscellaneous losses (ex Schedule D, Case VI loss) rules.[140]

---

[136] ITA 2007, s 767, ex TA 1988, s 776(9) (repealed because no application to corporation tax).

[137] ITA 2007, s 766 and CTA 2010, s 828, ex TA 1988, s 776(10); in practice, the Revenue confine this provision to companies already dealing.

[138] ITA 2007, s 760 and CTA 2010, s 822, ex TA 1988, s 776(6).

[139] ITA 2007, s 770 and CTA 2010, s 831, ex TA 1988, s 776(11).

[140] CTA 2010, s 91. TA 1988, s 396 was *sub silentio* authority for this: there was an express bar on losses arising under TA 1988, ss 34–36 but there was no mention of s 776.

The Revenue may direct that the payer is to deduct basic income tax if it appears to them that a person who is entitled to any consideration or other amount taxable under these rules was not resident in the UK.[141] This does not allow the Revenue to issue a notice before the person becomes entitled to any consideration.[142]

Example—*Yuill v Wilson*[143]

The taxpayer, T, and connected settlements controlled company X which owned two pieces of land. T set up a non-resident trust which controlled two other non-resident companies, C and M, which each bought a property from X for full market value. The trust then disposed of its shares in C and M to an overseas company in which neither the taxpayer nor his family had any interest; the consideration due to C and M was to be paid in instalments on the happening of certain contingencies.

The House of Lords held that TA 1988, section 776(2) (now ITA 2007, section 756) applied to the gains realised by C and M. The gains had been obtained for the companies either directly or through T's companies, with the aid of the trustees, and T remained liable notwithstanding the subsequent sale of his shares in C and M to the overseas company. However, the House of Lords also held that a right to money which could not be said to be effectively enjoyed was not yet taxable; it followed that as yet there was no liability in respect of the unpaid conditional instalments.[144]

12.8   Transfer of Right to Receive Annual Payments

The sale of the right to receive certain annuities or interest payments was at one time dealt with under provisions considered above at §12.2. Following a redrawing of boundaries in 2005, TA 1988, section 775A was inserted by F(No 2)A 2005.[145] This section applied both for income tax and for corporation tax, but was not rewritten for income tax and was repealed by FA 2009.

---

[141] ITA 2007, s 944, ex TA 1988, s 777(9).

[142] *Pardoe v Energy Power Development Corp* [2000] STC 286.

[143] [1980] STC 460, [1980] 3 All ER 7, 52 TC 674; for another example, see *Chilcott v IRC* [1982] STC 1, (1982) 55 TC 446.

[144] In *Yuill v Fletcher* [1984] STC 401, the taxpayer appealed again on the grounds that the contingent rights of the companies to the instalments were 'money's worth', capable of being valued and sold within a year of the contract. The appeal failed; the gains were realised only when the instalments were received and ceased to be subject to restriction.

[145] F(No 2)A 2005, Sch 7, para 4.

PART II

International and European Union Tax

13

International Tax: Prologue and Connecting Factors[1]

13.1 Prologue

International tax is concerned with the tax system as soon as it moves beyond the purely domestic scene. It is concerned with the taxation of non-UK source income accruing to residents (see chapter fifteen below) and with UK source income accruing to non-residents (chapter sixteen below). The problems posed by controlled foreign companies are considered in chapter seventeen. International aspects of capital gains tax are discussed in chapter eighteen. These issues often raise questions of double taxation, by which is usually meant the provision of relief when two (or more) countries try to tax the same income (see chapters nineteen and twenty below). By way of preface, this chapter is concerned with the connecting factors used in the UK system, while chapter fourteen deals with the question

---

[1] For a general critique and call to action, see Graetz, (2001) 54 *Tax L Rev* 261 (the Tillinghast lecture). Other possible starting points are Vogel (1988) 16 *Intertax* 216, 310, 393; Kingson (1981) 81 *Columbia L Rev* 1151; Avi-Yonah (1996) 74 *Texas L Rev* 1301; and Easson, in Krever (ed), *Tax Conversations* (Kluwer, 1999) 419. For a good practical introduction, see Arnold and McIntyre, *International Tax Primer*, 2nd edn (Kluwer, 2002). For further study, see Harris and Oliver, *International Commercial Tax* (CUP, 2010).

of the enforcement of foreign revenue laws. Tax lawyers usually treat these rules as giving rise to points of domestic law in an international context rather than as part of international law proper; such an attitude is incomprehensible to international lawyers.[2] Thus tax lawyers debate whether the International Court of Justice is a suitable way of resolving tax disputes and usually conclude that it is not.[3] The UK tax system, with its pragmatic approach to things, treats these issues as esoteric; however, the Continental European tradition may bring change through the EU.

National tax systems are truly national and are one of the ultimate expressions of national sovereignty. They are usually drawn up in the interests of the nation and not of the nation's neighbours, which indifference is, at least in common law systems, returned by the neighbours. Continental European systems find themselves able to consider their neighbours with politeness. National tax systems resemble the continental plates of the plate tectonic systems—they are massive, they collide, and the impact usually causes one to go under and the other to rise up. Those caught at the point of collision may be able to take advantage of opportunities,[4] but equally they may be trying to avoid injustices such as double taxation or non-relief. National sovereignty is no longer enough. It is one cliché that the world is getting smaller, and another that business is getting more integrated; research work by the OECD and EC (2001) shows how tax still gets in the way.[5] As trade gets more integrated, yesterday's concepts may need to be revised or scrapped. A system based on determining business profits of a multinational on the basis of source alone becomes unreal—especially as world trade becomes ever more involved in terms of intangible services and intellectual property—and it becomes tempting to move to other measures for dividing up the total profits of the multinational, such as the number of employees or the amount of capital investment in each State. This 'unitary' approach has its problems, but it is a symptom of an underlying fact which cannot be wished away. Another solution is to tax internationally by creating a supranational tax authority, such as the European Union may well have to create one day.

Tax law does not form part of that branch of study known as private international law; one of the most constant UK rules directs that the UK courts will not enforce a claim by another state which is of a revenue nature. However, international co-operation has developed through international institutions such as the OECD, the United Nations and various intergovernmental bodies in different parts of the world. These institutions develop appropriate tax policy for governments, but they generally fail to create beneficial tax rights for individual taxpayers. Tax plays an important role in world trade law, and the World Trade Organisation (WTO) has had to adjudicate on matters of impermissible and impermissible discrimination.[6] However tax policy issues arise quite outside the remit of the WTO. For example, it has been suggested that the increasing prevalence of integrating

---

[2] See Avi Yonah (2004) 57 *Tax L Rev* 483.

[3] See Van der Bruggen (2001) 29 *Intertax* 250.

[4] Rosenbloom (2000) 53 *Tax L Rev* 137.

[5] See *Taxing Profits in a Global Economy* (OECD, 1991) and *Tax Effects on Foreign Direct Investment* (OECD, 2007). For the EU, see the EC Commission Working Paper, *Company Taxation in the Internal Market*, COM(2001)582 and the ongoing work on the CCCTB (www.ec.europa.eu/taxation_customs/taxation/company_tax/index_en.htm). The impact of tax on business investment is also the subject of ongoing research by the Oxford University Centre for Business Taxation (www.sbs.ox.ac.uk).

[6] Warren (2001) 54 *Tax L Rev* 131; for a comparison of EU and WTO approaches, see Gaines, Olson and Sørenson, *Liberalising Trade in the EU and the WTO: A Legal Comparison* (CUP, 2012) and Ortino, *Basic Legal Instruments for the Liberalisation of Trade* (Hart Publishing, 2004).

shareholder and company taxation presents a major challenge to the international tax structure.[7] Another example is the challenge to traditional concepts by the development of electronic commerce.[8]

International tax has developed its own criteria, sometimes building on but always distinct from those outlined in *Revenue Law*, chapter one.[9] When a national government examines its international tax rules it wants to achieve three things:

(1)   to get a reasonable share of tax from international, ie transnational, business;

(2)   to maintain horizontal equity for its people, whether they have foreign or domestic income; and

(3)   to encourage its own businesses, or at least see that they are not unfairly discriminated against.

As usual in tax policy, it is not possible to do all these things. In the international tax context this is prevented by the absence of a universal flat rate tax on a uniform base with uniform (high) levels of administration.

Tax theorists talking about objective (1) use the term 'inter-nation equity'. The objective for the UK is to devise rules which collect enough tax on profits earned by foreigners in the UK, while enabling the UK to gather enough tax on profits earned by its own people abroad. This may be seen as an area either for crude international bargaining or, more rationally, for trying to develop principles within which the bargaining process may take place. The view that the role of inter-nation equity in international taxation is just about politics did not go without challenge.[10] A growing band of scholars, arguing from varying combinations of normative and empirical work, have argued that the concept must be understood more broadly and take account of poverty and international justice.[11] Some writers suggest that at present international income tax policy is irresponsive to inequalities between States[12] and so more weight—or at least more effectiveness—should be given to source-based taxation of, at least corporate, income.[13]

Objective (2) suggests that the state will want to ensure that the total tax burden on X's income will be the same whether X earns that income at home or abroad. Carried to its

---

[7] Warren, *op cit*, 139.

[8] Eg the various OECD Reports gathered together in the annual van Raad, *Materials on International and EU Tax Law*, vol 1 (International Tax Centre Leiden) and the Symposium (1997) 52 *Tax L Rev* 557. See Shalhav (2003) 31 *Intertax* 131.

[9] See Arnold and McIntyre, *op cit*, ch 1; Graetz , *op cit*; and Warren, *op cit*, 158–68.

[10] Musgrave and Musgrave suggested a redistributive mechanism for relations between developed and developing countries: see (1972) 'Inter-nation Equity' in Bird and Head (eds), *Essays in Honor of Carl S Shoup* (University of Toronto Press, 1973), 63, 70.

[11] Other writing emphasises that inter-nation equity requires allocation of fiscal jurisdiction in accordance with prevailing views of justice internationally: see Kaufman, 'Fairness and International Income Taxation' (1998) 29 *Law and Policy in International Business* 145, 194. For a lead into theories of inter-nation equity, see Vogel, 'Worldwide versus Source Taxation on Income: A Review and Re-evaluation of Arguments (part III)' (1988) 10 *Intertax* 394, and Peggy Brewer Richman (later Musgrave) *Taxation of Foreign Investment Income* (Johns Hopkins Press, 1963). Connections between international taxation and philosophical ideas of international justice are made by Cappellan (2001) 15 *Ethics and International Affairs* 97.

[12] On adjusting US international tax policy to the needs of developing countries, Brown (2002) 23 *U PA J Intl Econ L* 45.

[13] Vogel, *op cit* (1988). The source of income is a difficult concept, so a simpler mechanism to allow developing countries take a greater share of MNE (multinational enterprise) revenue has interested some writers: see Avi-Yonah (2000) 113 *H L Rev* 1573, esp 1648–49.

conclusion this has some surprising results. Thus, it will cover income whether or not it is remitted to the UK and whatever the cause of non-remittance; it may also apply whether the non-remittance is because a capital gain has not been realised or the wealth is in an insurance policy or bond, but only if the same principles had been enacted as part of the domestic system. The same journey to a conclusion suggests that, where the foreign tax charged on income is higher than the UK tax, the UK should refund the difference; it does not, and is not likely to.

The tensions within (3) are clear from the way it is formulated; the UK wants to ensure that its people are not discriminated against by other governments when they carry out transactions abroad. However, at home it may be torn between wanting to protect its own residents and ensuring a competitive economy, whether the competition comes from residents or non-residents. As the global economy becomes ever more closely integrated, the distinction between the home trader and the foreigner becomes unreal. As Nation States become increasingly desperate to attract investment, they compete with their neighbours and rivals. Within the European Union much of this competition is now controlled by rules on state aids, but this may simply switch the area of competition to that of tax. Agreements between Member States to control harmful tax competition have been reached but are based on international agreement rather than binding EU law (see below §19.1.2).

In resolving these problems, tax systems use different concepts and techniques. Thus, the connecting factors for the taxpayer may be citizenship, or residence or domicile; the connecting factor for the particular receipt will be that of source (however determined). The foreign income may be relieved from tax by allowing the foreign tax to be used as a deduction in computing the UK income, as a credit, or by simply exempting the foreign income (such as dividends) from UK tax. These solutions are discussed in the context of phrases about capital neutrality.[14]

Capital import neutrality (CIN) focuses on investment in the particular market and demands that non-residents investing in the market (those by whom the capital is imported) should be treated the same as those who are also resident. CIN thus stresses the importance of neutrality in the country of source. An international system based on source only and not on residence would satisfy CIN; so a system which simply exempted foreign income of UK residents from UK tax would meet this test. Continental European thinking finds CIN attractive for the respect it pays to the sovereignty of the other State.[15]

Capital export neutrality (CEN) focuses on investment by the particular individual and demands that residents investing in a foreign market (those by whom the capital is exported) should be treated the same as those who invest at home.[16] CEN thus stresses the importance of neutrality in the country of residence. An international system based on residence and not on source would satisfy CEN.

Early in the 21st century, economists have demonstrated that CIN and CEN do not exhaust the forms which neutrality might take.[17] So one comes across capital ownership neutrality (CON) and national ownership neutrality (NON). CON suggests that the tax

---

[14] For inadequacies of these and other concepts, see Graetz, *op cit*. See also Devereux and Pearson, *Corporate Tax Harmonisation and Economic Efficiency*, IFS Report Series No 35 (Institute for Fiscal Studies, 1989), 16–24, suggesting that achieving CEN may be more important than achieving CIN.

[15] Schön, *Tax Notes International*, 4 February 2008, 423; *in memoriam* Klaus Vogel.

[16] For critique, see Graetz, *op cit*.

[17] Desai and Hines (2003) 56 *National Tax Jo* 487.

system should strive for the same result whether assets are owned at home or abroad, ie tax rules do not distort the ownership of assets. This system too emphasises source. An international regime paying attention to world welfare in which all countries exempt foreign income satisfies CON, but so also may a credit system.[18] NON is satisfied when all activities within the national area are taxed alike, whether investment is by domestic or by foreign firms. Here too one finds a call for the exemption of foreign income no matter what other countries do. Additional outbound investment does not reduce domestic tax revenue, since the reduction in domestic investment is offset by an increase in foreign investment.

13.2   UK Connecting Factors: General

In general, UK residents are taxable in respect of all income no matter where it arises; non-residents are taxable on income arising from sources within the UK.[19] UK residents are taxed because, whether or not British subjects, they enjoy the benefit of our laws for the protection of their property; non-residents because, in respect of property in the UK, they enjoy the benefit of our law for the protection of that property.[20] The burden of proof is on the Revenue to establish that a taxpayer is resident in the UK.[21] The UK used to regard citizenship[22] as a suitable test of the jurisdiction for executing people, but not for taxing them. Citizenship does, however, have some tax consequences for the UK.[23] The United States uses citizenship as one of its bases of tax.[24] Every so often proposals are made to reform and tighten the UK rules on residence; these usually fail for fear of upsetting the large expatriate community in London, especially the Greek shipping community, which might otherwise sail away from the UK.[25]

13.3   UK Connecting Factors: Individual's Residence[26]

There is not yet a statutory definition of 'residence'—though one is presently under consideration in the UK, with legislation expected in Finance Act 2013.[27] In practice much turns on the Revenue Code, formerly in leaflet IR 20 and, from 2009, in guide HMRC6.[28]

---

[18]   *Ibid*, 494.

[19]   On definition of 'United Kingdom', see above at §2.1; for an example of this fundamental principle, see discussion of *Becker v Wright*, in *Revenue Law* at §31.4.2.3.

[20]   *Whitney v IRC* [1926] AC 37, 54, (1926) 10 TC 88, 112, *per* Lord Wrenbury.

[21]   *Untelrab v McGregor* [1996] STC (SCD) 1; see Oliver [1996] BTR 505.

[22]   A company incorporated abroad is a subject of that country (*Janson v Driefontein Consolidated Mines* [1902] AC 484). See also Vaughan Williams and Crussach (1933) 49 *LQR* 334; and Farnsworth, *The Residence and Domicile of Corporations* (Butterworths, 1939) 302–09.

[23]   Eg ITTOIA 2005, ss 831–839, ex TA 1988, s 65(4) remittance basis if not ordinarily resident; citizenship is also relevant to tax treaties.

[24]   The effects of this base are often reduced by double tax treaties; see Gann (1982) 38 *Tax L Rev* 1, 58–69.

[25]   On 1988 Inland Revenue Consultative Document, see Hauser [1989] BTR 29.

[26]   See Sumption, *Taxation of Overseas Income* (Butterworths, 1977), ch 1; Farnsworth, *op cit*, ch 1; Olowofoyeku [2003] BTR 306.

[27]   HM Treasury, *Budget 2012*, HC 1853 (21 March 2012), para 2.51. For the latest see <http://www.hm-treasury.gov.uk/consult_statutory_residence_test.htm>.

[28]   Inland Revenue leaflet IR 20 was first published in 1973.

The basis for this Code is uncertain since the cases on which it rests are, for the most part, illustrations of the principle that since residence is a question of fact, the courts cannot reverse a finding by the Tribunals (formerly Commissioners) simply because they would not reach the same conclusion. The Revenue practice is based on decisions in favour of the Revenue and conveniently ignores those in favour of the taxpayer. The more recent guidance in HMRC6 indicates, amongst many things, that HMRC will not take the 91-day practice (discussed further at §13.3.2.2 below) as a mechanical 'safe harbour' rule.

Gaines-Cooper[29] is an important Supreme Court decision on the proper construction of the Revenue's guidance in IR 20. By the time the case reached the Supreme Court, the Revenue had accepted that their guidance was binding on them and could found a case based on legitimate expectation. The taxpayers in the joined cases argued that an alleged benevolent interpretation of the law on ceasing to be resident and ordinarily resident in IR 20 and/or benevolent HMRC practice gave rise to legitimate expectations of benevolent treatment. These arguments were rejected by the Supreme Court (4:1). Lord Wilson, giving the lead judgment for the majority, concluded that the evidence adduced was too thin to support the taxpayers' assertions (at 49).

Residence is distinct from domicile in its legal nature and purpose. The tax system usually asks whether X is resident in the UK or not resident in the UK, and not whether X is resident in the UK or in another country; the conflict of laws asks where a person has his domicile. Hence, X may have two residences, but not two domiciles;[30] equally, X may have no residence—but must have a domicile.[31] In the rare contexts where it is important to determine whether a person is resident in a particular country, such as that of double tax treaties, special rules determine residence; these treaty rules have nothing to do with common law residence.[32]

13.3.1 Rules for Residence

13.3.1.1 Presence not Absolutely Necessary

A person who is absent from the UK for the whole tax year may still be resident;[33] however, the question is one of fact and the issue is not beyond doubt.[34] Thus, a master mariner whose wife and family lived in the UK throughout the tax year, while he was absent, was taxed as if still resident in the UK.[35] However, in *Reed v Clark*,[36] it was held that a person

---

[29] *R (on the application of Davies and another) v Revenue and Customs Commissioners and R (on the application of Gaines-Cooper) v Revenue and Customs Commissioners* [2011] UKSC 47. See also case note by Welsh and Eden [2011] BTR 643.

[30] *A-G v Coote* (1817) 4 Price 183, (1817) 2 TC 385; *Lloyd v Sulley* (1885) 2 TC 37.

[31] *Bell v Kennedy* (1868) LR 1 Sc & Div 307, 320.

[32] On double tax treaties, see below at §20.6.1; see also CFC legislation, below ch 17.

[33] *Reed v Clark* [1986] Ch 1, [1985] STC 323, (1985) 58 TC 528.

[34] *Iveagh v IRC* [1930] IR 386 is to the contrary, and most of the (few) cases relied on could be and perhaps were decided on the basis of the rule in TA 1988, s 334. *Revenue and Customs Commissioners v Grace* [2009] STC 213, [2008] EWHC 2708 (Ch) is an important, interesting and Revenue-friendly case on TA 1988, s 336/ITA 2007, s 831, on whether a person is in the UK for a temporary purpose only. On further appeal the Court of Appeal ([2009] EWCA Civ 1082, [2009] STC 2709) held that while Lewison J had been right on the law, he had been wrong in thinking that this entitled him to reverse the decision of the Special Commissioner, Dr Brice. The matter was remitted for rehearing.

[35] *Rogers v IRC* (1879) 1 TC 225. Contrast *Turnbull v Foster* (1904) 6 TC 206, where the merchant had not previously been ordinarily resident in the UK and so was held not resident. On ordinary residence see a more recent example in *Tuczka v Revenue & Customs Commissioners* [2011] STC 113, where the taxpayer's appeal failed.

[36] [1986] Ch 1, [1985] STC 323, (1985) 58 TC 528.

who was absent from the UK for the whole of a tax year, and who set himself up in another country in such a way as to acquire residence there, was not within the rules in what is now ITA 2007, section 829, as he was not in the other country for the purpose of 'occasional' residence. A person may thus escape section 829 even though his time abroad is limited and he always intends to return.

13.3.1.2 Place of Residence not Essential

In the normal case, 'residence' means 'the place where one dwells permanently or for a considerable time, where one has one's settled or usual abode or the particular place at which one lives',[37] but 'resident' indicates a quality of the person to be charged, not of his property.[38] A vagrant is not the less resident in the UK for preferring a different hedgerow or doss house each night; neither is a person with a place of abode abroad incapable of also being resident in the UK,[39] even though he should lack such a place here.

13.3.1.3 Intention or Desire not Conclusive

A person may be resident in the UK notwithstanding the absence of any element of intention or desire. An intention to depart at any moment is no hindrance to residence.[40] Thus, a person may be resident even if his presence is compelled by reasons of business,[41] military service,[42] attendance at school[43] or even ill-health.[44] A foreigner compelled to spend time here in prison is presumably also resident here. Among the factors the courts look at are past[45] and present habits of life,[46] the frequency, regularity and duration of visits to the UK,[47] possibly the purpose of such visits,[48] ties with this country,[49] nationality[50] and whether or not a place of abode is maintained here.[51]

13.3.1.4 Flexibility of Concept

In considering this test, however, it is essential to bear in mind that

> ...[residence] is not a term of invariable elements, all of which must be satisfied in each instance. It is quite impossible to give it a precise and inclusive definition. It is highly flexible, and its many shades of meaning vary not only in the contexts of different matters but also in different aspects of the same matter.[52]

---

[37] *Levene v IRC* [1928] AC 217, 222; (1926) 13 TC 486 at 505, *per* Viscount Cave LC.
[38] *IRC v Lysaght* [1928] AC 234, (1928) 13 TC 511, *per* Lord Sumner.
[39] *Ibid.*
[40] *Brown v Burt* (1911) 5 TC 667 (yacht in tidal water—resident).
[41] *Inchiquin v IRC* (1948) 31 TC 125.
[42] *Miesagaes v IRC* (1957) 37 TC 493.
[43] *Re MacKenzie* [1941] Ch 69, [1940] 4 All ER 310.
[44] *Egyptian Delta Land and Investment Co Ltd v Todd* [1929] AC 1, 12; (1929) 14 TC 119, 140, *per* Viscount Sumner.
[45] *Levene v IRC* [1928] AC 217, 227; (1928) 13 TC 486, 501, *per* Viscount Sumner.
[46] *Ibid.*
[47] *Ibid*; *IRC v Brown* (1926) 11 TC 292; and *IRC v Zorab* (1926) 11 TC 289.
[48] In *Lysaght v IRC* [1928] AC 234, 13 TC 511 it was stressed that volition was not necessary. Intention is relevant for TA 1988, ss 334, 336.
[49] *IRC v Lysaght* [1928] AC 234; *Kinloch v IRC* (1929) 14 TC 736.
[50] *Levene v IRC* [1928] AC 217, 224; (1928) 13 TC 486, 506; and TA 1988, s 334.
[51] *Cooper v Cadwalader* (1904) 5 TC 101.
[52] *Thomson v Minister of National Revenue* [1946] SCR 209, 224, *per* Rand J.

13.3.2 Revenue Rules

13.3.2.1 Spending 183 days in the UK—in the Tax Year—Extended Presence as Residence

Under ITA 2007, section 831, which supersedes and amends TA 1988, section 336(1), a person who is in the UK for a total period equal to 183 days in the tax year is treated as resident.[53] The previous rules expressed in months meant that the number of days could vary between 181 and 184 depending on the months in issue. The 183 days need not be continuous. As from 6 April 2008 this includes all days on which the taxpayer is present in the UK at the end of the day.[54] So a day of arrival will count but a day of departure will not.

For some time the practice has been that someone in transit at a UK airport and who stays 'airside', and so does not officially enter the UK, is not present in the UK at the end of the day. This exemption is widened and made statutory.[55] The person must leave the UK the next day and must not engage in activities substantially unrelated to his transit through the UK. This rule is wide, making the exemption apply to those who do not stay 'airside', eg because of changing terminals, airports or even modes of transport. However, a person who takes part in a business meeting at the airport will be doing something unrelated to his transit and so will be unable to use the transit exemption if still here at the end of the day. Presumably, lawyers caught reading tax books relating to the business to which they are going in the onward country may use the exemption. The word 'activity' is dangerous. The HMRC examples show that they may have had in mind things other than income-generating activities. So 'planned' visits to see grandchildren en route—or to consult a surgeon—will mean that the transit exemption does not apply. The wording is also apt to catch a lovers' tryst—but only if planned!

The concept of planning is not in the legislation but is in the HMRC examples. It is therefore not completely clear whether the 'planning' relates to the person's activity in the UK or to the presence in the UK at midnight. If a person arrives in London in the morning, visits grandchildren in the afternoon and leaves before midnight, the day is not a day of presence in the UK at all. If the person is scheduled to leave before midnight but the flight is delayed, the situation is not clear. Caution, reinforced by a broad reading of the words of the statute, suggests that this person cannot use the transit exemption.

The 183 days must be in the tax year. Therefore, a person who arrives on 6 April may, on the view taken in the code, stay only 183 days in the next 12 months, whereas a person who arrives on 5 October may stay almost a full 12 months and still not be resident.

ITA 2007, section 831(1) contains the corollary that a person who has not actually resided in the UK for 183 days is not treated as resident if he is in the UK for some temporary purpose only and not with any view or intent of establishing residence:

> The meaning of it is this, if a foreigner comes here for merely temporary purposes connected with business or pleasure, or something else, and does not remain for a period altogether within the

[53] The principal difference is that TA 1988, s 336 referred to six months, not 183 days—on which see *Wilkie v IRC* [1952] 1 All ER 92, (1952) 32 TC 495; however, ITA 2007, s 831 also refers to presence in the UK as opposed to being in the UK, which has issues of representative presence.

[54] ITA 2007, s 831(1A), as amended by FA 2008, s 24.

[55] ITA 2007, s 831(1B), added by FA 2008, s 24; the CGT rules are also amended.

year of [183 days], he shall not be liable for a certain portion of taxation ... He would have been liable but for this exemption.[56]

This rule exempts from UK tax income any relevant foreign source income within ITTOIA 2005 or certain parts of ITEPA 2003, Parts 2, 9 (foreign pensions) and 10 (foreign welfare payments), and states a special residence rule for ITEPA 2003, Part 2, Chapters 4 and 5.[57] It does not affect other aspects of residence. In applying these provisions, accommodation which may be available in the UK for the person's use is ignored.[58]

The Statement of Practice allowing some relaxation of time limits where a person's stay is prolonged because of exceptional circumstances beyond that person's control, eg illness, does not apply to this rule.[59]

13.3.2.2 Habitual and Substantial Visits

Visitors are normally regarded as resident in the UK if they visit it regularly, ie their visits after three years average 91 days or more in the tax year; such visitors becomes resident as from the fourth year.[60] If they intend to follow this pattern from the beginning, they are treated as resident from the beginning. Equally, a decision, say, in Year 3 that the visits will follow this pattern, will cause them to be resident as from 6 April of Year 3. The role of intention is of great importance in such cases. In calculating the periods of 91 days the Revenue will not take into account days spent in the UK because of exceptional circumstances, eg illness.[61] However, the 2008 rules on counting presence at midnight as giving rise to a day of presence in the UK apply here too. The more recent guidance in HMRC6 indicates, amongst many things, that HMRC will not take the 91-day practice as a mechanical 'safe harbour' rule.

The bases for this practice are the decisions of the House of Lords in *Levene v IRC*[62] and *IRC v Lysaght*,[63] each of which concerns an unsuccessful claim by a resident to have given up residence. In *Levene v IRC* the taxpayer had been resident in the UK in previous years but had left the country in 1919. He did not set up a place of abode overseas. From 1919–25, he spent five months in each year in the UK but had no fixed abode here. He was 'a bird of passage of almost mechanical regularity'.[64] The reasons for his visits were the obtaining of medical advice, visiting his relatives, taking part in certain religious observances and dealing with his income tax affairs. The Commissioners held that he was resident here, a decision not reversed by the House of Lords.

In *IRC v Lysaght* the taxpayer had resided in England where he lived with his family, and was managing director of the family business. In 1919 he went to live permanently in Ireland and set up a home there. He retained a seat on the board of the company and visited England once a month for meetings, but for no other purposes. On such visits he

---

[56] *Lloyd v Sully* (1884) 2 TC 37, 42, *per* Lord Inglis.
[57] ITA 2007, s 831(2), ex TA 1988, s 336(2). See also *Revenue Law*, §13.3.
[58] ITA 2007, s 832(1), ex s 336(3), added by FA 1993, s 208(1).
[59] HMRC6, para 2.2.1, Statement of Practice SP 2/91 (especially para 3).
[60] HMRC6, para 7.5. Inland Revenue leaflet IR 20 (2000), §3.3 formerly used a pattern of 91 days per year after four years, and see Statement of Practice SP 3/81.
[61] HMRC6, para 2.2.1; Statement of Practice SP 2/91; Inland Revenue leaflet IR 20 (1999), §3.3, as supplemented by Revenue Interpretation RI 72.
[62] [1928] AC 217, (1928) 13 TC 486.
[63] [1928] AC 234, (1928) 13 TC 511.
[64] [1928] AC 217, 226, 501, *per* Viscount Sumner.

was not accompanied by his wife and he usually stayed at an hotel. The Commissioners held that he was still resident in the UK. The House of Lords could find no reason for holding that there was no evidence to support that finding and therefore dismissed the appeal. For Viscount Sumner the crucial point appeared to be that the taxpayer was obliged to come to this country, that that obligation was continuous, and that the sequence of the visits excluded the element of chance and occasion.[65] For Lord Buckmaster, with whom Lord Atkinson agreed, the matter was one of fact and degree, and so, pre-eminently, one of fact.[66] Lord Warrington was not sure that he would have taken the same view as the Commissioners.[67] Viscount Cave dissented, arguing that the matter was one of mixed fact and law, and so could be interfered with; and if it were a matter of fact, that there was no evidence to support the conclusion reached by the Commissioners.[68]

IRC v Lysaght has generally been looked upon as marking the most extreme frontier of residence. However, the case concerned the two years immediately after the move to Ireland. The taxpayer was still involved in the running of the English business and had no business interests in Ireland. He remained a member of a London club and had a bank account in Bristol. Moreover, his visits, although only for company meetings once a month, lasted, on average, a week, and meant that he was physically present in England for 94 days in the one year and 101 days in the other. The fact that he had found a permanent home outside the jurisdiction was only one factor to be weighed against these.

The importance of recognising that in *IRC v Lysaght* the House of Lords merely declined to interfere with a finding of fact by the Commissioners is shown by a comparison of that case with *IRC v Brown*,[69] where the taxpayer's usual habit was to spend seven months in Mentone, two months in Switzerland or at the Italian lakes, and three months in the UK.[70] The Special Commissioners held that he was not resident, and Rowlatt J held that he could not interfere with that finding. The same judge later held that he could not interfere with the finding of fact by the Commissioners in *IRC v Lysaght*. Yet it is the *Lysaght* case, despite the doubts on the facts expressed in the House of Lords, which is taken as the basis of current Revenue practice under the Code.

13.3.2.3 Coming to the UK

A person coming to the UK to work for at least three years will be treated as resident from the day of arrival until the date of departure. A person coming for a purpose lasting less than three years, or not knowing how long the stay will be, will be treated as resident here only by spending 183 days or more in the UK in the tax year (ie coming within the rule set out at §13.3.2.1 above).[71]

13.3.2.4 Availability of Accommodation

At one time the Revenue took the view that people having accommodation available to them would be resident if they made even a single visit to the UK. This would mean that by contrast to the Revenue rules in §13.3.2.1 and §13.3.2.3 above, a visitor to the UK

---

[65] [1928] AC 234, 245; (1928) 13 TC 511, 529, *per* Viscount Sumner.
[66] *Ibid*, 247, 534.
[67] *Ibid*, 251, 537.
[68] [1928] AC 241, 533.
[69] (1926) 11 TC 292.
[70] Case stated, para 3(4). One difference from *Lysaght* is that Brown had no business interests here. This difference is not reflected in the Code.
[71] HMRC6, para 7.2; Inland Revenue leaflet IR 20 (2000), §3.7 formerly used two years.

would be resident here notwithstanding that the visit was for less than six months.[72] It also meant that a person who arrived in the UK and stayed would be treated as resident from the moment of arrival.[73] Conversely, a person wishing to cease to be resident would fail to achieve that objective in a year if accommodation was available, no matter how short-term, in the UK in that year, rather than being resident only if the average of his visits to the UK was 91 days a year or more.[74] It is unlikely that this rule survived FA 1993, and ITA 2007 gives little ground for any such Revenue arguments.[75] However, owning or leasing available accommodation indicates an intention to stay, and is therefore still relevant to the acquisition and giving up of residence (see §13.3.4 below) and for ordinary residence.[76]

13.3.3 Change of Residence during Tax Year

The Tax Acts make no provision for splitting a tax year. They make no effort to tax new residents or departing residents only for that part of the year for which they were resident,[77] but tax for the whole year in full. However, ESC A11 allows a split to be carried out where an individual, who has not, prior to arrival, been ordinarily resident in the UK, comes to the UK to take up permanent residence or to stay at least two years, regardless of the purpose, or who ceases to reside by leaving for permanent residence abroad.

This concession applies also to the year of departure and return where, subject to conditions, an individual goes abroad under a contract of employment. The conditions for the extension are:

(1)   the absence and the contract of employment must extend over a period covering a complete tax year; and
(2)   any interim visits must not amount to 183 days or more in any tax year, or an average of 91 days or more in a tax year.[78]

The time of departure or arrival may make a significant difference to total tax liability, since personal reliefs are not apportioned by reference to the duration of residence. As with all concessions, the benefit is withheld if the taxpayer is using it for tax avoidance.[79] The similar Concession D2 applies for CGT. On 1998 rules for capital gains disposals by individuals temporarily non-resident, see below at §18.1.2.

13.3.4 Giving up Residence

Under the Revenue Code, if a person goes abroad permanently[80] he is regarded as resident in the UK if he pays a visit to the UK during the tax year, and as ordinarily resident if he comes here in most years. If he claims that he has ceased to be resident and ordinarily

---

[72]   Inland Revenue leaflet IR 20 (2000), §3.3.
[73]   Inland Revenue leaflet IR 20 (1996), §3.3.
[74]   Inland Revenue leaflet IR 20 (2000), §2.5; accommodation may be available whether or not it is owned.
[75]   FA 1993, s 208; Inland Revenue Press Release, 16 March 1993, [1993] *Simon's Tax Intelligence* 468.
[76]   Below §13.4. HMRC6, paras 2.2, 7.7.3, 7.7.4, 7.8.3 Example 3, and 8.1. See also Inland Revenue leaflet IR 20 (2000), §§3.7 and 3.11; the lease must be for three years or more.
[77]   See *Neubergh v IRC* [1978] STC 181, (1978) 52 TC 79.
[78]   ESC A11; this does not apply to FA 1995, s 198, IHT or CTT, nor to trusts. See also HMRC6, para 8.1.1; Inland Revenue leaflet IR 20 (2000), §§1.5–1.7.
[79]   See *R v IRC, ex parte Fulford-Dobson* [1987] STC 344.
[80]   HMRC6, paras 8.1–8.3; Inland Revenue leaflet IR 20 (2000), §§2.7 *et seq.*

resident here, and can produce some evidence for this (for example, that he has sold his house and set up a permanent home abroad), his claim is usually admitted provisionally with effect from the date following his departure. Normally this provisional ruling is confirmed after the visitor has remained abroad for a period which includes a complete tax year and during which his visits to this country have not amounted to an annual average of three months. If he cannot produce such evidence, he will be assessed on the provisional basis that he is still resident here and a decision made after three years in the light of what actually happens in that period. If he is found to have lost his residence, his liability is reassessed on that basis. Once more the FA 2008 rules treating presence at midnight as meaning a day of presence in the UK apply here.

Under the Revenue Code, a person who leaves the UK to work full-time abroad under a contract of employment is treated as not resident and not ordinarily resident if both the absence from the UK and the employment last for at least a whole tax year. Analogous treatment is provided for trades, professions and vocations.[81] The Code also mentions visits back to the UK. These are ignored if they total less than 183 days in any tax year, and average less than 91 days a tax year. Again, the FA 2008 rules treating presence at midnight as meaning a day of presence in the UK apply here. Continuing to have property in the UK for one's use is not fatal if the reason is consistent with the stated aim of living abroad permanently.[82]

As mentioned in §13.3 above, *Gaines-Cooper*[83] is an important Supreme Court decision on the proper construction of the Revenue's guidance in IR20 in the context of giving up residence. Lord Wilson, giving the lead judgment for the majority (4:1; at 45), reviewed the guidance just discussed and concluded that an ordinarily sophisticated taxpayer would have interpreted it to mean that:

(1) giving up residence required leaving the UK in a more profound sense than travel;
(2) he was required to do more than to take up residence abroad;
(3) he must have relinquished his usual residence in the UK;
(4) any subsequent returns to the UK must be no more than visits; and
(5) any property retained by him in the UK was for the purpose of visits, not residence.

Although deciding that the answer demanded a multi-factorial evaluation of the taxpayer's circumstances, if invited to summarise the requirements in IR 20, Lord Wilson thought he could do so in three words—a distinct break.

13.3.5 *Concessionary Relief for Accompanying Spouses or Civil Partners*

Where a taxpayer, T, has a spouse or civil partner, S, the status of each is to be determined independently. However, where T goes abroad for purposes of whole-time employment and S goes either at the same time or afterwards but for a different purpose, T may cease to be resident and ordinarily resident as from the day after the date of departure to the

---

[81] HMRC6, paras 8.5 and 8.8; Inland Revenue leaflet IR 20 (2000), §§2.2–2.5.
[82] HMRC6, para 8.1; Inland Revenue leaflet IR 20 (2000), §2.7.
[83] [2011] UKSC 47. See also case note by Welsh and Eden [2011] BTR 643.

date of return, while S may find residence and ordinary residence persisting.[84] Concession A78[85] applies where S is abroad for a complete tax year and interim visits to the UK do not amount to 183 days or more in any one tax year, or to an average of 91 days or more in a tax year. In these circumstances the residence of S for tax liability for the years of departure and return will be determined by reference to T's actual residence during the year. An early return home because T's employment ends unexpectedly will not prevent ordinary residence from having ceased, provided it includes a complete tax year of absence and any visits to the UK average less than 91 days a tax year.

13.4 Ordinary Residence

For now, the Tax Acts also talk of 'ordinary residence'.[86] Following a period of consultation, however, the Government announced at Budget 2012 that it intends to abolish ordinary residence for tax purposes from 6 April 2013. Thus, the discussion that follows soon may be of historical interest only.

The Revenue view 'ordinarily resident' as 'broadly equivalent to habitually resident', and this is what Baroness Hale said in the conflict of laws case *Mark v Mark*.[87] The *Inspectors' Manual* states that a person is ordinarily resident in the UK if 'resident here year after year'.[88] Common sense would suggest that ordinary residence is narrower than residence. In *IRC v Lysaght*,[89] Viscount Sumner said: 'I think the converse to ordinarily be extraordinarily and that part of the regular order of a man's life, adopted voluntarily and for settled purposes, is not extraordinary'. People are ordinarily resident in the UK if they have habitually and normally resided lawfully in the UK from choice and for a settled purpose throughout the relevant period apart from temporary or occasional absences: a specific limited purpose, such as education, may be a settled purpose; it is irrelevant that their real house was outside the UK, or that their future intention and occupation might be outside the UK.[90]

On this view those who are resident within the Revenue rule at §13.3.2.1 above clearly would not be ordinarily resident, while those within the rule at §13.3.2.2 clearly would be ordinarily resident. Both Mr Levene and Mr Lysaght were held to be ordinarily resident in the UK. It would appear that physical presence is not necessary for ordinary residence, whatever the situation with regard to residence itself. It may also be that ordinary residence, unlike residence, at least for an adult,[91] is usually a voluntary matter; however, it might be that a foreigner imprisoned for life would be treated as ordinarily resident. Dealing with the question of

---

[84] Eg thanks to ITA 2007, s 832, ex TA 1988, s 335.

[85] Summarised in HMRC6, para 8.9; Inland Revenue leaflet IR 20, §2.6.

[86] For example ITTOIA 2005, s 857 (4) and TA 1988, s 334. For reviews of case law, see Smart (1989) 38 *ICLQ* 1715; and Wosner [1983] BTR 347.

[87] *Mark v Mark* [2006] UKHL 42, para 33; Inland Revenue note on Finance Bill 1974, [1974] *Simon's Tax Intelligence* 225, para 3. Contrast the precision of the Indian Income Tax Act 1961, s 6(6)—a person is not ordinarily resident if he has not been resident in nine of the 10 preceding years or if, during the preceding seven years, he has not been in India for a total of 730 days.

[88] *Manual*, para 35.

[89] [1928] AC 234, 243, (1928) 13 TC 511, 528.

[90] *Shah v Barnet London Borough Council* [1983] 1 All ER 226.

[91] *Miesagaes v IRC* (1957) 37 TC 493 (see above at §13.1.1.3) involved an infant; and see *Simon's Direct Tax Service*, Pt E6.130 for the treatment of spouses, civil partners and children.

the habitual residence of an illegal immigrant who was thereby guilt of a criminal offence, Baroness Hale said that it was possible that the legality of a person's residence might be relevant to the factual question of whether the residence was 'habitual'. She contrasted the position of someone 'on the run' with someone leading a perfectly ordinary life here for long periods despite having no permission to do so, eg an illegal immigrant.

Where an individual comes to the UK for the purpose of employment here, but does not acquire accommodation on a lease of more than three years, ordinary residence is treated by the Revenue as beginning at the start of the tax year following the third anniversary of the arrival. Individuals arriving in the UK for other purposes are now treated the same way. The purchase of accommodation outright for a lease longer than three years (or a change of intention with regard to the length of stay) causes ordinary residence to begin with the start of the year of arrival or, if later, the year of the purchase or change of mind.[92]

TCGA 1992, section 2(1) envisages that a person may be ordinarily resident but not resident. A person who has been resident here but who is absent from the jurisdiction for the purpose only of occasional residence abroad is treated as actually resident by ITA 2007, section 829 (ex TA 1988, section 334). At one time this rule applied only to a person who was a Commonwealth citizen or citizen of the Republic of Ireland, so that a person who fell outside those categories but who had been resident here and gone abroad for the purpose only of occasional residence, perhaps retaining a place of abode here, could be ordinarily resident. However, this rule was widened by ITTOIA 2005, section 831, and so has applied to all taxpayers as from 6 April 2005.

13.5   Domicile[93]

Persons are domiciled[94] where they have or are deemed by law to have their permanent home. Everyone must have a domicile, but cannot have more than one domicile. Subject to two qualifications, the test of domicile is that developed by the general rules of the conflict of laws.

The first qualification is that for tax purposes the question is whether or not a person is domiciled in the UK.[95] For general conflict of law purposes the question will be whether a person is domiciled in England and Wales, or Scotland or some other separate jurisdiction. Although, generally, a person domiciled in the UK will be domiciled in one of its constituent parts, this is not necessarily so, since a person with a domicile of origin in France who decides to live in the UK, but who is undecided as between Scotland and England, may have a UK domicile for UK tax purposes and a French domicile for conflict of laws purposes. However, it is understood that the Revenue do not take this point and would treat the person as still domiciled in France. The second qualification is that for tax purposes an

---

[92]   HMRC6, paras 7.7.3–7.7.4 ; Statement of Practice SP 17/91; Inland Revenue leaflet 20, §3.11.

[93]   For a discussion of possible reform and of some of the case law, see Fentiman, (1986) 6 *OJLS* 353 and [1999] *CLJ* 445; and, in a tax context, see Sheridan [1989] BTR 230; Green [1991] BTR 21; and Lyons [1993] BTR 42. See also Revenue guidance in HMRC6, ch 4.

[94]   For an example, see *Anderson (Anderson's Executors) v IRC* [1998] STC (SCD) 43; see also *Re Clore (No 2), Official Solicitor v Clore* [1984] STC 609. On the importance of domicile in tax matters, see the Law Commission, Joint Report on Domicile, Cm 200 (1987), but note subsequent changes, especially in relation to ITEPA 2003.

[95]   Eg ITEPA 2003, s 21, ITTOIA 2005, s 87 and ITA 2007, s 726 (ex TA 1988, s 739).

individual's registration on the UK electoral roll as an overseas voter is disregarded in determining domicile.[96] This rule may be disregarded if the individual so wishes.

13.5.1 Meaning of Domicile

People are domiciled where they have or are deemed by law to have their permanent home.[97] They must have a domicile, but may not have more than one. 'Domicile of origin' is the domicile which the law attributes to every individual at birth. If a child is legitimate, this is the domicile of the father at the date of the child's birth; if the child is illegitimate, this is the domicile of the mother.[98] 'Domicile of choice' is the domicile which people may acquire by leaving the country of their domicile of origin and taking up residence in another country with the intention of making their permanent home there. However, until there is both the intention to change the domicile and also the establishment of residence in the new territory, the domicile of origin remains. Mere length of stay in a country is not sufficient to establish a domicile of choice in that country. A domicile of choice is acquired by the combination of residence and intention of permanent or indefinite residence.[99] Thus, civil servants, missionaries and other persons whose domicile of origin was in one of the constituent countries of the UK and who reside abroad for vocational or business reasons, even for the greater part of their lives, retain that domicile unless they have abandoned the intention of ultimately returning to live in the country of their domicile of origin and have formed the definite settled intention of taking up permanent residence in the particular country in which they reside. The illegality of that presence is normally irrelevant.[100]

13.5.2 Change of Domicile

The domicile of origin continues until a domicile of choice is acquired. On the other hand, a domicile of choice is lost by departure from the country of such domicile without the intention of returning there to live; in that event, the domicile of origin revives unless and until a new domicile of choice is acquired.[101] The onus of proof of abandonment of the domicile of origin is upon those who seek to establish the acquisition of a domicile of choice, and very strong evidence is required for this purpose.[102]

13.5.3 Married Women, Civil Partners and Domicile

The law relating to the domicile of married women is governed by the Domicile and Matrimonial Proceedings Act 1973, which came into force on 1 January 1974. The domicile of a married woman is no longer the same as her husband's by virtue only of marriage but

---

[96] FA 1996, s 200.
[97] *Whisker v Hume* [1858] 7 HL Cas 124, 160, *per* Lord Cranworth.
[98] *Udny v Udny* [1869] LR 1 Sc & Div 441, 457.
[99] On nationality as a factor, see *Bheekhun v Williams* [1999] 2 FLR 229; noted by Stibbard (1999) *Private Client Business* 360.
[100] *Mark v Mark* [2005] UKHL 42 *per* Baroness Hale, paras 49–50 and *per* Lord Hope, para 13.
[101] See *Bell v Kennedy* [1868] LR 1 Sc & Div 307.
[102] Eg *F and F v IRC* [2000] STC (SCD) 1.

is ascertained by reference to the same factors as in the case of any other individual capable of having an independent domicile. This is necessarily true for civil partners, whose status did not exist in 1974.

Where, immediately before 1 January 1974, a married woman had her husband's domicile by dependence, she is treated as retaining that domicile (as a domicile of choice if not also her domicile of origin) unless and until it is changed by acquisition or revival of another domicile either on or after the coming into force of the Act. Prior to 1 January 1974 a woman, of whatever age, acquired at marriage the domicile of her husband, and her domicile followed his throughout their married life notwithstanding separation (even judicial separation). On termination of the marriage, by death of the husband or divorce, the woman reacquired the capacity to have an independent domicile. She did not, however, then revert automatically to her domicile of origin. The domicile which a woman acquired on marriage (where it was not her domicile of origin) ranked as a domicile of choice and, like any other domicile of choice, could be lost only by permanent departure from the country of domicile.

13.5.4 Domicile of Child

Normally, the domicile of a child changes automatically with that of the father, although the position may be different where the parents are deceased, separated or divorced. An individual is capable of having an independent domicile when he or she attains the age of 16, or marries under that age.

13.6   Residence of Corporations[103]

UK tax law imposes UK residence on (a) any company the central management and control of which is located in the UK; and (b) a company incorporated in the UK or, being a *Societas Europaea* (SE), registered in the UK—as from 1 April 2005.[104] Test (a) is a common law test; (b) is a statutory test introduced in 1988. Tests (a) and (b) overlap, in that a company which is both incorporated and managed here will be treated as resident here. Where, however, a company is incorporated here but managed abroad, it will be treated as resident here under test (b).[105] Test (a) will be much applied in issues like CFC rules. Tests (a) and (b) are subject to a third test, (c), introduced in 1994, under which a company which is resident in the UK on one of these tests, but which is treated as resident in another country and not resident in the UK for treaty purposes, will not be treated as resident for general purposes either.

---

[103] See Farnsworth, *The Residence and Domicile of Corporations* (Butterworth & Co, 1939); Pyrez (1973) 21 *Can Tax Jo* 374; Owen [2005] BTR 186 and 390; Fraser [2006] BTR 692; Harris and Oliver, *op cit*, 59–68.

[104] CTA 2009, s 14, ex FA 1988, s 66A, added by F(No 2)A 2005, s 60.

[105] CTA 2009, s 14, ex FA 1988, s 66(1).

13.6.1 Rule (a): The Common Law Test of Central Management and Control

13.6.1.1 The General Rule (a)

Since income tax originally applied both to individuals and to companies, it was perhaps inevitable that residence would be taken as the basis of taxation of companies. The long-established case-law test of residence was laid down by Lord Loreburn in *De Beers Consolidated Mines Ltd v Howe:*[106] '[A] company resides, for the purpose of income tax, where its real business is carried on ... and the real business is carried on where central management and control actually abides.' As Lord Radcliffe has remarked, 'this judgment must be treated today as if the test which it laid down was as precise and unequivocal as a positive statutory injunction.[107] However, while the test is treated as if it were statute, the issue is one of fact; it follows that if the Commissioners or Tribunals have understood the law, there is very little hope of getting a decision reversed by the courts.[108] For problems in applying this test, see §13.6.3 below.

In the *De Beers* case, South Africa provided the place of registration, the mines where the diamonds were extracted and which were marketed by the company, its head office and its shareholders' meetings. The diamonds were sold through a London syndicate. Directors' meetings were held both in South Africa and London, but it was in London that the majority of the directors resided. The Commissioners held that London was the place from which the directors controlled and managed the chief operations of the company. In challenging this conclusion, the company took as a point of law the proposition that, being incorporated and registered in South Africa, it must be resident in South Africa. That proposition was rejected by the House of Lords.

It did not automatically follow that, in the converse case, a company incorporated in the UK but managed and controlled from abroad was resident abroad. There was authority before *De Beers* for this view, but these cases were overruled in *Todd v Egyptian Delta Land and Investments Company Ltd* in 1929.[109]

13.6.1.2 Rule (c) Modifying Rule (a): Double Tax Treaty

Where a company would be treated as resident in the UK under rule (a), including the SE, but as non-resident under the terms of an applicable double taxation agreement, it is to be treated as non-resident for all UK tax purposes.[110] Clearly, this rule has no effect if the company would be treated as resident in the UK for treaty purposes. Less obviously, the rule has no effect if the treaty, because it has no tie-breaker clause, concludes that the company is resident in both countries for treaty purposes; treaties without a tie-breaker clause include those with Greece, the Isle of Man and the Channel Islands. The 2001 UK–US Treaty has a half-hearted tie-breaker clause under which the tie may be broken, but only by mutual

---

[106] [1906] AC 455, 458, (1906) 5 TC 198, 212.

[107] In *Unit Construction Co Ltd v Bullock* [1960] AC 351, 366; (1960) 38 TC 712, 738. The test was present, in the 1975 UK–US Double Tax Treaty, Art 4(1)(a)(ii), but is not part of the 2001 treaty. Other treaties, eg UK–Netherlands, Art 4(3), use the phrase 'effective management'; for discussion concluding that there is no distinction, see Owen [2003] BTR 296.

[108] Inland Revenue, *International Tax Handbook*, para 315.

[109] [1929] AC 1, (1929) 14 TC 119.

[110] CTA 2009, s 18, ex FA 1994, s 249; on the SE, see also CTA 2009, s 16.

agreement procedure; if they do not reach agreement only very limited benefits may be taken from the treaty, and so presumably the tie is not broken.[111]

Normally, the change of residence occurs as soon as the facts are satisfied; however, if the treaty applies the tie-breaker clause only when the two taxing authorities have reached agreement on the point, the change of residence is deferred until that agreement is reached.[112] Where rule (c) applies, the treaty provision prevents dual residence. The reason for this change was partly to relieve companies of unwanted burdens and partly to protect the exchequer. The principal burden of which companies were relieved was the liability to ACT when making a qualifying distribution. The protection of the exchequer arises mostly in connection with a company which is a member of a group. Such a company may be exempt from UK tax on its profits but, as a UK-resident company, may pass any loss to other UK-resident group companies; rule (c) prevents group relief from arising (subject to EU law considerations).[113] The Revenue have announced that they do not intend to invoke rule (c) in marginal cases where there is no mischief—unless the company invokes the treaty.[114]

The effect of the rule was to cause the company to cease to be resident as from 30 November 1993. Certain specific consequences of this change were addressed in FA 2004, section 250; these rules were repealed in 2010.

13.6.2 Rule (b): The Statutory Test of Incorporation in the UK

13.6.2.1 The General Rule (b)

FA 1988, section 66 introduced the second test, now in CTA 2009, section 14, that a company which is incorporated in the UK is resident here for tax purposes; if such a company has its central management elsewhere, it is treated as resident in the UK only.[115] This major change brings the UK tax system into line with many others. It applied as from 1988, generally regardless of when the company had been incorporated. As from 1 April 2005 a similar rule applies to an SE.[116] A subsequent transfer of the SE's registered office out of the UK does not of itself end the UK residence.[117] A company which ceases to carry on any business, or which is being wound up, is treated as retaining its prior residence.[118]

13.6.2.2 Rule (c) Modifying Rule (b)

Like the common law rule of residence, rule (b) is modified from 30 November 1993. Where a company would be treated as resident in the UK under this rule, but as non-

---

[111] Art 4(5). The previous (1975) treaty had no such clause.

[112] Eg, UK–Canada Treaty, Art 4(3).

[113] See CTA 2010, ss 130–134, which allow the non-resident company to use group relief if it is within the charge to UK tax; above §7.1.1.

[114] Thus, Inland Revenue, *International Tax Handbook*, para 453: 'For instance, the location of effective management of the holding company for the UK subgroup of an overseas group may be unclear in a case where a company is mainly managed here but some management decisions are taken abroad. We would not regard as objectionable the fact that the company exists to allow losses to flow as group relief between members of the UK subgroup and the benefit of any doubt on the location of effective management may be given to the company.'

[115] CTA 2009, s 14(2), ex FA 1988, s 66(1).

[116] CTA 2009, s 16(2), ex FA 1988, s 66A, added by F(No 2)A 2005, s 60.

[117] CTA 2009, s 16(4), ex FA 1988, s 66A, added by F(No 2)A 2005, s 60.

[118] CTA 2009, s 15, ex FA 1988, s 66(2).

resident under the terms of an applicable double taxation agreement, it is now to be treated as non-resident for all UK tax purposes.[119]

In looking at rule (b) it must be remembered that a company which is incorporated in the UK cannot change either its place of incorporation or its registered office; this is because it is domiciled in the UK. It may, of course, be struck off the Register of Companies and begin a new life as a new company in a new country, but under UK company law that is exactly what has happened—the UK company has not changed its residence; it has ceased to exist.

13.6.2.3 Reasons for Introducing Rule (b)

There were broadly three reasons for the introduction of the incorporation test.[120] The first was the possible threat posed by EC law to the provision in what became TA 1988, section 765, that UK resident companies could not lawfully cease to be resident without Treasury consent. This provision was repealed when the incorporation rule became law. The second was the realisation that the UK rules were out of line with those of other countries. The third reason is the most interesting and shows the world in which the Revenue have to work; this third was the growing use of what the Revenue called 'nowhere companies'. As the Revenue Handbook sadly puts it (at para 445), these were

> [c]ompanies incorporated in the UK by non-residents but non-resident under UK tax rules. Such a company was not subject to tax on worldwide income anywhere and was unlikely to suffer tax at all. In the 1970s, foreign operators began to realise that the UK provided an ideal opportunity for such companies. Traditional tax-haven countries such as the Channel Islands and Isle of Man have provided tax shelters for companies incorporated but not having real activity there on payment of a fee. In the UK there was no fee—only the cost of setting up and keeping the company on the register. All the operators had to do was to make sure that there was nothing like management and control or trading activity or income here. There was the added advantage of the respectability of UK incorporation. Before other countries got wise to the ploy they might even have assumed the company to be taxable here. Until 1979, exchange control was something of a hindrance because these companies had to get Bank of England permission to be treated as non-resident for exchange control—they obviously did not want their money in blocked sterling. The Bank of England would have given permission but might have asked awkward questions about the background which the operators would have been reluctant to disclose, even though bank officials would not have divulged anything to the Revenue or to anybody else.

> Our own attempts at getting information met with little success. Not only would this information identify the exceptional case of UK resident ownership, it could be passed on to the countries of the beneficial owners where this exchange of information is authorised by a Double Taxation Agreement. But some companies operating in low tax areas such as the Middle East used the UK for the benefit of recourse to its law and had no reason to hide anything. Representations on behalf of these companies were partly responsible for stifling the proposal for an incorporation rule in 1981. By 1988 the number of dubious companies had increased enormously, the Revenue authorities of some countries were complaining at our acquiescence and it was suspected that a number of companies were being used for criminal activities.

---

[119] CTA 2009, s 18, ex FA 1994, s 249.

[120] See Inland Revenue, *International Tax Handbook*, paras 357, 445; see also Edwardes Ker, *International Tax Strategy* (In-depth Publishing, 1974) 2, describing a UK incorporated but non-resident company as one of the best 'no-tax companies'.

13.6.3 Issues in Rule (a)

Two issues have been addressed by the courts:

(1)   What sort of control is needed?
(2)   Can control be split so that there is dual residence?

13.6.3.1 What sort of Control is Needed?

Relevant control: Revenue approaches. The control which is important, at least for a company under an English type of company law, is that of the directors rather than the shareholders.[121] The shareholders may, by virtue of their votes, control the corporation; they may compel the directors to do their will, but it does not follow that the shareholders are managing the corporation.[122] The control which the test requires is often equated with the place where the directors meet; however, this is subject to a test of genuineness. The Revenue adopt the following approach:[123] (i) they first try to ascertain whether the directors of the company in fact exercise central management and control; (ii) if so, they seek to determine where the directors exercise this central management and control (which is not necessarily where they meet);[124] (iii) in cases where the directors apparently do not exercise central management and control of the company, the Revenue then look to establish where and by whom it is exercised.

However, the mere fact that English company law takes this view is not conclusive. The question is one of the control of the business and, under a foreign system of company law, a different conclusion might be justified.

In such circumstances, the Revenue divide management up into (i) the pinnacle, (ii) the head office where the executives who make the company tick work and (iii) the shop floor itself. Rule (a) looks for level (i). The Revenue add that the distinction between (i) and (ii) may sometimes be hard to draw. They note that it is much easier for (i) to move than (ii). It is clear from the Revenue *Handbook* that the Revenue would really like to move from (i) to (ii),[125] and that their failure to achieve this has probably been one of the reasons for the introduction of the incorporation test.

Where the power to control is exercised—or ought to be exercised? The place of control and management means that of actual control and not merely the place where control should properly be exercised. In *Unit Construction Co Ltd v Bullock*,[126] three subsidiary

---

[121] *American Thread Co v Joyce* (1911) 6 TC 1, 32–33; cf *John Hood & Co Ltd v Magee* (1918) 7 TC 327, 351, 353, 358.

[122] *Automatic Self Cleansing Filter Syndicate Co Ltd v Cunninghame* [1906] 2 Ch 34, confirming that directors' mandate was the mandate of the whole body of shareholders, not of the majority only.

[123] Statement of Practice SP 1/90, para 15, but note para 18 on need for genuine commercial reasons.

[124] On this point see the Revenue win in *Laerstate BV v HMRC* [2009] UKFTT 209, when control was held to have been exercised in the UK by a sole Dutch director making decisions in the UK, despite board meetings taking place elsewhere. For commentary, see Loomer [2009] BTR 378.

[125] Eg the 1981 proposals for redefining residence, on which they say, at para 348 of the *Handbook*: 'At one time the view of the UK was that our domestic concept of central management and control meant the same thing as place of effective management and there was a note to this effect in the Commentary on the 1977 OECD Model Double Taxation Convention. We no longer believe that necessarily to be so and the note does not appear in the 1992 edition of the OECD Model. The place of effective management is generally understood to be the place where the Head Office is: the Head Office in the sense of—not the registered office—but the central directing source.'

[126] [1960] AC 351, (1960) 38 TC 712.

companies had been incorporated and registered in Kenya. Their articles of association placed the management and control of the business in the hands of directors and provided that meetings might be held anywhere outside the UK. The purpose of this scheme was to use the profits for development in Africa without becoming liable to UK taxation, and to forestall possible difficulties in the event of African nationalisation. Two years later the Kenya companies had incurred substantial losses, and the parent company took over the management and control of the subsidiaries in an attempt to save its investment. All decisions of major importance and many of minor importance were thereafter taken by the parent company. The House of Lords held that despite the admission by the Kenya companies that they were resident in Kenya, they were in fact resident in the UK. As Viscount Simonds put it: 'The business is not the less managed in London because it ought to be managed in Kenya.'[127]

A vigorous use of *Unit Construction* might[128] have enabled the Revenue to achieve their wish to move from the pinnacle level of control to that of effective management, but this did not happen and eventually was answered, in the negative, by the Court of Appeal in *Wood v Holden*.[129] It did not want to argue that large numbers of overseas subsidiaries of UK parent companies were resident here, nor that large numbers of UK incorporated companies, being the subsidiaries of foreign parents, were not resident here—after all, the companies were quite prepared to be treated as resident and their tax planning had been on that basis.[130] In *Wood v Holden* the Court of Appeal treated *Unit Construction* as a case in which the parent had usurped the powers of the subsidiary company.[131] The difficult practical question was just when the subsidiary company, by following a parent's advice, had surrendered control to that parent. Lord Cohen suggested that the facts of the case were most unusual;[132] parent companies do not usually usurp control but operate through the boards of the subsidiary companies. Modern methods of communication, combined with tight control from a group headquarters company, often make this view obsolete. In *Wood v Holden*, an elaborately choreographed series of transactions was given the effect wished for by its designers, but that was because each participant was a free agent simply doing what they had all agreed to do. The Revenue practice[133] is to invoke the *Unit Construction* case where the parent usurps the functions of the board of the subsidiary, or where that board merely rubber-stamps the parent company's decisions without giving it any independent consideration of its own; the Revenue treat the subsidiary as having the same residence as its parent. In applying the test to an international group, they place emphasis on the degree of autonomy which those directors have in conducting the company's business and ask about the extent to which the directors of the subsidiary take decisions on their own authority as to investment, production, marketing and procurement, without reference to the parent. So in *Wood v Holden* the Revenue did not believe the steps were independent; the Court disagreed.

---

[127] [1960] AC 351, 363; (1960) 38 TC 712, 736.

[128] But might not: see *Untelrab v McGregor* [1996] STC (SCD) 1; for discussion of the case, see Oliver [1996] BTR 505.

[129] [2006] EWCA Civ 26, [2006] STC 443; for comment see Fraser [2006] BTR 692, note also comment on Chancery Division in Owen [2005] BTR 390.

[130] Inland Revenue, *International Tax Handbook*, para 335.

[131] Eg para 27, Chadwick LJ agreeing with Park J at first instance.

[132] [1960] AC 351, 374, (1960) 38 TC 712, 744.

[133] Statement of Practice SP 1/90, paras 16, 17; but note para 18 on the need for genuine commercial reasons.

Today, the constitution of the company remains an important factor in determining where control is exercised, and the courts have not had any opportunity to show us how far they might delve back in the decision-making process. If major decisions are taken by a company only after consultations with a principal shareholder who lives in another jurisdiction, it may be that the company is resident where the shareholder is resident. One possible result of the decision might have been an increase in the number of corporations which have more than one residence, although *Unit Construction* is not itself such a case.

13.6.3.2 Can Control be Split so that there is Dual Residence?

Two House of Lords cases dominate this issue. It was not clear whether Lord Loreburn's test meant that a company could have only one residence,[134] but the matter came up in the difficult and unfortunate decision of *Swedish Central Rly Co Ltd v Thompson*.[135] The decision of the House of Lords four years later in *Todd v Egyptian Delta Land and Investment Co Ltd*[136] is not easy to reconcile with *Swedish Central*.[137] However the cases are reconciled,[138] they may be taken as authority for three propositions:

(1)   that the test of residence laid down in the *De Beers* case (§13.6.1.1 above) applies to all corporations regardless of the place of registration or incorporation;
(2)   that a company may be resident in two places; and
(3)   that a finding of dual residence is not to be made unless the control of the general affairs of the company is not centrally placed in one country but is divided among two or more.[139]

It is also clear that residence may be in one country and the company's sole trade carried on in another,[140] and, conversely, that the mere carrying on of trade in the UK is not sufficient to establish residence here.[141]

Where rule (b) applies and a company is resident in the UK through incorporation, a dual residence problem cannot arise since incorporation is the only test.[142] The same is true where rule (c) applies. The scope for dual residence problems has therefore been reduced.

13.6.3.3 How Effective are these Rules?

The Revenue are monitoring the return of 'nowhere companies',[143] which may be UK incorporated companies carrying on all their activities as trustee or nominee for a non-resident; only the trustee's remuneration appears in the accounts. The other

---

[134] It is now clear that the test is the same for all companies; see below. However, in practice the Revenue tend to rely on ITA 2007, s 720, ex TA 1988, s 739 to tax individuals who clearly are resident, rather than make direct assessments on companies incorporated abroad.

[135] [1925] AC 495, (1925) 9 TC 342.

[136] [1929] AC 1, (1929) 14 TC 119.

[137] See, among others, Farnsworth, *op cit*, 107–20; and Dixon J in *Koitaki Para Rubber Estates Ltd v Federal Commr of Taxation* (1940) 64 CLR 15.

[138] See *Revenue Law*, 1st edn (Butterworths, 1976), 779–81.

[139] See Farnsworth, *op cit*, 311.

[140] Eg *Saõ Paulo (Brazilian) Rly Co v Carter* [1896] AC 31, (1896) 3 TC 407; *New Zealand Shipping Co Ltd v Thew* (1922) 8 TC 208, HL.

[141] *A-G v Alexander* (1874) LR 10 Exch 20.

[142] CTA 2009, s 14(2), ex FA 1988, s 66(1).

[143] Inland Revenue, *International Tax Handbook*, para 446; see §13.6.2.3 above.

emerging trend is the use of a limited partnership rather than a company. See also §2.13 above.

13.6.4 Double or Dual Resident Investing Companies

Certain reliefs are restricted where a company is resident in two countries under the domestic tax systems of each—ie the UK and the other country.[144] The problem may be illustrated simply. When a company is incorporated in the US but has its central management and control in the UK, it will be treated as resident in the US under US rules and in the UK under UK rules. Before 2002, the company was not treated as not resident in the UK despite rule (c) above, since the UK–US treaty did not then contain a 'tie-breaker' clause.[145] The company is able to use many UK reliefs, such as loss relief and capital allowances, on the basis that it is a UK-resident company and will be able to pass the benefit of those reliefs to other companies within its group, notwithstanding that it is also resident in the US and so able to claim reliefs under that tax system as well. Particular problems arise from the payment of interest. The dual resident company may pass the benefit of such a payment to other companies in the US and UK groups, and so get relief twice. Where the borrowing is from another company within the multinational's structure, the recipient of the interest will perhaps pay tax once, but this will be more than offset by the double relief. The 2005 rules on tax arbitrage (above §4.7) address similar issues but are not confined to dual resident companies.

Restrictions now apply where the company is a 'dual resident investing company'.[146] The process of defining an investing company begins by saying that an investing company is one which is not a trading company; however, the term 'trading company' is itself defined so as to exclude a company the main function of which is to carry on all or any of various activities, such as acquiring and holding shares in dual resident companies or raising finance. This is backed up by the exclusion of other companies carrying on such activities to an extent which does not appear to be justified by any trade it does carry on, or for a purpose which does not appear to be appropriate to any such trade.[147] There is also a special definition of 'residence' in the other territory, so as to cover being subject to charge to tax in the other county by reason of almost anything other than source.[148]

The reliefs restricted are those relevant to group relief, ie losses, excess capital allowances, expenses of management and charges on income.[149] These rules should be seen as complementary to US rules.[150] The effect is to ban relief under the rules of both systems where a dual resident company makes the payment, and so to encourage the group to ensure that deductible payments are in future made only by companies which are resident in only one jurisdiction.

---

[144] The proposal to restrict these reliefs goes back to a consultative document issued by the Revenue in November 1984.

[145] On rule (c), see above at §13.6.1.

[146] CTA 2010, s 109, ex TA 1988, s 404(1), adapted for the 1996 loan relationship rules by FA 1996, Sch 14, para 21.

[147] CTA 2010, s 109(4), (5), ex TA 1988, s 404(6).

[148] CTA 2010, s 109(1), ex TA 1988, s 404(4); the wording is, however, different from that in s 749(1) (CFC legislation).

[149] CTA 2010, s 109(1), (2), ex TA 1988, s 404(2).

[150] IRC §1503(d), introduced by Tax Reform Act 1986, s 1249; for a comparison of the two sets of rules, see *Law Society's Gazette*, 11 March 1987, 713, 714.

13.6.5 Ordinary Residence

No point seems to turn now on the distinction between residence and ordinary residence of corporations. It was apparently admitted in *Union Corpn v IRC*[151] that residence and ordinary residence of companies were co-extensive, but it has been suggested that in cases of dual residence, ordinary residence is linked with the registered office.[152]

13.6.6 Domicile

The law of domicile can be applied to corporations only 'with a certain sense of strain'.[153] This connecting factor is used only occasionally.[154] A corporation is domiciled in its place of incorporation.[155] It would appear to follow that its domicile cannot change,[156] save for some exceptional circumstance such as a private Act of Parliament.

13.6.7 Tax Presence

In *Clark v Oceanic Contractors Inc*[157] the House of Lords invented a new connecting factor—tax presence. This is a presence sufficient to make the PAYE system applicable (see *Revenue Law*, §13.4).

13.6.8 Seat

In certain European countries the legislation refers to the legal 'seat' of the company, and so this concept is also found in various EU legislative acts.[158] Under German law a dual resident company was a conceptual impossibility, but the ECJ has compelled the German tax system to accept the legal personality of a foreign company that transferred its place of management, and so its residence, to Germany.[159]

The following extract comes from a Consultation Paper by the 'High Level Group of Company Law Experts' which was commissioned by the European Commission to develop ideas for EU-wide company law.[160] The experts acknowledged the difficulty of defining the 'real seat doctrine':

> 5. Other Member States adopt the real seat doctrine—the validity of incorporation and legal status of a company are recognised by reference to the law of claimed formation only if it maintains its 'real seat' or siege réel, siege effectif, etc within that jurisdiction. The meaning of 'real seat' varies; generally, if there is no substantial connection between the 'central', or 'controlling' operations (particularly the place where the governing organs meet) and the jurisdiction of formation, then

---

[151] [1952] 1 All ER 646.

[152] Hannan and Farnsworth, *The Principles of Income Taxation* (Sweet & Maxwell, 1952), 306.

[153] Morris, *Conflict of Laws*, 5th edn (Sweet & Maxwell, 2000) 29.

[154] See, eg F(No 2)A 1931, s 22(1)(b); and TA 1988, ss 739, 740, 761, 762.

[155] *Gasque v IRC* [1940] 2 KB 80, (1940) 23 TC 210.

[156] Farnsworth, *The Principles of Income Taxation*, 4th edn (Sweet & Maxwell, 1964) 273–74.

[157] [1983] STC 35; see Norfolk [1983] BTR 172.

[158] Ault *et al*, *Comparative Income Taxation*, 2nd edn (Kluwer, 2004), 349–56, ie Pt 4 A Residence Taxation, esp §§1.2, 2.2 and 2.3.

[159] *Ibid*, 356.

[160] Available at <http://europa.eu.int/comm/internal_market/en/company/company/modern/consult/>.

recognition by reference to that law is denied. Thus if a company is formed under the law of one Member State and moves its undertaking or central functions to another, which applies the real seat doctrine, without re-incorporation within that other, its legal security will be undermined. Similarly, if a company, which has been formed in a real seat doctrine state, makes a similar move to a second state but needs to maintain legal relations in the state of formation, then even if the new host state would apply the incorporation doctrine, its position will still be unsatisfactory, since its status in the formation state will be impugned. This will apparently be so even if the new host state would recognise the company's status and validity subject to the law of its original state of origin, thus applying the policy of the latter state (which is presumably what the real seat doctrine is designed to protect). Finally, even if both a state of origin and a host state apply the incorporation doctrine, the corporation's status may be nullified in a third state, if that third state applies the real seat doctrine.

13.7 Movement of Corporate Capital: Reporting and Penalties

Until 1988 it was a criminal offence for a company to change its residence without Treasury consent.[161] The same applied if a trade or business was transferred to a non-resident company by setting up a non-resident subsidiary company to run the trade in a foreign country.[162] These offences were part of an era which believed in exchange control and restriction on the free movement of capital. Exchange control was abolished in the UK in 1979; freedom of movement of capital within the European Community (now the EU) was established in 1992. The validity of these pre-1988 provisions as a restriction on freedom of establishment and freedom to provide services was challenged in *R v HM Treasury, ex parte Daily Mail Trust*,[163] and while the ECJ found in favour of the Crown, this was largely because of the undeveloped state of (then) EC company law.

The 1988 introduction of the incorporation rule of residence meant that it was no longer possible for a company incorporated in the UK to change its residence simply by changing the place of its central management and control. A company incorporated here but resident abroad under previous rules ceased to be so resident on 15 March 1993. Two of four criminal offences could be—and were—repealed. However, special rules were still needed to prevent companies moving too much out of the reach of the tax authorities. The Revenue's view of former TA 1988, section 765 is salutary:[164]

> These provisions go very deep and they really mean that a United Kingdom company must seek consent for almost any change in the structure of the overseas interests which it controls. One can only surmise the reason for this very sweeping approach. It is likely that our predecessors either realised or suspected that tax planning arrangements had been made or conceived which might have been very costly to the Revenue. The most effective course seen was a very fine net that would

---

[161] TA 1988, s 765(1)(a). A prosecution could be brought only with the consent of the Attorney-General; apparently no prosecution was ever brought. On history of s 765, see Dewhurst [1984] BTR 282; the subsection was repealed by FA 1988, s 105.

[162] TA 1988, s 765(1)(b); subsection repealed by FA 1988, s 105.

[163] [1988] STC 787—the freedom of establishment in Art 52 EEC Treaty (now Art 49 TFEU) was not breached. For more on EU law and exit taxes, see ch 21 below.

[164] Inland Revenue, *International Tax Handbook* (2003), para 1303, text superseded by new corporation tax and income tax manuals but still very relevant.

allow the Treasury, with Revenue advice, to inspect everything that was proposed and to have the opportunity of stopping transactions which it saw as objectionable before they were carried out.

Prior to 2009, if a body corporate which was resident in the UK wished to cause or permit its non-resident subsidiary to create or issue any shares or debentures, it was required to obtain the consent of the UK Treasury.[165] If this matter related to movements of capital within the European Community, there was simply a duty to report.[166] The Revenue views on the boundary between the duty to report and the need to obtain consent were explained in a Revenue document.[167] A similar consent or duty to report was needed if the resident body corporate wished to transfer shares or debentures of its non-resident subsidiary; this consent was needed only if the resident body owned or had an interest in the shares or debentures, and was not needed if the transfer was for the purpose of enabling a person to be qualified to act as a director.[168] On deemed disposals for capital gains, see below at §18.4. In addition, there was an obligation on a company to settle its tax matters before ceasing to be resident. A failure to do so gave rise to penalties.[169]

As part of the reform of the UK tax system to help international businesses, TA 1988, sections 765–767 and associated provisions were repealed altogether in 2009.[170] In their place, FA 2009, Schedule 17 imposes a duty to notify HMRC of reportable events or transactions of a value exceeding £100 million.[171]

13.8 Partnerships and European Economic Interest Groupings

13.8.1 Partnerships

Trading partnerships are resident where the control and management of the trade is situate, regardless of the residence of the partners.[172] Non-trading partnerships are presumably not treated as entities separate from their partners, and so each partner is liable according to his own residence or non-residence. There is no reported case on other unincorporated bodies.

13.8.2 European Economic Interest Groupings

A European Economic Interest Grouping (EEIG) is a form of business entity set up by enterprises of two or more Member States.[173] It is intended to be an attractive vehicle for international co-operation within the European Union among enterprises, which may

---

[165] TA 1988, s 765(1)(c). On history, see Inland Revenue, *International Tax Handbook*, ch 13.

[166] TA 1988, s 765A, added by FA 1990, s 68(2), (4). See also the Movements of Capital (Required Information) Regulations 1990 (SI 1990/1671).

[167] Statement of Practice SP 2/92; note the Revenue view that the investment must be made 'with a view to establishing or maintaining economic links'.

[168] TA 1988, s 765(1)(d).

[169] FA 1988, ss 130–131; other companies may be liable for unpaid tax, s 132.

[170] FA 2009, Sch 17, paras 1–3.

[171] FA 2009, Sch 17, paras 4–8. The list of events is in para 8(2) and the exclusions are in para 9. A group with more than one UK corporate parent must nominate a single reporting body (para 6).

[172] Inference from ITTOIA 2005, ss 6, 856(2) and 878(3). Much clearer in the superseded TA 1988, s 112; *Padmore v IRC* [1989] STC 493, (1989) 62 TC 352, CA.

[173] ITA 2007, s 842 and CTA 2010, s 990, ex TA 1988, s 510A, introduced by FA 1990, s 69, Sch 11, para 1; see Council Regulation (EEC) No 2137/85 of 25 July 1985; for information-gathering powers, see TMA 1970, s 12A.

include companies and other bodies subject to corporation tax, or partnerships or sole traders subject to income tax. The purposes for which an EEIG may be formed include such activities as packaging, processing, marketing or research which are ancillary to the business of and which are for the common benefit of members of the EEIG. An EEIG may not be formed in order to make profits for itself.[174] The scope for using EEIGs is therefore very limited.

The principle to be applied in charging an EEIG to tax is fiscal transparency; the grouping is simply an agent for its members.[175] Profits of the EEIG are taxed in the hands of the members only and not at the level of the EEIG. Where it carries on a trade or profession, an EEIG is treated as a partnership.[176] Subject to any contractual arrangements, shares are governed by the share of profits to which the members are entitled under the contract.[177] Where, however, no trade or profession is carried on, a member joining a EEIG is treated as acquiring a proportionate share in the assets of the EEIG; similarly, on disposal there is a disposal of a share in the assets then held. A disposal of the assets by the EEIG is treated as a disposal by the members of their shares in the assets.[178] Contributions towards running expenses and capital allowances for contributions towards capital expenditure are determined according to the normal rules.[179] However, this principle of fiscal transparency does not apply to machinery provisions. Thus, where the EEIG is a UK-registered company, it may have to deduct tax at source of making a payment of interest or other charge on income.[180] This simple outline of the legislation masks many conceptual and practical problems.[181] These entities are the subject of their own Revenue manual.

13.9 Trustees and Personal Representatives

The position with regard to trustees is now governed in part by legislation. By TCGA 1992, section 69, as amended as part of the trusts modernisation package in 2006, trustees are treated as a single body of persons. They are treated as resident in the UK if:

(1) all of them are so resident; or
(2) if at least one is resident and one is not resident, so long as the settlor fulfils the necessary condition. That condition is that the settlor (S) was ordinarily resident or domiciled in the UK; this is answered at the time the trust is made or, if made on death, immediately after S's death.

---

[174] Inland Revenue Press Release, 19 April 1990, [1990] *Simon's Tax Intelligence* 382, citing Art 3.1 of the Council Regulation 2137/85.

[175] ITA 2007, s 842(1), r 1 and CTA 2010, s 990(1), r 1, ex TA 1988, s 510A(2).

[176] ITA 2007, s 842(1), r 4 and CTA 2010, s 990(1), r 4, ex TA 1988, s 510A(6).

[177] ITA 2007, s 842(2) and CTA 2010, s 990(2), ex TA 1988, s 510A(4), (5).

[178] ITA 2007, s 842(1), r 3 and (4), and CTA 2010, s 990(1), r 3 and (4), ex TA 1988, s 510A(3)(b).

[179] Inland Revenue Press Release, 19 April 1990, [1990] *Simon's Tax Intelligence* 382, para 2.

[180] Under ITA 2007, ss 874–964, ex TA 1988, s 349 or 350; Inland Revenue Press Release, 19 April 1990, [1990] *Simon's Tax Intelligence* 382, paras 3–5.

[181] See Dixon and Morgan, *Tolley's International Tax Planning*, 4th edn (Tolley, 1999), ch 11; Anderson, *European Economic Interest Groupings* (Butterworths, 1990), chs 4 and 8; and Wales [1990] BTR 335.

In applying these rules, a trustee who would otherwise be treated as non-resident will be treated as resident in the UK if he acts as a trustee in the course of a business carried on in the UK through a branch, agency or PE.[182] Section 62(3) of TCGA 1992 directs that PRs should take the residence, ordinary residence and domicile of the deceased.

The income tax rules are the same. However, they have been rewritten as ITA 2007, sections 474–476, which means they say the same but in more words. Provocatively, these provisions are also to apply for corporation tax while still not applying for CGT.

The effect of these rules is that a settlement with a UK settlor will be taxed on its foreign income provided there is at least one UK resident trustee. Conversely, a foreign settlor will be able to appoint UK trustees and preserve non-resident status for the trust by retaining at least one non-resident trustee.[183] As a non-resident body, the provisions of ITA 2007, section 720 (Part 13, Chapter 2) may fall to be considered.[184]

At one time there was no direct provision for income tax. The Revenue view was that the residence of one trustee within the UK was enough to make the whole trust liable to UK income tax on the basis of residence. However, this view was rejected by the House of Lords in *Dawson v IRC*.[185] Parliament responded by passing FA 1989, sections 110 and 111, which are the basis for the rules just described.

13.10   Tax Havens

A tax haven is simply a place with a favourable tax climate.[186] Among the favourites are the Channel Islands, the Isle of Man or, with greater tax advantages, the Bahamas, the Turks and Caicos Islands, the Cayman Islands and Liechtenstein. All depend on the local rules with regard to tax, trust and company law. Even the UK has tax advantages for foreigners, as the continuing row over non-domiciles shows. Such fiscal prostitution is widespread. One country's tax incentive causes another country to brand it as a tax haven. Some countries need overseas earnings, and may accept it in fees for financial services rather than the profits of polluting plant and machinery. If other countries tax so highly as to encourage the flight of fiscal refugees, they have to take the consequences.

UK tax legislation has a number of rules directed against the use of controlled foreign companies resident in low tax countries (see chapter nineteen below). On steps to 'curb harmful tax competition', taken at the OECD and EU levels to limit the intensity of the prostitution, see §19.1.2 below.

---

[182] TCGA 1992, s 69(1), (2). For a decision on the different question of where a trust is effectively managed, a question which arises in the context of double taxation treaties, see *Wensleydale's Settlement Trustees v IRC* [1996] STC (SCD) 241.

[183] Hansard, Standing Committee G, cols 609, 610, 22 June 1989. If the non-resident trustee were to become a UK resident, eg by staying in the UK for more than six months in a year of assessment, would any action lie at the suit of the beneficiaries?

[184] Ex TA 1988, ss 739–746 . For transitional rules, see FA 1989, s 110(6)–(9); on 1989 changes, see Avery Jones [1989] BTR 249.

[185] [1989] STC 473; on the Court of Appeal decision, see Francis [1988] BTR 46.

[186] See also Orlov (2004) 32 *Intertax* 95.

14

Enforcement of Foreign Revenue Laws

14.1 General Rule: No Enforcement

In *Government of India v Taylor*,[1] the House of Lords held that the UK courts would decline to exercise jurisdiction to entertain a suit for the enforcement of the revenue law of another country, whether by direct or indirect means.[2] A foreign judgment for a sum payable in respect of taxes cannot be registered under the Foreign Judgments (Reciprocal Enforcement) Act 1933.[3] Following the same approach, it has been held that such a judgment is not a civil matter within Article 1 of the Brussels Convention.[4] Where a foreign government had successfully sued in its own courts for tax due to it and recovered the tax but not the costs, it was not able to sue for the costs in the UK since no separate claim lies for costs under English or Scots law.[5] The UK approach is adopted in other countries too, eg the US.[6] Interestingly, there has never been a mutual collection article in the main Model Tax Conventions.[7] It is becoming more common, however, for UK tax treaties to include an article based on Article 27 of the OECD Model Tax Treaty on assistance in the collection of taxes. In any event, the general rule is now subject to a major exception for taxation charged under the law of another Member State under EU law (see §14.3.1 below).

What is a revenue law is a matter for the *lex fori*. It has extended to compulsory contributions to a state insurance scheme, since a compulsory contribution levied by a state

---

[1] [1955] AC 491, [1955] 1 All ER 292; noted in 3 *ICLQ* 161, 465; 4 *ICLQ* 564. See, generally, Carter (1989) 48 *CLJ* 417; Smart, *Cross-Border Insolvencies*, 2nd edn (Butterworths, 1998), 197–211; Baker [1993] BTR 313; and Baker, in *Tolley's International Tax Planning*, 5th edn (2002), ch 33.

[2] [1955] AC 491, 510; on indirect enforcement, see Smart (1986) 35 *ICLQ* 704.

[3] Section 1(2)(b).

[4] Ie the Convention on Jurisdiction and Enforcement of Judgment in Civil and Commercial Matters; see QRS 1 *Aps and others v Fransden* [1999] STC 616.

[5] *A-G for Canada v William Schulze & Co* (1901) 9 SLT 4.

[6] Baker (2002) 30 *Intertax* 216.

[7] For reasons, see Prats (2002) 30 *Intertax* 56.

organisation is a revenue matter.[8] A payment for services supplied by the state[9] would seem to fall outside this definition, however, at least where there is some choice over whether to accept the services.

In the *Taylor* case the House of Lords also held that the foreign tax liability was not an allowable liability under the companies legislation. Current UK insolvency legislation provides for assistance between courts in territories designated by the Secretary of State. The matter arises where X is insolvent in one state, owing tax there, but has assets in another state. The legislation, as interpreted by the courts in other countries, allows the trustee in bankruptcy or the receiver to get at the assets in the other country; however, it should be noted that none of these cases concerns the situation in which the only creditor is the tax authority.[10] UK case law establishes that an assignee acting as nominee for a foreign tax-gathering authority may obtain the assistance of the English court in gathering evidence, but may not sue in England or otherwise recover assets in England.[11] The now lapsed European Convention on Insolvency Proceedings, Article 39 would have abolished the common law approach and allowed the enforcement of a claim by a foreign Revenue authority.[12] In one common law jurisdiction a judge declined to apply the basic principle in bankruptcy proceedings.[13]

The principle probably originates in a dictum of Lord Mansfield in 1775 where, upholding a vendor's claim for the purchase money due on goods sold in France and which the purchaser intended, to the vendor's knowledge, to smuggle into England, he said that 'no country ever takes notice of the revenue laws of another'.[14] The proper law of the contract being French, English law was irrelevant.

An attempt to enforce a foreign revenue law indirectly was made in the Irish case of *Peter Buchanan Ltd and MacHarg v McVey*.[15] The taxpayer, a director of a Scottish company, had disposed of his shares in two other companies and, after full disclosure to the UK Inland Revenue, was assured that the deal did not involve excess profits levy. Subsequently, the levy was retrospectively applied to the taxpayer. He therefore arranged to transfer his stock of whisky and his private assets to safe hands in Ireland, followed his wealth to Ireland and thought that 'he might safely snap his hands in the face of the disgruntled Scottish Revenue'. The liquidator of Peter Buchanan Ltd, a man chosen by the Revenue because of his potentialities as a financial Sherlock Holmes, then sued in the Irish courts on the ground that the stripping of the company's assets was ultra vires the company and a breach of his duty as director. The action was dismissed on the ground that it was in substance an indirect attempt to enforce the revenue laws of another country. At first instance, Kingsmill

---

[8] *Metal Industries (Salvage) Ltd v ST Harle (Owners)* 1962 SLT 114 (employer's contribution); issues which have been held not to be revenue matters include exchange control (*Kahler v Midland Bank Ltd* [1950] AC 24, [1949] 2 All ER 621) and a legal aid contribution (*Connor v Connor* [1974] 1 NZLR 632).

[9] See *Revenue Law*, ch 1.

[10] See Smart, *op cit*, 197–211; see also Baker, in *Tolley's International Tax Planning*, 33.4; and note Avery Jones [1991] BTR 109 on an unsatisfactory case from Florida.

[11] Smart, *op cit*, 200–01, referring to *Re State of Norway's Application* [1990] 1 AC 723, [1989] 1 All ER 745, HL; and the curious case of *Re Tucker* [1990] 1 Ch 148, CA, on which Smart refers to Fidler (1997) 5 *Journal of International Banking and Finance Law* 19.

[12] Smart, *op cit*, 209.

[13] Forsyth J in the Alberta, Canada case of *Re Sefel Geophysical Ltd* [1989] 1 WWR 251, 260.

[14] *Holman v Johnson* (1775) 1 Cowp 341.

[15] [1954] IR 89.

Moore J placed some weight on the fact that the Inland Revenue was the only unpaid creditor, but this point was not touched on by the Supreme Court of Eire.

14.2 Recognising Without Enforcing

14.2.1 Contract

The rule is that UK courts will not enforce a foreign revenue law, not that they must not recognise it. Thus, in *Regazzoni v KC Sethia (1944) Ltd*,[16] Viscount Simonds said that '[i]t does not follow from the fact that today the court will not enforce a revenue law at the suit of a foreign state that today it will enforce a contract which requires the doing of an act in a foreign country which violates the revenue laws of that country', a statement which may limit the initial decision of Lord Mansfield.

14.2.2 Evidence

In *Re State of Norway's Application*,[17] the House of Lords held that Norway could seek the assistance of the UK courts in obtaining evidence in relation to a tax case in Norway under the Evidence (Proceedings in Other Jurisdictions) Act 1975. The case did not concern a tax liability arising under a third country which had begun proceedings in Norway, neither did it deal with the recovery of assets as distinct from information.

14.2.3 Title to Goods

In *Brokaw v Seatrain UK Ltd*,[18] household goods were on the high seas on a US ship sailing from Baltimore to England when the US Treasury served a notice of levy on the shipowner and demanded the surrender of all property in its possession. When the ship reached England the US Government claimed possession; the consignees of the goods sued the shipowner in detinue. It was held that the service of the notice of levy was insufficient to reduce the goods into the possession of the US Government, and therefore that the Government had to rely upon its revenue law to support its claim to possession. If, however, the notice of the levy had been sufficient, under English conflict of law rules, to reduce goods into the possession of the US Government, that claim would have been enforced because the English courts would then be enforcing an actual possessory title and not a revenue law.[19] How this can be reconciled with those cases in which courts have refused indirectly to enforce a revenue law is a difficult matter.[20] Perhaps a proprietary claim cannot be an indirect enforcement, whereas a personal claim may be.[21]

---

[16] [1957] 3 All ER 286, 292.

[17] [1990] AC 723; for comment, see Lipstein (1990) 39 *ICLQ* 120.

[18] [1971] 2 QB 476, [1971] 2 All ER 98.

[19] *Ibid*, 482, 100. Cf *Singh v Ali* [1960] AC 167, [1960] 1 All ER 269.

[20] *Buchanan Ltd v McVey* (above at §14.1); see also *Jones v Boriand* (1969) 4 SA 29; and *Rossano v Manufacturer's Life Insurance Co Ltd* [1963] 2 QB 352, [1962] 2 All ER 214. If a foreign court made a person bankrupt for non-payment of tax, how far would the UK courts go in deciding the consequences of that status?

[21] Thus, if a foreign country holds X liable for Y's tax (cf TMA 1970, s 78), can X bring an action on an indemnity against Y in the UK courts? Such a claim succeeded in *Re Reid* (1970) 17 DLR (3d) 199.

14.2.4 Extradition

The English courts have held that a person may be extradited for an offence of fraud falling within the relevant treaty, even though the fraud relates to a tax matter.[22]

14.2.5 Trustee's Obligation to Pay

Since a foreign tax law cannot be enforced in the UK courts, it follows that it cannot give rise to a legal obligation enforceable here; it might, in turn, follow that for a trustee to pay such a tax would be a breach of trust. However, in deciding such issues the court must pay attention to the consequences for the trust of non-payment. These points emerge from *Re Lord Cable's Will Trusts*.[23] The issue was whether the court should grant an injunction to prevent the passing of money from the UK to trustees in India, given that the primary purpose of the payment was to enable the trustees to make payments due under the Indian exchange control legislation. If the payment was not made, the trustees were liable to imprisonment and to a penalty of up to five times the sum involved. Slade J refused to grant an injunction.

This leaves various questions open. First, would the position be the same for a tax as for exchange control? The answer appears to be 'Yes', since Slade J went on to consider obiter the position of payments of Indian estate duty.[24] Secondly, would it be a breach of trust for the trustees to pay? The refusal of an injunction to prevent the trustees from paying is not conclusive of this issue; however, Slade J said that the reimbursement of the trustees from the trust funds in respect of estate duty so paid would be a proper payment.[25] Thirdly, would it be a breach of trust not to pay? The effects for the trust fund would be so drastic that it would appear that the trustees' general duty to preserve the trust fund would require them to pay and so would make it a breach of trust not to pay. However, both in relation to this and the second point it must be remembered that this was a case of an Indian trust with funds and trustees in India; had there been no such connection with the country asserting a claim against the trust funds, a different result might have followed as, indeed, might have been the case if the consequences of non-payment had been minimal. Other problems arise when a foreign country will regard payment of UK tax as a breach of trust and the present UK trustees are trying to export the trust to that other country. There is considerable variation between different countries on these issues.[26]

---

[22] *R v Chief Metropolitan Stipendiary Magistrate, ex parte Secretary of State for the Home Department* [1988] 1 WLR 1204, [1989] 1 All ER 151, DC.

[23] [1976] 3 All ER 417.

[24] *Ibid*, 417, 435, 436.

[25] *Ibid*; citing *Re Reid* (1970) 17 DLR (3d) 199 (Canada) and explaining dicta of Lord Robertson in *Scottish National Orchestra Society Ltd v Thomson's Executors* 1969 SLT 325, 330. This would distinguish the payment of a foreign tax from the payment of a statute-barred debt.

[26] Baker, *Tolley's International Tax Planning, op cit*, para 33.6.

14.3 Exceptions

14.3.1 EU Law

Under EU law, various levies are now charged by the authorities of the Union rather than by the Member States.[27] There have long been extensive obligations with regard to the provision of information with regard to certain taxes. The ECJ gives full scope to these obligations; so there is no need for the Member State to have made an assessment to tax before a duty arises on other States to supply information.[28]

Since 2002 UK courts may enforce a claim to listed taxes arising in another Member State, and the list includes taxes on income and capital.[29] The UK revenue department litigates on behalf of the foreign tax authority. Recovery may be enforced even though the claim is contested, though at the risk of having to pay compensation, under human rights jurisprudence, to the extent that the claim proves to be unfounded.[30] The ECJ has held that the Directive is retroactive and affects claims arising before it was introduced. The Court reasoned that the change was procedural and not substantive; it did not set out rules about the accrual or scope of claims, and there was nothing in it to indicate that it was not to apply to pre-existing debts.[31]

Other UK legislation authorises the transfer of *information* to the competent authorities of another Member State, provided the officer is satisfied that the other State's confidentiality rules are at least as strict as the UK's.[32] Similarly, the Treasury is authorised to make regulations for obtaining information about various types of savings income for matters arising out of any Union obligation to ensure the effective taxation of savings under the law of the UK; this power applies also to non-Member States.[33] Further, there is an express provision imposing a duty on the relevant UK tax authorities to notify a person when the competent authority in another Member State requests the UK to inform that person of an 'instrument or decision' emanating from the other Member State and concerning taxes covered by the mutual assistance directive;[34] no doubt there are similar rules in other Member States. Looking ahead, one can see much more radical ideas. One is for multilateral tax auditing.[35] In 2011 the ECOFIN Council adopted an amended directive on mutual administrative assistance that may point towards new directions for exchange of information. The directive requires automatic exchange, permits spontaneous exchange, and allows information in certain circumstances to be passed on to non-tax authorities and to third States.[36]

---

[27] See Decision 70/243/EEC (OJ 1970 L94/19).

[28] Case C-420/98 *W N v Staatssecretaris van Financien* [2001] STC 974.

[29] Directive 76/308/EEC as amended.

[30] Baker, *op cit*, citing App No 349895/97 *Janosevic v Sweden*, para 106.

[31] Case C- 361/02, 362/02 *Greece v Tsaplois* [2004] STC 1220.

[32] FA 2003, s 197 (not rewritten), ex FA 1978, s 77 and FA 1990, s 125.

[33] TMA 1970 ss 18B–18E, inserted by TIOPA 2010, Sch 7, para 103, ex FA 2003, s 199.

[34] F(No 2)A 2005, s 68 (not rewritten).

[35] Van der Hel-van Dijk and Kaerling (2003) 31 *Intertax* 4.

[36] Council Directive 2011/16/EU of 15 February 2011 on administrative co-operation in the field of taxation, repealing Directive 77/799/EEC. For commentary, see Baker [2011] BTR 125, 126.

14.3.2 Tax Treaties

The rules at §14.3.1 are matters of EU law and therefore relevant only where EU principles apply. Most double tax treaties to be found around the world, including most of those made by the UK, attempt to counter some evasion techniques by providing for the exchange of information.[37] Some treaties, and recently some UK treaties, actually make provision for providing assistance to treaty partners in the collection of tax, as in Article 27 of the OECD Model Treaty.[38] The 2011 UK–South Africa treaty protocol added such an article and, interestingly, included a provision to the effect that there is no obligation to assist where the requested state considers that the taxes at issue are imposed 'contrary to generally accepted taxation principles'.[39] On whether the treaty requires the UK tax authorities to provide information to a foreign tax authority if there is no UK tax in issue, see below at §20.5.[40] Some treaties require mutual assistance in recovering tax due, to ensure that treaty benefits are not given to people who are not entitled to them.[41]

In 2006 the UK took a decisive, further step down this road. By FA 2006, section 173, the Crown was given powers to bring into effect the 1988 OECD Convention on Mutual Administrative Assistance. The Convention aims to help governments enforce their tax laws and provides an international legal framework for co-operation among countries in countering international tax avoidance and evasion. In 2010, the Convention was amended by protocol, which updated it to reflect developments internationally in this area (and particularly in the EU) and opened it up to all countries. FA 2006, section 175 allows the Treasury to make regulations for the recovery in the UK of debts relating to a foreign tax and to include such powers in future arrangements under section 173.[42]

Further developments in this area include the UK's 2009 tax information exchange agreement with Liechtenstein, which was accompanied by a somewhat controversial disclosure facility to allow UK taxpayers with undeclared investments in Liechtenstein to come forward and get their tax affairs in order.[43] While this arrangement is believed to have generated over £3 billion in tax receipts for the UK, the favourable terms provided (eg maximum penalty of 10% rather than 100%, and restricting the inquiry period to the past 10 years rather than the usual 20 years) may be viewed as overly-generous treatment of tax evaders, including ones who moved investments from other jurisdictions into Liechtenstein purely to make use of this facility. In addition, in 2011 the UK entered into a tax co-operation agreement with Switzerland, aimed at raising revenue from UK taxpayers on undeclared income and gains in Swiss banks.[44]

---

[37] OECD Model, Art 26; see generally McCracken (2002) 50 *Canadian Tax Jo* 1869–1912.

[38] See now OECD Model, Art 27, added 2003. On unhappy if dated US experience, see 50 *Columbia L Rev* 490. The US entered a reservation in relation to the OECD treaty of 1988, so far as it related to enforcement.

[39] See Baker [2011] BTR 125 for analysis. Baker notes that no assistance provisions were included in 2011 treaties with Bahrain or Hong Kong, which suggests to him that the UK policy on such articles is to include them only if the other negotiating state wishes to do so.

[40] *US v AL Burbank* 96 Sup Ct 2647; cited by Baker, in *Tolley's International Tax Planning*, para 34.67.

[41] OECD Model, Commentary on Art 27, para 2.

[42] On FA 2006, see Fraser and Oliver [2006] BTR 648.

[43] For details see <http://www.hmrc.gov.uk/disclosure/liechtenstein-disclosure.htm>.

[44] Available at <http://www.hmrc.gov.uk/taxtreaties/ukswiss.htm>.

14.4 Criminal Law

Despite these rules, one very difficult and important issue remains unresolved—whether a breach of a foreign revenue law giving rise to criminal liability under that foreign law can give rise to criminal liability in the UK under the 1993 amendments to the Criminal Justice Act 1988, which are concerned with money laundering.[45]

14.5 Policy and Reform

The result of the general rule considered in this chapter is to permit people to avoid tax due to a foreign country by bringing themselves and their wealth within the UK. Reasons for this rule are not completely convincing.[46] Sometimes the rule been based on the notion that tax, as an expression of the sovereign power of a state, should not be allowed to encroach on the sovereign power of another state,[47] a problem the logical solution of which is to allow the forum state a choice. Similarly, a state should be able to waive the argument that its presence in court is inconsistent with its sovereignty. Another argument equate taxes with fines and penalties,[48] which the UK courts will also enforce; however, this ignores the fact that for some offences a fugitive criminal may, unlike a prudent tax traveller, be extradited. Other, more practical explanations are the wish to avoid entanglements on questions of proof of foreign tax laws[49] and the real risk that there might be much litigation. Further, there are real political and economic risks when the courts are asked to decide which tax laws they will enforce and which not.[50] Clearly, some territorial limitations would have to be worked out if the present rule were to be abandoned; there is no real reason why English courts should uphold a claim by a foreign government to levy a poll tax on inhabitants in England. The solution of such problems has been the function of the conflict of laws. Even when territorial problems have been settled, there must remain the possibility of refusing to enforce a foreign revenue law on grounds of public policy;[51] the 1970s Russian tax on emigrating Jews might prove one such.[52]

Improvements in international co-operation have long been sought—by revenue departments and so by the OECD and the Council of Europe. An important developments on this front was the 1988 OECD Multilateral Convention on Mutual Administrative Assistance in Tax Matters, which was amended in 2010 to modernise it and open it up to all countries. Since the Convention was designed by revenue departments, no thought is given to protection for taxpayers. There is no requirement under the Convention that the external revenue department should display competence in its affairs, no requirement that the departments should devote earmarked resources to treating taxpayers as efficiently and courteously as they would in their countries of residence, and no obligation to open an office in its embassy so as to handle matters.

---

[45] See Bennett [1999] *Private Client Business* 159. On money laundering more generally, see Rider [1996] *Private Client Business* 134, 201, 265.

[46] For discussions, see Castel, 42 *Can BR* 277; Leflar (1932) 46 *HLR* 193, 215.

[47] Lord Keith in *Government of India v Taylor* [1955] AC 491, 511.

[48] *Ibid*, 506, *per* Viscount Simonds; Leflar, *op cit*, 193.

[49] Read, *Enforcement of Foreign Judgments* (Harvard University Press, 1938), 290.

[50] Eg Kingsmill Moore J in [1954] *IR* 89, 105–06.

[51] Perhaps retrospective legislation would not be enforced.

[52] However, emigration taxes were once a lively issue: see Bhagwati and Partington, *Taxing the Brain Drain* (North-Holland, 1976).

15

UK Residents and Foreign Income

15.1 General

Residents of the UK may find themselves taxable on overseas income under the following provisions, but the extent of liability may be affected by other connecting factors. A recent example is the treatment of 'non-doms', ie people who are not domiciled (nor ordinarily resident) in the UK and who benefit from certain tax advantages, most importantly the remittance basis of income taxation. The efforts of government to change the rules on the taxation of non-doms provide an interesting exercise in government advance and retreat; see §15.4 below. However, these are not the only rules which require discussion.

15.1.1 Income Tax

Under the income tax provisions, UK residents with foreign income will probably find themselves facing potential double taxation. While the UK wishes to tax the foreign income, the country of source, ie where the income arises, may also wish to do so. The basic principle that UK residents are taxable on their overseas income is to be found in the terms of ITEPA 2003, ITTOIA 2005 and ITA 2007. The charge on foreign source income in ITEPA 2003 arises under Part 2, Chapter 5.[1] ITTOIA 2005, Part 2, Chapter 2 contains the rules for trades carried on within and without the UK. ITTOIA 2005, Part 3, Chapter 2 deals with UK property businesses and Chapter 3 with overseas property business; Chapter 11 has further rules for overseas property income where the remittance basis applies.[2] The point is that the UK legislation deals with domestic and foreign matters side by side. This is not to say that the rules are identical—merely that they are treated in neighbouring bits of the statute book. Thus, the tax treatment of UK dividends received by individuals from UK companies is treated in Part 4, Chapter 3, while the very different rules for dividend income from non-UK resident companies are dealt with in Chapter 4.

A major feature of international tax systems is the obligation to deduct at source when income crosses a border. In the UK there have also been obligations on persons within the UK financial system to deduct tax on certain payments received from overseas and passing through their hands. These withholding rules have 19th-century origins, and have been rewritten several times in more recent years. These rules were reformed in 1996, 2000 and 2001, but were then reduced in a dramatic way in 2004 when the EC Savings Directive was implemented; they have been rewritten for income tax by ITA 2007, Part 15.[3] There are also special withholding tax rules, eg on payments to entertainers. Lastly, a charge may arise under an anti-avoidance rule. Under these withholding rules, UK residents may be liable to tax on certain foreign income accruing to non-residents.

Another rule that has not been rewritten for income tax is TA 1988, sections 756A–764, concerning offshore funds. In this area different avoidance rules have different objectives; some are aimed at deferral of liability and so try to tax on an accruals basis, while others, eg the offshore funds rules, deal with the conversion of income into capital gain, a conversion which at one time meant total freedom from tax.

15.1.2 Capital Gains Tax

Capital gains tax, as discussed in more detail in chapter eighteen, is levied on all gains accruing to a person resident or ordinarily resident in the UK regardless of the location of the asset, with a remittance basis for those not domiciled in UK. For charge on temporary non-residents arising when they resume UK residence, see below at §18.1.2.

15.1.3 Corporation Tax

Corporation tax was formerly levied on the income of the corporation as computed under the schedular system, eg Schedules A and D, Cases I–VI, on all income arising within the

---

[1] See *Revenue Law*, §13.3.

[2] For the list of foreign income heads under ITEPA 2003 and ITTOIA 2005 (in the remittance context), see below §15.4.3. The older heads of charge, now superseded for income tax by ITTOIA 2005, segregated foreign source income into (a) Sch D, Case IV—securities outside the UK; (b) Sch D, Case V—possessions outside the UK (TA 1988, s 18); and (c) Sch D, Case VI (see *Revenue Law*, ch 28). In addition, statute imposes liability in respect of offshore income gains. Sch D, Case V (but not Case IV) survived for corporation tax until the 2010 rewrite (see below).

[3] See TA 1988, ss 118A–118K, introduced by FA 1996 but superseded by FA 2000, s 111, which came into force in 2001; FA 2000, s 111. See further below at §16.6.4.

period. The corporation tax legislation, whilst still scheduler in design terms, has been rewritten and the rules are now spread across, primarily but not entirely, the Corporation Tax Act 2009, Corporation Tax Act 2010 and Taxation (International and Other Provisions) Act 2010. Neither the remittance basis nor the now obsolete percentage reductions (see below §15.4.1) apply to corporation tax. For rules on the taxation of the UK permanent establishment of a foreign company (introduced in 2003), see §2.9 above.

15.1.4 Credit for Foreign Dividends

The taxation of foreign dividends accruing to a company subject to UK corporation tax was reviewed by the ECJ in the cases discussed in more detail below in chapter twenty-one. A system under which credits were available for domestic but not for foreign dividends looked discriminatory, and certainly favoured investment in UK shares rather than in foreign ones. The ECJ indicated that this was not acceptable and so FA 2008 granted relief.[4] First, there must be an individual who is a UK resident, or UK or other EEA national. Secondly, the dividend must come from a company not resident in the UK. In these circumstances the normal credit of 1/9th is added, just as with a UK source dividend. So a dividend of 90 is grossed up by 1/9th to 100 and the dividend ordinary rate of 10% charged. The effective tax rate on the 90 is therefore nil. If the dividend upper rate is due (32.5%), this makes tax of 32.5 less 10 credit, so 22.50 net—which is 25% of the 90. At one time the credit was not going to be available if the total of such dividends accruing to an individual during the year was £5,000 or more. Happily this plan was aborted.

In general, the UK tax system respects the legal form in which investments overseas are made and allows deferral of tax until income arises from the investment or, in some situations, is actually received in the UK (the remittance basis). However, deferral is overridden in the case of the controlled foreign company (CFC) legislation; these are rules designed to prevent the use of foreign companies to defer liability to UK corporation tax (see chapter seventeen below). From 1956 until 1965 the UK tax system had a special category of 'overseas trade corporation'. These were UK-resident companies with foreign trading income, and were exempt from UK tax on that foreign income provided it was not distributed.[5]

15.1.5 Corporation Tax and Foreign Dividends

Prior to 2009, where a UK-resident company had dividend income from a UK-resident company, the dividend was not subject to UK corporation tax by virtue of TA 1988, section 208. Now, CTA 2009, Part 9A exempts most dividends received by a UK company, whether from another UK company or from a company overseas. If the distribution is not exempt it is subject to corporation tax; if it is exempt the company may elect to treat it as taxable. In determining eligibility for the exemption, different rules apply depending on whether the company is 'small' or 'not small'; these rules are discussed below at §19.3.

---

[4] ITTOIA 2005, s 397A, added by FA 2008, s 35 and Sch 12.
[5] See Royal Commission on Taxation of Profits and Income, *Final Report*, Cmd 9474 (1955), ch 24; and Ilersic [1957] BTR 7.

15.2   Issues in Foreign Income

15.2.1   Place of Trade

15.2.1.1   General

For income tax, the profits of a trade carried on by a UK resident are chargeable to tax under ITTOIA 2005, Part 2, Chapter 2 wherever the trade is carried on.[6] A non-resident, on the other hand, is taxable under ITTOIA 2005, Part 2, Chapter 2 on profits of a trade only if they arise from a trade wholly or partly carried on in the UK. Thus, a non-resident is not taxable on profits accruing from a trade carried on wholly outside the UK. An old example of the distinction in the law between former Schedule D, Case I and Case V is *Sulley v A-G*.[7] Here, the taxpayer bought goods in the UK for export to America, where they were resold by his partners; the trade was carried on wholly overseas, and so was within Case V (now relevant foreign income within ITTOIA 2005, sections 7(5) and 830), not Case I (now ITTOIA 2005, section 6(1)).

It will be more difficult for a sole trader to establish that the trade is carried on wholly overseas. In *Ogilvie v Kitton*,[8] the taxpayer, who was resident in Aberdeen, was the sole owner of a business of woollen warehousing carried on by his employees in Toronto. He had the sole right to manage and control his business, and although that right was not exercised, it could have been. The trade was therefore not wholly overseas.

Where a company wishes to trade overseas, it may do so by direct exporting, by a licensing system, by establishing a branch in the foreign country or by establishing a foreign subsidiary company.[9] In such instances, the profits will flow back to the UK in the form of dividends, interest, royalty payments and other forms, such as payments for services. The flow may be reversed by loans. The company may thus become an overseas incorporated pocket book—subject to any possible application of the CFC rules (see chapter seventeen below). Loans to overseas subsidiaries often have advantages over direct equity investment in that interest, unlike a dividend, is generally deductible in computing profits, and it is in general easier to reduce investment by repaying capital than by re-exporting it; hence the thin capitalisation problem—above §4.6.

15.2.1.2   Subsidiary Company not Necessarily a Stooge

Where the resident company sets up a wholly-owned subsidiary in the foreign country to carry on a trade there, it is a question of fact whether that subsidiary is carrying on its own trade or is simply acting as agent for its parent's trade.[10] The question is not concluded, however, by saying that the overseas company is a wholly-owned subsidiary.[11] The question depends on who manages the trade and not on who owns the shares.[12]

---

[6] ITTOIA 2005, s 6. Transfer pricing rules (see above at §4.6) may also apply here.

[7] (1860) 5 H & N 711, (1860) 2 TC 149.

[8] (1908) 5 TC 338.

[9] At one time conversion of a branch into a subsidiary fell within TA 1988, s 765 (see above at §13.7); today, it may cause a chargeable gain to arise (but see TCGA 1992, s 140; above at §4.3.3.4).

[10] *Apthorpe v Peter Schoenhofen Brewing Co Ltd* (1899) 4 TC 41.

[11] *Gramophone and Typewriter Ltd v Stanley* [1908] 2 KB 89, (1908) 5 TC 358; and see *Watson v Sandie and Hull* [1898] 1 QB 326, (1898) 3 TC 611.

[12] *Kodak Ltd v Clark* [1903] 1 KB 505, (1903) 4 TC 549.

15.2.1.3 Resident Company can Trade Wholly Overseas

A corporation may be resident in the UK because its central management and control abides in the UK. It might appear to follow that it cannot trade wholly overseas.[13] Despite this, the House of Lords held in *Mitchell v Egyptian Hotels Ltd*[14] that a company resident in the UK could be trading wholly abroad. The company was resident in England and carried on the business of hotel proprietors. It so amended its articles of association as to provide for the carrying on of the Egyptian business by a local board[15] in that country, which was to be wholly independent of the London board or any other part of the company. The only way in which the London board might have influenced its activities was by controlling the remuneration of the directors in Egypt. The Court of Appeal held that the company was carrying on a trade wholly outside the UK, and an evenly divided House of Lords could not reverse that decision.[16] Other cases[17] have shown that regular oversight of the foreign trade will prevent it from being one carried on wholly overseas, so it is important that on the facts of the case there was no power directly to control the Egyptian trade.

In *Mitchell v BW Noble Ltd*,[18] control was shared between London and Paris, and it was held that the trade did not fall within Schedule D, Case V. Where the trade was carried on partly in the UK and partly overseas, so that Schedule D, Case I applied, concessionary relief formerly was available for certain unremittable debts.[19] Where a trade or business is carried on by a partnership and the control and management is abroad, it is deemed to be carried on by a person resident outside the UK.[20] If the partnership trades in, as opposed to with, the UK, tax will become due in respect of the profits of that trade as with any other non-resident person, and an assessment may be made on the partnership in the name of any partner resident here.

15.2.2 Basis of Assessment: ITTOIA 2005—Trading, Savings and Property Income[21]

15.2.2.1 Trading

Under ITTOIA 2005, the foreign aspects of income are treated as part of the general charging rules which apply to domestic income too. It follows that the normal charging rules, including the basis period rules for opening and closing years, also apply here. Likewise, the charge under Part 2, Chapter 17 (adjustment income and expenses on a change of accounting basis) applies just as easily to the purely foreign trade as to a purely domestic one. Under the

---

[13] Eg *American Thread Co v Joyce* (1911) 6 TC 1, 18, *per* Hamilton J; see also Lord Halsbury in *Saõ Paulo (Brazilian) Railway Co v Carter* [1896] AC 38, (1895) 3 TC 410.

[14] [1915] AC 1022, (1915) 6 TC 542. For a similar result in relation to a trust, see *Ferguson v Donovan* [1929] IR 489. Inland Revenue, *International Tax Handbook*, para 343 suggests that the Revenue would now view the company as non-resident.

[15] The Egyptian Board controlled only the Egyptian business: *Swedish Central Rly Co Ltd v Thompson* [19251 AC 495, 523, 524, *per* Viscount Cave LC.

[16] Mere oversight regularly exercised is sufficient control, but merely to have the right to intervene and not to exercise that right is not (*Mitchell v Egyptian Hotels Ltd* [1915] AC 1022, 1040; 6 TC 542, 551, *per* Lord Sumner).

[17] *Saõ Paulo (Brazilian) Railway Co v Carter* [1896] AC 31, (1895) 3 TC 407.

[18] [1927] 1 KB 719, (1927)11 TC 372.

[19] Ex ESC B37.

[20] ITTOIA 2005, s 872(3), ex TA 1988, s 112 (but not for mixed partnership—see CTA 2009, s 1266 and Sch 1, para 364(3), ex TA 1988, s 115(5)).

[21] Before 1996–97 tax was charged on a preceding year basis; before 1926, Sch D, Case IV was charged on a current year basis and Case V on a three-year average—see Royal Commission on the Taxation of Profits and Income, *Final Report*, Cmd 9474 (1955), para 785.

schedular system an individual enjoying income arising from an overseas trade, profession or vocation was assessed to tax under Schedule D, Case V; however, the basis period was determined by the rules applicable to Schedule D, Cases I and II.[22] The opening and closing year provisions apply to overseas trades, etc, as they apply to UK trades, etc. Overlap profit charge and overlap profit relief are still relevant today under ITTOIA 2005.

15.2.2.2 Other

All other income assessable under ITTOIA 2005 (ex Schedule D, Case IV or V) is assessed on a strict fiscal year basis, unless it arises to a partnership. Thus, the basis period for 2012–13 is income arising from 6 April 2012 to 5 April 2013.[23]

15.2.2.3 Remittance

Where this basis applies (see below §15.4) the charge is on income remitted to the UK during the fiscal year.[24] This applies irrespective of the nature of the overseas income; so for a non-domiciled individual (and so taxable on the remittance basis) carrying on trade, the taxable profits from an overseas trade are the amount remitted to the UK in the fiscal year and not the accounting period.

15.2.2.4 Overseas Income of a UK Partnership

Where an individual is a member of a UK partnership which has profits assessable under ITTOIA 2005, the basis period which applies to that partnership income is applied to all other income arising to the partnership, eg overseas investment income. The income of that basis period is then allocated to the individual partners.[25] This overrides other basis period rules.

15.2.2.5 History: Schedule D, Case IV—Scope

Schedule D, Case IV charged income from securities. 'Securities' meant a debt or claim the payment of which was in some way secured, eg a debenture;[26] the term has been held to extend to a personal guarantee,[27] but not to stocks and shares. Case IV no longer applies for corporation tax and so is repealed by ITTOIA 2005. The location of the source of interest income has arisen only in cases where all the facts pointed one way.[28]

15.2.2.6 History: Schedule D, Case V—Scope of Possessions

Schedule D, Case V charged income from possessions, a phrase which it has been held includes any source of income,[29] presumably other than securities. A payment under a

---

[22] TA 1988, s 65(3), as amended by FA 1994, s 207 (repealed by ITTOIA 2005).

[23] TA 1988, s 65(1) (repealed by ITTOIA 2005).

[24] ITTOIA 2005, Pt 8, Ch 2, s 831, ex TA 1988, s 65(4).

[25] ITTOIA 2005, s 852, ex TA 1988, s 111(4) and (8).

[26] Viscount Cave LC in *Singer v Williams* [1921] 1 AC 41, 49; (1921) 7 TC 419, 431.

[27] *Westminster Bank Executor and Trustee Co (Channel Islands) Ltd v National Bank of Greece* [1971] 1 All ER 233, (1971) 46 TC 491, [1969] BTR 415. On location of source of interest, see Inland Revenue Interpretation RI58.

[28] See the exchange of views in *Offshore Taxation Review*, vol 8, 65 (Thornton), 115 (Simpson) and 235 (Venables); and Inland Revenue Interpretation RI 58.

[29] *Colquhoun v Brooks* (1889) 14 App Cas 493, 508, *per* Lord Herschel, and 514, *per* Lord MacNaghten. In *IRC v Reid's Trustees* [1949] AC 361, 371, Lord Simmonds suggested that 'income' for Sch D, Case V might be wider than income for the rest of the Taxes Acts.

discretionary trust becomes a possession at least once the trustees have exercised their discretion.[30] A foreign trade is also a possession.[31]

Maintenance payments which have a foreign source are not income under UK tax law.[32] This is regardless of the treatment of the payment under the foreign tax system, ie whether or not the payment is taxable to the payee or deductible by the payer. An alimony order by a foreign court was held to be a foreign possession.[33]

A foreign pension fell within Schedule D, Case V, but a foreign employment within Schedule E;[34] both now come under ITEPA 2003.[35] Income from a pension was held to be income from a foreign possession and not income from employment, even though the pension arose from contributions made to a fund as a result of a foreign employment.[36] Certain borrowings on life policies were treated as falling within Case V but are swept into the general rules in ITTOIA 2005, Part 4, Chapter 10.[37]

15.2.2.7 Income from Overseas Land

Today ITTOIA 2005, Part 3 applies to both UK and overseas property businesses.[38] From 1998 until 2005 income from overseas land was the subject of a statutory regime similar to that which prevailed for land in the UK.[39] Capital allowances are available.[40] It follows that interest payable on a loan to buy the property will be deductible, a major change from pre-1998 practice.[41] ITTOIA 2005, Part 2, Chapter 11 contains special rules relevant where the remittance basis applies. These rules apply where income arises from any business carried on for generating income from land outside the UK; the income must not be trading income.[42]

ITTOIA 2005, Part 3 excludes some Part 2 computational rules from applying to all property businesses, whether domestic or foreign. These include sections 94–96 on foreign travel. The rules in ITTOIA 2005, Part 3, Chapter 6 on furnished holiday accommodation apply only to a UK property.[43]

15.2.2.8 Foreign Savings Income: Dividends and Distributions

By ITA 2007, section 8, domestic dividends and distributions chargeable under Part 4, Chapter 3 now attract rates of 10% (dividend ordinary rate), 32.5% (dividend upper rate), or 42.5% (dividend additional rate and dividend trust rate). These rates also apply to equivalent distributions by foreign companies, called 'relevant foreign distributions', chargeable under Part 4, Chapter 4, ie if the distribution would be income chargeable under Part 4, Chapter 3 if the company were resident in the UK.[44] Whether such income is domestic or

---

[30] *Drummond v Collins* [1913] 3 KB 583, 594; (1913) 6 TC 525 at 532, *per* Horridge J.

[31] *Colquhoun v Brooks* (1889) 14 App Cas 493.

[32] ITTOIA 2005, s 730, ex TA 1988, s 347A(4).

[33] *IRC v Anderstrom* (1928) 13 TC 452; on concessionary double taxation relief, see ESC A12.

[34] TA 1988, s 19.

[35] ITEPA 2003, Pt 9, Ch 4, and Pt 2, Ch 5 respectively.

[36] *Apin v Estill* [1987] STC 723; followed in *Albon v IRC* [1998] STC 1181.

[37] ITTOIA 2005, s 501, ex TA 1988, s 554(1).

[38] On definition of 'overseas land', see s 356.

[39] Formerly TA 1988, s 65A, as amended by FA 1998. See also Inland Revenue, *Inspectors' Manual*, paras 1595 et seq.

[40] CAA 2001, s 15 as amended by ITTOIA 2005; before ITTOIA 2005 an ordinary Sch A business and an overseas property business were specified as separate qualifying activities.

[41] Inland Revenue Press Release, 29 November 1994, [1994] *Simon's Tax Intelligence* 1463.

[42] ITTOIA 2005, ss 261 and 263.

[43] Ex TA 1988, s 65A(6), (7); FA 1990, s 29 is also excluded.

[44] ITA 2007, s 19(3).

foreign, it is treated as the highest part of the person's income.[45] If the income is foreign, the 10% UK tax credit is available if the conditions in ITTOIA 2005, section 397A are satisfied. This in turns requires the satisfaction of one of three conditions in section 397(AA): (a) that the individual's shareholding in the distributing company is less than 10%;[46] (b) the distributing company is an offshore fund; or (c) the distributing company is resident in a qualifying territory. There are also rules on manufactured dividends.[47] There may be credit relief under other provisions for foreign tax paid.

It must not be overlooked that the definition of what is income under Part 4, Chapter 4 is very different from that for Chapter 3 (see below at §15.3). Section 13(1), when defining which foreign dividend income is subject to these rates of tax as opposed to the normal income tax rates, uses the Chapter 3 definition for domestic income. The dividend rates of 10%, 32.5% and 42.5% are also excluded if the income is taxable on a remittance basis (see below at §15.4).[48] On domestic rules, see *Revenue Law*, §7.7.

The taxation of foreign dividends accruing to a company subject to UK corporation tax is normally exempt from UK tax (see further §19.3 below).

15.2.2.9 Other Foreign Savings Income

ITA 2007, as amended for 2008 and later years, applies the 10% starting rate to domestic interest within ITTOIA 2005, Part 4, Chapter 2; the same applies to equivalent income from foreign sources.[49] There are the same exceptions for income which is charged under the remittance basis.

While the definition of 'savings income' in ITA 2007, section 18 covers many types of income from savings and investments (including purchased life annuities), it is expressly excluded from annuities and other annual payments which are not interest, and fails to mention various payments falling within ITTOIA 2005, Part 3, Chapter 8 (ex TA 1988, section 119); these exclusions presumably apply to analogous foreign income.

15.2.2.10 Deduction for Business Travel Expenses

An individual who carries on a trade, profession or vocation wholly outside the UK but who is not taxable on a remittance basis may claim the deduction of certain travel costs.[50] The allowable expenses are those for travel by the businessman from any place in the UK to any place where the business is carried on, or from any such place to any place in the UK, and for board and lodging.[51]

These rules are similar to those introduced for ITEPA 2003.[52] The similarity is taken further in that the ITTOIA 2005 rules allow also for the deduction of the costs of travel for a spouse, civil partner and child aged under 18.[53] In these cases the taxpayer's absence from the UK must be wholly and exclusively for the purpose of performing the functions

---

[45] ITA 2007, s 16.
[46] Defined in ITTOIA 2005, s 397C.
[47] ITTOIA 2005, s 397B.
[48] ITA 2007, s 16(7).
[49] ITA 2007, ss 10,12 and 18.
[50] ITTOIA 2005, s 94, ex TA 1988, s 80.
[51] ITTOIA 2005, s 94 (3), ex TA 1988, s 80(2).
[52] See *Revenue Law*, §13.3, but not identical, eg there is no need for separate reimbursement (because there is no one to do the reimbursing).
[53] ITTOIA 2005, s 96, ex TA 1988, s 80(5)–(8).

of the trade, profession or vocation or those of some other business, with apportionment between the different businesses.

Where there are two or more overseas locations, the taxpayer may deduct the cost of travel from one to the other; of the two, at least one must satisfy the rules, ie be that of a business carried on wholly outside the UK.[54] The absence from the UK must still be wholly and exclusively for the purpose of performing the functions of both activities, and the tax-payer must actually perform those functions at each location. The deduction is put against the trade carried on at the destination unless it is outside these rules, in which case the place of departure is taken instead. Where there are two businesses at the place of destination or departure, an apportionment is carried out.[55]

15.3   Characterisation of Receipts and Entities: The Role of Foreign Law

Two questions arise: (a) is a receipt income (or capital gain) for UK tax purposes; and (b) whose income is it? Both issues involve taking the legal rights and relations arising under a legal system different from that of the UK and classifying them in accordance with concepts used by UK tax law. In this process, the way in which the foreign country's tax system would treat the facts is at best of marginal relevance, although that treatment will be highly rele-vant to the very different question of double tax relief subsequently. The process considered here is the same as that known as 'characterisation' in the conflict of laws. The problems presented by different tax classifications of the same entity by different tax systems gave rise to planning opportunities—hence the tax arbitrage rules—above §4.7.

15.3.1 Receipts

The question whether a particular payment is income arising from a source within ITTOIA 2005 is a question for UK tax law, but that question must be determined according to the legal nature of the rights arising from the security or possession under the foreign law. In *Archer-Shee v Garland*,[56] a tenant for life was entitled under a New York trust, and the issue was whether money to which the taxpayer was entitled was income 'from stock and securities',[57] the alternative view being that a tenant for life had only a right to see that the property was correctly administered by the trustees. Under English law the former had already been held to be correct,[58] but on evidence being presented that under New York law the latter was correct, the House of Lords held that the rights of this beneficiary could not be said to be income arising 'from stocks and shares'. Since the UK tax liability turned on the nature of that foreign right, foreign trust law was relevant in determining that right.

These matters have arisen also in connection with payments by companies to share-holders. Under UK company law, the rights of shareholders are to participate in profits, to

---

[54] ITTOIA 2005, s 94(3)(d) and (4), ex TA 1988, s 81.
[55] ITTOIA 2005, s 95.
[56] [1931] AC 212, (1931) 15 TC 693.
[57] See Income Tax Act 1918, Sch D, Case IV, r 1.
[58] *Baker v Archer-Shee* [1927] AC 844, (1927) 11 TC 749.

participate in assets on liquidation and to have a reduction of capital. Of these the first is income for tax purposes, but the other two are capital;[59] this treatment is mirrored in UK tax law and provides the procrustean UK categories by reference to which foreign rights will be assessed. In *Reid's Trustees v IRC*,[60] the House of Lords held that a dividend from a foreign company might be classified as income even though the equivalent payment by a UK resident company would have been taxed quite differently—as a payment of capital and so, at that time,[61] not taxed at all. Lord Reid said that this was due to a peculiarity of the system for taxing domestic dividends at that time.[62] He noted the formal point that the payment did not alter the nature of the capital asset, ie the shareholding, but added that it clearly altered its value. On the other hand, there were other ways, such as the payment of a large dividend before sale, which also lowered that value and were clearly income. He therefore concluded that if a foreign company chose to pay a dividend it was taxable income, even though paid out of capital profits.

In *Reid's Trustees* the South African company declared what was fairly obviously a dividend, and in the absence of evidence of South African law, the foreign rights were assumed to be the same as under English company law. Other cases have concerned different ways of paying shareholders. In *Rae v Lazard Investment Co Ltd*,[63] a Maryland company carried out what we now know as a demerger; it transferred a business to a subsidiary company and then transferred shares in that subsidiary to the shareholders. Under Maryland corporate law the process was called a 'distribution in partial liquidation' and was regarded as a capital transaction. The Court of Appeal held that it was also a payment of capital for UK tax purposes. Again, in *Courtaulds Investments Ltd v Fleming*[64] the court held that a payment by way of repayment of a share premium was capital, even though under the relevant foreign law it could only be repaid out of profits accumulated in a special account. By contrast, in *Inchyra v Jennings*,[65] a direction in an American trust that a beneficiary should receive 1% of the trust capital each year was held to create annual payments[66] and so income for UK tax law.

Four lessons may be drawn:

(1) the court rejects a purely formal approach which would simply ask whether the foreign possession was intact;[67]
(2) the source of the payment is irrelevant;
(3) the question 'What is the nature of the rights?' is answered using the UK three-part test where appropriate, and otherwise seeking the relevant foreign law analogy; and
(4) the analogy of fruit and tree is unhelpful.[68]

---

[59] Buckley J in *Courtaulds Investments Ltd v Fleming* [1969] 3 All ER 1281, (1969) 46 TC 111, 124.
[60] (1949) 30 TC 431; Reid was applied by the *Privy Council in Bicber v IT Commrs* [1962] 3 All ER 294.
[61] Today it would come within CTA 2010, s 1000(1), ex TA 1988, s 209(2)(a).
[62] (1949) 30 TC 431, esp 449; a shareholder was not at that time directly assessable on a dividend paid out of profits which were not taxable in the hands of the company. Lord Reid could have added that the (pre-1965) system by which the shareholder was taxable on a dividend paid out of profits which were taxable in the hands of the company was unusual and not to be extended to foreign companies, which paid no UK tax on their profits.
[63] (1963) 41 TC 1; noted at [1963] BTR 121.
[64] [1969] 3 All ER 1281, (1969) 46 TC 111.
[65] [1965] 2 All ER 714, (1965) 42 TC 388.
[66] See *Revenue Law* at §29.2. Cf *Lawson v Rolfe* [1970] 1 All ER 761, (1970) 46 TC 199; see [1970] BTR 142.
[67] *Courtaulds v Fleming* (1969) 46 TC 111, 126.
[68] *Ibid*, 125H; see also Lord MacDermott in *Reid Trustees v IRC* (1949) 30 TC 431, 448.

15.3.2 Entities

The same approach is found when looking at the question whether a payment, which is clearly income for UK tax purposes, is income of A or B. The problem usually arises in connection with the distinction between companies and partnerships—income of the company being income of the company, while income of the partnership flows through to the individual partners. Of course there is the initial fact that a foreign company is not a legal entity under UK law, and so it was only by the comity of nations that it can be recognised.[69]

The issue whether a foreign entity is to be treated as a company or as a partnership for UK tax law is often described, these days, as one of 'transparency', but that simply reformulates the issue. The transparent taxation of UK partnerships is directed by ITTOIA 2005, section 849; there are special provisions on the remittance basis (section 858) and on double tax agreements (section 859). In this connection (as discussed in *Revenue Law*, §20.10.7), to counteract various schemes Parliament has enacted that the members of a firm include any person entitled to a share of income of the partnership. This rule applies for income tax, corporation tax and CGT; unusually the provisions are declared always to have had effect.[70]

However, this leaves the question, what is a partnership? The problem arises in connection with foreign associations or entities which are not clearly one or the other, and the court has to determine the characteristics which make a UK association one rather than the other.[71] The matter was considered in *Memec plc v IRC*.[72] Those characteristics of an English partnership, and so of transparency, are:

- no separate legal personality
- carrying on business together
- the ability of every partner to bind the firm and the other partners
- joint liability of every partner for all debts and obligations of the firm
- the fact that partners own the firm and are entitled to an undivided share of each partnership assets.

Although these characteristics have to be modified when discussing limited partnerships and Scottish partnerships, the overall idea of a partnership is reasonably clear. What is very clear is that the matter is treated as one of substance, and that the parties cannot determine the issue of transparency by the use of labels. In earlier case law the UK court held that a French *société en nom collectif* was a legal person separate from its members,[73] but this has been disavowed by the Revenue.[74] In France itself an EEIG has been characterised as a

---

[69] Eg Lord Hanworth in *Ryall v Du Bois* (1933) 18 TC 431, 440.

[70] ITTOIA 2005, s 858 (4), TA 1988, s 115(5C) and TCGA 1992, s 59(4), all added by FA 2008, s [55].

[71] See Avery Jones *et al* [2002] BTR 375–436.

[72] [1998] STC 754, esp 764–66, *per* Peter Gibson LJ. For comment, see [1999] BTR 153; and Venables (1998) 8 *The Offshore Taxation Review* 189. In the case, M had been receiving dividends from a German subsidiary (GS) and got credit relief for the tax paid by GS's German subsidiaries. Under a new arrangement they got a better or more secure deal under German tax, but eventually lost out at the UK end because they lost the right to credits for tax paid by the subsidiaries. See also *Newstead v Frost* [1980] STC 123, (1980) 53 TC 525, HL.

[73] (1929) 14 TC 560; see esp 577–78, *per* Lord Hanworth MR.

[74] Inland Revenue, *International Tax Handbook*, para 1673. For effects of Revenue advice on borderline cases, see *R v IRC, ex parte Bishopp and ex parte Allan* [1999] STC 531.

partnership and not a company.[75] The area will become one of fine distinction, and there is much to be said for the US approach which allows taxpayers to select the characterisation of their choice in borderline cases.[76]

There is no reason why a classification reached for UK domestic rules has to be applied for treaty purposes too. This may be desirable from the point of view of symmetry and elegance but is not necessary. The Revenue view is that a US limited liability corporation (LLC) is a corporate entity and not a partnership (following US rules), but it does not accept that an LLC is a US corporation as defined in the UK–US Double Tax Treaty.[77]

15.4 Remittance Basis for Relevant Foreign Income and Chargeable Gains

15.4.1 *The Concept and the Basics*

FA 2008 inserted Part 14, Chapter A1 into ITA 2007; this runs from section 809A to section 809Z7 and revolutionised the UK rules for the remittance basis of taxation. ITA 2007, Chapter A1 provides one coherent and modern scheme for taxation on a remittance basis; it aligns the administrative arrangements for—and applies similar rules as to what is a remittance to—the various different types of foreign income and to capital gains (hence FIGs). It removes the rules under which Irish income could not benefit from the remittance basis.[78] It also introduced the special £30,000 charge for long-term residents (LTRs), called the remittance basis charge (RBC) (see below at §15.4.7). Section 809Z7 contains interpretations. It cannot be pretended that these rules are always easy to grasp, but that is because they are a compromise designed to improve the remittance basis. Others may well feel that it should either have been abolished altogether or left alone. One might also note the perils for a government being bounced into a change because of a wish to trump a proposal from an opposition party.

An individual (T) is not obliged to use the remittance basis, but the consequence of not doing so is that the FIGs are taxed on an arising basis, ie whether or not remitted to the UK. If the arising basis does apply, however, T becomes entitled to the personal allowances set out in ITA 2007, Part 3, Chapter 2 (personal and blind person's allowances), tax reduction as per Chapter 3 (married persons and civil partners) or life assurance (sections 457–459) that are disallowed for those subject to the remittance basis by section 809G. Further, the annual exempt amount for CGT (TCGA 1992, section 4) is available. If instead the remittance basis is chosen, these may not be available.

---

[75] *Société Kingroup*, Conseil d'état, 4 April 1997; on treatment of Swiss general partnerships, see *Oxnard Financing SA v Rahn* [1968] 1 WLR 1465; and Kent [1999] BTR 125.

[76] Ault *et al*, 278.

[77] Fraser [2001] BTR 153; see also *Engineer v IRC* [1997] STC (SCD) 189. On such companies, see Freedman 63 *MLR* 317.

[78] HMRC Notes to Finance Bill, paras 99 *et seq*.

The Revenue practice of entering into forward agreements with individual taxpayers, under which their liability to tax was agreed as a fixed sum for a certain number of years, was held to be ultra vires.[79]

FA 2009 Schedule 24 made a few changes in the light of one year's experience of the new rules, including amendments to the relevant person test in section 809M. The value of a remittance where property forming part of a larger set is remitted was redefined in the Revenue's favour (paragraph 8). There were some procedural changes to do with self-assessment (paragraphs 3 and 4). Property is now 'remitted to the UK' if used to pay interest on a debt—and not just the debt itself (paragraph 6)—and the scope of the exemption in section 809X was widened slightly (paragraph 10).

15.4.1.1 Categories of Income—or Capital Gains—Eligible for Remittance Basis Treatment

The categories of remittances which are charged to tax are set out in the legislation (see below §15.4.3).

Statute also provides rules to determine the order in which sums are to be taken to be remitted from a mixed fund (ITA 2007, section 809Q). If sums are not mixed but kept isolated and distinct, the actual source will give the answer. Usually the issue will be whether the sum remitted is income (maximum rate of tax 50%) or capital gain (now 18%/28%). The order is as follows:

(1) relevant foreign earnings (ITEPA 2003, sections 22 and 26);[80]
(2) foreign specific employment income (ITEPA 2003, section 41A);
(3) relevant foreign income (ITTOIA 2005, section 830);
(4) foreign chargeable gains (TCGA 1992, section 12);
(5) relevant foreign earnings subject to a foreign tax;
(6) foreign specific employment income subject to a foreign tax;
(7) relevant foreign income subject to a foreign tax;
(8) foreign chargeable gains subject to a foreign tax;
(9) other income or capital.

This order for remittances from a mixed fund is mandatory (see also, in relation to CGT, §18.2 below). This gives rise to a need, not so much for planning opportunities, but for caution in arranging one's affairs to avoid unnecessary charges. The (extensive) use of separate accounts may become the norm. A mixed fund may arise either because it contains different sorts of FIGs chargeable on a remittance basis, or because it contains both chargeable FIGs and non-chargeable sums.

15.4.1.2 Remittances

Where income is eligible to be taxed on a remittance basis, it is taxed only when remitted to the UK and not when it arises. The question whether the foreign income, etc has been remitted to the UK is the subject of rules in ITA 2007, sections 809T–809U (§15.4.6).

---

[79] *Al Fayed v Advocate General for Scotland* [2004] STC 1703; the judgment of the Lord Justice Clerk [2002] STC 910 contains a fascinating account of the way in which the Revenue exercised the power.
[80] Section 809Z(3).

15.4.1.3 Exempt Remittances

In certain situations the arrival of the money or property in the UK does not cause the remittance basis to apply. These are the subject of rules in ITA 2007, sections 809V–809Z6. See §15.4.6.3.

15.4.1.4 Migrant Exemption

ITA 2007, sections 828A–828D are designed to exempt from UK tax altogether people not wanting to use the remittance basis. The person in mind is the migrant worker employed seasonally in agriculture in the UK and other countries in the same tax year, and whose non-UK income is subject to tax where it is earned. By granting the exemption these rules remove the duty to file a self-assessment return. Relevant foreign income for the year must not exceed £10,000, and relevant foreign investment income must not exceed £100. The worker must have been liable only to basic or starting-rate income tax.

15.4.2 Using the Remittance Basis: Categories of Taxpayers

15.4.2.1 Long-term Residents

Only long-term residents (LTRs) are liable to the £30,000 charge. An individual is an LTR if he or she is age 18 or over and has been a UK resident for at least seven of the last nine tax years. So a person continuously resident in the UK since attaining the age of 10 will become an LTR on his or her 18th birthday and will be an LTR for the whole of that tax year. Such a person is required to nominate income or gains for the application of the £30,000 charge (section 809C(2) and (3)). Only LTRs are required to make a nomination. See further below at §15.4.7.

15.4.2.2 De Minimis (Section 809C)

A de minimis rule applies where C, an individual, is entitled to the remittance basis. C comes within this rule if the total of unremitted FIGs does not exceed £2,000. The de minimis person *is* entitled to the various allowances normally forbidden by section 809G (see §15.4.1 above). C may simply apply this basis in making the self-assessment—there is no need for a claim under section 809B.

15.4.2.3 Neither De Minimis Nor LTR

Such an individual (C) is entitled to use the remittance basis but in its 2008 form. If money is actually remitted, a claim must be made under section 809. C is not entitled to the various allowances forbidden by section 809G and set out at §15.4.1 above.

15.4.2.4 Claims According to the Finance Bill Notes

Section 809E is designed to ensure that an individual does not have to complete a self-assessment form if entitled to the remittance basis but no tax liability will result. So it applies where T has neither remitted foreign income nor taxable UK income—assuming that T is not an LTR.

15.4.3 *FIGs*

The categories of FIGs with charging provisions are:

- relevant foreign earnings—ITEPA 2003, sections 22 or 26
- foreign specific employment income—ITEPA 2003, section 41a
- relevant foreign income—ITTOIA 2005, sections 830 and 832
- foreign chargeable gains—TCGA 1992, section 12.

All these provisions have been amended or replaced by FA 2008.

'Relevant foreign income' categories, as set out in ITTOIA 2005, section 830, ie income accruing from a source outside the UK, are:[81]

Part 2: Trading Profits

- Chapter 2 Trade Profits (including Chapter 17 charges on adjustment income and expenses on a change of accounting practice)

Part 3: Property Income

- Chapter 3 Overseas Property Business and Chapter 11 Overseas Property Income Where Remittance Basis Applies

Part 4: Interest and Savings

- Chapter 2 Interest
- Chapter 4 Dividend Income for Non-UK Resident Company
- Chapter 7 Purchased Life Annuity Payments
- Chapter 8 Deep Gain Securities
- Chapter 14 Sales of Foreign Dividend Coupons

Part 5: Miscellaneous

- Chapter 2 Annual Payments
- ITTOIA 2005, section 579 Royalty Payments etc from Intellectual Property
- Chapter 4 Films etc
- Chapter 5 Telecommunication Rights
- ITTOIA 2005, section 649 Estate Income
- Chapter 8 Income Not Otherwise Chargeable

ITTOIA 2005, section 830(4) adds, inter alia, a list of other income treated as relevant foreign income, including a partner's share of a firm's trading income (ITA 2007, section 857(3)), a distribution by the Commonwealth Development Corporation, certain foreign pensions within ITEPA 2003, sections 575(3), 613(4), 631(3) and 635(4), and foreign social security income (ITEPA 2003, section 679(2)).

---

[81] ITTOIA 2005, s 830(1); see also s 830(4).

ITTOIA 2005, like TCGA 1992 (below §18.1.2), is now backed up by a rule to catch temporary non-residents.[82] The purpose is to prevent avoidance. A person with unremitted foreign ITTOIA 2005 income might decide to become non-resident for a year and during that year remit all that income to the UK. Neither the arising basis nor the remittance basis would apply. Section 832A applies if the individual was resident and: (a) there are fewer than five years between the year of departure and the year of return; and (b) the individual was resident in the UK for at least four of the seven years before the year of the departure.

15.4.4 History of the Remittance Basis[83]

A remittance received in the UK may be exempt from UK tax under a double tax treaty.[84] Before 1914[85] all income accruing to a resident from a foreign source, ie one wholly outside the UK, was taxed on a remittance basis. In 1914 the remittance basis was replaced by the arising basis for income from stocks, shares and rents—hence the *Archer–Shee* litigation (see §15.3.1 above); this was extended in 1940[86] to a few remaining categories of investment income, such as income on foreign bank deposits and income arising to beneficiaries under foreign trusts.[87] In 1974 the remittance basis was effectively abolished for residents, although it remains of importance to those who are not domiciled in the UK or who are not ordinarily resident here.[88] When the UK abolished the Schedule E remittance basis for residents, special percentage reductions in the amount falling to be taxed (100%, 50%, 25% or 10%) were introduced; since then, reductions have in turn been removed as a result of the general lowering of tax rates. The only survivors are the 100% reduction for seafarers[89] and 10% for foreign pensions.[90] At one time a 25% percentage reduction applied to income from trades and professions.[91] The pre-2008 remittance basis was full of holes and anomalies—many are discussed in the notes to the Finance Bill 2008.

The remittance basis does not apply for corporation tax.[92] However, if a foreign trade is run through a subsidiary company resident in that other country, the profits will not generally be taxed in the UK until they are transferred to this country as dividends, interest or royalty payments.[93] The CFC legislation (below, chapter seventeen) provides the exceptions.

15.4.5 What must be Remitted; Pre-2008 Law—The Need for Reform

ITA 2007, sections–809Z6, added by FA 2008, determine whether there has been a remittance—and so a charge to tax—and how it is to be valued. In order to appreciate the scope of these rules it is worth just noting the pre-2008 situation first.

---

[82] ITTOIA 2005, s 832A, added by FA 2008.
[83] Avery Jones, in Tiley (ed), *Studies in the History of Tax Law* (Hart Publishing, 2004), 15.
[84] *Lord Strathalmond v IRC* [1972] 3 All ER 715, (1972) 45 TC 537.
[85] FA 1914, s 5; FA 1940, s 19—as recommended by Royal Commission (1920), §27.
[86] FA 1940, s 19.
[87] Thus, undoing *Archer-Shee v Garland* (see above at §15.3.1).
[88] The restriction to Commonwealth citizens or citizens of the Republic of Ireland was removed by ITTOIA 2005 as from 6 April 2005.
[89] TA 1988, s 192A, Sch 12.
[90] *Ibid*, s 196.
[91] FA 1978, s 27, Sch 4; repealed by FA 1984, s 30. For transitional effects, see TA 1988, Schs 29, 30.
[92] TA 1989, s 70(2).
[93] Debt is usually easier to repatriate than equity. On CFC legislation, see ch 17 below.

15.4.5.1 Alienation before Remittance

Where the remittance basis applied, the sum received had to be received as the income of the recipient in the UK; that is, it must not only have been income according to UK tax law, but must have been received in the UK by the taxpayer in whose hands it was subject to UK tax. So the remittance basis could be avoided by making sure that what was remitted was not income of the taxpayer but money belonging to another person, eg another family member to whom the one-time income was passed by way of gift. The leading case illustrating this was *Carter v Sharon*.[94] Here the taxpayer arranged for a banker's draft to be sent to her daughter from California. It was shown that by Californian law the gift was complete not later than when the draft was posted; the money therefore was not a remittance of income to the taxpayer. Had the mother simply sent her daughter a cheque drawn on her California bank account, the money, when it arrived in England, would still have been taxable since it belonged to the taxpayer as she could have revoked the cheque.[95] The question of the effectiveness of the gift is judged according to the foreign law. Today this is stopped by the 'relevant person' rules, which treat a remittance by the individual or by someone in a detailed list in section 809M as a taxable remittance.

15.4.5.2 Conversion

Another line of reasoning accepted by the Revenue was that unless there was an express provision directing otherwise, the conversion of the foreign unremitted income into something else, eg an object, meant that the remittance of the object to the UK did not amount to a remittance of the original income. It followed that if foreign income was converted into a car which was then brought into the UK, no liability would arise under the remittance basis. If, however, the car were then sold, the proceeds might be taxable.[96] If, by that time, the car had been given to someone else, the proceeds might not be taxable under ITTOIA 2005.[97] Such distinctions and traps brought no credit on the system.

For income falling within ITEPA 2003, ex Schedule E, Case III, it was expressly provided[98] that emoluments shall be treated as received in the UK if—and when—they are paid, used or enjoyed in the UK, or in any manner or form transmitted or brought to the UK. The wording of this ITEPA 2003 rule was much wider, and clearly contemplates the possibility of transmission in kind, while the ITTOIA 2005 rule did not. The rule was confined to emoluments received in kind but which had not altered their form. The point remained untested by litigation.

---

[94] [1936] 1 All ER 720, (1936) 20 TC 22; cf *Thomson v Bensted* (1918) 7 TC 137. Accepted by the CA as good law in the professional negligence case of *Grimm v Newman* [2002] EWCA Civ 1621, [2002] STC 1388. The Court considered the possible impact of *Harmel v Wright* [1974] STC 88 on *Carter v Sharon* but distinguished that case (paras 51–62); it also discounted any application of the *Ramsay* principle in the light of *MacNiven* (para 60).

[95] As in *Timpson's Executors v Yerbury* [1936] 1 All ER 186, (1936) 20 TC 155.

[96] In the year in which the car was sold (*Scottish Provident Institution v Farmer* (1912) 6 TC 34). On tracing, see Coles [1979] BTR 238. Other relevant cases include *Patuck v Lloyd* (1944) 26 TC 284.

[97] *Bray v Best* [1989] 1 All ER 969, [1989] STC 159, (1989) 61 TC 705, HL. This was a decision under Sch E, Case I and involved no international element; it has since been reversed by legislation (FA 1989, s 36(3)); see *Revenue Law*, §14.1.1.The 1989 change affected what is now ITEPA 2003 but not ITTOIA 2005.

[98] ITEPA 2003, s 33(2), ex TA 1988, s 132(5).

15.4.5.3 Exporting Debt

Then there was the device under which a taxpayer, with funds overseas taxable on a remittance basis, borrowed money in the UK and the loan was then repaid from the fund overseas. The problem is whether the economic value accruing to the taxpayer results from the receipt of income in the UK or from the export of a debt from the UK. Statute intervened to widen or render certain the scope of remittance when the taxpayer is ordinarily resident in the UK.[99] However, taxpayers who were not ordinarily resident had to rely on the old case law.

15.4.5.4 Source

There was the further rule that the original source had still to exist in the year in which the income was remitted. This was reversed in 1989 for what became ITEPA 2003, but not, until 2008, for ITTOIA 2005.[100]

15.4.6 What is a Remittance? 2008 Rules

15.4.6.1 Remittances

In a turgid and hard-to-read style, the 2008 rules consign all these situations in which FIGs escaped, or have at some time escaped, liability to history. The purpose is clear: it is to keep FIGs safe from being taxed as a remittance only where they remain genuinely outside the UK.

Section 809L is a long and complicated provision, and deals with the various problems of alienation, conversion and exporting debts set out in §15.4.5 above. In form it has four conditions, (A)–(D). The receipt is taxable as a remittance if it comes within (A) and (B) and either (C) or (D) considered below. As from 6 April 2008, FIG is remitted first if money or property is brought into the UK, or received or used in the UK by or for a 'relevant person'; this is condition (A). Condition (A) then goes further and reaches a benefit consisting not of money or property but a service provided in the UK by or for a relevant person. Condition (A) specifies—and widens—the type of receipt.

Under section 809M, a person is 'relevant' if being the person with the income or gain (E), or a close relative of that person. Close relatives include spouses and civil partners (and people living together as husband and wife or civil partners). They also include children and grandchildren under 18,[101] and extend to entities related to E, such as a company in which E is a participator (whether or not a close company), or a settlement in which E is a settlor or beneficiary or a body connected with a settlement.[102] The definition of 'close company' now includes subsidiaries, and there is a new definition of 'participator'.[103] FA 2010 extended this to include certain subsidiaries of a non-resident company. It will be noted that the list of 'relevant' persons does not include children over 17. Attempts to take advantage of this situation may be vulnerable under the associated operations rule. The same is true of schemes involving parents, who are not relevant persons either. It seems that

---

[99] ITTOIA 2005, ss 833 and 834, ex TA 1988, s 65(6)–(9), as amended by FA 2008, Sch 7.
[100] ITEPA 2003, s 30, ex FA 1989, s 36(3). The reversal seems to be by ITA 2007, ss 832 *et seq*.
[101] Child or grandchild may be of any person within ITA 2007, s 809M(2)(a)–(c).
[102] ITA 2007, s 809M(1)–(3).
[103] ITA 2007, s 809M(3)(ca).

a child under 18 who marries does not cease to be a relevant person. It should also be noted that, as the result of a late change, trustees of a settlement are relevant persons only if their beneficiaries include persons relevant under other paragraphs of section 809M(2).

Condition (B) provides the link to the FIG. It is satisfied if the property—or consideration for the service—is wholly, or in part, the FIG. Condition (B) then goes on to deal with 'relevant debts'. It is also satisfied if the FIG—or anything derived from the FIG—is used outside the UK (directly or indirectly in respect of a relevant debt). Looking at what we have covered so far, a debt is relevant if it is a debt relating to the property or service mentioned above under condition (A).

Gift recipients.[104] Condition (C) deals with gifts (alienation). It is satisfied if qualifying property of a gift recipient is brought into the UK and enjoyed by a relevant person. The various terms are defined.[105] So a gift recipient is someone, other than a relevant person, to whom E gave the property, and it is, or represents, the FIGs. Qualifying property is the property given or derived from it.[106]

Needless to say, the rules are framed to cover not only property brought into the UK, but also property used as consideration for a service in the UK or to pay a relevant debt outside the UK.

Connected operation.[107] The final condition (D) is an alternative to (C). If the sum, etc is to be taxable as remitted FIG, it must have met conditions (A) and (B). Condition (D) applies where the property is not a qualifying property of a gift recipient (so (C) cannot apply anyway) but the property is brought into the UK and enjoyed by a relevant person in circumstances where there is a connected operation (CO). There are exceptions for full consideration or enjoyment on the same terms as the general public. There is also an exception if the property or service is enjoyed virtually to the entire exclusion of the relevant person.[108]

Connected operations are defined by section 809O. An operation is connected if effected with reference to a qualifying disposition (QD), or with a view to enabling or facilitating a QD; a QD is one made by a relevant person.[109]

15.4.6.2 Timing and Valuation

The amount remitted is governed by section 809P. Where the property or consideration caught is the foreign income or gain itself, the amount of the FIG remitted is taken. If it derives from that FIG, the value of the underlying FIG is taken, not the value of the derived property. When used to pay a relevant debt, the amount remitted is that used to pay the debt, not the value of the liability.

Further, but similar, rules apply where the remittance comes within conditions (C) and (D).[110]

The statutory list in section 809Q(4) setting out order in which sums remitted to the UK are taxed was discussed above in §15.4.1.

---

[104] ITA 2007, s 809L(4).
[105] ITA 2007, s 809N.
[106] ITA 2007, s 809N(7) and (8).
[107] ITA 2007, s 809L(5).
[108] ITA 2007, s 809O(6).
[109] ITA 2007, s 809O(3).
[110] ITA 2007, s 809(6).

One curious timing provision deserves mention. Under section 809U, if the normal remittance rules give one timing outcome but a deeming provision would make it earlier, the normal timing rule prevails.

15.4.6.3 Exempt Property

Having widened the net so comprehensively, Chapter A1 then has to narrow it (sections 809V–809Z6). Section 809V excludes certain payments to HMRC where the taxpayer is a long-term UK resident. The idea is, presumably, to allow the taxpayer to pay the £30,000 charge (RBC) from untaxed foreign income or gains to HMRC without incurring further liability. The HMRC notes to the Bill are very restrictive—thus the money must come direct from the overseas account to HMRC, whether by cheque or electronic transfer, and not via UK bank account.

Another exemption, section 809W, a late addition to the Bill, deals with sum used to pay for certain services relating to property outside the UK, eg legal fees. The sums must be paid to a bank account outside the UK.

Property, defined so as to exclude money (section 809Y), will be exempt even though brought into the UK or used in the UK if it satisfies one of four tests. The link provision in section 809X provides the exemption, which sets out the categories of exempt property and gives references to the detailed rules. Property ceasing to satisfy these tests—whether because it breaches the conditions or is sold—is treated as remitted (section 809U). The categories are:

(1) *Property consisting of works of art or collector's pieces.* Such property will be exempt if meeting a public access test (section 809V). Normally the property must be in a museum or gallery, in storage at such a place or in transit from such a place between there and outside the UK. Normally the work must be on public display, but this is softened to being available on request for works which are too fragile. Works on public display in connection with their sale also qualify for this rule. However, a charge will arise if the property is actually sold in the UK (section 809U(3)).

(2) *Personal use items.* Clothing, footwear, jewellery and watches derived from relevant foreign income will be exempt if they meet a personal use rule (sections 809X3, 809Z and 809Z1).

(3) *Temporary presence.* Property of any kind will be exempt if it meets a rule for repairs (sections 809 X(5) and 809Z3) or more generally the temporary importation rule (sections 809X(5) and 809Z4); the latter uses the concept of 275 'countable days'. Days on which the property meets the rules for personal use or repair are not countable days; further conditions apply where public access is in issue (section 809Z4).

(4) *De minimis.* Property of any kind will be exempt if the notional remitted amount (NRA) defined in section 805Z5 is less than £1,000. The NRA is defined as being the income that would have been treated as remitted if it had not been exempt. The rules direct a just and reasonable valuation where property is part of a set, only part of which is in the UK (section 809Z5(2)).

15.4.6.4 Exception Interest on Grandfathered Loans

It has been common for a person, T, wanting to buy property in the UK to borrow money from abroad. If the loan were made in the UK, T would need to pay interest and, in due course, pay off the capital, eg out of FIGs. Before FA 2008 the UK tax treatment of a payment to the bank by T would depend on whether it was to pay interest or repay capital. A repayment of capital was treated as being remitted income or gain, while a payment of interest was not.

The FA 2008 changes abolished this distinction, and so a transitional clause (119) was added. No charge arises where the loan was made before 12 March 2008 with the sole purpose of enabling the individual to buy a residential property in the UK. The money lent has to be received in the UK and used to acquire the property before 6 April 2008. Repayment of the debt must be secured on the property. In the circumstances, interest payment will not be treated as remittance—for the period of the loan or until 2028 if sooner. Any variation of the terms of the loan or any further loan will cause the exception to end forthwith—unless the new terms would satisfy these rules.

15.4.7 Special Rules for Long-term Residents

The remittance basis charge—or RBC—applies if T (a) is an individual resident in the UK and is 18 or over in that year, and (b) has been resident for at least seven of the last nine tax years immediately before the current year (section 809H). Section 809C directs that T must nominate an amount of unremitted offshore income or gains which will be subject to the charge. For a tax at 50% to generate £30,000 of tax there must be £60,000 of underlying income—with gains now taxed at a maximum rate of 28% a much larger figure is needed (£107,143).

The point of nominating—or identifying—these FIGs is that when in a later year those identified income or gains are actually remitted to the UK, they will not be taxed again. However, it is not quite as simple as that. If in the later year there are FIGS which have *not* been nominated (and so not taxed in the UK by the RBC), any sums received in the UK will be attributed first to untaxed—and so now taxable—FIGs; only when the untaxed FIGs are exhausted will the sums be attributed to the nominated FIGs.[111] In view of these rules, it is not surprising that section 809C directs that the nominated income or gains must not be such that tax on the relevant FIGs exceeds £30,000.

When the nomination is made, the effect of this is laid out by section 809H(2) and (3)—the technicalities make the sum due (on the nominated income or gains) taxable on an arising basis. Where the amount of tax due would be £30,000 or more, the £30,000 ceiling applies.[112]

If the income tax due on the nominated income or gains is less than £30,000, the tax system increases the liability to £30,000 anyway.[113] The only way to avoid the charge is not to be taxed on the remittance basis for that year—ie to be taxed on all income or gains, whether or not remitted.

The £30,000 payment is a payment of income tax or, if the nominated profits are capital gains, CGT. It follows that it may be used for gift aid purposes under UK tax law.[114] It should also be recognised by a foreign tax system as such a payment, and so be available

---

[111] ITA 2007, s 809H—the full order is in s 809I.
[112] ITA 2007, s 809G(2) and (3)
[113] ITA 2007, s 809G(4) and (5).
[114] ITA 2007, s 809H(2).

for credit or other double taxation relief purposes; this is, initially at least, a question for the foreign tax system.

At Budget 2011, the Government announced it intended to increase the existing £30,000 annual charge to £50,000 for non-domiciles who have been UK-resident for 12 or more years and who wished to retain access to the remittance basis. The higher charge was implemented by Finance Act 2012, Schedule 12, adding new Chapter A1 of ITA 2007, Part 14, with effect from 6 April 2012. The £30,000 charge was retained for those who have been resident for at least seven of the past nine years and fewer than 12 years. In 2011 and 2012 the Government also consulted on reforms to the taxation of non-domiciled individuals, with a view to simplifying the rules and encouraging investment in the UK, whilst ensuring that non-doms make a 'fair tax contribution'. Following on from that consultation, an incentive for business investment by non-doms[115] and a series of technical simplifications to the taxation of non-doms were introduced in Finance Act 2012,[116] with effect from 6 April 2012.

15.5 Reliefs for Unremittable (Stranded) Foreign Income

15.5.1 Arising Basis

This deals with a quite different question. UK income and corporation tax may be postponed where income taxed on an arising basis, whether in full or on a reduced sum, cannot be remitted, whether because of laws, executive action or the impossibility of obtaining foreign currency, and the taxpayer has not realised the income outside the territory for a consideration either in sterling or in a currency which might be converted into sterling.[117] Impossible means that it is impossible to obtain currency which may be transferred to the UK.[118] In view of this redefinition of impossibility, it is not clear whether the export to the UK of an object paid for with the foreign currency will end the relief before it is sold. The consequences of spending the income within the foreign country are also unclear. Taxpayers must show that they were not able to remit it. When this can no longer be shown, they, or their estates, become liable to income tax or corporation tax,[119] which will be assessed by reference to the year in which it first arose. There are specific rules for valuing the unremittable income.[120] Separate but similar rules apply to ITEPA 2003.[121]

---

[115] ITA 2007, ss 809VA–809VO.

[116] FA 2012, Sch 12, Pts 2–4.

[117] ITTOIA 2005, Pt 8, Ch 4 and CTA 2009, Pt 3, Ch 12 (trading income) and Pt 18, ex TA 1988, s 584, originally FA 1953, s 21; on which see Royal Commission on the Taxation of Profits and Income, First Report, Cmd 8761 (1952). Distinguish the situation where the income, although due, has not been paid.

[118] ITTOIA 2005, s 841 (3)(c); Explanatory Notes Change.

[119] For corporation tax a slightly different rule applies and it is treated as income when the conditions no longer apply: CTA 2009, s 175 (for trading income) and s 1276 (ex TA 1988, s 585(2A)).

[120] ITTOIA 2005, s 845, based on TA 1988, s 585(8).

[121] ITEPA 2003, ss 35 and 36.

15.5.2 Remittance Basis

Where the unremittable foreign income is taxable on a remittance basis, the tax liability is inevitably postponed until the income is actually remitted, but then the tax may be much higher by reason of the sudden remittance of the income of several years. When the income becomes remittable, it is chargeable, if the taxpayer so elects, by reference to the year in which it arose. If, for some reason, no liability is incurred in the year in which the income arose, as where the taxpayer was not then resident, no tax is due.[122] Separate but similar rules apply for ITEPA 2003.[123] The relief applies to persons rather than just to individuals, and so is available, for example, to trusts. Since the remittance basis has no application to corporation tax, this relief cannot either, and so the provision in TA 1988 is repealed by ITTOIA 2005.

15.6 Anti-avoidance: Transfers of Assets Abroad—Attribution of Income for Income Tax

15.6.1 Introduction

15.6.1.1 Overview

This is a difficult area, not least because, as has been said, no argument has been too esoteric for the Revenue to pursue in administering these rules.[124] The taxation of residents, coupled with the non-taxation of non-residents, might encourage residents to arrange for income which would otherwise come to them to be held by non-residents, and especially by such artificial entities as trusts[125] and companies. Legislation was introduced in 1936[126] (now ITA 2007, Part 13, Chapter 2, sections 714–751, ex TA 1988, sections 739 *et seq*) to counter devices whereby assets would be transferred to persons abroad, ie resident or domiciled outside the UK, in whose hands the income would not be subject to UK tax, and where some benefit of that income would or might accrue to the original resident. In this legislation references to individuals include references to their spouse or civil partner, but not to cohabitees.[127] The term 'person abroad' (to whom the property is transferred) is defined in ITA 2007 as meaning a person either resident or domiciled outside the UK; in applying these rules, a body incorporated outside the UK is treated as if resident outside the UK.[128] The legislation applies only for income tax; corporation tax has more far-reaching rules for CFCs, considered in chapter seventeen below. In 2011, the European Commission formally requested the UK to amend these rules, which it views as contrary to EU Treaty fundamental freedoms, namely the freedom of establishment and free movement of capital. At Budget 2012, the Government confirmed its intention to consult on amending this

---

[122] ITTOIA 2005, Pt 8, Ch 2, ss 835–837, ex TA 1988, s 585(3), (4).
[123] ITEPA 2003, s 37.
[124] Ashton [1990] BTR 251 at 252 ; see also Boyd [1980] BTR 442 on history of early cases.
[125] Eg *Astor v Perry* [1935] AC 398, (1935) 19 TC 255.
[126] FA 1936, s 18; for debates on clause, see *Whiteman on Income Tax*, 3rd edn (Sweet & Maxwell, 2008), §§23.03 *et seq*.
[127] ITA 2007, s 714(4).
[128] ITA 2007, s 718; for trusts and estates, see s 718(2).

regime with a view to implementing changes in Finance Act 2013. The changes are not expected to be to a taxpayer's disadvantage, and generally will have retrospective effect to 6 April 2012.

There are three heads of charge, of which the first two go back to 1936. These two impose a charge on the transferor and are:

(1) the receipt of a benefit derived from a power to enjoy the income (ITA 2007, section 720, ex TA 1988, section 739(2)); or

(2) the receipt of a capital sum (ITA 2007, section 727, ex TA 1988, section 739(3)).

The third head of charge was added in 1981 and applies to certain non-transferors who receive a benefit as a result of 'relevant transactions' (ITA 2007, section 731, ex TA 1988, section 740). FA 2008, in its revolution of the remittance basis, made changes to the remittance rules in relation to each head of charge. The purpose is to ensure that the taxpayer may claim the benefit of the remittance basis in the same circumstances as if the payment had been received direct, while taking full account of the new remittance rules which allow the payments to remain untaxed only so long as they remain genuinely offshore.[129]

Each head will cause the UK tax system to attribute the income accruing to the non-resident to the UK resident. It is not necessary for the transferor to receive the income.[130] In the absence of such a provision, a resident might transfer shares to a non-resident company, which would gather in the income free of UK tax and then distribute money to the transferor either by way of dividend, ie when it chose to, or by way of a capital payment which might be tax free. The rules apply whether or not the transferor was ordinarily resident in the UK at the time of the transfer.[131]

The CFC rules introduced in 1984 apply only to companies and not to individuals. However, the presence of a CFC may reduce the charge under the first head.[132]

Origin of the third head. These rules have given rise to major issues of statutory construction.[133] In particular, they were given a very wide construction on one aspect by the House of Lords in *Congreve v IRC* in 1945.[134] This was reversed in 1979 by the House of Lords in *Vestey v IRC*.[135] Many cases between 1945 and 1979, giving a wide construction to other parts of these rules, have cited *Congreve* as part of their background reasoning. *Vestey* has not stopped the Revenue from taking strong positions in such litigation on section 739, eg in *IRC v Willoughby* in 1997.[136] The *Vestey* case held that the first two heads of charge applied only where the person with the power to enjoy the income or who had received the capital sum was the transferor (or spouse or civil partner).[137] The primary reason for this

---

[129] HMRC Notes to Sch 7, para 88; the provisions changed and strengthened are ss 726, 730 and 735, backed up by s 735A.

[130] See Carswell LJ in *IRC v McGuckian* [1994] STC 888, 916; (1994) 69 TC 1, 41, CA (NI).

[131] ITA 2007, ss 21(5) and 728(3), ex TA 1988, s 739(1A), added by FA 1996.

[132] But see ITA 2007, s 725, ex TA 1988, 474(4) and ITA 2007, s 718(2), ex TA 1988, s 742(8), as amended by FA 1990, s 66 and FA 1994, s 251(3).

[133] See also *Revenue Bulletin*, Issue 40, [1999] *Simon's Weekly Tax Intelligence* 829.

[134] [1945] 1 All ER 945, 30 TC 163.

[135] [1980] AC 1145, [1980] STC 10, 54 TC 503; see Sumption [1980] BTR 4, reversing the earlier House of Lords decision in *Congreve v IRC* [1945] 1 All ER 945, 30 TC 163. On the scope of the *Vestey* decision, see Venables (1991) 1 *The Offshore Tax Planning Review* 19.

[136] [1997] STC 995.

[137] ITA 2007, s 714(4).

decision was the absence of any provision in the section whereby the income of the foreign entity could appropriately be attributed to the beneficiaries, and reluctance on the part of the court to allow that attribution to be carried out simply by Revenue discretion. Similarly, in *IRC v Pratt*,[138] the court held that these rules did not apply to multiple transfers if the respective interests of the assets transferred could not be separated and clearly identified. The rules in ITA 2007, sections 731–733 (ex TA 1988, section 740) are designed to fill the resulting gap by making persons other than the transferor liable when—and to the extent that—they receive a benefit which is not otherwise chargeable to income tax; to meet the objections of the judges, further rules allow HMRC to allocate the charges.[139] See below at §15.6.1.4.

15.6.1.2 The First Head of Charge—Power to Enjoy Income

ITA 2007, section 720 (ex TA 1988, section 739(2)) applies where there has been a transfer of assets, and charges: (a) any individual[140] who (b) has, by virtue of the transfer or any associated operations, (c) the power to enjoy income which (d) in consequence of the transfer (e) becomes that of a person resident or domiciled outside the UK. Such income is deemed to be that of the person with the power to enjoy and is taxed under the relevant parts of ITTOIA 2005—previously under Schedule D, Case VI.[141] It is in this context that the decision of the House of Lords in *IRC v McGuckian*,[142] characterising as income a sum received for the sale of a right to a dividend, assumes its importance. In *IRC v Brackett*,[143] the concept of income becoming payable to a non-resident was held to include the profits of a non-resident trader. This decision involved a tax haven company employing an individual resident in the UK but not domiciled in the UK, and so potentially able to use the remittance basis.

Under the first head there is a special rule where the benefits are provided out of the income of a person abroad; here there will be a charge on the value of the benefit received, except to the extent that the individual has been taxed already.[144]

The elements of this head of charge are considered further below at §15.6.2.

15.6.1.3 The Second Head of Charge—Capital Sum

ITA 2007, section 727 (ex TA 1988, section 739(3)) applies where there is a transfer of assets and, whether before or after the transfer, an individual ordinarily resident in the UK receives a capital sum. This sum must be connected with the transfer and be either (a) a sum paid or payable by way of loan,[145] or (b) any other sum paid or payable otherwise than as income and which is not paid or payable for full consideration in money or money's

---

[138] [1982] STC 756, 57 TC 1.

[139] ITA 2007, s 743, ex TA 1988, s 744.

[140] Ie the transferor or spouse or civil partner, but not a widow (*Vestey's Executors v IRC* [1949] 1 All ER 1108, (1949) 31 TC 1).

[141] ITA 2007, s 735(3)(4), ex TA 1988, s 743(1)–(1B).

[142] [1997] STC 908, (1997) 69 TC 1; see Revenue Law, §5.6.4. For comment, see Venables (1997) 7 *The Offshore Taxation Review* 69.

[143] [1986] STC 521, 60 TC 134.

[144] See Ashton [1990] BTR 251.

[145] Unless wholly repaid before the beginning of the year (ITA 2007, s 729(2), ex TA 1988, s 739(6)). Leaving money outstanding on a purchase is not a loan (*Ramsden v IRC* (1957) 37 TC 619).

worth. Thus, this does not apply where a resident simply sells assets for full market value to a non-resident.

'Capital sum' is widened by section 729(4) (ex TA 1988, section 739(5)) to cover sums paid to third parties at the direction of the individual or by assignment from him, and sums received jointly.

Where there is a capital sum as defined, the income accruing from the assets to the person outside the UK is treated by section 727 as that of the individual who received the capital sum. It will be noticed that tax under this section is not limited to the capital sum[146] but goes on forever—or at least for the duration of the life of the individual, or so long as income accrues to the non-resident. All that is required is a capital sum connected with the transfer.

15.6.1.4 The Third Head of Charge: Benefit Received by Non-Transferor

Where a non-transferor receives a benefit as a result of a relevant transaction, tax cannot be charged under the first two heads and is charged under ITA 2007, section 731 (ex TA 1988, section 740). There must be a relevant transfer and the receipt of a benefit by an individual ordinarily resident in the UK; the charge arises to the extent that the receipt falls within 'relevant income'.[147] 'Relevant income' is income accruing to a person resident or domiciled outside the UK and which may, by virtue or in consequence of the transfer or associated operations, be used directly or indirectly for providing a benefit for the individual, or for enabling a benefit to be provided for him.[148] The benefit must be provided out of assets available for the purpose as a result of the transfer or one or more associated operations. The allocation system in section 733 requires a comparison of (a) the total untaxed benefits, and (b) the available relevant income. The income arising which is to be charged under section 733 is the smaller of (a) and (b).[149] ITA 2007, section 735 (ex TA 1988, section 740(5)) provides a limited role for the remittance basis if the individual receiving the benefit is not domiciled in the UK; this was amended by FA 2008.[150]

Thus, as with section 720, there must be an initial transfer of assets, either alone or in conjunction with associated operations, and, as a result, income must become payable to a person resident or domiciled outside the UK; further, the person chargeable must be an individual ordinarily resident in the UK. Also like section 720, various supporting provisions, including ITA 2007, sections 748–749 on information powers, are made expressly applicable (discussed below at §15.6.2). In addition, the general defences such as an innocent purpose apply to section 731. The payment may also include a capital gains element; on interaction, see below at §18.5.4.

15.6.1.5 No Tax Avoidance Purpose Tests

Under a test inserted by FA 2006, and applying to transactions on or after 5 December 2005, none of the above provisions will apply if the individual meets an interesting test based on objective factors, viz that it would not be reasonable to draw the conclusion, from all the circumstances of the case, that the purpose of avoiding liability to taxation

---

[146] *Vestey v IRC* [1980] AC 1145, [1980] STC 10, (1980) 54 TC 503.
[147] ITA 2007, ss 731–733, ex TA 1988, s 740(2).
[148] ITA 2007, s 718(1) and 733(1), ex TA 1988, s 740(3).
[149] ITA 2007, s 724, ex TA 1988, s 743(5).
[150] ITA 2007, s 735, replaced by FA 2008 as ss 735 and 735A.

was the purpose or one of the purposes for which the relevant transaction or any of them was effected.[151] There is an alternative test under which all the relevant transactions were genuine commercial transactions, ie effected in the course of trade or business and for its purposes (the test also applied to a transaction with a view to setting up a trade or business). There is also an arm's-length test (ITA 2007, section 738). 'Tax' means any revenue within the ambit of HMRC's responsibilities and 'revenue' means taxes, duties and NICs.[152] Foreign taxes are therefore not within the definition.

An older test still applies where transactions were carried out before 5 December 2005.[153] Here the person must show[154] to the satisfaction of an officer of HMRC that: (a) the purpose of avoiding tax liability was not the purpose or one of the purposes[155] for which the transfer or associated operations were made; or (b) that the transfer was a bona fide commercial transaction and not designed for the purpose of avoiding liability to taxation.[156] This was one of the first legislative attempts at an anti-avoidance clause; later clauses prefer references to objects over those to purposes.[157] The test of purpose is subjective.[158] Although the purpose test provides a defence to a charge under these rules, one cannot turn that round and say that the presence of a tax avoidance motive is a condition precedent to their applying.[159]

In *IRC v Willoughby*,[160] Lord Nolan said that it would be absurd to describe as tax avoidance the acceptance of an offer of freedom from tax which Parliament had deliberately made. A UK resident might opt not to own investments directly but to profit from the investments through the medium of the personal portfolio bond. The former would be liable to income tax at both basic and higher rates on the income from the investments, and also to CGT on chargeable gains realised on disposal. The latter, under the tax regime applicable to overseas life policies, would pay no tax on the income or capital gains until the maturity of the bond or the occurrence of one of the other specified chargeable events. Taking the option so offered was not tax avoidance.[161]

This pre-5 December 2005 test of purpose is applied only to the transfer in question, ie the one which conferred on the taxpayer the power to enjoy the income of the non-resident or the capital sum; it is not clear whether a subsequent tax-induced associated operation may infect the initial transfer.[162] Taxation includes taxes other than income tax, eg death duties,[163] but, it appears, not foreign taxes.[164] The burden is on the taxpayer to bring the facts within the defence. There is no formal clearance procedure. Under self-assessment the

---

[151] ITA 2007, s 738, ex TA 1988, s 741A(5)–(7).

[152] ITA 2007, s 737(7).

[153] ITA 2007, ss 739 (all relevant transactions before 5 December 2005) and 740 (some transactions before that date), ex TA 1988, ss 741A–741C, added by FA 2006.

[154] On importance of burden of proof on the taxpayer, see *Philippi v IRC* [1971] 3 All ER 61, 47 TC 75.

[155] The 1936 test was one of the 'main purposes', but this was amended in 1938; contrast, eg ITA 2007, s 685, ex TA 1988, s 703 and TCGA 1992, s 30.

[156] ITA 2007, ss 739(2)–(4), and 751, ex TA 1988, s 741.

[157] See Avery Jones [1983] BTR 9, esp 18–30, arguing that they are the same; see also [1983] BTR 113.

[158] *A Beneficiary v IRC* [1999] STC (SCD) 134.

[159] *Carvill v IRC* [2002] EWHC 1488; [2002] STC 1167.

[160] [1997] STC 995.

[161] *IRC v Willoughby* [1997] STC 995, 1001–02, *per* Lord Nolan; the question whether the transaction came within (b) as a bona fide commercial transaction was deliberately left open.

[162] See *IRC v Herdman* [1969] 1 All ER 495, 45 TC 394.

[163] *Sassoon v IRC* (1943) 25 TC 154.

[164] *IRC v Herdman* [1969] 1 All ER 495, (1969) 45 TC 394.

taxpayer must disclose any income or benefit assessable under these rules and whether reliance is placed on the purpose defence.[165] A court looking for a person's purpose is entitled to look at what he did subsequently.[166]

15.6.2 Elements

15.6.2.1 Transfer of Assets

For all three heads of charge there must be a transfer of assets or operations associated with the transfer.[167] Further, the income accruing to the non-resident must accrue by virtue of, or in consequence of, that transfer or those operations.[168] It is not necessary that the income should come from the transferred assets. The situs of the assets is unimportant. The term 'asset' is defined to include property or rights of any kind;[169] it has been construed in a way similar to that for CGT, and so includes rights under a contract of employment.[170] The term 'transfer' is defined to include the creation of rights or property.[171]

15.6.2.2 Connecting Factors

The transferee must be either not resident or not domiciled in the UK when the income accrues, so disregarding questions of residence when the transfer is made.[172] Whether ITA 2007, section 718 (ex section 739(2) and (3)) applies if the transferor becomes ordinarily resident in the UK only after the transfer is not completely clear, but it is unlikely that it does.[173] They clearly do apply whether or not the particular individual, ie the one with the power to enjoy or in receipt of a capital sum, was ordinarily resident in the UK at the time of the transfer.[174]

15.6.2.3 Associated Operations

The associated operations may be by the transferor, or the transferee or any other person.[175] The scope of an 'associated operation' is widely defined in ITA 2007, section 719 (ex TA 1988, section 742(1)) as operations of any kind affected by any person in relation to any of the assets, or income or assets representing those assets or that income. Thus, the transfer of shares or a partnership to a company,[176] taking up residence or domicile

---

[165] Revenue Interpretation (April 1999).
[166] Salmon LJ in *Philippi v IRC* (1971) 47 TC 75, 113–14.
[167] Now defined by ITA 2007, ss 715–719.
[168] See *Vestey's Executors v IRC* [1949] 1 All ER 1108, 31 TC 1; and see below §15.6.4.
[169] ITA 2007, s 717, ex TA 1988, s 742(9)(b).
[170] *IRC v Brackett* [1986] STC 521, 60 TC 134.
[171] ITA 2007, s 716(2), ex TA 1988, s 742(9)(b).
[172] *Congreve v IRC* [1946] 2 All ER 170, 30 TC 163.
[173] But in pre-(1980) *Vestey* days a person within s 739(2) who acquired UK ordinary residence after the transfer was caught (*IRC v Herdman* [1969] 1 All ER 495, 45 TC 394). For discussion, see Venables (1991) 1 *The Offshore Tax Planning Review* 19.
[174] ITA 2007, s 718, ex TA 1988, s 739(1A)(a); added 1997 to reverse, in part, *IRC v Willoughby* [1997] STC 995.
[175] Eg *Lord Chetwode v IRC* [1977] STC 64, [1977] 1 All ER 638.
[176] *Latilla v IRC* [1943] 1 All ER 265, (1943) 25 TC 107.

overseas,[177] an exchange of debentures[178] and the making of a will,[179] have all been held to be associated operations; mere inactivity resulting in intestate succession is not.[180] The issue of debentures may be associated with an acquisition of rights.[181]

15.6.2.4 Power to Enjoy (First Head Only)

Under the first head—and only under that head—there has to be a power to enjoy income. This requirement is satisfied if any of the following sets of circumstances exists:[182]

(1)   The income is in fact so dealt with by any person as to be calculated, at some point of time and whether or not in the form of income, to enure for the benefit of the individual (whom we will call A). 'So dealt with' denotes some element of dealing;[183] something passive, such as retention and investment of income for future use, may qualify.[184]

(2)   The receipt or accrual of the income operates to increase the value to A of assets held by A or for A's benefit. The income need not be received by the transferor, but it must increase the value of the transferor's assets, as where assets were transferred to a non-resident company in return for promissory notes; income subsequently accruing to the company increased the value of the notes.[185] Similarly, where a vendor transferred shares to a company but left the purchase money outstanding, it was held that he had the power to enjoy the income accruing to the company in the form of dividends, since the income of the company increased by the value of the right to recover the debt.[186] This seems open to question, at least where the company could always meet its obligations—but the legislation directs attention to substance not form (see below).

(3)   A receives or is entitled to receive, at any time, any benefit provided or to be provided out of that income, or out of moneys that are or will be available for the purpose by reason of the effect or successive effects of the associated operations on that income and on any assets which directly or indirectly represent that income. This turns on actual receipt or entitlement to receipt by the transferor. The possession of shares in a company gives a right to any dividends that may be declared.[187] There is some doubt whether loans fall within this rule.[188] In *IRC v Brackett*,[189] the benefits provided included the provision of liquidity through the purchase of assets the taxpayer could not otherwise dispose of easily, the provision of money for repairs he could not otherwise afford and the payment of money in discharge of his moral obligations. These were held sufficient. Where liability arises under this head, the extent of liability is

---

[177] *Congreve v IRC* [1946] 2 All ER 170, (1946) 30 TC 163.
[178] *Earl Beatty's Executors v IRC* (1940) 23 TC 574.
[179] *Bambridge v IRC* [1955] 3 All ER 812, 36 TC 313.
[180] *Bambridge v IRC* (1955) 36 TC 313, 328, *per* Jenkins LJ.
[181] *Corbett's Executrices v IRC* [1943] 2 All ER 218, 25 TC 305.
[182] ITA 2007, s 723, ex TA 1988, s 742(2).
[183] Lord Simonds in *Lord Vestey's Executors v IRC* [1949] 1 All ER 1108, 31 TC 1.
[184] *IRC v Botnar* [1999] STC 711, 727 (para. 33).
[185] See *Lord Howard de Walden v IRC* [1942] 1 KB 389, (1942) 25 TC 121.
[186] *Ramsden v IRC* (1957) 37 TC 619; *Earl Beatty's Executors v IRC* (1940) 23 TC 574.
[187] *Lee v IRC* (1941) 24 TC 207.
[188] See Lord Normand in *Lord Vestey's Executors v IRC* [1949] 31 TC 1, 90.
[189] [1986] STC 521.

probably limited to the value of the benefit received and does not extend to the whole of the income accruing to the transferee.[190]

(4) A may, in the event of the exercise or successive exercise of one or more powers by whomsoever exercisable and whether with or without the consent of any other persons, become entitled to the beneficial enjoyment of the income. This is designed to apply where foreign trustees of a discretionary trust own shares in an overseas company controlled by persons other than the trustees. The term 'power' is undefined and therefore unlimited, save that it means something other than rights that come from pure dominion over the property.[191] The income which accrued to B will almost certainly have ceased to have that character before it reaches A; there is no rule of law which requires it still to have the character at that time.[192]

(5) A is able in any manner whatsoever, and whether directly or indirectly, to control the application of the income. For this, it will be noted, there is no need for the control to be for A's own benefit. It has, however, been held that a right to control investments is not a right to control the application of the income. Control of a company gives control over income through control over the directors.[193] However, the donee of a special power of appointment among a defined and ascertainable group of persons does not have the power required for this head,[194] a decision since extended to the donee of an intermediate power, that is a power to appoint among the whole world subject to the exclusion of a defined class of persons which included the donee.[195] Where a settlor has a power to appoint and remove trustees, it should not be assumed that the trustees will disregard their fiduciary duties and simply act as the settlor directs.[196]

As if (1)–(5) were not wide enough, it is further provided that when these tests are applied, regard is to be had to the substantial results and effects of the transfer or the operations, and all benefits accruing as a result of the transfer are to be taken into account regardless of the nature or form of the benefits and whether or not the individual had any rights.[197] This clause was intended to counteract the Cayman Islands legislation[198] reducing the legal character of interests of beneficiaries under trusts subject to Cayman Island law to that of mere spes or chance.

In determining whether a person has this power, the terms of any relevant instrument must be construed to ascertain their true legal effect; thus, if a person apparently able to exercise a power in his own favour would find such an appointment barred by the doctrine of fraud on a power, there is no power to enjoy under this head. The fact that the resident has no power to enjoy the income of the transferee is not conclusive. One must ask whether

---

[190] *IRC v Botnar* [1999] STC 711, 731 (paras 52–53).
[191] *Ibid*, 729 (para. 40).
[192] *Ibid*, 730 (para 45).
[193] *Lee v IRC* (1941) 24 TC 207.
[194] *Vestey's Executors v IRC* [1949] 1 All ER 1108.
[195] *IRC v Schroder* [1983] STC 450, 57 TC 94.
[196] *Ibid*.
[197] ITA 2007, s 733, ex TA 1988, s 742(3).
[198] *IRC v Botnar* [1998] STC 38, 41; this was reversed on appeal but on a different construction of the terms of the trust ([1999] STC 711).

A has the power to enjoy any income of any person; thus, control over the transferee is sufficient.[199]

HMRC officers have the most extensive power to demand information[200] in applying this section, both from the transferor and from any other person. There is some protection for solicitors[201] and bankers.[202]

15.6.3 The Charge

Under the first head the whole of the income of the non-resident person may be treated as that of the transferor, even though the 'power to enjoy' does not extend so far.[203] Logically, this should extend to all income, whether or not from the assets transferred; but in practice the Revenue appear to take a less exacting line. Under the second head the Revenue treat as taxable only the income of the non-resident derived from the transfer or associated operations.[204] As already seen, where the individual is not domiciled in the UK a remittance basis is used—where the third head applies.[205]

ITA 2007, section 731 (ex TA 1988, section 740) charges on a different basis—by reference to the benefit received to the extent that it falls within relevant income.[206] 'Relevant income' is income accruing to a person resident or domiciled outside the UK and which may, by virtue or in consequence of the transfer or associated operations, be used directly or indirectly for providing a benefit for the individual, or for enabling a benefit to be provided for him.[207] The section then proceeds along lines similar to ITTOIA 2005, section 641 (see *Revenue Law*, §31.6). To the extent that the benefit falls within the amount of relevant income up to and including that year, it is taxable as income of the individual. If the benefit should exceed that income, it is carried forward and may be made liable to tax in later years by reason of the existence of relevant income in those later years.[208] Where the person is not domiciled in the UK, a remittance basis is applied.[209] There is no charge if the benefit is not received in the UK. On a literal interpretation, a benefit received abroad and later brought to the UK escapes charge as it is not received in the UK.

These rules are deeming provisions and the courts will not allow one to deem too far, especially if this would mean that a person they deem fraudulent would otherwise escape prison. In *R v Dimsey* and *R v Allen*,[210] the accused had been found guilty of cheating the public revenue by committing certain offences in relation to the profits of companies liable to, but not declared for, corporation tax. Under these rules the profits of the companies

---

[199] *Earl Beatty's Executors v IRC* (1940) 23 TC 574, 590.

[200] ITA 2007, s 748(1), (2), ex TA 1988, s 745(1); eg *Clinch v IRC* [1973] 1 All ER 977, 49 TC 52.

[201] ITA 2007, ss 748(4) and 749(1)–(5), ex TA 1988, s 745(3).

[202] ITA 2007, s 749(6), ex TA 1988, s 745(4); strictly construed in *Royal Bank of Canada v IRC* [1972] 1 All ER 225, 47 TC 565.

[203] The Revenue view derives some support from the now overruled decision in *Congreve v IRC* [1945] 1 All ER 945, 954; (1945) 30 TC 163, 199, *per* Cohen LJ.

[204] *Whiteman and Wheatcroft on Income Tax*, 2nd edn (Sweet & Maxwell, 1976) §§19.57–19.59.

[205] ITA 2007, ss 726(1)–(3) and 730(1)–(3), ex TA 1988, s 743(3).

[206] ITA 2007, s 731, ex TA 1988, s 740(2).

[207] ITA 2007, s 733(1), ex TA 1988, s 740(3).

[208] ITA 2007, s 731, ex TA 1988, s 740(2).

[209] ITA 2007, s 735(1)–(6), ex TA 1988, s 740(5).

[210] [2001] UK HL 46, [2001] STC 1520 and also [2001] UK HL 45, [2001] STC 1537. On the Court of Appeal's consideration, see Morgan [2001] BTR 13 regarding the problem of double taxation.

could have been taxed to another person, and so the accused argued that there was no tax liability on the companies and so no criminal liability on their part. The judges reasoned that, although these rules deemed the income of the foreign entity to be that of someone else, it did not follow that it ceased to be the income of the foreign entity. The risk of double taxation was thought to be too unrealistic to worry about.[211]

The income caught is that 'which becomes payable' to the non-resident, and the House of Lords has held that no deduction may be made for the non-resident's management charges.[212] Expenses of collection are allowable, as are deductions and reliefs that would be allowed if the income belonged to the individual.[213]

When the income of the non-resident is in the form of a dividend from a UK company, that person will, as a non-resident, not be entitled to the tax credit, unless qualifying as an 'eligible non-UK resident'.[214] However, the resident whose income it is deemed to be is presumably so entitled. In the heyday of offshore funds it appears that the UK tax authorities were not very active in using TA 1988, section 739 even to charge a UK resident on his proportionate share of the income, apparently because these funds had a favourable effect on the UK balance of payments.[215]

To prevent double charges, ITA 2007, section 743 (ex TA 1988, section 744) provides that no amount of income may be charged more than once under these rules. The problem arises, for example, if the transferor who has a power to enjoy then receives a benefit. In such circumstances, the Revenue attribute the income as appears to them just and reasonable; this is one of several Revenue decisions under this Chapter specifically made reviewable by the Tribunal (section 751).

There is also a provision (section 747) governing the interaction of these rules with those on accrued income profits under ITA 2007, Part 12, Chapter 2 (see Revenue Law, §26.4).

15.6.4 Limitations

ITA 2007, section 718 is not completely unlimited:

(1) The provision applies only where the power to enjoy income or the receipt of a capital sum or of a benefit rests in or accrues to an individual. Intermediaries, such as UK trusts and companies, are not individuals, although, of course, transfers by such bodies may be associated with earlier or later transfers by individuals.

(2) The income must accrue to the non-resident person in consequence of the transfer or the associated operations. In *Fynn v IRC*,[216] an individual had a right to demand repayment of a loan from a foreign company which he had set up. He also had a charge on the company's assets. It was held that he had no power to enjoy the income accruing to the company in consequence of the charging of the assets of the company.

---

[211] See Lord Scott in *R v Allen* [2001] STC 1520, [57].
[212] *Lord Chetwode v IRC* [1977] STC 64, [1977] 1 All ER 638; on the meaning of 'payable', see also *Latilla v IRC* [1943] 1 All ER 265, 25 TC 107.
[213] ITA 2007, s 746, TA 1988, s 743(2).
[214] ITTOIA 2005, s 397, ex TA 1988, s 231(1). The term 'eligible non-UK resident' is defined in s 397(4) by reference to s 56(3), and includes EEA nationals.
[215] Edwardes Ker, *International Tax Strategy* (In-depth Publishing, 1974), ch 23, at 12.
[216] [1958] 1 All ER 270, 37 TC 629.

(3) The section applies only where the individual is ordinarily resident in the UK; non-residence short of ordinary residence does not suffice.

(4) All three heads are limited to situations where income accrues to the non-resident person. Investment of assets transferred abroad so that no income is produced therefore avoids these provisions.[217] The question whether a particular receipt is income is presumably to be decided by UK tax law in the light of the rights and duties arising under the foreign law.[218]

---

[217] For CGT anti-avoidance provisions, see below at §18.3.

[218] See above at §15.3. On inclusion of guaranteed returns on transactions in futures and options, see ITTOIA 2005, s 569, ex TA 1988, Sch 5AA, para 8, inserted by FA 1997, Sch 11, extended to options by FA 1998, s 97.

16

Source: The Non-resident
and the UK Tax System

16.1 Basic Rules

The taxation of the non-resident on income[1] arising in the UK is governed by three sets of rules:

(1) rules embodying the doctrine of the source: these limit but do not deny the non-resident's liability to income arising in the UK;

(2) rules limiting the non-resident's liability to basic rate or the dividend rate according to the type of income concerned, so making no attempt to charge the income to higher rates of tax: the converse of this is to limit the non-resident's rights to recover tax where total income is very low; and

(3) rules requiring a person paying the income to the non-resident to withhold tax.

The effect of these rules may be modified by applicable double tax treaty rules (see chapter twenty below). There are other administrative rules defining the ways in which the non-resident may be made liable for the tax, and especially when the tax may be collected from the non-resident's UK agent (see below at §16.6).

The changes to the tax treatment of non-resident companies made by FA 2000 were designed to go some way to equating the treatment of the UK branch or agency of a non-resident company with that of a resident company by recasting rules in terms of liability to UK corporation tax rather than simple residence (see above §§2.9 and 7.1, and below §19.4.1). Thus, the corporation tax references to 'branch' or 'agency' were replaced

---

[1] For capital gains, see below at ch 18.

by references to 'permanent establishments' (PEs) by 2003. Income tax retains the terms 'branch' and 'agency'. The overall effect does not disturb the three principal rules just outlined. See also chapter three above.

16.2   Source—General

It is a basic principle of UK income tax that tax is charged on income arising to non-residents from sources within the UK.[2] This is so stated for ITTOIA 2005, Part 2 (section 6), Part 4 (section 361) and Part 5 (section 621). Unfortunately ITTOIA 2005 does not use the simple technique for Part 3. In Part 3 (property income), section 260 tells us that this Part will tax income from a UK property business and from an overseas property business. Then section 269 tells us that both the UK resident and the non-UK resident may carry on a UK property business but—and here at last is the point—that only a UK resident may carry on an overseas property business. ITEPA 2003 has its own rules—Part 2, Chapters 4 and 5.

Previously these principles were expressed in the following provisions:

(1)   Schedule A—land in the UK (TA 1988, section 15);
(2)   Schedule D, Cases I and II—profit from any trade or profession carried on within the UK to the extent of the profits there arising (TA 1988, section 18(1)(a)(iii);
(3)   Case III—from any property (as defined) within the UK (TA 1988, section 18(1)(a)(iii)); however, certain types of interest are exempt (TA 1988, sections 47 and 48);
(4)   Case VI—any annual profits or gains not falling under any other Case or Schedule;
(5)   distributions by companies resident in the UK (TA 1988, section 20). However, the view of the ECJ is that, correctly analysed, the UK rules do not attempt to charge these dividends to UK tax at all (see above at §§3.3.3 *et seq*).

Corporation tax is charged on non-resident companies trading through a PE in the UK on the profits attributable to the PE.[3] The profits of a trade carried on in the UK but without a PE are chargeable to income tax, but this is subject to override by an applicable double tax treaty that would likely bar the UK, as source country, from imposing tax in this situation.

CGT is charged on the trade assets situated in the UK of non-residents trading through a PE.[4] Otherwise, an non-resident is not subject to UK CGT, unless ordinarily resident. The UK's refusal to use the source basis of taxation for CGT means that the boundary between income and capital gain acquires greater importance, and that when the legislature moves a receipt from capital gain to income, eg for premiums on leases[5] or transactions

---

[2] A UK patent is a UK source (CTA 2009, ss 914–915, ex TA 1988, s 524(2)); but see ESC B8. For another concession see ESC A12 (alimony paid by a person no longer resident under UK court order). For criticisms of source concept in multinational context, see Green (1993) 79 *Cornell LR* 18.

[3] CTA 2009, s 5, ex TA 1988, ss 6 and 11.

[4] CTA 2009, s 19(3)(c) and TCGA 1992, s 10(B).

[5] ITTOIA 2005, Pt 3, Ch 4 and CTA 2009, ss 243 and 244, ex TA 1988, s 34.

in land,[6] there are substantial implications for non-residents.[7] At Budget 2012, however, the Government announced it is considering new plans to tax non-resident companies, trusts, etc (not individuals) on capital gains on the disposal of UK residential property, from April 2013.

Example

John Smith is neither resident nor ordinarily resident in the UK, neither does he have a UK domicile. His five UK sources of income are as follows:

(1)	Rent from UK property	£3,000
(2)	Dividends from UK companies	£10,000 net
(3)	Duties performed outside UK with non-resident employer	£10,000
(4)	Duties performed in UK under employment with a non UK-resident employer	£2,500
(5)	Interest in the following UK government stocks: 3% War Loan (interest £3,500) 6% Funding Loan (interest £1,200)	£4,700

John Smith's items of assessable income would be (1), (2) and (4) (total £15,500). Item (3) is not subject to UK tax and (5) is exempt because of the non-resident status. In calculating his tax liability two further rules need to be noted:

(a) *personal reliefs*—on whether he is entitled to these, see ITA 2007, section 56 (*Revenue Law*, §11.1.1);

(b) *dividends*—assuming there is no double taxation treaty and that Smith is not entitled to personal reliefs, he is not entitled to claim any credit on UK company dividends; there is no grossing up but there is no liability to dividend ordinary or upper rates. On this basis, the ECJ held that the UK did not attempt to charge these dividends to UK tax at all (see above at §3.3.3).

16.3   Place of Trade

A non-resident is taxable under ITTOIA 2005, Part 2 on profits from a trade within, as opposed to one with, the UK.[8] So, if the non-resident establishes a branch in the UK from which the trade is carried on, he is trading in the UK; by contrast, the presence of a mere administrative office, or perhaps a representative office supplying information in London, will not give rise to tax—provided the office does not trade. Although corporation tax has

---

[6] ITA 2007, s 755 and CTA 2010, s 819, ex TA 1988, s 776.

[7] On whether such re-designations are effective for treaty purposes, see Avery Jones in Vogel, Raad, Van Raad and Kirchhof (eds), *Essays in Honour of Klaus Vogel* (Kluwer, 2002).

[8] ITTOIA 2005, s 6(2), ex TA 1988, s 18(l)(a)(iii); see, generally, Norfolk [1980] BTR 72. This is subject to the application of a double tax treaty, which would likely deny the UK the right as source country to tax such trading profits.

moved to the concept of a PE, it still asks whether the trade is being carried on in the UK through the PE.

In asking where the trade is carried on, the UK has used two tests: the first, which is particularly appropriate to the sale of goods, asks where the contract was made; the second, and broader, test asks where, in substance, the operations take place from which the profits in substance arise. Both tests place the source in one, and only one, place. This all-or-nothing approach applies to determine the source of the income for the purposes of the UK's schedular system; however, this is quite separate from the question where the income arises. Although the trade is the source and therefore must have only one place, its income may arise in more than one place, as is shown by a 1991 decision on a double tax treaty point relying in part on a 1990 Privy Council decision.[9]

The mere purchase of goods in this country for export and resale abroad is not enough to amount to trading here.[10] What is enough was defined by Brett LJ in *Erichsen v Last*:[11]

> I should say that wherever profitable contracts are habitually made in England, by or for foreigners, with persons in England, because they are in England, to do something for or to supply something to those persons, such foreigners are exercising a profitable trade in England, even though everything to be done by them in order to fulfil the contract is done abroad.

16.3.1 Sale of Goods: Where is the Contract Made?

Most of the cases have concerned the sale of goods by a non-resident to someone in the UK, and the basic test has been that the trade is carried on where the contracts of sale are made.[12] The place of a contract is determined according to English domestic law—the place at which the acceptance of an offer is communicated. It follows that an acceptance by post completes the contract at the place of posting, whereas an acceptance by telex completes the contract at the place of receipt. This principle is comparatively simple to apply when a foreigner deals directly with the customer, but difficult questions of fact arise when an intermediary is employed. The fact that the foreigner uses an agent or stations an employee[13] in England is not sufficient to create a trade within, as distinct from with, the UK. Here, too, great attention is paid to the place of the contract.[14] The arrival of e-commerce might seem to put these simple concepts under strain, since the physical process by which the contract is created may take place through servers in many different parts of the globe. However, it is best to approach these problems simply and regard the Internet as just one more step in a process which began with telex machines—or even the telephone. Websites are little more than passive agents and should therefore be disregarded.

---

[9] *CIR v Hang Seng Bank Ltd* [1990] STC 733; *Yates v CGA* [1991] STC 157, 64 TC 37.

[10] *Sulley v A-G* (1860) 5 H&N 711, (1860) 2 TC 149n; cf *Greenwood v FL Smidth & Co* [1922] 1 AC 417, (1922) 8 TC 205 where the goods were sold in England; and *Taxation Commrs v Kirk* [1900] AC 588, PC, where the goods were manufactured here for export and not simply bought. The danger in the rule in *Sulley v A-G* is that a foreigner may employ an agent here to buy goods and yet the agent may have an undisclosed interest in the business. This may lead to evasion, especially when the agent is a relative of the principal.

[11] (1881) 8 QBD 414, 418; 4 TC 422, 425; see also *Neilsen, Andersen & Co v Collins* [1928] AC 34, 13 TC 91.

[12] Eg *Maclaine & Co v Eccott* [1926] AC 424, (1926) 10 TC 481. On importance of place of delivery, see Wills J in *Thomas Turner (Leicester) Ltd v Rickman* (1898) 4 TC 25, 34; but cf Lord Cave in *Maclaine & Co v Eccott*, 432, 575.

[13] As in *Greenwood v FL Smith & Co* [1922] 1 AC 417, (1922) 8 TC 205.

[14] Eg *Thomas Turner (Leicester) Ltd v Rickman* (1898) 4 TC 25, 34, *per* Will J.

Where a contract is made through an agent, the normal principles of offer and acceptance must be applied to determine where the contract is made. Where an agent merely has to consult his foreign principal before accepting contracts, the trade is carried on here. If, however, his sole function is to pass the offer to head office, which communicates directly with the customer, the foreigner is trading with, and not within, the UK.

In *Grainger & Son v Gough*,[15] Louis Roederer canvassed orders for champagne in the UK through the firm of Grainger and Son, which would pass on all orders and money received from the customers in the UK to Rheims, from where Roederer would despatch the champagne. The contracts for the sale of wine being made in France and both the property and the risk passing to the purchasers in France, the House of Lords held, reversing the Commissioners, that Roederer was not trading in, but with, the UK. There being no liability on Roederer, Grainger and Son was not accountable for tax as agents of Roederer.

The place of the contract distinguished *Grainger v Gough* from the earlier cases in which the courts had that a trade was carried on in the UK. In *Pommery and Greno v Apthorpe*,[16] the London agents of Pommery held stocks of wine in London which were used for all save orders for 'considerable quantities', and paid monies received into Pommery's London bank account. The court had little difficulty upholding the Commissioners' finding that the trade was carried on in England. The fact that Pommery had a principal establishment outside the UK, and that its sales in the UK amounted to only a small part of its total trade, was irrelevant.

16.3.2 Operations from which Profits Arise

The notion that the place of the contract determines the place of the trade is a very English notion since it combines the obsession with sale as the paradigm contract with the doctrine of the source. As Esher MR put it in *Werle & Co v Colquhoun*: '[T]he contract is the very foundation of the trade. It is the trade really.'[17] There has to be some practical limit saying how far the courts will go back in locating profits. The question is where the profits are made, and not why. So the courts do not go beyond the business operations from which the profits derive. Once again, the arrival of e-commerce does not change the nature of the issue to be resolved, although it may make the factual background against which the decision has to be made more fragmented.

The cases also show that the place of the contract is not a touchstone. In *Maclaine & Co v Eccott*,[18] while describing the place of the contract as the most important and, indeed, the crucial question, Lord Cave listed other factors, such as the place where payment is to be made for the goods sold and the place where the goods are to be delivered, and disclaimed any exhaustive test. The place of contract was further downgraded by Lord Radcliffe,[19] who described it as capable of being somewhat ingenuous in modern (1950s) business conditions.

---

[15] [1896] AC 325, (1896) 3 TC 462.
[16] (1886) 2 TC 182; cf *Werle & Co v Colquhoun* (1888) 20 QBD 753, (1888) 2 TC 402.
[17] (1908) 2 TC 402, 410, PC. See also Rowlatt J in *FL Smidth & Co v Greenwood* (1920) 8 TC 193, 199.
[18] [1926] AC 424, 432. To the same effect, see Scrutton LJ in *Balfour v Mace* (1928) 13 TC 539, 558.
[19] *Firestone Tyre and Rubber Co v Lewellin* (1957) 37 TC 111, 142.

The place of contract, although useful as a test in the area of simple sale, is less appropriate in the manufacturing sphere.[20] In *FL Smidth v Greenwood*, Atkin LJ said[21] that it was perfectly possible for a manufacturing business to be carried on here even though the contracts for the sale of goods are made abroad:

> The contracts in this case were made abroad. But I am not prepared to hold that this test is decisive. I can imagine cases where the contract of resale is made abroad and yet the manufacture of the goods, some negotiation of the terms and complete execution of the contract take place here under such circumstances that the trade was in truth exercised here. I think the question is where the operations take place from which the profits in substance arise.

In *Firestone Tyre and Rubber Co Ltd v Lewellin*,[22] the UK subsidiary (Brentford) of a US parent (Akron) made tyres in the UK and supplied them to foreign subsidiaries at cost plus 5%. The court held that the US parent was trading in the UK, as was the UK subsidiary, and that the location of the master agreement governing the trade between the parent and its subsidiaries was not conclusive. The operations, the supply of the tyres and delivery alongside ship in a UK port, took place in England, constituted the carrying on of a trade in England, and that trade, the Commissioners had correctly held, was the trade of Akron, not Brentford.[23] The obligation on Brentford to account to Akron for any profit in excess of 5% was of crucial importance here. It followed that Brentford, as the regular agents of Akron, could be assessed to the tax due from Akron.

16.4 Computation of Profits—Transfer Pricing

16.4.1 The Problem

Profits of a trade carried on within the UK will be computed according to the normal principles applicable to ITTOIA 2005.[24] TIOPA 2010, Part 4 (ex TA 1988, section 770A and Schedule 28AA) enables both the Revenue and the taxpayer to allocate profits arising from a business with concerns in several countries between those different concerns. The transfer-pricing regime in TIOPA 2010, Part 4 also enables the Revenue to counteract traders who seek to prevent profits arising in this country through the manipulation of prices; in such circumstances the price that would have been paid if the parties had been at arm's length will be taken.[25] Other ways of reducing profits are to establish in the UK

---

[20] Cf Lord Salvesen in *Crookston Bros v Furtado* (1910) 5 TC 602, 623.

[21] [1921] 3 KB 583, 593; (1921) 8 TC 193, 209. Cf Lord Esher in *Grainger & Son v Gough* (1896) 3 TC 311, 317. For an example, see *IRC v Brackett* [1986] STC 521, 60 TC 134; B was a property consultant working for a Jersey company created by a settlement of which he was the settlor. B was held assessable under TA 1988, s 739 (see above at §15.5) on his own account and on behalf of the company under the now superseded TMA 1970, s 79 (see below at §16.6).

[22] (1957) 37 TC 111.

[23] (1957) 37 TC 111, 143, *per* Lord Radcliffe.

[24] For example of problem, see *Taxation Commissioner (NSW) v Hillsdon Watts Ltd* (1937) 57 CLR 36, esp 51–52, *per* Dixon J. On application in purely domestic UK transactions, see *Revenue Law*, §21.10 and above ch 4. For material on the position in EU countries, see *Company Taxation in the Internal Market*, COM (2001) 582, Part II, Chapter 5.

[25] TIOPA 2010, s 147, ex TA 1988, Sch 28AA, para 1. On treaty practice, see Vogel, *Klaus Vogel on Double Tax Conventions*, 3rd edn (Kluwer, 1997), Art 9, paras 18–45. On Revenue practice, see the Revenue's *International Tax*

other aspects of business of an inherently loss-making character, such as administration or research. These are not necessarily harmful to the UK even though induced by considerations of tax saving. One must remember, however, that transfer pricing is not just, or even primarily, a tax issue. It is a vital part of business planning and management in any international concern. The scope of the UK transfer-pricing regime was radically altered by FA 2004, not only by being extended to domestic transactions but also by excluding many SMEs (see §4.6).

Before plunging into the current rules on transfer pricing, a different method of taxation should be noted, ie taxation of a group on a unitary basis by means of formulary apportionment. This abandons the present attempt to attribute particular profits to particular sources and takes a global (or unitary) view. Once the profit of the group as a whole has been ascertained, this method allocates the profits among the different entities by reference to a formula using criteria such as payroll, property and receipts.[26] This method has caused much anguish between the United States and the rest of the world, partly because it means that the worldwide profits of a group as taxed in each state are likely to exceed 100% in total, and partly because of the substantial compliance costs involved in negotiating the basis of taxation.[27]

16.4.1.1 Methods[28]

The international standard used in determining transfer prices for tax purposes is the arm's-length principle as stated in Article 9 of the OECD Model Tax Convention, which allows enterprise profits to be adjusted and taxed accordingly where conditions are made or imposed between associated enterprises that differ from those which would be made between independent enterprises. The OECD has published a list of its approved transfer pricing methods for implementing the arm's-length principle in its Transfer Pricing Guidelines.[29] The issue of transfer pricing has become highly topical, not least because of extreme US legislative reaction to a small-scale problem. The problem arises in various contexts. In connection with the sale of goods, the problems generally concern the method by which the goods are priced. In some situations there will be an actual market in which identical goods are dealt in at arm's length. Where this is not so, another method must be sought. A figure may give a profit similar to that of the other companies in the same sector

Handbook, ch 15. On whether the Revenue's powers under the now superseded TA 1988, s 770 could be widened by a double tax treaty, see Oliver [1970] BTR 388, 396. For important OECD guidance, see the latest version of the OECD *Transfer Pricing Guidelines for Multinational Enterprises and Tax Administrations* (22 July 2010, referred to in this chapter as the 'OECD Guidelines'). In 2012, the UN released a *Practical Manual on Transfer Pricing for Developing Countries*—see <http://www.un.org/esa/ffd/tax/documents/bgrd_tp.htm>.

[26] See Kaplan [1983] BTR 203; and McLure (ed), *The State Corporation Income Tax* (Hoover Foundation, 1984); reviewed in [1984] BTR 191.

[27] See above at §3.3.3.

[28] See generally Hamaekers, *Rivista di Diritto Tributario Internazionale* 3/1999, Staaten and Steuern, *Festschrift for Klaus Vogel* (Muller, Heidleberg 2001) 1043–65 and the *International Transfer Pricing Journal* published by IBFD Amsterdam. Many of the issues were discussed in OECD publications *Transfer Pricing and Multinational Enterprises* (OECD, 1979), and *Transfer Pricing and Multinational Enterprises: Three Taxation Issues* (OECD, 1984) 73–91. These have now been superseded by the ongoing OECD Guidelines, the current version of which are reprinted in the annual edition of van Raad, *Materials on International and EU Tax Law* (International Tax Centre Leiden).

[29] OECD Guidelines, Ch I discusses the arm's-length principle and Ch II discusses transfer pricing methods.

(the comparable uncontrolled price or 'CUP'),[30] or the yield on the capital involved may be employed. CUP, though attractive, requires great attention to detail in order to ensure that true comparability exists.

However, both these methods make a series of assumptions which may be misplaced, and the more usual methods are either cost plus or resale price, the latter being more correctly described as 'price minus'. Cost plus involves taking the cost of production and adding an appropriate percentage. This involves many problems in determining cost and the appropriate mark-up.[31] It may, however, be useful where semi-finished goods are sold, or when the subsidiary is, in essence, a subcontractor. It may also be useful for services. The resale price method begins with the price at which the goods are sold on to an independent purchaser and then reduces that price by a percentage to reflect the vendor's costs, expenses and a reasonable profit.[32] Here, problems arise over the appropriate mark-up, save where the goods are sold on very quickly with little risk to the person reselling and without having been subjected to any intermediate process.

Problems also arise in connection with royalty and trademark licence payments,[33] with the allocation of R&D,[34] head office and other central administration costs.[35] There are also many problems in connection with banking enterprises.[36] However, one of the principal current problems is the effect of a loan by one company to another within the same group but usually, although not necessarily, in different jurisdictions. This is known as the thin capitalisation problem (see above at §4.6). The UK now deals with the thin capitalisation through its transfer pricing rules.

16.4.1.2 Administration: The Taxpayer as Shuttlecock

Where problems of this nature arise, there will be obvious difficulties in negotiating with the Revenue to see whether TIOPA 2010, Part 4 should apply and, if so, how it should be applied. There are, however, even more substantial problems where the income tax folk may take one view but the revenue authorities in another jurisdiction—or even indirect tax folk in the same country—may take a different view. Where double tax treaties apply, it may be possible to use the mutual agreement and competent authority provisions to resolve these problems to avoid double taxation, but the time taken may be substantial.[37] Since 1995 a multilateral Arbitration Convention has been in force within the European Union (see below at §16.4.3).

16.4.1.3 Information Powers; Taxpayer Costs

The Revenue have extensive information-gathering powers. These are potentially extremely expensive for taxpayers in view of the compliance costs involved. It has been held that the

---

[30] Comparability must extend to many things, eg market conditions (comparable levels of demand), the market level (ie wholesale or retail), comparable goods, comparable volume (a large order attracts a discount) and contract terms (ie are there warranties, is delivery cif or fob, etc?): OECD Guidelines, Ch II, Pt II, B.

[31] OECD Guidelines, Ch II, Pt II, D.

[32] OECD Guidelines, Ch II, Pt II, C.

[33] OECD Guidelines, Ch VI.

[34] OECD Guidelines, Ch VIII.

[35] *Transfer Pricing and Multinational Enterprises: Three Taxation Issues* (OECD, 1984), 73–91; OECD Guidelines, Ch VII.

[36] *Transfer Pricing and Multinational Enterprises: Three Taxation Issues* (OECD, 1984), 45–70.

[37] *Ibid*, 21, ch 42. See more generally OECD Guidelines, Ch IV.

court has jurisdiction to allow a taxpayer to challenge a demand for information, not least because the taxpayer, under the statutory code, has no way of appealing against the demand for information, and a failure to comply with the demand entails a penalty.[38]

16.4.1.4 US Attitudes

Reference has been made to the US rules as reformed in 1986 and subsequently. There are two main problems for the rest of the world. The first is that the United States has decided to reject the OECD approach and provide that taxpayers should adopt a 'best method' approach. If the taxpayer has not adopted what the Internal Revenue Service (IRS) (eventually) regards as the best method, it is open to the taxpayer to use a comparable profits method (CPM). This may involve looking at a number of average-operating profits earned by uncontrolled distributors and seeing how their profits ratios compare. The taxpayer will be safe if the operating profit-to-sale ratio comes within the middle 50% of the range of figures established, ie between 25% and 75%. As so often with the United States, there are further incentives to compliance (ie overpayment to the United States) in the shape of semi-automatic penalties. The OECD approach rejects the idea of a 'best' method and prefers CUP, cost plus and resale price to profit adjustments. It also, very sensibly, states that administrators should refrain from making minor adjustments.[39]

Another problem concerns the transfer of intangible property. Here the US Internal Revenue Code (IRC) §482 requires the Internal Revenue Service (IRS) to make periodic adjustments to the sums received, ie to use hindsight. This is also completely contrary to OECD principles. Apparently, it arose because US rules allowed US companies to transfer intangibles to Puerto Rica at cost, so ensuring that all future income arose outside the mainland United States. The simple solution of stopping the transfer of such assets at such a low cost was not pursued as Congress got excited by the prospect of making multinationals pay a 'fair share' of US tax.

16.4.2 Current UK Transfer-pricing Rules[40]

Dissatisfaction with the existing transfer-pricing rules, when combined with the realisation that the change to corporate self-assessment in 1999 required changes, led to a detailed consultation exercise followed by proposals for reform which were implemented as part of FA 1998. The rules took effect for the first accounting period ending on or after 1 July 1999;[41] the new rules avoid some of the defects of the old. These rules, now rewritten as TIOPA 2010, Part 4, were amended in three directions by FA 2004. First, in response to ECJ rulings in discrimination cases, it was decided to extend the rules to purely UK-domestic transactions. Secondly, the rules were narrowed by excluding most SMEs; this change applies both transnationally and domestically. Thirdly, these rules were extended to cover

---

[38] *Beecham Group plc v IRC* [1992] STC 935, (1992) 65 TC 219.

[39] On non-OECD approved methods, see OECD Guidelines, Ch III.

[40] FA 1988, s 108 and Sch 16. The Inland Revenue Consultative Document was announced on 9 October 1997, [1997] *Simon's Weekly Tax Intelligence* 911. For comment, see Hadari (1998) *Can Tax Jo* 29. For similar proposals for change in Canada, see Vincent and Freedman (1998) 46 *Can Tax Jo* 1213.

[41] Transitional rules allowed existing joint venture arrangements to remain outside the scope of the new rules for a maximum period of three years from 17 March 1997 (FA 1998, s 108(5), (6)).

all cases of thin capitalisation; these had previously been dealt with, at least in part, by TA 1988, section 209(2)(da), which treated excessive interest as a distribution.

TIOPA 2010, Part 4 (ex TA 1988, Schedule 28AA) uses the arm's-length rule for transfer-pricing events. Under the self-assessment system, taxpayers must use this rule in making their returns and not, as previously, sit back and wait to see if the inspector raised questions on the accounts, and then ask the Board to make a direction. This change makes matters more equitable between taxpayers of different degrees of conscientiousness, as well as making the UK system more like those in other countries. The legislation applies to each transaction (or 'provision') separately[42] rather than having the broad sweep of the US Code (IRC §482). Payments of excessive interest by a thinly-capitalised UK taxpayer company under finance arrangements guaranteed by affiliates come within these rules. However, control is defined in a different way from the usual definition in CTA 2010, section 450; not only is a 40% interest treated as giving control, but also, as from 2005, persons acting together in relation to financing arrangements.[43]

The legislation applies only if the arm's-length principle means a potential tax advantage for UK taxpayers, ie it applies only to reduce a loss or increase a profit.[44] The legislation does not include provision for *secondary* adjustments to other taxpayers, but does enable the parties to make tax-free payments to each other to bring their cash position into line with the tax result.[45] An HMRC central monitoring system is intended to ensure uniformity of application of these rules. Board involvement is still needed in that adjustments to profits under these rules requires a Board determination unless there is a written agreement between the Revenue and the taxpayer.[46]

Before 2004, TA 1988, Schedule 28AA was excluded for all transfers between UK taxpayers.[47] This was achieved by saying that the actual provision was not treated as conferring a potential advantage in relation to UK tax if various conditions were met, ie the person was chargeable to UK tax and not exempt. However, FA 2004 changed this by removing that exemption. TIOPA 2010, Part 4 does not apply to foreign exchange and financial instrument legislation since these have their own rules,[48] neither does it apply for the purposes of calculating capital allowances, balancing charges or capital gains and losses.[49]

16.4.2.1 Adjustments

Where a company, A, resident in X, sells goods to B, a company resident in Y, the price may be increased by the X revenue authorities under TIOPA 2010, section 147. A 'corresponding' adjustment ought then to be made by state Y when dealing with the same company. Where both A and B are resident in the UK, the transfer-pricing rules give a right to the

---

[42] TIOPA 2010, s 147, ex TA 1988, Sch 28AA, para 1.

[43] TIOPA 2010, ss 148 and 160, ex TA 1988, Sch 28AA, paras 4 and 4A. added by F(No 2)A 2005, Sch 8, para 1.

[44] Potential advantage is defined in TIOPA 2010, s 155, ex TA 1988, Sch 28AA, para 5.

[45] TIOPA 2010, ss 195–196, ex TA 1988, Sch 28AA, paras 6 and 7.

[46] FA 1998, s 108, esp subss (5), (6) (not rewritten); for procedures to inform disadvantaged persons of rights of appeal, etc, where both are UK persons but the exemption in ex TA 1988, Sch 28AA, para 5(3) does not apply, see FA 1998, s 11. This also applies for persons within ex TA 1988, Sch 28AA, para 12(4): see now TIOPA 2010, s 212.

[47] Ex TA 1988, Sch 28AA, para 5(2)–(6).

[48] CTA 2009, ss 447 and 694, ex TA 1988, Sch 28AA, para 8.

[49] TIOPA 2010, ss 213–214, ex TA 1988, Sch 28AA, para 13; on oil companies, see ss 205–206 and 217, ex paras 9–11.

corresponding adjustment.[50] This may, in turn, lead to an adjustment to a right to treaty relief, for example where B is a foreign branch of a UK company.[51]

Corresponding adjustments, which are relatively straightforward, are to be distinguished from 'secondary' adjustments. These arise where A, a UK resident, buys goods from B, a foreign company, and the price paid by A to B is later reduced; there is no machinery for making B repay A and many good commercial reasons why B should not do so, but how should that part of the sum which has ceased to be a price for goods be treated for tax purposes? Under the 'secondary' adjustment the sum could be treated as a payment by A to B by way of dividend if B is shareholder in A, and as a loan in other circumstances. If the sum is a dividend, withholding tax may be due under a tax treaty; if it is a loan, A may be deemed to receive interest. These secondary adjustments are much loved by countries where theory prevails over pragmatism, ie not the UK.

16.4.2.2 Interpretation

The UK transfer-pricing rules contain express reference to the OECD Guidelines for construction purposes.[52] Some see this as a dubious delegation of a rule-making power to an inter-governmental quango; others express more practical objections to having to refer to a document published in an ever-changing loose-leaf format.[53] The UK precedent has now been followed by The Netherlands.

16.4.2.3 Administration

Transfer pricing may be financially important to government and fascinating to academics but is, potentially, hugely expensive and time-consuming to business. In response to a consultation exercise in 2007 following HMRC's Review of Links with Large Business, a team of transfer-pricing specialists was assembled at HMRC, charged with the goal of resolving transfer pricing enquiries within 18–36 months.[54]

16.4.3 The EU Arbitration Convention

The EU Arbitration Convention was to last for five years in the first instance, was extended to 2005 and is now renewed every five years unless a Contracting State objects in writing.[55] A compulsory arbitration procedure does not usually feature in double tax treaties, and the various technical committees, eg of the OECD and the United Nations, have usually been unable to support one. The US–German Treaty contains an

---

[50] TIOPA 2010, s 174, ex TA 1988, Sch 28AA, para 6.

[51] TIOPA 2010, ss 188–189, ex TA 1988, Sch 28AA, para 7.

[52] TIOPA 2010, s 164, ex TA 1988, Sch 28AA, para 2; see also IR Notes to Finance Bill 1998, paras 49–54, esp para 49, which states that the Schedule cannot be interpreted in a way which goes beyond Art 9 of the OECD Model Treaty. On story of OECD Guidelines, see articles by Elliott, Self and Morton [1995] BTR 348–77.

[53] Ault (1994) 22 *Intertax* 144.

[54] HMRC website, 'transfer pricing'.

[55] 90/436/EEC of 23 July 1990 and Code of Conduct 2695/5/04, with materials and related documents on the EU website at <http://ec.europa.eu/taxation_customs/taxation/company_tax/transfer_pricing/arbitration_convention/index_en.htm>. See also van Raad, *Materials on International and EC Tax Law, 2007–08*, vol 1 (International Tax Centre Leiden, 2007), 1809 *et seq*; Oliver [1998] BTR 389; Oliver (1990) 18 *Intertax*, 437. For critical EU Commission comments, see COM (2001) 582, Pt III, esp at 5.5. For detailed analysis, see Hinnekens [1996] BTR 154 and 272; and, on interpretation issues, see (1998) 8 *EC Tax Law Review* 247.

arbitration process—but only where both States agree. Article 27(5) of the OECD Model Tax Convention now provides for arbitration if the competent authorities are unable to resolve disputes within two years. Several recent UK double tax treaties also include an arbitration provision in Article 27.[56]

The Convention is concerned only with transfer pricing and builds on the mutual agreement procedures in double tax treaties. It does not mention 'transfer pricing' as such, but concerns 'the elimination of double taxation in connection with the adjustment of profits of associated enterprises'. The enterprise must be an enterprise of a Contracting State. Interestingly, the Convention is based on the former Article 220 of the EC Treaty. Interpretation is to be done by the national court. The enterprise may not use the Convention if it is liable to serious penalties.[57] Despite its name, the Convention does not provide for binding arbitration, as the April 1990 draft directive had proposed, but instead for the appointment of an independent advisory commission which is to advise the competent authorities in the Member States. The taxpayer may require the authorities to establish a commission if they fail to agree within two years of the matter being put before them. The authorities will make their decision in the light of that advice; they may ignore that advice only if they are agreed on an alternative outcome. The Convention is backed up by a Joint Transfer Pricing Forum, comprising Member State and business representatives with an independent chairperson, and a detailed Code of Conduct; the Code is not part of the Convention and is a political document.

The UK legislation implementing the Convention goes further than is required and compels the Commissioners to give effect to the agreement or decision made under the Convention by HMRC and any other competent authority or any opinion of the advisory commission.[58] This is to override any other rule of law.[59] Normal time limits for claiming reliefs are overruled.[60] The Revenue are given statutory authority to provide the advisory commission with information required under a request from the commission.[61] Any member of the advisory commission who discloses information acquired by him in this capacity is guilty of an offence unless it has already been made public or the disclosure is with the consent of the party supplying; it is a defence for that person to prove that he believed that the information had already been made public and that he had no reasonable cause to believe otherwise.[62] A prosecution requires the consent of the Commissioners or the appropriate DPP.[63]

---

[56] See Baker [2011] BTR 125 at 130. Baker draws the inference that the inclusion of an arbitration provision is now part of UK treaty policy, at least if the other negotiating party is willing to agree to it.

[57] Art 8.

[58] TIOPA 2010, s 126–128, ex TA 1988, s 815B, added by F(No 2)A 1992, s 51; on need to implement, see Inland Revenue, *EC Direct Measures: A Consultative Document* (1991).

[59] TIOPA 2010, s 127(3), ex TA 1988, s 815B(2).

[60] TIOPA 2010, s 127(5), ex TA 1988, s 815B(3).

[61] TIOPA 2010, ss 128(1), ex TA 1988, s 816(2A), added by F(No 2)A 1992, s 51.

[62] FA 1989, s 182A (not rewritten), added by F(No 2)A 1992, s 51(3); such provisions are authorised by Art 9(6) of the OECD Model Treaty.

[63] FA 1989, s 182A(5).

16.5 Advance Pricing Arrangements

TIOPA 2010, Part 5 contains statutory authority for advance pricing arrangements between the Revenue and the taxpayers[64]—as is practised elsewhere, most frequently in the United States.[65] The Revenue will make these agreements only if there is significant doubt about how the arm's-length principle should be applied;[66] the agreement must be bilateral but there may be multiple bilateral agreements.[67] The procedure is important because it goes wider than TIOPA 2010, Part 4. The agreement must be in writing and made as a consequence of an application by the taxpayer, T, to the Commissioners.[68] The matters which may be covered are: (a) the attribution of income (actual or prospective) to T's branch or agency in the UK; (b) and (c) the attribution of income (actual or prospective) to T's permanent establishment in the UK (if T is foreign) or elsewhere (and T is resident in the UK); and (d) the extent to which T's income is to be taken to be income arising in a country or territory outside the UK (this last is expected to be important where credit relief for foreign tax may be in issue).[69] The Revenue notes seem to assume that the presence of a double tax treaty will prevent the need for such agreements; however, T may wish to secure his position under unilateral credit relief. The list extends to (e) the treatment for transfer-pricing tax purposes of any provision made or imposed between T and any associated person.[70] This last category also applies to (f) any provision between T's North Sea ring-fenced trade and other activities.[71] If a mutual agreement is reached with the tax authorities of another country, the legislation imposes a duty on the Commissioners to make consequential adjustments to its agreement with the taxpayer.[72] Where a provision made between T and another party is the subject of an agreement, the equivalent consequential transfer-pricing rules are made to apply.[73] These enable the other party to use the price established in accordance with the agreement.

The advantages of such arrangements are that they remove late confrontation with one or other tax authority, they are binding on the Revenue and mean that there can be no penalties provided they are adhered to. They provide certainty and avoid double taxation, assuming that the other country also accepts them. The disadvantages are the amount of time, effort and costs incurred in assembling the information and making disclosure, the fact that the arrangements may be cancelled by the Revenue and the fact that some countries, eg France and Germany, will not participate. The French dislike is based partly on a

---

[64] TIOPA 2010, ss 218-230, ex FA 1999, ss 85–87; for practice, see Statement of Practice SP 3/99. See also Inland Revenue Press Release, 31 March 1999; [1999] *Simon's Weekly Tax Intelligence* 722.

[65] See also OECD Transfer Pricing Guidelines, Ch IV, Pt F.

[66] See Statement of Practice SP 3/99, para 19.

[67] *Ibid*, paras 11–14.

[68] TIOPA 2010, s 218(1), ex FA 1999, s 85(1).

[69] TIOPA 2010, s 218(2), ex FA 1999, s 85(2)(a)–(c).

[70] TIOPA 2010, s 218(2)(e), ex FA 1999, s 85(2)(d); on associated persons, see s 219, ex s 85(6); the limitation to transfer-pricing rules is in s 220, ex s 85(4).

[71] TIOPA 2010, s 218(2)(f), ex FA 1999, s 85(2)(e).

[72] TIOPA 2010, s 229, ex FA 1999, s 86(3); for penalties, see TIOPA 2010, s 227, ex FA 1999, s 86(4)–(9) and Statement of Practice SP 3/99, paras 55, 56.

[73] TIOPA 2010, s 222, ex FA 1999, s 87, applying TA 1988. Sch 28AA, paras 6, 7. FA 1998, s 11 (notice to the other party) also applies (s 223, ex s 85(5)).

dislike of other parts of the US system, notably the CPM which is designed to increase the US take at the expense of other countries.[74] The UK Revenue see a very limited role for such agreements.[75]

16.6   Administration: Assessing and Collecting the Tax

16.6.1 General

The rules for collecting tax from non-residents, introduced in 1995 and rewritten into ITA 2007, Part 14, Chapters 2B and 2C, have two limbs.[76] The first defines rules for taxing a trade carried on through a branch or agency here (see below at §16.6.2), and defines the circumstances in which the UK representative of a non-resident cannot be made liable for UK tax due from that non-resident.[77] Similar rules (see below at §16.6.3) apply for CGT. Further rules (see below at §16.6.4) limit the liability of the non-resident for income and corporation tax; other rules apply to paying and collecting agents.[78]

Many general UK rules impose an obligation on a person paying income to another to withhold income tax; some apply only to transnational transactions (see below at §16.6.4). In addition to these rules, a special rule applies to entertainers and sportsmen (see below at §16.6.5).

16.6.2 Trade Carried on Through a Branch or Agency: Income Tax

Where a non-resident carries on a trade, profession or vocation in the UK through a branch or agency, that branch or agency is treated as the UK representative of the non-resident and as a person distinct from the non-resident.[79] Liability for sums received continues even after the end of the agency.[80] If the branch or agency is a partnership, the partnership is the agent.[81] The income of the branch or agency comprises the amount arising directly or indirectly through or from the branch or agency, and the amount of any income from property or rights used or held by or for the branch or agency;[82] these expressions echo the words of the OECD Model Double Tax Treaty, Article 7. There are further rules for capital gains and insurance companies.

It is possible for a non-resident to carry on a trade in the UK without having a branch or agency. Such a non-resident is liable to UK tax under the self-assessment rules.

Three principal categories of agents are excluded. The first is the occasional agent, ie not in the course of carrying on a regular agency for the non-resident. This repeats words

---

[74] See, generally, Bertram and Lymer, Tax Research Network Conference.

[75] SP3/99 and Inland Revenue Bulletin, October 1999, 697.

[76] Smith [1995] BTR 241.

[77] On transitional relief preserving ESC B40 up to 2005, see Inland Revenue Press Release, 17 February 1995, paras 5–10, [1995] *Simon's Weekly Tax Intelligence* 283.

[78] Ex TA 1988, ss 118A *et seq*; see Southern [1996] BTR 375.

[79] ITA 2007, s 835E, ex FA 1995, s 126(2), (4); for definition, see s 126(8).

[80] ITA 2007, s 835E, r 1, ex FA 1995, s 126(3).

[81] ITA 2007, s 835E, r 3, ex FA 1995, s 126(5)–(7).

[82] ITA 2007, s 835(2), ex FA 1995, s 126(2). See also Inland Revenue Tax Bulletin (August 1995), 237.

found in earlier legislation, where they were described by one judge as 'apparently very vague'.[83] The second category is the defined broker.[84] A broker, unlike an agent, acts for both sides.[85] If the conditions are satisfied, the broker is not liable even though he acts regularly for the non-resident. There is no definition of the term 'broker'.[86]

The third category is the investment manager carrying out investment transactions for the non-resident.[87] The manager must be carrying on a business of providing investment management services, have carried out the transaction in the ordinary course of business and have received not less than the customary charge for the service. Further, the manager must have acted in an independent capacity.[88] Other rules may disqualify the manager from protection if he and any connected persons are beneficially entitled to more than 20% of the taxable income of the non-resident from transactions carried out through brokers and investment managers.[89] The 20% rule is softened to exclude situations where this percentage is exceeded owing to matters outside the manager's control (assuming the manager takes reasonable mitigating steps); this is primarily to prevent the agent from becoming liable just because of a sudden swing in the market. These rules are modified for collective investment schemes.[90] The reasons for allowing even 20% participation are concerned with managers wanting to put 'seed money' into investment schemes.

16.6.3 Capping Tax on Investment Income

16.6.3.1 Background

In principle a non-resident is liable to UK income tax in full on profits arising from a trade, profession or vocation carried on in the UK and from land in the UK. The same is true of other sources of income, provided the non-resident has a UK representative under the rules in ITA 2007.

However, if there is no chargeable UK representative, ITA 2007, Part 14, Chapter 1 (ex FA 1995, section 128) directs that the non-resident's tax liability to income tax on these other sources is limited to the tax deducted at source. It also directs that the income subject to such deduction is not to be aggregated with the non-resident's other income to calculate the tax due in respect of that other income.[91] As was seen above, not all UK intermediaries are representatives; the purpose of the rule is to prevent exposure to extra UK tax just

---

[83] ITA 2007, s 835G, ex FA 1995, s 127(1)(a); *TL Boyd & Sons Ltd v Stephen* (1926) 10 TC 698, 747, *per* Rowlatt J. For another example, see *Willson v Hooker* [1995] STC 1142, 67 TC 585.

[84] ITA 2007, s 835H, ex FA 1995, s 127(1)(b), (2).

[85] *Wilcock v Pinto & Co* [1925] 1 KB 30, 42; 9 TC 111, 130, *per* Bankes LJ.

[86] In general, the words of ITA 2007, s 835J, ex FA 1995, s 127 re-enact TMA 1970, s 82(1); however, s 82 defined a broker as including a 'general commission agent'. In *Fleming v London Produce Co Ltd* [1968] 2 All ER 975, 985–86, Megarry J said that 'general commission agent' must be construed eiusdem generis with broker, and that such an agent held himself out as willing to act for others. Rowlatt J once said that a general commission agent generally negotiates for commission; in that case the agent was held not to be a general commission agent when he paid for the goods as soon as he received them instead of waiting to pay the principal out of the proceeds of the sale (*TL Boyd & Sons Ltd v Stephen* (1926) 10 TC 698, 746).

[87] ITA 2007, s 835I, ex FA 1995, s 127(1)(c), (3); such transactions are defined in s 127(12).

[88] On which, see ITA 2007, s 835M, ex FA 1995, s 127(18).

[89] ITA 2007, s 835N, ex FA 1995, s 127(4)–(8); see Smith [1995] BTR 241, 244.

[90] ITA 2007, s 835Q, ex FA 1995, s 127(9)–(11).

[91] ITA 2007, s 811, ex FA 1995, s 128(1).

because the non-resident uses a UK investment manager.[92] FA 2008 brought a welcome flexibility by giving HMRC the power to make an order designating transactions as investment transactions for the purpose of these rules.[93] The list is published on the HMRC website.[94]

16.6.3.2 The Income

The limit applies to income under:

(1) ITTOIA 2005, Part 4, Chapters 2 and 3;
(2) ITTOIA 2005, Part 4, Chapter 11(transactions and deposits);
(3) ITEPA 2003, Part 9 or section 660 (certain employment-related annuities or social security benefits, etc); and
(4) income within ITA 2007, section 812, ie income arising from a business carried out through a broker or investment manager; here there is an exception for income chargeable under FA 1993, section 171(2) (profits of the underwriting business of a member of Lloyd's).[95]

The effect of these rules is to limit the non-resident's liability to tax. However, where the non-resident is entitled to personal allowances, the effect is to set those allowances against these heads of income first. Only if the allowances are not fully absorbed may they be set against any other income chargeable to UK tax.

16.6.3.3 Other Rules

The limit does not apply to a non-resident trust if there is a UK-resident individual or company as a beneficiary.[96] ESC A11, which allows the splitting of a tax year, has no application to ITA 2007, section 811, which applies only where the NR is non-resident for the whole year.[97] There was a similar limit for corporation tax but this was repealed.[98] It did not apply to profits of a corporate member at Lloyd's.

16.6.4 Deduction at Source

Various provisions require deduction by the person making the payment where the payee is non-resident, eg rent (ITA 2007, sections 971–972, ex TA 1988, section 42A), yearly interest (ITA 2007, section 874(1)(d), ex TA 1988, section 349(2)(c)), sale of patent rights (ITA 2007, section 910, ex TA 1988, section 349ZA), and copyright royalties and public lending rights (ITA 2007, sections 906–909, ex TA 1988, sections 536 and 537). These are a vital part of the system of taxing non-residents.

---

[92] ITA 2007, ss 813 and 814, ex FA 1995, s 128(2), (3); for earlier years, see ESC B13.
[93] ITA 2007, ss 827(2) and 835S, ex FA 1995, s 127(12), introduced by FA 2008, s 35 and Sch 12. Investment Manager (Specified Transactions) Regulations 2009 specifiy such transactions, including any transaction in stocks or shares, units in a collective investment scheme, securities or foreign currency. The regulation does not carry the usual SI number, but is nevertheless secondary legislation with full statutory force.
[94] HMRC international manual INTM269070.
[95] In addition to ITA 2007, ss 813 and 814, see ss 825 *et seq*.
[96] ITA 2007, ss 811–814, ex FA 1995, s 128(5), (6).
[97] ESC A11. The previous version was 'clarified' by Inland Revenue Press Release, 19 January 1996.
[98] FA 1995, s 129, repealed by FA 2003, s 155.

In this connection one must note the major changes made in the last decade reducing the scope of deduction at source for payments of interest and public revenue dividends. These should be seen in conjunction with other provisions on the exchange of information and as part of the UK view that tax on interest accruing to non-residents is better protected by the exchange of information than by a withholding tax. This view is consistent with UK attitudes but not with Continental ones, where bank secrecy has been treasured not so much as a way of evading tax as a way of protecting oneself against the power of the State, a problem which has of course been much more acute on the Continent than in the UK.

16.6.5 Entertainers, etc

This part of the law does not show the rewrite in a good light; the provisions which used to be TA 1988, sections 555–558 are now spread between ITTOIA 2005, ITA 2007 and CTA 2009. A charge is imposed on the profits arising where a non UK-resident performer, as defined, performs a relevant activity in the UK in the tax year.[99] The need for such a provision and its history are well explained by Lord Scott in *Agassi v Robinson*.[100] ITA 2007, Part 15, Chapter 18, sections 965–970 (ex TA 1988, section 555) provide for the deduction of tax from any payment or transfer made which is connected with the relevant activity.[101] Performers caught include entertainers and sportsmen. The task of prescribing and refining is carried out by regulations.[102] The Revenue accept that the obligation to deduct is subject to the provisions of the relevant double taxation agreement; thus, the UK–US Treaty grants an exemption where the gross receipts of the person do not exceed $20,000 in the tax year concerned.[103]

The regulations contain considerable scope for problems of interpretation and timing, but their main thrust is clear and they are widely drawn. Among matters to be noted is the rule that while the maximum amount to be withheld is the basic rate of tax, now 20%, the amount paid may be treated by the Revenue as a net sum, thus causing the sums to be grossed up,[104] a process which makes the effective rate of tax on the net sum 28%.

The scope of these rules was considered in *Agassi v Robinson*.[105] A, the well-known tennis player not resident in the UK, set up a controlled company to handle endorsements, etc. Sums were paid to the company by other non-resident companies, Nike and Head, under such contracts. A came to the UK to play in tournaments such as Wimbledon. It was not disputed that these payments could properly be attributed to his time playing tennis in the UK. However, A argued that what is now ITA 2007, section 966 had a territorial limitation; since it imposed a duty to withhold tax, it could apply only where the payer could be made to deduct tax, ie if the payer had a tax presence in the UK. Head and Nike had no such presence. Agreeing with Lightman J and reversing the Court of Appeal, the House of Lords held that it would be absurd to attribute to the legislature the intention that liability

---

[99] ITTOIA 2005, s 13 and CTA 2009, s 1309, ex TA 1988, s 555.
[100] [2006] UKHL 23, [2006] STC 1056 at paras 8 *et seq*.
[101] See comparative study by Sandler (1995), research sponsored by the Chartered Institute of Taxation (Kluwer, 1995).
[102] Income Tax (Entertainers and Sportsmen) Regulations 1987 (SI 1987/530).
[103] Art 16 of the UK–US Treaty (2001).
[104] SI 1987/530, reg 17.
[105] [2006] UKHL 23, 2006 STC 1056.

could in any and all cases be avoided by the simple expedient of channelling the payment through a foreign company with no tax presence here. If this were the case, the tax would effectively become voluntary.[106] Lord Walker dissented. The case concerns the liability of A; no attempt was made to use these rules to recover the tax from Nike or Head, a view which seems consistent with principle.

Then there is the European law issue. A similar provision of the German tax code imposing a flat rate tax on visiting entertainers and sportsmen was held to break Article 43 EC (now Article 49 TFEU) unless it gave rise to a lower tax burden.[107] As an American national, Mr Agassi was not able to use this line of argument.

---

[106] Eg Lord Manc, *ibid*, at [32].
[107] Case C-234/01 *Arnoud Gerritse v FinanzAmt NeuKoln-Nord Gerritse* [2003] ECR I-5933; see Hinnekens [2003] 12 *EC Tax Rev* 207.

17

Controlled Foreign Companies Resident
in Low Tax Areas

17.1   Introduction

17.1.1 The Current State of Play

Chapter IV of Part XVIII of TA 1988 is (still) entitled 'Controlled Foreign Companies' (CFCs). Its rules may be traced back to FA 1984. For reasons dealt with at §17.1.2 below, these rules look at particular non-resident companies and treat the income arising in those companies as subject to UK corporation tax in the hands of those with the right level of interest in the company. This is done even though the income has not been passed to the shareholders, and in particular shareholders resident in the UK, by way of dividend. It will be seen that the rules look at income and not capital gains; moreover, the regime applies to companies and not to individuals (or trusts or partnerships). As we shall see, the CFC regime has a number of other limiting features.

Since 1984 the rules have been changed both in detail and in substance on a number of occasions. In 2007, section 751A was added to deal with the situation in which the CFC had a business establishment in an EEA territory; this was to give effect to the important decision of the ECJ in *Cadbury Schweppes plc v IRC*[1] (see below §17.6). One may contrast the rather fierce tone of this proviso and the accompanying UK Draft Guidance with the

---

[1] Case C-196/04 [2006] STC 1908.

less strident approach of the European Commission.[2] Whereas HMRC see it as a rule to be carried out vigorously, the Commission seem to see it as the start of a dialogue.

The Government's 2007 discussion document on the taxation of foreign profits, which envisaged a move to an exemption system for foreign dividends (since implemented, see below §19.3), also contained proposals for major changes in the CFC area. The original proposal was to move from the present 'entity' approach—which looks at particular companies or entities—to a 'tainted income' approach. This proposal was ultimately rejected as unworkable, and replaced with one focusing again on entities.

At Budget 2011, the Government announced its intention to introduce a new mainly entity-based CFC regime that would levy a charge on only that portion of overseas profits that had been artificially diverted from the UK. The new CFC regime, introduced in Finance Act 2012, Schedule 20, includes a finance company partial exemption, resulting in an effective UK tax rate of one-quarter of the main rate on profits derived from overseas group financing arrangements. Interim changes to the existing CFC regime intended to pave the way to the final reforms were made by FA 2011, Schedule 12. These included a new exemption for companies with limited UK connection, and a further de minimis exemption from apportionment of income (subject to anti-avoidance rules). Draft legislation was issued in 2011 and revised in 2012 following yet more discussions. The new regime, which is to take effect for CFCs with accounting periods beginning on or after 1 January 2013, is discussed below at §17.7 after discussion of the (for now) existing regime.

17.1.2 Purposes

The recognition of a company as an entity separate from its shareholders, even of a 100% subsidiary separate from its parent, gave rise to many opportunities to defer the payment of UK tax on foreign profits leaving them in the hands of the foreign subsidiary which earned them. This could be viewed as a breach of capital export neutrality, and so many countries, including the UK, now have special rules designed to undo the effect of the deferral in certain circumstances. Some countries, including the UK, also concentrate on the type of jurisdiction in which the profits arise; in the UK these are low tax areas (a combination of the entity approach and the designated jurisdiction approach). The UK CFC legislation has a second objective which is to counter harmful tax competition by allowing the withdrawal of various exemptions from particular territories (see below §17.5).

The UK's CFC regime applies if, in any accounting period, a company is 'resident' outside the UK but is controlled by persons resident in the UK, and the company is subject to a lower level of taxation in that country of residence.[3] The CFC rules apportion the total income profits of the foreign company computed as for UK corporation tax (its chargeable profits) and any creditable tax, among all the persons who had an interest in the company during the accounting period. The ECJ has considered, and is considering, the applicability of the UK rules not only in respect of profits arising in EU Member States but also from

---

[2] EC Commission communication of 10 December 2007.
[3] Introduced by FA 1984, ss 82–108. See, generally, Arnold, *The Taxation of Foreign Controlled Companies: An International Comparison* (Canadian Tax Foundation, 1986); and Arnold [1985] BTR 286, 362. There is useful updating material in Sandler, *Pushing the Boundaries* (IFS, London, 1994). For an interesting critique of the very different US rules known as sub part F as they were, see US Treasury Policy Study December 2000 (available in electronic format from the US Treasury website).

sources outside the EU. A decision against the UK rules which applies to non-EU source profits would have the most serious implications.

17.1.3 Outline

A charge may be made only on a company resident in the UK which has a minimum 25% interest in the CFC.[4] The UK company must include the amount chargeable under these rules in its self-assessment return.[5] The inspector may not issue a closure notice or make a discovery assessment without Commissioner approval.[6] This means that the company's return may not be amended by an inspector without Commissioner approval—or with the company's written agreement. The normal self-assessment information rules apply.[7] The minimum 25% interest rule might seem to encourage schemes under which holdings are divided among other companies. However, the legislation used to have a 10% minimum, so showing that the Revenue saw no threat from such schemes. The answer is likely to be that commercial considerations prevented such schemes from getting off the ground unless they were very artificial, in which case other doctrines would apply.

The CFC rules apply only if the CFC is controlled by persons (not just companies) resident in the UK. This slightly confusing position means that not only companies but also individuals and trusts are taken into account when deciding whether the company is controlled by persons resident in the UK, but it is still the case that the actual charge is on a company. Thus, if a company is resident outside the UK but has 30% non-UK shareholders, 40% UK corporate shareholders and 30% UK individual shareholders, the company is controlled by persons resident in the UK and the CFC rules can apply; however, they apply only to the 40% UK corporate shareholders.

Further rules apply to dual resident companies.[8] The first is concerned with the question whether a company is a person resident in the UK, and refers to CTA 2009, section 18 (ex FA 1994, section 249) which concerns dual resident companies which are given single residence in the other country under the tie-breaker clause of a double tax treaty (above §13.6); section 18 makes such companies non-resident for general tax purposes. Section 747(1B) provides that section 18 is *not* to apply for almost all CFC purposes.[9] Its effect, therefore, is that the dual resident company is still resident in the UK for CFC purposes, eg it is a company to which profits of the CFC may be attributed. Although the effect of these rules may be discerned, the purpose behind them is obscure. The rules were originally proposed as protection for the UK tax base from possible effects of the 2002 changes exempting UK-resident companies from corporation tax on the capital gains arising on the disposal of large shareholdings, but the final link is not clear.[10]

Whether obscure or not, the rules applied only where the company became a dual resident after 31 March 2002. Unfortunately it emerged that pre-2002 companies were

---

[4] TA 1988, s 747(5), as amended by FA 1998, Sch 17, para 3.
[5] TA 1988, s 747(4)(a) and FA 1998, Sch 18, para 8, third step.
[6] TA 1988, s 754B, added by FA 1998, Sch 17.
[7] Earlier specific powers were repealed by FA 1998, Sch 17, para 12; see Inland Revenue Notes on the Finance Bill, para 15.
[8] TA 1988, s 747(1B), added by FA 2002, s 90.
[9] The only purpose for which it does apply is s 747(1)(a)—is it resident outside the UK?
[10] *Simon's Finance Act Handbook 2002* (Butterworths, 2002), 84; the *Handbook* contains other subtle points.

continuing to be used, and so such companies are treated as resident in the UK if they fulfil either of two conditions after 21 March 2006; the details of these conditions are beyond the scope of this book.[11] A further rule was added in 2008. In determining the chargeable profits to be attributed, account must be taken of any profits held by trustees of a settlement in relation to which the company is a settlor or beneficiary.[12] Supplementary rules are designed to prevent a double charge to tax when the trust income is later distributed.[13]

There are a number of major exceptions to the CFC rules[14] (see below at §17.5).

Where profits are apportioned to a UK company in this way, ITA 2007, section 720 (ex TA 1988, section 739) must also be considered. When the ITA 2007 rules would treat the profits of the CFC attributed to the UK-resident shareholders as the profits of an individual, the ITA 2007 rules are excluded.[15]

In order to prevent the avoidance of the 25% minimum by fragmentation of share ownership, it is provided that shares held by connected or associated persons are to be taken into account in calculating the extent of the interest.[16] This does not mean that the connected or associated persons are liable to tax under these rules, or that the amounts apportioned to them are taxable in the hands of the UK-resident taxpayer.

The rules impose a charge on the UK-resident company to a sum equal to UK corporation tax. They do not allow the Commissioners to go further and attribute the UK-resident company profits amongst those with interests in the UK company.

Tax on the amount apportioned to, and chargeable on, a UK company is attributed to the accounting period of the UK company in which the relevant accounting period of the CFC ends.[17]

Where the CFC keeps its accounts in a currency other than sterling, the chargeable profits are calculated in that foreign currency for the purpose of these rules.[18] The figures are translated into sterling by reference to the London closing exchange rate for the two currencies concerned for the last day of the accounting period concerned.[19]

17.2 Definitions

17.2.1 Residence

The legislation applies only where the company is not resident in the UK but is resident in a country with a lower rate of tax.[20] This is one of the unusual situations in which the UK tax system, having decided that a company is not resident in the UK, must determine exactly where the company is resident; the rules are therefore artificial. The basic rule is

---

[11] FA 2002, s 90, as amended by FA 2006, s 78.
[12] TA 1988, s 747(6), para (ab); added by FA 2008, s 64.
[13] TA 1988, s 747(7)–(9), added by FA 2008, s 64.
[14] TA 1988, s 748.
[15] TA 1988, s 747(4)(b).
[16] TA 1988, s 747(5)(b).
[17] TA 1988, s 754(2).
[18] FA 1993, ss 92–92E as added by FA 2004 (see above §5.4); the addition of these rules meant that s 747A was superfluous and it was repealed by FA 2005, Sch 7, para 24.
[19] TA 1988, s 747(4B), 748(5), 750(8), Sch 24, para 11A(5)–(7), added by FA 1995.
[20] TA 1988, s 747(1)(c).

that a company is regarded as resident in any territory in which, throughout the relevant accounting period, it is liable to tax (whether or not it actually pays any) by reason of its domicile, residence or place of management.[21] These phrases are designed to distinguish tax on the basis of residence from tax on the basis of source. Presumably, this question is determined by reference to the UK tax system's assessment of the foreign tax law; the question whether the entity is a company is, again, presumably to be decided by UK tax law.

Where the company is liable to tax in more than one country, those people with more than 50% of the interests which are chargeable under TA 1988, section 747 may select the territory.[22] This test is not straightforward because of the reference to those chargeable under section 747. If all those with interests in the CFC are companies resident in the UK, those with 51% will be able to elect. If only 60% of those with interests in the company are companies resident in the UK, one looks to find a majority in that 60%. The selected majority are very accurately described as those with 'the majority assessable interest'.[23] In order to prevent over-nice (and expensive) arguments, the question whether there is an assessable interest is framed in terms of whether it is 'likely' that the company would be chargeable.[24] Failing such an election one looks first to the place of effective management, followed by the situs of the majority of the assets; as a last resort the Revenue officer may designate the country.[25] These elections and designations are irrevocable.[26]

If no territory of residence can be found under these rules, the company is presumed to be resident in a territory with a lower rate of tax.[27]

17.2.2 Control

17.2.2.1 Overview

For the purposes of defining control, the close company rules are generally used.[28] It is necessary to examine whether 51% of those with interests in the company are resident in the UK as opposed to the company being in the hands of five or fewer participators.[29]

The control rules have had to be widened. First, and following the example of the transfer-pricing rules, the CFC rules provide that the test of control is satisfied if a single UK-resident person controls 40% of the CFC while another person controls at least 40%. This is aimed at certain joint venture structures. However, this extension does not apply if the non-resident controls more than 55% of the interests' rights and powers.[30] Moreover, the fact of joint venture partnership does not make them partners for these rules. Secondly,

---

[21] TA 1988, s 749(1); these words are familiar to international tax specialists in other contexts: see OECD Model Treaty, Art 4(1).

[22] TA 1988, ss 749(4), 749A(1); for procedures, see s 749A generally.

[23] TA 1988, s 749(8).

[24] TA 1988, s 749(9).

[25] TA 1988, s 749(2), (3), (6).

[26] TA 1988, s 749A(1)(b).

[27] TA 1988, s 749(5).

[28] TA 1988, s 756(3), referring to CTA 2010, s 882, ex TA 1988, s 416. The definition of 'loan creditor' is in CTA 2010, s 453, ex s 417(7)–(9).

[29] TA 1988, s 756(3).

[30] TA 1988, ss 747(1)(A), 755D, added by FA 2000, Sch 31, paras 2, 4.

it is provided that in determining whether UK residents control the company, account is taken of any rights to income, proceeds of disposal on a disposal of all the share capital and/or assets on a winding up. This was to counter a situation in which UK residents were entitled to all the company's profits but an offshore trust held more than 50% of the shares.[31]

17.2.2.2 Interests

Close company rules are also used to see whether a person has an 'interest' in a company. Rights considered to establish interest are share capital, voting rights, a right to receive distributions, or a right to secure that income or assets may be applied directly or indirectly for someone's benefit.[32] Apart from the exclusion of loan creditors,[33] the only softening is that where entitlement to secure the application of a company's income or assets for a person's benefit is contingent upon a default of the company under any agreement, this is an 'interest' only if the default has occurred.[34]

17.2.2.3 Other

The rules include both indirect control[35] and the close company attributed ownership provisions (see above §10.2.2).[36]

17.2.3 Other Definitions

17.2.3.1 Accounting Periods

These are defined as for corporation tax; however, a period begins when a company comes under the control of UK residents and ends when it ceases to be so.[37]

17.2.3.2 Creditable Tax

This is defined to comprise:

(1) any double taxation relief which would be available if the foreign company's chargeable profits were liable to corporation tax, in respect of any foreign tax attributable to income comprised in those chargeable profits;
(2) income tax deducted at source from income received by the company which could be set off against such corporation tax; and
(3) income or corporation tax actually charged on or borne by the chargeable profits and not repayable.[38]

---

[31] TA 1988, s 755D(1A), added by FA 2008, s 64.
[32] TA 1988, s 749B(1), (3), (4).
[33] TA 1988, s 749B(2); defined by CTA 2010, s 453, ex s 417(7)–(9).
[34] TA 1988, s 749B(4).
[35] TA 1988, s 749B(5).
[36] CTA 2010, s 451; these rules are important where relatives, etc, are not UK residents.
[37] TA 1988, s 751(1)–(5A); note procedural rights and obligations of the Revenue in TA 1988, s 751 (4)–(5A).
[38] TA 1988, s 751(6).

17.2.3.3 Trading Company

This is a company the business of which consists wholly or mainly of the carrying on of a trade or trades.[39] Companies dealing in shares, securities, land, trade, or commodities or financial futures are therefore classed as trading companies.

17.3 Territories with a Lower Level of Taxation

A company is subject to a lower level of taxation only if the local tax paid is less than three-quarters of 'the corresponding UK tax';[40] before 1993 the fraction was one-half. The change was a delayed reaction to the general reduction in UK corporation tax rates since 1984. Some foreign tax systems responded to this rule by creating so-called designer tax rates, eg making a company pay just enough tax to reach the 75% limit, either by letting the company choose its rate of tax or by setting two rates of tax for two types of income and then allowing the company to allocate its income between the two categories.[41] Such devices were stopped by FA 2000 with effect from 6 September 1999.[42] The friendly countries indulging in this behaviour were Guernsey, Jersey, the Isle of Man, Gibraltar and Ireland.

The 'corresponding UK' tax is the hypothetical corporation tax on the chargeable profits of the foreign company computed on the assumptions described in TA 1988, Schedule 24[43] (see below). UK income or corporation tax actually charged on chargeable profits is deducted from the corresponding UK tax. Double taxation relief attributable to the local tax is not taken into account.[44] In applying these rules, any application under section 751A is disregarded.

Where the CFC has income which is not subject to UK tax, the foreign tax paid in the territory is reduced proportionately.[45] This is to ensure that the right amount of foreign tax is taken into account. For the same reason the total foreign tax paid by the CFC is reduced by any repayment of the tax (or credit) made to a person other than the CFC.[46]

Local tax is confined to tax paid under the law of the CFC's territory of residence[47] and does not include tax paid or suffered in a third territory. Since the CFC is assumed to be resident in the UK for the purposes of computing its chargeable profits, third territory taxes are taken into account under the normal double taxation relief rules in computing the corresponding UK tax with which the local tax is being compared. The local tax paid by the CFC excludes those taxes which are computed on some basis other than profits. A list of those territories not regarded by the Revenue as low tax countries was published in 1984.[48] A list of countries outside the CFC rules is now set out in a statutory instrument (see below at §17.5.5).

---

[39] TA 1988, s 756(1).
[40] TA 1988, s 750, as amended by FA 1993, s 119(1), (2); on accounts in foreign currency, see s 750(5)–(8), added by FA 1995, Sch 25, para 5.
[41] Inland Revenue Press Release, 6 September 1999.
[42] TA 1988, s 750A, added by FA 2000, Sch 31, para 3.
[43] TA 1988, s 750(3).
[44] TA 1988, s 750(3)(b).
[45] TA 1988, s 750(1A), added by FA 2005, s 120 with effect from 1 December 2004.
[46] TA 1988, s 750(1B), added by FA 2005, s 120 with effect from 1 December 2004.
[47] TA 1988, s 750(1).
[48] See [1985] *Simon's Tax Intelligence* 469.

17.4   The Apportionment Process and its Assumptions

17.4.1 *Apportioning among Interests*

The CFC rules on apportionment now use the concept of 'relevant interests'.[49] They begin with the simple case where all the 'relevant interests' in the CFC are held by persons who have been resident or non-resident (in the UK) throughout the relevant accounting period;[50] in addition, a company with an intermediate interest[51] in the CFC must also have the character of an ordinary shareholding in the CFC itself. In such a case, the apportionment is in direct proportion to the percentage of the issued ordinary share capital of the CFC, as represented in accordance with rules in TA 1988, section 752B,[52] which direct how the apportionment is to be carried out where the shares are held indirectly[53] or are not held throughout the period—or both.[54] Direct and indirect interests are defined.[55]

Where the same interest in a CFC is held directly by one UK-resident company and indirectly by another, or others, the rules treat the interest as held solely by the one with the more direct interest.[56]

Shares may be held by a person, eg an individual or a trust, who is not a UK-resident company but is connected or associated with such a company having a relevant interest in the CFC. Such persons are called 'related persons'.[57] Related persons may have relevant interests, so rules are required to determine when profits can be attributed to them and when to the company to which they are related. Thus, if R, the related person, has an interest in the CFC, it will not be 'relevant' if held indirectly through another UK-resident company or through another related person. Since the concept of related person may be extended to a company, R's interest is also ignored if a UK-resident company has a relevant interest in R.[58]

Any interest held in a fiduciary or representative capacity may be treated as held by the person or persons for whose benefit it is held.[59]

17.4.2 *Assumptions in Calculating CFC's Chargeable Profits*

17.4.2.1 Basics[60]

The CFC is deemed to be resident in the UK. The company's income is computed under the rules in TA 1988, Schedule 24. The company may also be treated as using a foreign currency in computing its profits.[61]

---

[49] TA 1988, s 752; 'relevant interests' are defined in s 752A; different rules applied before self-assessment.
[50] TA 1988, s 752(2).
[51] Defined in TA 1988, s 752C(4).
[52] TA 1988, s 752(3).
[53] TA 1988, s 752B(1)–(3).
[54] TA 1988, s 752B(4), (5).
[55] TA 1988, s 752C(1).
[56] TA 1988, s 752A(3).
[57] TA 1988, s 752A(4)–(8).
[58] TA 1988, s 752A(6).
[59] TA 1988, s 752C(5), (6).
[60] TA 1988, Sch 24, paras 1–4. On accounting periods of insurance companies, see ss 755A–755C.
[61] TA 1988, Sch 24, para 11A, added by FA 1995, Sch 25, para 6.

17.4.2.2 Continued Residence

To allow certain reliefs and allowances to be carried forward, rules ensure the continuation of assumed UK residence over a number of accounting periods. The assumed residence begins with the first accounting period for which an apportionment under section 747(3) falls to be made, and continues until the company is no longer under UK control, whether or not a direction is made. For the purposes of carry forward of loss relief, the corresponding UK tax is assumed to have been computed for each accounting period since that for which the first direction was made, even if no directions have been made for subsequent periods. Losses incurred during any of the six years before the first period for which an apportionment falls to be made can be used.[62] Because capital gains are not attributed, capital losses are not allowed. The company, despite its deemed UK residence, is deemed not to be a close company.[63]

17.4.2.3 Reliefs[64]

It is assumed that the company has claimed or is to be given the maximum amount available of those reliefs which have to be claimed and allowances which are given automatically but which may be disclaimed in whole or part, unless any UK company or companies holding a majority interest disclaims any such relief or claims a smaller amount.[65]

Group relief and related provisions are excluded for the purposes of computing chargeable profits. Accordingly, the foreign company is not treated as a member of a UK group or consortium. TA 1988, section 343 does not apply on the transfer of a trade by another company to the foreign company. Relief may, however, be available on the transfer of a trade by the foreign company to a UK company.

17.4.2.4 Capital Allowances[66]

The full range of capital allowances, including scientific research allowances, is treated as available. Allowances for pre-apportionment periods are also available.

17.4.2.5 TA 1988, Section 584[67]

Relief may be given for unremittable foreign income (see above at §15.5).

17.4.3 Reliefs Available to the Chargeable UK Company

17.4.3.1 Own Reliefs

When the chargeable profits of the CFC have been calculated along with the right proportion to be attributed to the UK company, further rules permit the UK company to reduce its liability by using reliefs available to it. These include its own excess relevant allowances, such as loss relief.[68]

---

[62] But only in accordance with the rules in TA 1988, Sch 24, para 9.
[63] TA 1988, Sch 24, para 3.
[64] TA 1988, Sch 24, paras 5–9.
[65] The time limit of 20 months from the end of the accounting period may be extended under TA 1988, Sch 24, paras 4(2), 9(4).
[66] TA 1988, Sch 24, para 10.
[67] TA 1988, Sch 24, para 12.
[68] TA 1988, Sch 26, para 1.

17.4.3.2 Dividends from the CFC

Relief has to be given when the UK company having paid a CFC charge then receives a real dividend from the CFC[69]—assuming the dividend is not already exempt from UK tax under CTA 2009, Part 9A. Where a dividend is paid by the CFC out of profits from which the apportioned chargeable profits are derived, the gross amount of UK tax charged on UK companies in respect of those profits—'the gross attributed tax'—is treated as tax paid in respect of the profits concerned and, accordingly, as underlying tax for the purposes of double taxation relief under ITOPA 2010, Part 2. The full amount of gross-attributed tax qualifies for relief, even though some or all of that tax may have been reduced following a claim in respect of relevant allowances. This rule applies only where the dividend comes from the profits which have already been charged under these rules.

Any excess tax (such as a withholding tax but exclusive of underlying tax) qualifying for tax credit relief may be set against the gross amount of tax assessed on the UK-resident companies. On a claim by any of those companies, the amount of tax assessed on the claimant in respect of the chargeable profits of the company is reduced and, where necessary, repaid.

Relief for underlying tax is generally confined, under the terms of a double taxation agreement or the unilateral relief provisions in TIOPA 2010, section 14, to UK-resident companies that have a particular degree of control (normally 10% or more of the voting power) in the foreign company. This condition is deemed to be satisfied in considering whether any such company is entitled to the relief in respect of any of the gross-attributed tax.

Gross-attributed tax is not added to the amount of the dividend in determining the liability to tax of the person who receives that dividend. The effect is that when the UK company owns all the shares in the foreign company, UK tax on the dividends received should be completely offset by the tax already paid under these rules; subsequent dividends thus become tax free. Naturally, more complex results ensue when there is more than one person with an interest in the foreign company.

Special rules deal with dividends paid otherwise than out of specified profits in cases where only part of the chargeable profits of the foreign company are apportioned to UK-resident companies liable for tax thereon. In such circumstances, the gross-attributed tax is regarded as attributable to a corresponding proportion of the chargeable profits of the CFC (the taxed profits), and so much of the dividend as is received by, or by a successor in title of, any such UK-resident company is to be regarded as paid primarily out of taxed profits. For this purpose, a person may be a successor in title in respect of the whole or any part of the interest held by a UK-resident company in the CFC by virtue of which an amount of its chargeable profits was apportioned to that company.

17.4.3.3 CGT

Rules provide relief against any capital gains charge in respect of tax paid under these provisions when shares in the foreign company are subsequently disposed of.[70]

---

[69] TA 1988, Sch 26, para 4.
[70] TA 1988, Sch 26, paras 3, 6.

17.4.3.4 Double Tax Treaties and the CFC Legislation

In *Bricom Holdings Ltd v IRC*,[71] the UK company had 100% control of a company resident in The Netherlands. The profits of the Dutch company attributed to the UK company included interest received by the Dutch company from a UK source; under the UK–Netherlands Treaty, such interest income of the Dutch company would be exempt from UK tax. The Revenue argued that the Treaty did not have this effect and so the CFC charge could apply to the UK company.[72] The UK courts have agreed.

The Special Commissioners held that the charge arising under section 747 was not corporation tax as such but a charge of a sum equal to corporation tax on the various hypotheses set out above. The process involved three stages: (a) calculating the amount of profits of the foreign company on the various hypotheses; (b) apportioning the profits among the various interest companies; and (c) calculating the tax for each UK company. The interest received by the Dutch company lost its character as interest at the first stage.

The case went straight to the Court of Appeal from the Commissioners. The Court agreed that the interest could not be excluded from the CFC calculation just because it might or might not fall within the Treaty—but on different grounds. Millet LJ said that the CFC legislation was to be applied by assuming that the CFC was resident only in the UK and not as resident in both countries. Under the deeming exercise which followed, the interest was simply a measure by which an element in the notional sum was calculated and then apportioned to the UK parent. On this basis it was not necessary to decide whether the CFC charge was corporation tax or a separate tax, although Millet LJ doubted whether he would have agreed with the Commissioners on this point. Leave to appeal to the House of Lords was given but no appeal was made.

The *Bricom* case was a subtle exercise which avoided the fundamental question. That question has since been addressed in other countries. The general approach is that there is no conflict between the CFC rules and the Treaty, but a dissenting voice has come from France.[73] It should also be noted that the 2003 revisions to the OECD Commentary Article 1 (paragraph 23) expressly acknowledge that CFC rules are a legitimate instrument to protect the domestic tax base.

17.5 Exclusions

Some exclusions are structural. Thus, the rules apply only:

(1)　to income, and not to capital gains;

(2)　to bodies subject to corporation tax, and not to income tax;

(3)　where the minimum of 25% of the chargeable profits may be attributed to this company (and to persons connected or associated with it);

(4)　where the local tax burden in the territory of residence is less than 75% of the corresponding UK tax;

---

[71] [1997] STC 1179, dismissing appeal from [1996] STC (SCD) 228.

[72] On general problems of CFC legislation and tax treaties, see Sandler, *Pushing the Boundaries* (IFS, 1994); and Lang *et al*, *CFC Legislation, Tax Treaties and EC Law* (Kluwer, 2004).

[73] The *Schneider Electric* case (French *Conseil d'Etat* No 232276 of 28 June 2002).

(5)   if the CFC's profits do not exceed a de minimis threshold currently set at £50,000; or
(6)   if the CFC's 'relevant profits' do not exceed a de minimis threshold of £200,000.

However, in addition, TA 1988, section 748 gives specific exclusions where the CFC's profits come from exempt activities (see §17.5.3), or it satisfies a motive test (see §17.5.4). There is also an immensely important list of excluded countries (see §17.5.5) which is probably based on the motive test. The former, but now repealed, exclusions for an acceptable dividend policy (see §17.5.1) or where the company satisfies a public quotation condition (§17.5.2) are briefly mentioned. The rules in section 751A dealing with the situation in which the CFC had a business establishment in an EEA territory, are outlined at §17.6. FA 2011 introduced both full and partial exemption for companies with limited UK connection or with IP profits that cannot be regarded as diverted from the UK (see §17.5.6).

   TA 1988, section 748A allows the Treasury to disapply the exemptions in section 748 by a statutory instrument creating a 'territorial exclusion'.[74] The power to make such instruments applies where the company is: (a) incorporated in the territory; or (b) is liable to tax by reason of domicile, residence or place of management; or (c) carries on business through a PE. Condition (c) is subject to a *de minimis* clause. The instrument specifies the territory to which the exemptions are not to apply and is designed to counter harmful tax competition.

17.5.1 Acceptable Distribution Policy (Repealed)

Until the 2009 introduction of the dividend exemption regime in CTA 2009, Part 9A, the CFC rules did not apply if the foreign company followed an acceptable distribution policy. The following conditions needed to be met to satisfy this test:[75]

(1)   A dividend, which was not paid out of specified profits, was paid for the accounting period in question.
(2)   A dividend was paid during or within 18 months after that period (the Revenue could extend the time allowed for this).
(3)   A company distributed by way of dividend an amount not less than 90% of its available profits for the accounting period to UK residents. Where there was only one class of shares and all the interests were share interests held by UK residents,[76] only 90% of profits attributable to the UK shareholders must have been distributed.[77] A similar relief applied if one class was voting shares and the other was non-voting, fixed-rate preference shares.

Where the company fulfilled these conditions for a particular accounting period, that period was called an 'ADP exempt period'.[78] The time-limit for making a claim was

---

[74] Added by FA 2002, s 89; see Cussons [2002] BTR 317.
[75] TA 1988, Sch 25, paras 1–4; see also Inland Revenue Decision RD 2.
[76] TA 1988, Sch 25, para 2(4) does not apply, as para 2(4)(b) is not satisfied.
[77] At one time a trading company only needed to distribute 50% of its profits, but this was changed by FA 1995, Sch 36, para 4.
[78] TA 1988, Sch 24, para 1(6), added by FA 1996, Sch 36, para 3; the legislation contains further amendments using this concept.

20 months from the end of the ADP exempt period.[79] CFCs could make distributions out of profits of earlier accounting periods, provided they had not been taxed already under the CFC provisions. For this purpose the profits of a later period were taken before those of an earlier one.[80] Detailed rules attributed dividends to particular periods (and so to particular profits). There were also rules dealing with payments through intermediate companies, the avoidance of double counting and others countering the avoidance of liability through the manipulation of accounting periods. A payment of dividend to a company was not relevant unless it was taken into account in computing the company's income for corporation tax.[81] Additional anti-avoidance rules also applied. For further detail, see *Revenue Law*, 5th edition.

17.5.2 The Public Quotation Condition (Repealed)

Pursuing the analogy of domestic close companies yet further, the legislation, through a late amendment, originally provided that those powers would not apply if the CFC fulfilled a public quotation condition closely modelled on TA 1988, section 415 (see above at §10.2). In order to prevent abuse, this was repealed for accounting periods beginning on or after 6 December 2006.

17.5.3 Exempt Activities[82]

The objective of this test is to exclude automatically from the charge those foreign companies which, because of the nature of their activities in their territories of residence, can reasonably be regarded as being located there for purposes other than reducing UK tax. However, as the Revenue repeatedly make clear in their information releases, it is still open to a company simply to invoke the motive test set out below at §17.5.4. The purpose of the exempt activities test is to ensure that the CFC legislation will not apply to a company which, say, simply runs a hotel on a beach or provides financial services in that territory. Although the legislation refers to territories, express provision is made for the 'special administrative regions' of Hong Kong and Macao.[83]

A foreign company carries on exempt activities if it satisfies four, or sometimes five, conditions throughout the accounting period:

(1) It must have a 'business establishment'[84] in its territory of residence; this means having premises with a reasonable degree of permanence, not just a name plate, and with sufficient and local staff, not merely a formal presence such as a registered address in the territory.

(2) Its business affairs must be effectively managed there;[85] thus, the number of persons employed by the company must be adequate to deal with the volume of business.

---

[79] TA 1988, Sch 24, para 4(2A), inserted by FA 1996, Sch 36, para 7.

[80] TA 1988, Sch 25, para 2A(4), (5).

[81] TA 1988, Sch 25, paras 2(1A), 4(1A), added by FA 1990, s 67(3).

[82] TA 1988, Sch 25, paras 5–12.

[83] TA 1988, Sch 25, para 5(3)–(5), as amended by FA 2003, s 201; the changes are retrospective but are designed to ensure that subsidiaries of UK companies can take advantage of the exempt activities exemption as was always intended. Inland Revenue Document IR CE1, issued 27 November 2002, [2002] *Simon's Tax Intelligence* 1580.

[84] TA 1988, Sch 25, paras 6(1)(a), 7.

[85] TA 1988, Sch 25, paras 6(1)(b), 8.

Less obviously, the rules state that services provided by the company for persons resident outside the territory must not be performed in the UK. Companies resident in an EEA territory have a special test of 'effectively managed' for this exempt activities rule. The test is directly related to the rule in section 751A, and requires that there be enough individuals working for the company with authority and competence to undertake all or substantially all of the company's business.[86] See §17.6 below.

(3)   Its main activity must not be investment business,[87] such as leasing, holding of securities or intellectual property, dealing in securities or the receipt of income such as dividends, interest, or royalties, and must not be such that the company may be used as an invoicing route. It has been made clear that banks are not barred from this exclusion on the ground that they carry on an investment business; the definition of intellectual property for this purpose is meant to be simply illustrative and includes the holding of patents, trademarks, registered designs, copyrights as well as industrial, commercial or scientific know-how.[88]

(4)   Its main business must not be dealing in goods for delivery to or from the UK, or to or from connected or associated persons.[89]

(5)   If the company is carrying on a wholesale distributive or financial business in that accounting period, less than 50% of its gross trading receipts from that business must be derived, directly or indirectly, from connected or associated persons or persons with a 25% assessable interest in the company in that accounting period.[90] Rule (5) is aimed at transfer pricing and similar devices, such as captive insurance companies, and withholds the exemption where 50% or more of the receipts come from transactions with specified forbidden persons. FA 2000 widened the disqualifying business in rule (5) to cover the provision of any services.[91] FA 2003 widened the category of forbidden persons. So far as insurance business is concerned, this widening did not apply to long-term insurance but only to 'protection' insurance.[92] The particular concern was that companies were using their liabilities under extended warranties, credit protection policies and similar products to UK customers as income from exempt activities.

Special rules apply to holding companies (which, inter alia, can separate out their own exempt activities). As from 1 July 2009 the rules are concerned simply with 'local holding companies'; the former references to 'superior' and 'non-local' holding companies were removed. The rules for local holding companies are strict. The company must receive at least 90% of its income from non-resident subsidiaries meeting the CFC exempt activities rules. The income must be received by the holding company in the territory in which it

---

[86] TA 1988, Sch 25, paras 5(1A) and 8(5) and (6).
[87] TA 1988, Sch 25, paras 6(2)(a)(i), 9.
[88] TA 1988, Sch 25, para 9(1A).
[89] TA 1988, Sch 25, paras 6(2)(a)(ii), 10.
[90] TA 1988, Sch 25, paras 6(2)(b), 11.
[91] TA 1988, Sch 25, paras 6(2)(b), (2A), 11(1)(h), as added by FA 2000l, Sch 31, paras 5, 8.
[92] FA 2003, Sch 42.

is resident.[93] FA 2008 refined the 90% rule. The rule states that at least 90% of its gross income must come from subsidiaries carrying on these exempt activities. Planners argued that income would not form part of the gross income of a company if it accrued to a partnership in which the holding company had a major interest. The rules now state that 'gross' income includes any income to which it is entitled and so whether or not received, eg the partnership income, and any trust income in relation to which the company is a settlor or beneficiary.[94]

17.5.4 Motive Test

A company which fails to satisfy any of the above tests will nevertheless escape the charge if it meets the requirements of the motive test.[95] No apportionment is made for an accounting period in so far as any of the transactions, the results of which are reflected in the profits arising in the accounting period, or any two or more of those transactions taken together, achieved a reduction in UK tax which was no more than minimal. The apportionment is also excluded if (a) it was not a main purpose of any of those transactions (either alone or taken together) to achieve that reduction, and (b) a reduction in UK tax by the diversion of profits from the UK was not a main reason for the company's existence in that accounting period.

A transaction achieves a reduction in UK tax[96] (meaning income tax, corporation tax or CGT)[97] if any person would have been liable for more tax, or would have been entitled to less relief or a smaller repayment, if the transaction had not taken place. A 'transaction' for this purpose may comprise one or more transactions which are reflected in the company's profits in any accounting period. The definition of 'associated operations' was tightened up by FA 1996.[98] The purpose in question in this test is that of the foreign company and any person who had an interest in that company in the relevant accounting period.

A reduction in UK tax by a diversion of profits[99] from the UK is achieved by the existence of a company if the whole or a substantial part of the receipts making up the foreign company's profits in that period could reasonably have been expected to be received by a UK resident and been subject to UK tax without any relief, had it not been for the existence of the foreign company in question or another foreign company connected or associated with it and capable of fulfilling the same functions relative to any UK resident company. Companies are meant to fall foul of this test only if the diversions achieve a loss of UK tax and are a main reason for the existence of the company.

---

[93] TA 1988, Sch 25, para 6(3).

[94] TA 1988, Sch 26, para 6(5C), added by FA 2008, s 64.

[95] TA 1988, s 748(3). For a rare example of litigation, see *ABTA v IRC* [2003] STC (SCD) 194 (satisfied part of test but not all) and comment by Shiers [2003] BTR 212.

[96] TA 1988, Sch 25, para 16.

[97] TA 1988, Sch 25, para 17(2); the inclusion of CGT is noteworthy, as capital gains are excluded from the CFC attribution process.

[98] See FA 1996, Sch 36, para 4(6).

[99] TA 1988, Sch 25, para 19.

17.5.5 The Revenue List of Excluded Countries

The Revenue publish a list of countries which are regarded as either wholly or completely outside these rules; with the introduction of self-assessment the list has taken the form of a statutory instrument.[100] A company which is resident in and carrying on business in a country in Part I of the list is outside these rules, while a similar relief is given for a country in Part II of the list only if it does not benefit from one of the reliefs specified. A company is regarded as carrying on a business in a country if 90% of its commercially quantified income is local source income.

This is not a list of countries which are regarded as not having a low level of taxation. The basis for the exclusion of the rules must be sought in the motive test (§17.5.4). The point is explained by Arnold thus:

> [T]he reason … appears to be that low taxation is determined only for the country in which the company is resident. By adding the requirement that a company derive at least 90% of its income from the country, the list permits inclusion of high tax countries (such as France) that exempt foreign income.[101]

The excluded countries exemption was found to be subject to abuse, and so amendments were made by FA 2005, withdrawing the exemption where the company had been involved in a scheme or an arrangement to reduce UK tax.[102] Further changes made at the same time:

(1) required the company not simply to be incorporated in the territory but also to be liable to tax there;

(2) amended the rules on CFC control to take account of bodies which are not companies but are involved in economic activity; and

(3) provided that income is not to be treated as local source income if at least 50% of the CFC's income derives from transactions with persons who are connected or associated.[103]

17.5.6 Limited UK Connection and not UK-diverted IP Profits

FA 2011 introduced TA 1988, section 748(1)(ba) and Part 2A of Schedule 25, providing a full exemption from the CFC regime for a company resident in the same foreign territory in which it has a business establishment, if it principally trades with non-UK customers and has a limited amount of finance and IP income. In addition, section 748(1)(bb) and Part 2B provide a full exemption for an overseas company that derives IP profits which cannot be regarded as having been diverted from the UK. FA 2011 also introduced partial exemption where some but not all of the conditions are satisfied in section 748(1)(ba) or (bb): see section 751AB.

---

[100] Controlled Foreign Companies (Excluded Countries) Regulations 1998 (SI 1998/3081), [1999] *Simon's Weekly Tax Intelligence* 85.

[101] [1985] BTR 302; see also Arnold, *Taxation of Controlled Foreign Corporations: an International Comparison* (Canadian Tax Foundation, 1986) 321.

[102] FA 2005, s 87.

[103] Controlled Foreign Companies (Excluded Countries) (Amendment) Regulations 2005, SI 2005/186.

17.6   Net Economic Value Arising in a Relevant EEA Territory[104]

TA 1988, sections 751A and 751B allow a company to escape from a CFC liability in so far as it is attributable to 'net economic value' arising in a relevant EEA territory. The provisions were introduced by FA 2007 in response to the decision of the ECJ in *Cadbury Schweppes plc v IRC*.[105] In that case the ECJ ruled that the Revenue's application of the UK's CFC rules could be, and often would be, in breach of the EU principle of freedom of establishment. The case is one of 22 cases which have been the subject of a group litigation order. It concerned the profits of an Irish subsidiary of the well-known UK company; these were attributed by the Revenue to the UK parent under the CFC rules. It was agreed that the Irish tax on the Irish profits was lower than the UK tax would have been. The Court held that Articles 43 TEC and 48 TEC (now Articles 49 and 54 TFEU) prohibiting restrictions on the freedom of establishment of companies must be interpreted as allowing the application of the CFC rules only where the taxpayer's arrangements were wholly artificial and intended to escape the UK tax normally payable. Accordingly, the CFC rules could not be applied where it was shown, on the basis of objective factors which were ascertainable by third parties, that despite the existence of tax motives, the controlled company was actually established in Ireland and carried on genuine economic activities there. The resident company had to be given an opportunity to produce evidence that the CFC was actually established and that its activities were genuine.

The purpose of sections 751A and 751B is to provide a framework in which that opportunity can be given. They apply where an apportionment falls to be made under these rules and throughout that period the CFC had a business establishment in an EEA territory and there are individuals who work for the CFC in that territory. To prevent pointless application, another condition is that a company resident in the UK ('the UK-resident company') must have a relevant interest in the CFC in that period. 'EEA territory' is defined as a territory which is an EEA state at that time, but excluding the UK. The legislation distinguishes 'Member States', ie members of the EU, from EEA states. EEA states qualify only if international tax enforcement arrangements are in force under FA 2006, section 173 (above, chapter fourteen). So Iceland and Norway qualify but Liechtenstein does not.

The company must apply for the apportionment to be reduced by a specified amount. HMRC may grant the application only if they are satisfied that the specified amount does not exceed the amount (if any) equal to so much of those chargeable profits as can reasonably be regarded as representing the net economic value which (a) arises to the appropriate body of persons (taken as a whole) and (b) is created directly by qualifying work.

These terms are then defined. So 'net economic value' cannot include any value which derives directly or indirectly from the reduction or elimination of any liability of any person to any tax or duty imposed under the law of any territory. The definition of 'appropriate body of persons' is concerned with both single CFCs and groups. 'Qualifying work' means work that (a) is done in any EEA territory in which the CFC has a business establishment throughout the relevant accounting period, and (b) is done in that territory by individuals working for the CFC there. Individuals are regarded as working for a company in any

---

[104]   See Taylor and Sykes [2007] BTR 609.
[105]   Case C-196/04 [2006] STC 1908; for a detailed analysis, see Simpson [2006] BTR 677.

territory if they are employed by the company in the territory, or are otherwise directed by the company to perform duties on its behalf in the territory. The HMRC Guidance includes nine examples of net economic value.

Meanwhile the group litigation proceeds. It is self-evident that the approach from Luxembourg is rather abstract. No doubt we shall soon see how many other companies decide to reopen CFC apportionments. It will be interesting to see whether claims may even be brought for losses sustained by companies which made a distribution to satisfy the former acceptable distribution test (TA 1988, Schedule 26, Part II). Whether such claims succeed is another matter.

17.7   CFC Reform

As noted in the introduction to this chapter, at Budget 2011 the Government announced its intention to introduce a new CFC regime. The new rules in Part 9A of TIOPA 2010 are effective for CFCs with accounting periods beginning on or after 1 January 2013. The rules, it is fair to say, remain exceedingly complicated, and what follows is only a general summary of the key provisions.

To begin, as Richardson notes,[106] much of the architecture of the new regime is similar to that of the existing regime just described. A charge is levied on UK resident companies holding a significant interest in non UK-resident companies controlled by one or more UK persons. Companies not subject to a lower level of taxation still will not be CFCs; under the new rules this is by the operation of an exemption. Similarly, there are some mechanical exemptions, which, like the old regime, include a form of low profit exemption and an exemption for excluded countries. One important and obvious difference from the old regime is that companies carrying on financial trades may qualify for a partial finance company exemption, with only one-quarter of the company's relevant profits eligible for apportionment (an effective tax rate of 6% assuming a 24% corporation tax rate).

TIOPA 2010, Part 9A, Chapter 2 sets out the basic details of the CFC charge. The centerpiece of the new CFC regime is the 'Gateway' that is used to identify situations with a significant mismatch between key business activities undertaken in the UK and the profits arising from those activities which are allocated outside the UK. The Gateway, found in Chapters 3–8, effectively replaces the old motive test, and limits the CFC's chargeable profits to only so much of its profits as pass through the Gateway (section 371BA). Chapter 3 operates as an initial filter and begins by laying down rules for determining which, if any, of Chapters 4–8 apply for an accounting period (section 371BB). Non-financial profits that meet any one of the four conditions in section 371CA will be outside the CFC charge:

- *Condition A* (UK activities)—at no time during the accounting period does the CFC have any UK-managed assets or bear any UK-managed risks. Assets or risks are 'UK-managed' if (a) the acquisition, creation, development or exploitation of the asset, or (b) the taking on, or bearing of, the risk, is managed or controlled to any significant extent by way of activities carried on in the UK by the CFC (otherwise than through a UK PE) or by companies connected with the CFC operating on a non arm's-length basis.

---

[106] Richardson [2012] BTR 3.

- *Condition B* (Capability and commercial effectiveness)—throughout the accounting period the CFC has itself the capability to ensure that its business would be commercially effective were its UK-managed assets or risks no longer UK-managed.
- *Condition C* (Tax purpose)—at no time during the accounting period does the CFC hold assets or bear risks under an arrangement (a) the main purpose, or one of the main purposes, of which is to reduce or eliminate UK tax, and (b) in consequence of the arrangement the CFC expects its business to be more profitable. In addition, there must not be an expectation that, as a consequence of the arrangement, a person's tax liabilities in any territory will be reduced and it is reasonable to suppose that, but for that expectation, the arrangement would not have been made.
- *Condition D*—the CFC's assumed profits consist only of one or both of non-trading finance profits or property business profits.

If none of these four conditions is satisfied then the remaining chapters of the Gateway or, alternatively, the exemptions which apply to the CFC as a whole, will need to be considered. Chapter 4, the primary remaining Gateway chapter, seeks first to identify the share of the CFC's assets and risks that would be attributed to a UK PE of the CFC, assuming that all the significant people functions (SPFs) relevant to those assets and risks were undertaken by a single enterprise. If there are no relevant UK SPFs then there are no Chapter 4 Gateway profits. If there are relevant UK SPFs, the Chapter 4 Gateway profits are those which the CFC would not earn if its ownership of the assets and its bearing of the risks were correspondingly reduced.[107] Various exclusions may also apply. Chapter 5 applies for a CFC's accounting period if the CFC has non-trading finance profits. Chapter 6 concerns trading finance profits of the CFC where the CFC has funds or other assets which derive from UK-connected capital contributions. Chapter 7 relates to captive insurance businesses and Chapter 8 deals with solo consolidation waivers under section BIPRU 2.1 of the FSA Handbook.

Turning now to the exemptions, Chapter 9 begins by providing both partial and full exemption for qualifying loan relationships. Chapter 10 contains the excluded territories exemption for CFCs resident in a territory with a headline tax rate of >75% of the UK main corporation tax rate that satisfy a number of further conditions. The low profits exemption in Chapter 11 applies if the CFC's accounting profits (a) are not more than £50,000, or (b) are not more than £500,000 and the amount of those profits representing non-trading income is not more than £50,000. Chapter 12 is an entirely novel exemption for low profit margins, where the CFC's accounting profits basically represent 10% or less of relevant operating expenditure. Lastly, Chapter 13 sets out the 'tax exemption', which replaces the former lower level of tax test and applies if the CFC is subject to local tax of at least 75% of the corresponding UK tax.

---

[107] As described in HM Treasury and HMRC, 'Controlled Foreign Companies (CFC) reform: a Gateway update' (February 2012) 10.

18

Capital Gains

18.1 General Rules

18.1.1 Residence and Non-residence

A person is chargeable to CGT if resident or ordinarily resident in the UK for at least part of the year of assessment.[1] If the person is not so resident, a charge arises only if:

(1) a trade or profession is being carried on through a branch or agency; and
(2) the asset was both situated in the UK and either used in or for the trade when or before the gain accrued, or used by or for the branch or agency when or before the gain accrued.[2]

The corporation tax principles are similar, though the legislation refers to a 'permanent establishment' rather than a 'branch or agency'.[3]

These rules preserve the basic premise that a person is taxable either because of residence or source, but curiously restricts the source to the one type—through a branch or agency. Thus a non-resident without such a trade or profession bears no CGT even though the asset is in the UK. Equally, T, a resident individual with a substantial liability to CGT could,

---

[1] TCGA 1992, s 2(1). On residence for year of commencement or cessation, see ESC D2 (as modified; see Inland Revenue Press Release, 17 March 1998, [1998] *Simon's Weekly Tax Intelligence* 428).
[2] TCGA 1992, s 10; he may also be exempt by treaty (*ibid*), and see below at §20.6. On post-cessation disposals, see *ibid*, s 10(2).
[3] TCGA 1992, s 10B.

until 1998, go overseas, cease to be resident and ordinarily resident, and then dispose of the assets free of all UK tax—at least if the disposal was in the next year of assessment.[4] This reluctance to tax the non-resident is the norm in other countries.[5]

Today, this approach is subject to a number of qualifications:

(1) Special rules apply to individuals who cease to be resident but then resume their UK residence (TCGA 1992, section 10A; see below §18.1.2).
(2) There is a general deemed disposal rule for companies ceasing to be resident (TCGA 1992, section 185).
(3) There is a similar rule for trusts (TCGA 1992, section 80).
(4) Certain non-residents with chargeable assets in the UK will be deemed to dispose of them when the assets cease to be chargeable (TCGA 1992, section 25).
(5) Certain gains of non-resident companies may be attributed to UK members (below §18.3).
(6) Certain gains of non-resident trusts may be attributed to relevant UK persons (below §18.5).

Residence and ordinary residence have the same meanings as for income tax.[6] One who is in the UK for some temporary purpose and not with a view to establishing residence here is treated as resident only if the period of residence in the UK is at least 183 days.[7] On this point it should be noted that at Budget 2012, the Government announced it intends to abolish 'ordinary residence' for tax purposes, with effect from April 2013.

Where an asset is acquired and disposed of in foreign currency, acquisition cost and disposal proceeds are calculated at the exchange rates prevailing at the acquisition and disposal (*Revenue Law*, §43.1.2).[8] On foreign currency as a chargeable or exempt asset, see *Revenue Law*, §33.7.

In a major policy shift that would bring the UK a little closer to the OECD norm of source taxation of capital gains in respect of land located in the source country, at Budget 2012 the Government also announced it was considering extending the CGT regime to gains on disposals by non-resident non-natural persons of UK residential property and shares or interests in such property. The new rules are expected to take effect from April 2013 following a period of consultation.

18.1.2 Temporary Non-residence and Capital Gains

The relative ease with which properly-advised taxpayers with mobile lifestyles could achieve non-resident status[9] gave rise to Revenue worries. The resulting legislation, TCGA 1992, section 10A,[10] is specific; it is not concerned with migrants so much as with temporary

---

[4] On dangers of relying on ESC D2 when carrying out an avoidance scheme, see *R v IRC, ex parte Fulford-Dobson* [1987] STC 344; discussed by Williams [1987] BTR 271.

[5] Exceptions include India and Japan. The reluctance is based on the difficulty in collecting the tax, but has not stopped the UK expanding income tax to catch certain receipts.

[6] On residence of partners, see TCGA 1992, s 59 and TA 1988, s 112.

[7] TCGA 1992, s 9(3).

[8] *Capcount Trading v Evans* [1993] STC 11, CA; reaffirming *Bentley v Pike* [1981] STC 360, (1991) 53 TC 590.

[9] Eg *Reed v Clark* [1985] STC 323, (1985) 58 TC 528.

[10] Introduced by FA 1998, s 127.

non-residents. It applies if B, an individual and one-time resident of some duration, having become a non-resident, then reacquires resident status; the charge arises only in the year of return,[11] and only where B has been non-resident for fewer than five complete tax years of assessment. Further, it applies only where B has been resident for four of the seven years immediately before the non-residence; for this purpose residence for any part of the year suffices.[12]

Section 10A charges gains realised during the period of non-residence, including any liability in respect of section 13 (see below at §18.3) and section 86 (see below at §18.4) which would have arisen if B had been resident.[13] Relief is given for any losses.[14] Gains and losses on assets acquired after becoming non-resident are, in general, excluded. Further rules deny relief where the new asset exploits a deferral of or exemption from UK tax, eg the acquisition was one on which neither gain nor loss accrued to the disposer or roll-over relief reduced the cost of the asset, or the asset was acquired from a spouse or civil partner or was an interest in the settlement.[15] Provision is made to ensure that the tax position of a non-resident carrying on a trade or profession in the UK through a branch or agency is not affected.[16]

Some of the problems presented by double tax treaties were addressed in 2005. The original version of section 10A expressly preserved the effect of double tax treaties. This meant that where the treaty contained a capital gains clause, B was usually protected from section 10A, so giving rise to avoidance.[17] FA 2005 addresses this by saying that a person who is resident (or ordinarily resident) in the UK under UK domestic rules but a non-resident for tax treaty purposes, is not resident for the purposes of section 10A; on treaty non-residence, see §20.6.1.[18] Consistently with this approach, it also provides that when the taxpayer returns, the gains are not to include gains in respect of assets acquired while the person was resident in the UK but non-resident for treaty purposes.[19] Also consistently with this approach, the legislation provides that nothing in any double tax treaty is to prevent the UK from charging tax in the year of return.[20] The original 1998 provision preserving the effect of double tax treaties has been repealed.[21]

Where the relevant treaty does not have a capital gains article in the appropriate form, the foreign state may not give credit for the UK tax charged later and the UK may not give

---

[11] On period during which assessment may be made, see TCGA 1992, s 10A(7); the rules apply to individuals becoming non-resident on or after 17 March 1998 (FA 1998, s 127(4)).

[12] TCGA 1992, s 10A(1), (8), (9).

[13] TCGA 1992, s 10A(2).

[14] TCGA 1992, s 10A(2).

[15] TCGA 1992, s 10A(3), (4). The no gain, no loss disposals are those in ss 58 (husband and wife), 73 (death) and 258(4) (works of art); the reductions are those under ss 23 (reinvestment of compensation money), 152 (acquisition of business asset), 162 (transfer of business) and 247 (compulsory acquisition). There are further rules for reorganisation of bonds and gilts (s 116), acquisition of compensation stock (s 134) and rollover relief where the new assets are depreciating assets (s 154).

[16] TCGA 1992, s 10A(5).

[17] Such clauses usually gave the States of treaty residence exclusive right to tax, so that the UK could not tax someone who was resident under normal UK rules but non-resident for treaty purposes.

[18] TCGA 1992, s 10A(9)–(9B) as inserted by F(No 2)A 2005, s 32. The various changes took effect from 26 March 2005 or the start of 2005–06 as appropriate.

[19] TCGA 1992, s 10A(3)(a), as amended by FA 2005, s 32.

[20] TCGA 1992, s 10A(9C), inserted by FA 2005, s 32.

[21] TCGA 1992, s 10A(10), repealed by FA 2005, s 32.

relief for the foreign tax charged earlier.[22] This shows the haphazard nature of treaty relief and the unsatisfactory nature of CGT, with its insistence on asset and disposal.

18.1.3 Delayed Remittances

Where a gain arises from the disposal of an asset situated overseas, but the gain cannot be remitted to the UK, the taxpayer[23] may make a claim for deferral of CGT on conditions analogous to income tax relief (see above at §15.5). The inability to remit gains to the UK must arise from the laws of the territory where the asset was situated, from the executive action of its government or from the impossibility of obtaining foreign currency there. Since tax is levied as soon as the conditions cease, gains accruing over several years may come into charge at one time. In such circumstances, unlike income tax, there is no charge by reference to the years in which the gain accrued. This may mean the loss of the annual exemption for the years in which the gains actually arose. Similar Revenue reasoning means that this relief does not apply where the taxpayer is chargeable on a remittance basis.

18.1.4 Foreign Bank Accounts

TCGA 1992, section 252A and Schedule 8A, added by FA 2010, aim to prevent the creation of an allowable capital loss when there has been no economic loss. Schedule 8A, paragraph 1 provides that the Schedule applies where:

(1) an individual disposes of a non-sterling debt owed by a bank (ie a positive (credit) balance in a bank account denominated in a foreign currency) (a 'section 252 debt');
(2) the debt is situated outside the UK; and
(3) TCGA 1992, section 37 acts to exclude income chargeable on the individual under the remittance basis from the consideration for the disposal. Section 37 excludes consideration that is chargeable to income tax from the computation of a chargeable gain. Where the whole consideration is excluded by section 37, new Schedule 8A, paragraph 2 provides that any loss accruing to the individual from the disposal is not to be an allowable loss.

There are further rules for part disposals.

18.2 Remittance Basis

As already seen (above §15.4), the FA 2008 remittance rules apply both to income and to chargeable gains (FIGs). The remittance basis applies to capital gains realised by an individual resident or ordinarily resident, but not domiciled, in the UK; however, this applies only to gains from the disposal of an asset outside the UK.[24] In computing the

---

[22] Avery Jones [1999] BTR 325.
[23] TCGA 1992, s 279.
[24] TCGA 1992, s 12.

amount of the gain, any liability to foreign tax is deductible in full.[25] The scope of remittance is widened in the same way as for income tax.[26]

The availability of the remittance basis is thus governed by the status of the person rather than simply by the location of the asset. The rule is analogous to the treatment of investment income. One consequence of the rule is that a disposal for less than acquisition cost, eg a gift, cannot be charged in this country.

TCGA 1992, section 16(4), now repealed, actually barred loss relief where the remittance basis was available. After FA 2008 the situation is more complex. An individual who is resident but not domiciled in the UK may simply decide to use the arising basis and not the remittance basis. Such a person is entitled to loss relief under the normal CGT rules.

If, however, he elects to use the remittance basis, more complex rules (TCGA 1992, sections 16ZA–16ZD) apply. Section 16ZA directs that they apply once the individual has elected, irrevocably, to be taxed on the remittance basis under ITA 2007, section 809B; any year during which this election is in force is called a 'relevant tax year'. So sections 16ZA–16ZD apply for all later years, save only for those in which the individual is domiciled in the UK.

If the gains are remitted in the year in which they accrue, they are charged (under section 12) in the normal way. However, if losses arise in Year 1 but gains are remitted in Year 3 so that they become chargeable in Year 3 under TCGA 1992, section 12, the normal remittance basis rule, section 16ZB, applies to determine the amount that will be taxable. Section 16ZC deals with the order in which losses are set off against gains, and does so on a two-step basis familiar in modern UK tax legislation. Section 16ZC also sets out what is to happen when the gain and loss arise in the same year.

The essence of the scheme in section 16ZB is that the loss may be set off against the gain which is remitted and so becomes taxable in the UK under section 12. However, if the taxpayer still has unremitted gains from any previous year or that year, the loss is set off against those other still unremitted gains. This result is not unlike the old rule in section 16(4) (now repealed).

18.2.1 Remittance from Mixed Fund

Also as seen above (§15.4), where the fund from which money consideration or service has been funded is mixed, FA 2008, section 809Q(4) lists the order in which remittance is taken to come. This is the familiar order:

(a) relevant foreign earnings if not subject to a foreign tax (ITEPA 2003, sections 22 and 26);

(b) foreign specific employment income if not subject to a foreign tax (ITEPA 2003, section 41A);

(c) relevant foreign income if not subject to a foreign tax (ITTOIA 2005, section 830);

(d) foreign chargeable gains if not subject to a foreign tax (TCGA 1992, section 12);

and then

---

[25] TCGA 1992, s 278, unless relief is given under s 277.
[26] TCGA 1992, s 12(2).

(e) relevant foreign earnings subject to a foreign tax;
(f) foreign specific employment income subject to a foreign tax;
(g) relevant foreign income subject to a foreign tax;
(h) foreign chargeable gains subject to a foreign tax;
(i) income or capital not within paragraphs (a)–(h).

The list is intended to benefit the Revenue. Taking sums which have not borne tax (paragraphs (a)–(d)) before those which have (paragraphs (e)–(h)) takes into account the fact that the UK may have to give relief for the foreign tax, whether by credit of deduction.

Placing income or capital in (i) and so last is a major change. Previous HMRC practice was to treat it as comprising capital and capital gain in proportion to their presence in the account.[27] This is now enacted as treating the fund as containing income or capital if and to the extent that it is just and reasonable to do so.[28]

Separate problems arise where the fund includes receipts from the sale of two assets. Thus, if one asset is sold with a gain of £500 and another asset for a loss of £500, it is presumably open to argue that the loss should be set off against the gain. Further issues arise might have arisen if the gains were treated differently, eg if one is exempt and the other not, but this will usually be anticipated by noting that the legislation in framed in terms of chargeable gains.

18.2.2 Location of Assets—CGT Rules

The situs of assets is important, as the remittance basis applies only to foreign assets. TCGA 1992, section 275, widened in 2005,[29] contains 14 rules, including the following:

(1) Most rights over immovable property follow the location of the immovable property. Similarly, most rights in or over tangible movable property follow that of that property. However, debts, secured or unsecured, are generally situated in the UK if and only if the creditor is resident in the UK.[30]

(2) Registered shares or debentures are generally situated where they are registered; and if registered in more than one register, where the principal register is situated. If the company does not have share capital, the rule looks to the interests of the members of the company.

(3) Intangible assets subject to UK law are always treated as located in the UK for CGT.[31] Futures and options have their own rules which relate to the location of the underlying subject matter.[32]

(4) Co-owners have their own provision.[33] Their interests are located where the asset in which their interests subsist is located.

---

[27] Inland Revenue, *Capital Gains Manual*, paras CG 25380, 25400–401.
[28] FA 2008, s 809Q(3).
[29] F(No 2)A 2005, s 34 and Sch 4.
[30] See Oliver [1991] BTR 189, n 1.
[31] TCGA 1992, s 275A(1)–(3) and 275B, added by FA 2005, Sch 10, para 5.
[32] TCGA 1992, s 275A(4)–(9) and 275B added by FA 2005, Sch 10, para 5.
[33] TCGA 1992, s 275C added by FA 2005, Sch 10, para 6.

18.3   Gains Realised by Certain Closely-held Non-resident Companies

It will be remembered that the CFC legislation discussed in chapter seventeen does not apply to capital gains. Gains accruing to a company are not usually attributable to those with interests in the company, but an exception is made by TCGA 1992, section 13 (as much amended in 1996) where the company would be a close company but for being non-resident.[34] The gain will be attributed to participators as defined for the close company legislation (see above §10.2); as a de minimis rule the gain will be attributed only if it is more than one-tenth of the relevant gain.[35] The participator must be either resident or ordinarily resident and, if an individual, domiciled in the UK. Gains to be attributed are determined on corporation tax principles.[36] Special rules apply to determine the place of this gain in the hierarchy of the participator's total income.[37] Before 1996 the test was based not on being a participator but on being a shareholder, which gave rise to much planning.[38] Until 2008, section 13 did not apply to a participator who did not have a UK domicile. As from 6 April 2008, the part of the gain treated as accruing to the individual is deemed to be a foreign chargeable gain.[39] If a gain arises when the individual disposes of the interest in the company, relief may be claimed for any tax paid under section 13.[40]

Section 13 applies also to trustee participators.[41] Where a participator is a beneficiary of the trust, and the intermediate trustee participators do not make any payment to the participator, only the trustees are vulnerable under section 13.[42] However, there are many problems where the trustee or the settlor is already at risk under one of the other attribution rules.[43]

The charge cannot be avoided by placing another company (or several companies) between the participator and the company to which the gain accrues, since the Revenue are given power to attribute the gain down through any number of intervening companies to the real shareholders.[44]

The participator can use the tax paid under section 13 as a credit against any tax due on a later disposal of the shares or other asset giving rise to participator status.[45] If not already so used, it may be used as a credit against any tax due on a later distribution by the company, whether a distribution of income or capital, or on a winding up;[46] for this rule the distribution must occur within two years of the gain accruing to the company. These rules are well-intentioned but incomplete; the substitution of participator status for shareholder

---

[34] See generally, McCutcheon [1996] BTR 379. On original version, see Bennion [1983] BTR 74.
[35] TCGA 1992, s 13(4) amended by FA 2001 s 80; see also TCGA 1992, s 13(10B), added by FA 2001 s 80.
[36] TCGA 1992, s 13(10A), added by FA 1998.
[37] TCGA 1992, s 13(7A).
[38] McCutcheon, *op cit.*
[39] TCGA, s 14A, added by FA 2008, Sch 7, para 104.
[40] HMRC Notes to Finance Bill.
[41] TCGA 1992, s 13(10).
[42] TCGA 1992, s 14; see McCutcheon, *op cit*, 381.
[43] TCGA 1992, ss 86, 87.
[44] TCGA 1992, s 13(9).
[45] TCGA 1992, s 13(7); on time limits see TCGA 1992, s(5A) and (5B), added FA 2001 s 80.
[46] TCGA 1992, s 13(5A). Before 1996 the s 13 assessment was undone if the company distributed the gain to the shareholder; this is inappropriate in a world of self-assessment.

status, and the fact that attribution does not follow the precise legal chain of ownership, means that the person liable to tax under section 13 and the persons receiving the distribution may be different.[47]

Example

X Ltd is a non-resident close company. Smith buys 25% of the share capital in X Ltd. X Ltd realises a gain of £10,000; £2,500 is attributed to Smith, making a tax liability (but for any exemption) of £750. If Smith later sells the shares realising, say, a gain of £1,000, that gain will be reduced by the £750 to £250. If the shares are sold for a gain of £400, the gain is simply reduced to zero.

It was found that section 13 could be circumvented where offshore assets were held by an offshore company owned by a trust and a double tax treaty gave an exemption for such gains, even though the offshore company would have been a close company (and the UK resident trustees would have been participators) if it were resident in the UK. So where gains of non-resident companies arise, section 13 is now to be applied without regard to such a treaty.[48]

The amount of gain or loss accruing to the company is calculated on the basis that the company was within the charge to corporation tax on capital gains.[49] Presumably, this assumption may be extended to other companies so that a no gain, no loss rule applies, for example, on an intra-group transfer even though both companies are non-resident.[50]

The section does not apply to gains accruing on the disposal of tangible property or foreign currency, used only in a foreign or partly foreign and partly UK trade.[51] Losses may be attributed to attributable gains, provided the loss would have been taxable under these rules if it had been a gain instead, ie in the same accounting period.[52]

The section carries the very real risk of taxpayers having to pay CGT without being able to secure any payment from the company. If the tax is reimbursed by the company, it will reduce any credit available to be set against other tax. Relief for unremittable gains[53] does not extend to gains which cannot be got at simply because of minority shareholder status.[54] Further provisions adapt these rules for non-resident groups (TCGA 1992, section 14).

In 2011, the European Commission formerly requested the UK to amend these rules, which it views as contrary to EU treaty fundamental freedoms, namely, the freedom of establishment and free movement of capital. At Budget 2012, the Government confirmed its intention to consult on amending this regime with a view to implementing changes in Finance Act 2013. The changes are not expected to be to the taxpayer's disadvantage, and generally will have retrospective effect to 6 April 2012.

---

[47] *Simon's Direct Tax Service Handbook to FA 1996*, s 174.
[48] TCGA 1992, s 79B, added by FA 2000, s 94.
[49] TCGA 1992, s 13(11A).
[50] Revenue Interpretation RI 43.
[51] TCGA 1992, s 13(5), as amended FA 2001 s 80.
[52] TCGA 1992, s 13(8).
[53] TCGA 1992, s 279; see above at §18.1.3.
[54] One solution may be to sell the shares in the non-resident company before the company disposes.

18.4 Trading Non-residents

18.4.1 Overview

Non-residents are subject to CGT if they carry on a trade, etc, in the UK through a branch or an agency.[55]

Gains or losses are within the scope of CGT if they arise in respect of UK assets:

(1) used for the purposes of the branch trade, etc; or
(2) held for the purposes of the branch.

The allowable costs of such assets are established in the normal way.[56] If the branch assets are transferred to a UK-resident company controlled by the non-resident, they are deemed to have been disposed of at their open market value and a charge to tax may therefore arise.[57] However, the disposal is treated as made for a consideration giving rise neither to gain nor loss if the whole or part of the branch trade is transferred and the disposal falls within TCGA 1992, section 171.[58] No gain, no loss treatment may also be claimed for transfers of a UK trade between companies resident in other EU Member States, where the consideration is satisfied by the issue of securities in the transferee company (see further above at §4.3.5).[59]

A number of anti-avoidance provisions counter the transfer of such assets outside the CGT net. These are the transfer of assets abroad prior to disposal;[60] a disposal after cessation of UK trade (unless the trade is transferred in circumstances falling within TCGA 1992, section 139);[61] a rollover of gains against non-UK assets;[62] and the use of tax treaty relief by persons resident both in the UK and in another country.[63]

As just seen, rollover relief under section 152 is restricted for non-residents;[64] if the old assets are 'chargeable assets in relation to a person' at the time of the disposal, the new assets must be similarly related. This exclusion of rollover relief is not needed—and does not apply—if the person acquiring the new asset is within the UK tax net by reason of personal status, ie by becoming resident or ordinarily resident in the UK, when the asset was acquired.[65] However, this (logical) generosity is withheld (logically) from dual residents in whose hands the assets are safe from the UK tax charge by reason of a double tax agreement.[66]

---

[55] TCGA 1992, s 10.
[56] Even if acquired from another non-resident, but subject to TCGA 1992, s 17 if the non-residents are connected persons.
[57] By TCGA 1992, ss 17(1), 286 or, alternatively, 25(3).
[58] TCGA 1992, s 172 was repealed for disposals after 31 March 2000; this had confined the no gain, no loss treatment to situations in which both companies were resident in the UK; see FA 2000, Sch 29, para 3.
[59] TCGA 1992, s 140A(4)(a).
[60] TCGA 1992, s 25(1).
[61] TCGA 1992, s 25(3), modified by s 28(3A) for disposals after 31 March 2000.
[62] TCGA 1992, s 159(1).
[63] TCGA 1992, s 159(3).
[64] TCGA 1992, s 159.
[65] TCGA 1992, s 159(2).
[66] TCGA 1992, s 159(3).

As for income tax, the UK branch or agency of a non-UK resident is treated as the non-UK resident's UK representative under new Part 7A of the TCGA 1992 (sections 271A–271J). These rules are a rewritten and updated version of the former rules in FA 1995, sections 126–127. The scheme in Part 7A parallels and refers to the analogous income tax rules in ITA 2007, Part 14, Chapter 2B. Part 7A Chapter 2 imposes various obligations and liabilities in respect of the assessment, collection and recovery of CGT, etc on the UK representative branch or agency. Under section 271F, the obligations and liabilities of the non-UK resident are to be treated as if they were also the obligations and liabilities of the UK representative. Section 271G provides certain exceptions to the rule in section 271F in respect of notices and information requests to the non-UK resident unless the branch or agency has itself been given notice, and does not require an independent agent acting as UK representative to do anything except 'as it is practicable for the representative to do so.' Section 271H provides further exceptions to section 271F in the case of criminal offences and civil penalties.

18.4.2 Deemed Disposals

A non-resident, N, is liable to CGT only if holding chargeable assets in the UK, ie the assets are connected with a trade or profession being run through a branch or an agency here. By TCGA 1992, section 25(1), N is treated as making a disposal of any chargeable assets when the assets are removed from the UK and so cease to be chargeable.[67] If N is also ceasing, contemporaneously, to carry on the trade or profession through a branch or an agency in the UK, section 25(1) does not apply[68] but section 25(3) does. Section 25(3) directs a deemed disposal when the trade ends or the asset ceases to be a chargeable asset; hence there is no deemed disposal if the asset remains a chargeable asset. The transfer of a branch or an agency to a UK-resident company under the same control can now give rise to a deferral of liability.[69]

18.5   Settlements and Trusts

18.5.1 Introduction and Residence

18.5.1.1 Introduction

There are four sets of special rules affecting settlements:

(1)   the first set applies on the migration of settlements (§18.5.2);
(2)   the second set applies on the disposal of a beneficial interest (§18.5.3);
(3)   the third set attributes all trust gains to a settlor who retains an interest (§18.5.4); and
(4)   the fourth set attributes gains realised by foreign trustees to UK beneficiaries (in contravention of the normal principle that only the trustees are liable for CGT) (§18.5.6).

---

[67] TCGA 1992, s 25(1), (7).
[68] TCGA 1992, s 25(2), or, if the asset is an exploration or exploitation asset, as defined by s 25(6).
[69] TCGA 1992, s 171, as widened by FA 2000; for disposals before 1 April 2000, s 172 applied.

The normal CGT definition of 'settlement' applies for (1) and (2); the wider income tax definition in ITTOIA 2005, section 620 applies for (3) and (4). The third set of rules is backed up by rules for transfers of value linked with borrowing (see §18.5.5). These scope of these rules is not affected by the repeals of the general settlor-interested provisions formerly in TCGA 1992, sections 77–79.

These rules represent a growing awareness on the part of the UK tax system that trusts are not just for the support of aged relatives and young children but avoidance devices of a very sophisticated type.[70] The rules offer sophisticated responses to sophisticated schemes, and so reinforce a climate in which sophistication may be attempted. These rules were first introduced in 1991 but have since been amended.[71] This was one of those areas in which the rate of CGT might be higher than the income tax charge. Before 2008 these rates might reach 64% or, in unlucky combination, 104%.[72]

18.5.1.2 Residence

In 2006 the capital gains rules on residence of trustees were aligned with those for income tax (under TCGA 1992, section 69; above §13.9). A trustee who is not resident will be treated as being so if acting as a trustee in the course of a business carried on in the UK through a branch, an agency or a PE here (section 69(2D)). It can be appreciated that there will be major fiscal consequences from a quite small change in the way such trustees run their businesses. The trustees are a single body of persons (under section 69(1)).

In *Roome v Edwards*,[73] an assessment on UK trustees of part of the fund was upheld even though the gain accrued to the trustees of another part—all those trustees being non-resident. FA 2006 introduced an election by which a sub-fund may elect to be taxed as a separate settlement; such an election may preclude such an assessment, but it will mean that there may be a disposal and consequent CGT charge where a transfer is made to a sub-settlement.

Trustees may cease to be resident in the UK. This might happen because of a change in the residence status of a trustee, or by a transfer of the property from one set of trustees to a new set. The concession allowing individuals to be treated as non-resident for the remainder of the year in which they migrate does not apply to trustees in their capacity as trustees.[74] A migration within six years of the creation of the settlement may cause the tax held over on the creation of the settlement to fall due.[75] TCGA 1992, section 10A, which applies to temporary non-residents, applies only to individuals and so not to trusts; this is because there is an exit charge when a trust migrates, but not where an individual does, and this was thought to be sufficient. Section 10A may become relevant where a settlor is charged under section 86.

---

[70] For the Australian response to these problems, see Burns and Krever, *Interest in Non-Resident Trusts* (Australian Tax Research Foundation Study No 28).

[71] FA 1991, ss 83 *et seq*; see Inland Revenue Press Release, 19 March 1991, [1991] *Simon's Tax Intelligence* 290. On 1998 changes, see McCutcheon [1998] BTR 476.

[72] McCutcheon (1998) *Taxation* 617.

[73] [1981] STC 96, [1981] 1 All ER 736, (1981) 54 TC 349.

[74] ESC A11.

[75] TCGA 1992, s 168. The holdover will have been under ss 165 or 260, on which see *Revenue Law*, §§36.3–36.5.

It was found that the deemed disposal rule was not sufficient where a double tax treaty was involved. A rule added in 2005 tries to address this problem.[76] Where a chargeable gain accrues to trustees during a year of assessment for which they are 'within the charge to CGT' but at a time when they are 'non UK resident', nothing in a double tax treaty is to prevent the normal CGT tax charge from arising. Trustee are 'within the charge' for a year if for any part of that year they are resident (or ordinarily resident) and, in a glorious double negative, 'not Treaty non-resident'. A person is treated as a Treaty non-resident if he is non-resident for the purpose of that tax treaty (see §20.6.1).

18.5.2 Deemed Disposal on Trustees Becoming Non-resident: Section 80

Where trustees cease to be resident in the UK there is a deemed disposal of all 'defined assets';[77] assets are defined assets unless they stay within the UK CGT net, or if they were already outside that net by reason of a double tax treaty.[78] Rollover relief will be excluded in analogous circumstances.[79]

Death is not regarded as a tax avoidance device, and so special rules apply where the migration is caused by the death of a trustee. If the trust resumes its UK residence within six months from the death of the trustee, the deemed disposal is excluded, save for assets which have been the subject of an actual disposal in the meantime[80] or which would have been protected by a double tax treaty in any case.[81] Conversely, a trust which has become UK resident by reason of such a death will not be the subject of a deemed disposal (save for assets which have been the subject of holdover relief) if it resumes its non-resident status within six months.[82]

Tax due under a deemed disposal may be collected from any person who ceased to be a trustee within the period of 12 months ending with the migration; the ex-trustee has a right of indemnity in such circumstances.[83] This potential liability does not apply to trustees who establish that they ceased to be trustees before the end of the relevant period and that, at that time, there was no proposal that the trustees might become non-resident.[84]

There is a similar deemed disposal if the trust, while remaining resident under UK ordinary tax rules, ceases to be so thanks to the application of a double tax treaty.[85] There is also a restriction on rollover relief where the new asset is acquired by such trustees.[86]

---

[76] TCGA 1992, s 83A, added by F(No 2)A 2005, s 33, with effect from 16 March 2005.

[77] TCGA 1992, s 80(1), (2). For definitions, see TCGA 1992, ss 169E–169G, added by FA 2004; cross-references from s 80 added by FA 2008. On practice under ss 80–85, see Statement of Practice SP 5/92, paras 4–6.

[78] TCGA 1992, s 80(3), (4), referring to assets remaining in a UK branch or agency.

[79] TCGA 1992, s 80(3), (5).

[80] TCGA 1992, s 80(6), (7).

[81] TCGA 1992, s 81(1), (3).

[82] TCGA 1992, ss 81(5)–(7), 84.

[83] TCGA 1992, s 82.

[84] TCGA 1992, s 82(3).

[85] TCGA 1992, s 83.

[86] TCGA 1992, s 84.

18.5.3 Disposal of Beneficial Interests in Non-resident Settlement: Section 85

The disposal of a beneficial interest does not usually give rise to a charge to CGT,[87] the charge on disposals by the trustees being thought sufficient. However, the disposal of a beneficial interest by a UK-resident beneficiary under a non-resident trust is expressly made chargeable[88] since, in such cases, there will be no charge at the trustee level.

With effect from 6 March 1998, the disposal of a beneficial interest became chargeable where the trust is treated as resident in the UK but has been an offshore trust at any time during its history.[89] Where there is a charge on the migration of the trust under section 80 and that migration was after the beneficiary had acquired the interest, whether by purchase or having the interest conferred, the gain accruing on a subsequent disposal of that interest is calculated on the assumption that it was acquired for market value at the time of the migration, the so-called uplift.[90] The effect will be to give relief for those gains charged at the trustee level when the trust migrates, assuming that there are gains; where there are losses the same rules apply, so that the real function of the rule is simply to mark the boundary between trustee taxation and beneficiary taxation. There is no provision allowing the beneficiary to use losses sustained by the trust.

This approach must be modified where the trust continues to be resident under normal CGT rules but is treated as non-resident by a double tax treaty. Where this occurred before the beneficial interest was acquired by the beneficiary, no relief applies; otherwise, there is a deemed acquisition when the treaty migration occurs.[91]

There is no uplift for 'relevant offshore gains', a phrase preferred by the legislation to the more common 'stockpiled gains'.[92] The relevant gains are those which would have been available to become chargeable if there had been capital payments to UK-resident beneficiaries.[93] The avoidance scheme at which the charge is aimed arose where a non-resident trust had such gains but had not made any chargeable payments; the gains remained 'stockpiled'. The trust would become resident in the UK before being taken offshore again, allowing the trust to take advantage of the uplift as it left the UK. This change applies to trusts becoming non-resident on or after 21 March 2000.[94]

18.5.4 Attribution of Gains under Non-resident Trust to Settlor with Interest in Non-resident or Dual Resident Settlements: Section 86

Under section 86, gains of a non-resident trust are attributed to the settlor who is domiciled in the UK at some time in the year and is either resident in the UK during part of the year or ordinarily resident during the year in which the gain arises.[95] The term 'settlement' is defined in the same way as for income tax legislation and so covers a whole variety of

---

[87] TCGA 1992, s 76.
[88] TCGA 1992, s 85(1); and see *Revenue Law*, §40.6. On practice, see Statement of Practice SP 5/92, paras 4–6.
[89] TCGA 1992, s 76, (1A) and (1B), added by FA 1998, s 128.
[90] TCGA 1992, s 85(3).
[91] TCGA 1992, s 85 (4)–(8).
[92] TCGA 1992, s 85(10), added by FA 2000, s 95.
[93] Ie those within TCGA 1992, s 89(2) and Sch 4C, para 8(3) (s 85(11)).
[94] FA 2000, s 95(5).
[95] TCGA 1992, s 86(1), (3); details of the charge are set out in s 86(4), (5). On practice, see Statement of Practice, SP 5/92, paras 7–10.

situations in which property originates from the settlor.[96] These rules have been progressively widened. In 2008, thought was given to widening this provision to cover a settlor who was not domiciled in the UK but was resident and possibly a remittance basis user, but this did not happen. Other widenings did occur to take account of the new remittance basis.

18.5.4.1 Qualifying Settlement

The charge applies if the settlement is a 'qualifying settlement', ie (a) created on or after 17 March 1998, or (b) created before that date but in relation to which various 'triggering events' occur on or after that date.[97] The first event is that property is provided for the settlement otherwise than by way of bargain at arm's length.[98] The second event is the migration of the trust, or the trust acquiring non-resident status under a double tax treaty.[99] The third event is a variation of the terms of the trust so that any one of a list of people becomes for the first time a person who will or might become entitled to a benefit from the settlement.[100] The fourth event is where a person falling within that list enjoys a benefit from the settlement for the first time and that person is not one who (looking at the matter before that date) might be expected to enjoy a benefit on or after that date.[101]

18.5.4.2 Interest

The settlor is taken to have an interest in a very wide variety of circumstances. The definition covers circumstances in which income or property is, or will or may become applicable, in any circumstances whatsoever, for the benefit of or payable to defined persons. The list of defined persons includes the settlor and a long list of others—the settlor's spouse or civil partner, children and grandchildren,[102] the spouse or civil partner of any such child or grandchild, any company controlled by such persons and any company associated with such a company.[103] There are exclusions for certain types of interest.[104] The charge is avoided if the settlor dies during the year, or if the only listed person giving rise to such an interest dies (or all such persons die) in the year.[105]

The settlor has a statutory indemnity against the trustees,[106] but this may not be worth very much. Of course, it is not likely to be less successful than a claim by the Revenue, but the point of this provision is that because the trustees are non-resident, there is no charge on them in respect of the gains. The Revenue are given extensive information powers.[107]

---

[96] TCGA 1992, ss 169E–169G and Sch 5, paras 7, 8.
[97] TCGA 1992, Sch 5, para 2A.
[98] TCGA 1992, Sch 5, para 9(4); the section is not in terms confined to property being provided by the settlor, but the definition of 'settlement' is confined to property originating from the settlor. On practice, see Statement of Practice SP 5/92, paras 11–37.
[99] TCGA 1992, Sch 5, para 9(4).
[100] TCGA 1992, Sch 5, para 9(5).
[101] TCGA 1992, Sch 5, para 9(6).
[102] TCGA 1992, Sch 5, para 2(3)(da), (db), added in 1998.
[103] TCGA 1992, Sch 5, para 2(1)–(3).
[104] TCGA 1992, Sch 5, para 2(4)–(6).
[105] TCGA 1992, Sch 5, paras 3–5.
[106] TCGA 1992, Sch 5, para 6.
[107] TCGA 1992, Sch 5, paras 11–14 were replaced by Sch 5A in 1994 (Sch 5, para 10 was not replaced).

18.5.4.3 Trusts Created before 17 March 1998

These are subject to different rules, in that the class of disqualifying beneficiaries included children but not grandchildren. The existence of grandchildren will therefore not cause section 86 to apply unless a triggering event occurs on or after 16 March 1998.

18.5.4.4 Trusts Created before 9 March 1991

The attribution to settlor rules were introduced in 1991 and did not apply to trusts created before 19 March 1991 unless one of the triggering events happened on or after that date. However, these trusts were brought within section 86 with effect from 6 April 1999.[108] Such trusts might be saved from the change if they were 'protected settlements'.[109] In order to avoid capital gains being charged on a UK-resident settlor, it became necessary for the children of the settlor, children of the settlor's spouse or civil partner and any spouses or civil partners of such children to exclude themselves as beneficiaries (or, alternatively, for the trust to be wound up or to become resident in the UK). A child under the age of 18 does not have the legal capacity to exclude himself as a beneficiary without consent of the court. Hence, the charge on the settlor does not apply where the only members of the settlor's immediate family who can benefit are children who are under the age of 18 as at 5 April 1999.[110] Unborn children and future spouses or civil partners of the settlor or of his children being within the class of potential beneficiaries are also ignored in applying this test.[111] The presence of the settlor's grandchildren among the beneficiaries is not fatal to the trust's claim to be a protected settlement and so outside these rules.[112] Anti-avoidance provisions covered the period from the Budget Day announcement on 17 March 1998 to 5 April 1999.[113]

18.5.4.5 Section 86 and the Returning Settlor: Section 86A

Section 86 treats the gains realised by a non-resident trust as attributable to the resident settlor. If the settlor is non-resident, section 86 has no application, though section 87 may. If a settlor has become non-resident but then becomes resident again in circumstances falling within TCGA 1992, section 10A, rules are needed to settle the status of gains which have been realised by the trust during the period of non-residence. These gains will have been 'trust gains' for the purposes of section 87 when realised, but now should cease to be so because of being attributed to the settlor under section 10A. The trust gains when the settlor ceases to be resident are calculated first; this sum should be nil since section 86 excludes section 87.[114] Where distributions have been charged to beneficiaries under section 87 they are not also taxed to the settlor; where they are taxed to the settlor on resuming residence, they cease to be trust gains under section 87.[115]

---

[108] TCGA 1992, Sch 5, para 9(1A), added by FA 1998, s 132.
[109] TCGA 1992, Sch 5, para 9(1B).
[110] TCGA 1992, Sch 5, para 9(10A)(a).
[111] TCGA 1992, Sch 5, para 9(10A)(b)–(d).
[112] Revenue Interpretation RI 198 (December 1998)
[113] FA 1998, Sch 23.
[114] TCGA 1992, s 87(3).
[115] TCGA 1992, s 86A, applying where year of departure is 1997–98 or later (FA 1998, s 129(1)).

18.5.5 *Transfer of Value Linked with Borrowing; Attribution of Gains to Beneficiary: Schedules 4B/4C*

Trennery v West,[116] decided by the House of Lords in 2005, held that flip-flop schemes did not work. Under these schemes, taxpayers attempted to mitigate CGT liability on sales of unquoted trading company shares by first transferring the shares to interest in possession trusts, which at that time were liable to CGT at a rate of only 25% (compared to the then 40% top rate of CGT for individuals). Since Parliament could not be absolutely sure that the Revenue would win, special legislation—TCGA 1992, Schedule 4B—was added by FA 2000. This imposes a charge where transfers of value by trustees are linked with borrowing by trustees. Among the trusts caught by Schedule 4B are those within TCGA 1992, sections 87 or 88, ie offshore trusts with one or more UK beneficiaries.[117] Schedule 4B is backed up by Schedule 4C; this ensures that the rules in Schedule 4B apply in these circumstances rather than the rules in TCGA 1992, sections 86–98. These rules were supplemented by FA 2003, which added a new section 85A and made many revisions to Schedule 4C;[118] taxpayers had decided to use the stringent new rules to create a suspension of the operation of sections 87—89. In view of the decision of the House of Lords, it is thought unnecessary to go into this special legislation further.

18.5.6 *Attribution of Gains Arising under Trusts and Other Arrangements to Beneficiaries Receiving Capital Payment: Section 87*

Section 87 was the subject of much discussion in connection with the reform of the remittance basis; eventually many of the wilder ideas were discarded.[119]

18.5.6.1 Which Settlements?

Gains realised by overseas trustees of a settlement are attributed to beneficiaries; this treatment is now applied irrespective of the domicile and residence of the settlor when the trust was created.[120] For this purpose, the term 'settlement' receives not its narrow, CGT meaning but its wide, income tax meaning of arrangement.[121] These provisions also apply to trusts which are resident in the UK for domestic purposes, but which are treated as non-resident by a double tax treaty; in such circumstances the trust gains giving rise to potential attribution to the settlor will be the lesser of (a) the actual gains, and (b) gains protected by the treaty; these are called dual resident settlements.[122]

18.5.6.2 The Statutory Scheme

As chargeable gains accrue to non-resident trustees, they are cumulated as trust gains of the particular year,[123] including those which have been attributed to the settlor under section 77.[124] Capital payments received by the beneficiaries are then attributed to the trust

---

[116] [2005] UKHL 5. See *Revenue Law*, §40.2.2.
[117] TCGA 1992, Sch 4C, para 1; Schedule added by FA 2000, s 92, Sch 25.
[118] See Revenue BN33, [2003] *Simon's Tax Intelligence* 752, and Chamberlain [2003] BTR 396.
[119] See HMRC Finance Bill Notes, Sch 7, paras 50 *et seq*.
[120] TCGA 1992 s 87(10), as amended by FA 1998, s 130.
[121] TCGA 1992, s 97(7), ie ITTOIA 2005, s 620.
[122] TCGA 1992, s 88.
[123] Ie such gains as would have been chargeable if they had been resident or ordinarily resident in the UK.
[124] TCGA 1992, s 87(8).

gains, which become chargeable gains in the hands of the beneficiaries.[125] This applies to all beneficiaries, whether domiciled in the UK at some time during the year or not, but the remittance basis may apply in certain situations, ie when the non-UK domiciled beneficiary comes within sections 809B, 809C or 809D (see above at §15.4).[126] When a capital payment is made to a beneficiary in one year and a trust gain arises in a later year, a charge may arise in that later year. Relief may be claimed for trust losses.[127] Under the pre-2008 rules all such trust gains were placed in one big pool. The 2008 rules make a welcome change to a year-by-year basis; matching rules are provided on a last in, first out basis (see below).[128] The location of the asset from which the trust gains arise does not matter.[129]

The gains are attributed to beneficiaries in proportion to the capital payment received by them, but are not to exceed those payments.[130] This obscure provision seems to mean that if the only payments made to the beneficiaries are made to A, then A can be assessed for all the gains accruing to the non-resident trustees up to the amount A has received; A is thus at risk for up to 28% of the entire sum received.

18.5.6.3 Capital Payment: Section 97(1), (2)

A capital payment is defined as one which is not chargeable to income tax. The term covers the transfer of an asset, a loan and various indirect payments. It does not cover a payment by way of bargain at arm's length.[131] An interest-free loan repayable on demand has been held to be a payment—and so a capital payment—for the purposes of this rule.[132] The court should prefer a bold interpretation to a narrow one if the latter would reduce the legislation to futility; the value of the payment could be determined retrospectively.[133]

18.5.6.4 Transition: Non UK-domiciled Beneficiaries and 6 April 2008

There are several important transitional rules. No charge arises where such beneficiaries receive capital payments before 6 April 2008 which are matched to trust gains accruing after 5 April 2008. Similarly no charge arises in the converse case—where payments received after 5 April are matched with trust gains accruing before 6 April 2008.[134]

18.5.6.5 Rebasing Option

FA 2008 included an option under which trustees on non UK-resident trusts might rebase their assets as at 6 April 2008. This would make compliance with the UK rules much easier. It will be seen that the election was given to the trustees, not the beneficiaries.[135] Rebasing was to be effective for capital gains but not for income tax. During the passage of the Finance Bill 2008 a number of changes were made to soften this approach.[136]

---

[125] TCGA 1992, s 87(4).
[126] TCGA 1992, s 87B, added by FA 2008.
[127] TCGA 1992, s 97(6).
[128] TCGA 1992, s 87A, added by FA 2008, para 108; ss 92–95 are all repealed by para 113.
[129] HMRC Notes, para 51.
[130] TCGA 1992, s 87(5).
[131] TCGA 1992, s 97(1), (2); on valuation, see s 97(4).
[132] *Billingham v Cooper* [2001] STC 1177 (CA).
[133] *Ibid, per* Robert Walker LJ at para 35, quoting a passage from Lord Simon LC in *Nokes v Doncaster Amalgamated Collieries* [1940] AC 1014, 1022.
[134] FA 2008, Sch 7, paras 119 *et seq.*
[135] FA 2008, Sch 7, para 126.
[136] See Public Bill Committee, 19 June 2008, col 873 (Jane Kennedy, MP).

18.5.6.6 'Interest' Charge on Matched Payments to Beat Deferral: Section 91

In an effort to discourage the use of settlements as devices to retain gains rather than distribute them, the charge under section 87 is supplemented.[137] Increased tax is due if a capital payment is made and the payment can be matched to trust gains from an earlier period (referred to as the qualifying amount).[138] Now that the general matching approach is 'last in, first out', it follows that payments matched with gains of the same year are not subject to this rule. The exclusion applies to the trusts gains of the previous year as well.

The increased tax is equal to the amount of interest that would be chargeable on a sum equal to the tax in respect of the chargeable amount for a period beginning on 1 December in the year of assessment following that for which it is the chargeable amount, and ending on 30 November in the year of assessment following that in which the capital payment is made. The rate of interest is currently set at 10%, but may be varied by Treasury order.[139] Thus, if a capital payment was made in 2010–11 and the payment is matched with trust gains accruing in 2005–06, there would have been 50% supplementary charge for the five-year period 1 December 2006 to 30 November 2011. This charge will now be related to the flat 28% rate of CGT, and runs regardless of when in 2010–11 the capital payments are made. The extra tax is not to exceed the amount of the capital payment.[140] In reckoning the period for the calculation of interest, it is not possible to go back before 1 December falling six years before 1 December in the year of assessment following that in which the payment is made (making a maximum of four chargeable years).[141]

Matching etc, section 87A. As already seen, rules matching capital payments with trust gains generally adopt a last in, first out approach.[142] HMRC have produced worked examples for their Notes to the Finance Bill.

18.5.6.7 Payment by Controlled Company

The idea of a chargeable payment includes a payment by a company controlled by the trustees; a payment received from a qualifying company controlled by the trustees is treated as if it had been received direct from the trustees. A company is a qualifying company if it is a close company, or if it would be close if it were resident in the UK.[143] In consequence, the definition of 'beneficiary' is amended to include people who receive capital payments from the settlement. However, the trustees of a settlement are not treated as beneficiaries, a rule which prevents appointments or advances to sub-trusts being capital payments.[144] It was found that the definition of 'control' was too loose, and so the requirement that persons with control had to be resident or ordinarily resident in the UK was removed.[145] This change in determining control does not affect the rules about the extent of the interest which the UK resident is treated as having and so the extent to which the capital payment would be chargeable.

---

[137] TCGA 1992, s 91.
[138] TCGA 1992, s 91(2).
[139] TCGA 1992, s 91(3), (6); the charge cannot affect payments made before 6 April 1992.
[140] TCGA 1992, s 91(2).
[141] TCGA 1992, s 91(4), (5).
[142] TCGA 1992, s 87A; reversing the previous rule in TCGA 1992, s 92(4).
[143] TCGA 1992, s 96(10).
[144] TCGA 1992, s 97(8)–(10).
[145] TCGA 1992, s 86(5), as amended by FA 2000, s 96.

18.5.6.8 Interaction with ITA 2007, Section 731 (ex TA 1988, Section 740)

ITA 2007, section 731 treats a capital payment as income to the extent that there is relevant income. Where a payment falling within section 731 exceeds the then relevant income, the excess may be taxed in future years under section 731 should relevant income arise; however, it may also be taxed immediately under these rules (including the rules for migration of settlements).[146] When this occurs, the excess reduces the amount liable to be taxed under section 731 in later years, ie the charge under these rules excludes the subsequent charge under section 731.[147]

Section 731 does not apply if there is no tax avoidance motive. Moreover, since the top income tax rate is higher than the top capital gains tax rate, there is no longer any point in a beneficiary arguing that he should come within section 731 rather than the TCGA 1992 provision.[148]

18.5.6.9 Migration: Section 89

The charge under these rules must take account of the migration of the trust from the UK complete with trust gains. Capital payments subsequent to the distribution are treated as chargeable gains of the beneficiaries.[149] Payments made before it ceases to be resident are treated only as capital payments (thus causing a liability in respect of subsequent gains) if made in anticipation of a disposal by the trustees in the non-resident period.[150]

18.5.6.10 Transfer between Settlements: Section 90

Where property is transferred to other trusts, whether or not the latter were made by the original settlor, the infection of 'trust gains' will be transferred with the property so far as not already attributed to the beneficiaries and so far as not made for a consideration in money or money's worth.[151] UK charities may be able to claim exemption from TCGA 1992, section 87 under section 256.[152]

On transfer of value linked with borrowing, see §18.5.5.

---

[146] TCGA 1992, ss 87 or 89.

[147] ITA 2007, s 734, ex TA 1988, s 740(6).

[148] Butterworth's Finance Act 1998, Commentary to FA 1998, s 130, points out two other differences: (a) that a distribution to a non-resident will wash out the gain for s 87 but not for s 731; and (b) that s 87 does not apply if the beneficiary is resident but not domiciled, whereas s 731 is excluded for such people only if the relevant income is foreign and the capital distributed is kept abroad.

[149] TCGA 1992, s 89(2). This appears to be in addition to any liability that may arise under the deemed disposal rule in s 71.

[150] TCGA 1992, s 89(1).

[151] TCGA 1992, s 90.

[152] Revenue Interpretation RI 189 (1998).

19

Unilateral Relief Against Double Taxation

19.1 Introduction: The Problems of Double Taxation

The UK taxes income if it arises here, or if the person entitled to it is resident here. This leaves untaxed only foreign income[1] arising to a non-resident. If other countries adopt a similarly generous view of their own taxing powers—as they often do—it is inevitable that some income will be taxed twice. Double taxation may also arise in connection with capital gains, but this is reduced because the UK taxes gain on the basis of residence only; a non-resident does not pay CGT even in respect of assets sited in the UK. UK rules have for many years allowed the UK resident a credit for the foreign tax paid. The rules for credit relief were based on the idea of the individual source and individual country rather than pooling, and so could be quite restrictive. FA 2000 allowed pooling for certain dividends (§19.5.4) and FA 2005 allows it for royalty income from the same source but different countries.

---

[1] See above §16.1.

However, FA 2005 also introduced several new rules to restrict relief in ways which marked the end of the idea of the credit system as something which needed little justification.

With the credit system having been brought into disrepute, voices were raised in support of a system which exempted foreign source dividends from UK tax altogether. A discussion document was issued in 2007, and a new regime was introduced by FA 2009. The relevant legislation on the exemption for foreign (and domestic) dividends received by a UK-resident company is found in CTA 2009, Part 9A. This was followed in 2011 by the introduction of an election to exempt profits of foreign permanent establishments of UK residents. Foreign tax credit and other relief, formerly in TA 1988 and written into TIOPA 2010, are still available, but are less important than they once were now that the vast majority of foreign dividends are exempt from UK tax.

19.1.1 Costs

19.1.1.1 Background

Double taxation of cross-border income is thought to be objectionable since, by making overseas profits accruing to UK residents more expensive than domestic profits, it discourages a person from trading overseas and so interferes with international trade, a breach of capital export neutrality (CEN). It will also cause extra costs to persons resident in other countries but with UK source income. The extra costs to business were examined by the OECD in 1991[2] (the OECD report) and formed the focus for much of the work of the Ruding Committee's report on EC countries in 1992 (the Ruding report) and the later EC Commission Staff Working Paper on Company Taxation in the Internal Market (2001).[3] The reports of 1991 and 1992 showed first that in order to achieve a 5% return on an investment after tax, the domestic tax system produces its own costs—requiring an average pre-tax return of 5.8%. However, they showed that the required pre-tax rate of return rose to 7.5% once international factors were considered; the UK figures were 5.9%, 6.7% for investment from the UK into all other OECD countries and 7.0% for investment from other countries into the UK. These UK figures were reached after taking account of tax treaties; without such treaties the figures were 8.2% and 9.0%.[4] Tables 23 and 24 of the 2001 report, based on figures from 1999, showed it was still the case that neither CEN nor capital import neutrality (CIN) was respected in the EU; outbound and inbound investments were still taxed more heavily than domestic investment.[5] In the absence of a will to have one tax system common to all countries (though slow progress is being made on a common consolidated corporate tax base), steps may be taken towards the less glamorous goal of reducing these costs by domestic and bilateral action. It is worth noting that for a multinational, compliance costs came to 1.9% of tax payments, while for a medium-sized enterprise with international business they came to 30.9%.

On the role of the European Union (EU) in making of treaties and on the relation between EU law and treaties, see below at §20.1 and chapter twenty-one.

---

[2] *Taxing Profits in a Global Economy* (OECD, 1991).
[3] Ruding (chair), *Report of the Committee of Independent Experts* (EC Commission, 1992) and EC COM(2001) 582.
[4] OECD report, table 5.9; see *ibid*, ch 2, Pt D, ch 5, ch 6, Pt C; and Ruding report, chs 2, 5.
[5] For much useful technical background, see Loretz (2007) 28 *Fiscal Studies* 227.

19.1.1.2 The FA 2000 Modernisation of the Credit System

FA 2000 contained many changes to the rules for double taxation relief (DTR) as a result of the consultation process begun in 1999.[6] It has to be said that this process was very unprofessional and the resulting legislative wrangle one of the least edifying of recent memory. The most public problems revolved around the proposal to stop the use of mixer companies, ie foreign companies with UK parents, which were used to mix receipts from various parts of the world before they were transmitted to the UK as dividends. This enabled companies to get round one of the then universal principles of the system, that foreign tax should be set against UK tax on the same source, ie no pooling.

The problems were two-fold. First, the proposal had not been part of the consultation process. Secondly, it ran into such heavy opposition that it had to be scrapped. However, the form in which it was scrapped was not a simple abandonment of the proposal, or even a brand new provision allowing pooling. Instead the section which was going to outlaw mixing was amended so as to become one which allowed pooling in prescribed circumstances.

This wrangling meant that other important changes have tended to get overlooked. Many of the changes made by FA 2000 were beneficial to the taxpayer, either enacting existing practice or making significant changes, such as the excess credit loss rules for dividends. Of the 21 paragraphs, 15 could be seen as beneficial. One such was the revision of time limits for claiming relief; this had been made necessary by the 1996 loan relationship and similar rules which would mean that with the UK accounting-base rule, the UK would have taxed interest long before the foreign tax system did.[7] More controversial are the relationship between treaty relief and unilateral relief, and the rule requiring taxpayers to take reasonable steps to minimise their foreign tax in TIOPA 2010, section 33.

19.1.2 Harmful Tax Competition

While much effort has been expended over the last few decades to try to remove discrimination against non-residents, the attention of the OECD is now turning to the opposite problem—tax discrimination in favour of non-residents. This practice has developed as states scramble for inward investment. Where this goes too far it is referred to as 'fiscal dumping'; the use of the term 'dumping', which is also used for practices banned under GATT and now the World Trade Organisation, is deliberate. The OECD has developed rules which would prevent, or at least limit, harmful tax competition; the European Commission has set up a code of practice.[8] The OECD has set up a Forum on Harmful Tax Practices, with a soft approach to compliance based on periods of self-review followed by peer review; its powers are limited to financial services and similar mobile service activities.[9] It is not concerned about a state's right to charge lower rates of tax than other states, provided

---

[6] See Inland Revenue, *Double Taxation Relief for Companies—a discussion paper*, March 1999 and *Double Taxation Relief for Companies: Outcome of Review*, March 2000. See also the articles in [1999] BTR by Waters at 448, Oliver at 459 and Harris 469.

[7] On time limits see TIOPA 2010, ss 19, 79 and 80, ex TA 1988, s 806, amended by FA 2000, Sch 30, para 13.

[8] See introductory article by Weiner and Ault (1998) 51 *National Tax Jo* 601. See OECD Reports for 1998, 2000, 2001 and 2004, van Raad, *Materials on International and EC Tax Law, 2004–05*, vol 1 (International Tax Centre Leiden, 2004) 811–1002, and see, generally, Schön (ed), *Tax Competition in Europe* (IBFD, 2003).

[9] See OECD website for progress reports at <www.oecd.org>.

that rate is applied generally; so, a 20% corporation tax would not be objectionable, but a general rate of 20% and a 3% rate on these mobile activities is likely to be, especially if such companies are allowed to provide these services only to people outside the state and, almost conclusively, if the state has refused to supply details of these transactions to other states. The OECD has made a certain amount of progress but is still concerned with transparency and exchange of information. The original OECD report of 1998 also considered what defensive measures Member States might take, including the introduction of CFC rules. Progress reports were published in 2001 and 2004; by 2004 countries previously described as 'tax havens' had become 'participating partners', but this was because they had joined the project—up to a point. More recently, the OECD has focused on exchange of information on request on tax matters. In the OECD's Global Forum on Transparency and Exchange of Information for Tax Purposes most recent (2011) progress report, all jurisdictions surveyed have committed to implementing the OECD's international standard on exchange of information, with only Guatemala, Nauru and Niue yet to implement it substantially.[10]

The EU harmful tax competition scheme is wider in that it concentrates on any type of activity and not just mobile services. However, it is concerned with competition within the EU, and so would find nothing wrong with a low rate of tax on some services if other Member States charged similarly low rates. A Code of Conduct for business taxation was adopted by the Council of Economics and Finance Ministers (ECOFIN) on 1 December 1997. By adopting this Code, the Member States undertook to (a) roll back existing tax measures that constitute harmful tax competition, and (b) refrain from introducing any such measures in the future.[11] A survey of Member State practices was completed in 1999.[12] The Code is not legally binding but has political force. It is monitored by a Code of Conduct Group that reports regularly to the Council. The EU scheme also makes allowances for state aid factors in favour of outermost regions and small islands.

19.2 Methods for Reducing or Eliminating Double Taxation[13]

19.2.1 Exemption[14]

A tax system could achieve the avoidance of double taxation in a number of ways. One is not to tax overseas income, either generally or particularly. Such was, in effect, the case when the remittance basis was at its height, before 1914,[15] and until 1974 when the remittance basis was available to UK residents in respect of income earned overseas.

---

[10] The 2011 report is available at <http://www.oecd.org/site/0,3407,en_21571361_43854757_1_1_1_1_1,00.html>.

[11] For recent developments, see the Commission's website on harmful tax competition at <http://ec.europa.eu/taxation_customs/taxation/company_tax/harmful_tax_practices/index_en.htm>.

[12] Inland Revenue Press Release; for (earlier) reservations, see House of Lords Select Committee on European Union Legislation, HL-92, 15th Report, 1998–1999 session, paras 119–46.

[13] On history, see Harris [1999] BTR 469.

[14] The merits of credit and exemption are considered in Inland Revenue, *Double Taxation for Companies—a discussion paper* (March 1999), chs 3, 4; here, the Inland Revenue came down in favour of the status quo, ie credit not exemption (see para 4.18).

[15] FA 1914, s 5; for history, see Royal Commission on the Taxation of Profits and Income, *1st Report*, Cmd 8761 (1953), §§15–20 and Inland Revenue discussion paper (1999), *op cit*, Annex 5.

The special status afforded to overseas trade corporations, whereby they were exempt on trading income reinvested overseas, was another example.[16] Many countries give substantial exemptions for overseas trade in an attempt to assist their own balance of trade and general level of economic activity.[17] Today, France practices an extensive but not universal exemption system for foreign income. Some countries operate an exemption system for income from a country which is a tax treaty country (Canada, Germany and in part Australia).[18] The Netherlands is closer to France on this matter but applies a principle of exemption with progression. Under this approach the foreign income is not itself taxed but, because it is in effect treated as the bottom slice of overall income, it will, assuming a progressive rate structure, increase the rate of tax charged on that part which is chargeable.[19] For the UK's 2009 move to exempt participation dividends and profits of foreign PEs, see §19.3 below.

Short of abandoning the taxation of overseas income, the Government has three other options, examined in §§19.2.2–19.2.4 below.

19.2.2 Credits: Direct and Indirect

The first option for the Government is unilaterally to allow the foreign tax paid as a credit against the UK tax liability. This is permitted by TIOPA 2010, section 18 (ex TA 1988, section 790). Similar provisions apply to CGT[20] and to corporation tax on capital gains.[21] The rules which the foreign tax must satisfy in order to qualify as a tax credit are generally, but not always, the same whether the credit arises under treaty or unilaterally.[22] It is customary to talk about 'direct' and 'indirect' credits. Direct credits are credits for tax charged directly on the income, eg rent from land or a dividend on shares. Indirect credits are credits for tax paid on the profits out of which the direct income has emerged. Thus, while a tax on the dividend paid by a company carries a direct credit, the tax paid by the company on the profits out of which the dividend is paid is available for indirect credit against the tax on the dividend itself. The same point is made by saying that the indirect credit is credit for the tax on the underlying profits. The UK refers to this by the formula 'relief for the underlying tax', rather than 'indirect tax credit'; the UK formula may be long-winded, but it is precise and avoids problems of confusion with relief for indirect taxes. In order to qualify for the relief for the underlying tax it is usually necessary to have a significant—or 'investment' or 'participating'—shareholding; holdings falling short of this are often referred to as 'portfolio' holdings. The boundary between the two is often 10%.

---

[16] See above at §15.1.

[17] See Royal Commission (1953), *op cit*; and Royal Commission on the Taxation of Profits and Income, *Final Report*, Cmd (1955), app III.

[18] See Arnold, Li and Sandler, *Working Paper 96-1 for the Technical Committee on Business Taxation* (Canada Department of Finance, 1996). Australia has moved from a listed country approach to a general exemption for branch income and non-portfolio dividends (otherwise a foreign tax credit). This is used in conjunction with the CFC rules under which the credit system is used.

[19] There is much valuable material on the rules in 10 foreign countries in Inland Revenue discussion paper (1999), *op cit*, Annex 6.

[20] TIOPA 2010, ss 31–33, ex TCGA 1992, ss 277, 278; on which, see Statement of Practice SP 6/88; and [1989] BTR 105. A treaty may be useful in providing its own rules for the situs of assets.

[21] TIOPA 2010, s 18, ex TA 1988, ss 788(1), 790(1).

[22] Eg the rules in TIOPA 2010, ss 2–9 (treaty) versus 8–17 (unilateral), both giving rise to the credit in s 18; ex TA 1988, ss 794–806.

If the foreign tax is available as a credit at a rate which wipes out any UK tax liability, it might appear that there is very little difference between a credit system and an exemption system. However, under a credit system the foreign income will still be relevant in calculating the person's total income and so the marginal rate of tax. However, this distinction is itself blurred if the country still takes account of the foreign income in computing taxable income—exemption with progression.

19.2.3 Deduction

The second option for the Government is to specify that the foreign tax shall be deductible in computing the profits of the business, thus treating the foreign tax like any other business expense. A foreign tax may be deductible under the principles applicable to ITTOIA 2005, Part 2/CTA 2009, Part 3, but case law establishes that this cannot be true of an income tax (*Revenue Law*, §22.3.2). Deduction for income tax and corporation tax purposes in respect of non-UK tax paid on overseas income and profits is permitted in the UK by TIOPA 2010, section 112 (ex TA 1988, section 811). Section 113 provides a deduction from a capital gain for foreign tax on the disposal of an asset. Such foreign tax may not be deducted in respect of income charged on a remittance basis.

19.2.4 Treaty

The third option for the Government is to enter into a double taxation agreement with the other country, a process authorised by TIOPA 2010, section 2 (ex TA 1988, section 788). Treaty relief may exempt some income from tax in one country and give credit for foreign taxes on other income (see further below at §20.3).

19.2.5 Electing Against Credit

Under UK tax law, a person may elect not to take the credit relief.[23] There are circumstances in which this may be advantageous. Thus, if the foreign tax arises on part of a source of income but there is an overall loss in respect of that source, credit relief will be useless; a deduction will, however, increase the loss and the loss, unlike unused credits, may be set off against other income or rolled forward to later years. Taxpayers may not elect to treat a part of the foreign tax as a credit and the balance as a deduction.[24] However, they may treat one foreign tax as a credit and another as a deduction. For new rules on unused credits, see below §19.6.

19.2.6 UK as Source

As country of source, the UK may wish to levy income tax on income accruing to a non-resident. Here it may decide not to tax at all (eg certain government securities held by non-residents), give credit for tax paid in the country of residence (not a feature of the UK tax system) or, under a treaty, levy a reduced rate of tax, often called a withholding tax, leaving the other country to give credit if it wishes.

---

[23] TIOPA 2010, s 27, ex TA 1988, s 805.
[24] TIOPA 2010, s 31(2), ex TA 1988, s 795(2).

19.2.7 Further Issues

It should not be thought that the selection of the appropriate method of avoiding double taxation completes these issues. Enough has been said in this book about different ways of taxing income to warn one that many complexities remain. If one country taxes a particular receipt and the other does not, there is no problem of double taxation; however, if one country allows a particular deduction in computing income and the other does not, the two systems will achieve different levels of income and so another but different reason for variable amounts of tax. Again the two systems may disagree about when the income arises. More fundamentally, they may disagree about where the taxpayer resides, where the income arises, what sort of income it is (eg business income or royalties) or even whose income it is. At this point the plate tectonics analogy for the collision of tax systems (above §13.1) becomes ever more apt, and the analogy of three-dimensional chess to provide solutions may have to add the fourth dimension of time.

19.3 Foreign Dividend and Foreign PE Profits Exemptions

19.3.1 Introduction

Prior to the FA 2009 reforms, the UK double tax relief system for foreign-sourced income was based on the concept of granting a credit under a treaty for foreign taxes, although the UK also offered a comprehensive form of unilateral tax credit and a deduction. In June 2007 a discussion document raised the possibility of replacing the credit system with an exemption system for shareholdings of 10% or more.[25] The first argument was that the credit system had become too complicated for multinationals and other large businesses, especially in relation to calculating the indirect credit, so compliance costs would be reduced. One might add that there was still the risk of uncredited foreign taxes. The second was that with an exemption system, these businesses would be encouraged to repatriate foreign profits without having to worry about UK taxes instead of leaving the profits offshore awaiting reinvestment, so life would be simpler. To simplicity and reduced compliance costs the supporters added the politically essential argument that it would enhance UK competitiveness, and that the cost in terms of lost tax revenue would not be substantial.

For such a major reform, the time between discussion proposals and legislative enactment was relatively short.[26] From July 2009, most dividends received by a UK-resident company from foreign companies (and other UK companies) are exempt from UK tax. Non-exempt foreign dividends may be eligible for relief from double tax under the existing tax credit system, along with various forms of foreign income other than dividends. As part of the package of reforms, including the move to exemption, the UK introduced a worldwide debt cap to limit group interest expense deducted in the UK and is reforming its CFC rules. The Government also studied the case for a reduced rate of corporation tax applied to income from patents, which has led to the introduction of the so-called 'patent box', discussed above at §4.8.

---

[25] See ch 3, above.
[26] The regime was inserted by FA 2009, s 34 and Sch 14: see Voisey's FA 2009 note in [2009] BTR 533 for more details.

The detailed rules governing the dividend exemption system (sometimes called the 'dividend participation system') are in CTA 2009, Part 9A. Companies have the option to elect out of the exemption regime, such as where a relevant double tax treaty provides for a lower rate of withholding tax on dividends if the dividends are 'subject to tax' in the UK.[27] The regime begins by prescribing that all dividends and other distributions are chargeable to corporation tax unless they qualify for at least one specified category of exemption (CTA 2009, section 931A(1)).[28] The legislation provides different regimes for 'small companies' (defined in section 931S by reference to a European test) and for 'non-small' companies. The discussion that follows begins with non-small companies, before moving on to consider the rules applicable to small companies.

19.3.2 Non-small Companies

The exemption regime as it applies to 'non-small companies' is in CTA 2009, Part 9A, Chapter 3. There are five 'exempt classes' of distribution, which should cover most distributions received by UK-resident companies, whether from other UK companies or from non-UK companies. It is necessary to fall into only one of these classes in order to qualify for exemption.

The exempt classes are:

- section 931E—distributions from controlled companies (ie subsidiaries);
- section 931F—distributions in respect of non-redeemable ordinary shares (ie most ordinary dividends);[29]
- section 931G—distributions from portfolio shareholdings (no more than 10%);
- section 931H—distributions that are not designed to reduce UK tax; and
- section 931I—distributions in respect of shares accounted for as liabilities for loan relationships (there is a cross-reference to section 521C).

Excluded from these exemptions are any amounts of interest which are deemed to be distributions under CTA 2010, section 1000(1)E or F.[30] Also excluded are distributions where the paying company is able to claim a tax deduction in the country of origin (section 931D(c)).

Lastly, dividends are excluded from exemption if they are made 'as part of a scheme the main purpose, or one of the main purposes, of which is to obtain a tax advantage', or if the scheme is one of the specific prescribed schemes in the legislation.[31] Sections 931J to 931Q contain eight categories of schemes which will prevent an exemption from applying. These are schemes involving:

(1)   the manipulation of the controlled company rules;
(2)   quasi-preference or quasi-redeemable shares;

---

[27] Voisey [2009] BTR 533, 540.
[28] F(No 3)A 2010 removed a somewhat confusing exemption for dividends 'of a capital nature' (ex s 931A(2)); see Tank, Weston and Melia [2011] BTR 47.
[29] CTA 2009, s 931U sets out the meaning of 'ordinary share' and 'redeemable' for this purpose.
[30] Ex TA 1988, s 209(2)(d) or s 209(2)(e)). The exclusion is in CTA 2009, s 931D(b).
[31] CTA 2009, s 931V sets out the meaning of 'scheme' and 'tax advantage scheme'; 'tax advantage' is defined in TA 1988, s 840ZA (not rewritten).

(3) manipulation of portfolio holdings;
(4) arrangements in the nature of loan relationships;
(5) distributions for which deductions are given;
(6) payments for distributions;
(7) payments not on arm's length terms; and
(8) the diversion of trade income.

In summary, from 2009, the vast majority of distributions received by large (more precisely 'non-small') UK companies should be covered by at least one of these exemptions. As a result, the UK rules should comply with the requirements of EU law, and also provide analogous treatment where a non-Member State is involved.

19.3.3 Small Companies

The rules applying to dividends received by 'small' companies are in CTA 2009, Part 9A, Chapter 2. A small company for this purpose is defined in section 931S as one with fewer than 50 full-time employee equivalents and turnover or a balance sheet total of €10 million or less.[32] Certain investment companies, eg an authorised unit trust, cannot be small. Under section 931B, dividends received by a small company will be exempt if:

(1) the payer is a resident of (and only of) the UK or a qualifying territory at the time that the distribution is received;
(2) the distribution is not a deemed distribution in respect of interest under CTA 2010, section 1000(1)E or F;
(3) no deduction is allowed to a resident of any territory outside the UK under the law of that territory in respect of the distribution; and
(4) the distribution is not made as part of a tax advantage scheme.

The vast majority of dividends received by a small company will satisfy these conditions for exemption. A list of qualifying territories for the purposes of requirement (3) above is available on the HMRC website. These are countries with which the UK has double tax treaties that contain a non-discrimination clause, ie normally countries which levy tax on corporate profits as opposed to tax havens.

19.3.4 Exemption for Foreign PE Profits

FA 2011 introduced a new optional exemption from corporation tax on profits arising from foreign PEs of UK-resident companies (CTA 2009, sections 18A *et seq*).[33] The introduction of the new exemption is consistent with the UK's move towards a territorial approach to taxation of foreign dividends, as just discussed. Absent an election into the new regime, a UK-resident company with a foreign PE is taxed in the UK on its worldwide income, including income attributable to the activities of the PE. Consequently, the UK-resident

---

[32] Adopting by reference the definition in the Annex to Commission Recommendation 2003/361/EC of 6 May 2003.
[33] For more detail, see Ball [2011] BTR 424. Note also the implementing no gain/no loss rule in TCGA 1992, 276A, where an exemption election has been made under CTA 2009, s 18A.

company gets immediate relief in the UK on any losses attributable to the activities of the PE.[34] Any profits of the PE, on the other hand, are likely to be subject to tax in the foreign jurisdiction. To address the risk of double taxation of the foreign PE profits, the UK allows relief for foreign tax by way of credit against the UK tax on those profits, either under a tax treaty or under the UK's unilateral relief rules in TIOPA 2010, Part 2, Chapter 1 (discussed in §19.4 below).

Should the UK resident company elect (irrevocably) into the new exemption regime, any profits attributable to its foreign PEs are exempt from UK corporation tax. The downside is that no relief is given in the UK for losses attributable to foreign PEs either (CTA 2009, sections 18A and 18F). The decision whether to elect for exemption treatment rather than tax credit relief will depend on the particular circumstances of the UK-resident company and its foreign PEs.

19.4   Credit Relief: The Framework

19.4.1 Introduction

Although FA 2009 introduced an wide-ranging exemption system for dividends (see §19.3), there will be many circumstances in which that system does not apply and the existing credit system does. The unilateral tax credit is a generous relief; indeed, its generosity can weaken the UK Government's bargaining power when negotiating treaties. The main rules on unilateral relief were written into TIOPA 2010, Part 2, Chapter 1, and, subject to some caveats discussed next, generally apply even though treaty relief may also be available.

Situations in which unilateral relief will be particularly important are where:

(1)   there is no double tax treaty with the country of source;[35] or
(2)   there is such a treaty, but it does not cover this particular tax;[36] or
(3)   taxes have been levied by municipalities or other constituent parts of the state and the relevant treaty applies only to the national state;[37] or
(4)   treaty relief applies only to certain classes of income.[38]

Treaty relief of course remains vital when considering a non-resident with UK-source income.

19.4.1.1 Treaty Relief Excluding Unilateral Relief

The interaction of unilateral and treaty relief was changed fundamentally but not completely in 2000. TA 1988, section 793A provided that treaty rules will exclude unilateral

---

[34] The details of the exemption are discussed in Ball, *op cit*.
[35] On interaction with treaties, see TIOPA 2010, s 11. On application to dividend income, see Statement of Practice SP 12/93.
[36] TIOPA 2010, s 6(1)–(4), ex TA 1988, s 788(3).
[37] TIOPA 2010, s 8(3), ex TA 1988, s 790(12), refers to 'territory' not 'State'.
[38] See ex TA 1988, s 800, repealed by FA 2000, Sch 30, para 9.

relief in two situations.[39] These rules may provide an interesting example of a treaty impos-ing a charge to tax which would not otherwise arise. The situations are:

(1)   where the treaty (or the law of the foreign country implementing the treaty) expressly grants a credit for foreign tax paid; and
(2)   where the treaty expressly denies a credit.

In each case unilateral relief will not be available. This new relationship applies only to future treaties. It is not clear that this change is justified in principle. The section 793A rules are now found in TIOPA 2010, sections 10 and 25.

    In *Bayfine UK v Revenue & Customs Commissioners*,[40] the Court of Appeal considered the relationship between unilateral credit relief under TA 1988, section 790 and relief under the US–UK Treaty, Article 23. Arden LJ held that since the purpose of the treaty was to eliminate double taxation and prevent evasion, a construction under which both States had to give relief was wrong. In the present case this was avoided by paying proper attention to Article 1(4).[41] The overall result was that the UK was not obliged to give credit relief for the US tax, but the US authorities were. She also held that HMRC were not obliged to allow unilateral relief as treaty relief was available.[42]

19.4.1.2 History

Unilateral relief was introduced into the UK in 1950, although relief for tax charged in a dominion had been known since 1916.[43] In 1950 the credit was to be for three-quarters of Commonwealth taxes and for one-half of foreign taxes. This may have been because of the notion of imperial preference, or because to give full credit unilaterally would weaken the hand of the UK negotiators as they worked towards a full set of bilateral arrangements. The pace of negotiation was slow, and in 1953 these limits on credit were abolished.[44]

    There is something profoundly unhistorical in treating unilateral relief before treaty relief. The 1950 unilateral relief rules built on the rules which had been introduced for treaties in 1945. The present legislative framework governing relief by way of credit in TIOPA 2010, Part 2 applies both to unilateral credit[45] and to treaty relief.[46]

19.4.2 Residence

The taxpayer generally must have been resident in the UK—whether or not also resident in another country—for the chargeable period.[47] One effect of this was that until FA 2000,

---

[39] Added by FA 2000, Sch 30, para. 5.
[40] [2011] STC 717, [2011] EWCA Civ 304.
[41] *Ibid*, [57].
[42] *Ibid*, [67]. There are many further issue lurking here, including some involving TA 1988, s 793A (now TIOPA 2010, s 25). In view of Arden LJ's decision on these points it was not necessary for her to decide whether the taxpayer was bound to take steps to reclaim UK tax under then TA 1988, s 795A, but she considered these at [68–77].
[43] For an account of the History of DTR, see Inland Revenue discussion document (1999), *op cit*, Annex 5.
[44] As recommended by Royal Commission (1953), *op cit*, §§40–42.
[45] TIOPA 2010, Pt 2, s 18(1)(b), ex TA 1988, s 788(3).
[46] TIOPA 2010, Pt 2, s 18(1)(a), ex TA 1988, s 788(4).
[47] TIOPA 2010, s 26, ex TA 1988, s 794.

the UK branch of a non-resident company was not entitled to credit relief. Moreover, the branch was unlikely to be able to invoke the treaty's non-discrimination clause, since this statutory provision overrides anything the treaty might say.[48] A foreign branch of a company resident in the EU might, however, be able to rely on EU Treaty non-discrimination rules, such as Article 49 TFEU (ex Article 43 TEC) and Article 56 TFEU (ex Article 49 TEC).

The residence rule is relaxed for certain banks with a branch or agency in the UK for foreign tax paid on certain types of interest accruing to the branch. It is also relaxed for tax paid in the Channel Islands or Isle of Man, to a person resident in the UK or the Isle of Man or the Channel Islands, and for tax due under ITEPA 2003 in respect of foreign tax where the duties are performed wholly or mainly in the foreign country and the person is resident here or in that country.[49]

The denial of relief to the UK branch of a person resident in another EU Member State was likely to be challenged successfully under EU law. FA 2000 therefore provides that for accounting periods ending after 20 March 2000 the restriction ceases to apply. The branch may claim credit relief for foreign tax paid, but not for tax paid in the home state. The total relief is not to exceed what could have been claimed if the branch had been a person resident in the UK.[50] This legislation is still framed in terms of branches.

19.4.3 Foreign Tax

Four principal rules apply, to which FA 2005 added a fifth which is relevant only when tax is withheld at source and the business is that of a financial trader: see §19.4.3.5 below.

19.4.3.1 Payable

First, the tax payable must have been chargeable under the laws of the foreign territory.[51] The foreign tax is that chargeable rather than that paid; credit is given only to the extent of the tax properly payable to the foreign country. Thus, if a relief had to be claimed in due time under the foreign tax system and is not so made, the UK will grant relief only on the basis that the claim had been made in time. A curious exception arises when there is a transfer of a non-UK trade by a person resident in the UK to a person resident in another EU Member State; here, double tax relief may be given for tax which has not been actually paid.[52] Another such exception, known as 'tax sparing', arises only in the treaty context (see below at §20.2.3.1).

There is now a statutory obligation to take all reasonable steps to minimise the foreign tax payable.[53] This applies to claims made after 20 March 2000 and has been the cause of much unhappiness among practitioners, who have good cause to wonder what it means. The Revenue think that people should claim reliefs such as capital allowances but would

---

[48] *Sun Life of Canada v Pearson* (1986) 59 TC 250; this point was not considered beyond the High Court.
[49] TIOPA 2010, ss 28–30, ex TA 1988, s 792(2).
[50] TIOPA 2010, s 30(5), ex TA 1988, s 794(2)(bb), added by FA 2000, Sch 30, para 4.
[51] TIOPA 2010, s 8(2), ex TA 1988, s 792(1). On interpretation of chargeable or payable, see *Sportsman v IRC* [1998] STC (SCD) 289.
[52] TIOPA 2010, ss 122–123, ex TA 1988, s 815A, added by F(No 2)A 1992, s 50 (see above at §2.9).
[53] TIOPA 2010, s 33, ex TA 1988, s 795A, added by FA 2000, Sch 30, para 6.

not be expected to carry a loss forward rather than back.[54] The rational basis for this distinction is not clear. Where relief is claimed for foreign tax by the taxpayer but a payment is made by a tax authority to the taxpayer or to a person connected to the taxpayer by reference to the foreign tax, the credit is reduced by the amount of the payment.[55]

19.4.3.2 Correspond to UK Income Tax

Secondly, the tax must be a tax on income which corresponds to UK income tax.[56] In *Yates v GCA International Ltd*,[57] a Venezuelan tax charging 90% of the gross receipts was held to be a tax corresponding to income tax. At first sight a tax on 90% of the receipts would, as the Revenue argued, seem to be a tax on turnover rather than on income, but in the particular case Scott J said that there was no evidence that the 10% reduction was unrealistic for the majority of businesses falling to be taxed under the Venezuelan rule; he accepted that it was unrealistic for this taxpayer, but that was not the point.[58] The Revenue's apparent aversion to treating a gross profits tax as a tax on income is presumably to be taken only in the context of business profits, since the UK's domestic income tax system allows no deduction for expenses in connection with interest income under ITTOIA 2005, Part 4, Chapter 2, or dividend income under Chapter 3. The Revenue publish a list of admissible and inadmissible taxes.[59]

Accepting *Yates*, the Revenue announced that they would solve this issue by examining the foreign tax in its legislative context in the foreign territory and deciding whether it served the same function as income and corporation tax serve in the UK in relation to the profit of a business. Turnover taxes as such are still excluded, but taxes on gross receipts or on a percentage of gross receipts are not necessarily excluded.[60]

19.4.3.3 In Respect of Income Arising There

Thirdly, the tax must be payable in respect of income arising in that territory.[61] *Yates* establishes that this is determined as a matter of UK law using UK concepts, and is not determined by the local law.[62] The test is that profits arise where the operations take place from which those profits in substance arise.[63] Further, it must be accepted that profits may arise in more than one place, so that an apportionment may be necessary.[64]

The *Yates* case raises another issue—the correct measure of the foreign income. Where the foreign income is investment income, it is not too difficult to measure it; the gross amount of the dividend or interest will usually be accurate. Problems arise when consideration turns from free-standing income, to income which is taxed on the gross amount

---

[54] Outcome of Inland Revenue Review, March 2000, paras 1.40–1.41.

[55] TIOPA 2010, s 34, ex TA 1988, s 804G, introduced by FA 2009, s 59(2).

[56] TIOPA 2010, s 8(2), (3), ex TA 1988, s 790(12).

[57] [1991] STC 157, (1991) 64 TC 37; on the *Yates* case generally, see Oliver [1993] BTR 201.

[58] [1991] STC 157, 168j; (1991) 64 TC 387, 53A.

[59] See HMRC website, formerly Inland Revenue booklet IR 146; see Inland Revenue Press Release, 27 March 1995, [1995] *Simon's Weekly Tax Intelligence* 518.

[60] Statement of Practice SP 7/91.

[61] TIOPA 2010, s 9(1)–(3), ex TA 1988, s 790(4).

[62] [1991] STC 157, at 170d; (1991) 64 TC 37, 54H.

[63] *Smidth v Greenwood* [1922] 1 AC 417, 8 TC 193; and *IRC v Hang Seng Bank Ltd* [1990] STC 733.

[64] [1991] STC 157, 172; 64 TC 37, 570, Scott J said that if he had not been allowed to apportion he would have said that the profits arose in the UK (*ibid*, 173; 57I).

in the foreign country but on a net amount in the UK. Baker[65] puts forward the following scenario: A UK-resident company has total receipts of £1,000, which includes foreign royalties of £100 on which foreign tax of £25 has been paid. The company has deductible expenses of £600 and profits of £400, and so UK corporation tax of £120. How much of the £25 foreign tax is available for credit? Is it (a) £25 (the tax paid on the receipt of £100), or (b) £12 (100/1,000 × 120) or (c) £10 (this takes 100/1,000 of the net profit of £400 and infers that only £40 of the business profit is doubly taxed; £10 is the foreign tax at 25% on £40). The current state of UK law is uncertain. In *Yates*, the Special Commissioner decided that £12 would be the right answer. Although this is likely to be particularly striking in cash terms where one is dealing with income taxed on the gross amount in the foreign country, but only as part of a net amount in the UK, it is likely to arise whenever the two systems adopt different measures of the income.

19.4.3.4 By Claimant

Fourthly, where underlying tax is concerned, the tax must have been paid by the person claiming the credit. While this might seem to be obvious, it actually raises a number of problems. Thus, in the area of relief for underlying tax, no claim may be made for tax paid by a company which has been merged into the group if it ceases to exist as a result of the merger, a metaphysical concept depending on the precise analysis of the effects of the merger under the foreign company law system.[66] Similarly, there are issues if one person, often a company, is made liable for the tax due from another, but related, person.

The situation was addressed in 2000. If company A has paid the tax on the underlying profits and the profits have become the profits of company B otherwise than by a dividend payment, any dividend payment by B to company C will carry a right to the tax paid by A.[67] There is a cap on the amount of relief; this is set at the amount B would have been able to claim if A had paid the sums by way of dividend.

The axiom that the foreign tax must have been paid by the taxpayer was also softened by FA 2000 at some other points, eg where foreign groups or certain foreign entities are concerned.[68] Here the group may be treated as a single entity if it is so treated by the foreign tax system.

19.4.3.5 Tax Withheld at Source

Further rules apply where tax is withheld at source from income taxed as a receipt of a trade, ie interest and dividends received by financial traders and certain royalties. These were the results of a Revenue consultation which started from the premise that certain expenses were relevant, eg changes in the value of the underlying asset (if that was a revenue asset), borrowings and overheads. However, determining the amount of those costs referrable to a particular piece of income was not straightforward.

---

[65] (1998) 52 *Bulletin for IBFD*, 445.
[66] See also Inland Revenue, *Outcome of Review* (2000), para 1.20. In practice relief was often given.
[67] TIOPA 2010, s 69(1)–(3), ex TA 1988, s 801B, added by FA 2000.
[68] TIOPA 2010, s 71, ex TA 1988, s 803A, added by FA 2000, Sch 30, para 15.

19.4.3.6 Minor Points

The exchange rate to be used to calculate the amount of foreign tax paid is that in force at the time of payment.[69] Later fluctuations, which may go either way, are ignored. The problem of calculating the correct amount of tax in California has been the subject of Revenue guidance.[70] If the amount of the foreign tax liability changes, so that relief given becomes excessive, there is now an explicit obligation on the taxpayer to inform the Revenue.[71]

One UK statutory rule added in 2005 was at first applied only to companies but was extended to income tax in 2008.[72] The changes conform to HMRC practice, but were necessary to remove doubts arising from the case law.[73] The 'doubts' arose because the court did not agree with the HMRC view of the law. The case arose in connection with portfolio dividends received as part of a financial company's trade. The Special Commissioners held that the general rule in TA 1988, section 787 meant that one should look at the UK corporation tax on the financial trade as a whole. The HMRC view, now enacted as statute, was that one should just look at the dividend income, less any expenses attributable to that dividend. The purpose was to ensure that credit relief was not given against tax due on other trade profits unrelated to the payment of the foreign tax. The 2008 change also extended to income tax the rule that the credit must be computed by reference to the UK tax on the profit, and that in doing so account must be taken of any deductions or expenses that would be allowable in computing the taxpayer's liability.[74]

Although the provisions added in 2005 are headed 'trade income', this is slightly misleading. In income tax terms the rules cover not only ITTOIA 2005, Part 2, Chapter 2, but also Chapter 18 (post-cessation receipts) and property business income taxable under Part 3, Chapters 3, 10 and 11.[75] For corporation tax they cover profits chargeable under CTA 2009, Part 3 and also Part 4 post-cessation receipts and any other income computed in accordance with trading principles.[76] The key point is that all these sources use trading principles to compute income. However, they become relevant only if the receipt from which the tax is withheld is a trading receipt. Most dividends and most interest payments will not be trading receipts. All the Revenue literature in 2005 suggested that they were focusing on withholding tax and that the rules do not go wider—which is why this section of the text has the heading it does. So withholding tax must be deducted in computing the foreign tax available for credit, and the credit is limited to the UK tax on those profits. Royalties paid in respect of asset in more than one jurisdiction are treated as a single asset.[77] Any disallowed credit may be taken as a deduction.[78]

---

[69] *Greig v Ashton* (1956) 36 TC 581.
[70] Revenue Interpretation RI 102.
[71] TIOPA 2010, ss 45–46, ex TA 1988, s 798B, introduced by FA 1998, s 105; see Inland Revenue Press Release, 17 March 1998, [1998] *Simon's Weekly Tax Intelligence* 466 on timing.
[72] TIOPA 2010, ss 37(2)–(4) and 44(1)–(5), ex TA 1988, s 798(1A) for income tax and s 798A(2) for corporation tax.
[73] *Legal and General Assurance v Thomas* [2005] Sp 461; see generally Cussons [2005] BTR 371.
[74] TIOPA 2010, ss 37-38 , ex TA 1988, s 798.
[75] TIOPA 2010, s 37(7), ex TA 1988, s 798(5).
[76] TIOPA 2010, s 44(6), ex TA 1988, s 798A(4).
[77] TIOPA 2010, s 47, ex TA 1988, s 798(4).
[78] TIOPA 2010, s 35, ex TA 1988, s 798C.

Four further special rules apply for corporation tax. Three are asset identification rules:

(1)   Where the asset is a hedging relationship with a derivative contract, this may be treated as one asset.[79]
(2)   As with income tax, royalties paid in respect of assets in more than one jurisdiction are treated as a single asset.[80]
(3)   A portfolio of investments is treated as a single asset where it is not reasonably practical to treat the investments separately.[81]

The fourth special rule acts as an anti-avoidance rule, undoing any scheme of arrangement between A, a trader, and B, a main purpose of which is to alter the effect of the tax credit rules; the income is to be treated as B's not A's.[82] There is an anti-fragmentation rule for banks designed to clarify the existing rules and ensure that such schemes do not work.[83]

The FA 2005 corporation tax rules apply to any payment of a foreign tax on or after 16 March 2005, or to income received on or after that date but under deduction of tax at source; the income tax rules use 6 April instead.

19.4.4 UK Taxable Income

The credit is allowed against the UK tax on that income; this requires first the calculation of the UK income on which the UK tax would be due.[84] This being the purpose of the exercise, the income is calculated according to UK tax rules.[85] Foreign income taxed on an arising basis is taken gross, ie without any deduction for the foreign tax.[86] It follows that any withholding tax must be added back. Where the income is a dividend and credit relief is due for the corporation tax underlying it, the sum must be grossed up to take account of the underlying tax. Income which is taxed on a remittance basis is grossed up to include the foreign tax payable.[87] One cannot remit a sum net of tax and ask to have the foreign credit set against the UK tax on the net sum.

19.4.5 UK Tax

The UK tax payable in respect of that income is now calculated; the expression *in respect of that income* articulates the UK's source doctrine for DTR. Naturally, the calculation of UK tax is done in accordance with UK tax rules. The Revenue view is that relief for foreign income tax may not be set against Class 4 NICs.[88]

---

[79] TIOPA 2010, s 46, ex TA 1988, s 798B(1) and (2).
[80] TIOPA 2010, s 47, ex TA 1988, s 798B(3).
[81] TIOPA 2010, s 48, ex TA 1988, s 798B(5).
[82] TIOPA 2010, s 45, ex TA 1988, s 798B(4).
[83] TIOPA 2010, s 45, ex TA 1988 ss 798A(3A)–(3C) and B(4A)–(4C), introduced by FA 2009, s 60.
[84] TIOPA 2010, ss 31–32, ex TA 1988, s 795; on loan relationships, see TIOPA 2010, s 31(5), ex TA 1988, s 795(4), overriding FA 1996, s 80(5).
[85] The *Bowater* case (see below at §19.5.2) has no application here.
[86] TIOPA 2010, s 31(2), ex TA 1988, s 795(2); s 795(1) contained the treaty rule. On tax sparing, see TIOPA 2010, ss 31(4) and 32(5), ex TA 1988, ss 788(5), 795(3).
[87] TIOPA 2010, s 32(2), ex TA 1988, s 795(2).
[88] Inland Revenue, *Double Taxation Relief Manual*, para 601.

19.4.6 The Credit

Where credit is to be allowed against any of the UK taxes chargeable in respect of any income, the amount of the UK taxes so chargeable shall be reduced by the amount of the credit.[89] This simple rule masks many problems.

19.4.6.1 Different Basis Periods

Problems arise where profits accrue over a period (eg business profits) and the foreign tax system and the UK have different basis periods, as where the UK operates on its year of assessment financial year while the foreign system operates on a calendar-year basis. Here an apportionment of the foreign tax must be made. Thus, if X has foreign income for the year 2009–10, relief will be given against UK tax for three-quarters of the foreign tax paid in the calendar year 2009 and one-quarter of that paid for 2010; the fact that X may not know the amount of foreign tax paid in 2010 when making the return for 2009–10 is immaterial save at the practical level.[90] This problem should not arise where a withholding tax is levied at source, since here the withholding tax will be the tax on the income.

19.4.6.2 Business Income—Overlap Profits

The purpose of the current-year rules (*Revenue Law*, §20.1) is broadly to ensure that all relief available for foreign tax is given over the life of the business. Under this system, relief is given against the UK tax on the overlap profits even though it has been given effect as a credit once already. It will be seen that the concept of the overlap profit is central to the new solution. Therefore, the credit may be used in respect of the overlap profit, notwithstanding that it has been allowed as a credit against income taxed in a previous year of assessment.[91]

   Where such double relief has been given, a compensating reduction must be made if the original income of the overlap period becomes deductible under ITTOIA 2005, section 205 or section 220. The first step is to ascertain the total amount of credit that was set off over the two years of assessment when the original income was taxed twice, and deduct from it the amount that would have been set off if that income had been taxed only once.[92] This original excess is now used to reduce any double tax credit which would have been allowed in respect of that source in the final period under section 220, and only the balance, if any, is available for set off as a foreign tax credit.[93] If the original excess exceeds the credit for the final period a special charge to income tax is made—the person chargeable is treated as having received in that year a payment of an amount such that income tax on it at the basic rate is equal to that excess.[94] Where there is an overlap period and a deduction under section 220, ie not on the discontinuance of the trade, the double tax credit in relation to each element of the overlap is treated in the proportion which the overlap profit bears to that aggregate of taxable profits.[95]

[89] TIOPA 2010, s 18, ex TA 1988, s 793(1), on credit for banks, sees s 30 (ex s 794).
[90] For Revenue practice, see Inland Revenue, *op cit*, para 651.
[91] TIOPA 2010, s 22, ex TA 1988, s 804(1), amended by FA 1994, s 217; on overlap profile, see ITTOIA 2005, Pt 2, Ch 15.
[92] TIOPA 2010, s 24(1)–(3), ex TA 1988, s 804(5A), added by FA 1994, s 217.
[93] TIOPA 2010, s 24(5), ex TA 1988, s 804(5B)(b), added by FA 1994, s 217
[94] TIOPA 2010, s 24(4), ex TA 1988, s 804(5B)(a), added by FA 1994, s 217.
[95] TIOPA 2010, s 24(7), ex TA 1988, s 804(5C), amended by FA 1994, s 217.

19.4.6.3 (Old) Preceding Year

Further problems used to arise owing to the preceding-year basis of assessment. Where, under that system, income earned in the foreign country in Year 5 was used as the basis of UK tax in Year 6, unilateral credit was given for the Year 5 foreign tax in calculating UK tax for Year 6.[96]

19.4.7 The Relief

19.4.7.1 Income Tax and Capital Gains Tax

Once the amount of the credit has been ascertained, it is set against the UK tax chargeable, which is reduced by the amount of the credit. This means that foreign income taxes on the income from the foreign source are allowed against the UK tax charged on the income from that source. Care may have to be taken in identifying the source.

19.4.7.2 The Source

In *George Wimpey International Ltd v Rolfe*,[97] a company (GW) tried, unsuccessfully, to widen this rule. GW had paid foreign tax in respect of foreign profits from foreign branches of its trade, but made an overall trading loss when all its operations, including the UK operations, were taken into account. It argued that it should be entitled to set off the foreign tax against the UK corporation tax in respect of its non-trading income. Hoffmann J, upholding the decision of the Special Commissioner, held that the taxpayer company was not entitled to DTR. He referred to the scheme of the legislation and said that that led to the need to identify exactly the fund charged to overseas tax with a fund also chargeable to UK tax. He said:[98]

> The reference in [TA 1988, section 790(4), now TIOPA 2010, section 9(1)(b)] to United Kingdom tax being computed by reference to income on which the foreign tax had been computed was … intended to ensure that the identity was not between funds which might notionally be regarded as taxable income in that foreign territory and the UK but between the actual funds by reference to which the computation of tax was made … [I]t seems to me the income in respect of which the taxpayer company became liable to corporation tax was its non-trading income notwithstanding that the computation of that income was made subject to deduction for losses which took into account the company's trading in the three territories. The company was not chargeable to any tax in respect of the income which had been subject to foreign tax and accordingly no credit can be allowed.

19.4.7.3 Restriction on Credit

The amount of the credit must not exceed the difference between:

(1) the amount of income tax which would be borne by the taxpayer if he were charged to income tax on his total income from all sources, including the foreign income grossed up as necessary; and

(2) the tax borne by him on his total income but minus the foreign income as computed.[99]

---

[96] On old form of treaty, see *Duckering v Gollan* [1965] 2 All ER 115, 42 TC 333; the effect of this case was undone for treaties by a change in treaty practice, and for unilateral relief by substituting 'by reference to' the foreign income for 'in respect of'.

[97] [1989] STC 609, 62 TC 597.

[98] *Ibid*, 616, 606.

[99] TIOPA 2010, s 36, ex TA 1988, s 796(1).

The effect of this rather inelegant, but taxpayer-friendly formula is to treat the income as the top slice of income; this means that the UK tax against which the foreign tax is credited is that taxed at top slice rate and not an overall average rate.

Although the foreign tax must be paid in respect of the same source, it does not have to be paid by the same taxpayer. Thus, if state A taxes the income of a child as income of the child, and the UK taxes it as income of the parent, the parent may use the foreign tax paid.

Where more than one foreign source is involved, each is treated separately but in order—the order being at the taxpayer's option.[100] In such circumstances it obviously pays to take the income taxed at the highest foreign rates first. In any event, the total tax credit must not exceed the total income tax payable.[101]

19.4.7.4 Capital Gains Tax

Equivalent relief is given[102] for foreign tax charged on the same disposal. Where credit relief is not available, or not available in full, the unused foreign tax may be treated as an allowable deduction. Owing to the variety of systems of taxing gains around the world, this relief may be lost. Thus, different events may give rise to a tax liability in respect of what is, in substance, the same gain. For example, a capital asset in a foreign branch may incur a tax charge in that country if, without being sold, it is written up in the books and the foreign country charges tax on the unrealised gain. If, in a later year, the asset is sold and UK CGT liability arises, it seems that, strictly, DTR should not be available in respect of the earlier foreign disposal. However, a Statement of Practice provides that the foreign tax credit will be given on the occasion of the subsequent disposal which gives rise to UK CGT.[103] The Statement does not cover the converse situation where the UK tax becomes due before the foreign tax.

19.4.7.5 Corporation Tax

Equivalent relief is also given for income and capital gains subject to corporation tax; the amount of credit must not exceed the corporation tax attributable to that income.[104] Since all the income chargeable is charged at one rate, companies with high overseas income from countries with high rates of tax may decide to expand their UK operations.

19.4.7.6 Allocation of Charges, etc

Where a company has overseas income and domestic income, it is necessary to allocate such items as expenses of management and charges on income among the different sources, so as to calculate the amount of UK corporation tax attributable to that foreign income. The general approach is to allow the company to allocate these as it sees fit.[105]

These rules are adapted for non-trading deficits on loans relationships.[106] TIOPA 2010, section 50 provides first that non-trading credits are calculated on their own, ie without any deduction for non-trading debits. The non-trading debits must be calculated by taking

---

[100] TIOPA 2010, s 36(3), ex TA 1988, s 796(2).
[101] TIOPA 2010, s 41, ex TA 1988, s 796(3).
[102] TIOPA 2010, s 40, ex TCGA 1992, s 277.
[103] Statement of Practice SP 6/88.
[104] TIOPA 2010, s 42, ex TA 1988, s 797(1), (2).
[105] TIOPA 2010, s 52, ex TA 1988, s 797(3).
[106] TIOPA 2010, s 50, ex TA 1988, ss 797, amended by FA 1996, and 797A, added by FA 1996.

the debits for the period and then deducting any which have been relieved in other ways or which have been carried forward from an earlier period. In accordance with the general scheme for loan relationships in CTA 2009, Part 5 (see above §5.1), those carried forward may be set only against non-trading profits. Provision is made to exclude deficits which have been set off against general profits of the same or the preceding period. The purpose of section 50 is to permit the operation of section 42 even though the foreign interest is no longer separately distinguished. Where section 50 does not apply, TIOPA 2010 still allows the company to allocate these deficits as it thinks fit, subject to three qualifications. First, any decision by the company to set off a non-trading deficit against trading profits of the same period must be respected here too.[107] Secondly, if the deficit is carried forward from an earlier period, it may be set only against non-trading profits.[108] Thirdly, it is not open to a company to allocate excess charges to UK income greater than the amount of that income so as to set up a loss which might be carried forward.[109] This treatment applies to all non-trading credits and not just interest.[110]

It remains the case that when loss relief is available it will be applied first, thus cancelling the tax credit for any double tax relief. As unused double tax relief may not be carried forward as double tax relief but only, when relevant, as a deduction, and so perhaps a trading loss, the point is of some importance.

There was much legislation dealing with ACT; here, the rule eventually established was that the foreign tax credit was deductible before the ACT.[111] As a result, it has ceased to be necessary to set ACT against domestic source income rather than foreign source income.

19.4.7.7 International Companies; Getting the Source Right

Since, subject to the rules in §20.4, each source is taken separately and credit is given only on a yearly basis with no carry forward of unused credit reliefs, the problem of unused foreign tax credits is a very real one in the UK system. The use of an overseas company through which the foreign income may be channelled has two potential advantages. First, the source is the foreign company, so enabling the income from the different sources and possibly different rates to be pooled; pooling leads to the averaging of the foreign taxes and prevents a loss of tax credit where the foreign tax on some of the sources is higher than the UK rate. Secondly, the foreign income may, subject to the CFC legislation, be accumulated in the foreign company and then remitted back into the UK when there is enough UK tax to make use of the credits. The first advantage is particularly useful where dividends from a number of overseas countries are involved and the company is known as a 'dividend mixer company'; the second leads to the description of a 'Case V trap company'.[112]

---

[107] TIOPA 2010, s 55, ex TA 1988, s 797(3A), added by FA 1996.

[108] TIOPA 2010, s 53, ex TA 1988, s 797(3B), added by FA 1996.

[109] *Commercial Union Assurance Co plc v Shaw* [1998] STC 386.

[110] TIOPA 2010, s 50, ex TA 1988, s 797A, as amended by FA 2000, Sch 30, para 7.

[111] Ex TA 1988, s 797(4), (5); see also *Collard v Mining and Industrial Holdings Ltd* [1989] STC 384, 62 TC 448, HL.

[112] On which see Collier, Hughes and Payne, *Tolley's International Tax Planning*, 4th edn (Tolley, 1999), paras 27.38–27.57 and Inland Revenue discussion paper (1999), *op cit*, ch 6. Revenue Interpretation RI 149 assumes that these schemes work.

19.5   Indirect Credit: Dividends and Underlying Tax

Where a UK-resident company receives a dividend from a non-resident company, liability to corporation tax will arise under CTA 2009, Part 9A (ex Schedule D, Case V), which then provides an exemption from UK tax where specified conditions are met; the vast majority of dividends will qualify for exemption.[113]

For the small minority of foreign dividends received by UK companies that will not be exempt, and for foreign dividends received by individuals, a tax credit under TIOPA 2010 may be available instead. The tax deducted in the country of source will have been a withholding tax, probably at the rate of 5% or 15% where a treaty exists and at the full domestic withholding rate if there is no applicable treaty. These taxes may be taken as credits against the UK tax due, whether income tax or corporation tax. Where the foreign tax system has charged a separate tax on the profits of the company, it would be equitable to allow credit not only for the income tax charged on the dividend but also for at least a proportion of the tax levied on the profits of the company which underlie the dividend—hence the UK expression 'relief for underlying tax'. Relief for underlying tax is governed by TIOPA 2010, sections 14–16 (unilateral relief) and 63–66 (tax treaty relief).

Example

In 2011 Y Ltd, a UK-resident company, has trading profits of £400,000 and receives a dividend of £864,000 net (£960,000 gross) from one of its overseas subsidiaries. Foreign tax on the profits and local withholding tax on dividends paid are 40% and 10% respectively. Y Ltd pays dividends (net) of £750,000 to its shareholders.

UK source income is £400,000, making tax liability of £100,000 @ 25%.

The foreign dividend of £864,000 must first be grossed up at 10% to give the gross dividend (taking account of the withholding tax) and then at 40% to take account of the foreign tax on the profits out of which the dividend has been paid. This gives a gross figure of £1.6 million, on which the UK tax at 25% will be £400,000. The foreign tax available for credit relief is £640,000 (40% of £1.6m) plus £96,000 (10% of £960,000), making a total of £736,000. Since this exceeds the UK tax of £400,000, there will be no more UK tax to pay on the foreign income; the tax liability of £100,000 on UK-source income remains unaffected. Since Y Ltd is not a financial trader there is no room for the restrictions on credit relief where there is withholding tax to apply.

No underlying relief may be claimed if a tax deduction is given in another country by reference to the dividend.[114] This change was made in 2005 to counter schemes which used payments characterised as interest for tax purposes in another jurisdiction but as dividend for UK tax purposes. If, as normally happens, the interest is deductible in full in the foreign system, it cannot give rise to underlying relief. The thinking behind this is similar to that behind the tax arbitrage rules above at §4.7, but the rule is quite distinct.

---

[113] See §19.3 above. Under the former rules, the payment was not exempt from corporation tax through TA 1988, s 208 as the payer was a non-resident.

[114] TIOPA 2010, s 57(3), ex TA 1988, s 799(2A), added by FA 2005, s 85 as from 16 March 2005.

19.5.1 Related Company

Indirect relief applies only to companies.[115] The foreign company (FR) must be a 'related' company of the UK parent company (UKP), ie UKP must control at least 10% of the voting power of FR.[116] The figure of 10% is historically low; it was originally 50% in 1930, and reduced to 25% in 1965. An alternative test by reference to ordinary share capital applies to dividends paid on or after 1 January 2005; this is to satisfy the new revised EU Parent and Subsidiary Directive but is not confined to EU States.[117]

UKP may hold that 10% either directly or indirectly through an intermediate subsidiary company (SUB). SUB will be a subsidiary of UKP if UKP controls at least 50% of the voting power of SUB.[118]

Thus, if UKP has a 9% direct stake in FR it is not entitled to relief. If, however, SUB has a 1% stake in FR, UKP will become entitled to indirect relief if it controls 50% or more of the voting power of SUB. It must be noted that this is a simple test for UKP. If UKP controls 50% of the voting power of SUB, this will entitle UK to the underlying relief. The legislation does not say, as it does in many other tax contexts, that because UKP has only 50% of the shares in SUB it may therefore include only 50% of the 1% holding in FR (and so fall short of the magic 10%).

Although the 10% threshold is a magic figure, provision is made for the preservation of this relief where a 10% holding is reduced by dilution.[119] Where treaty relief applies only to certain classes of dividend, eg ordinary shares, unilateral relief for the underlying tax may be claimed for other classes, eg preference dividends.[120]

19.5.2 Relevant Underlying Profits: Source of Dividends

Where relief for the underlying tax is given, the next step is to ascertain the profits underlying the dividend, the rate of tax available for credit depending on a comparison of the tax paid with the profits.

The relevant profits are:

(1) if the dividend is paid for a specified period, the profits of that period;
(2) if the dividend is not specified for a period but is stated to come out of specified profits, those profits; and
(3) if the dividend is neither for a specified period nor from a specified source, the last complete internal accounting period of the company before the payment.

If under rules (1)–(3) the dividend exceeds the profits, profits from previous years may underlay the dividend unless they have already done so.[121] Case law established that

---

[115] TIOPA 2010, ss 14(3) and 57(2), ex TA 1988, ss 790(6)(a), 801.
[116] TIOPA 2010, ss 14(4) and 63(2), ex TA 1988, s 801(5); on control, see CTA 2010, s 1124, ex s 840.
[117] TIOPA 2010, s 64(6), ex TA 1988, s 801(5A) added by F(No 2)A 2005 s 43.
[118] TIOPA 2010, ss 14(5) and 63(6), ex TA 1988, s 792(2).
[119] TIOPA 2010, s 15(6), ex TA 1988, s 790(6)(b)–(10); eg nationalisation.
[120] TIOPA 2010, s 14, ex TA 1988, s 800.
[121] TIOPA 2010, s 59, ex TA 1988, s 799. Where, under the tax law in a foreign country, a dividend is increased for tax purposes by an amount which may be set against T's own tax liability (or, if in excess thereof, paid to him) then any such increase is to be subtracted from the underlying tax (TIOPA 2010, s 58, ex TA 1988, ss 788, 799, 808). It is thus clear that foreign imputation credit is excluded from the calculation of credit relief for underlying tax.

the profits are those appearing in the company's accounts, and not those which are the basis upon which the foreign tax is assessed; a statutory basis for this was supplied by FA 2000.[122] If distributable profits are restricted, the average rate of foreign tax payable will be increased.

19.5.3 Subsidiaries as Related Companies

In the example at §19.5.1 above, UKP, the first company, resident in the UK, had a 10% stake in FR, and so FR became a related company of UKP. However, FR may have a subsidiary of its own (FRS1). If FR controls at least 10% of the voting power of FRS1, FR and FRS1 will be related; more importantly, UKP will be able to claim the indirect credit relief for the tax paid by FRS1. It does not matter that UKP does not control 10% of the voting power of FRS1; what matters is that FR has such control over FRS1 and that UKP has such control over FR. A company may, in turn, be related to another company, the third company, and so on, down a chain.[123]

The UK permits an indefinite number of links in the chain, and requiring only a 10% stake at each link; this is most unusual (and generous) in comparative terms. Since 1971 the first company has been able to claim credit relief in respect of the tax borne by the third company on its profits when those profits are passed back up the chain in the form of dividends. It is necessary that the general UK conditions for tax relief would have been satisfied at each stage up the chain.[124] It is also necessary that the appropriate degree of relationship exists at each link stage. The relationship requires that either the second company controls, directly or indirectly, not less than 10% of the voting power of the third company, or that it is a subsidiary of a company which controls 10% of that voting power.

FRS1, the third company, may be resident in some third country or even in the UK. Where any company in the chain is resident in the UK, the tax on its profits for which relief is claimed is not to include income tax paid in respect of dividends received by that company from other companies resident in the UK.[125]

19.5.4 Mixer Companies and Onshore Pooling

19.5.4.1 Introduction

As just seen, the principal use of the dividend mixer company was to allow the foreign profits which would have been taxed at various rates to be mixed together in one pot out of which the dividend would come. Since the UK tax system regarded the dividends as coming from the immediate source, ie the mixer company, relief could be given for the underlying tax at whatever rate that tax had actually been paid. This practice allowed companies to circumvent the basic principle of UK credit relief, which was that where the foreign tax exceeded the UK tax, credit relief was restricted to the amount of the UK tax. As a result of the review of DTR for companies, the Government decided to try to end this

---

[122] *Bowater Paper Corpn Ltd v Murgatroyd* [1969] 3 All ER 111, 46 TC 3, and FA 2000, Sch 30, para 8, adding ex TA 1988, s 799(5)–(7), now ITOPA 2010, s 59.

[123] TIOPA 2010, s 64, ex TA 1988, s 801(1) and s 802 for insurance business.

[124] TIOPA 2010, s 65, ex TA 1988, s 801(2).

[125] TIOPA 2010, s 66, ex TA 1988, s 801(4).

circumvention. The rules eventually enacted apply to claims on or after 31 March 2001, unless the dividend was paid by the mixer company to the UK company before that date.

What the rules do, as finally enacted, is explicitly to allow mixing in defined circumstances; to move from implicit tolerance of offshore pooling through foreign mixer companies to explicit acceptance of on-shore pooling in restricted circumstances. There are three principal forms of restriction. The first is that the extent to which dividends may be pooled is restricted by the use of a cap on the amount of credit that may be used. The second is that while onshore pooling is available to companies resident in the UK through and to certain UK branches or agencies of persons resident elsewhere,[126] it is not available to individuals or trusts. The third is that onshore pooling is not open to dividends which escape the CFC legislation because they satisfy the acceptable distribution test; these dividends must always be streamed separately. There is a suspicion that it was these CFC dividends which caused the real problems for the Revenue, and that much anxiety would have been avoided if that problem, and only that problem, had been addressed directly at the beginning. However, by then, too much political capital had been invested for the simple solution to be acceptable to the Government.

19.5.4.2 Three Rules (Two Now Repealed)

The first rule: Normal UK corporation tax rate cap. Where there is a chain of companies including a UK company, any dividends paid by companies in the chain below the UK company will have the foreign tax credit capped by reference to M, the maximum relievable rate, which is the normal corporation tax rate (currently 24%).[127] A very great deal depends on the way in which the tax is calculated. Where underlying tax is involved, the formula in TIOPA 2010, section 58 is:

$$(D + PA) \times M$$

where D is the amount of the dividend, PA the underlying tax properly attributable to the proportion of the relevant profits represented by the dividend and M the corporation tax rate of the recipient for the accounting period in which the dividend is received.[128]

The company may make a claim to exclude a certain amount of the underlying tax (U) if it wishes;[129] it might wish to do so if this will bring the amount of tax down below the cap level and so avoid 'tainting' the dividend.[130] The foreign tax cannot be used as a deduction.[131]

At one time a further deduction could be made where the amount given by the formula exceeded U. In calculating U it was at one time possible, before 2005, to bring UK tax into account. This would happen if the foreign company had shares in a UK company and the UK company paid a dividend out of profits charged to UK tax; here the underlying UK

---

[126] Through ex ss 806A and 806K respectively.

[127] TIOPA 2010, s 58, ex TA 1988, s 799(1A) as added by FA 2001, Sch 27, para 2 and superseding the version originally added by FA 2000, Sch 30, para 8. On the old 28% rate and HMRC error, see HMRC Note, 4 July 2008.

[128] For examples, see *Simon's Finance Act Handbook 2001* (Butterworths, 2001) 176–78.

[129] TIOPA 2010, s 60, ex TA 1988, s 799(1B), added by FA 2001.

[130] See Inland Revenue Press Release 8 November 2000, [2000] *Simon's Weekly Tax Intelligence* 1593 and Budget Note 24/01, [2001] *Simon's Weekly Tax Intelligence* 460.

[131] TIOPA 2010, ss 60(3) and 57(3), ex TA 1988, s 811, as amended by FA 2001, Sch 26, para 6.

was treated as if it were foreign underlying tax.[132] This was used as the basis for avoidance and therefore abolished in 2005.

The second rule: pooling with 45% maximum (now repealed). The effect of the first rule is to deprive the UK company of the benefit of any foreign tax above the normal UK corporation tax rate. The second rule, prior to its repeal in 2009 with the introduction of the dividend exemption system, was therefore all-important. Despite the normal UK corporation tax rate restriction, relief might have been available under the second rule for foreign tax, whether underlying or on the dividend itself, which was above the cap but below a maximum of 45%.[133] This foreign tax might have been credited against the UK tax payable on certain other foreign dividends and so gave us the official pooling—at the expense of additional complexity.

The third rule: not from CFC, now also repealed. For the purposes of these pooling rules, the dividends must have met various criteria but, in particular, must not have been a dividend paid by a CFC which escaped the CFC legislation because, and only because, of the acceptable distribution test, or which represented such a dividend.[134] Such dividends were required to be separately streamed.[135] For further detail on the operation of the onshore pooling system, and the calculation of eligible unrelieved foreign tax (EUFT), see *Revenue Law*, 6th edition.

19.5.5 Restriction of Relief for Underlying Tax

Rules apply to dividends paid to a company resident in the UK to counter devices which artificially increased the underlying tax. These rules[136] apply where a UK company (UKA) makes a claim for this relief in respect of a dividend paid by the overseas company (FB), that dividend includes tax paid by FB or one of the other companies further down the chain and is paid 'at a high rate'.[137] A rate is high if it exceeds the 'relievable rate', ie the rate of UK corporation tax in force when the dividend is paid.[138] So far these rules would have a dramatic effect of reducing the availability of relief for underlying tax. It is therefore essential to appreciate that these rules apply only if there is an avoidance scheme.[139]

An avoidance scheme is defined as one where there is a specified relationship between the companies and there is a scheme or an arrangement the parties to which include those companies, and the purpose, or one of the main purposes, of the scheme or arrangement is an amount of underlying tax taken into account in a claim for a tax credit.[140] Further rules cover the relationship between the companies, and provide that the term 'arrangement' covers an arrangement of any kind and need not be in writing.[141]

---

[132] Ex TA 1988, s 801(4B)–(4D), added by FA 2001, Sch 27, para 3, but repealed by FA 2005; for Revenue explanation of original rule, see Revenue Briefing Note BN 24 (7 March 2001) 2.

[133] Ex TA 1988, s 806B; on upper percentage, see ex s 806J. On the repeal of these rules by FA 2009, see Voisey [2009] BTR 533, 540.

[134] Ex TA 1988, s 806C(1).

[135] Ex TA 1988, s 801C.

[136] TIOPA 2010, ss 67–68, ex TA 1988, s 801A, added by FA 1997, s 90(2) as from 26 November 1996; see Oliver [1997] BTR 250.

[137] TIOPA 2010, s 67, ex TA 1988, s 801A(1).

[138] TIOPA 2010, s 67(7), ex TA 1988, s 801A(5).

[139] TIOPA 2010, s 67(4),(5), ex TA 1988, s 801A(1)(c).

[140] TIOPA 2010, s 68, ex TA 1988, s 801A(6), (7).

[141] TIOPA 2010, s 68(9), ex TA 1988, s 801A(8)–(11).

Where these conditions are met, the amount of credit is restricted to the amount of tax that would be paid at the relievable rate on 'the relevant profits'.[142] An example of the sort of scheme at which these rules are aimed is where A receives a dividend from B at a normal rate, but A then arranges for B to acquire from some unconnected person a stake in another company (C) which is proposing to pay out a dividend from an income taxed at a high rate. A will, in these circumstances, claim DTR in respect not only of the direct tax on the dividend from B but also the indirect tax paid by B and C on the profits out of which B's dividend to A is paid.[143] These rules restrict the relief for the underlying tax to what it would have been at normal UK corporate rates on the profits used to pay the dividend. The rules do not go further and restrict the credit to the amount of tax that would have been paid if the only profits had been those of company B ignoring the acquisition of the stake in company C.

In 1997 the Minister stated, long before FA 2000, that the section was not intended to catch the acquisition of a dividend mixer company, or to interfere with reorganisation—unless there was a scheme of the sort under attack.[144]

19.5.6 Banks and Underlying Tax

The purpose of TIOPA 2010, section 70 (ex TA 1988, section 803) is to bolster sections 37–38 where the claim is for indirect tax credit. Without this rule companies would circumvent the rules by the simple device of inserting an overseas subsidiary between them and the source of the interest or dividends. Unlike the old rule, it covers both interest and dividends, and also covers associates of financial traders. Its scope was greatly reduced in 2005.

19.6   Schemes and Arrangements to Increase Credit Relief

TIOPA 2010, sections 81 *et seq* (ex TA 1988, section 804ZA) empower HMRC to issue a notice counteracting schemes and arrangements to increase foreign tax credit relief in connection with schemes set out in section 83.[145] The legislation prescribes various things that must be included in the notice, and may include HMRC's view about the adjustments required.[146]

Section 81 applies where an officer of HMRC considers, on reasonable grounds, that the conditions in section 82 are or may be met, namely: (a) a credit is allowable for the period, (b) there is a scheme or an arrangement of which the (or a) main purpose is to cause an amount of foreign tax to be taken into account, and (c) the scheme is in the list prescribed in section 83. The legislation does not apply to schemes the purpose of which is to cause

---

[142] TIOPA 2010, s 67(6), ex TA 1988, s 801A(3), (4).

[143] *Simon's Finance Act Handbook 1997* (Butterworths, 1997), 121.

[144] Hansard, 13th Sitting, cols 458–460; [1997] *Simon's Weekly Tax Intelligence* 278. See also Revenue Interpretation RI 171.

[145] Added by FA 2005, s 87; formerly in TA 1988, Sch 28AB.

[146] TIOPA 2010, ss 81(2) and 89(2), ex TA 1988, s 804ZA(8), (9).

an amount of underlying tax to be taken into account.[147] The provisions are excluded if the amount of tax claimed by the taxpayer—and any connected persons with corresponding chargeable periods—is minimal.[148]

The section applies whether the tax credit claimed is the normal direct tax credit, or the indirect or underlying tax credit where a foreign dividend is paid out of profits which have borne tax. The legislation expressly authorises an adjustment to the foreign tax which the specified foreign company is treated as having paid; the foreign company is treated as having paid only so much as would qualify for relief if it were UK resident.[149]

Section 83 refers to situations described in sections 84–88, which may be described broadly as follows:[150]

(1) where the foreign tax is properly attributable to another source of income or chargeable gain which is really unrelated to the foreign tax;

(2) where a foreign tax payment is less than the amount allowable as a credit (usually this is where the payment of the tax does not increase the overall tax liability of the scheme participants, eg because the tax payment is matched by a tax-saving elsewhere);

(3) where a claim, election or other arrangement under the foreign law increases the claim to the foreign tax credit (the claim may arise under the domestic law of the foreign territory or some treaty);

(4) where under the scheme the amount of UK tax is less than if the scheme were disregarded (eg where the credit not only covers the tax on the scheme income but is also set against other income, thereby reducing total UK tax liabilities); and

(5) there are tax deductible payments by A in return for which A or a person connected with A receives income for which credit relief is available.

The way in which the scheme applies to the underlying tax relief has to be spelt out. Here the scheme is prescribed if it would be prescribed if the foreign company were resident in the UK but making no different assumptions about where its activities are carried on.[151]

The rules in TIOPA 2010, sections 81 *et seq* were widened and strengthened in 2010. Manufactured overseas dividends are now subject to section 85A—where deemed overseas tax deducted is not to be treated more favourably than tax credits on real dividends. There were also revenue-protecting changes to section 86 and also to section 112 (ex TA 1988, section 811), which provides for a deduction from income for foreign tax instead of a credit.

---

[147] TIOPA 2010, s 83(2), ex TA 1988, Sch 28AB, para 1(3); on (staggered) commencement, see FA 2005, s 87(3)–(5).

[148] TIOPA 2010, s 82(5)–(7), ex TA 1988, s 804ZA(5)–(7); periods correspond if they have at least one day in common.

[149] TIOPA 2010, s 89(3), ex TA 1988, s 804ZA(10).

[150] The explanatory instances are taken from the Inland Revenue Notes to the Finance Bill.

[151] TIOPA 2010, s 83(3)–(7), ex TA 1988, Sch 28AB, para 1(2)–(5).

19.7   Miscellaneous Matters: Accrued Income Scheme

The accrued income scheme for income tax (see *Revenue Law*, §26.4) contained its own DTR rules. Thus, credit relief was given if the sums treated as received under that scheme would have fallen under ex Schedule D, Case IV or V. When a payment which had been received was reduced for tax purposes by these rules, the foreign tax available for relief was also reduced.[152] With the introduction of the 1996 rules for loan relationships for corporation tax (now in CTA 2009, Part 5), the accrued income scheme no longer applies to companies falling within that tax.[153] Separate (but similar) provision was made for accrued income credits in such situations, but it was found to be abused and so was repealed by FA 2008.[154]

---

[152] TIOPA 2010, ss 10, 39 and 112, referring to the relevant ITA 2007 provisions; ex TA 1988, s 807.
[153] Ex TA 1988, s 807(6), added by FA 1996, Sch 14.
[154] Ex TA 1988, s 807A(3), added by FA 1996, Sch 14, but repealed by FA 2008, s 59 and Sch 22, para 2.

20

Double Taxation: UK Treaty Relief

20.1   The UK Treaty Network[1]

The UK today has treaties with over 115 countries,[2] including (separately) the Isle of Man, Jersey and Guernsey (including Alderney). In 1997 the UK was the first country to reach this century. At that time there were over 1,300 treaties worldwide;[3] by 2012 that number had nearly doubled to over 2,500.[4] The UK has treaties with nearly all Western European countries, with most members of the Commonwealth and with all other OECD countries, such as Japan. There are no treaties with many of the Arab countries such as Yemen,[5] nor with some tax havens such as Liechtenstein, though a treaty was signed in 2010 with the Cayman Islands. Arrangements with some countries are limited to transport profits and

---

[1] Discussions of tax treaty problems require the reader to consult Baker, *Double Taxation Conventions* (Sweet & Maxwell, 2001); Vogel, *Klaus Vogel on Double Tax Conventions*, 3rd edn (Kluwer, 1997). One must also consult the invaluable if now slightly dated Edwardes Ker, *Tax Treaty Service* (In-depth Publishing, 1994) and the accompanying book, Edwardes Ker, *Tax Treaty Interpretation* (In-depth Publishing, 1995). HMRC have their own *Double Taxation Manual*, available on the HMRC website. See also Harris and Oliver, *International Commercial Tax* (CUP, 2010).

[2] More correctly, the agreements are with 'territories' (TIOPA 2010, s 2, ex TA 1988, s 788).

[3] Inland Revenue Press Release, 10 April 1996, [1996] *Simon's Weekly Tax Intelligence* 701.

[4] See HMRC website at <http://www.hmrc.gov.uk/taxtreaties/dta.htm>.

[5] The Agreement with Saudi Arabia covers air transport profit and dependent personal services.

employees, eg Brazil and Iran. Countries which exempt foreign income from tax often have treaties with the UK, finding this useful for matters such as rules on the location of sources and administrative arrangements.

Bilateral treaties are a palliative for an understandable failure to reach international agreement on the principles of tax law. They have been well-described as a bolt-on exercise in damage limitation.[6] They do not solve all problems of the interaction of tax systems, and give rise to particularly acute problems when payments from or to third countries become involved.[7] How well they work may be assessed more generally by asking how far they reduce the distortions otherwise imposed on business.[8]

Although the UK has prided itself on its network of treaties and has often proclaimed *pacta sunt servanda* ('treaties are to be observed'), FA 2005 marked a determined effort to introduce a significant number of 'treaty overrides' or provisions designed to overrule the normal effect of tax treaty provisions. When considered along with some of the FA 2005 changes to credit relief considered in chapter nineteen above (and which apply to UK treaty credit relief), it is as though tax treaties are now seen as another part of the tax avoider's armoury rather than as a necessary way of helping UK-based international business or even as a civilised way of dividing taxing power with treaty partner States.

20.1.1 EU Aspects

The EU does not, as yet, have a multilateral convention for Member States. Article 293 TEC formerly imposed an obligation on Member States to eliminate double taxation within the Community, but this was too broad to give rise to direct effect and so could not be invoked by an individual taxpayer.[9] In any event, Article 293 TEC was not reproduced in the TEU or TFEU post-Lisbon Treaty. At one time the EU expressed an interest in co-ordinating the work of individual governments in treaty matters by looking at major issues, and especially at limitation of benefit clauses, but nothing was done at institution level.[10]

The Court of Justice of the European Union (CJEU) has indicated that it will not regard the division of taxing rights between Member States as automatically giving rise to unjustified discrimination. However, this does not mean that the Court will simply waive its non-discrimination jurisprudence in the face of a tax treaty. Thus, where a state invokes the need to protect the cohesion of its tax system, it may find that the effect of the treaty between it and the other Member State is to deprive its cohesion argument of any force.[11]

In addition there is the big question whether a treaty made by state A, which gives its resident entities certain rights *vis-à-vis* another state, whether or not a member of the EU, is bound to give the same benefits to an entity resident in another Member State, B,

---

[6] This does not mean that one should not think about better concepts, eg Verdoner (2003) 31 *Intertax* 147.

[7] See Harris and Oliver, *op cit*, ch 5 (on 'beyond the bilateral').

[8] For an outline of areas in which parts of the OECD Model Treaty do not fit well together, see Avery Jones (1999) 53 *Tax Law Review* 1, 25–37. The now dated figures from the 1991 OECD survey are given above at §19.1.

[9] Case C-336/96 *Gilly v Directeur des Services Fiscaux du Bas-Rhin* [1998] STC 1014, [1998] All ER (EC) 826. On other aspects of *Gilly*, see ch 21 below.

[10] Institute of Taxation TR6/93, [1993] *Simon's Tax Intelligence* 350.

[11] See Case C-80/94 *Wielockx* [1995] STC 876, discussing the effect of Case C-204/90 *Bachmann v Belgium State* [1994] STC 855.

but which has a branch in A.[12] In the *St Gobain* case,[13] state A was Germany and state B was France. A French company with a German branch was held entitled to the protection of a clause in a German treaty with a non-Member State. However, this was not because the relief arose directly from the treaty but because German domestic law incorporated that treaty relief into its own domestic law. The ECJ allowed the French company to claim the relief. The UK Government accepted the wide approach in FA 2000 by allowing non-resident companies to claim DTR if they had a branch, now a PE, in the UK (see above at §19.4.1). The ECJ has now ruled on the 'most favoured nation' issue and held that there is no obligation on the Member State to extend treaty rights to someone resident in a state which is not a party to the treaty.[14]

Today the dominant influence in UK tax treaty design is the OECD Model Treaty, which is revised periodically, most recently in 2010.[15] The OECD is an intergovernmental organisation with some 34 Member States (as of 2012). Since the OECD consists of States with 'advanced' economies, its Treaty was not as suitable for developing countries; the United Nations came to the assistance with its own model. The UN Model Treaty, however, is based heavily on the OECD version. Today, the OECD Model Treaty is used by many non-OECD Member States, and the views of non-Member States may sometimes now be found in the commentaries to the OECD Model Treaty. The OECD Model Treaty consists of clauses to which commentaries are attached. The status of these commentaries in the interpretation of tax treaties is a matter of great importance. It must, however, be remembered that those at the OECD who approve changes to the treaty or its commentaries are government representatives and not disinterested experts. The OECD Model Treaty does not purport to be comprehensive; thus, there is no article dealing with trust income as such.[16]

The UN Model Treaty for the benefit of developing countries was first published in 1988 and revised in 2011.[17] The United States and The Netherlands have published their own model treaties. Multilateral treaties are relatively rare.[18]

Having got through all this activity one is faced with another instance of the question raised earlier about the roles of principle and equity as opposed to brute negotiating strength.[19]

---

[12] See discussion by Kessermann (1997) 6 *EC Tax Review* 146 (before *Gilly*); and de Graaf (1998) 7 *EC Tax Review* 258.

[13] Case C-307/97 [2000] STC 854; and see Oliver [2000] BTR 174 and Kostense [2000] 9 *EC Tax Review* 220.

[14] Case C-376/03 *D v Inspecteur van de Belastingdienst/Particulieren/Ondernemingen Buitenland te Heerlen* [2005] STC 1211.

[15] See <www.oecd.org>. See also discussion in Avery Jones (1999) 53 *Tax Law Review* 1, 2. The Treaty is the subject of an excellent book by Baker, *Double Taxation Agreements and International Tax Law*, 2nd edn (Sweet & Maxwell, 2001).

[16] For an attempt to fit income from trusts into the existing treaty framework, see Avery Jones *et al* [1989] BTR 41 and 65; on accumulation trust and tax treaties, see Prebble [2001] BTR 69.

[17] For a comparison of the treaties, see van Raad, *Materials on International and EC Tax Law 2007–08*, vol 1 (International Tax Centre Leiden, 2007), 391.On the 2001 version, see Bruggen [2002] BTR 119; on 1978 version, see Surrey (1979) 19 *Harvard Intl L J* 1, 4.

[18] They are to be found in Africa and in the Nordic countries: see Vogel, *op cit*, 11; see also Lang *et al*, *Multilateral Tax Treaties: New Developments in International Tax Law* (Kluwer, 1998).

[19] Eg Bird and Mintz in Cnossen and Sinn (eds), *Public Finance and Public Policy in the New Century* (MIT Press, 2003) 405–47.

20.2 The Nature of UK Treaty Relief

20.2.1 Treaty-Making Power

Under UK law treaties do not have direct effect. Tax treaties, or more correctly 'arrangements', are made in relation to a territory (so avoiding problems over states the UK did not recognise)[20] and take effect under statutory authority,[21] being incorporated into domestic law by statutory instrument.[22] In accordance with general UK constitutional principles, these treaties may only include the matters permitted by the legislation.[23] TIOPA 2010, section 6(2) and (3) (ex TA 1988, section 787(3)) state that double taxation arrangements have effect so far as they provide, inter alia:

- for relief from income tax or corporation tax;
- for taxing income of non UK-resident persons that arises from sources in the UK;
- for taxing chargeable gains accruing to non UK-resident persons on the disposal of assets in the UK;
- for relief from CGT; and
- for taxing capital gains accruing to non UK-resident persons on the disposal of assets in the UK.

On the relationship between unilateral relief and treaty relief, see §19.4.1 above.

TIOPA 2010, section 7 allows the Revenue to propose Orders in Council only if they are consistent with the purposes spelt out in sections 2 to 6. Since sections 2 to 4 refer to granting relief for foreign taxes, it is thought that the UK treaties may only relieve from tax and not increase it.[24] However, the former version of these rules in TA 1988, section 788 had less happy aspects for taxpayers; its limited nature was used, before FA 2000, to deny credit relief for foreign taxes to the UK PE of a non-resident company and repayment supplement.[25]

A double taxation treaty provision being made under statutory authority[26] becomes part of municipal law; it follows that where the text of the Order in Council does not agree with that of the treaty, the former prevails.[27] The Order may override the normal rules of UK tax

---

[20] TIOPA 2010, s 2(1)(a), ex TA 1988, s 788(1), as amended by FA 2002 s 88 to reach an agreement with Taiwan. Similar problems have arisen over the precise area to be covered, eg the Israeli-occupied West Bank of the Jordan, or where the two governments both claim *de jure* sovereignty over the same territory (eg Northern Ireland).

[21] TIOPA 2010, s 2, ex TA 1988, s 788; IHTA 1984, s 155.

[22] Explained in TIOPA 2010, s 2(1), ex TA 1988, s 788(2).

[23] TIOPA 2010, s 6, ex TA 1988, s 788(3).

[24] The Revenue were known to be interested in the question whether use of the Article 9 in the OECD Model Treaty on associated enterprises could increase the burden of tax on companies as compared with the application of the former UK statutory transfer-pricing rules in TA 1988, s 770; the switch to the OECD Model in s 770A, now TIOPA 2010, Pt 4, should mean that this particular issue has now gone away. Contrast IHT, where the Revenue view is that the treaty cannot enlarge the tax—see *Manual on Inheritance Tax Double Tax Conventions*, para 7.

[25] Avery Jones [1991] BTR 407; citing *Sun Life Assurance of Canada v Pearson* [1984] STC 461, 516b (on which see also Oliver [1986] BTR 195) and *R v IRC, ex parte Commerzbank* [1991] STC 271.

[26] On process of implementation, see Bartlett [1991] BTR 76. For criticism of some of Bartlett's views, see Edwardes Ker *Tax Treaty Interpretation*, §44.03, who argues that the treaties are made under the Crown's prerogative power and given effect by Order in Council. Moreover, since the Crown has no prerogative power to tax, this provides another reason why a treaty cannot widen the charge to tax.

[27] See Oliver [1970] BTR 388, 398–400.

law, but whether it does so or not is a matter of construction.[28] Where a treaty assigns a tax exclusively to the UK, this is not a direction that the UK *shall* tax but rather the recognition of a *power* to tax.

The treaty-making power in TIOPA 2010, section 2 is limited to relief for income tax, corporation tax, CGT, petroleum revenue tax and any taxes of a similar character imposed by the laws of that territory. It is usual for the treaty to state precisely the taxes which may be claimed for credit, so avoiding the problem of having to convince the Revenue some time later that the particular tax is of such a character. A hypothetical question is how the court would view an attempt by the Revenue to argue that a tax which had been mentioned in the treaty was not eligible for credit relief because it was not of the right character and that the Revenue had been in error in agreeing with the other state that it was. The Revenue argument would have to be that section 2 did not authorise it to make such a treaty.

A problem arose over development land tax (DLT). The Revenue took the view that this was not a tax of a similar character. As the DLT legislation had no enabling clause, it followed that no treaty relief was available for DLT.[29] If the UK had tried to incorporate DLT into one of its treaties, a person not resident in the UK but resident in the other state would have been without remedy. Then TA 1988, section 788 prevented any claim under domestic law, and the individual could not claim any relief in international law since states, not individuals, are parties to treaties in international law.

Another example concerns the days of the advance corporation tax (ACT) regime (now repealed)—*Boake Allen and other test claimants v IRC*[30] (at the lower level of appeal this case was known as the *NEC Semi-Conductors* case). Here, a majority of the House of Lords held that TA 1988, section 788 did not apply to ACT. Section 788(3) spelt out the parts of the Treaty which would be incorporated into domestic UK tax law. Section 788(3)(a) referred to a 'corporation tax in respect of income or chargeable gains', and the ACT did not fit that description.[31] Naturally this depends on the finding that ACT was not a corporation tax. The case makes a nice contrast with non-discrimination under EU law.

UBS AG v HMRC[32] is a case that involved another part of the pre-1999 UK corporation tax system, viz a claim to release a credit from surplus franked investment income under the now repealed TA 1988, section 243. UBS was a bank resident in Switzerland but with a branch in London. Moses LJ said that the claim for relief under section 243 of the 1988 Act did not fall within TA 1988, section 788(3)(a), as a claim for the release of the credit under section 243 was not a relief from corporation tax. UBS had no liability; it sought payment of a tax credit in an amount calculated by reference to the distributions it had received. UBS was not seeking 'relief … from corporation tax' because there was no liability to an amount of tax which would otherwise be payable.[33] Neither was it within section 788(3)(d) as it was not a right to a tax credit.[34] The judges disagreed on the scope of the non-discrimination clause, but the decision on section 788 was enough to make the Revenue win.

---

[28] *IRC v Collco Dealings Ltd* [1961] 1 All ER 762, 39 TC 509; and see *Ostime v Australian Mutual Provident Society* [1960] 1 AC 459, 38 TC 492 (TA 1988, s 445 excluded by treaty).
[29] Oliver [1984] BTR 193.
[30] [2007] UKHL 25, [2007] STC 1265.
[31] [2007] UKHL 25, [45] *et seq*.
[32] [2007] EWCA Civ 119, [2007] STC 588.
[33] [2007] EWCA Civ 119, [42] *et seq*; Arden and Sedley LJJ agreed, [51 and 87].
[34] *Ibid*, [49–50]; Arden and Sedley LJJ agreed, [51 and 87].

20.2.2 Who can Invoke a Treaty?[35]

While under general UK law individuals cannot claim the benefit of a treaty, the fact that the tax treaty has become part of domestic law by reason of the Order in Council does give rise to such rights, but only so far as that incorporation allows. A treaty based on the OECD Model will usually say that it applies to persons who are resident. 'Person' is then defined to 'include' an individual, a company or any other body of persons, and a 'company' as including any body corporate or other entity treated as a body corporate for tax purposes, a process which requires a reference back to the internal law of the state concerned.[36]

The question whether rights arising under a bilateral treaty may be used by a person who is resident only in a third country depends on the construction of the agreement. Thus, in *IRC v Commerzbank AG*,[37] dividends paid by a US corporation to the UK branch of a German bank were not subject to UK corporation tax because of the terms of the 1975 US–UK Treaty. Today, a different decision would be reached.[38]

20.2.3 The Credit

Where a treaty provides for relief by way of credit for the foreign tax paid, the way of giving relief is a matter for UK law, and the rules are stated in TIOPA 2010, sections 2–7 and 18.[39] The UK Treasury has power to deny tax credit refund under a treaty to companies which have, or are associated with companies which have, a qualifying presence in a state which practises unitary taxation (called a 'unitary state').[40] This power would have been exercised in relation to California, but happily that dispute was resolved.[41]

20.2.3.1 Credit for Tax not Paid: Pioneer Relief or Tax Sparing[42]

The logic of the tax credit scheme of relief means that concessions, whereby the country of source lowers its tax rates, are cancelled out since it results simply in a lower credit to set against the tax liability in the country of residence. Since 1961,[43] provisions allow the taxpayer to treat the amount in respect of which the relief was given by the foreign country as if that tax had been paid.[44]

---

[35] See Edwardes Ker, *Tax Treaty Interpretation*, chs 50–52, 56.

[36] See *Padmore v IRC (No 1)* [1989] STC 493 (CA), dismissing appeal from [1987] STC 36; Avery Jones [1987] BTR 88. See also Harris [2011] BTR 188.

[37] [1990] STC 285, decided under the 1945 Treaty. On interpretation techniques in this case, see Avery Jones [1990] BTR 388; and White and Avery Jones [1991] BTR 35.

[38] See US–UK Treaty 1975, Art 1(1), confining the 1975 Treaty to persons resident in one or other country; there was no such clause in the 1945 Treaty and the 1975 Treaty did not come into force until 1980. The 1977 Treaty excludes not only branches of companies resident in third countries but also branches of a company resident in the other Contracting State.

[39] Ex TA 1988, ss 788(2) and 792–806; see above at §19.4.

[40] TA 1988, ss 812–814 (not rewritten).

[41] Treasury Press Releases, 13 May 1993 and 15 September 1993, [1993] *Simon's Tax Intelligence* 858 and 1250.

[42] See OECD, *Tax Sparing: A Reconsideration* (OECD, 1998); summarised by Gosselin (1999) 47 *Can Tax Jo* 405. The statutory basis for tax sparing in TA 1988, s 788(5) was amended by FA 2000, Sch 30, para 1; see rewritten version in TIOPA 2010, ss 4 and 20.

[43] FA 1961, s 17; then TA 1988, s 788(3), now TIOPA 2010, s 6(1)–(4). Section 17 was amended in 1976; TIOPA 2010, s 32(1), (2) (ex TA 1988, s 795(1)) contains the treaty rule. On tax sparing, see TIOPA 2010, ss 4 and 20 (ex TA 1988, ss 788(5), 795(3)).

[44] Treaties containing such clauses include ones with Barbados, Israel, Jamaica, Malaysia, Malta, Pakistan, Portugal, Singapore, and Trinidad and Tobago.

FA 2000 made changes for certain overseas dividends paid to a UK company. Relief may be claimed for the underlying tax on the profits out of which the dividends are paid in only two situations, the second of which has two limbs. The first is where the treaty specifically provides such relief. The second is where the relief sought is unilateral and either both the overseas company and the subsidiary are resident in the same country, or the sparing relief is provided by the treaty between the UK and the territory from which the profits arose.[45]

The device of tax sparing has been heavily criticised in—and scarcely used by—the US. The main objection is that by giving a positive advantage to the citizen trading overseas, it breaks the fundamental principle underlying the notion of the tax credit, which is neutrality between citizens trading abroad and those trading at home.[46] Other objections are that it gives the largest tax benefits to the countries with the highest nominal tax rates[47] without any necessary relationship to the fundamental economic needs of the country. It should not, however, be inferred that the United States ignores the problem; it gives relief in a different way by, in effect, granting capital allowances in respect of expenditure outside the United States, something permitted under the UK capital allowance system only if the trade is carried on at least partly in the UK. A more substantial objection is that tax sparing is a very inefficient way of achieving its goals unless carefully targeted.[48]

20.3 Interpretation of Treaties[49]

20.3.1 Approaches to Interpretation

The correct approach to the interpretation of a treaty is controversial.[50] There are several distinct issues—thus, should treaties be interpreted in the same way as domestic tax legislation, and what materials should the court look at when interpreting a treaty? Some would like the courts simply to resolve the immediate dispute in a pragmatic fashion; others would like the courts of all countries to develop a supranational interpretation, if necessary with a supranational court.[51]

What is clear is that interpretation issues can be complex. A treaty regulates the interaction of two tax systems which are complex in themselves, and the answer has to make sense in terms of the tax systems involved. There is no reason why a term should be interpreted in the same way in each system. The OECD reports on financial instruments and on software showed how divergent these views could be.[52] Even if the system can agree on how a

---

[45] FA 2000, Sch 30, para 2, amending s 788(5) (treaty relief), and para 3, adding TA 1988, s 790(10A)–(10C) (unilateral relief); see rewritten version of s 790(10A)–(10C) in TIOPA 2010, s 17(1)–(5).

[46] See Surrey (1956) 56 *Col LR* 815; and (1958) 11 *National Tax Jo* 156.

[47] Counter-measures taken by developing countries include conditional withholding tax (Jamaica) and the raising of the tax level (Panama).

[48] See OECD, *op cit*, 31.

[49] See the works cited above in n 1.

[50] See, generally, Avery Jones [1984] BTR 14 and 90, and the long list cited by Sandler and Li (1997) 45 *Can Tax Jo* 893, 898. For an interesting Australian example, see *Lamesa Holdings Ltd BV v FCT* [1997] FCA 785, see also [1999] FCA 612, dealing with the capital gains article in the Australia–Netherlands Double Tax Treaty and whether the term 'real property' could extend to shares in a company owning real property.

[51] On history of such ideas see Edwardes Ker, *Tax Treaty Interpretation, op cit*, ch 2; and Avery Jones [2001] BTR 382-84.

[52] *Issues in International Taxation No 4* (Software) (1992); and *Taxation of New Financial Instruments* (1994).

particular receipt should be classified for treaty purposes, there will still be more funda-mental characterisation problems, such as whether income can be attributed to this person or to someone else, how anti-abuse doctrines should apply or how the entity receiving the income should be classified (as a partnership or a company), as well as issues as to the source of the income or the problem of quantifying branch income.[53]

The Vienna Convention on the Law of Treaties 1969[54] requires that a treaty be interpreted in good faith in accordance with the ordinary meaning to be given to the terms of the treaty in their context, and in the light of their object and purpose.[55] It then defines 'context' as including any associated agreements and instruments, and goes on to permit reference to subsequent agreements and practices between the parties directed to interpretation and to *travaux préparatoires*. Where the treaty is authenticated in two languages, each is of equal weight unless the agreement states otherwise.[56] The English courts have authorised reference to *travaux préparatoires* and to the commentaries to the OECD Model Treaty.[57] *Travaux préparatoires* may extend to an interpretative document prepared by state A which is part of the negotiating process, or which is shown to the representatives of state B before the treaty is promulgated.[58]

Authorising reference to the commentaries is a long way from being bound by them.[59] However, the question arises whether the court should look at such materials to resolve an ambiguity, or more permissively whether or not there is an ambiguity.[60] The Vienna Convention suggests the less permissive approach is likely; US practice prefers the more permissive approach, but then the United States has not ratified the Vienna Convention. It is not clear how the OECD Model Treaty can be fitted in with the words of the Vienna Convention.[61]

UK tax treaties are not necessarily to be interpreted as though they have been drafted in Lincoln's Inn.[62] However, it does not follow that a purposive approach is to be preferred to a textual one, and it should be noted that the Vienna Convention prefers a textual approach.[63] Moreover, the OECD commentaries do not claim too much for themselves[64] and are all too often self-serving.[65] The actual results reached are consistent with the traditional English approach of strict interpretation. Looking at the result reached in

---

[53] See Avery Jones *et al* [1996] BTR 212.

[54] The leading work on the Treaty is Sinclair, *The Vienna Convention of the Law of Treaties*, 2nd edn (Manchester University Press, 1984).

[55] Article 31; on good faith and treaty interpretation see Bruggen [2003] BTR 25-68.

[56] Articles 31-33.

[57] *Sun Life Assurance Co of Canada v Pearson* [1986] STC 335, CA. In *The Queen v Crown Forest Industries Ltd* [1995] 2 CTC 64, (1995) 95 DTC 5389 the Canadian Supreme Court gave the OECD Model Treaty (and com-mentaries) high persuasive authority; for critical discussion, see Ward *et al* (1996) 44 *Can Tax Jo* 408; but see also Vincent (1996) 44 *Can Tax Jo* 38.

[58] See Arnold, Edgar, Li and Sandler, *Material on Canadian Income Tax*, 11th edn (Carswell, 1996), 207.

[59] However, for an example of UK tax law expressly incorporating OECD principles, see the transfer pricing rules in TIOPA 2010, s 164.

[60] The Canadian Supreme Court took the more permissive approach in the *Crown Forest* case [1995] 2 CTC 64, 77.

[61] Arnold *et al, op cit*, 206.

[62] Peter Gibson LJ in *Memec plc v IRC* [1998] STC 754, 766; approving Mummery J in *IRC v Commerzbank* [1990] STC 285, 297-8, (1990) 63 TC 218, 235-6.

[63] See Smith (1996) 49 *The Tax Lawyer* 845.

[64] See Avery Jones (1999) 53 *Tax Law Review* 1, 19.

[65] Sandler and Li (1997) 45 *Can Tax Jo* 893.

Commerzbank (see §20.2.2 above), one commentator concluded that while the article was meant to mean something else, there was no admissible evidence to contradict the plain words interpretation, which all goes to show that it is what one says, rather than what one means, that matters.[66]

On the broader question of the role of public international law, Edwardes Ker concludes, depressingly:[67]

> Unfortunately even those judges who have recently focused on the applicability of the [Vienna] Convention have done little more than just cite it. Just as unfortunately some of those judges who have focused on principles of public international law have applied them with insensitivity as inappropriate as their colleagues' lack of focus.

The English approach was summarised by Mummery J as follows:[68]

(1) It is necessary to look first for a clear meaning of the words used in the relevant article of the convention, bearing in mind that 'consideration of the purpose of an enactment is always a legitimate part of the process of interpretation': a strictly literal approach to interpretation is not appropriate in construing legislation which gives effect to or incorporates an international treaty. [Such an] interpretation may be obviously inconsistent with the purposes of the particular article or of the treaty as a whole. If the provisions of a particular article are ambiguous, it may be possible to resolve that ambiguity by giving a purposive construction to the convention looking at it as a whole by reference to its language as set out in the relevant United Kingdom legislative instrument.

(2) The process of interpretation should take account of the fact that the language of an international convention has not been chosen by an English parliamentary draftsman. It is neither couched in the conventional English legislative idiom nor designed to be construed exclusively by English judges ...

(3) Among those principles is the general principle of international law, now embodied in art 31(1) of the Vienna Convention on the Law of Treaties ...

(4) If the adoption of this approach to the article leaves the meaning of the relevant provision unclear or ambiguous or leads to a result which is manifestly absurd or unreasonable recourse may be had to 'supplementary means of interpretation' including *travaux préparatoires*.

(5) Subsequent commentaries on a convention or treaty have persuasive value only, depending on the cogency of their reasoning. Similarly, decisions of foreign courts on the interpretation of a convention or treaty text depend for their authority on the reputation and status of the court in question.

(6) Aids to the interpretation of a treaty such as *travaux préparatoires*, international case law and the writings of jurists are not a substitute for study of the terms of the convention. Their use is discretionary, not mandatory, depending, for example, on the relevance of such material and the weight to be attached to it.

---

[66] Avery Jones [1990] BTR 388, 392.

[67] Edwardes Ker, *Tax Treaty Interpretation, op cit*, §1.03.

[68] In *IRC v Commerzbank* [1990] STC 285, 297–98; (1990) 63 TC 218, 235–36; approved by Peter Gibson LJ in *Memec plc v IRC* [1998] STC 754, 766. Mummery J's starting point was the decision of the House of Lords in *Fothergill v Monarch Airlines Ltd* [1981] AC 251; the cross-references to that case have been removed here. On *Commerzbank*, see Avery Jones [1990] BTR 388; and White and Avery Jones [1991] BTR 35.

20.3.2 *Whose Meaning?*

Some of the problems thrown up are familiar to students of private international law. Thus, Article 3(2) of the OECD Model Treaty provides that any term which is not defined shall, unless the context otherwise requires, have the meaning that it has at that time under the law of the relevant state for the purposes of the taxes to which the convention applies, the tax meaning being preferred to that under other laws of the state.[69] It is anything but clear what is meant by 'context' or what meaning is to be assigned to the term if the context excludes the domestic meaning.

However, Article 3(2) is seen as one of the 'really clever' things about the OECD Model Treaty, since it enables the two systems to work together even though each has a different set of rules defining 'income'. It does not require that the words should have the same meaning in each system; instead it enables the treaty relieving provisions to correspond to the tax system in force in each.[70] It is generally assumed that the sort of problem addressed by Article 3(2) arises where the state of residence (R) is trying to give credit for tax in the state of source (S). Article 3(2) encourages R to give its own meaning to the tax paid in S. It has, however, been used to suggest that R should apply its own rules where it is giving relief as the state of residence. Thus, if R says that if it had been S it would not have taxed this item, it may follow that it is not obliged to give relief for the tax paid by S.[71]

Problems will arise when the two domestic systems give different meanings; in the absence of a common meaning, double taxation may ensue. If countries A and B agree on a meaning, it would seem to follow that B will want to use the same meaning when dealing with country C; this means that the accidents of litigation, rather than systematic and thorough analysis, may shape the answer. One solution lies in the development of autonomous interpretations, perhaps developed by a body attached to the OECD. It is hard to fit such ideas into traditional common law notions of procedure, but it certainly is easier following the Woolf reforms of 1999.

A word used in more than one article in a treaty does not necessarily mean the same in each article—even though the courts of the other party have so held; arguments framed in terms of trying to achieve symmetry or harmonisation are not conclusive.[72]

20.3.3 *Ambulatory?*

Another problem is that of choosing the right interpretation if the domestic meaning is A when the treaty is signed, but B by the time the relevant year is reached. Canadian courts have favoured the static approach over the ambulatory, but have been almost instantly reversed by the legislature.[73] If OECD commentaries are looked at, it may be inferred that this may extend only to those commentaries existing at the time of ratification of the

---

[69] See discussion by Avery Jones *et al* [1996] BTR 212 (also in (1996) 36 *European Taxation* 118); see also Avery Jones (1993) 33 *European Taxation* 252; and Edwardes Ker, *Tax Treaty Interpretation, op cit*, ch 8.

[70] Avery Jones (1999) 53 *Tax Law Review* 1, 18.

[71] For criticisms of such an approach, see Avery Jones *et al* [1996] BTR 212.

[72] See divergence of view in *Memec plc v IRC* [1998] STC 754 between Sir Peter Gibson LJ (at 768) and Sir Christopher Staughton (at 771).

[73] Tax Conventions Interpretation Act (Canada) 1984, reversing *R v Melford Developments Inc* (1982) 82 DTC 6281.

particular convention.[74] The UK position is undecided.[75] The ambulatory position is to be preferred as a matter of theory, and has been part of the OECD commentary on Article 3(2) since 1995.[76]

20.4   Relief by Exemption

Clauses may simply provide that income of the type stated shall be exempt from tax in one country.[77] Whether and to what extent it will be taxable in the other country is a matter for the revenue law of that other country. For example, income earned overseas by a visiting teacher there for temporary purposes may be exempt from tax in the country of service but is taxed in the country of residence.[78] Until 1998, that income might also escape UK tax.[79]

A more common form of exemption will exempt a person from tax in the country where the income arises if he is subject to tax in respect of the income in the other country. It appears to be the generous practice of some foreign countries to regard income taxed in the UK on preferential reduced or remittance bases as being 'subject to tax' in the UK and so not liable to the foreign tax. Examples of income which is often given exemption in either of these forms include trading profits arising otherwise than through a PE, and pensions and salaries paid by governments.

The effect of the exemption is that these receipts are not included in the receipts of the taxpayer's business. This might, in turn, mean that the business had a loss rather than a profit. A further rule applies, therefore, where the person is not resident in the UK but is carrying on a business in the UK. Receipts accruing to such persons would not be excluded where they consisted of interest, dividends or royalties.[80]

20.5   General Matters

Treaties are based on the twin poles of residence and source. This was because when treaties began, some countries, like the UK, taxed income on a worldwide basis, while others appeared to have collection of taxes levied on sources within their territory.[81] The meaning

---

[74] See Ward *et al* (1996) 44 *Can Tax Jo* 408, discussing the decision of the Canadian Supreme Court in *The Queen v Crown Forest Industries Ltd* (1995) 95 DTC 5389, giving the OECD Model (and commentaries) high persuasive authority.

[75] However Baker, *Double Taxation Agreements and International Tax Law, op cit,* 27, points out that the Canadian Supreme Court in the *Melford* case placed some reliance on dicta in *IRC v Collco Dealings Ltd* [1962] AC 1 and *Woodend (KV Ceylon) Rubber and Tea Co Ltd v Commr of Inland Revenue* [1971] AC 321, PC.

[76] See Baker, *Double Taxation Agreements and International Tax Law, op cit,* 29–31.

[77] Receipts by a non-resident carrying on a banking, insurance or share-dealing business in the UK, although exempt from UK tax, are not excluded in computing the profits of that business so as to give rise to a loss for corporation tax purposes. This ends a 'fascinating anomaly' by which UK branches of US banks and insurance companies could claim treaty exemption on US-source interest without restriction on the right to offset interest paid on the corresponding borrowing against their other UK income.

[78] For example UK–US Treaty 1975, Art 20. See *IRC v Vas* [1990] STC 137, (1990) 63 TC 430; and the more straightforward case of *Devai v IRC* [1997] STC (SCD) 31.

[79] Ex TA 1988, s 193, Sch 12, para 3; on 1998 repeal of the 100% reduction with immediate effect, see *Revenue Law,* §13.3.

[80] CTA 2010, s 54, ex TA 1988, s 808, as amended by FA 1994, s 140.

[81] See Avery Jones [2001] BTR 382.

of 'residence' for treaty purposes is explored below. The equally fundamental concept of 'source' contains an ambiguity: does it mean the origin or actual source from which the income arises (as the term has been used throughout this book), or simply the territory in which it originates, ie from what or just from where? This may be tested by asking whether the UK gives credit for tax paid by a PE abroad.[82] The matter is addressed in modern treaties by express provision, and so 'source' means taxable in the other state in accordance with the treaty. Older treaties had no such clause; however, Article 3(2) of the OECD Model Treaty may be used to infer that the context required the rejection of the normal tax concept of tax origin in favour of the broader territory meaning, so giving relief.

20.5.1 Discrimination

The OECD Model Treaty[83] prohibits the government from discriminating against citizens of other countries with sources in the first country.[84] This does not prevent the first country raising or lowering its own tax rates, but only from discriminating against non-residents. The purpose of this clause is to prevent discriminatory legislation, not to prevent unfairness.[85] The UK Revenue allow taxpayers to invoke such a provision only sparingly (for examples, see above at §2.4.2).[86] The clause has an odd history[87] and is very narrow; by being confined to tax, it does not apply to a rule barring repayment supplement to a taxpayer resident in the other signatory territory,[88] a point which makes a nice contrast with the vigorous jurisprudence of the ECJ (now CJEU).[89] Many UK treaties with former colonies do not include a non-discrimination clause. Where enterprises of a Contracting State are concerned, a comparison is made with the treatment of other similar enterprises, a phrase which enables comparison of the treatment of one enterprise with that of enterprises controlled by persons in the other state or in some third state altogether.[90]

Whether there is a breach of the non-discrimination article will depend not only on a close examination of the different situations covered by the article, but also on finding the right comparator. In *Boake Allen (previously NEC Semi-Conductors Ltd) and other test claimants v IRC*,[91] the taxpayer companies were UK subsidiaries of a parent based in Japan. Under TA 1988, section 247 (since repealed), UK-resident companies could make a group income election, as a result of which there was no liability to pay the now-repealed ACT. This election was not available where the payment was made to a parent resident outside

---

[82] Avery Jones [1994] BTR 191.

[83] Art 24. For comments on earlier version, see [1981] BTR 47; and Avery Jones *et al* (1990) 30 *European Taxation* 309; and Avery Jones [1991] BTR 359 and 421. For 1993 survey of country practices, see International Fiscal Association, *Cahiers* 78b. On (dismal) performance by US authorities, see Goldberg and Glicklich (1992) 1 *Florida Tax Review* 51.

[84] See, generally, Avery Jones *et al* [1991] BTR 359 and 421. For earlier comment, see Oliver [1977] BTR 148; and van Raad [1981] BTR 43.

[85] *Sun Life Assurance Co of Canada v Pearson* [1984] STC 461.

[86] There is much valuable comparative material in Arnold, *Canadian Tax Foundation Paper No 90* (1991); see also Friedlander [2002] BTR 71.

[87] Van Raad, *Non-Discrimination in International Tax Law* (Kluwer, 1986); this book is a slightly dated but still very useful analysis of the US and Netherlands laws.

[88] Arnold *et al*, *op cit*, 220.

[89] On German courts' move towards bringing EC principles into tax treaties, see (2004) 32 *Intertax* 134.

[90] On meaning of 'other similar enterprises', see Oliver [1989] BTR 141, pointing out that the OECD report on transfer pricing takes a much broader view.

[91] [2007] UKHL 25.

the UK; such restrictions had been held to be in breach of EC non-discrimination law principles in the *Metalgesellchaft* case,[92] but did they breach the treaty? The House of Lords held that there was no breach.

Following on the intervening decision of the House in *Pirelli Cable Holding NV v IRC*,[93] their Lordships held that what the group income election was concerned with was deciding how to allocate the liability to ACT between the two companies. It followed that the section had no meaning where the parent was not subject to ACT. This was why the election, with its cash-flow advantages, was rightly denied. This reason had nothing to do with the control being in foreign hands, and so there was no breach of the non-discrimination article.

The House of Lords decision in *Pirelli* left open the question—one of fact—whether the Pirelli company would have made a group income election. Despite the clarity of the House of Lords decision, the taxpayers returned to court to argue the question whether they were entitled to tax credits and so should not have to bring them into account. The taxpayers' argument was rejected at first instance and by the Court of Appeal.[94]

UBS AG v HMRC[95] involved another part of the pre-1999 UK corporation tax system, viz a claim to release a credit from surplus franked investment income under the now repealed TA 1988, section 243. UBS was a bank resident in Switzerland but with a branch in London. As seen in §20.2.1 above, the Court unanimously rejected the claim since it did not come within TA 1988, section 788(3)(a) or (d). Moses LJ held that the matter had to be dealt with under the dividend article (Article 10) and that the non-discrimination article (Article 23) could not intervene. Arden LJ thought that Article 23 could still apply. Moses LJ agreed with the Special Commissioners, but they had reached their decision with great reluctance and had been scathing of the failure of the Government properly to implement a treaty (see paragraph 41 of their decision). They invited HMRC to revisit section 788; the FA 2006 changes, below, did not address these issues.

In 2008 the OECD, as part of the ongoing review project, included major changes to the OECD commentary on non-discrimination. One may read this in part as an effort to make sure that the OECD approach to non-discrimination remains very different from that prevailing under EU rules.

20.5.2 Administration; Mutual Agreement, Exchange of Information and Mutual Assistance in Collecting Tax

There will be a mutual agreement procedure article enabling the competent authorities in the Contracting States to resolve issues by agreement.[96] The competent authorities are usually the tax departments—often acting under an authorisation from the relevant Ministry of Finance. Such a clause authorises them to act without having to go through diplomatic channels or international court process. Such an article usually covers not only procedures for specific cases involving specific individuals, but also more general interpretative

---

[92] Joined Cases C-397/98 and C-410/98 *Metallgesellschaft Ltd v IRC and AG; Hoechst AG v IRC and A-G* [2001] STC 452.
[93] [2006] UKHL 4, [2006] STC 548.
[94] *Pirelli Cable Holding v HMRC* [2008] EWCA Civ 70.
[95] [2007] EWCA Civ 119, [2007] STC 588.
[96] OECD Model, Art 25. On old law on nature of legal rights under the mutual agreement procedure, see Avery Jones *et al* [1979] BTR 329; [1980] BTR 13; and [2001] BTR 9.

problems, and even allows the competent authorities to consult together for the elimination of double taxation in cases not provided for in the convention (a legislative role). Unfortunately, the individual taxpayer does not usually have any rights in this process, and often ends up as a pawn in a battle between two revenue machines.[97] Interestingly, the US–Germany Treaty contains an arbitration provision,[98] while the Austrian–German treaty provides for matters to be put before the ECJ, though whether that Court can take jurisdiction is another matter.[99]

Interpretative agreements are general rather than specific. In *IRC v Commerzbank*,[100] Mummery J held that a joint statement by the two signatory states on a point of interpretation did not make that interpretation binding on the courts. However, the wording of the treaty in that case was not based on the OECD Model Treaty.

The Revenue have statutory authority to give effect to the solutions and agreements reached under this procedure; statute also provides for claim for reliefs and various time limits.[101] The normal time limit for claiming the relief as determined by the agreement is 12 months after being notified of it. The claim itself, which may give rise to the mutual agreement, must at present be made six years from the end of the period to which it relates. The agreement is not binding on the taxpayer, who may then use the normal appeals procedure. The OECD reviewed the effectiveness of the mutual agreement procedure and produced a draft manual in 2006 and proposals on arbitration in 2007; the changes finally agreed in 2008 include a change to the treaty itself for arbitration (new clause 5). Under Article 25(5), where the competent authorities of the Contracting States have been unable to reach agreement to resolve a taxpayer's case within two years from the presentation of the case to one of the competent authorities, the taxpayer may request any unresolved issues to be submitted to binding arbitration. Furthermore, in a major change of practice, the commentaries suggest a mechanism for arranging for arbitration under *existing* treaties.[102] For the EU Arbitration Convention for transfer pricing, see above at §16.4.3. Of seven UK tax treaties or amending protocols signed in 2010 and 2011, three contain such an arbitration provision—Germany, Bahrain and Armenia—but four others do not.[103]

The treaty will likely include a clause providing for the exchange of information.[104] Some, but not all, recent UK treaties also include a provision based on Article 27 of the OECD Model Treaty, providing for mutual assistance in the collection of tax.[105] The 2011 UK–South Africa Treaty protocol added such an article and, interestingly, included a provision to the effect that there is no obligation to assist where the requested state considers

---

[97] On the nature of legal rights under such articles, see Avery Jones *et al, ibid.*

[98] On arbitration generally in tax treaties, see Groen (2002) 30 *Intertax* 3.

[99] On Germany–US Treaty, see Fogarasi, Gordon and Venuti (1989) 18 *Tax Management Intl J* 317. On German–Austrian Treaty, see van der Bruggen [2002] 11 *EC Tax* 52-64.

[100] [1980] STC 285, 392.

[101] TIOPA 2010, ss 124–125, ex TA 1988, s 815AA, added by FA 2000, Sch 30, para 20; changes to TCGA 1992, s 278 are made by para 21.

[102] In van Raad, *Materials on International and EC Tax Law, 2007–08*, vol 1 (International Tax Centre Leiden, 2007) 796–835, also available from OECD website along with country profiles.

[103] Baker [2011] BTR 125, 129–30 and Baker [2011] BTR 626, 627. This suggests to Baker (at 627) that the inclusion in UK tax treaties of the provision for arbitration 'depends upon the position taken by the other Contracting State, and some states (China is an example) do not appear to be very enthusiastic about arbitration'.

[104] OECD Model Art 26. See McCracken (2002) 50 *Canadian Tax Jo* 1869.

[105] See now OECD Model, Art 27, added 2003. On unhappy if dated US experience, see 50 *Columbia L Rev* 490. The US entered a reservation in relation to the OECD Treaty of 1988, so far as it related to enforcement.

that the taxes at issue are imposed 'contrary to generally accepted taxation principles'.[106] It is not yet clear whether the treaty requires the UK tax authorities to provide information to a foreign tax authority if there is no UK tax in issue[107] (see above at §14.3.2). On obligations to exchange information with other EU Member States, see above at §14.3.1.

The powers to make treaties including such matters are now to be found in FA 2006 (not rewritten). This Act not only provides the basic authority in this area but widens the Revenue powers to obtain information (in TMA 1970) needed for 'a relevant foreign tax', ie one imposed in the foreign territory and covered by the treaty. The Treasury is allowed to make regulations allowing the recovery in the UK of debts arising from these relevant foreign taxes. In negotiating treaties covering these matters, the Revenue officer must be satisfied that the confidentiality rules in that state are no less strict than those in the UK.[108]

20.5.3 Changes to Treaties

Double tax treaties are not immutable. The usual method of change adopted is renegotiation, a process which may be accelerated by announcing that a particular country will no longer be bound by its present treaties after a certain date.[109] Changes in the domestic tax law are not inhibited by the presence of a treaty,[110] and some changes may have the effect of altering completely the basis of a treaty, eg the adoption of the imputation system of corporate taxation in 1973.[111] These are, of course, only UK rules; other countries, especially those which incorporate treaties into domestic law directly, may well take a different view. It may also be noted that the 1998 changes which extended the CGT charge to temporary non-residents originally contained express provision to ensure that it did not override treaties; seven years of experience convinced the Revenue of the need for change and so a treaty override provision was introduced in 2005.[112]

An interesting example of this process is TA 1988, section 112(4) and (5) (now ITTOIA 2005, section 852), originally passed in 1989, which was designed to reverse the decision in *Padmore v IRC*.[113] That case had held that where a partnership was resident in Jersey, the effect of the UK–Jersey Treaty was that not only was the Jersey partnership as such exempt from UK tax on its profits, but, more surprisingly, that a UK-resident individual partner was exempt from UK income tax on his share of the profits. The rules were amended to

---

[106] See Baker [2011] BTR 125 for analysis. Baker notes that no assistance provisions were included in 2011 treaties with Bahrain or Hong Kong, which suggests to him that the UK policy on such articles is to include them only if the other negotiating state wishes to do so.

[107] In *State of Norway's Application* [1990] AC 723, the English courts exercised their discretion under the Evidence (Proceedings in Other Jurisdictions) Act 1975.

[108] FA 2006, ss 173 and 175; s 173 supersedes the separate provision in TA 1988, s 815C and IHTA 1984, ss 158 and 220A.

[109] Eg Dominica in 1986, or the UK ending the agreement with the Netherlands Antilles in 1989; on new Antilles regimes, see Arts (2002) 30 *Intertax* 153.

[110] Whether the new domestic law is excluded by the treaty is a question of construction (*IRC v Collco Dealings Ltd* [1961] 1 All ER 762, (1961) 39 TC 509). See, generally, Edwardes Ker, *Tax Treaty Interpretation, op cit*, ch 9.

[111] Taylor [1973] BTR 174; on 'erosion' of US treaties by domestic changes made by congress and the courts, see Kaplan [1986] BTR 211.

[112] TCGA 1992, s 10A(1). On s 10A, see above at §18.1.

[113] [1989] STC 493, CA, dismissing appeal from [1987] STC 36. For comment on first-instance decision, see Avery Jones [1987] BTR 88.

reverse this decision (with retroactive effect[114]) and now provide that the treaty is not to affect any liability to tax in respect of the resident partner's share of any income or capital gains of the partnership.[115] An argument that the 1989 change was ineffective failed.[116]

20.5.4 Beneficial Ownership

Several treaty articles require that the person claiming the benefit of the treaty provision should be beneficially entitled to the particular receipt. This may be partly intended to prevent treaty shopping (§20.7.1 below), but it is capable of having a meaning for the tax avoidance situation outside. The meaning of the expression beneficial ownership came before the English Court of Appeal in *Indofoods International Finance v JP Morgan Chase Bank*.[117] The Court held that on the facts a company was not the beneficial owner. Bizarrely, the case concerned a contract dispute between two non-UK companies as to what the Indonesian view of beneficial ownership might be—and whether it was reasonable to expect a company to indulge in a restructuring which would succeed only on one answer to the beneficial ownership question. The Court held that the expression had an established meaning in international tax law, and produced an interpretation which gave great pleasure to the taxing authorities.

The case law on the meaning of beneficial ownership continues to develop, see eg the Canadian case *Prevost Car Inc v R*, where the court took a narrow view of beneficial ownership, holding that a company that receives dividends is the beneficial owner unless the company is a conduit with absolutely no discretion over the use or application of the income.[118] This narrow interpretation in *Prevost Car* was applied in the taxpayer's favour in a 2012 case involving IP royalties, *Velcro Canada Inc v The Queen*.[119] In 2011 the OECD issued a discussion document proposing changes to the commentary on the meaning of 'beneficial ownership' in Articles 10, 11 and 12 of the OECD Model Treaty.[120] With respect to Article 10, the OECD proposed adding that the recipient of a dividend is the beneficial owner of that dividend 'where he has the full right to use and enjoy the dividend unconstrained by a contractual or legal obligation to pass the payment received to another person'.

20.6 Specific Clauses

The treaty will usually begin by specifying the taxes covered and its personal scope (eg whether it is confined to persons resident in each state).[121] Other definitions of terms used in the treaty follow. UK treaties often state that the party to the treaty is the UK, and

---

[114] The provision is deemed always to have been made, save that it is not to affect any court decision before 25 October 1988 or the law to be applied by an appellate court where the judgment of the High Court or Court of Session was given before that date (from which it can be inferred that no litigation was concluded in Northern Ireland).

[115] Such a formula had already been employed in other treaties, eg Art 11(3) of the UK–Switzerland Treaty 1955.

[116] *Padmore v IRC (No 2)* [2001] STC 280.

[117] [2006] EWCA (Civ) 158, [2006] STC 1195 CA, reversing Evans Lombe J [2005] EWHC 103 (Ch), [2006] STC 192; see generally Fraser and Oliver [2006] BTR 424 and, on HMRC draft guidance, [2007] BTR 39.

[118] 2008 TCC 231.

[119] 2012 TCC 57.

[120] Available on the OECD website. See also Collier [2011] BTR 684.

[121] As the current US–UK Treaty does; however, the old treaty as interpreted in *IRC v Commerzbank* [1990] STC 285 did not.

go on to define what the UK means, ie to determine its territorial scope. Sometimes the definition changes, as with the UK deciding to extend its view of itself for treaty and other fiscal purposes by including the Continental Shelf.[122]

However, these questions raise a more fundamental question,[123] which is whether a tax treaty can have any territorial scope or whether it is universal. If a treaty is universal it will protect against all attempts by the state of source to tax the person resident in the other state, ie it applies to the same geographical area as that to which the state's tax laws are applied, unless the treaty provides otherwise. Thus, if the tax jurisdiction changes, the scope of the treaty changes too. On a territorial view, a change in the tax jurisdiction does not automatically change the scope of the treaty's application.

20.6.1 Residence

The interpretative section of the treaty establishes the meaning of the term 'resident' for the purposes of the treaty rules which follow. A person must be a resident of one Contracting State—and not of the other—to make the treaty work. To this end there are usually tie-breaker clauses. The terms used are much more familiar to civil lawyers than to common lawyers.[124] Thus, the civil law test of residence outside the tax area was probably closer to the UK's concept of domicile than to our concept of residence. Unlike the civil law systems, the OECD Model Treaty provides an order in which the tests are to be applied, and has made the outcome less abstract and more fact-based than in civil law systems.[125] Naturally, these definitions are quite distinct from the normal rules of residence.[126] There are definitions of 'residence' for both individuals and other entities such as companies. The treaty will often refer to a company's 'place of effective management' (POEM); effective management is usually found where the managers of the actual business are, as opposed to the central management and control exercised by directors.[127] Astonishingly, the 2008 changes to the commentary state that effective management is, after all, to be found at director level where the key decisions on the conduct of the entity's business *as a whole* are to be found. This is close to referring to central management and control after all, but then the commentary, in what is close to an act of cowardice, leaves it to the competent authorities to settle disputes as to the POEM. Settlement by agreement rather than purely on a tie-breaker such as POEM is becoming more common in treaties, including recent UK treaties with the Netherlands (2008) and Hong Kong (2010). The absence of agreement brings a restriction of treaty benefits—though with the possibility of arbitration under Article 25.

---

[122] On differences between UK and Norway, see Oliver [1990] BTR 303.

[123] Skaar [1993] BTR 189.

[124] Avery Jones *et al* [1981] BTR 14 and 104; see discussion by Venables (1998) 8 *Offshore Taxation Review* 189.

[125] *Ibid*, 119.

[126] *IRC v Exxon Corpn* [1982] STC 356. For an example of the importance of such definitions, see *Lord Strathalmond v IRC* [1972] 3 All ER 715, (1972) 48 TC 537; and compare *Avery Jones v IRC* [1976] STC 290, [1976] 2 All ER 898. See, generally, Avery Jones *et al* [1981] BTR 15 and 104. On ordinary rules, see c 13 above.

[127] See Statement of Practice SP 1/90; and Inland Revenue, *International Tax Handbook*, paras 347 *et seq*.

Although treaty provisions are usually intended to be effective only for treaty purposes, the treaty may have an effect in domestic law, as where a company which is non-resident for treaty purposes is treated as not resident for other purposes as well.[128]

Re Trevor Smallwood Trust[129] concerned the capital gains article in the UK–Mauritius Treaty (Article 13(4)), but the case turns on the tie-breaker rules for residence. The Court of Appeal disagreed with Mann J, preferring instead the conclusion of the Special Commissioners that 'residence' for purposes of the Treaty was not to be determined on a 'snapshot' basis. The issue then fell to be resolved by the application of the test of POEM in the tie-breaker. Patten LJ (in dissent), relying on *Wood v Holden*,[130] concluded that the Mauritius trustees retained their right and duties as trustees to consider the matter at the time of alienation of the shares, and, consequently, the Special Commissioners' conclusions were not ones which were open to them on the evidence or on the findings of fact which they made. Hughes LJ (and Ward LJ agreeing), on the other hand, held that the Special Commissioners were entitled to find that the POEM of the trust was in the UK in the fiscal year in question on the facts before them: '[T]here was a scheme of management of this trust which went above and beyond the day to day management exercised by the trustees for the time being, and the control of it was located in the United Kingdom.'

This case is an important win for HMRC on the meaning of residence of trustees (and, to some extent, companies). It is also, at last, an endorsement by the Court of Appeal of the Special Commissioners' recent approach (viz *Wood v Holden, Laerstate BV*[131]) to determining residence not merely by considering where the formal decisions of the board of directors or trustees are made, but by engaging in a detailed factual inquiry in order to ascertain where the 'real' top-level management decisions were made (see §13.6 above).

20.6.2 Trader and Professional: Permanent Establishment

Traders resident in the UK and carrying on a trade partly inside and partly outside the UK are taxable under ITTOIA 2005, Part 2/CTA 2009, Part 3 on the profits as they arise. Whether they are taxable in the foreign country depends first on that country's tax law. If no foreign tax is payable, no double tax problem arises. If, however, foreign tax is payable, the next step is to look at the treaty, which will probably permit the foreign country to tax the industrial and commercial profits allocable to the enterprise's 'permanent establishment' (PE) in that state.[132] This last term is separately defined in each treaty, but generally includes[133] a branch, place of management,[134] factory or other fixed place of

---

[128] FA 1994, s 249; treaties usually have a tie-breaker clause, but this practice has not been invariable: eg the US–UK Treaty 1975, Art 4 had no tie-breaker clause for companies. Above, §13.6.

[129] [2009] STC 1222, [2009] EWHC 777 (Ch) (reversed [2010] EWCA Civ 77).

[130] [2006] EWCA Civ 26.

[131] In *Laerstate BV v HMRC* [2009] UKFTT 209, control of a non-UK incorporated company was held to have been exercised in the UK by a sole Dutch director making decisions in the UK, despite board meetings taking place elsewhere. For commentary, see Loomer [2009] BTR 378.

[132] For case law down to 1997, see Edwardes Ker, *International Tax Treaties Service, op cit.*

[133] See OECD Model Treaty, Art 5. A PE in the foreign country will also give rise to tax on capital gains and may result in a heavier tax on dividends from that country if the business is incorporated there. On some divergent definitions in European countries, see Skaaar [1997] BTR 494; on history, see Huston and Williams, *Permanent Establishments: A Planning Primer* (Kluwer, 1993).

[134] This derives from the UK test of residence. A person may have a PE in the UK and yet not be resident here (*Greenwood v FL Smidth & Co Ltd* [1922] 1 AC 417, (1922) 8 TC 193. See also *OECD Discussion Draft on Place*

business, but not an agency (unless the agent has and habitually exercises a general power to negotiate and conclude contracts on behalf of his principal), a bona fide broker or a general commission agent.[135] It has been suggested, convincingly, that these clauses are an inaccurate translation from a French original.[136] Often, treaties will also state that certain activities, such as the display of goods, do not amount to having a PE.[137] The 2008 changes to the commentary to Article 5 (paragraphs 42.11 *et seq*) include a new test for PE in relation to services. In 2011 the OECD issued a discussion document containing a number of draft proposed changes to the Commentary on the OECD Model Treaty in relation to the interpretation and application of the definition of PE in Article 5. The proposed changes address technical issues such as whether 'goods or merchandise' covers digital products or data, and other questions such as when a home office, farm, shop on a ship, and development property can be a PE.

Assuming a PE does exist in the foreign state, that state will usually be allowed to tax only so much of the investment income and profits as are attributable to the PE,[138] and the treaty may say how the profits are to be allocated to that establishment. There have been serious problems about applying this important concept to the world of electronic commerce. Formerly, the rules emphasised the making of contracts, but this focus began to look inadequate when applied in a world where, increasingly, the only physical manifestations of business were servers, websites, Internet service providers and telecommunications infrastructure.[139]

The OECD undertook a detailed study into the attribution of profits to PEs[140] that led to amendments to Article 7(2) in the 2010 version of the OECD Model Treaty. The changes to the Article 7 commentary and treaty provision represented major and profound changes to the way in which profits are to be attributed to a PE. The concept of the related business activity was replaced by that of the functionally separate enterprise. Article 7(2) now provides that profits are to be attributed 'taking into account the functions performed, assets used and risks assumed by the enterprise through the permanent establishment and through other parts of the enterprise'. As only some of the OECD member countries so far

---

of Effective Management (OECD, 2003); van Raad, *Materials on International and EC Tax Law, 2007–08*, vol 1 (International Tax Centre Leiden, 2007) 580–84; and Hinnekens (2003) 31 *Intertax* 314.

[135] OECD Model Treaty, Art 5(5), (6); on agency, see Pleijsier (2001) 29 *Intertax* 167 and 218.

[136] See discussion by Avery Jones *et al* [1993] BTR 341.

[137] OECD Model Treaty, Art 5(4).

[138] Eg see OECD Model Treaty, Art 7. For an interesting Canadian example of the problems of application, see *Cudd Pressure Control Inc v The Queen* [1995] 2 CTC 2382: the case draws attention to tensions in the OECD commentary shown by the different approaches adopted in Art 7 on permanent establishment and Art 9 on associated enterprises; both articles create a fictional independence for the establishment and company. The court disallowed notional deductions apparently permitted by Art 7 on the basis that they would not have been allowed under Canadian domestic law. On *Cudd Pressure*, see van Raad (2000) 28 *Intertax* 162 and 253; and Ward (2000) 48 *Can Tax Jo* 559.

[139] See, *inter alia*, Doernberg and Hinnekens, *Electronic Commerce and International Taxation* (Kluwer, 1999); Bourgeois and Blanchette (1997) 45 *Can Tax Jo* 1127 and 1378; Thorpe Emory (1997) 11 *International Law Review* 633. For official UK revenue views, see Customs and Excise Press Release 6 October 1998, [1998] *Simon's Tax Intelligence* 1436. The OECD Commentary to Art 5 states that the mere presence of a server in a state does not give rise a PE in that state. The Revenue have indicated that in their view neither websites nor servers are PEs: Inland Revenue Press Release, 11 April March 2000, [2000] *Simon's Weekly Tax Intelligence* 625.

[140] The OECD's *Report on the Attribution of Profits to Permanent Establishments* (OECD, 2008) was reissued with minor revisions in 2010.

have accepted the new wording, it is likely that it will only be new UK treaties and protocols with those states which will have this wording for some time to come.[141]

20.6.3 Business Profits

Where a business is carried on through a PE in a foreign country, business profits earned by that PE are taxable in the country of source.[142] Profits earned otherwise than by the establishment are taxable in the country of residence. If the trader decides to set up a subsidiary company in the country of source, OECD Model Treaty, Article 9 will apply. The words of the business profits article mask an important difference between civil law and common law countries: in civil law countries all income of the PE is treated as business income; whereas in common law countries this is not necessarily so.[143]

Some UK residents had tried to use foreign trusts and partnerships to avoid tax (see *Revenue Law*, §20.10.7 and above at §15.3.2), relying on treaty provisions that provided that the trading profits of a non-resident enterprise are taxable in the UK only to the extent that they are attributable to a business carried on by or through a PE in the UK. TIOPA 2010, section 130 ensures that this treaty provision does not prevent persons resident in the UK from being liable to tax in the UK. This rule, which applies to income arising on or after 12 March 2008, is to prevent avoidance where partnerships are not involved.[144]

Shipping and similar sources of profits have their own article.[145] At one time there was a separate article dealing with independent personal services—Article 14—but this was removed from the OECD model in 2000, largely on the ground that Article 7 was sufficient.[146] However the article remains in force in many, as yet unrenegotiated, treaties.[147] Under such treaties the country of residence has the exclusive right to tax unless there is a 'fixed base' in the other Contracting State; so much of the profit as was attributable to that fixed base is taxed there.[148] The article was modified for artistes and sportsmen.[149] The change to Article 7 also meant rewriting of the concept of the PE.

In considering these matters it is important to remember the role of the PE concept to allocate profit to the operations of a person resident in one country to activities carried on in the other. It does not give the PE legal personality.

20.6.4 Associated Enterprises

Article 9 of the OECD Model Treaty imposes an arm's-length principle and is the basis of the UK's rules for transfer-pricing legislation. Like Article 7 dealing with the profits of

---

[141] Baker [2011] BTR 625, 626. Baker notes that none of the seven most recent UK treaties signed in 2010 and 2011 used the new wording.

[142] OECD Model Treaty, Art 7(1); for an interesting discussion of the problems which arise, see the report on the International Seminar held at Harvard in late 2002; the report is by Arnold, de Sasseville and Zolt and is published in (2002) 50 *Can Tax Jo* 1979–2024. On relationship between Art 7(2) and (3), see commentary added 1994.

[143] Avery Jones *et al* [2003] BTR 224.

[144] TIOPA 2010, s 130, ex TA 1988, s 815AZA, added by FA 2008, s 56.

[145] Art 8. On history, see Maisto (2003) 31 *Intertax* 232.

[146] De Kort (2001) 29 *Intertax* 72.

[147] Oliver (2001) 29 *Intertax* 204.

[148] OECD Model Treaty, Art 14.

[149] OECD Model Treaty, Art 17, Nitikman (2001) 29 *Intertax* 268. There are also many domestic law problems; see generally, Sandler, *Taxation of International Entertainers and Athletes* (CIOT and Kluwer, 1995).

a PE, this creates a fictional independence for the entities involved. Article 9 deals with enterprises under common control, and allows an adjustment of profits by one state and then directs the other state to make a corresponding adjustment if, and only if, it agrees. Double tax problems may arise when interest payments are made to the parent company and when the profits earned by the subsidiary leave that country in the form of dividends.

20.6.5 *Dividends, Interest and Royalties*

The OECD Model Treaty provides for a withholding tax of a maximum of 10% on payments of interest[150] and of 15% on dividends, except where the recipient is a company holding at least 25% of the shares in the paying company when the rate is 5%.[151] Royalty payments are taxable only in the country of residence, except where there is an effective connection between the PE in the source country and the property giving rise to royalties.[152] By contrast, the old Mexico model gave the taxation of dividends to the place where the capital was invested,[153] of interest to the place of indebtedness[154] and of royalties to the place of exploitation[155]—that is the country of source. Many of these provisions in the OECD Model Treaty, particularly those relating to dividends, were simply unacceptable to less 'developed' countries.

The definition of 'interest'[156] is a matter for the UK courts, but statute now provides special rules.[157] Treaties often provide that where, owing to a special relationship, the amount of the interest paid exceeds the amount that would have been paid in the absence of the relationship, only that hypothetical amount is treated as interest. Where such a clause is relevant, under TIOPA 2010, section 131 the special relationship is to take account of all factors, but express mention is made of whether the loan would have been made at all, the amount of the loan, the rate of interest and other terms that would have been made. The burden is then on the taxpayer to establish that there is no such special relationship. Section 131 further provides that where the company making the loan does not have a business of making loans generally, that fact is to be disregarded.[158] It also provides that the direction to regard all the factors does not apply where the relationship expressly requires regard to be had to the amount of the debt on which the interest is paid and it limits the factors to be taken into account.[159]

Where relief from UK tax in respect of interest is in issue, it is essential that a claim is made as soon as possible in order that tax is not deducted at source. Notice of exemption

---

[150] OECD Model Treaty, Art 11. Some treaties exempt interest on normal intra-group loans.

[151] OECD Model Treaty, Art 10; on OECD history, see Harris in (2000) 15 *Australian Tax Forum* 1–72 and 75–224.

[152] OECD Model Treaty, Art 12.

[153] Mexico Model, Art IX.

[154] Mexico Model, Art II.

[155] Mexico Model, Art X (copyright royalties were excluded).

[156] On problems of the source of interest, see Avery Jones (1999) 53 *Tax Law Review* 1, 31.

[157] TIOPA 2010, s 131, ex TA 1988, s 808A, added by F(No 2)A 1992, s 52. For the correspondence between The Law Society and the Inland Revenue, see [1993] *Simon's Tax Intelligence* 307.

[158] TIOPA 2010, s 131 (5), ex TA 1988, s 808A(4).

[159] TIOPA 2010, s 131(4), ex TA 1988, s 808A(5). See also Inland Revenue Press Release, 15 May 1992, [1992] *Simon's Tax Intelligence* 519.

from such deduction may have retroactive effect, but only to the date that the certified treaty claim is received by the proper officer of the Revenue.[160]

20.6.6 Royalties

References to 'special relationships' are found not only in articles on interest but also in those on royalties. The factors to be taken into account are equivalent to those for interest.[161]

The definition of 'royalty' gave rise to a famous US case involving Pierre Boulez, the composer and conductor. Boulez was resident in Germany and received payments for fees for making recordings in the United States with US orchestras. The US Tax Court[162] held that these were payments for personal services, even though the German tax authorities viewed them as royalty payments. The German view became part of a revised treaty.

A company making a payment of a royalty to a non-resident is now allowed to deduct tax at the treaty rate and not the normal 20%.[163] The risk that the treaty does not in fact apply falls on the paying company.

20.6.7 Employees

UK residents going to work for a foreign company overseas will usually be taxable under the UK tax rules on foreign earnings. Under the treaty they may well be declared to be taxable only in the country of their residence and not in the country of the employment if the employment is exercised there. Some treaties tax in the country of source only if the taxpayer spends a certain number of days in that country.[164] The 2008 Commentary changes clarify the way the days are counted.

20.6.8 Capital Gains

Subject to three exceptions, Article 13 of the OECD Model Treaty gives the right to charge capital gains exclusively to the country of residence. The three exceptions which allow the country of source to tax are: (a) gains from immovable property; (b) gains from assets held as part of the business property of a PE; and (c) gains from certain ships and aircraft. The scope of the capital gains article can be uncertain. As this book shows, the distinction between capital and income is deeply ingrained in the UK tax system, but some capital receipts are regarded as income for income tax purposes. It is a nice question whether for treaty purposes such receipts should be governed by the article to which they belong as income, the present article or the 'other income' article. A pragmatic approach would suggest that when the UK redefines a receipt for domestic purposes in a way which is more precise, eg as part of employment income under ITEPA 2003 or trading income under ITTOIA 2005, Part 2, that redesignation should apply for treaty purposes too. Where the item is simply lobbed into miscellaneous rules (eg ex Schedule D, Case VI), the other

---

[160] Revenue Interpretation RI 79; that officer is now the Financial Intermediaries and Claims Office (FICO) (International), formerly the Inspector of Foreign Dividends.

[161] TIOPA 2010, s 132, ex TA 1988, s 808B, added by FA 2000, Sch 30, para 17.

[162] (1984) 83 TC 584.

[163] ITA 2007, ss 911–913, ex TA 1988, s 349E, added by FA 2002, s 96.

[164] For example US–Belgium Treaty (90 days).

income article may be relevant but ought to yield place to the more precise capital gains article.[165] Of course, UK rules also include situations in which what had been income was moved to capital gain, eg where a company buys its own shares in circumstances coming within CTA 2010, section 1033. The decision by ITTOIA 2005 no longer to use the miscellaneous provisions (ex Schedule D, Case VI) as a dumping-ground reformulates the issues—but does not solve them.

20.6.9 Other Income

Not every treaty contains another income article, which means that gaps can sometimes occur.[166] This may be because the treaty fails to mention certain categories of income, or because the income mentioned arises in the other state and in a third country. The presence of such an article does not solve all problems; thus the article does not cover payments to or by transparent entities such as partnerships.[167]

20.7   Other Problems and Issues

20.7.1 Treaty Shopping

No chapter on treaties would be complete without a reference to the practice of treaty shopping.[168] This practice consists in a resident of a state, which is not a party to the treaty, establishing an entity within a state which is party to the treaty in order to take advantage of its provisions.[169] An OECD report concluded that the practice is consistent with treaty law but should be countered by express provisions in the treaties themselves, or by the extension of domestic anti-avoidance legislation.[170] The general attitude of the UK has been to avoid over-hasty provisions of wide ambit.[171] The United States, by contrast, has been active in seeking to limit the benefits of its treaties to persons genuinely resident in the other state; the famous article dealing with this matter in the Netherlands–US Treaty covers nine pages.[172]

20.7.2 Anti-avoidance Rules

There are two distinct issues in relation to the application of anti-avoidance rules.[173] One is whether, when the domestic system reclassifies a particular receipt, that reclassification is also accepted for treaty purposes. Thus, CTA 2010, Part 18 redesignates certain capital

---

[165] See conclusion to Avery Jones [2001] BTR 382.

[166] See Ward *et al* [1990] BTR 352; also in (1990) 38 *Can Tax Jo* 233.

[167] On tax treaties and partnerships, see the commentary to Art 1 of the OECD Model Treaty.

[168] For an early survey, see Becker and Wurm (eds), *Treaty Shopping* (Kluwer, 1988).

[169] Baker, *Double Taxation Agreements and International Tax Law, op cit*, 52; see also Edwardes Ker, *Tax Treaty Interpretation, op cit*, chs 58–60.

[170] OECD, *International Tax Avoidance and Evasion—Four Related Studies* (1987). For literature and discussion, see Baker, *op cit*, 52–63.

[171] Beighton (1994) *FT World Tax Report* 2.

[172] US–Netherlands Double Tax Treaty, Art 26; on which see Troup [1993] BTR 97; and, on compatibility with EC (now EU) law, see Hinnekens (1995) 4 *EC Tax Review* 282, and Jimenez (1996) 5 *EC Tax Review* 76.

[173] See Edwardes Ker, *Tax Treaty Interpretation, op cit*, chs 57–60.

receipts as income; does this shift matters from the capital gains article to the income from land (or some other income) article?

The second issue is whether doctrines such as the composite transaction doctrine have effect for treaty purposes. After the *Barclays BMBF* case,[174] there is no reason why they should not.

To these two issues a third may be added—if the UK were to adopt a GAAR, how would it apply in the treaty context?

20.8   Reform and Planning

20.8.1 *General*

Relieving double taxation with a foreign tax credit—whether by treaty or unilaterally—at first sight appears fair and reasonable. If the foreign tax is lower than the domestic tax, as will usually be the case (since the domestic tax rate reflects the person's total income from all sources as opposed to his income from one country where he is not resident), the effect is to deprive the country of residence of part of its tax but enable it to preserve equality of tax rates between the person with foreign income and his fellow resident with only domestic income (unless the foreign rate exceeds the UK rate). However, the tax credit has attracted some increasingly debated consequences, particularly where the profits of incorporated business are concerned. Historically, the extensive use of the tax credit by the US[175] has had two consequences: first, it has encouraged other countries to put a tax on the profits of companies, at a time when, in the US, the wisdom of taxing such profits was coming increasingly into question; secondly, it encouraged the countries of source to pitch their corporate tax rates as high as those in the United States, since this would simply increase their share of the tax which the company had to pay anyway, thus causing a loss to the US Revenue without any disincentive for the company.[176]

One alternative would be to extend the relief to indirect taxes—a course which has some attractions for those who believe that an indirect tax on the turnover of companies is to be preferred to a direct tax on their profits. Other courses of action would be simply to abolish the credit, thereby penalising the resident with foreign income, or at the other extreme, to abolish the taxation of foreign income, thereby penalising the stay-at-home. As was seen at the beginning of chapter nineteen above, there is often not much difference between an exemption system and a credit system where the other country has a similar system with similar or higher rates. Another possibility would be differential tax rates, as was in effect done through the percentage reductions. Other devices include deferment of tax in the country of residence until the income has been repatriated (an extension of the remittance basis) and the use of investment credits.

---

[174] *Barclays Mercantile Business Finance Ltd v Mawson* [2005] STC 1 (HL); and see *Revenue Law*, §5.6.
[175] On the role of Thomas Sewell Adams, see Graetz and O'Hear (1997) 46 *Duke Law Journal* 1021.
[176] Eg Panama.

20.8.2 Particular[177]

(1) The band of taxes against which the tax credit works, viz income and corporation taxes, and CGT and foreign taxes similar in character,[178] is narrow. Indirect taxes are regarded traditionally as deductible in computing the profits and so as a part of the costs of the enterprise. A different explanation for the restriction may be that historically the demand was for relief against the double taxation of income. This causes trouble where the country of source, knowing that it can levy only low withholding rates of tax on dividends and interest, decides to levy taxation by means of royalties, or devices such as the famous Middle-Eastern posted prices for oil[179] which have sometimes charged local tax on an inflated price. The argument against this extension would be that to allow relief now would simply encourage the source countries to raise their rates of indirect tax.

(2) The operation of foreign tax credit regimes in practice can be narrow. Despite the FA 2000 rules for companies and underlying tax, the premise of the UK tax credit regime—of less importance since the move in 2009 to exemption treatment for most foreign dividends—is that it may be used only against the UK tax on that source and only against income from that source in that year.[180] If the foreign tax is higher, that excess may not be set off against other income, not even against UK tax on other foreign income. There is thus generally no pooling of foreign income for credit relief, nor may a net loss be carried forward to the next year against income from the same or any other source.[181] The credit is thus distinct from an expense item or a trading loss. There is, of course, no reason why the UK revenue should refund tax collected by another country, unless it is to encourage exports, and for this there may be more efficient methods. Other countries have sometimes granted much more generous relief, but tend now to allow pooling on a 'basket' rather than an unrestricted basis.[182]

(3) There remain many problems over differences between the fiscal concepts used in different systems. One example is that under Australian law, that part of a director's fees in excess of reasonable remuneration may be treated as dividend. The tax paid on this notional dividend would be ineligible for relief in the UK where, if tax were levied, the whole of the director's fees would be taxable as such.[183] Another example is the characterisation of sums paid under a finance lease, whether these are payment of rent (as in the UK) or part of the sale price (as in most other countries). Prickly problems may arise where the two states differ as to how they characterise the particular receipt. Thus, if state S, the source state, classifies the receipt in a way which gives it the right to tax, and R classifies the receipt differently in a way which gives it the exclusive right to tax, is R obliged to give credit for the tax paid in S?[184]

---

[177] See Shelburne [1957] BTR 48 and 143—still, astonishingly, relevant; and Inland Revenue, *Double Taxation Relief for Companies: a Discussion Paper* (1999).

[178] TIOPA 2010, s 2, ex TA 1988, s 790(6) and ex TCGA 1992, s 277.

[179] See Public Accounts Committee 1972–1973, First Report, §§14, 57. There are no full double tax treaties with these countries.

[180] See Inland Revenue, *Double Taxation Relief for Companies: a Discussion Paper* (1999), paras 6.1–6.5.

[181] Pooling is considered in Inland Revenue, *Double Taxation Relief for Companies: a Discussion Paper* (1999), ch 6.

[182] See Ault *et al*, *op cit*, 396–97.

[183] Shelburne [1957] BTR 53.

[184] See Avery Jones *et al* [1996] BTR 213.

(4)   There are problems where a third country enters the scene, since treaties are bilateral arrangements and very few lay down how each party is to give credit for taxes paid in a third country. While the UK may give unilateral relief, or even treaty relief, under an arrangement between it and the third country,[185] such rules do not solve the interaction of the relief with the third country and the relief with the second.[186]

(5)   The present tax treaties often frustrate the domestic purposes of the source country, save where pioneer relief or tax sparing may apply.

---

[185] Eg the 1955 UK–Denmark Treaty, Art XVII, para 4; and Royal Commission on the Taxation of Profits and Income, *Final Report*, Cmd 9474 (1955), para 759. The 1980 Treaty with Denmark does not contain this provision.

[186] For an example, see *IRC v Commerzbank* [1990] STC 285.

21

European Union Tax Law

21.1   EU Law Restraints on Member States Fiscal Sovereignty: The Basic Position

The operation of EU law has important implications for the domestic direct tax regimes of the Member States, including the UK. It is no longer possible to consider domestic tax rules, like those of the UK corporation tax regime, without turning one's mind to the effect EU law might have on those rules. Since the beginning of the 21st century, EU law has taken on an ever-increasing role in the direct tax sphere, and the law in this area continues to evolve, sometimes rapidly, occasionally fundamentally. This chapter aims to give the reader a background to important EU law principles of relevance to direct tax, and a framework for analysing the key cases of the European Court of Justice (ECJ) in direct tax matters. It also seeks to provide a snapshot of the present (but constantly developing) state of the case law on the application to selected corporation tax topics of the fundamental freedoms under the Treaty on the Functioning of the European Union (TFEU).

To begin, EU law[1] limits the rights of the UK government to levy taxes by taking precedence over Acts of Parliament.[2] This supremacy does not apply to those areas in which sovereignty has not been ceded. Supremacy issues first arise in connection with UK legislation. The UK Parliament may find that its legislation conflicts with principles of the

---

[1] The literature on EU (ex EC) tax law has become vast. For a broad, technical, overall account of EU tax harmonisation policy, see Terra and Wattel, *European Tax Law*, 6th edn (Kluwer, 2012). For an overview of EU law and the Union institutions, see Dashwood *et al*, *Wyatt & Dashwood's European Union Law* (Hart Publishing, 2011), and on tax set in a wider context see chs 17 and 20. Other interesting, but dated, sources include Williams, *EC Tax Law* (Longman, 1998); Farmer and Lyal, *EC Tax Law* (OUP, 1994); and Radaelli, *The Politics of Corporate Taxation in the European Union* (Routledge, 1997), esp chs 5 and 6.

[2] *Stoke-on-Trent City Council v B&Q plc* [1991] 4 All ER 221, 223.

EU law,[3] or that it has not followed the proper procedure, for example by not consulting the Commission,[4] so that in either case its legislation is of no effect. However, issues also arise when an individual taxpayer is accorded rights under EU law through the doctrine of direct effect.[5] A provision giving rise to direct effect must be clear and concise; it must be unconditional and unqualified, and not subject to the taking of any further measures on the part of a Union or national authority; and must leave no substantial discretion in its implementation to a Union or national authority.[6] Several Treaty provisions have been given direct effect in taxation. The ECJ has asserted a pre-emptive jurisdiction to forestall divergent interpretations of a directive by allowing a reference by a national court on what is actually a domestic tax issue but which arises from legislation based on an EU law.[7]

A failure to implement directives properly and in time will enable a taxpayer to assert the rights set out in the directive against the Member State,[8] if the conditions for direct effect apply. In addition, the citizen may be able to recover damages from the state under the principle in *Francovitch*[9] for failure to implement the directive—this right may arise even though the principle required for direct effect is not satisfied.[10]

21.1.1 State Aids[11]

Some of the provisions, eg Article 107 TFEU (ex Art 87 TEC) concern state aid, and case law establishes clearly that tax provisions which are in substance state aid fall foul of these provisions unless clearance has been obtained for them from the Commission under Article 108 TFEU (ex Art 88 TEC).[12] So, when the UK Parliament increased the rate of insurance premium tax for certain types of insurance sold through travel agents without obtaining clearance from the Commission, the English court held that this differential taxation would distort competition and intra-Community trade and so breached (now) Article 107 TFEU.[13] The Court of Appeal has held that the detriment imposed on personal service companies by the IR35 legislation in ITEPA 2003, Part 2, Chapter 8 could be found to be an unlawful state aid only if it favoured other competing businesses; the applicants had not established this.[14] These rules may apply where a state's legislation deliberately favours a non-resident over a resident. The distinctions are subtle. The FA 2008 changed the limits for reliefs for venture capital trusts (VCTs) via the Corporate Venturing Scheme

---

[3] As in the famous *Factortame* case: *R v Secretary of State for Transport, ex parte Factortame* [1991] 1 AC 603.

[4] As in *R v Customs and Excise Commrs, ex parte Lunn Poly Ltd* [1999] STC 350.

[5] Case 26/62 *Van Gend en Loos v Nederlandse Tariefcomissie* [1963] ECR 1.

[6] Edward and Lane, *European Community Law* (Butterworths, 1995), para 133.

[7] Case C-28/95 *Leur Bloem* [1997] STC 1205; see Betten (1999) 36 *CML Rev* 165.

[8] The so-called 'vertical' direct effect of directives allows the enforcement of rights against the Member State but not against other citizens: Edward and Lane, *op cit*, para 148.

[9] *Ibid*, para 141.

[10] Case C-91/9 *Faccinni Dori v Recreb* [1994] ECR I-3325.

[11] See, especially for case law, P Werner, *The Cambridge Yearbook of European Legal Studies*, vol 9 (CUP, 2007) 481. See also Evans, *State Aid* (OUP, 1998) and Schön (1999) 36 *CML Rev* 911.

[12] There is a helpful notice on tax and state aid by the Commission, Notice of 11 November 1998, 98/C384/03 and an EC Commission Report C (2004) 434.

[13] *R v Customs and Excise Commrs, ex parte Lunn Poly Ltd* [1999] STC 350.

[14] *R (Professional Contractors Group) v IRC* [2001] EWCA Civ 1945; [2002] STC 165.

and for Enterprise Investment Schemes (EISs). The EISs required state aid approval but the others did not.[15]

21.1.2 Indirect Taxes and Similar Charges

Article 110 TFEU (ex Art 90 TEC) prohibits discrimination against imports from other Member States by the levying of charges higher than those imposed on domestic products. Article 111 TFEU (ex Art 91 TEC) prohibits refunds on exports exceeding the actual taxation imposed on the goods. Article 113 TFEU (ex Art 93 TEC) addresses how the legislation of turnover taxes may be harmonised, a process which has given us the famous Sixth Directive imposing a common tax base to VAT throughout the Union, enacted in the UK as the VATA 1984, now consolidated as the VATA 1994. This surrender of sovereignty in relation to turnover taxes does not extend to taxes which are not turnover taxes, eg insurance premium tax.

21.1.3 Direct Taxes—No Compensation for Effects on Trade

Article 112 TFEU (ex Art 92 TEC) extends the principle of Article 111 TFEU (ex Art 91 TEC) to direct taxation and prohibits Member States from operating systems of compensation for the effects of direct taxation on trade within the EU. However, this is subject to a right of derogation, provided the Government obtains authorisation from the Commission.

21.2 Positive and Negative Harmonisation

21.2.1 Positive Harmonisation

Article 115 TFEU (ex Art 94 TEC) provides for the approximation of laws by directives, and it is on this basis that the Commission has tried to achieve harmonisation of company taxes. No article *requires* harmonisation of direct taxes in the way that Article 113 TFEU does for indirect taxes. Directives under Article 115 TFEU require unanimity in the Council. There has been regular UK legislation to implement directives, as in 1990 when the Revenue were placed under a duty to provide information about liabilities to tax in another Member State.[16] The Single Market programme provided its own impetus, leading to the Ruding Committee's 1992 report on the distortions caused by different corporation tax systems, the extent to which those could be removed by market forces and the desirability of legislation towards harmonisation should those forces not be enough.

Two Directives were enacted in 1990, the Parent–Subsidiary Directive and the Mergers and Acquisitions Directive, designed to grant to cross-border transactions the same favourable treatment as is provided for equivalent purely domestic transactions.[17] The UK introduced the appropriate implementing legislation, but the Revenue conceded that

---

[15] FA 2008, s 31 and HMRC Budget Technical Note BN16 (12 March 2008).
[16] FA 1990, s 125.
[17] Directive 90/435 [1990] OJ L225/6 and Directive 90/434 [1990] OJ L225/1 respectively.

the Directives would probably have had direct effect anyway.[18] In addition, a multilateral convention on transfer pricing is now in force, along with a Council regulation on administrative co-operation in the field of indirect taxation.[19] The new millennium has seen directives on interest and royalties, and on savings income.[20] These directives are discussed in the relevant chapters of this book and in *Revenue Law*. A proposed directive on losses has been withdrawn.[21]

It is work on the common consolidated corporate tax base (CCCTB) which has perhaps been the most tantalisingly slow. However, there was a very detailed paper in 2001 and subsequent further work, leading to a 2011 Commission proposal for a Council Directive (COM(2011) 121/4).[22] It is quite possible, should a directive fail to be passed by the Council, that a CCCTB will be agreed and operated by a number of the Member States under the enhanced co-operation rules in Article 20 of the Treaty on European Union (TEU), with the UK remaining resolutely outside. The ever-closer operation of the European single market is undermining many traditional assumptions and techniques of international tax. This should cause no surprise to students of history of the United States, Germany or Italy. The UK is developing a halfway house between international tax and domestic tax to encompass the EU.

21.2.2 Negative Harmonisation

21.2.2.1 Background

The starting point has to be that the EU treaties leave direct taxes as matters for the Member States. As a result, the Court cannot offer to citizens of the Union transferring their activities to another Member State any guarantee that this will be neutral as regards taxation.[23] However, the ECJ has said again and again that those powers must be exercised in a manner consistent with EU law. The ECJ has gone on to make what some see as erratic, narrow and often destructive contributions to Member States' tax law on the basis of the non-discrimination principle. This important principle is embodied for tax purposes in the Treaty fundamental freedoms, including the free cross-border movement of employees (Article 45 TFEU; ex Art 39 TEC); freedom of establishment for businesses (Article 49 TFEU; ex Art 43 TEC); freedom to provide services (Article 56 TFEU; ex Art 49 TEC); and free movement of capital (Article 63 TFEU; ex Art 56 TEC).

One of the points most often made by the ECJ was that national legislation should not have one set of rules for a purely domestic situation and another for cross-border operations. Related to this is the series of cases stemming from the famous *Avoir Fiscal*

---

[18] *EC Direct Tax Measures: A Consultative Document* (December 1991), para 2.13.

[19] [1992] *Simon's Tax Intelligence* 161.

[20] EC 2003/49/EC and EC 2003/48/EC respectively.

[21] Com (90) 505.

[22] For the latest status see <http://ec.europa.eu/taxation_customs/taxation/company_tax/common_tax_base/index_en.htm>. Background work includes COM (2001) 582 and supporting study SEC (2001) 582, COM (2003) 726 European Tax Survey SEC 2004, 1128/2 and Report of CEPS Task Force Brussels, November 2001. For analysis, see Panayi, *The Common Consolidated Corporate Tax Base and the UK tax system*, IFS Tax Law Reform Committee Discussion Paper No 9 (Institute for Fiscal Studies, 2011) and Mitroyanni [2011] BTR 246.

[23] Eg, A-G Geelhoed in Case C-403/03 *Schempp v Finanzamt Munchen* [2005] ECR I-06421, para 33 (January 2005).

or *French Tax Credits* case,[24] which rather routinely said that a Member State should not have one rule for a branch and another for a subsidiary. These simple mantras opened Pandora's Box, and case after case was decided against the revenue authorities of the Member States.[25] Supporters of the ECJ argue that it has been consistent in its approach, and that Member States have to pay through court cases for their failure to adjust their legal systems to take account of the thinking of the Court. Critics of the ECJ say that it has not been consistent, that it has widened the basis on which it has acted, and that it has created and then abandoned a number of limitations on its jurisdiction.[26] What has encouraged critics of the Court is the way in which the language used falls short of what one might expect from such an important body. An interesting report for the European Parliament, published in March 2008, not only assesses the Court judgments in this area, but also tries to assess how far the Members States have amended their laws in response to the Court's decisions.[27]

More and more frequently, tax provisions which breach, or may breach, these provisions are being challenged in court actions brought by taxpayers in the national courts and referred to the ECJ for advice under the reference procedure in Article 267 TFEU (ex Art 234 TEC). They are also often the subject of investigation by the European Commission, which may bring its own court proceedings against a Member State under Articles 258 and 260 TFEU. The Commission also exercises its right to make submissions to the Court in cases brought by taxpayers.[28] It is thought that these specific powers prevent the Court from relying on the more general anti-discrimination rule in Article 18 TFEU (ex Art 12 TEC).[29] While some tax theorists and government departments shake their heads in disbelief at what the Court has been doing, taxpayers and their advisers had several years of sunshine days while those with a different set of assumptions argue that the Court has simply been doing what it was meant to do.[30]

---

[24] Case 270/83 *Commission v French Republic (Avoir Fiscal)* [1986] ECR 273.

[25] Until 2005 the decisions in favour of the Member States were Case 81/87 *R v HM Treasury, ex parte Daily Mail* [1988] ECR 5483, Case C-204/90 *Bachmann v Belgium* [1992] ECR I-249, Case C-250/953 *Futura Participations SA* [1997] ECR I-2471, and Case C-336/96 *Gilly v Directeur des Services Fiscaux du Bas-Rhin* [1998] ECR I-2793.

[26] For criticism of the Revenue for not taking steps earlier see Martin, *The Tax Journal* (10 January 2005), 7. See also Vanistedael (ed), *EATLP International Tax Series, Vol 2, EU Freedoms and Taxation* (IBFD, 2006); Schön (ed), *Tax Competition in Europe* (EATLP IBFD, 2003); Park, [2006] BTR 322; and Ghosh, *Principles of the Internal Market and Direct Taxation* (Key Haven, 2007).

[27] Malherbe *et al*, *The Impact of the Rulings of European Court of Justice in the Area of Direct Taxation 2010* (European Parliament, 2011). See also de la Feria and Fuest, 'Closer to an Internal Market? The Economic Effects of EU Tax Jurisprudence' (July 2011), Oxford University Centre for Business Taxation WP 11/12.

[28] Usually these are in support of the taxpayers, but in Case C-168/01 *Bosal Holding BV v Staatssecretaris van Financien* [2003] STC 1483 the Commission made some submissions in support of the Member State—to no effect.

[29] See Richardson [1998] BTR 281, 291, citing Case C-112/91 *Werner v FZA Aachen-Innenstadt* [1993] ECR I-429, para 20. While the case law has been concerned to make sure that a non-national is treated at least as favourably as a national, attention is now being paid (but not yet by the Court) to the opposite problem—where the non-resident is treated more favourably, and the Member States compete unfairly for business. The EU has an (unenforceable) code of conduct for Member States in such matters: see generally Schön (ed), *op cit*.

[30] For a rare example of practitioner expressing concern, see Airs, *The Tax Journal* (28 June 2004) 15–19. See also *Marks & Spencer v Halsey* [2003] STC (SCD) 70, where two of the UK's foremost tax practitioners and scholars, sitting in their capacity as Special Commissioners, try to establish some rational limits to the non-discrimination doctrine.

21.2.2.2 The General Approach[31]

Acting under this power (or duty) the ECJ has considered a number of standard tax rules, and in particular those considered below at §21.3. What matters for present purposes is that defeats presented problems for Member States. The loss of revenue might be addressed by increasing tax rates or providing new taxes. The rules regarding non-discrimination might be addressed by removing the discrimination; so when thin capitalisation rules were thought to have been declared generally unlawful by the Court of Justice—and so probably transfer-pricing rules too—Member States such as Germany and the UK reacted by making the restrictive rules apply to arrangements between domestic companies as well as to foreign ones. The result of all these pressures might, however, be less good domestic tax systems.

The ECJ has usually taken a broad approach to the non-discrimination principle and a narrow approach to any attempted justification. In the *French Tax Credits* case,[32] an Italian insurance company had set up a branch in France. The branch received dividend income from French sources. Under French tax law, companies could reclaim the tax credit accompanying the dividend from the French Revenue; however, repayment was refused if the company was not resident in France. The refusal was held to breach the freedom of establishment. Even if the disadvantage to the Italian company under the present rule was compensated for by other advantages, the French Government could not justify this breach of the duty under (now) Article 49 TFEU, which was to accord foreign companies the same treatment as was accorded to French companies. The extent of the disadvantage could not be in issue since the treaty prohibits all discrimination, even if only of a limited nature. Moreover, the fact that the Italian company could have got the benefit of the credit if it had established a French subsidiary (rather than a branch) was irrelevant, since this interfered with the freedom to trade in another Member State in a vehicle of its own choice—whether branch or subsidiary. (The idea that a branch and a subsidiary are somehow interchangeable has been seen as economically illiterate, but it has not stopped the Court from developing a stream of case law in which distinctions between the two have been struck down.)

What was wrong with the mantras above was that the Court too readily accepted that the domestic and cross-border situations had to be treated alike, instead of addressing the more subtle question of how to achieve equality of treatment of the two situations after allowing for the fact that domestic and cross-border situations are not alike.[33] The first hints of new thinking may be found in the *Manninen* case.[34] The need for a more nuanced approach was recognised by the Court,[35] especially following a major change in personnel, as in the case of *D*.[36] The story is well told by Kingston, who was legal secretary to Advocate General Geelohoed.[37] All these uncertainties create difficulties for the self-assessment system.[38]

---

[31] See Lyons [1994] BTR 554; Stanley (1997) 34 *CML Rev* 713.
[32] Case 270/83 *Commission v French Republic* [1986] ECR 273.
[33] CEPS Task Force Report (November 2005) 7.
[34] Case C 319/02 *Manninen v Finland* [2004] ECR-I-07477.
[35] Se eg Case C-141/99 *AMID v Belgium* [2000] ECR I-11619 and Case C-374/04 *Test Claimants in Class IV of the ACT Group Litigation* [2006] ECR I-11673.
[36] Case C-376/03 [2005] ECR I-05821.
[37] Kingston (2007) 44 *CML Rev* 1321
[38] On which see *HMRC v Vodafone 2* [2006] EWCA Civ 1132 [2006] STC 1530.

The principal cases involving the UK decided since the change are *Marks & Spencer*[39] on group losses, *Cadbury Schweppes*[40] on CFC legislation, and three group litigation cases—*Group Litigation Class IV ACT*,[41] *Group Litigation Franked Investment Income*[42] and *Group Litigation Thin Capitalisation*.[43] What these cases have in common is an approach by the Court which avoids a blanket condemnation of a state's tax rules just because of the possible restrictions. It accepts that the Member States have an interest in limiting the avoidance of tax, provided that appropriate objective tests are in place or can be designed to determine when the anti-avoidance provisions should apply and when not. Equal treatment of the two situations after allowing for the fact that domestic and cross-border situations are not alike was achieved by a new mantra, by which the Court accepts the need for a balanced allocation of taxing power between the Member States and that the Court is not there to destroy them one by one.

These disputes are good illustrations of the problems that arise from the nature of the European venture. Without genuine agreement about the goals and fundamental principles of the venture itself, it is not surprising that the result is a mess. The Commission's view that the Court of Justice will rein itself in when a common base for corporate tax has been achieved has been overtaken by the new approach. More kindly perhaps, one might say that what the Commission is trying to do is not to enjoy itself at the expense of Member States, but to remove obstacles to the doing of business in the single market, and that of the remaining obstacles it is the tax ones which are among the most urgent. Moreover, one does not want to see the restoration of a Member State's right to discriminate through direct taxation.

21.2.2.3 Freedom of Establishment

Article 49 TFEU (ex Art 43 TEC) guarantees freedom of establishment and expressly bans restrictions on the setting-up of agencies, branches or subsidiaries by nationals of any Member State in the territory of any other Member State. This is extended to companies and firms by Article 54 TFEU (ex Art 48 TEC). It has been interpreted broadly so as to ban not only overt discrimination by reason of nationality or, in the case of a company, its seat, but, for a time at least, all covert forms of discrimination which, by the application of other criteria of differentiation, lead to the same result.[44] Here too, joint assessment issues have arisen.[45] The wide scope of protection offered the freedom of establishment has already been seen in the *French Tax Credits* case.

The taxpayer also won in *R v IRC, ex parte Commerzbank AG*.[46] Here, a German bank with a UK branch had successfully argued that it was entitled to exemption from UK tax on interest received from US corporations;[47] its claim to repayment supplement was successful,

---

[39] Case C-446/03 *Marks & Spencer plc v Halsey (Inspector of Taxes)* [2006] STC 237.

[40] Case C-196/04 [2006] ECR I-07995.

[41] Case C-374/04 [2006] ECR I-11673.

[42] Case C-446/04 [2006] ECR I-11753.

[43] Case C-524/04 [2007] ECR I-02107.

[44] Judgment of the ECJ in *Commerzbank* (below, para 4, citing Case 152/73 *Sotgiu v Deutsche Bundespost* [1974] ECR 153, para 11; *R v IRC, ex parte Commerzbank AG* [1993] STC 605, 621, para 14 (ECJ).

[45] Case C-329/05 *Finanzamt Dinslaken v Meindl (Meindl-Berger, third party)* [2007] STC 314.

[46] [1993] STC 605 (ECJ). For subsequent action, see [1993] *Simon's Tax Intelligence* 1091, 1264. For speculation about ambit, see Sandler [1993] BTR 517.

[47] *IRC v Commerzbank AG* [1990] STC 285; unusually the applicable treaty was not confined to residents.

even though the UK domestic legislation clearly did not allow repayment supplement to a non-resident. The UK had argued that it was entitled to withhold the repayment supplement since Commerzbank, unlike resident companies, was exempt on the income originally in issue. This was swept aside: 'The argument cannot be upheld. The fact that the exemption in question was available only to non-resident companies cannot justify a rule of a general nature withholding the benefit. That rule is therefore discriminatory.'[48] This seems to leave it open to the UK to introduce a rule barring repayment supplement where the repayment claim arises in respect of income which is exempt from tax only by reason of non-residence; however, the UK statute was amended more generously, by removing the restriction altogether.[49] Meanwhile, it should be noted that the ban on repayment supplement remains effective for individuals, etc, not entitled to invoke EU rules, eg persons not resident in a Member State.

In the *St Gobain*[50] case, the German branch of a French company sought to take advantage of certain clauses in treaties made by Germany with other states (ie, not France). The Court held that the French branch was entitled to do so. The UK legislature, perhaps wisely, took it as its cue to extend various double taxation reliefs to UK branches of foreign companies; see §20.1.1 above.

21.2.2.4 Freedom of Movement of Capital[51]

Free movement of capital is protected under Article 63 TFEU (ex Art 56 TEC). A straightforward case on free movement of capital is provided by *Ministre des Finances v Weidert*.[52] The taxpayers, a married couple resident in Luxembourg, had subscribed for 200 shares in a Belgian company. If they had acquired shares for cash in fully taxable capital companies while resident in Luxembourg, they would have been entitled to a relief from Luxembourg income tax. The Court held that the relief was discriminatory and so the taxpayers were entitled to the benefit of the relief. The effect of the Luxembourg rules was to discourage Luxembourg nationals from investing their capital in companies established in another Member State; the provision also constituted an obstacle to a Belgian company seeking to raise capital in another Member State.

This article has given the Court problems. First, there is the inconvenient fact that Article 63 TFEU, unlike its neighbours, protects free movement of capital not only between Member States but also, subject to a condition, between Member States and third countries. The condition relates to restrictions existing on 31 December 1993 (Article 64 TFEU, ex Art 57 TEC). Secondly, Article 65 TFEU (ex Art 58 TEC) directs that the freedom of movement of capital is without prejudice to the rights of Member States to apply provisions of their tax law which distinguish between taxpayers who are not in the same situation with regard to their place of residence or with regard to where their capital is invested. Thirdly, Article 63 TFEU is without prejudice to the rights of Member States to take all requisite

---

[48] [1993] STC 605, 622 (ECJ).

[49] FA 1994, Sch 19, amending TA 1988, s 824 (income tax) and TA 1988, s 826, superseding s 825 for corporation tax as from start of pay and file (1993).

[50] Case C-307/97 *Compagnie de Saint-Gobain v Finanzamt Aachen-Innenstadt*; see [1999] *Simons Weekly Tax Intelligence* 1856. See also Oliver [2000] BTR 174.

[51] For a general discussion, see the chapter by Peers in Barnard and Scott (eds), *The Law of the Single Market: Unpacking The Premises* (Hart Publishing, 2002); Peers criticises (at 348) Case C-35/98 *Verkooijen* [2002] STC 654.

[52] Case C-242/03 [2005] STC 1241; see also Case C-334/02 *EC Commission v French Republic* [2007] STC 54.

measures to prevent infringement of national law with regard to various specific areas, including taxation.

These points might have made the courts wary in applying Article 63 TFEU, but instead they have treated the scope of discrimination just as widely as in the other articles. However, this has raised the question of the relationship between Article 63 TFEU and the others. Faced with a case which could have been decided under what are now Articles 49, 56 or 63 TFEU, the ECJ could simply have declined to rule on the application under Article 63 on the ground that its decision was already covered by the other Articles. However, the Court sometimes went further and tried to develop boundary rules, such as that where the case concerned a shareholding which gave a significant amount of control—not necessarily 50%—then the case belonged under (now) Article 49 and not Article 63 TFEU.[53] Fortunately this appears no longer to be so.[54] However, in the *FII* case, the ECJ started another line of reasoning to the effect that the justification that a court might accept might be different where the transfer was to a third country.[55]

The first case to be decided solely on the basis of freedom of movement of capital was Case C-35/98 *Secretaris van Financien v Verkooijen*.[56] This freedom was then set out in Article 73(1)(d) of the Treaty (now Article 63(1)(a) TFEU) and was implemented by Directive 88/361/EEC of 24 June 1988. In this case V, a Dutch resident, received dividend income from a Belgian company, which was subject to 25% withholding in Belgium in the usual way. If the dividends had been from a company with its seat in The Netherlands, V would have been entitled to an exemption on the first NLG 1,000 of dividend income. V appealed on the basis that (then) EC law did not allow Dutch tax law to restrict the exemption to companies resident in The Netherlands but should apply it to companies resident in all Member States. On a reference from the Hoge Raad under ex Article 177, the ECJ agreed with V. The first purpose of the exemption was partly to increase interest in equity shareholdings—and so the amount of capital subscribed to Dutch companies—and the second was to compensate in some small way for the effect of the Dutch classical system of corporate taxation, which meant that no part of the corporate tax was imputed through to the shareholder.[57] This was treated by the Court as a clear breach of EC law, since it constituted an obstacle to a Belgian company raising capital in The Netherlands.

In *EC Commission v Belgium*,[58] the Belgian Government had issued a public loan on the Eurobond market. Under the terms of the issue, withholding tax on interest payable on loan was waived but residents of Belgium were prohibited from subscribing for the loan. Not surprisingly, this restriction was held to breach (now) Article 63 TFEU. This free movement article was originally quite rudimentary and took effect in its present expansive form only in 1992. At that time a clause was added to the effect that the provision on free movement of capital was to be without prejudice to the rights of Member States to apply the relevant provisions of their tax law which distinguish between taxpayers who are not in the same situation with regard to their place of residence or with regard to where their capital is invested.

---

[53] Case C 251/98 *Baars* and Case C-436/00 *X and Y*.
[54] See eg Case 446/04, AG Geelhoed, para 34 and the full court at 58 *et seq*.
[55] Case C-446/04, para 121.
[56] Case C-35/98 *Verkooijen* [2002] STC 654. For the Directive, see [1988] OJ L178/5. Art 56 was raised in *Bachmann*, Case C-204/90 [1994] STC 855 at para 34—see also §21.2.2.6 below.
[57] Case C-35/98 *Verkooijen* [2002] STC 654, para 11.
[58] Case C-478/98 [2000] STC 830.

21.2.2.5 Application of the Non-Discrimination Principles[59]

Proceeding analytically, one might say that taxpayers face a two-stage test:

(1)   Has the threshold test of discrimination been met?
(2)   If there is discrimination, can it be justified by the Member State?

If a measure is justified, an additional question (or perhaps a third-stage test) then needs to be asked:

(3)   Is the measure proportionate?

Non-discrimination is at the heart of the TFEU and the law, including case law, which has developed the fundamental freedoms of movement of goods, services/establishment, persons and capital as set out in the TFEU. In the tax cases considering the application of this fundamental principle, discrimination is usually on grounds of nationality. Moreover, while Treaty articles concern nationals and non-nationals, case law often concerns non-residents, and sometimes requires Member States to treat non-residents either as if they were residents or at least not worse than residents. This is because the most frequent example of the non-national is the non-resident. It should be understood that when passages in cases refer to non-residents, they are actually concerned only with nationals of the EU.

As already seen, the concept of discrimination is not straightforward. The case law of the ECJ began by distinguishing direct discrimination from indirect or covert discrimination. The language used by the Court is not always precise, but the distinction seems to be between those measures which breach the non-discrimination principle on their face, eg rules applying only to nationals of a certain state, and those which simply have that effect. The importance of the difference is that if a measure falls within the direct category then justification must be sought within the words of the Treaty itself.[60] Not only are there few such justifications,[61] but the Court also has interpreted them strictly. In *Danner*, the Advocate General invited the Court to revisit this distinction and allow direct discrimination to be justified by reference to matters of overriding general interest, but this invitation was not accepted in terms by the ECJ.[62] However, most tax discrimination problems arose in the context of residence rather than nationality, and so normally belonged in the covert or indirect discrimination category

Indirect or covert discrimination may be justified provided:

(1)   the discriminatory measure pursues a legitimate objective compatible with the Treaty; and
(2)   the national rules are proportionate, in that the rules are appropriate to attain that objective and go no further than what is necessary for that purpose.[63]

---

[59]   Good starting points are Terra and Wattel, *op cit*; Kingston, *op cit*; and Park, *op cit*. See also Vanistedael (ed), *op cit*; Schön (ed), *op cit*; and Ghosh, *op cit*.
[60]   *Bond van Adverteerders v Netherlands* [1988] ECR 2805, para 34.
[61]   Eg Art 52 TFEU (ex Art 46 TEC) lists public policy, public security and public health.
[62]   Case C-136/00 I [2002] STC 1283, Opinion of AG Jacobs, paras 32–42. See Lyons [2003] BTR 98.
[63]   Case C-19/92 *Kraus v Land Baden-Wurtemburg* [1993] ECR I-1663, para 32.

It has to be said that in many of the cases the Member States have failed on test (2). Article 54 TFEU (ex Art 48 TEC) makes it clear that when one is dealing with the right of establishment of enterprises, ie companies or firms as opposed to individuals, those with a registered office or central administration within the community are to be treated the same way as natural persons who are nationals of Member States. This means that what may be covert discrimination for an individual may be overt discrimination for an enterprise.

The Court then decided to take a more expansive test of discrimination. This new test was that the Court could review national measures which, although not actually discriminatory, were liable to hinder or make less attractive the exercise of the fundamental freedoms guaranteed by the Treaty.[64] The 'making less attractive' threshold was significantly lower;[65] it came close to saying that any difference between tax systems was a source of discrimination.[66] UK case law has a direct and demonstrable inhibiting effect on the particular right.[67]

Eventually the obstacles/restriction itself came under attack by Advocate General Tizzano.[68] Such a broad approach to the 'restrictions' allowed economic operators, both national and foreign, to abuse the Treaty to oppose any national measure that, solely because it regulated the conditions for pursuing an economic activity, could in the final analysis narrow profit margins and hence reduce the attractiveness of pursuing that particular economic activity. He therefore advocated a return to a non-discrimination plus market access approach: where the principle of non-discrimination is respected, a national measure cannot be described as a restriction on the freedom of movement of persons *unless* the measure 'directly affects market access'. He added that this approach makes it possible to reconcile the objective of merging the different national markets into a single common market with the continuation of Member States' general powers to regulate economic activities. Such a completely articulated approach has appealed to Advocates General rather than the Court, but the overall effect has been substantial, at least in language.[69]

21.2.2.6 Justifications

The cases cited in the preceding paragraphs assert that it is open to any Member State to justify its discriminatory provision either in accordance with Article 65 TFEU or, if the discrimination is covert rather than overt, on more general grounds.[70] We now turn to the justifications which have succeeded—justifications (1)–(4) and (6)–(8) below—and an important but problematic limitation (at (5) below). It will be seen that some of these limiting principles created by the ECJ did not live long, a fact which does little for the ECJ's reputation. These taxpayer defeats—or Member State victories—are of different sorts. Some, eg (4) and (5), are inherent in the nature of EU law; (1) is temporary. In *Marks & Spencer*

---

[64] Case C-55 /94 *Gebhard* [1996] ECR I-1416, para 37; discussed by Richardson [1998] BTR 302, who also cites the opinion of the Advocate-General in Case C-80/94 *Wielockx* [1995] ECR I-2493, para 17.

[65] *Airs, op cit.*

[66] See *Marks & Spencer v Halsey* [2003] STC (SCD) 70, paras 59 *et seq.*

[67] *R (Professional Contractors Group) v IRC* [2001] EWCA Civ 1945; [2002] STC 165.

[68] Advocate General Tizzano, Case C-442/02 *Caixa-Bank v Ministère de l'Économie, des Finances and de l'industrie* [2004] ECR I-8961

[69] Examples of cases in which the ECJ has held that Member State rules were not restrictive are Case C-298/05 *Columbus Containers* [2007] ECR I-10451 and Case C-293/06 *Deutsche Shell GmbH* [2008] ECR I-1129.

[70] On the evolving law of these 'mandatory' requirements see the chapter by Scott, in Barnard and Scott, (eds), *op cit*, 269-93.

v Halsey,[71] the ECJ considered several justifications together (balanced allocation of taxing rights, preventing double deduction of losses, and tax avoidance). In later cases the Court held that it was not necessary for all of those justifications to be present; one or more would be sufficient.[72]

The ECJ has also spelt out reasons which are *not* sufficient to justify discrimination. The most important for tax lawyers is that, as the Court has consistently said, the need to protect tax revenues of a Member State does not justify discrimination. While the judges have also said that protecting the tax base against avoidance is a sufficient justification, they have gone to insist that the provision relied on by the Member State must then meet the test of proportionality; the rules have usually failed.[73] Other clearly unacceptable grounds of justification have included arguments that tax rates are lower in other Member States, compensating advantages exist taking into account other rules, administration would be difficult, and other avenues are available to avoid the discrimination.

(1)   *Community law insufficiently developed.* In the *Daily Mail* case,[74] a UK-resident company failed to circumvent the then UK rule requiring the company to obtain Treasury consent before emigrating because the UK consents could insist on the settlement of tax liabilities prior to departure. However, this was partly because of the undeveloped nature of European company law rules on freedom of movement, eg the diversity of rules in different Member States on matters such as whether the company's personality could continue in the new country.[75] It is unlikely that this justification would be of much assistance now, given that EU law has developed considerably since the early days of *Daily Mail*.

(2)   *The need to protect cohesion of B's tax system: Bachmann.* This is one of the principles which, although formulated by the Court, lay undeveloped and despised for many years. In *Bachmann v Belgian State*,[76] the ECJ allowed Belgium to maintain rules necessary to the 'cohesion' of its system. Here Belgium allowed X to deduct sickness and invalidity insurance contributions only if paid to a company recognised by the authorities in Belgium. Belgium established an objective reason for the refusal; under Belgian law, any income eventually paid out under the policies would be taxed in Belgium,[77] and this could be monitored by restricting the deduction to contributions made to a Belgian company. Moreover, where contributions had not been deducted, the sums paid out were not subject to tax. The restriction of the right to deduct to payments made in Belgium was therefore justified in the interests of the cohesion of its tax system. No less crucially, Belgium had established

---

[71] [2003] STC (SCD) 70.

[72] Case C-414/06 *Lidl Belgium* [2008] ECR I-6373. See also Case C-231/05 *OyAA* [2007] ECR I-6373 and Case C-337/08 *X Holding*.

[73] Eg Case C-330/91 *R v IRC, ex parte Commerzbank AG* [1993] STC 605. In *R (on application of Professional Contractors Group Ltd) v IRC* [2001] STC 629, the UK legislation countering the use of personal service companies (text at p 205) was held not to break EC law; not only was it non-discriminatory, but it was also proportionate to the legitimate objective of countering tax avoidance.

[74] *R v HM Treasury and IRC, ex parte Daily Mail and General Trust plc* [1988] STC 787.

[75] *Ibid*, 807, para 21.

[76] Case C-204/90 [1994] STC 855.

[77] The Court assumed that tax was paid by the company; this was not correct: see Lyons [1995/96] *EC Tax J* 27, 47.

that there was no other way of protecting that cohesion, and that the provisions met the principle of proportionality. Where, in a later case, double tax treaty provisions were in place, the ECJ said that those provisions were sufficient to protect the cohesion of Belgium's system.[78]

The *Bachmann* case was distinguished in the *Verkooijen* case.[79] The ECJ said that in *Bachmann* there had been a direct link in the case of one and the same taxpayer between the grant of the tax advantage and the offsetting of that tax advantage by a fiscal levy, both of which related to the same tax. Some see the approach of the ECJ in cases like *Marks & Spencer v Halsey*,[80] where it talks of the balanced allocation of taxing powers, as a reassertion of the cohesion justification. It will also be remembered that in that case the Advocate General suggested that *Verkooijen* was too strict.[81]

(3) *Need to provide effective fiscal supervision.* This was recognised, but then not applied for reasons of proportionality, in *Futura Participations SA and Singer v Luxembourg*.[82] The taxpayer was the Luxembourg branch of a French company. In such circumstances Luxembourg taxed only the profits attributable to the branch (or PE) and did not insist that accounts be kept in Luxembourg. Stricter rules applied, however, when the branch sought to use trading losses from a previous year. Here Luxembourg insisted that accounts had to be kept in Luxembourg. The Court held that this requirement did breach (now) Article 49 TFEU as it went further than necessary to achieve the legitimate purpose advanced by the tax authorities. It did not follow, however, that Luxembourg had to accept a simple apportionment basis.

Although the need to provide effective fiscal supervision looks promising from the Member State's point of view, it must be remembered that the ECJ takes the view that the exchange of information powers in double tax treaties or under EU law, along with mutual assistance by Member States in the collection of tax, may well suffice.[83]

(4) *Territoriality.* The decision in *Futura Participations* (see (3) above) had another point. Luxembourg insisted that the loss had to be economically related to the income. The Court held that this did not breach (now) Article 49 TFEU as the Luxembourg position was completely reasonable. However, this potentially sensible doctrine was not applied by the court in *Bosal*.[84] In *Marks & Spencer* (above), the Advocate General said that the purpose of the territoriality principle was to prevent conflicts in tax jurisdiction between Member States, and suggested that territoriality could be seen as an aspect of the cohesion principle.[85] In the Court's decision this becomes the famous

---

[78] Case C-80/94 *Wielockx* [1995] STC 876; however, it has been pointed out that the particular article of the OECD Model Treaty on which the Court relied did not apply to pensions from self-employment: see Richardson [1998] BTR 283, 284. On use of treaty to avoid cohesion problems, see *Danner* Case C-136/00 [2002] STC 1283, para 41. On coherence/cohesion generally, see also Case C-418/07 *Papillon* [2008] ECR I-08947 and Case C-157/07 *Krankenheim* [2008] ECR I-08061.

[79] Case C-35/98 *Verkooijen* [2002] STC 654.

[80] Case C-446/03, paras 43 *et seq*.

[81] AG Maduro's suggestions are at para 71 of his Opinion. See also Case C-397/98 *Metallgesellscahft/Hoechst* [2001] ECR-1727 and Case C-324/00 *Lankhorst-Hohorst GmbH* [2002] ECR I-11779.

[82] Case C-250/95 [1997] STC 1301.

[83] As in eg Case C-371/10 *National Grid Indus BV v Inspecteur van de Belastingdienst Rijnmond/kantoor Rotterdam* [2012] STC 114.

[84] Case C-168/01 *Bosal Holding BV v Staatssecretaris van Financien* [2003] STC 1483, paras 37 *et seq*.

[85] *Marks & Spencer v Halsey*, Case C-446/03, paras 62 and 64.

490 International and European Union Tax

phrase about the need for the Court to protect 'a balanced allocation of the taxing powers between the Member States'.[86]

(5) *Treaty-making powers.* The ECJ has said that these freedom articles do not prevent states from making tax treaties which allocate tax jurisdiction on the basis of nationality, at least where they are in accordance with international norms. This was reasserted by the Court in its ground-breaking decision in *Re D*,[87] where it recognised the need for a balanced allocation of taxing powers between the states. Moreover, it recognised that a treaty gave rise to reciprocal rights and obligations for residents of the two states concerned; the rights could not be invoked by someone resident in a third country. The case involved the Dutch wealth tax; the taxpayer was resident in Germany and was trying, unsuccefully, to invoke the benefit of the treaty made between The Netherlands and Belgium. Ghosh sees the reasoning as articulated in this case as inconsistent with other decisions of the Court.[88]

This approach may be seen as justification for the older case of *Gilly v Directeur des Services Fiscaux Bas Rhin.*[89] Unfortunately, the boundary between *Gilly*, on the one hand, and *Schumacker*[90] and *Wielockx*,[91] on the other, was not easy to determine.[92] The view taken here is that the Court quite deliberately—and, some might say, wisely—backed off from a decision which could have been used to unpick the tax treaty network. *Re D* follows that approach.

(6) *Interpretation of national law still a matter for national court.* In *ICI plc v Colmer*,[93] the House of Lords was faced with two ways of interpreting UK tax law. The first would have prevented a breach of EU law; the second would not. The ECJ ruled that there was no EU law obligation on a national court to prefer the first construction to the second. In *Vodafone 2*,[94] the UK Court of Appeal concluded that the UK's CFC legislation could be interpreted so as to be compatible with EU law by 'reading in' a new exception applying retrospectively to companies actually established in another EEA state which carry on genuine economic activities there.

(7) *Nationals of Member State only.* In general, the purpose of the treaty and so of this case law is to protect nationals of other Member States; residence has been equated with nationality, because most non-residents will be nationals of other Member States, so that covert discrimination is revealed. Nationals of states outside the EU are not entitled to protection under these rules, as shown by the UK litigation involving

---

[86] *Ibid*, para 43.

[87] Case C-376/03 *D v Inspecteur van de Belastingdienst/Particulieren/Ondernemingen Buitenland te Heerlen* [2005] STC 1211.

[88] Ghosh, *op cit*, 73.

[89] Case C-336/96 [1998]ECR I-2793; [1998] STC 1014; see comments in [1998] *IBFD Journal* 328.

[90] Case C-279/93 *Finanzamt Koln-Alstadt v Schumacker* [1995] ECR I-225.

[91] Case C-80/94 *Wielockx v Inspecteur der Directe Belastingen* [1995] STC 876.

[92] See, generally, Hedemann-Robinson [1999] BTR 128, 135–38; see also Avery Jones [1999] BTR 11, suggesting that if *Gilly* is right, and the Schumackers had been resident in France, the *Schumacker* decision would have been different for the year in which Mrs Schumacker had some earned income, but the same for the year in which she had none.

[93] Case C-264/96 [1998] All ER (EC) 585; [1998] STC 874; on treatment of outstanding cases, see Inland Revenue Press Release, 26 February [1999] *Simons Weekly Tax Intelligence* 312.

[94] *Vodafone v Revenue & Customs Commissioners (No 2)* [2009] STC 1480, [2009] EWCA Civ 446.

NEC, a Japanese company.[95] Therefore, a US company with a branch in the UK cannot complain about being discriminated under, say, French law. However, some care is needed where subsidiaries are involved. If a US company establishes a UK subsidiary, it will be open to the subsidiary to complain of discrimination under French law since, as a company established under UK law, it has UK nationality. The reason why this paragraph begins with the words 'In general' is to remind one that the free movement of capital can affect non-EU countries.

(8)   *Targeting tax avoidance.* While the ECJ has held that a 'blanket' tax avoidance provision cannot be justified,[96] other forms of tax avoidance rules may be. In *Marks & Spencer* and *Cadbury Schweppes*, the Court accepted that group relief restrictions and controlled foreign company rules, respectively, aimed at 'wholly artificial arrangements' could be justified, subject to proportionality. These cases are discussed in more detail in §21.3 below.

21.3   The ECJ Case Law on Selected Cross-Border Corporation Tax Topics

Acting under its power (or duty), the ECJ has attacked or is faced with considering a number of standard elements of corporation tax that have cross-border implications. Many of these cases have already been mentioned in the discussion of their particular topics, but are brought together here as an aid to understanding the broader context of the development of the ECJ's growing body of non-discrimination case law.

21.3.1   Taxation of Dividends and Imputation

The first issue is the imputation system of corporation tax itself. In *Manninen*,[97] the ECJ suggested that a Member State may use an imputation system only if it gives its resident shareholder taxpayers credit for tax paid in another Member State. Member States, including now the UK, are increasingly achieving non-discrimination status by granting partial dividend relief with respect to foreign dividends, eg in the exemption system in CTA 2009, Part 9A. The UK also now allows the UK-resident shareholder the same one-ninth credit as accompanies the domestic qualifying distribution (see above §§15.2–15.3). In *Hoechst AG v IRC* and *Metallgesellschaft Ltd v IRC*,[98] the UK imputation system's group income election was held to discriminate against groups in other (then) EC states, since it conferred a tax cash-flow advantage which was available only if the parent was resident in the UK. In turn, this led to actions based in restitution to recover the costs, principally financial costs, of having had to pay money earlier than was right.

---

[95]   Now called *Boake Allen and others v HMRC* [2007] UKHL 25, [2007] STC 1265, above at §20.2.1; compare Case C-446/04 *Test Claimants of the FII Group* [2006] ECJ 326.

[96]   Case C-324/00 *Lankhorst-Hohorst GmbH* [2002] ECR I-11779

[97]   Case C 319/02 *Manninen v Finland* [2004] ECR I-07477.

[98]   [2001] STC 452; for comment, see Richardson [2001] BTR 273 and Dourado (2002) 11 *EC Tax Rev* 147.

On dividends, there are two more recent free movement of capital cases. *Amurta SGPS v Inspecteur van den elastingdienst/Amsterdam*[99] concerned the Dutch tax system's 25% withholding tax on dividends. Company A receiving a dividend from Company B could claim exemption if Company A's seat or PE was in The Netherlands and it had at least 5% of the shares of Company B. In other situations, a higher percentage (25%) was required. The ECJ had little difficulty in finding that there was a breach of (then) Article 56 TEC where the percentage was less than 25% and the seat was not in The Netherlands. In a case concerning (then) Articles 56 and 57 TEC, *Holböck v Finanzamt Salzburg-Land*,[100] the taxpayer, H, was an Austrian who was the sole shareholder in a Swiss company. Under Austrian tax law, dividends from an Austrian company were taxed at half rate, while dividends from companies in non-Member States were taxed at the ordinary rate. The relevant years were from 1992 to 1996. The Court held that it was a pre-existing restriction within Article 57 TEC. The Court also held that the Austrian legislation was not intended to apply only to those shareholdings which enabled the holder to have a definite influence on a company's decisions and to determine its activities—this meant that (then) Article 43 TEC did not apply but Article 56 TEC did, and Article 56 TEC was excluded by Article 57 TEC.

21.3.1.1 Outbound Dividends

In Case 374/04 *Test Claimants in Class IV of the ACT Group Litigation*,[101] the Court considered the compatibility of the UK rules on the taxation of outbound dividends with EU principles under (then) Articles 43 and 56 TEC. It upheld the right of the UK to refuse credits on such dividends. The essence of the case was an argument by the companies that there was a difference between the treatment accorded to dividend payments to other UK-resident companies (TA 1988, section 208 made them exempt) and that accorded to non-resident companies (where section 208 did not apply). The Court examined TA 1988, section 233 and concluded that the effect of that provision was that the UK did not attempt to tax the outbound dividend. This was acceptable to the Court and the companies' argument was rejected. The conclusion that the UK did not even attempt to tax the outbound dividend is what distinguishes the UK case from the *Denkavit* case on dividends outbound from France. In *Denkavit*,[102] the French system taxation of dividends differed depending on whether the dividends were going to domestic parent companies or foreign parent companies; this was held contrary to (then) Article 43 TEC.

Other aspects of the ACT system were considered in Case 446/04 *Test Claimants of the FII Group*.[103] Under the ACT rules then in force but repealed in 1999, when a UK company was making a qualifying distribution, eg a dividend, to a shareholder, the company had to pay ACT. The company could use the ACT against its own liability to mainstream corporation tax on its profits for the period in respect of which the dividend had been paid. A problem arose if the company had foreign income which benefited from foreign tax credit relief—the effect of the credit, especially if the taxpayer had a holding of at least 10% and so benefited from the credit relief for tax on the underlying profits, would be that

---

[99] Case C-379/05 [2008] STC 2851.
[100] Case C-157/05 [2008] STC 92.
[101] Case C-374/04 *Test Claimants in Class IV of the ACT Group Litigation* [2006] ECR I-11673.
[102] On Case C-170/05 *Denkavit International BV* [2006] ECR I-11949, see Cussons, *The Tax Journal* (15 January 2007), 10-12.
[103] Case C-446/04 *Test Claimants of the FII Group* [2006] ECJ 326.

there would be no mainstream corporation tax against which to set the ACT. This was the surplus ACT problem.

There was also the franking problem. If the shareholder was a company resident in the UK and made a distribution of its own, it could, for example, set the credit accompanying the dividend (called franked investment income) against its own liability to pay ACT when it made its own dividend payment, so 'franking' the dividend; there were other ways of using the credit, eg in relation to losses, but what the company could not generally do was to reclaim the tax from the Revenue. The franking problem was a timing problem.

One argument in the case was that the Court should reject the whole UK two-track approach which distinguished so sharply between purely domestic dividends and foreign dividends. However the Court upheld the two-track approach, but with conditions which could be, as far as the UK Revenue were concerned, expensive. The Court held that having an exemption system for domestic distributions (then TA 1988, section 208) while subjecting incoming dividends to the UK's imputation system, might breach EC principles in (then) Articles 43 and 56 TEC. The question was to be answered by looking at the tax burden. The UK rules would satisfy Articles 43 and 56 TEC if the rate on inbound dividends was not greater than that on domestic dividends *and* that the credit was at least equal to the amount paid in the Member State of the company making the distribution up to the limit of the tax charged in the Member State on the company receiving the dividends. It is cases like *FII* that contributed to the UK's move in 2009 to an exemption system for most domestic and foreign dividends received by a UK company.

The case also involved the foreign income dividend (FID) scheme. This was introduced in 1994 (FA 1994, Schedule 16) to help companies with surplus ACT problems. A company was allowed to match the FID with foreign profits. However, the company had first to pay the ACT in the usual way; when it then matched the foreign dividend, it could get the ACT repaid by the Revenue—but not until the mainstream corporation tax became due, usually nine months after the end of the period. The vulnerability of this scheme to an argument based on the cash-flow advantage which succeeded in *Metalgesellchaft* is obvious. However, the companies went further and argued that some companies should be compensated for the enhanced dividend they had to pay to those shareholders, eg pension funds, who lost out on the tax credits normally accompanying the dividends (and which were not available to FIDs). The Court also held that the FID scheme breached (then) Articles 43 and 56 TEC because of the denial of the tax credit.

The question of the appropriate remedy, and in particular whether the UK was liable in damages, was left to the UK courts—as were very many other loose ends.[104] The Court of Appeal then referred many of the tax issues back to the ECJ for further clarification, and the restitution issues to the Supreme Court.[105]

21.3.2 Exit Charges

A deemed disposal charge for CGT when a taxpayer moves to another Member State may violate EU law. In *Lasteyrie du Saillant v Ministère de l'Economie*,[106] the Court ruled that the capital gains exit charge levied by France on a business person emigrating from France

---

[104] See Morgan and Bridges, *The Tax Journal* (8 January 2007), 8–10 and (15 January 2007), 13–14.
[105] [2010] EWCA Civ 103, [2010] STC 1251.
[106] Case C-9/02 *Lasteyrie du Saillant v Ministère de l'Economie* [2005] STC 1722.

to another Member State breached (then) Article 43 TEC (freedom of establishment). The Court expressly approved the UK rule in TCGA 1992, section 10A (see above §18.1.2), which imposes a charge on a temporary non-resident when the non-residence ends; but of course while that applies for CGT itself, it does not apply for corporation tax, where TCGA 1992, section 185 directs a deemed disposal.

In an important 2011 case directly concerning the application of exit taxes to companies, *National Grid Indus BV*,[107] the ECJ held that The Netherlands' attempt to tax an unrealised exchange gain when the company moved its place of management from The Netherlands to the UK was a restriction on the company's freedom of establishment. While the Court accepted that the restriction might be justified on the ground of balanced allocation of taxing powers, which gave The Netherlands the right to tax the amount of the gain (as ascertained at time of exit), it held that requiring immediate payment of the tax on that amount was disproportionate. The Court suggested that it would be less harmful to the freedom of establishment if the company had the option to pay the tax immediately or defer payment of tax (possibly with interest) until the gain was realised, if the company was prepared to accept the administrative burden of tracing that that would entail.

21.3.3 Thin Capitalisation

Rules which apply differently according to the residence of taxpayer or its companies attract frequent attention. In *Lankhorst-Hohorst GMBH v Finanzamt Steinfurt*,[108] a German rule treated the waiver of a debt repayment due from a subsidiary to its parent as a constructive dividend; however, while this rule applied to non-resident subsidiaries and some domestic ones, it did not apply to most domestic ones. Thin capitalisation/transfer pricing rules were extended by Germany to domestic transitions—as in the UK.[109] In *Bosal*,[110] a Dutch rule said that finance costs, such as interest, incurred by the parent company to finance subsidiaries in other Member States could be deducted only if they contributed to profits which were taxable in The Netherlands. This rule was held to be discriminatory and so the parent was entitled to deduct the cost. The result was that UK's transfer-pricing and thin capitalisation rules were clearly at risk.

The ECJ also ruled on the UK thin capitalisation rules in its group litigation. In Case C-524/04 *Thin Capitalisation GLO Test Case*,[111] the Court used its customary approach, asking whether the rules were a restriction, whether they might be justified and whether they were proportionate. There were three sets of UK rules. The original rule in TA 1988 directed that where the thin capitalisation rules applied, the whole payment was treated as dividend and not as interest. This bizarre all-or-nothing rule was held to break EC law. The original rule was amended by FA 1995, which concentrated on the amount of interest as opposed to the rate and directed that only the excess over the amount that would have

---

[107] Case C-371/10 *National Grid Indus BV v Inspecteur van de Belastingdienst Rijnmond/kantoor Rotterdam* [2012] STC 114.

[108] Case C-324/00 [2003] STC 607; Korner (2003) 31 *Intertax* 162; and Gutman and Hinnekens (2003) 12 *EC Tax Rev* 90.

[109] German transfer pricing reaction, Endres (2004) 32 *Intertax* 137 and de la Feria and Fuest, 'Closer to an Internal Market? The Economic Effects of EU Tax Jurisprudence', Oxford University Centre for Business Taxation WP 11/12 (July 2011).

[110] Case C-168/01 [2003] STC 1483.

[111] Case C-524/04 *Thin Capitalisation GLO Test Case* [2007] ECR I-2107.

been paid if there had been no connection between the parties was to be treated as interest. These rules were in turn amended by FA 2004 following the decision of the ECJ rejecting the German thin capitalisation rules in Case 324/00 *Lankhorst Hohorst* (above). The 2004 changes use the transfer-pricing rules instead of a separate provision, and apply to certain domestic situations as well.

Importantly, the Court did not reject the 1995 rules as necessarily contrary to EC law principles. Rather, it used the abuse approach developed in *Cadbury Schweppes* (see below §21.3.5). The taxpayers had a right to arrange intra-group finance as they wished, but the states had interests in preventing artificial transfers of profit across borders. Ultimately the Court held that taxpayers must be allowed to show that non arm's-length prices may be justified commercially. So, as in *Cadbury Schweppes*, the rule must be applied on a case-by-case basis. When the ECJ's decision was sent back to the UK courts for implementation, the Court of Appeal interpreted the ECJ's 'commercial reasons' test simply to mean that intra-group finance had to be on arm's-length terms. As the UK rules allowed a deduction for arm's-length financing costs, the Court of Appeal concluded that there could be no further remedy for amounts in excess of that.[112] The ECJ has not yet considered the 2004 rules. Some commentators dare to hope for the repeal of the 2004 rules in the light of this decision—probably in vain.[113]

The case contains other important—and controversial—comments on the scope of (then) Article 56 TEC as opposed to Article 43 TEC, and on the role of the justification of cohesion.[114]

21.3.4 Cross-Border Loss Relief

The UK legislation in response to the ECJ decision in *Marks & Spencer*[115] was considered briefly above (§7.6.7). In *Marks & Spencer*, the UK taxpayer sought to deduct from UK profits a loss sustained in France. If the loss had been sustained by a French branch, the loss would have been allowable. In fact, it had been sustained by a French subsidiary and so could not be used under UK tax rules. It is axiomatic in tax planning that foreign ventures begin as branches, so that full relief may be obtained against the parent's income for the almost inevitable start-up losses, and then switch to subsidiaries to shield the foreign income from UK tax until actual distribution. Here the foreign subsidiary's venture had ended badly and the loss was a liquidation loss.

It became conventional to say the ECJ's ruling was, in football parlance, a 'score draw'. The ECJ held:[116]

As Community law now stands, arts 43 EC and 48 EC do not preclude provisions of a Member State which generally prevent a resident parent company from deducting from its taxable profits losses incurred in another Member State by a subsidiary established in that Member State although they allow it to deduct losses incurred by a resident subsidiary. However, it is contrary to arts 43 EC and 48 EC to prevent the resident parent company from doing so where the non-resident subsidiary has exhausted the possibilities available in its state of residence of having the losses

---

[112] [2011] EWCA Civ 127.
[113] See eg Mahalingham [2012] BTR 134.
[114] See Morgan and Bridges, *The Tax Journal* (19 March 2007), 7 *et seq*.
[115] Case C-446/03 *Marks & Spencer v Halsey* [2006] STC 237.
[116] *Ibid*, 268.

taken into account for the accounting period concerned by the claim for relief and also for previous accounting periods and where there are no possibilities for those losses to be taken into account in its state of residence for future periods either by the subsidiary itself or by a third party, in particular where the subsidiary has been sold to that third party.

The UK Court of Appeal remitted the question whether there was 'no possibility' of the loss being used in another way to the First Tier Tribunal.[117] The Court of Appeal also held that the date when that issue must be determined is the end of the period within which the company may make the claim for relief.[118] The litigation on implementation continues on in the UK courts, now 10 years and running.[119] The European Commission considers that the UK's group relief legislation, as amended following the ECJ decision in *Marks & Spencer*, still infringes the freedom of establishment, and has referred the matter to the ECJ.

The ECJ has already had one foreign loss case—*AMID*[120]—but it adds nothing to *Marks & Spencer*. In *Lidl v Finanzamt Heilbronn*,[121] the Court agreed with Advocate General Sharpston on the general principle but disagreed with her on the question of proportionality. The Court upheld the Member State rule in question.[122]

21.3.5 Controlled Foreign Company Rules

The UK's CFC rules (discussed in chapter seventeen above) attribute the profits of certain overseas companies to UK corporate shareholders. In *Cadbury Schweppes v IRC*,[123] the taxpayer was such a shareholder and the overseas subsidiaries were such companies. The subsidiaries had been set up in Ireland under the terms of the relevant Irish legislation and paid tax at 10%, being within the International Financial Services Centre in Dublin. A previous structure had involved a Jersey company. The question referred to Luxembourg was whether the application of the CFC legislation interfered with the taxpayer's rights under the free movement provisions in (then) Articles 43, 49 and 56 TEC.

The Court's first principle was that measures to counter potential abuse were legitimate if aimed at 'wholly artificial arrangements'. Such conduct undermined the right of the Member States to exercise their tax jurisdiction in relation to the activities carried out in their territory and thus jeopardised a balanced allocation between Member States of the power to impose taxes (referring to *Marks & Spencer*, at [46]). However, in deciding whether the arrangements were wholly artificial, the Member State could not say just that the burden of tax was lower in the other state. So the CFC rules would not be compatible with EU law if they applied where, despite the existence of tax motives, the incorporation of a CFC reflected economic reality and the incorporation corresponded with an actual establishment intended to carry on genuine economic activities in the host Member State. Any finding of artificiality had to be based on objective factors ascertainable by third parties with regard, in particular, to the extent to which the CFC physically exists in terms

---

[117] *Marks & Spencer v Halsey* [2007] EWCA Civ 117, [43] *et seq.*
[118] *Ibid*, [25] *et seq.*
[119] At the time of writing the latest instalment is [2011] EWCA Civ 1156.
[120] Case C-141/99 [2003] STC 357.
[121] Case C-414/06 *Lidl Belgium GmbH v Finanzamt Heilbronn* [2008] ECR I-3601.
[122] For criticism of AG Sharpston's opinion, see Airs, *The Tax Journal* (21 April 2008), 9–11.
[123] Case C-196/04 [2004] STC (SCD) 342.

of premises, staff and equipment, such as a 'letterbox' or 'front' subsidiary.[124] As noted in §21.2.2.6(6) above, in *Vodafone 2*, the UK Court of Appeal concluded that the UK's CFC legislation could be interpreted so as to be compatible with EU law by 'reading in' a new exception applying retrospectively to companies actually established in another EEA state which carry on genuine economic activities there.[125]

21.3.6 The Relationship Between EU Law and Bilateral Tax Treaties

There was already a duty on Member States to take the most-favoured-nation principles into account when negotiating with third parties in the field of aviation.[126] In the direct tax context, *Bouanich v Skatterverket*[127] concerned a rule which allowed resident shareholders to deduct certain items from dividends. A non-resident shareholder was not allowed to do so. The Court held that this was a breach of (then) Article 56 TEC. The Court also considered national legislation derived from a double tax treaty between France and Sweden, and held that it too could breach EC non-discrimination principles in appropriate circumstances. Similarly, *Meilicke v Finanzamt Bonn-Innerstedt*[128] concerned a rule under which a resident was allowed a tax credit for dividends from a resident company but not from a non-resident company. The Court held that this was a breach of (then) Article 56 TEC. More cases on this particularly challenging topic are awaited with interest.

21.4   Other Aspects of EU Law

21.4.1 Interpretation

In EU law the courts adopt a purposive interpretation and treat VAT law, in particular, as a matter of principle and purpose.[129] The courts state the principle and then work down to the facts. Moreover, literal interpretations are rejected in favour of the purpose of the directive;[130] only if all else fails do the courts proceed to a literal approach.[131] This approach comes naturally when UK courts face problems of interpreting EU law as such, or UK rules based on EU directives: see, for example, the Court of Appeal reading in a new exemption to the controlled company rules in *Vodafone 2* as just discussed in §21.3.5 above. However, the schizophrenic state under which tax matters are tested on a literal basis in a domestic context and on a purposive basis in a European context may become

---

[124] See Case C-341/04 *Re Eurofood IFSC Ltd* [2006] All ER (EC) 1078, paras 34 and 35. For a more detailed analysis, see Simpson [2006] BTR 677 and practical comments by Dodwell, Williams and Pleasant, *The Tax Journal* (13 November 2006), 7. See further ch 17 above.

[125] *Vodafone v Revenue & Customs Commissioners (No 2)* [2009] STC 1480, [2009] EWCA Civ 446.

[126] Cases C-466/98–476/98 *Commission v UK* ('the *Open Skies* case') [2002] ECR I-09427. The remarks of AG Tizzano are particularly wide-ranging. See Panayi [2003] BTR 189.

[127] Case C-256/04 [2008] STC 2020.

[128] Case C-292/04 [2008] STC 2267.

[129] See Avery Jones (1996) 17(3) *Fiscal Studies* 63; see further *Revenue Law*, §3.1.2.

[130] For example, Case 154/80 *Staatssecretaris van Financiën v Coöperatieve Vereniging Coöperatieve Aardappelenbe-waarplaats GA* [1981] 3 CMLR 337 (the *Dutch Potato* case), and Case 89/91 *Staatssecretaris van Financiën v Hong Kong Trade Development Council* [1983] 1 CMLR 73 (ECJ).

[131] Case 139/84 *Van Dijk's Boekhuis BV v Staatssecretaris van Financiën* [1986] 2 CMLR 575 (ECJ), distinguishing the creation of a new article from the thorough repair of an old article.

unstable, especially as the volume of EU material expands. The idea of English courts finding they are championing a minority tradition in a sea of other ideas is particularly piquant for Scots lawyers, who have had to suffer this since the Act of Union. A related phenomenon is the practice, already seen in UK legislation implementing the Mergers Directive, of ensuring that cross-border transactions are not favoured at the expense of purely domestic ones.[132]

21.4.2 The Role of the Commission—and its Views

Since the Commission has enforcement powers under the EU Treaty, one must pay particular attention to its views. For example, one view is that current EU law does not oblige a Member State to grant the withholding tax rate of its most favourable bilateral agreement automatically to taxpayers of another state which is not covered by the agreement.[133] However, the Commission was largely instrumental in pressing the *French Tax Credits* case (see §21.2.2.2 above) and the refusal to allow the Court to weigh the advantages and disadvantages of doing business as a branch rather than as a subsidiary; many see this as the false start of the Court's adventures into this area.

---

[132] Inland Revenue, *EC Direct Measures—A Consultative Document* (1991), paras 2.4, 2.5, 2.10.
[133] Written Answer, 9 November 1992 ([1992] OJ C40/93); reported in *Simon's Tax Intelligence* 302.

PART III

Tax-preferred Savings

22

Favoured Methods

The UK has a number of tax rules designed to encourage saving. These rules are considered in this chapter and in chapters twenty-three and twenty-four below. One interesting side-effect of this encouragement to save has been that people often end up with a larger estate when they die. The tax rules are designed to give relief from income tax and/or CGT, not IHT. So the Chancellor may take three times as much in IHT as he gives away in the other taxes.[1]

This chapter covers the UK tax treatment of certain favoured forms of saving. The treatment of—and of income from—investment intermediaries is discussed in chapter twenty-three below. The division between chapters twenty-two and twenty-three is not precise. The extent of these rules, and in particular the extent of the exemptions and reliefs, is made very clear by the gathering together of the material in ITTOIA 2005, Part 4 (savings and investment income) and Part 6 (exempt income). However, the boundary between a rule prescribing the limits of a section, and so to be found in Part 4, and an exemption, to be found in Part 6, is not precise, and so the arrangement adopted in previous editions has largely been followed here. The treatment of the biggest tax privileges of all, those for pension arrangements, was completely rewritten by FA 2004 and took effect in April 2005; this treatment is outlined in chapter twenty-four below. It should also be noted that Finance Act 2012 introduced a new favourable investment scheme—the Seed Enterprise Investment Scheme (SEIS).[2] Individuals who invest in shares in qualifying seed companies issued on or after 6 April 2012 and before 6 April 2017 are eligible for income tax relief of 50%[3] as well as CGT relief on disposal of the shares.[4] Gains realised on the disposal of assets in 2012–13 that are reinvested through SEISs qualify for a CGT exemption.[5]

---

[1] *Sunday Times*, 4 February 2007, Money Section.
[2] ITA 2007, Part 5A, ss 257A *et seq.*
[3] ITA 2007, s 257AB.
[4] TCGA 1992, ss 150E–150G.
[5] TCGA 1992, Sch 5BB.

22.1   General

The correct tax treatment of income from savings is a highly contentious issue, marking, as it does, the divide between comprehensive income tax (CIT) and expenditure tax (ET). Thus the debate is a reflection of that larger debate: partly a belief that income from saving is doubly taxed, since savings are usually made out of taxed income; and partly a belief that saving is a good thing and so should be encouraged. The 1995 OECD report *Taxation and Household Savings* showed that most countries' systems penalise savings.[6] However, if tax-efficient ways of saving are introduced, it must be expected, as US and UK experience shows, that there will be long transitional phase during which money is simply moved from existing savings into the new accounts. The OECD report also showed that countries with the most generous interest deductions, then the United States and Scandinavia, had the lowest rate of savings (2%); the least generous group (most other large industrial economies) had a savings rate of 11.5%. Perhaps the most dramatic experiment concerned New Zealand where, in the late 1980s, pension contributions ceased to receive any privileged treatment; deductions to pension funds ceased to be deductible and tax was charged on the income of the funds, although not on the eventual pension. The effect was a sharp fall in pension savings, small firms winding up their pension schemes and large firms reducing promised benefits. Household saving dropped from 1.3% of GDP in 1987 to −1.9% in 1989–90.[7]

In the UK there is a strong government wish to encourage saving for retirement, and one strand of the debate is whether such savings should be compulsory. The strongest objection to compulsion comes from the very people whom the Government sees as most in need of having such savings, ie those at the lower end of the income scale. These people not only understand that their disposable income would be reduced while working, they also realise that any benefit from their saving is likely to be swallowed up by the pension credit mechanism (below). This leaves those who would save anyway as the people who object much less to compulsion. Thus government policy confounds itself.

Tax encouragement to save may take many forms:

(1)   the annual return received by the investor may be free, in whole or in part, from income tax;
(2)   there may be an income tax deduction, in whole or in part, for the sum invested;[8]
(3)   the sum received on disposal may be exempt, in whole or in part, from CGT.

In addition:

(4)   the entity with which the money is invested may be free of tax on its income and or capital gains; and
(5)   the CGT liability normally arising on a disposal may be deferred on a reinvestment.

---

[6] See comment by Robson (1995) 16(1) *Fiscal Studies* 38. For a broad economics-based survey of theories on saving, see Boadway and Wildasin (1994) 15(3) *Fiscal Studies* 19.

[7] Davis, *Pension Funds*, (OUP, 1998), 87–88; citing Fitzgerald and Harper (1992) 9 *Australian Tax Forum* 194.

[8] There is no CGT deduction until the disposal—unless, perhaps, rollovers are treated as a form of deduction since the investment is greater by the amount of the tax not charged.

22.2 Current UK Savings Incentives

Income and capital gains from certain forms of savings are exempt from tax, as follows (the ITTOIA provisions apply for income tax, while TA 1988 and later legislation still apply for corporation tax where relevant):

(1)   Interest and bonuses on National Savings Certificates; maturity bonuses on defence bonds, British savings bonds and national development bonds; and, for persons resident and ordinarily resident in Northern Ireland, Ulster Savings Certificates.[9]

(2)   SAYE interest and bonuses under certain certified contractual savings schemes; for schemes certified on or after 1 December 1994,[10] exemption is limited to savings-related arrangements linked to share option schemes within ITEPA 2003.[11]

(3)   Capital gains from government stocks and qualifying corporate bonds.[12]

(4)   Income and capital gains of authorised pension and retirement benefit schemes.

(5)   Income and capital gains on investments held under an individual investment plans, ie individual savings accounts (ISAs) and formerly personal equity plans (PEP) and TESSAs[13] (see §22.3 below).

(6)   Income and capital gains from funds invested with a venture capital trust,[14] enterprise investment scheme, corporate venturing scheme or real estate investment trust (REIT) (see §§22.5, 22.6 and 23.10 below).

(7)   Pension funds (chapter twenty-four below).

(8)   Unit trusts, etc (see §23.3 below).

(9)   Securities which are free of tax to residents abroad (FOTRA) securities.[15]

Other tax privileges include the following:

(10)   Tax deductions for investments by an individual in shares in certain qualifying trading companies (the Enterprise Investment Scheme (below §22.5), venture capital trusts (below §22.6), and the Seed Enterprise Investment Scheme discussed in the introduction to this chapter).

(11)   An individual's contribution to a pension scheme is deductible from income, for income tax purposes, within limits: see chapter twenty-four below.

(12)   CGT exemptions and deferrals of gain if reinvested (see *Revenue Law*, CGT chapters and especially chapter thirty-two).

---

[9]   ITTOIA 2005, Pt 6, Ch 2, ss 692 and 693, ex TA 1988, s 46 (still in force for corporation tax). See Explanatory Notes Draft Bill, changes 122 and 123. ITTOIA 2005, s 693 makes statutory the former concessionary relief for accumulated interest on Ulster Savings Certificates following the death of the holder (ex ESC A34). An exemption for National Savings Bank interest up to £70 on ordinary accounts (formerly ITTOIA 2005, s 691, ex TA 1988, s 325) was repealed by FA 2011.

[10]   ITTOIA 2005, Pt 6, Ch 4, ss 702–708, ex TA 1988, s 326 and Sch 15A (not relevant for corporation tax).

[11]   ITTOIA 2005, s 703 refers to ITEPA 2003, s 516(4).

[12]   TCGA 1992, s 115.

[13]   ITTOIA 2005 generalised the PEP regulation-making powers in TA 1988, ss 333 *et seq* and repealed the TESSA regulation-making powers in TA 1988, ss 326A *et seq* (added by FA 1990, s 28)—not relevant for corporation tax.

[14]   ITTOIA 2005, Pt 6, Ch 5, ss 709–712.

[15]   ITTOIA 2005, Pt 6, Ch 6, ss 713–716, FA 1996, s 154 (still in force for corporation tax).

22.3   Individual Savings Accounts[16]

As from 6 April 1999 the former favoured savings devices of tax exempt special savings accounts (TESSAs) and personal equity plans (PEPs) ceased to be available for new investment. They were succeeded by individual savings accounts (ISAs). TESSAs were time limited and therefore have expired; PEPs were not time limited, but as from 6 April 2008 all existing PEPS become stocks and shares ISAs. Unlike the predecessor schemes, the ISA includes a number of voluntary standards designed to make some schemes attractive to savers as distinct from fund managers; these are the 'CAT standards', which set levels for charges, access and terms.[17] There was much delight in certain circles when ISAs had a slow start; since investors had just rushed to save with TESSAs and PEPs for the last time, some savings fatigue was not surprising. Later figures suggested that ISAs were actually quite popular.[18]

An ISA is a scheme of investment which may be used by a qualifying individual.[19] A qualifying individual must be aged 18 or over and either resident or ordinarily resident in the UK.[20] The individual must not break the rules for the number of ISA investments in the year.[21] There are provisions on ceasing to qualify.[22] For many years ISAs had maxi accounts and mini accounts. This has now been simplified, and investors now have a choice of two types of ISA:

(1)   a stocks and shares ISA; and
(2)   a cash ISA.

Moreover, they may invest in both in the same year, whether with the same provider or different providers, The overall maximum subscription level per tax year is £11,280, of which a maximum of £5,640 may be saved in a cash ISA and the rest in a stock and shares ISA (figures for 2012–13). Money in Child Trust Funds may be rolled over into ISAs, but the first child will not reach the relevant age until 2020. From 2011, Junior ISAs are available for children aged under 18 who do not have a Child Trust Fund.[23]

Like TESSAs and PEPs, ISAs allows individuals to hold various investments free of income tax and CGT.[24] Unlike those schemes, ISAs allow investors to use an insurance policy. An ISA, by abolishing the PEP distinction between qualifying and non-qualifying funds, has a slightly wider geographical spread than a PEP, and permits investments in gilts. Like a PEP, but unlike a TESSA, an ISA has no lock-in period to qualify for tax relief.

---

[16] Regulations were made under FA 1998, s 75, which refers to TA 1988, ss 333 and 333B, TCGA 1992, s 151. The principal regulations are the Individual Savings Account Regulations 1998 (SI 1998/1870) (hereafter 'ISA Regs'), [1998] *Simon's Weekly Tax Intelligence* 1200; and the Individual Savings Account (Amendment) Regulations 1999 (SI 1998/3174), [1999] *Simon's Weekly Tax Intelligence* 97. See also Inland Revenue Press Release, 1 April 1999, [1999] *Simon's Weekly Tax Intelligence* 730.

[17] See Treasury Press Release, 22 December 1998, [1999] *Simon's Weekly Tax Intelligence* 32.

[18] Chennells, Dilnot and Emmerson (eds), *Green Budget 2000* (Institute for Fiscal Studies, 2000), 78.

[19] ISA Regs 1998, reg 4(1).

[20] ISA Regs 1998, reg 10; Crown employees within TA 1988, s 132(4)(a) also qualify.

[21] ISA Regs 1998, reg 10(2)(b), (c).

[22] ISA Regs 1998, reg 11.

[23] ISA Regs 1998, regs 4ZA–4ZE.

[24] ISA Regs 1998, reg 22.

An ISA may be opened by someone on behalf of the qualifying individual and does not have to be opened in writing. The tax credit repaid in respect of dividends was limited to 10% and has now expired.[25] There are, however, disadvantages of an ISA compared with TESSAs and PEPs. The maximum sums which may be invested each year are lower.

Interest in cash held as part of the stocks and shares component of an ISA will be taxed at the basic rate of 20%.[26] This cannot be a tax since ISAs are tax free, but it will be taken by the Revenue anyway.[27] There are many rules for accounts managers,[28] and for transfer of accounts to other managers.[29] There are also many administrative and information rules.[30] Another provision adapts the CGT rules, eg by directing a disposal and acquisition at market value when the administrator transfers assets to the investor.[31] There are separate regulations for insurance companies[32] and the overseas life assurance business of such companies.[33]

When investors in Northern Rock withdrew the money from ISAs with that company, they thereby forfeited their ISA tax advantages in 2007–08 and earlier years. They should have arranged for a transfer to another provider to be made by Northern Rock. FA 2008, section 40, amending ITTOIA 2005, section 701, allows HMRC to amend the regulation so that particular people may avoid forfeiture. The retrospective regulation must be wholly beneficial and may be to specific groups or circumstances.

22.4   Venture Capital Trusts[34]

Rules for venture capital trusts (VCTs) were first introduced in 1995, but were extensively revised by FA 2004 and have been occasionally modified since then. The income tax legislation gives relief from income tax for qualifying investments by individuals in approved VCTs; as from 6 April 2007 these are to be found in ITA 2007, Part 6 (previously TA 1988, section 332A and Schedule 15B). Exemption from CGT was given both to the VCT itself in respect of its gains (TCGA 1992, section 100) and to the individual on a disposal of the qualifying shareholding (TCGA 1992, section 151A); these remain part of TCGA 1992. There is no charge to income tax on distributions by the VCT to the shareholders. The conditions to be satisfied by a VCT seeking approval and as to the holding it may acquire are now set out in ITA 2007, Part 6, Chapter 3 (previously TA 1988, section 842AA and

---

[25] FA 1998, s 76.
[26] ISA Regs 1998, reg 23.
[27] Redston (1999) *Taxation Practitioner*, 10, 12.
[28] ISA Regs 1998, regs 14–20.
[29] ISA Regs 1998, reg 21.
[30] ISA Regs 1998, regs 24–33, 35.
[31] ISA Regs 1998, reg 34.
[32] Individual Savings Account (Insurance Companies) Regulations 1998 (SI 1998/1871), [1998] *Simon's Weekly Tax Intelligence* 1230; and Individual Savings Account (Amendment) Regulations 1999 (SI 1998/3174), reg 13, [1999] *Simon's Weekly Tax Intelligence* 97.
[33] Insurance Companies (Overseas Life Assurance Business) Regulations 1998 (SI 1998/1872), [1998] *Simon's Weekly Tax Intelligence* 1235.
[34] See Shirley (1994) 15(2) *Fiscal Studies* 98, arguing that the legislation should have subsidised debt, not equity. On practice, see Stratton, *Tolleys Tax Planning 2003–04*, ch 64, 1841. For instructive information on US and Canada, see Sandler, *Venture Capital and Tax Incentives: A Comparative Study of Canada and the United States*, Tax Paper No 108 (Canadian Tax Foundation, 2004).

Schedule 28B). The VCT is liable to tax on its income as distinct from its realised capital gains; the practice of using borrowings to fund acquisitions means that there may well be no taxable income. The following account relates to the year 2012–13. The VCT must be approved by the Commissioners; loss of approval has tax consequences.[35] The 2004 changes followed a review of VCTs and enterprise investment schemes (EISs) (§22.5 below).

The individual investor may claim relief from income tax; as at 6 April 2012 an individual could claim at the maximum of 30% (earlier years allowed relief at 20% or even 40%) for sums up to £200,000 invested in the VCT;[36] relief for investors applies only in relation to shares for which the individual has subscribed. For CGT reliefs, see *Revenue Law*, §41.7. Many, but not all, of these changes bring the VCT relief closer to that for EISs (§22.5 below). Immediately before 2004 there was a reinvestment relief for gains otherwise chargeable to CGT if the gains could be matched with an investment in the VCT (the serial investor relief), but this was repealed since the 40% income tax relief was then made available.[37]

Income tax relief[38] is given for the cost of eligible shares issued by a VCT. The maximum amount qualifying for relief in one year is now £200,000; shares are eligible if they carry no preferential rights to dividends or assets, nor any right to be redeemed.[39] The shares must not be loan-linked; a loan is linked if it is one made to the individual (or an associate) which would not have been made if the individual had not subscribed for the shares.[40]

The relief must be claimed and takes effect at step 6 of the process set out in *Revenue Law*, §12.2.5.[41] For shares issued after 5 April 2006 the relief is lost if there is a disposal within five years of the issue or certain other events occur; the benefit of the relief may be recovered by an assessment to income tax.[42] (For shares issued after 5 April 2000 and before 6 April 2006 the period was three years.[43]) A disposal is ignored if between spouses or civil partners living together.[44]

FA 2001 also provided that VCT relief was not lost when the VCT went into liquidation or merged; rules to facilitate mergers were added in 2002.[45] A rule that 100% of the funds raised must be put to work within 12 months was softened to 80% within 12 months and the balance within 24 months, by FA 2001.[46] The rule that the trade had to be carried on by the same company throughout the period was softened in 2004 to allow the trade to be carried on by another qualifying group company.[47] There are restrictions on the type of

---

[35] ITA 2007, ss 259, 274–275, 283, ex TA 1988, s 842AA(1)–(4); the rules on withdrawal of approval and its consequences begin in s 281, ex s 842AA(6).

[36] ITA 2007, ss 261 *et seq*, ex TA 1988, Sch 15B, para 1, as amended by FA 2008, s 32.

[37] TCGA 1992, Sch 5C, repealed by FA 2004, Sch 19.

[38] ITA 2007, s 261, ex TA 1988, s 332A, added by FA 1995 and enacting TA 1988, Sch 15B.

[39] Definition of 'eligible share' ITA 2007, s 273, ex TA 1988, Sch 15B, para 6.

[40] ITA 2007, s 264, ex TA 1988 Sch 15B, para 2.

[41] ITA 2007, ss 263 and 271–273.

[42] ITA 2007, ss 266–270, ex TA 1988, Sch 15B, paras 3, 4; on information, see s 271, ex Sch 15B, para 5.

[43] See also changes made by FA 2000, Sch 18 for shares issued on or after 6 April 2000.

[44] ITA 2007, s 267, ex TA 1988, Sch 15B, para 3.

[45] ITA 2007, ss 314–325; the merger rules (ss 321 *et seq*) were added by FA 2002, Sch 33.

[46] ITA 2007, ss 293–294, ex TA 1988, Sch 28B, para 6(1)–(2A).

[47] ITA 2007, ss 290–292, ex TA 1988, Sch 28B, para 3, as amended by FA 2004.

business which the company may carry on; FA 2008 added shipbuilding, coal production and steel production.[48] The relief is also lost if the VCT approval is withdrawn.[49]

Extensive rules define the qualifying holdings rules for the trust.[50] Since 17 March 2004 these rules have allowed more subsidiaries to qualify, in particular:

(1) a 51% subsidiary rather than a 75% subsidiary; and
(2) in certain circumstances a 90% property management subsidiary; the 90% test also applies if the subsidiary carries on the trade R&D which benefits the VCT investment.[51]

These and other changes mirror those made to the EIS scheme.[52] The trust is obliged to distribute income and capital gains regularly to its investors.[53] There is no charge to income tax on a dividend from the trust[54]; this extends to dividends paid to assignees, provided they were acquired for bona fide commercial purposes and not as part of an avoidance scheme. The exemption from income tax should not be given too much weight; there is no exemption from corporation tax for the companies in which the trust invests.

The VCT income must derive wholly or mainly from shares or securities;[55] it is thought that this test will be satisfied at 70%. The same test applies to the value of qualifying holdings as a proportion of the trust investments. At least 30% of the trust's holdings must be in eligible shares.[56] The VCT's ordinary shares must be listed on a regulated market, but the relevant company in which the qualifying activity is carried on must be unquoted.[57] No one holding by the VCT must exceed 15% of its total investments.[58] There are also rules limiting the amount of money raised which is not invested (it must not exceed £1 million) and on the maximum value of the assets of the company invested in.[59] Various trades do not qualify.[60] There are rules to ensure the independence of the company invested in.[61]

The VCT offers better tax incentives than PEPs and, unlike the EIS, allows the investor to spread the risk over a number of companies. It was thought that a typical trust would invest in between 20 and 40 companies, including those on the AIM.

F(No 3)A 2010 introduced additional changes to ensure that these favoured venture capital schemes are not in violation of EU state aid rules. Collectively, these amendments eased the requirement that an investee company must carry on its trade wholly or mainly in the UK, introduced a financial health requirement for investee companies which receive funds from either a VCT or through the EIS, allowed a VCT to list on any EU regulated

---

[48] ITA 2007, s 303 (VCT) or s 192 (EIS).
[49] ITA 2007, s 268; on assessment, see s 270.
[50] ITA 2007, Pt 6, Ch 4 (ss 286–313), ex TA 1988, s 842AA, Sch 28AB.
[51] ITA 2007, ss 301 and 299, ex TA 1988, Sch 28B, paras 5A and 10ZA.
[52] Revenue Notes to Finance Bill 2004, cls 88 and 89.
[53] ITA 2007, s 275(2).
[54] ITTOIA 2005, Pt 6, Ch 5, ex TA 1988, Sch 15B, para 7.
[55] ITA 2007, s 276. There are also rules on the receipt of royalties or licence fees as a qualifying trade; ITA 2007, s 306, ex TA 1988, Sch 28B, para 4(5), (6), amended by FA 2000, Sch 18, para 5.
[56] ITA 2007, ss 275 and 277–279.
[57] ITA 2007, s 295, TA 1988, Sch 28B, para 2. For problems, see Stratton, *op cit.*
[58] ITA 2007, ss 275 and 277.
[59] ITA 2007, ss 287 and 297, ex Sch 28B, paras 7 and 8. These limits are £15 million before the issue of the relevant holding and £16 million afterwards.
[60] ITA 2007, ss 303 *et seq*, added to by FA 2008, s 33.
[61] ITA 2007, ss 296 and 310.

market and increased the VCT minimum equity investment in eligible shares from 30% to 70%. Lastly, Finance Act 2012 introduced a new disqualifying purpose test in ITA 2007, s 299A to exclude companies set up for the purpose of accessing relief, and provided further exclusions for the acquisition of shares by a qualifying company in another company, as well as investment in some Feed-in Tariff businesses.

22.5   Enterprise Investment Scheme

The EIS, introduced by FA 1995, is the latest version of a device which began in 1983; it too was revised by FA 2004, but changes over the years have been frequent, with particularly major revision in 2001. The income tax legislation has been rewritten and is now ITA 2007, Part 5 (sections 156–257). In this chapter the older references are retained but preceded by the term 'ex'. However, TA 1988, Part VII, Chapter II (sections 289–312) still applies to shares issued before 6 April 2007 and 'ex' must be understood in this sense. None of the rules has been affected by ITTOIA 2005. Although the relief shares many rules with VCT, it is quite distinct. EIS is a relief from income tax for sums invested in shares issued by a qualifying company carrying on a qualifying business. Any gain made by the investor is exempt from CGT, provided the shares are held for at least three years; if the shares are sold below cost, the cost for capital loss purposes is reduced by any EIS relief given.[62] There is no relief from income tax for distributions by the company. Increases in EIS investment limits have to go through the EU Commission system to check for compliance with state aid rules.

Income tax relief is given for the cost of eligible shares in and issued by a qualifying company.[63] The maximum amount which may be subscribed in one year is now (2012–13) £1,000,000; it was set at £400,000 in 2006, having been £200,000 in 2004.[64] Relief is given at the EIS rate of 30%, but may not create any right to repayment.[65] Shares must be ordinary shares and carry neither preferential rights to dividends or assets, nor any right to be redeemed.[66] The share must be subscribed for wholly in cash and be fully paid-up when issued.[67] There are rules for allocating the relief to the different shares.[68] The relief must be claimed and takes effect at step 6 of the process set out in *Revenue Law*, §12.2.5.[69]

On the part of both the investor and the company, the shares must be subscribed for genuine commercial reasons and not for tax-avoidance purposes;[70] the shares must be issued by the company for the purpose of a qualifying business activity.[71] Individuals must

---

[62] On relevant CGT rules, see TCGA 1992, s 150A; and on taper relief, s 150D applying Sch 5BA.

[63] ITA 2007, ss 156 *et seq*, the share requirements are in Pt 5, Ch 3 and the issuing company conditions are in Ch 4, ex TA 1988, ss 289, 289A, 293 and 297. See Way, *Tolley's Tax Planning 2007–08*, ch 19.

[64] ITA 2007, s 158, ex TA 1988, s 290(2); there is also a minimum subscription of £500 (s 157(2), ex s 290(1)).

[65] ITA 2007, s 158(2), ex TA 1988, s 289A(2); renamed by FA 2008, Sch 3.

[66] ITA 2007, s 173 (2), ex TA 1988, s 289(7).

[67] ITA 2007, s 173, ex TA 1988, s 289(1).

[68] ITA 2007, ss 201 *et seq*.

[69] ITA 2007, ss 158(3) and 201–207.

[70] ITA 2007, ss 165 and 178.

[71] ITA 2007, s 175.

not be connected with the company; a director is not necessarily connected, provided no unreasonable payments are received from the company.[72]

The company must be a qualifying company, ie unquoted and carrying on one or more qualifying trades.[73] Qualifying trades are elaborately defined by excluding many trades;[74] the exclusions include not only share dealing but also running a nursing home.[75] The company must also be independent.[76] The courts have held that a company providing accounting services to a firm of accountants was not providing independent accountancy services and so did not qualify; in a similar vein they have held that the payment of a dividend was not a qualifying business activity.[77]

As with VCTs, the rules as to the percentage of the money raised which must be put to work in the qualifying activity within 12 months is 80%, having been reduced from 100%.[78] More than one company may carry on the activity.[79] Also as with VCTs, there is a gross assets limit—the company's assets must not exceed £15 million before the issue or £16 million afterwards.[80] The annual investment limit for qualifying companies is £5 million. The company may have subsidiaries, but these must meet various conditions; some rules refer to 51% subsidiaries and others to 90% subsidiaries.[81] As with VCTs, shares must not be loan-linked.[82] There must be no prearranged exit.[83]

Relief may be reduced or withdrawn, and a charge to tax arises if the individual disposes[84] of the shares before the end of the relevant period as now designated (a maximum of five years; it was seven years for shares issued before 6 April 2000).[85] If the disposal is otherwise than by way of bargain at arm's length, the relief is simply withdrawn; in bona fide disposals the maximum recovered may be reduced.[86] The benefit of the relief may be recovered by an assessment to income tax under ITA 2007.[87] However, ITA 2007, Part 4, Chapter 6 (section 131), formerly TA 1988, section 574, giving relief against income tax for the loss on the disposal of the shares, may apply.[88]

---

[72] ITA 2007, ss 163 and 166–171, ex TA 1988, ss 291, 291A, 291B; the permitted payments are listed in s 168(2), ex s 291A(3). *Taylor v Revenue & Customs Commissioners* [2010] UKUT 417, [2011] STC 126 concerned the question whether the investor was connected with the company, viz whether the investor had to have (a) 30% of the share capital and 30% of the loan capital, or (b) 30% of the amalgamated capital. Roth J preferred (b).

[73] ITA 2007, ss 181–184, ex TA 1988, s 293; on effect of land holding, but note s 188 on property managing subsidiaries. The parent company of a trading group qualifies.

[74] ITA 2007, ss 192 *et seq*, ex TA 1988, ss 297, 298. On effect of IP rights, see s 195 continuing changes made by FA 2000.

[75] ITA 2007, s 198, ex TA 1988, s 297(fe).

[76] ITA 2007, s 185, ex TA 1988, s 293(8).

[77] The cases are *Castleton Management Service Ltd v Kirkwood* [2001] STC (SCD) 95; and *Forthright (Wales) Ltd v Davis* [2004] EWHC Civ 524; [2004] STC 875.

[78] ITA 2007, s 175, ex TA 1988, s 289(1)(c). *Blackburn v Revenue & Customs Commissioners* [2009] STC 188, [2008] EWCA Civ 1454 is an interesting case on proving that money had been subscribed for shares when it had been left with the company and allowed to build up.

[79] ITA 2007, s 183, ex TA 1988, s 289(1A)–(1E), as substituted by FA 2004.

[80] ITA 2007, s 186.

[81] ITA 2007, ss 189–191, ex TA 1988, s 308 and ss 293(6ZA), 300(2)(b) as added by FA 2004.

[82] ITA 2007, s 164, ex TA 1988, s 299A.

[83] ITA 2007, s 177, ex TA 1988, s 299B.

[84] Other than on a disposal between spouses or civil partners living together (see ITA 2007, ss 245–246, ex TA 1988, s 304).

[85] On 'designated' periods, see TA 1988, s 291(b), as amended by FA 2000, Sch 17, para 2.

[86] ITA 2007, ss 209 *et seq*, ex TA 1988, s 299(1).

[87] ITA 2007, ss 234 *et seq*, ex TA 1988, s 307.

[88] ITA 2007, s 131, ex TA 1988, s 305A.

A charge also arises where an individual who has subscribed for the shares receives value from the company within the designated period.[89] The charge is to recover the benefit of the tax relief and so does not apply to the extent that the value received exceeds the benefit of the relief.[90] 'Value received' is widely defined, but here too it has been softened over the years, eg by ignoring receipts which are insignificant or which are returned.[91] The repayment of certain short-term loans is also ignored.[92] Further charges may arise where capital is replaced, a new trade begun, new share capital acquired or value is received by persons other than the claimants.[93]

Further rules are provided for corporate reorganisations, the acquisition of the share capital by a new company and its application to subsidiaries, and where there are nominees, etc.[94]

Enterprise investment schemes are also of importance because of the rules allowing CGT to be deferred when gains have been realised and the proceeds are reinvested in an EIS.[95] These rules date from 1998 and replace the old CGT general reinvestment relief; they also broaden an earlier relief which allowed deferrals on an investment in an EIS. CGT deferral relief is useful as it is available in cases where the CGT exemption is not available, eg when the investor is connected or the subscription limit is exceeded.

The rules reflect much experience with the business expansion scheme (BES) (1984–93). About one-quarter of BES projects failed in the first two or three years, and more than £196 million was sunk into assured tenancy companies just before the worst slump to hit the property market since 1945. Making money only came from offers in the early 1990s, especially when accompanied by loan-back schemes (now blocked as loan-linked transactions). Original investments were farmland, hotels and even wine. In 1988 the assured tenancy companies had attracted £100 million; other investments £5 million.[96]

In 2009, ITA 2007, section 175 was simplified—all the money must be employed within two years of the date of issue. The changes to EIS income tax relief applied also to reinvestment relief. In addition, there was a technical change on share-for-share exchanges; the change was beneficial to taxpayers and was designed to prevent a taxable gain arising in relation to the old shares.[97] F(No 2)A 2010 amended paragraph 1 of Schedule 5B to the TCGA 1992 to deny EIS reinvestment relief when a claim to entrepreneurs' relief is made. F(No 3)A 2010 introduced additional changes to ensure that these favoured venture capital schemes are not in violation of EU state aid rules. These amendments eased the requirement that an investee company must carry on its trade wholly or mainly in the UK, and introduced a financial health requirement for investee companies which receive funds either from a VCT or through the EIS. As with VCTs, Finance Act 2012 introduced a new disqualifying purpose test, to exclude companies set up for the purpose of accessing

---

[89] List begins in ITA 2007, ss 213 *et seq*, ex TA 1988, s 300.

[90] ITA 2007, s 220.

[91] ITA 2007, ss 213 *et seq*, ex TA 1988, s 300(2); on 'insignificant' value, see ss 214 and 215; on timing of value, see s 216 and on amount, see s 217; on receipt of replacement value, see ITA 2007, ss 221 *et seq*, ex TA 1988, s 300A.

[92] ITA 2007, s 216 (2), ex TA 1988, s 300(2)(b).

[93] See list in ITA 2007, ss 224–236, ex TA 1988, ss 302, 303.

[94] ITA 2007, ss 247–249, 191 and 250, ex TA 1988, ss 304A, 305, 308, 311.

[95] TCGA 1992, Sch 5B, added by FA 1998. On 1998 changes, see Hutton [1998] *PCB* 285; and McKie [1998] *PCB* 174.

[96] See *The Economist*, 3 December 1988.

[97] See Finance Bill 2009, HMRC Notes on Clauses, paras 1–6.

relief,[98] and provided further exclusions for acquisition of shares by a qualifying company in another company as well as investment in some Feed-in Tariff businesses.

22.6 Corporate Venturing Scheme

It is something of a relief, after wading through the statutory provisions on VCTs and EIS, to come across the more modern rules on the corporate venturing scheme (CVS) which took effect on 1 April 2000 and are contained in FA 2000, Schedule 15 (not rewritten). Unlike the previous reliefs in this chapter, it is aimed at investment by companies and so applies only for corporation tax. However, many of the rules have been changed along with those for VCTs and EIS, eg as to the gross capital, the number of employees and the limits on the amount invested in the issuing company in any 12-month period.[99] The investing company gets relief at 20% of the amount it subscribes for new ordinary shares which are held throughout the qualification period, which is usually three years.[100] There are also reliefs against income for losses on these shares, net of any investment relief remaining after the disposal,[101] and provision for deferring any capital gains liability on reinvesting in another such scheme.[102] There are further rules about the application of corporate reorganisation provisions; these are to be applied to these shares separately from other shares.[103]

The investing company[104] must not at any time during the qualification period (three years) have a material interest in the issuing company, nor may it control it. The issuing company must carry on only non-financial trades. The investment must be subscribed for commercial reasons and not for tax-avoidance purposes.

The rules on the company issuing the shares[105] are similar to those for EIS and VCTs. Such a company must be small, independent, unquoted and trading. It must not carry on certain prohibited activities, eg nursing homes.[106] It must not derive a substantial part of its income from licence fees and royalties, save where these have been generated by its own R&D.[107] The relief is not lost if the company becomes quoted within the three-year period, provided this was not imminent when the shares were issued. The relief is lost if the shares are disposed of within the qualification period.[108] Further restrictions apply if value is received from the company by the investing company or other persons.[109] Loss of relief is tempered in certain circumstances.[110] The relief is not lost if the company goes into liquidation or receivership within the three-year period. The relaxations which we have

---

[98] ITA 2007, s 178A.
[99] FA 2000, Sch 15, paras 22 (amended 2006), 22A (added 2007) and 35A (added 2007). For further examples, see paras 23A and 29(3).
[100] FA 2000, Sch 15, para 39.
[101] FA 2000, Sch 15, para 67.
[102] FA 2000, Sch 15, para 73.
[103] FA 2000, Sch 15, para 80.
[104] FA 2000, Sch 15, paras 4–14.
[105] FA 2000, Sch 15, paras 15–33.
[106] FA 2000, Sch 15, para 32.
[107] FA 2000, Sch 15, para 29.
[108] FA 2000, Sch 15, paras 3 and 46
[109] FA 2000, Sch 15, paras 47 and 56.
[110] FA 2000, Sch 15, para 60.

seen for VCTs and EIS apply here too. So FA 2004 allows a subsidiary to be a qualifying subsidiary if it is a 51% subsidiary of the CVS company, although the 90% test applies to a property management subsidiary and to subsidiaries whose activities benefit most from the money raised through the CVS.[111] Some of the 2001 changes to VCTs and EIS, eg rules on ignoring insignificant repayments,[112] had been part of the CVS as first enacted in 2000, but some changes were made to CVS in 2001, eg: (a) the change to the period within which the money raises had to be put to use;[113] and (b) the amendment of the rule on ignoring replacement value when considering whether the benefit of the relief should be withdrawn where the investing company received value from the issuing company.[114]

22.7 Purchased Annuities

There are several types of purchased life annuity, which may be immediate or deferred and may be for life or for a period of years (or a mixture with life but a guaranteed five-year period). Their attraction is that they are an insurance against outliving capital. Their weakness, apart from the risk that the annuitant dies the day after the purchase without any minimum period of payment, is that they will either be eroded by inflation or, if proofed against inflation, will be lower than the purchaser may expect.

22.7.1 Theory and Avoidance

The investment of one's capital in the purchase of an annuity meant that one was buying income with capital and that income tax was therefore due on the whole of each payment received, even though, in commercial reality, one was receiving back each year a part of one's capital together with interest. A number of ways around this all-income treatment were devised. The first, which lasted until 1949, provided for an advance by way of interest-free loan each month, which was to be extinguished by set-off against a capital sum due under the contract on death. The Revenue's argument that these were in substance annual payments was rejected.[115] Such loans are now treated as income.[116] A second way, which still survives, applies to an annuity certain, ie an annuity payable for a stated number of years, not depending on the survival of the annuitant. The Court of Appeal held that tax was chargeable only on so much of the payment as represented interest and not on the whole sum.[117] This split treatment was not accorded to normal annuities, which terminated on the death of the annuitant, and so companies would issue 'split annuities', meaning an annuity certain for a stated number of years, to be followed by a deferred annuity. The

---

[111] FA 2004 does this principally by adding FA 2000, Sch 15, para 21A, and amending paras 5 and 23.
[112] FA 2000, Sch 15, para 57.
[113] Amendment to FA 2000, Sch 15, para 15.
[114] FA 2000, Sch 15, para 54.
[115] *IRC v Wesleyan and General Assurance Society* (1946) 30 TC 11; see *Revenue Law*, §27.3.
[116] TA 1988, s 554.
[117] *Perrin v Dickson* [1930] 1 KB 107, (1930) 14 TC 608; but doubted in *Southern-Smith v Clancey* [1941] 1 All ER 111, (1941) 24 TC 1.

payments under the former annuity would be divided into capital and interest. While the latter would be taxable in full, it was arranged that the sum payable under the contract would be higher and, in any case, the cost of it would be lower in view of the more advanced age of the annuitant.

22.7.2 Current Law—Splitting

The premise that a purchased life annuity is taxed in full is maintained by the charging rule in ITTOIA 2005, Part 4, Chapter 7. This is, however, subject to the partial exemption in Part 6, Chapter 7, which allows splitting and has been part of the law since 1956. Only those who love the Rewrite can understand why these two batches of provisions, consisting of five and eight sections, are separated in this way. The statute includes procedural rules, eg on claims and appeals, and a regulation-making power.[118] The rules in TA 1988, sections 657 *et seq* that formerly applied for corporation tax were repealed by FA 2008 when life insurance contracts were brought into the loan relationship rules. The relevant legislation is now in CTA 2009, Part 6, Chapter 11, sections 560–569. The discussion below focuses on the income tax treatment.

Under the splitting procedure, that part which represents the estimated capital content is exempt from tax and only the balance is income. This approach does not apply where the annuity is already given some relief or is not purchased by the annuitant. An annuity is not split if, apart from Part 6, Chapter 6, it is treated as having a capital element, or if the premiums have qualified for life insurance premium tax relief.[119] Also taxable in full are annuities purchased or provided for under a will or settlement, out of income of property disposed of by the will or settlement (whether with or without resort to capital).[120] Annuities provided under schemes such as those for retirement benefits or personal pensions—under which the contributors have already received tax reliefs—are also outside the apportionment rules, but this is because of the provisions in ITEPA 2003, Part 9 (pension income) which have priority.[121] Apportionments are made if the sums paid are partly for the annuity and partly for other reasons.[122]

The method of apportionment between income and capital—or, as ITTOIA 2005, now puts it, between income and the exempt amount—is carried out by dividing the sum spent by the normal expectation of life according to government mortality tables, regardless of the individual.[123] The rules contain two variables, thus creating four situations. The first variable is whether or not the amount of the annuity depends solely on the duration of a

---

[118] ITTOIA 2005, ss 717, 723 and 724.

[119] ITTOIA 2005, s 718 (2)(a), ex TA 1988, s 657(2).

[120] ITTOIA 2005, ss 718 (2)(b) and (c).

[121] ITTOIA 2005, Pt 4, Ch 1, s 366 and explanatory notes. The same goes for a sum taxable in full under Pt 2 or Pt 10.

[122] ITTOIA 2005, s 722.

[123] The tables are authorised under ITTOIA 2005, s 724, ex TA 1988, s 658; the manner of computing them was put under statutory authority only in 1991 (with retroactive effect) (FA 1991, s 76). The tables must be obeyed (*Rose v Trigg* (1963) 41 TC 365). This is hard, since a person with lower-than-average life expectancy may get special terms from a company.

human life or lives;[124] the second variable is whether the term of the annuity depends solely on the duration of a human life or lives.[125] The four situations are:

- Situation 1: where the amount of the annuity payments depends solely on the duration of a human life or lives. Here the statutes direct how one calculates the exempt proportion.[126]
- Situation 2: where the amount also depends on another contingency. Here each payment is exempt only in so far as it does not exceed a fixed sum; shortfalls in payments may be carried over to other years.[127]
- Situation 3; where the term depends solely on the duration of human life or lives. Here the exempt proportion and the exempt sums are calculated under rules in sections 720 and 721.[128]
- Situation 4: where the term of the annuity depends on other factors too. Here the rules in sections 720 and 721 are applied, and a just and reasonable apportionment is made.[129]

If one spouse, H, transfers an annuity to the other spouse, W, with whom H is living, the transfer will be ineffective for tax purposes since the transfer is of a right to income and so the settlement rules discussed in *Revenue Law*, chapter thirty-one will apply.[130]

If the annuitant cashes in the policy, the same charge to tax may arise as under the chargeable event rules (below §23.5.3).

The calculation of the taxable income element and the tax-free capital element used to be done by HMRC. This is not really appropriate in the days of self-assessment, and so FA 2007, section 46 amended TA 1988, sections 656 and 658, and ITTOIA 2005, sections 717 and 623 remove this HMRC role.

---

[124] ITTOIA 2005, s 719(2)–(5).
[125] ITTOIA 2005, ss 719(2) and (6)–(8).
[126] ITTOIA 2005, s 719(3).
[127] ITTOIA 2005, ss 719(4) and (5).
[128] ITTOIA 2005, ss 719(6) and (7).
[129] ITTOIA 2005, s 719(8).
[130] ITTOIA 2005, s 625(3), ex TA 1988, s 660A(6).

23

Investment Intermediaries

23.1 Introduction

At first sight there should be no need for special legislation to deal with investment companies, and also almost no need for anyone to create such a company. An individual who wishes to hold investments is usually much better advised to hold them directly rather than through a company. Although the corporation tax rate may be lower than the income tax rate, a closely-held investment company cannot use the lower corporation tax rate; money extracted as dividends will be subject to a further layer of tax if the investor is a higher-rate taxpayer, and the close company rules designed to penalise loans may apply. In the unlikely event that money is extracted by way of capital gain, as by the sale of shares, there will be the further problem of a double charge on capital gains already realised by the company. Without special reliefs, the addition of investment intermediaries would mean triple or quadruple taxation of capital gains.

However, this is to see things simply in terms of the individual wealth holder. Investment companies are important parts of the investment market. Some, such as approved investment trusts, open-ended investment companies and approved unit trusts (which are taxed as if they were companies), receive special reliefs from some or all of these consequences. They will not be close companies, and are usually exempt from corporation tax on their profits and gains. This chapter begins with special expenses rule for all investment companies and then considers the specially-approved intermediaries. Reliefs for VCTs and EISs have been mentioned in chapter twenty-two above.

23.2 Management Companies with Investment Business—Deduction of Management Expenses

CTA 2009, Part 16 (ex TA 1988, section 75) allows companies with investment business to deduct certain expenses of management from their profits in addition to those already deductible, eg under CTA 2009, Parts 3 or 4. Pursuant to section 1218, a 'company with investment business' means a company whose business consists wholly or partly of making investments (and is not a credit union).[1] The reason why Part 16 is needed lies in the schedular system. Most revenue expenses incurred in earning trading profits or income from property are deductible from gross receipts in arriving at the net income assessable, under the rules now in CTA 2009, Parts 3 and 4. However, relief was not normally given for expenses incurred in earning investment income, such as company dividends, and interest. TA 1988, section 75 was first introduced in 1915 in response to increased taxation during the First World War; it was substantially amended by FA 2004 which added section 75A and a new section 75.[2] The new rules widened the situations in which expenses may be claimed, and made the timing of the deduction depend on accounting principles and not when the payment is made.

The relief to a 'company with investment business' applies not only to companies whose business consists wholly of making investments, but also to those whose business partly so consists, eg companies which have a trade of their own but also hold shares in subsidiaries. The definition of 'investment company' in TA 1988, section 130 is still there after the Rewrite, as it has a role to play in other rules.[3] In *IRC v Tyre Investment Trust Ltd*,[4] the phrase 'the making of investments' was held to mean 'investing'. It was not necessary for an investment company to buy and sell investments regularly, provided it takes some active interest in the investments which it has made. The asset must be held in order to produce a profitable return and not be merely incidental to some other activity; for this reason a property management company might well not be an investment company.[5] A holding company formed to hold shares in subsidiary companies can be an investment company and can be a company with investment business.[6] The effect of the 2004 change may be seen when considering a trading company deriving income from the investment of large amounts of surplus cash. It will not be an 'investment company' unless it can establish that the main part of its business consists in the making of investments, and the principal part of its income is derived from it. It will, however, be a company with an investment business, and so come within this regime as from 2004.

---

[1] CTA 2009, s 1218, ex TA 1988, s 130.

[2] FA 1915, s 14; later ITA 1918, s 33. On FA 2004, ss 38–46, see Inland Revenue Notes to Clauses 38 *et seq.*

[3] The Revenue Notes, para 26, suggests TA 1988, s 573 (now in CTA 2010, ss 69–73) and the transitional rules in ss 42 and 43.

[4] (1924) 12 TC 646—where the effect of the decision was to bring the company within the charge to Excess Profits Duty.

[5] *100 Palace Gardens Terrace v Winter* [1995] STC (SCD) 126, 129f; distinguished on the facts in *Cook v Medway Housing Society Ltd* [1997] STC 90.

[6] In *IRC v Tyre Investment Trust Ltd* (1924) 12 TC 646, the company was formed to acquire shares in two companies and sell them on. More recently, in *Dawson Group plc v Revenue & Customs Commissioners* [2010] STC 1906, [2010] EWHC 1061 (Ch), Mann J held that a company was an investment company and that certain expenses were not deductible as they were not expenses of management.

23.2.1 Qualifying Expenses of Management

The term 'expenses of management' was not defined by TA 1988, section 75 and has been said to be 'insusceptible of precise definition'.[7] Nevertheless, CTA 2009, section 1219 makes an attempt, describing such expenses as in respect of so much of the company's investment business as consists of making investments that are not held for an allowable purpose. Capital expenditure is not deductible.[8] These will include staff costs, indirect costs, including repairs to equipment, legal and other professional fees,[9] and property maintenance costs, including rents, rates, maintenance and repairs of premises occupied for business purposes. Sums paid to purchase investments are not management expenses since they are part of the costs of buying investments, not managing them. However, it does not follow that only expenses incurred in the function and process of management may qualify. Relief is available for expenditure incurred in evaluating an investment, such as the legal costs of investigating title, as well as for expenditure on an abortive investment. Judges have indicated that a broad view may be taken of what is an (allowable) expense of investigation as opposed to a (non-allowable) expense of acquisition.[10] In an ideal world one might think that an expense was either an expense of management allowable under this rule, or an expense allowable for capital gains under TCGA 1992 rules. The pre-2004 version of section 75 expressly included commissions;[11] today the matter is left to general principles.

Among the items that will not qualify are capital expenditure, entertainment expenditure, other specifically barred payments, such as bribes, and losses on the disposal of investments.[12] In addition, the expense must not be in respect of an investment held for an unallowable purpose, a phrase defined as a purpose which is not a business or commercial purpose of the company, or for the purpose of activities which are outside the charge to corporation tax.[13] Following Revenue guidance, one may say that 'unallowable purposes' therefore covers social or recreational purposes. The insistence that the investment be within the charge to corporation tax means that an investment held by a non-resident company with a UK PE will qualify if the management is part of the activities of the PE of a company, but not otherwise. Expenses of a members' club will not qualify since the club is outside the charge to tax by reason of mutuality.[14]

These rules now have their own anti-avoidance provision. Expenses are excluded if the main purpose (or one of the main purposes) of incurring the expense or of surrounding arrangements is to obtain a tax advantage.[15] Where both this rule and that on manufactured payments apply, this rule has precedence.[16]

---

[7] *Sun Life Assurance Society v Davidson* [1958] AC 184, 196; 37 TC 330, 354, *per* Viscount Simonds.

[8] CTA 2009, s 1219(3), ex TA 1988, s 75(3) added to reverse the Court of Appeal decision in *Camas v Atkinson* [2004] STC 860. Draft Guidance on these changes, and in particular the exclusion of capital expenditure, is discussed in a Revenue Guidance Note, 15 June 2004, [2004] *Simon's Tax Intelligence* 1472.

[9] *Holdings Ltd v IRC* [1997] STC (SCD) 144.

[10] Carnwath LJ in *Camas v Atkinson*, above, para 32.

[11] TA 1988, s 75, but not everything called a commission qualifies (see *Hoechst Finance Ltd v Gumbrell* [1983] STC 150, (1983) 56 TC 594).

[12] Unless CTA 2010, ss 68–71, ex TA 1988, s 573 applies—certain losses on the disposal of shares in unquoted trading companies.

[13] CTA 2009, s 1220, ex TA 1988, s 75(3) and (5). These words are becoming common, see eg the loan relationships legislation in chapter 5, above.

[14] Revenue Notes to Clauses 39 *et seq*, paras 14–16.

[15] CTA 2009, s 1220(2)–(5), ex TA 1988, s 75, as amended by FA 2007, s 28, for accounting periods beginning after 19 June 2007.

[16] Ie CTA 2010, s 799, ex TA 1988, Sch 23A, para 7A.

23.2.1.1 Dual Purpose

There is no requirement that expenses must be 'wholly and exclusively' incurred for the purposes of the company's business. Apportionment of expenditure is therefore possible. In particular, if expenditure is excessive, only amounts reasonably incurred will qualify as expenses of management.[17]

23.2.1.2 Relief

Relief is given by deducting expenses of management first from income not otherwise charged to tax as held in the course of the company's investment activities.[18] The balance of expenses remaining is then deducted from other income and chargeable gains of the company. Expenditure still unrelieved may be carried forward, without time limit, against future income, from whatever source, of the company,[19] or it may be relieved by way of group relief.[20] Excess management expenses, unlike trading losses, cannot be carried back to previous accounting periods.

Since 2004 the expense must be 'referable to an accounting period' as opposed to the earlier 'disbursed'. The rules for this are set out in sections 1224–1227, the basic one being when an expense is debited in the company's accounts in accordance with GAAP.[21] Because this means that an expense may be allowed before it is paid, the rules provide for a charge to tax to arise where sums have been credited in the accounts to reverse a previous deduction, eg section 1228.

Restrictions are imposed on the carry-forward of unused expenses where there has been a change in the ownership of a company with an investment business. In addition to the usual references to increases in the scale of the company's activities or revival from quiescence, the rules refer to a 'significant increase' in the amount of the company's capital. There is a 'significant increase' in the amount of an investment company's capital if, in the three years after the change of ownership, the company's capital is either at least double, or greater by £1 million than, the amount of capital before the change.[22] The rules also aim to prevent avoidance by the manipulation of capital at or around the time of the change of ownership.

23.2.2 *Investment Dealing Companies*

If the company crosses the line to become an investment dealing company, its profits will be computed under the trading rules in CTA 2009, Part 3 (ex Schedule D, Case I principles). However (since 1997), it has had to treat a dividend or other qualifying distribution falling within ex TA 1988, section 209 as arising under its trade and not under ex Schedule F to prevent tax credit being used in various ways under the old corporation tax system.[23]

---

[17] *LG Berry Investment Ltd v Attwooll* [1964] 2 All ER 126, (1964) 41 TC 547; see also *Fragmap Developments Ltd v Cooper* (1967) 44 TC 366.

[18] CTA 2009, s 1219–1222, ex TA 1988, s 75(6).

[19] CTA 2009, s 1223, ex TA 1988, ss 75(8) and (9).

[20] CTA 2010, ss 99(1)(f), (4), 103 and 105(1)–(4), ex TA 1988, s 403(4), (5).

[21] CTA 2009, s 1225, ex TA 1988, s 75A(2).

[22] CTA 2010, s 672 *et seq*, and in particular s 682, ex TA 1988, s 768B and Sch 28A, Pt I, added in 1995 and updated by FA 2004, Sch 6.

[23] Ex TA 1988, s 95.

23.3   Unit Trusts and Open-ended Investment Companies

Unit trusts and open-ended investment companies (OEICs) operate in the same sector of the market; both provide a form of pooled investment. Unit trusts have been established for many years; OEICs are a relatively recent invention. Some unit trust managers are changing from unit trust status to OEICs, presumably in the hope of attracting more clients through greater clarity and lower costs. For investors, the biggest difference concerns pricing. Unit trusts offer a dual pricing system, with an offer price and a bid price—'offer' for sale to the client and 'bid' to buy from the client. Shares in an OEIC will have only one price, with the costs of buying and selling appearing as separate items on the transaction. There are, however, other differences, for example one is a trust and the other is a company.

23.3.1 Unit Trusts[24]

Unit trusts are trusts in the strict legal sense of the word, and operate in accordance with the terms of their trust deed. The trustee is usually a bank or an insurance company, but the management of the trust is carried on by a separate management company. The unit holders are simply beneficiaries under the trust whose rights are regulated by the trust deed. Unit holders dispose of their units by selling them to the trust manager at a price equal to asset value, less a small discount. The manager may either hold the units for sale to an investor, or it may sell them back to the trustee, when they are cancelled. It follows that there is no 'discount' as there is for shares in an investment trust; equally, because the trust is not allowed to borrow, there is no 'gearing'.

23.3.1.1 Authorised Unit Trust[25]

An authorised unit trust is treated, in relation to income received by the trustees, as though it were a UK-resident company, and as if the units were shares in the company.[26] Profits consist of income less expenses of management. Capital gains are not chargeable to tax.[27] Corporation tax is charged at a rate equal to the basic rate of income tax, ie 20%.[28] CTA 2009, section 1218, allowing the deduction of management expenses, applies whether or not the trust would be accompanied by investment business within section 1219. Some unit trusts operate under an umbrella scheme, under which unit holders may switch from one type of unit to another. Although the different funds are treated as one for the purposes of the Financial Services Act 1986, each must be taken separately for tax purposes.[29]

 HMRC v Smallwood[30] shed light on the intricacies of TCGA 1992, sections 38, 39, 41 and 99 in the context of unit trusts. The taxpayer, T, subscribed £10,000 for units in an enterprise zone property unit trust. Capital allowances of 100% were available for money

---

[24] See Leslie, *Tolley's Tax Planning 2007–08*, ch 6.
[25] Financial Services Act 1986, s 78. The relevant tax rules are in CTA 2010, Pt 13, Ch 2, ss 616–619, ex TA 1988, s 468(6). ITTOIA 2005, ss 389–391.
[26] CTA 2010, s 617, ex TA 1988, s 468.
[27] TCGA 1992, s 100(1).
[28] CTA 2010, s 618, ex TA 1988, s 468(1A), added in 1996; immediately before 1996 it had been the basic rate, the change marking the introduction of the lower rate for basic- and lower-rate taxpayers.
[29] CTA 2010, s 619(3), ex TA 1988, s 468(7)–(9), added in 1994 and TCGA 1992, s 99A added by FA 2004, s 118.
[30] [2007] EWCA Civ 462, [2007] STC 1237.

invested in buildings (£9,678), which T claimed as a deduction against his general income for 1988-89. Ten years later T received distributions of £5,000 and £125, which were treated as part disposals of his holding and generated a capital loss of £4,865. The Court of Appeal held that because section 99 deemed the relevant asset to be the shares in the unit trust, the capital allowances given in respect of the buildings were not relevant to the calculation of the loss under sections 38 and 39. As a result, the Revenue's challenge failed. Sedley LJ remarked that he had an uncomfortable sense that the taxpayer was doing better than he should out of the tax system.

23.3.1.2 Income Distributions

The tax treatment of income distributed or available for distribution by an authorised unit trust to its unit holders depends on what the trustees want to do. The trust may treat the distribution as:

(1)   a franked payment under ITTOIA 2005, Part 4, Chapter 3, referred to as a 'dividend distribution';[31] or
(2)   an interest distribution under ITTOIA 2005, Part 4, Chapter 2, ie yearly interest subject to deduction of basic rate income tax at source (referred to as an 'interest distribution').[32]

The choice is restricted, in that (2) may be chosen only if the trust has sufficient (60%) of its investments in relevant securities. The purpose of (2), introduced in 1994, is to enable the UK-based bond and money funds to compete on roughly equal terms with Continental counterparts.

23.3.1.3 Unauthorised Unit Trust

This is taxed as a trust.[33] In the first instance, income received is taxed as the income of the trustees, who are liable to pay income tax on it at basic rate.[34] Actual distributions of income to unit holders are deemed to have been paid as annual payments under deduction of income tax at the basic rate;[35] any income not actually distributed at the end of the accounting period is treated as having been distributed on that date. ITTOIA 2005 rewrote the distribution part of these rules for income tax.[36] One minor mistake made by ITTOIA 2005 was corrected as from 6 April 2008.[37]

FA 2010, section 490 and Schedule 13 added ITA 2007, sections 943A–943D to prevent tax loss through conversion of foreign income subject to withholding tax into associated UK dividends (with tax credits).

---

[31] ITTOIA 2005, s 389.
[32] ITTOIA 2005, s 376.
[33] CTA 2010, ss 621–622, ex TA 1988, s 469(1).
[34] CTA 2010, s 621, ex TA 1988, s 469(2).
[35] ITA 2007, s 941, ex TA 1988, s 469(3), (4); on CGT consequence, see TCGA 1992, s 100(2).
[36] ITTOIA 2005, Pt 4, Ch 11, ex TA 1988, s 469(3)–(6).
[37] FA 2008, s 66.

23.3.2 *Open-ended Investment Companies*[38]

FA 1995 made provision for the taxation of OEICs;[39] the rules have been rewritten in CTA 2010, sections 612–615. These companies are open-ended in that their shares may be continuously created or redeemed depending on the net demand by investors. As with existing authorised unit trusts (and unlike investment trusts), the transactions will be undertaken at a price derived from the net asset value of the OEIC's underlying investments.[40] These companies are common elsewhere in the EU, where they are used for a variety of purposes; in the UK, however, it seems that they will be permitted only as collective investment vehicles. Broadly, the investor buys redeemable share capital in the company, and realises the value either by selling the shares to another person or by requiring the company to redeem them.

An OEIC is taxed in broadly the same way as unit trusts.[41] There is no charge on the OEIC in respect of capital gains, and income is subject to tax at the basic rate.[42] The shareholders are taxed each year on the full net income earned for them (whether or not distributed).[43] A unit trust may convert itself into an OEIC without incurring a tax charge on the transfer.[44] FA 2005 authorises the Revenue to rationalise the provisions on OEICs by regulation.[45]

23.4 Investment Trusts[46]

An investment trust is a company, not a trust. It has share capital and wide powers of investment, although these are usually narrowed to achieve 'approved investment trust' status in the eyes of the Revenue. The company will usually be prohibited from trading in securities. The form is very flexible, and investment trusts therefore range from conservative to the exotic. Some trusts issue only ordinary shares, but others offer split capital trusts which may be repaid at different dates. Some trusts offer income, others only a capital sum on redemption. ISAs may invest in investment trusts only if the trusts meet certain conditions, eg that at least one half of the shares are ordinary shares in EU-resident companies.

The ordinary shares in the investment trust company may be bought and sold on the stock exchange. Because of the way companies are structured, the price paid for the shares is at a discount to the value of the underlying securities; this discount applies equally when the shares come to be sold. This means that in a declining stock market the discount may get greater; such discount will be exacerbated if the investment trust has borrowed money

---

[38] See Leslie, *op cit*, 1323. Also, more generally, Grimmett in Wright, *Zurich Investment and Savings Handbook 2004–05* (Zurich, 2004), ch 8.

[39] FA 1995, s 152.

[40] [1994] *Simon's Tax Intelligence* 1492.

[41] CTA 2010, ss 614–615, ex FA 1995, s 152(1), ITTOIA 2005, ss 373–375 (interest payments) and 386–389 (dividend distributions).

[42] CTA 2010, s 614 and TCGA 1992, s 99. Ex TA 1988, s 468A1 added by F(No 2)A 2005, s 17.

[43] ITTOIA 2005, ss 386 *et seq*; Open-ended Investment Companies (Tax) Regulations 1997 (SI 1997/1154).

[44] Open-ended Investment Companies (Tax) Regulations 1997 (SI 1997/1154), reg 25.

[45] F(No 2)A 2005, ss 17–19.

[46] Macleod [1994] BTR 111; Watson and Bullock, *Tolley's Tax Planning 2007–08*, ch 33.

(through debentures) to finance purchases. If the company has borrowed a relatively large sum of money it is said to be highly geared (in US terminology, 'highly leveraged'). In the conventional part of the UK investment trust industry, gearing of 10–15% is moderate, and 30% or more is high.[47] Investors wishing to avoid the risks of discounting and gearing may prefer unit trusts.

If an investment company is an approved investment trust, it is allowed to switch its investments without worrying about capital gains liability; the company is exempt.[48] All other income of the company is taxed in the usual way. The shareholders will pay tax on any income they receive from the company in the usual way. If the company has 'approved' status, its memorandum and articles of association must prohibit the distribution by way of dividend of surpluses arising on the realisation of investments. The exemption from CGT for the company does not extend to the shareholders.

An approved investment trust must meet various conditions: it must be UK resident; it must not be a 'close' company; every class of its ordinary share capital must be quoted on a recognised stock exchange; and its income must be derived wholly or mainly from shares or securities. The Revenue regard this final condition as satisfied if 70% of gross income, before expenses, is so derived.[49] Further, the company must not retain, for any accounting period, more than 15% of the income it derives[50] from shares and securities (or, if greater, £10,000).[51] In general, no holding of shares and securities in a company must represent more than 15% by value of the investing company's investments.[52]

FA 2009, section 45 granted the Treasury regulation-making power, duly exercised,[53] to give these companies the option to treat dividends as distributions of interest instead. This treatment shifts the tax point from the company to the shareholder and makes investment by such companies in interest-bearing assets more efficient. It also means no accompanying tax credit and tax at 40% rather than 32.5% for higher-rate taxpayers.

23.5 Insurance Policies

23.5.1 Introduction

Life assurance presents the UK tax system with various problems. First, the funds held by insurance companies are huge. Assets held by UK insurance companies and pension funds in 2010 came to £2,599 billion, of which £1,010 billion were in securities other than shares, £368 billion in UK company securities, £468 billion in UK mutual fund shares, £430 billion in non-UK companies and £152 billion in loans.[54] Secondly, those funds are held for a variety

---

[47] Wright, *Zurich Investment and Savings Handbook 2004–05, op cit*, para 7.6.5.
[48] TCGA 1992, ss 100, 288.
[49] By agreement with the Association of Investment Trust Companies.
[50] This rule does not apply to income, which cannot be distributed because of a legal restriction.
[51] CTA 2010, s 1161 and ITA 2007, s 276; ex TA 1988, s 842(2A)–(2C) inserted by FA 1990, s 55.
[52] This condition does not apply where the holding, when it was acquired, was worth no more than 15% of the then value of the investing company's investments; the 15% condition does not apply if the company is itself an investment trust—or would be if its ordinary share capital were quoted. On unit trusts, see Statement of Practice SP 5/91.
[53] Investment Trusts (Dividends) (Optional Treatment as Interest Distributions) Regulations, SI 2009/2034.
[54] See National Accounts (Office for National Statistics, 2011), Table 4.4.9.

of purposes—of which some are long-term, known as 'life business', eg pensions, annuities and life assurance, while others are short-term, known as 'general business', eg motor, accident and property. Various types of business are recognised for tax purposes.[55] Thirdly, some of the companies are 'mutual', ie all the profits accrue to the members of the company (ie the policyholders), as opposed to 'proprietary' where profits are shared between the policyholder members and the owners of the company (the shareholders). It is noteworthy that in the last decade a number of companies have moved from mutual to proprietary status. While some of the arguments are controversial, it is beyond doubt that among the effects of the change have often been large pay increases for those who previously ran the companies but continue to do so. Members were bribed with their own money to enable other people to make more—a very odd result, but typical of its time. The subsequent need to divide the profits of the company between shareholders and policyholders has exacerbated the decline in returns on investments in this sector.

Lastly, while the principles of taxation of these companies were originally worked out on the basis of established principles, recent years have seen ever more precise tranches of legislation to secure for the UK a proper share of the profits of an increasingly international business.

Much of the language of insurance—and so of insurance taxation—is unique or, if one prefers, obscure.[56] However, certain basic distinctions need to be borne in mind. First, there is the distinction between assurance and insurance. Under an *assurance* contract, a sum of money will definitely become payable, the only question is when, eg at age 60 or on prior death; under an *insurance* contract, the sum will become payable only if the event occurs, eg if rain forces the cancellation of a cricket match. This is close to, but not identical with, the distinction between life business and general business.

In connection with life policies of assurance it is customary to talk of 'endowment policies' (with a strong savings element), under which the sum will be payable at a certain age or on prior death, of 'whole life policies' (payable only on death) and of 'term' or 'temporary' policies of insurance, under which the sum is paid only if the person dies within the term of years specified. These three categories reflect the different ways of achieving the basic goals of life assurance, which are the provision of capital for later years and protection of the family against premature loss of the contribution (whether financial or in kind) of the life assured. Endowment policies are often 'with profits'. Here the policyholder receives not only the sum assured, but also a share of the profits earned by the company in the intervening years. Profits may be attached to the policy each year, called 'reversionary' or 'annual' bonuses, in which case they become guaranteed to be paid when the assured is paid. They may also be declared on the termination of the policy, when they are called 'terminal' bonuses. Because of the success of the stock market in the 1980s and 1990s, these profits could be very substantial and might be three or four times the sum originally assured. These were often linked with mortgages, in which the building society lent the borrower the sum originally assured. Because house prices rose very fast, endowment policies became an expensive way of borrowing; as a cost-cutting expedient, people would borrow a sum and take out a policy on which the sum assured would be less than the sum borrowed, in the hope that the profits would bridge the gap. These 'lean' or low-cost

---

[55] TA 1988, ss 431–431F, 458.
[56] For a glossary, see a general work such as Wright, *Zurich Investment and Savings Handbook 2004–05, op cit.*

endowment options came unstuck when the bonuses declined along with the stock market. A second form is the 'without-profit' policy—naturally, the premiums on these were lower than for with-profits policies. A third form began as an alternative to with-profits policies; companies began to offer unit-linked polices, which would still offer sums assured, but the money not needed to cover that risk was put directly into units instead of being placed in a large pot. The policyholder could see the value of the units each day of the week. The choice between these was matter of temperament and need. What the story shows is the flexibility of the life assurance policy as an element of prudent financial management. What the story, as told so far, does not show is the lack of flexibility which stems from the essence of these as long-term arrangements; they suit the investment patterns of civil servants or academics rather than entrepreneurs in that they reward regular saving. While the policy could be cancelled by surrendering to the assurance company, there were major financial disadvantages—not only would those terminal bonuses be missed out on, but the sum received back from the company would, in the early years, be much less than the sums already contributed. This reduction would occur because of the sums paid by way of commission to an agent, eg £4,000 out of £75,000 paid for a single premium policy.

From the point of view of the tax system, life assurance began as a good thing and attracted a special relief for premiums. By 1984, the industry was competing in the investment and savings market with its products, and the Chancellor saw it as competing unfairly because of the tax relief.[57] The relief was stopped for new policies. Already, however, the tax system had felt it necessary to counter certain dealings in the first 10 years of a life policy—these rules remain in place and concern policies which do not meet certain criteria (non-qualifying policies); these rules were rewritten by ITTOIA 2005.

Today, the question whether an individual investor should use these products depends, so far as tax is concerned, on whether the investor pays tax at or above the higher rate, and whether the policy is a qualifying policy.[58] The advantage of the qualifying policy is that there is no income tax or CGT charge on the policy itself and the company pays tax at a rate below 40%; income tax will be charged on most transactions involving non-qualifying policies, however, and on some transactions involving qualifying policies. Premium relief for pre-1984 policies applied only to qualifying policies.

The UK tax system accords special treatment to the life insurance industry. The pre-1984 income tax relief on premiums remains in force, for now, for existing policies, although the Government announced at Budget 2011 that it intends to abolish this relief. A special system of taxing income and gains applies to insurance companies. Other companies may find a life policy useful as way of investing surplus funds.[59]

The legislation talks a great deal of qualifying and non-qualifying policies. The advantages of qualifying policies are that there may be some tax relief on the premiums (if the policy was taken out before 1984) and that the proceeds are tax-free if maintained for at least 10 years (or three-quarters of its term) and the policy has not been paid up within that period. Non-qualifying policies do not attract premium relief and are subject to charges on the occurrence of various chargeable events whenever they may be. Whether the policy is qualifying or non-qualifying, there is no charge to income tax on the policyholder while the

---

[57] See Lawson, *The View from No 11: Memoirs of a Tory Radical* (Bantam Press, 1992) 355–56.
[58] Potter and Monroe, *Tax Planning* (Sweet & Maxwell, 1982) §5-01.
[59] Wright, *Zurich Investment and Savings Handbook 2004–05, op cit*, para 14.3.7.

policy continues intact. There is also an exemption from CGT on a disposal by the original beneficial owner or an assignee otherwise than for value. The 10-year rule has become relevant recently where people have under-invested in 'lean' endowment policies in connection with mortgages and are invited to increase their premiums in the last 10 years of the policy.

Lastly, it should be noted that the special income tax and CGT rules applicable to life insurance policies have been targeted by tax avoidance schemes (see also *Revenue Law*, §43.2). In *Drummond v Revenue & Customs Commissioners*,[60] the taxpayer (D) carried out a CGT loss avoidance scheme. D had bought a second-hand life policy in 2001 for £1.962 million. He then surrendered the policy and obtained its surrender value of £1.75 million (based on the premiums paid); the surrender cost him £210,000. He claimed, invoking TCGA 1992, section 37, that in calculating his gain he could exclude the £1.75 million of surrender value from the proceeds of sale because this was liable to the special rules for income tax in TA 1988, section 541. This would leave him with the large loss now claimed. Today this would be countered by TGCA 1992, section 16A, added in 2007. The Court of Appeal held that this was not a correct application of section 37. Rimer LJ was not going to be party to any 'black letter literalism' (paragraph 23); the purpose of these rules was to avoid double taxation and not to avoid tax altogether.

23.5.2 Income Tax Relief for Premiums on Pre-14 March 1984 Policies

23.5.2.1 The Relief

As just noted, the Government announced at Budget 2011 that it intends to abolish this relief, which remains in TA 1988 and was not rewritten. As things currently stand, the claimant, T, is entitled to deduct from the premium a sum equal to 12.5% of the premium;[61] thus, if the premium is £100, the actual payment is £87.50. There is a ceiling of £1,500, or one-sixth of total income, whichever is the greater.[62] When T receives the commission in respect of the policy, the 12.5% deduction must be applied to the net sum paid.[63] A premium is paid even if the payer borrows the money to pay it, and even if the lender is the insurer.[64]

The policy must be on the life of T or T's spouse, or on their joint lives;[65] it must secure a capital sum payable on death, whether or not in connection with other benefits, so that a temporary term policy is not eligible.[66]

23.5.2.2 'Qualifying' Policy[67]

The purpose of these conditions is to ensure that premiums are paid each year and with a reasonably even spread. Although aimed at the single premium policy, the rules go much wider. For endowment assurances the term must be at least 10 years. The premiums must

---

[60] [2009] EWCA Civ 608, [2009] STC 2206.
[61] TA 1988, s 266, not rewritten.
[62] TA 1988, s 274.
[63] CCAB Press Release, 26 April 1977, [1977] *Simon's Tax Intelligence* 97.
[64] Certain borrowings may be treated as income (TA 1988, s 554).
[65] TA 1988, s 266(2)(b); on year of marriage, see s 280.
[66] TA 1988, s 266(3)(a), but note exceptions in *ibid*.
[67] The rules were relaxed for certain industrial insurance policies (TA 1988, Sch 15, para 7), but these policies have fallen into disfavour. ITTOIA 2005 rewrites para 20 on replacement of qualifying policies (see ITTOIA 2005, s 542), but only for income tax.

be payable at yearly or shorter intervals for at least 10 years or until the event specified, whether death or disability. The total premiums payable under the policy in any period of 12 months must not exceed twice the amount payable in any other 12-month period, or one-eighth of the total premiums payable if the policy were to run for the specified term.

The policy must guarantee that the sum payable on death will be at least 75%[68] of the total premiums payable if the policy were to run its term. Broadly similar principles apply to whole life and term assurances.[69] A temporary assurance for a period of not more than 10 years may be a qualifying policy, but only if the surrender value is not to exceed the total premiums previously paid. A term policy of less than 12 months cannot be a qualifying policy.[70]

The legislation also contains a number of special rules. Any exceptional mortality risk is disregarded.[71] A policy issued in connection with another policy cannot qualify if either policy provides unreasonable benefits.[72] Certain policies issued outside the UK are treated as non-qualifying; they may become 'qualifying' policies subsequently.[73] At one time the issuing life assurance company had to certify that a policy was a qualifying policy, but this was changed with effect from 5 May 1996. Today, under the self-assessment regime, tax-payers must report gains from non-qualifying policies on their tax returns.[74] Special rules apply to determine whether a policy is a qualifying policy where one policy is substituted for another or the terms of a policy are varied.[75] Some variations of terms are prevented from having this effect.[76]

23.5.2.3 Clawback of Relief

These rules apply only to qualifying life policies issued after 26 March 1974 but before 14 March 1984. Some, applied only to the first four years of existence, are not of current interest;[77] their purpose was to prevent the taxpayer from realising a quick profit due simply to the tax relief obtained. Events more than four years after the issue of the policy give rise to clawback only if two conditions are satisfied:[78]

(1) that the event is either—
    (a) the surrender of the whole or part of the rights conferred by the policy, or
    (b) the falling due (other than on death or maturity) of a sum payable in pursuance of a right conferred by the policy to participants in profits; and
(2) that either of these events has already happened, whether more or less than four years after the issue of the policy.

---

[68] There is a 2% reduction for every year by which the person exceeds 55 years of age (TA 1988, Sch 15, para 2(1)(d)(i)). The conditions imposed by FA 1975 apply to policies issued after the appointed day, 1 April 1976.

[69] There is no relaxation for those over 55, including the 75% rule, unless the policy makes no provision for payment on surrender and the term does not run beyond age 75. Where the capital sum may be taken as a single sum or a series of sums, the 75% rule is applied to the smallest sum that may be taken—an obvious anti-avoidance measure (TA 1988, Sch 15, para 1(9)).

[70] TA 1988, Sch 15, para 10.

[71] TA 1988, Sch 15, para 12.

[72] TA 1988, Sch 15, para 14.

[73] TA 1988, Sch 15, para 24.

[74] FA 1995, s 55; replacing old certification system in paras 21and 22.

[75] TA 1988, Sch 15, para 25.

[76] FA 2006, s 87, amending TA 1988, Sch 15, para 18(3)—the change in the method of calculating returns on qualifying policy does not cause a charge.

[77] TA 1988, s 268.

[78] TA 1988, s 269.

The effect of (2) is one may make a single such arrangement—but not two. Its purpose is to prevent the payment of premiums out of the proceeds of periodic partial surrenders.[79]

The sum clawed back is the lesser of 12.5% of (a) the total premiums payable during the year of assessment, and (b) the sums payable on surrender or otherwise falling due.[80]

23.5.3 Sums Payable on Chargeable Events: Liability to Tax in Excess of Basic Rate—Non-qualifying Policies

The investments caught by these rules are not only life insurance policies, but also contracts for life annuities and capital redemption policies.[81] However, many areas of life insurance are excluded from these rules. These are certain older policies, mortgage repayment policies, pension policies, exempt group life policies and credit union life policies.[82] Some reliefs apply only for qualifying policies, while further rules apply to portfolio bonds (see §23.6) and foreign policies and contracts.[83] It is here that ITTOIA 2005 has rewritten the rules—but only for income tax. TA1988, sections 539–554 have been replaced by ITTOIA 2005, Part 4, Chapter 9, sections 461–566. The rules as they formerly applied for corporation tax were repealed by FA 2008 when life insurance contracts were brought into the loan relationship rules.[84] The relevant legislation is now in CTA 2009, Part 6, Chapter 11, sections 560–569. The brief account which follows focuses on income tax and is intended very much as an introductory outline.

The purpose here is to charge the policyholder on profits made by the insurance company for the policyholder and passed to the holder in some form (including a loan), notwithstanding that the company will already have paid tax on the profits;[85] there is no indexation relief. However, in broad terms, the charge applies to non-qualifying policies at any time and to qualifying policies only within a certain period. There is usually a charge only to the extent that a rate higher than basic rate is due from the holder; top-slicing relief may reduce that burden further.

Examples of such policies are single premium property bonds and policies; the rules do not apply to mortgage protection policies, retirement annuity policies or to policies forming part of pension schemes. At present these are charged to tax at $(40 - 20)\% = 20\%$. Chargeable events are death, maturity, surrender, assignment for money or money's worth and the drawing-down of money by way of payment or loan in excess of permitted limits.[86]

The rules are softened for qualifying policies. In the case of death and maturity, the charge arises only if the policy is converted into a paid-up policy before the expiry of 10 years from the making of the insurance or, if earlier, three-quarters of the term for which the policy was to run if not ended by death or disability (no charges arises on the surrender of a 12-year policy after nine years). In the case of the other events, the question

---

[79] Inland Revenue Press Release, 10 December 1974, [1974] *Simon's Tax Intelligence* 518.

[80] TA 1988, s 269(2); if there is more than one event, s 269(3) applies.

[81] ITTOIA 2005, s 473(1).

[82] ITTOIA 2005, ss 477–483.

[83] ITTOIA 2005, ss 474–476.

[84] See HMRC Explanatory Notes to Finance Bill 2008, cl 33 and Schs 13 and 14.

[85] However, companies are able to defer realisations of assets over a long period—as their many investments in office buildings and shopping centres show.

[86] ITTOIA 2005, s 484, ex TA 1988, s 540(1)(a).

is simply whether those events have occurred within that same 10-year or three-quarter time-frame.[87] No charge arises for a qualifying policy simply because the death occurred within 10 years—dealing is also needed.

Tax at higher rates may be applied if the company's profits will not have been charged to UK tax.[88] Where a non-resident individual who owns a non-resident policy becomes resident in the UK, any tax charge arising, subsequently, on the non-resident policy will be limited, proportionally, to the period of UK residence.

When a charge arises, ITTOIA 2005, section 530 treats basic rate income tax as paid. ITA 2007, sections 152 and 153 deal with losses arising (ex Schedule D Case VI). According to the HMRC Notes on Clauses, schemes tried to 'create loss relief from offshore life insurance policies against offshore income gains'. This was stopped by FA 2009, section 69 amending ITA 2007, section 125(8), which directs that gains from polices, etc, whether foreign or not, will not be eligible for claiming income tax loss relief. Some parts apply from 2008–09 (section 69(3)).

23.5.3.1 Chargeable Events[89]

The chargeable events are:

(1)   death giving rise to benefits under a life policy;[90]

(2)   maturity of the policy;[91]

(3)   total surrender[92] of the rights under the policy including bonus;[93] and

(4)   assignment of the rights for money or money's worth.[94] However, an assignment between spouses living together is ignored, as is an assignment by way of security for a debt or the discharge of a debt secured by the rights under the policy.[95]

Rules have been added to deal with rebated or reinvested commissions.[96]

23.5.3.2 Calculating the Charge by Calculating the Gain[97]

On death, the gain is the amount by which the surrender value immediately before the death,[98] plus what TA 1988 called the 'relevant capital payments' and ITTOIA 2005 calls

---

[87] ITTOIA 2005, s 485, ex TA 1988, s 540(1)(b).

[88] ITTOIA 2005, s 530, ex TA 1988, s 547(6) as amended; sometimes only the 20% charge applies (s 547(6A), added in 1995).

[89] ITTOIA 2005, s 462 and 484, ex TA 1988, s 540(1); s 540(3), preserved by ITTOIA 2005, Sch 2, para 53, had a transitional exception for certain second-hand bonds issued before 1982. Liability in respect of such bonds may still arise (see s 544 and ITTOIA 2005, Sch 2, para 53).

[90] ITTOIA 2005, s 484(1)(b).

[91] Ex TA 1988, s 540(2) allowed a deferral of liability if a replacement policy was taken out, but this was repealed by FA 2003, s 173 and Sch 34, Pt 4. No chargeable event arises where a qualifying policy is substituted for a new non-resident policy (*ibid*, Sch 15, para 26).

[92] On when events are treated as part surrender, see ITTOIA 2005, s 500, ex TA 1988, ss 539(4), 542(2) and 548(1). See Explanatory Note Change 100.

[93] Payment of a bonus may be treated as a surrender (ITTOIA 2005, s 500, ex TA 1988, s 539(4)), as may loans (see below).

[94] ITTOIA 2005, s 484(1)(a)(ii), ex TA 1988, s 540(1).

[95] ITTOIA 2005, s 487, ex TA 1988, s 540(4).

[96] ITTOIA 2005, ss 541A and 541B, ex TA 1988, ss 548A and 548B, added by FA 2007, s 29. Changes affect policies only where the premiums paid exceed £100,000 a year (there is a nice anti-fragmentation rule) and the policy is not held for at least three complete years. The rules are aimed at schemes described in the Revenue Notes.

[97] See also ITTOIA 2005, s 476, ex TA 1988, s 553(3) for certain foreign policies.

[98] ITTOIA 2005, s 493(7).

'compendiously total benefit value', such as bonuses, exceeds the total amount paid by way of premiums, plus any sums already treated as gains on some previous partial surrender or assignment.[99] These provisions are backed up by five further sections containing rules on valuing the policy, calculating the deductions, disregarding certain amounts, a special rule on qualifying endowment policies held as securities for a company's debts and—an ITTOIA 2005 innovation—a rule expressly disregarding trivial inducement benefits.[100] These basic rules also apply on maturity or surrender in whole, and on an outright assignment.[101]

Partial surrenders[102] and partial assignments are also chargeable events. Many modern policies allow partial surrenders at frequent intervals, and such surrenders gave rise to complex calculations. In an attempt to reduce the work involved, both for life offices and the Revenue, a different system of determining both whether there has been a gain and its extent applies.[103] At one time partial assignments were chargeable events only if for money or money's worth, but this was changed in 2001.[104]

The chargeable amount under TA 1988 was the excess of 'reckonable aggregate value', ie the sum of all the values of surrender and assignments not brought into account,[105] over 'allowable aggregate amount',[106] ie the sum of all appropriate portions of premiums paid.[107] The effect of these rules was to allow withdrawals of up to 5% of premiums paid without attracting any charge. This 5% drawdown was of great practical importance. In ITTOIA 2005 these rules are greatly spread out. They start with rules for events requiring periodic calculations, such as part surrender and assignments (including certain loans),[108] and then provide the relevant calculation rules.[109] These are followed by further rules for 'transaction-related' calculations; these calculations are required only if the first set of calculations produces a particular situation.[110]

23.5.3.3 Relief by Top-slicing

Individuals may claim top-slicing relief, a process which first requires the calculation of the slice of the gain, which is now called the 'annual equivalent' of the gain.[111] To do this the gain is spread back over a number of years by multiplying it by one over the number of complete years (a) on the first chargeable event—back to the start of the policy, (b) on any later chargeable event other than final termination—back to the previous chargeable event, (c) on final termination—the number of whole years from the start of the policy.[112]

---

[99] ITTOIA 2005, ss 491(1), 493 (1), ex TA 1988, s 541(1)(a).

[100] ITTOIA 2005, ss 492–497.

[101] ITTOIA 2005, s 491(1)(a) refers to events within s 484(1)(a)(i)–(iii) and (b)–(e), so omitting only (a)(iv)–(vi), ie ITTOIA 2005, ss 509, 514 and 525(2).

[102] Payment of a bonus may be treated as a surrender (ITTOIA 2005, s 539(4)); as may loans (see below).

[103] Inland Revenue Press Release, 10 December 1974, [1974] *Simon's Tax Intelligence* 518.

[104] ITTOIA 2005, s 507(4), Step 1(b), ex TA 1988, s 546(1)(a)(ii).

[105] Ex TA 1988, s 546(2).

[106] Ex TA 1988, s 540(1)(a)(v).

[107] Ex TA 1988, s 546(3).

[108] ITTOIA 2005, ss 498–506.

[109] ITTOIA 2005, ss 507–509.

[110] ITTOIA 2005, ss 510–514; the situation is defined in s 510(1).

[111] ITTOIA 2005, ss 535–537, ex TA 1988, s 550. This relief is not affected by the abolition of the general top-slicing relief in *ibid*, Sch 2 by FA 1988, s 75.

[112] ITTOIA 2005, s 463(1) (Step 1).

The slice of the gain is then added to T's other income to discover the amount of extra tax payable by reason of its addition.[113] If the addition of that sum does not give rise to anything but tax at the basic rate, no tax is, usually, payable.[114] If, however, extra tax is payable, the amount of that tax is then calculated. The average of that tax rate is then ascertained, the basic rate deducted and the resulting rate applied to the whole gain.[115] Although a policy gain is not liable to basic rate income tax, the amount is part of total income and so may restrict the amount of age relief.

When a chargeable event occurs through death or maturity and there is a loss or, as the statute has it, a deficiency, an individual may deduct that loss from total income so far as it does not exceed gains taxed in earlier partial surrenders or assignments;[116] this allows the tax on gains made earlier to be recovered. The relief does not apply to losses on assignments, neither does it make any allowance for inflation. It applies only to the extent of any 'excess' or 'extra' liability.

Basic rate tax is payable in certain situations to do with certain foreign policies or policies issued by friendly societies in connection with tax-exempt business.[117] The foreign policy rules are subject to special reliefs for EEA insurers where a comparable EEA tax charge has been levied, and to another rule for a more general foreign tax relief.[118] Further rules apply to multiple interests.[119]

Example

It will be seen that T's liability is tied to that of the year of the chargeable event. Thus, if T is able to delay the surrender until a period of low income, such as retirement, the charge may be avoided altogether. Suppose T has a non-qualifying policy which has run for 12 years and a gain of £12,000; the slicing rule will take one-twelfth as the right slice (£1,000). If T is more than £1,000 below the higher rate threshold, there will be no charge under these rules. If T is already paying tax at 40%, then 20% of the £1,000 will be taxed and the same proportion applied to the remaining £11,000, making a total of £2,160. If T is just £500 below the higher rate threshold, so that £500 will be taxed at 20%, the tax on the £1,000 slice will be £100 and the total tax £1,200.

23.5.3.4 Trusts, Estates and Companies

Where a chargeable event happens in relation to an individual but the policy is held by trustees, the trustees may be liable for the tax in certain prescribed situations,[120] although there is an indemnity against the trustees.[121] These rules are supplemented by others where the trustees are not resident.[122]

---

[113] *Ibid*, Steps 2 and 3.
[114] ITTOIA 2005, s 530. However, if the effect is to increase total income and so cause the withdrawal of age relief, some liability may arise.
[115] Ex TA 1988, s 541(1).
[116] ITTOIA 2005, ss 539–541, ex TA 1988, s 549.
[117] ITTOIA 2005, s 531.
[118] ITTOIA 2005, ss 533 and 534.
[119] ITTOIA 2005, ss 469–472, ex TA 1988, s 547A, added in 1998.
[120] ITTOIA 2005, s 467, ex TA 1988, s 547(1)(a).
[121] ITTOIA 2005, s 530 (indemnity), ex TA 1988, s 551 (indemnity).
[122] ITTOIA 2005, s 468.

Where X, the individual, dies, X's personal representatives will not usually be liable to tax since they do not pay tax at the higher rates.[123] Special rules therefore apply where the gain would have been liable to basic rate tax.[124]

There were also rules for gains accruing to companies, which were repealed in 2008 when life insurance contracts were brought into the loan relationship rules.[125] For policies issued to a company, close or otherwise, after 13 March 1989, or existing policies which were varied or extended after that date, the entire gain, ie the excess of the surrender value of the policy over premiums paid, was treated as taxable under Schedule D, Case VI.[126] A company was similarly liable in respect of a policy which secured a debt owed by the company, as well as a policy settled by the company on trust. Special rules applied to the calculation of a policy gain where the policy secures a debt.

23.5.3.5 Loans as Surrenders

If money were able to be withdrawn in the form of loans instead of by the normal surrender of policy rights, these rules might be frustrated. It is therefore provided that loans are in general equivalent to a surrender of rights.[127] There are exceptions, eg for interest payable at a commercial rate or when the loan is for a qualifying purpose such as to provide a life annuity and the interest qualifies for relief under TA 1988, section 365 (not yet rewritten).[128] Any repayment of the loan is treated as a premium.[129] This counters the common, borrow-all arrangement under which T, the policyholder, paid the first few premiums out of his own resources and then borrowed from the insurance company—at interest—to pay subsequent premiums.

23.5.3.6 Life Annuity Contracts and Guaranteed Income Bonds

The rules prescribing excess liability on chargeable events in relation to endowment policies are adapted to the surrender of life annuity contracts.[130] Unfortunately, ITTOIA 2005 no longer deals with them in discrete sections but scatters them through the single code.[131] Sometimes a charge to basic rate income tax is made.[132]

Payments under a guaranteed income bond are treated as partial surrenders, except for the final one, which is treated as a total surrender.[133]

23.6 Personal Portfolio Bonds

Rules[134] were introduced to reverse the decision of the House of Lords in *IRC v Willoughby*.[135] In that case, the House of Lords held that a UK resident who had purchased

---

[123] ITTOIA 2005, s 467(4).
[124] ITTOIA 2005, s 467.
[125] Ex TA 1988, s 547(1)(b).
[126] Ex TA 1988, s 541(4A)–(4B) added in 1989 and repealed by FA 2008.
[127] ITTOIA 2005, s 501.
[128] ITTOIA 2005, ss 502 and 503(2), ex TA 1988, s 548.
[129] ITTOIA 2005, 494(1)(c), ex TA 1988, s 548(1).
[130] By ITTOIA 2005, ss 484 *et seq*, TA 1988, ss 542–544.
[131] Eg ITTOIA 2005, s 484(1)(d) and (e).
[132] ITTOIA 2005, s 531, ex TA 1988, s 547(6).
[133] ITTOIA 2005, ss 593 and 490, ex FA 1997, s 79(3).
[134] SI 1999/1029, made under ex TA 1988, s 553C. For useful guidance, see Redston (1999) 143 *Taxation* 114.
[135] [1997] STC 995.

a single premium personal portfolio bond at a time when he was a non-resident of the UK was not taxable on the income arising on the bond until its maturity. The rules reversing that result apply to the gain deemed to accrue on such bonds on an annual basis, save for the final year when the actual proceeds are used.[136] The rules adapt the life policy chargeable event rules described above.[137] These have been rewritten as primary legislation for income tax by ITTOIA 2005.[138]

23.7   Friendly Societies

The products offered by friendly societies are broadly similar to those offered by other life assurance companies. However, friendly societies are usually exempt from corporation tax on the profits of certain life and annuity business, a fact which enables them to offer better rates of return. This advantage was reduced by an obligation to hold 50% of their assets in narrow-range securities as defined by the now superseded Trustee Investment Act 1961.

The conditions under which policies and contracts constitute exempt business of friendly societies have been the subject of frequent changes in recent years. Life policies and contracts issued after 30 April 1995 are exempt policies if the premiums or premiums payable in any 12-month period do not exceed £270.[139] Annuity contracts are exempt if the annual sum payable does not exceed £156. Surrenders of policies may be chargeable events.[140] A friendly society is taxed as a mutual life assurance company in respect of its taxable insurance business, ie insurance business which is not tax-exempt under TA 1988, section 461.[141] A change to the definition of life or endowment business made by FA 2007 was found to have unintended effects for friendly societies and was therefore reversed retrospectively by FA 2008. FA 2008 also modified the rules on transfer between friendly societies.[142]

23.8   Insurance Companies

Although the taxation of insurance companies is far too detailed a topic for this book, three points are of general interest. The first is that for many years the fundamental principles underlying the liability to tax of insurance companies were unsettled and uncertain. The second point is that the life assurance business must be separate from other (general) business. The third point is that there were broadly two ways in which insurance companies were taxed—under the Schedule D, Case I trading principles,[143] or on the basis of income

---

[136] SI 1999/1029, reg 5.

[137] *Ibid*, reg 6.

[138] ITTOIA 2005, Pt 4, Ch 9, ss 475 and 515–526.

[139] FA 1995, s 54, Sch 10. Lower figures applied to earlier years; see also TA 1988, s 460(2) (not rewritten).

[140] Ex TA 1988, s 539(3), now dealt with under the loan relationship rules.

[141] TA 1988, s 463(1). Regulations modify the way in which the legislation on life assurance taxation, in TA 1988, Pt XII, is applied: Friendly Societies (Modification of the Corporation Tax Acts) Regulations 1992 (SI 1992/1655).

[142] FA 2008, s 44.

[143] *Sun Life Assurance Company of Canada (UK) Ltd v Revenue & Customs Commissioners* [2010] STC 1173, [2010] EWCA Civ 394 is a case on the application of trading loss rules in TA 1988 s 393 to insurance companies—and on FA 1989, s 89.

as computed under the various Schedules plus capital gains,[144] minus allowed expenses[145] (the I–E). Until 2007 the choice between the two lay with the Revenue, which generally preferred I–E. The Schedule D, Case I rules included provisions for the deduction of reserves and matching receipts when the reserves were drawn down.[146] The investment income and capital gains must have been allocated between two classes of business: (a) basic life and general annuity business; and (b) pension business. There were further rules for foreign business.[147] The rules on management expenses were modernised by FA 2004. A company with insurance business and other investment management business may find itself using TA 1988, section 76 for its insurance business and CTA 2009, section 1218 (ex TA 1988, section 75) for its other business.

Every year we now have statutes continuing the ongoing process of revising insurance company taxation in consultation with the industry. The year 2005 saw further rules for simplifying the taxation of different forms of life assurance business,[148] and 2006 saw changes principally to apply where assets are no longer needed for policy holders.[149] 2007 produced a major change of principle, in that (as just noted) HMRC ceased to be able to choose the basis of taxation to be applied to such companies.[150] From 2007, insurance companies are normally taxed on the I–E basis; some of the details of that basis are adjusted to ensure that the 'correct' amount of tax is paid and a 'clear' definition of the I–E basis is supplied. The I–E basis does not apply in two situations: (a) where the company is a pure reinsurer, and (b) where the business is purely of a particular type of life assurance; here normal trading profit principles apply.[151] Also in 2007 a separate category of life assurance business called 'Gross Roll Up Business', or GRB, was created, and rules introduced for corporation tax on the transfer of long-term business from one life assurance company to another.[152] FA 2007, section 42 and Schedule 9 contained other rules restricting the amounts general insurers may set aside; these replaced the rule in FA 2000, section 107. FA 2008 continued the revolution of this area by treating three types of life insurance contracts as falling within the loan relationship regime.[153] These are, subject to conditions, (a) a life insurance policy with a surrender value (or capable of having one); (b) a contract for a purchased life annuity; and (c) capital redemption polices. FA 2008, section 43 and Schedule 17 also made a whole series of changes to deal with funding arrangements, reinsurance and expenses, interest on 'deposit backs' and foreign currency assets.

FA 2009, section 46 and Schedule 23 made further changes. Perhaps the most important was the provision of a clear statutory framework for the tax treatment of additions by a life insurance company to its long-term insurance fund. FA 2010, section 47 modified the apportionment rules by adding TA 1988, section 432CA. As the Notes to Clauses say, the purpose was 'to prevent manipulation of liabilities in a non-profit fund to avoid tax when

---

[144] See TCGA 1992, ss 212 (as amended in 1993) and 213.
[145] TA 1988, s 76 (not rewritten); FA 1989, s 86.
[146] See TA 1988, ss 82, 83, 83AA, 83AB, added in 1996. See also *Prudential Assurance Co v Bibby* (1999) STC 952.
[147] TA 1988, s 442.
[148] F(No 2)A 2005, s 42 and Sch 9.
[149] FA 2006, s 86 and Sch 11.
[150] FA 2007, s 39 and Sch 8, adding TA 1988, ss 431G and 431H.
[151] TA 1988, s 431G(3).
[152] FA 2007, s 40 and Sch 9.
[153] FA 2008, s 36 and Schs 13 and 14.

previously unrecognised profits are recognised'. F(No2)A 2010, section 9 added a rule on the transfer of a business involving excess assets (TA 1988, section 432CB). FA 2011, section 56 further amended the rules governing apportionment of amounts brought into account. FA 2012 continued this seemingly-unstoppable trend, with further technical amendments in sections 25–30, eg abolishing relief for equalisation reserves.

23.9   Offshore Income Gains

As with insurance, the taxation of offshore funds is a difficult, technical subject and what follows is merely an overview. Various entities or funds may be formed offshore (ie outside the UK) with which an investor, T, may place money. Since these are not resident in the UK they are not subject to UK tax. Since they are not controlled from the UK they cannot be swept into the CFC legislation (and in any case often take the form of a trust rather than a company). Since T not only provides the funds but also expects to realise all the profits and gains in due course, there is no scope for those settlement provisions aimed at diversion of income or gains. So why is the tax system bothered?

The system is concerned, first, because the offshore entity, being outside the UK, will not be subject to UK tax and will often be located in a territory where it pays no tax at all; this will enable the funds to grow faster than if placed an equivalent UK-based entity.[154] The second concern is that the fund will 'roll up' the income it receives every year, leaving T with a single payment at the end. Although T will suffer from being kept out of the money because of its time value, T will usually gain, because what is eventually received will be capital and not income. Since 1984, when the offshore fund rules were first introduced, the consequence of this has been greatly reduced—but not eliminated. Investors are subject to tax under ITTOIA 2005, Part 5, Chapter 8 (income tax) or CTA 2009, Part 10, Chapter 8 (corporation tax). The description that follows focuses on the income tax charge and is intended as an outline. The relevant rules for determining the tax on returns to UK-resident investors holding interests in offshore funds are now found principally in the Offshore Funds (Tax) Regulations 2009 (hereafter the 'Offshore Funds Regulations').[155]

Under the Offshore Funds Regulations, the realisation of an interest in an offshore fund is taxed as income rather than gain, unless certain conditions are met. The term 'offshore fund' is defined in TIOPA 2010, Part 8, section 355. If the offshore fund is a 'reporting fund' under Part 3 of the Regulations, UK-resident investors are taxable each year on their share of the fund's reported income (distributed or not), with any gain or loss on the disposal of their interest taxed under the CGT rules If the offshore fund is a non-reporting fund, UK-resident investors generally are chargeable to income tax or CGT on actual distributions. In addition, there is a charge to tax under Part 2 of the Offshore Funds Regulations if a person disposes of an interest in a non-reporting fund (or a fund that formerly was one) and an offshore income gain arises. It will be noted that the charge is a charge to income tax, but the principles used to calculate that amount of income are those from CGT; FA 2008 adapted these rules to ensure that the changes to the CGT rules for the remittance

---

[154] If it takes the form of an insurance policy the gain may be taxed under TA 1988, s 540 as a non-qualifying policy.

[155] SI 2009/3001 as amended by SI 2011/1211, ex TA 1988, ss 757–764, Schs 27, 28, originally FA 1984, ss 92–100.

basis are taken into account.[156] Late changes were made by FA 2008 to deal with offshore income gains accruing to trusts which are taxed under TCGA 1992, sections 87 or 89(2). This had to do with order of matching—offshore income gains are matched before other chargeable gains.[157] Rules take account of any indexation allowed on an earlier no gain, no loss disposal. The holdover reliefs for gifts of business assets and rollover relief on the transfer of a business are not available. If the computation produces a loss, the unindexed gain is deemed to be nil and there is no material disposal. If the material disposal also gives rise to a charge to CGT, the consideration taken into account for CGT is reduced by the offshore income gain.[158] Special rules apply to persons resident and domiciled abroad, insurance companies and trustees.[159] Charities are exempt.[160]

A process to review and modify this regime began in December 2007. FA 2008, sections 41–42 contained extensive regulation-making powers which in due course were used to replace large parts of the TA 1988 rules. These powers are now in TIOPA 2010, section 354. In respect of distributions, FA 2009, section 39 inserted ITTOIA 2005, section 378A, a rule designed to prevent funds gaining an advantage through having a corporate structure. Where the fund is substantially invested in interest-bearing (or economically similar) securities (as defined in CTA 2009, section 494), the distribution is treated as interest for income tax purposes. This means no accompanying tax credit and tax at 40% rather than 32.5% for higher-rate taxpayers. 'Substantially' is defined in ITTOIA 2005, section 387A as meaning, broadly, when the value of the interest-bearing assets, widely defined, exceeds 60% of market value of all the investments (excluding cash awaiting investment). FA 2009, section 44 and Schedule 22 amended FA 2008, section 40, inserting sections 40A–40G. The purpose was to make the offshore fund more like a unit trust (§23.3) and treat the interest in the funds as the chargeable assets—and not the underlying investments.

23.10   Real Estate Investment Trusts

CTA 2010, Part 12, sections 518–609[161] allow qualifying companies or groups of companies to give notice under sections 523–524 that they wish to be treated under this regime. The legislation results from a long period of consultation. The company may elect to end the treatment (section 571); section 570 also lists other terminating events, eg automatically for breach of the conditions (section 578) or notice by HMRC (sections 573–577); on effects of termination, see sections 579–582. There is a very interesting HMRC power (sections 561–569) to overlook minor or inadvertent breaches; this may involve some payment of tax as opposed to termination (see HMRC Notes on Clauses).

Under the regime, the company is exempt from corporation tax on its property rental business profits (section 534). A separate rule (section 535) exempts some or all of the gain arising from the disposal of an asset used, which has been used for the purpose of the property rental business. The assets within the real estate investment trust (REIT) are

---

[156] Changes to ex TA 1988, ss 761 and 762 and the addition of ss 762ZA and 762ZBwere made by FA 2008, Sch 7, paras 92 *et seq*.

[157] As promised by HMRC Notes to Finance Bill, Sch 7, para 47.

[158] Offshore Funds Regulations, Pt 2, ex TA 1988, s 763.

[159] Offshore Funds Regulations, Pt 2, ex TA 1988, s 764; see also ex TA 1988, ss 663(2), 687(3).

[160] Offshore Funds Regulations, paras 31 and 101, ex TA 1988, s 761(6).

[161] Ex FA 2006, Pt 4, ss 103–145.

ring-fenced and rules apply to assets moving over the fence, whether moving outwards (sections 555–556), inwards (section 557) or on a demerger (section 558). When the profits are distributed to the shareholders, the burden of tax falls on them under CTA 2009, Part 4 or ITTOIA 2005, Part 3 (sections 548–549). The dividends are paid under deduction of basic rate income tax of 20% (ITA 2007, sections 973 and 974 is now the regulation-making power). The regime seeks to avoid problems of economic double taxation for companies which invest in properties as sources of rental income as opposed to development.

FA 2009, section 65 and Schedule 34 introduced new rules to prevent exploitation of the relief when a company restructures (now CTA 2009, section 600), removed an obstacle to entering the regime and allowed the company to issue convertible preference shares. F(No 3)A 2010, section 10 and Schedule 4 provided new rules to cover scrip dividends paid by REITs to satisfy the 90% test for distribution of ring-fenced profits. The script dividends will be taxed in the same way as a cash dividend. If the market value of the scrip dividend shares differs by more than 15% from the cash dividend that would have been paid, market value is substituted. FA 2012, Schedule 4 added yet more changes covering the conditions where close companies are involved and on trading of shares on recognised stock exchanges, on the distributable profits condition, and the balance of business condition.

23.10.1 Company Conditions

There are many conditions. First, the company must carry on a property rental business (sections 518–519); the property may be in the UK or abroad. Certain businesses, eg lettings incidental to a development business, and certain types of income, eg rent from siting a wind turbine, are excluded. Further conditions apply (sections 527–531) to make sure the company has the right balance of business. Thus, the property rental business must involve at least three properties, and no single property may represent more than 40% of the total value of properties involved (section 529). There is also a distribution requirement; normally at least 90% of the profits must be distributed by the normal tax filing date of the company (usually 12 months from the end of the accounting period, section 530). Profits of the property rental business must be at least 75% of the aggregate profits of the group or company (section 531). It will be clear from this that a company may qualify for the REITs regime even though only a part of its income is tax exempt; profits arising from the residual business are subject to corporation tax in the usual way (section 534).

The company—in the case of a group, the parent company—must meet conditions (section 528). Thus it must be UK-resident for tax purposes, it must not be an OEIC, its shares must be listed on a recognised stock exchange—and so not the AIM—it must not be a close company and it must have a relatively simple share structure (ordinary and non-voting, fixed-rate preference shares, and only one class of ordinary share).

23.10.2 Entry and Exit

A company entering the regime will find rules directing a deemed disposal of assets going into the exempt part, which will in future be ring-fenced, and regulating the capital gains and capital allowance consequences (sections 536–537). Conversely, when a company moves an asset from the tax-exempt part to the non-tax-exempt part, section 535 directs a similar deemed disposal at market value.

Formerly, a company joining the scheme was required to pay an entry charge of 2% of the market value of its investment properties at the date the company or group joined the regime (ex sections 538–540) This charge was abolished by FA 2012, Schedule 4, paragraph 33.

23.10.3 Restrictions

Section 541 ring-fences the tax-exempt business so that all its profits, losses and gains are separate from those of the other parts of its activities. Section 542 provides that the REIT is subject to the transfer-pricing rules in TIOPA 2010, Part 4, even though it is technically a small or medium-sized company. CTA 2010, section 66 is also disapplied, so requiring any loss on a foreign exempt property to be set off against profits of a UK property and vice versa.

Two further restrictions should be borne in mind. First, no one investor may be beneficially entitled to 10% or more of distributions, or control directly or indirectly 10% or more of the share capital or voting rights (section 553). Secondly, the ratio of interest on loans to fund the tax-exempt business to rental income of that business must be less than 1.25:1 (section 543). This is to stop the company borrowing money which effectively gives the lender a share of the profits. FA 2009, section 66 added now CTA 2010, section 543(7), which allows HMRC to waive the charge that would otherwise arise because the REIT company breaches the profit finance costing ratio where the company is in severe financial difficulties owing to unexpected circumstances and the company could not reasonably have taken action in time.

Section 545 contains a mini GAAR and gives HMRC the power to cancel a tax advantage, collecting tax to counteract that advantage. Section 546 outlines the appeal process against such counteraction. There is also an interesting anti-avoidance rule (section 582), designed to stop a company engineering its own departure from the regime, eg because it is facing a significant loss in the tax-exempt business which is only tax-effective if the company leaves the group. Section 582 enables HMRC to trap the loss by changing the normal cessation date.

The rules for groups of companies are set out in sections 601 and 606.

23.11   Authorised Investment Funds

The Financial Services Authority introduced a regime for Regulations made in 2008 which apply where authorised investment funds (AIFs) invest in REITs and related securities. Building on the REIT model, these may elect to have a property AIF regime, under which the tax point is moved from the fund to the investor.[162]

Although Property Authorised Investment Funds (PAIFs) are subject to tax treatment in some ways similar to REITs, the tax treatment in other ways is quite different.

Readers are referred to the relevant HMRC manual (CTM48811) for more information on PAIFs.

---

[162] HMRC BN 34, March 2008.

24

Pensions

24.1 Background

24.1.1 General[1]

A key government choice, made in 1980, was to increase the basic state retirement pension in line with inflation and not, as previously, in line with average earnings. This provided a major saving to the Treasury, and even more encouragement for people (and their employers) to take out private (and expensive) arrangements, eg with insurance companies. The result was a bonanza for pension advisers, who received commission income, and, for those running the schemes, huge bonuses paid in real money out of paper gains. The stock market declines of 2000 combined with drops in the interest rates and so in annuity values coincided with the start of tougher accounting valuations, which for the first

---

[1] For some very practical background, see Reardon, *Zurich Pensions Handbook*, 9th edn (Pearson, 2004). There is much background literature on this topic, eg the papers from the British Association Economics Section printed in (2005) 26 *Fiscal Studies* 1–134, Pensions Commission, *Pensions: Challenges and Choices. The First Report of the Pensions Commission* (2004), an independent body established by the Government following the Pensions Green Paper of December 2002, and a major study for the World Bank—Mitchell, *Trends in Retirement Systems and Lessons for Reform* (World Bank, 1993). The Report of the Committee on the Taxation Treatment of Provisions for Retirement, Cmd 9063 (1954) tells the story to 1954 and contains many proposals for reform, most of which were later implemented. Among broader books there is much of value and interest in Davis, *Pension Funds* (OUP, 1995) and Dilnot, Disney, Johnson and Whitehouse, *Pension Policy in the UK* (Institute for Fiscal Studies, 1994).

time made some companies fully realise what they had undertaken to provide for their employees in the shape of terminal salary schemes.

Companies decided to close their terminal salary schemes to new employees and, in some cases, even for existing employees for future years of employment. This led to a pensions crisis which was as much as anything a crisis of confidence; this in turn led to very cautious investment policies, which in turn missed out on the subsequent rise in stock market values. Subsequent legislation to provide some degree of protection through the Pension Protection Fund is controversial since it is unclear whether the protection will be sufficient.[2] What was bad enough for those companies which had not made full and proper provision for their liabilities was writ large for government, which ultimately ran away from trying to change the public sector schemes from a final salary scheme to a lifetime average salary scheme. The balance sheets of many governments around the world will look very bad if properly-valued pension liabilities are taken into account; fools' paradises are rarely comfortable places in which to live. When healthcare costs are also taken into account, the figures can look even worse.[3]

Behind this lies the problem of the dependency ratio, ie the ratio between those in work and those in retirement. It has been calculated that, as a result of changes in the birth rate and the increased life expectancy of those now coming up to pensionable age, by the year 2035 each pensioner will be supported by only 1.6 persons in employment as against 2.3 persons in 1985.[4] The practical solution to this problem is seen as extending the working life or by increasing contributions. It actually involves more fundamental matters, such as inter-generational equity and what one might in quasi-socialist periods have called a 'duty to work'. Those who regard the obligation to work as fundamental to a social welfare system, such as the UK tax credits system described in *Revenue Law*, chapter nine, will presumably accept that entitlement to pensions may also be tied to an obligation to work longer—and to have a proper reduction in pension benefits for those who retire early. The different pattern of pension entitlement is regarded as the main reason why by the age of 69 virtually no men are working in Belgium, whereas in Japan almost 50% of men are still in the labour force.[5] There is, however, also an even more basic economic point here. As argued by Eatwell, there have to be enough people to whom the generation in retirement can sell the financial rights and assets (stocks and shares) in return for the annuities on which they need to live.[6] This takes us back to the question whether the tax system should do more to encourage the relevant generation to have more children.

Few areas provide better examples of the problems of tax policy than pensions. Having decided that pension provision was a good thing and that tax advantages should be provided to encourage it, the UK legislature proceed to pile rule upon rule—and to widen existing rules. Change had to come, and so FA 2004 introduced new rules, which replaced all the old rules with one basic set and came into force on 1 April 2006 (see §24.9 below). Amendments have been made each year since, with particularly significant changes made

---

[2] Besely and Prat (2005) 26 *Fiscal Studies* 119, 130.

[3] Wise (2005) 26 *Fiscal Studies* 5.

[4] The same applies to the basic retirement pension.

[5] Wise (2005) 26 *Fiscal Studies* 5, 21; the different pattern in Denmark is attributed by Sefton, Van de ven and Weale (2005) 26 *Fiscal Studies* 83 *et seq* to strong government policies in favour of work.

[6] See <www.cerf.cam.ac.uk/publications>.

in FA 2011. It should also be noted that the Coalition Government pledged to restore the earnings link to state pensions.

The legislation governing the tax treatment of pension income is found primarily in ITEPA 2003, Part 9. ITEPA 2003 provides one single chapter, Chapter 5A, on the taxation of benefits (below §24.2). Chapter 15A exempts certain lump sums. Other exemptions are to be found in Chapters 17 (any taxpayer) and 18 (non-residents).

24.1.2 Privileges and Patterns

Employees, with or without financial assistance from their employer, are encouraged to set money aside for retirement. Sums set aside under a scheme approved by HMRC will not be treated as income for the year in which they are so set aside, and the fund in which the money is saved will usually be allowed to accumulate free of tax. In return for these privileges,[7] savers are taxed on their eventual pensions; income is spread forward to retirement years. This pattern of exemption for the sums saved, exemption for the income in the fund in return for eventual taxability of the pension (often reduced to 'EET'), may also be seen in some other countries. However, the UK has not had a pure EET since 1997, when pension funds lost the right to claim repayment of the tax credit on dividends.

A pension is a provision for old age, and therefore its provision is one of the prime functions of life assurance. Indeed, until 1916 there were no special rules concerning pensions as distinct from life assurance, and premiums under life assurance policies were deductible. However, in 1916[8] the relief for life assurance policies was restricted, even for policies already in force, to a deduction for income tax only (and not what shortly after became surtax) and to those premiums that secured the payment of a capital sum on death. The full relief was, however, still made available to certain superannuation and bona fide pension schemes for employees and the self-employed, even though commenced after 1916. Superannuation funds were made exempt in 1921.[9] Following the Report of the Committee on the Taxation Treatment of Provisions for Retirement (Cmd 9063 (1954)— the Tucker Report) further changes were made; in particular, provision was made for the self-employed, who were allowed complete deduction for premiums paid to secure a retirement annuity (see below at §24.6).[10] The more limited life assurance relief was abolished, but not for existing policies, in 1984. Life assurances had the attraction that one might buy an annuity with the proceeds and take advantage of ITTOIA 2005, Part 6, Chapter 7 (ex TA 1988, section 656); however, the attractions of this were reduced in a time of high inflation. For the self-employed an alternative is a life consultancy, although here not only do the payments have to be justified in order to be deductible for tax by the payer, but no protection is provided for dependants.

As seen above, reform has continued through to the new millennium and beyond.[11] Responsibility for providing for the cost of living in old age is a major political and economic issue in our society.[12] Long ago it could be regarded as a private matter (not

---

[7] On whether these incentives actually cost the government money, see Ruggeri and Fougere (1997) 18 *Fiscal Studies* 143.

[8] FA 1916, s 36; the special rules for pre-1916 policies were repealed in 1976.

[9] FA 1921, s 32.

[10] FA 1956, s 22; TA 1970, s 226.

[11] See also Disney and Emmerson (2005) 26 *Fiscal Studies* 55, 63 listing a number of apparently minor changes.

[12] On pensioners' (financial) behaviour, see Symposium (1998) 19 *Fiscal Studies* 141.

least because life expectancy was so low). Those wanting to make that provision might take out a life assurance policy. An entrepreneur would build up a business and then sell it to provide the necessary funds. A partner in a firm of solicitors would not retire but carried on (and on), worked as a consultant or sold his (almost invariably his) share of the firm to an incoming partner. For those fortunate enough to have family wealth behind them there was the possibility of having an annuity from the family settlement. War, inflation, taxation, social change and market forces have swept away some of these ways of providing for old age, but the need is still there. The cost of meeting that need is exacerbated by greater life expectancy and by a refusal to index-link the retirement age to that expectancy. As the state realises the cost of providing for people in old age, it is very anxious to encourage thrift—and then to penalise the rewards of thrift by taking money away for residential care in old age. The role of taxation in this has been twofold. First, very high rates of tax, especially income tax and estate duty, made some of these sources of support unreliable; the chances of saving much from earned income (with rates up to 83%) were remote, while the destruction of the family trust may be attributed to a combination of income tax and estate duty. Secondly, the granting of reliefs from tax for certain types of support, beginning with life assurance relief in 1799, meant that funds were channelled into tax-favoured forms of provision rather than other forms. The story of these reliefs has been one of change—and not always in one direction. In recent years the changes have been in the direction of choice and flexibility. Despite this, the non-approved pension scheme (which attracts no special tax subsidies) was still a standard part of the remuneration package for very important people in the private sector.

For the majority of the people in the UK these options were not at first available. The state was looked to, to provide support through the system of National Insurance. In the UK the state provides a basic retirement pension. Employees qualify through payments of Class I NICs charged on employer and employee, although the pension is related to the number of years of contribution; the self-employed qualify by paying Class 2 NICs. The basic state pension is below the poverty line. Those who retire and have no other source of income rely on the state for supplementary, income-related (ie means-tested) benefits. Former Chancellor Gordon Brown's belief in credits (see *Revenue Law*, chapter nine) shows up here too—with the Pension Credit. This has two elements: the Guarantee Credit element and the Savings element. It is not, in form, a tax credit and is not administered by the tax authorities.[13] Today one is meant to talk about 'targeted resources', not 'means-tested benefits'.[14]

It is in the interests of both the individuals and the state that people should save for retirement. Employees were at one time covered by the State Earnings Related Pension Scheme (SERPS) unless an approved employment-related pension scheme or private pension plan was taken out.[15] SERPS was regarded as still the scheme of last resort, and the state not only provided subsidies to persuade people to take out private cover instead

---

[13] It is administered by the Department of Works and Pensions.
[14] For an economic analysis of take-up of means-tested benefits, see Hancock *et al* (2004) 25 *Fiscal Studies* 279.
[15] Introduced by Social Security Act 1975; from 1961 to 1975 there was also a graduated pension scheme.

but also reduced the value of the benefits to be provided.[16] A state second pension (S2P)[17] superseded SERPS in 2002, but only for future years, so that anyone retiring between 2002 and 2050 may well have rights under both schemes. These are aimed primarily at low and moderate earners. Like SERPS, the S2P is not available to the self-employed. The state charges a rebate or lower (contracted-out) rate of NICs when the employee has contracted out of S2P.[18] As company schemes began to fold or close, some experts even advised their people to return to the state system, but without offering to reimburse all the commissions they had earned in the meantime.

24.1.3 Types of Provision

There are two major types of pension provision—the terminal salary scheme (TSS) sometimes called 'defined benefit' (DB), and the money purchase scheme (MPS), some-times called 'defined contribution' (DC).[19] These govern the size of the pot available for deployment on retirement, but in different ways. The TSS is tied to the value of the final salary (measured in various ways over various periods) and the maximum contributions are geared to the sums needed to meet this target. The MPS provides no limit on the pot available on retirement but has a ceiling on the amount which may be contributed each year. In the UK, until relatively recently, many occupational pension schemes were exam-ples of the TSS, while personal pensions schemes and retirement annuities are examples of the MPS.

From a labour economist's point of view, there may be important differences between these two schemes. TSS (or DB) may

> sort stayers from quitters and help match stayers to long-tenure firms … strengthen worker-attachment firms, enabling investments of firm-specific skills … reward, through pay-back loading, high achievers at zero cost to the firm.[20]

The disadvantages include the need to provide long-term contracts and the requirement of a normal retirement age. There are also advantages and disadvantages for the employee, and general economic issues. Thus, does the investment policy of a defined benefit scheme become unnecessarily conservative? Given the great weight of money in these funds, what are the effects of rules which favour investment in equities rather than bonds, or vice versa, and what would be the consequences for capital markets of changing them?[21]

24.1.4 Types of Benefit

24.1.4.1 Annuities and Lump Sums Versus Annuities

The normal benefit payable is an annuity, which is to last for the life of the assured but may be for the life of that person and another (eg a surviving spouse). Under a TSS, the amount of the annuity is fixed by reference to the terminal salary retirement age; under a

---

[16] Reardon, *op cit*, §11.5.
[17] Introduced by Child Support, Pensions and Social Security Act 2002; see Disney and Emmerson, (2005) 26 *Fiscal Studies* 55.
[18] Set by the Government Actuary. However, new age-related rebates have now come in.
[19] FA 2004, s 164 *et seq* and Sch 28.
[20] See Davis, *op cit*, ch 10.
[21] See, generally, Davis, *op cit*, ch 10.

MPS, the annuity is fixed by the annuity rates prevailing at the relevant time. The fall in interest rates in recent years has encouraged those affected to lobby (successfully) for some flexibility over the time by which they must acquire their annuities. Although T may take the pension annuity, T may also receive a (tax free) lump sum.

24.1.4.2 Flexible Annuities

An additional type of personal pension scheme was introduced in FA 1995, which gave members the right to elect to defer the purchase of an annuity and to take income withdrawals from their pension fund in the meantime. Today this is achieved by means of the alternatively secured pension (or 'ASP'), or withdrawal from the 'alternatively secured fund.[22]

24.2 Approved Retirement Benefit Schemes

The major influence on the development of approved retirement benefit schemes has been the Civil Service model; basically, no one should get a better deal than civil servants.[23] This, perhaps cynical, view ignores the major influence the Civil Service model has had in improving levels of pension provision, especially since railway companies and other large commercial concerns of the 19th century used that model for their own schemes.

24.2.1 Types of Scheme

Today schemes are governed by the rules in FA 2004, sections 149–284 (not rewritten) and secondary legislation. For earlier schemes, see the 5th edition of *Revenue Law*.

24.2.2 Taxation of Pensions

ITEPA 2003, section 570 states that the word 'pension' includes a pension which is paid voluntarily or is capable of being discontinued. The charge is on the full amount accruing during the year; the liability is on the person receiving or entitled to the pension.[24] FA 2004 does not rewrite this part of ITEPA 2003. The rules in Chapter 3 and 4 apply only if one of the more specific sets of rules later in the chapter do not. As from 2006, payments under all registered pension schemes are governed by ITEPA 2003, Part 9, Chapter 5A.

The term 'pension' has not been defined by statute or judicially; indeed, judges have refused to attempt such a definition. In *McMann v Shaw*,[25] a series of payments was held to be compensation for loss of office as opposed to a pension, the deciding factor being that they were not payments for services past or present—they were in fact payments to the former Borough Treasurer of Southall whose position was abolished under the

---

[22] FA 2004, s 165, rr 6–7 and Sch 28, paras 5, 7, 11 and 12.
[23] When the 'old code' of approval was brought in by FA 1921, the Revenue, in exercising their discretionary power to approve schemes, looked to the rules of the state schemes in deciding what might be accepted: hence, such rules as the maximum pension payable being 40/60ths of final salary became part of the code.
[24] ITEPA 2003, ss 571 and 572.
[25] [1972] 3 All ER 732, (1972) 48 TC 330.

London Government reorganisation in 1963, and the payments were made from the time the employee became redundant until he became entitled to a pension in respect of his previous service. In *Johnson v Holleran*,[26] it was held that retirement was not an essential condition for certain payments to be a pension, but that the former employment must have ceased. In *HMRC v Barclays Bank*,[27] the Bank had provided various services tax free to some of its pensioners. The Bank withdrew the concession and compensated the pensioners for their loss; the compensation payments were held to be relevant benefits and so chargeable under TA 1988, section 596A(1).

If the pension is payable under the rules of an approved scheme, whether or not an exempt approved scheme, it is charged to tax under ITEPA 2003, Part 9, Chapter 3 and so under PAYE.[28] Foreign pensions are chargeable under ITEPA 2003, Part 9, Chapter 4;[29] today, the chargeable amount is reduced by 10%; at one time the remittance basis applied.

24.2.2.1 Tax—Free Lump Sums

Under the Civil Service superannuation arrangements introduced in 1973, the lump sum gratuity which had previously been discretionary was made payable as of right, and it was thought desirable to declare that lump sums payable on retirement were not taxable, whether or not payable as of right.[30] In this way the lump sum was assimilated to the proceeds of a life assurance policy.

24.2.2.2 Restrictions

Tax-free status does not apply to an unjustified payment of compensation for early retirement unless due to ill-health; such a payment falls within ITEPA 2003, section 401.[31] Neither does it apply to unauthorised payments from a fund, or to payments after the cessation of tax exemptions.[32] The scheme in question must be an approved scheme, a statutory scheme or a foreign government scheme; or a funded, unapproved retirement benefits scheme where the lump sum is attributable to employer contributions to the scheme on which the employee has been charged to tax.[33] The sum may not exceed 3/80ths of final salary for each year of service up to 40.

24.2.2.3 Other Lump Sum Tax Rules

If consideration is received for a restrictive covenant given in connection with an office or employment, past, present or future, there may be liability under ITEPA 2003, section 225. Sums payable for termination of the office may be chargeable under section 401 to the extent that they exceed £30,000. An ex-gratia lump sum payment given on retirement will now be regarded as a benefit provided by an unfunded, unapproved pension

---

[26] [1989] STC 1, (1989) 61 TC 428.
[27] [2006] EWHC 2118 (Ch), [2007] STC 74, considering the meaning of a relevant benefit for the purposes of TA 1988, ss 596A and 612.
[28] ITEPA 2003, s 683(3), ex TA 1988, s 597(1).
[29] ITEPA 2003, s 575(2), as amended by ITTOIA 2005, ex TA 1988, s 65(2).
[30] Ex TA 1988, s 189, rewritten as ITEPA 2003, Pt 9, Ch 16 and superseded by Ch 15A.
[31] Ex TA 1988, s 189(2) and Sch 11, para 4. A payment is justified if it is properly regarded as a benefit earned by past service.
[32] Ex TA 1988, s 600.
[33] Ex TA 1988, ss 189, 595, 596A(8).

scheme and so be taxable in full.[34] Concessionary relief is given for lump sums paid by overseas pension schemes.[35]

24.2.3 Correction of Surpluses

In his review of pensions, Nigel Lawson decided to act against those funds which had sums of money beyond what was needed to meet future obligations. The precise position depended on the method of actuarial valuation, which was consistently followed. TA 1988, sections 601–603 and Schedule 22 addressed pension scheme surpluses. They applied only to exempt approved schemes. Many of the substantive rules were contained in supporting regulations dealing with valuation and administration respectively.[36] It is arguable that these rules were almost as damaging to pension schemes as former Chancellor Gordon Brown's decision to remove the repayment of tax credits on dividends in 1997. They do not survive FA 2004; for further details, see the 5th edition of *Revenue Law*.

24.3   Additional Voluntary Contributions

Before 2006 many employees used the additional voluntary contributions (AVCs) scheme.[37] Although the maximum contribution to an exempt approved scheme for which an employee may make and obtain deduction is normally limited to 15% of annual remuneration, very few schemes have this level of funding. Moreover, although qualifying remuneration has been capped since 1989–90, most employees are still below this cap. This is now absorbed into the general scheme in FA 2004, which came into force in 2006. For further details, see the 5th edition of *Revenue Law*.

24.4   Simplified Occupational Schemes

Simplified occupational schemes have now been absorbed into the general scheme in FA 2004, which came into force in 2006. For details, see the 5th edition of *Revenue Law*.

24.5   Approved Personal Pensions

Approved personal pensions have now been absorbed into the general scheme in FA 2004, which came into force in 2006. For details, see the 5th edition of *Revenue Law*.

---

[34] Exceptions are made for redundancy and compensation for loss of office, including the case of forced voluntary resignation, unless the employee does not belong to an approved scheme (see Statement of Practice SP 13/91); in such a case a lump sum ex-gratia payment may be made on retirement, but subject to normal Revenue limits and subject to a de minimis limit for which prior approval is not required.

[35] ESC A10.

[36] Pension Scheme Surpluses (Valuation) Regulations 1987 (SI 1987/412); and Pension Scheme Surpluses (Administration) Regulations 1987 (SI 1987/352).

[37] Social Security Act 1986, s 12 made it mandatory for members of exempt approved schemes to be given this opportunity as of right.

24.6   Retirement Annuity Contracts

As from 2006, these ceased to exist as a separate category.[38] For details see the 5th edition of *Revenue Law*. This scheme was frozen in 1988;[39] no new schemes were permitted. Originally proposed by the Millard Tucker Committee Report.[40]

24.7   Flexible Annuities—Income Drawdown

The idea of income drawdown is important in retirement planning; the individual may draw down some of the income while leaving the capital in the fund untouched and not having to turn that sum into an annuity. For pre-FA 2004 rules, see the 5th edition of *Revenue Law*.

24.8   Stakeholder Pensions

Another important part of the story of pensions is the stakeholder pension scheme; this cut the link between pension provision and relevant earnings. As paragraph 4 of the Revenue Notes to the Finance Bill 2000 proudly states: 'The changes mean that for the first time non-earners can contribute to a pension. This opens up pension savings to groups such as carers and parents taking career breaks to bring up children.' This is built on the importance of saving regularly and over a long period to build up a really significant fund. Indeed one wonders whether these people were really the object of the Chancellor's concern rather than the lower-paid. It was also intended that stakeholder pensions should have low administration costs and be open to a wider range of pension provider.

During the passage of the Finance Bill 2000, a late amendment allowed stakeholder pensions to be used by most but not all employees who were already in an occupational pension scheme, ie to contribute to the stakeholder scheme in addition to their existing scheme.[41] For details, see the 5th edition of *Revenue Law*.

24.9   FA 2004, Part 4 Rules

From 6 April 2006 (known as 'A day'), the general tax rules on pensions changed dramatically. As from that date, there has been one set of, at times necessarily complex, rules instead of the eight or nine previously in force. What follows is an outline of the legislation. FA 2011 made some important changes to the FA 2004 rules, as discussed below.

---

[38] FA 2004, Sch 24, Pt 3.
[39] For transitional rules, see TA 1988, s 618. On interaction, see *ibid*, s 655(1) and Revenue Interpretation RI 76, ss 4.10–4.13; see also Tiley and Collison, *UK Tax Guide 1998–1999* (Butterworths, 1998) paras 30.33 *et seq*.
[40] Report of the Committee on the Taxation Treatment of Provisions for Retirement, Cmd 9063 (1954), ch 6.
[41] TA 1988, s 632B.

24.9.1 Introduction

As can now be seen, the pension scheme rules had become so numerous and expansive that the whole structure was about to collapse under its own weight. Another report, a set of proposals and finally legislation—FA 2004—followed. One of the main attractions for the FA 2004 regime was that once it was in force, on 6 April 2006, all rights under existing schemes could be transferred across. This regime, as initially drafted, was generous, but it represented a new beginning. FA 2004 has been much amended by later Acts. These rules are not affected by the Rewrite and provide one example of income tax charges arising outside the three main income tax Acts.[42]

The objective is simplification. The FA 2004 rules apply uniformly to all personal pension arrangements. All schemes must be registered (Part 4, Chapter 2).

24.9.1.1 Benefits

There is flexibility of benefits (Part 4, Chapter 3). So all pensioners are entitled to take up to 25% of their fund as a tax-free lump sum. Personal pension schemes have always allowed pensioners to take up to 25% of the value of the fund as a lump sum (retirement annuities were more generous still at 33.3%). However, the maximum lump sum for members of occupational schemes was a multiple of their pension—this is what changed.

There is a greater flexibility of benefits when one considers the transition from work to retirement. Under FA 2004, one may draw a pension and still work. Again, this change is primarily of benefit to the members of occupational schemes. It was a condition of retiring from an occupational schemes that one retired—ie did not work—hence all the litigation in *Venables v Hornby*.[43] The self-employed were under no such restriction, as they could draw down their personal pension scheme benefits as required. The minimum retirement age rose from 50 to 55 in 2010.

24.9.1.2 Contributions—Limit 1 (Total Value)

Tax reliefs and rules about maximum contributions are contained in Part 4, Chapter 4. Employers may deduct contributions to a registered pension scheme. There is, however, flexibility regarding contributions: the 2004 rules restrict tax relief for contributions in just two ways (see also §24.9.1.3 below). First, there is a maximum lifetime contributions allowance: set initially at £1.5 million, it rose to £1.8 million in 2010, before it was cut back to £1.5 million again from 6 April 2012 (for other years, see below at §24.9.6.3). This has caused some anguish for some people who would see themselves as moderately, rather than immoderately, well-off. It has to be said that the drop in interest rates and so the annuity rate means that £1.5 million generates a lower pension now than it would have done in 2000. Those on defined benefit salary-linked schemes carry out a simple process of multiplying the pension by 20; so a pension of £70,000 gives a value of £1.4 million (and is safe), while one of £80,000 gives a value of £1.6 million (and becomes overfunded). It is also the case that sums generated in private pension schemes, where the old limitations were on the annual percentages of relevant earnings contribution not the value of the fund, could have grown above this figure. One solution was to retire before the new rules came in—as many

---

[42] See ITA 2007, s 3(2), referring to FA 2004, Pt 4, Ch 7.
[43] [2003] UKHL 65, [2004] STC 84.

of Her Majesty's judges felt compelled to do but for special treatment—or take advantage of the limited transitional rules, see §24.9.10.

24.9.1.3 Contributions—Limit 2 (Annual)

Secondly, there is an annual restriction on amounts added to the fund—this used to be a percentage (the basis allowance being 25%) of annual earnings but is now a simple annual sum. Originally £215,000, the annual allowance rose to £255,000 for 2010–11 before being cut back to £50,000 from 6 April 2011. Unused annual allowance from the previous three years may be carried forward if pension savings were made in those years. In considering whether this limit might be exceeded, it must be remembered that one can now put into the fund not only cash but also shares or land, the values of which may be matters of dispute.

24.9.1.4 Investments

The ability to put property into the fund was welcome news for wealthier savers with big pension funds and other sources of income, but it may prove dangerous for others. It must be appreciated that once the property is in the scheme, it must be treated as an investment asset like any other. So if a person puts a holiday home into the fund, there would have to be a charge at full market rent if it is occupied by the would-be pensioner and family. If a buy-to-let house is transferred, there will be CGT and stamp duty to pay, and then, as there is no taxable income, there will be no deduction for any interest either. Eventually rules were added restricting the powers of an investment-regulated pension scheme (defined in FA 2004, Schedule 29A, paragraphs 1–3) to acquire certain types of property, including residential property. A scheme acquiring such property is treated as making an unauthor-ised payment—and so is liable to a charge.[44] An occupational pension scheme is outside this embargo, whereas an individual member may not be.[45]

24.9.1.5 Charge

A tax charge arises (FA 2004, Part 4, Chapter 5) once the value of the fund (not of the contributions) passes the lifetime allowance. A tax charge of 25% is imposed (to remove the benefit of the tax exemption on the lifetime allowance). If money is taken out of the fund in an unauthorised way—paid back to the member to bring the value of the fund down—a 55% charge is imposed to claw back the allowance. This may look severe, but there is nothing to stop the person adding further sums if the value of the fund drops below the lifetime allowance—and there will be further relief in that year.

24.9.2 Basic Concepts and Overview

FA 2004, Part 4, Chapter 1 (sections 149–152) defines basic concepts; Chapter 2 (sections 153–159) covers the registration and de-registration of pension schemes; Chapter 3 (sections 160–185) provides for the payments that may be made by registered pension schemes and related matters; Chapter 4 (sections 186–203) deals with tax reliefs and exemp-tions in connection with registered pension schemes; Chapter 5 (sections 204–242) imposes tax charges in connection with registered pension schemes; Chapter 6 (sections 243–249)

---

[44] FA 2004, s 174A and Sch 29A, added by FA 2006.
[45] See amendment by FA 2008, Sch 29, para 3.

covers certain schemes that are not registered pension schemes; Chapter 7 (sections 250–274) makes provisions regarding compliance; and Chapter 8 (sections 275–284) contains interpretation and other supplementary provisions.

All references in this section of the chapter are to FA 2004, Part 4 unless otherwise stated.

24.9.3 Pension Schemes and Their Registration

A pension scheme is one which provides specified benefits to or in respect of persons on retirement, on death, on having reached a particular age, on the onset of serious ill-health or incapacity, or in similar circumstances.[46] Any scheme properly registered is a 'registered pension scheme'.[47] Other terms used are 'public service pension scheme',[48] 'occupational pension scheme'[49] and 'overseas pension scheme', this last having a subset of 'recognised overseas pension scheme' which means recognised by the UK tax authorities.[50]

There are several categories of member, viz active member, pensioner member, deferred member or pension credit member of the pension scheme.[51] A pension credit member is someone whose rights under the scheme are attributable (directly or indirectly) to pension credits.

Lastly, FA 2004 refers to 'arrangements', ie arrangements between the scheme and the person. Here we find not only defined benefits[52] and money purchase,[53] but also cash balance benefits.[54] Hybrid arrangements consist of a mixture of these three benefits.[55]

The registration of pension schemes is governed by Chapter 2, which starts by setting out how applications are to be made.[56] Section 153(8), added in 2005, ensures that only insurance companies may provide deferred annuities. FA 2005 also provides for members who have been duped into liberating funds from a scheme; if the courts or the Pension Regulator then direct the 'repatriation' of fund back to a pension scheme, the annuity contract is to be treated as a registered scheme.[57] Sections 266A and 266B provide relief from the unauthorised payment charge in these circumstances. Section 154, backed up by section 155, directs that the scheme must either be an occupational pension scheme, or be established by a defined body such as insurance company. The scheme administrator may appeal against a Revenue decision not to register.[58] The Revenue power to de-register is contained in section 157, which also contains the procedure. The grounds for de-registration are set out in section 158—these are mostly for serious breaches of the rules. The list includes excessive unauthorised payments, eg if the scheme chargeable payments are 25% of the assets of

---

[46] FA 2004, s 150.
[47] FA 2004, s 150(2).
[48] FA 2004, s 150(3), (4).
[49] FA 2004, s 150(5), (6).
[50] FA 2004, s 150(7), (8).
[51] FA 2004, s 151.
[52] FA 2004, s 152(6).
[53] FA 2004, s 152(3).
[54] FA 2004, s 152(5).
[55] FA 2004, s 152(8).
[56] FA 2004, s 153.
[57] FA 2004, s 153(8A).
[58] FA 2004, s 156.

the fund. An appeal against de-registration is available.[59] There is charge—at 40%—on all the assets in the fund on de-registration.[60]

24.9.4 Permitted Payments

24.9.4.1 Expressly Permitted Payments

Chapter 3 (sections 160–185) defines various categories of payments and has two functions, one being to list the payments which properly may be made, and the other being to identify those which may not be made and so attract penalties. The only payments which a registered pension scheme is authorised to make to or in respect of a member of the pension scheme are those specified in section 164 (section 160); it follows that all other payments are unauthorised. Each permitted payment is subject to detailed statutory amplification; the list comprises pensions (sections 165 and 167), lump sums (sections 166 and 168), recognised transfers (section 169) scheme administration member payments (section 171) and payments pursuant to a pension-sharing order or provision. Also expressly permitted are payments of a description to be prescribed by regulations made by the Board. Sections 161–163 contain definitions and cover payments, loans and borrowing. The definition of 'payments' covers rules not only about what amounts to payment but also about the person to whom or for whose benefit the payment is treated as being made. 'Loans' are defined, as they may be or become unauthorised payments (sections 171, 178 and 179) and so attract penalties. 'Borrowings' are defined because section 182 limits the number of borrowings that a scheme may make.

24.9.4.2 Pensions

Among the pension rules in section 165 are:

(1)   that a pension may be taken before normal minimum pension age only if ill-health is established;
(2)   that if the member dies within 10 years of entitlement, a cash sum may be paid (if the rules allow it).

There are also rules, added in 2005, on the abatement of public service pensions during re-employment. There are several rules for death benefit pensions,[61] eg: payment may be made only to a dependant of the member (rule 1), the payment must be a dependant scheme pension in respect of a defined benefit arrangements (rule 2); other rules apply to money purchase arrangements (rules 3 and 5). There are also limits on secured pensions (rule 4) and on ASPs (rule 6). ASPs are a very important feature of the new regime as they get round the pre-2006 absolute insistence on converting any money in a fund into an annuity at age 75. Funds left in the plan on death must be used for dependants or charity, or, sometimes, other pension group members. FA 2004, Schedule 28, amended by FA 2005 and 2006, supplements these rules. FA 2007 contains rules on the interaction of the ASP rules and IHT.

---

[59] FA 2004, s 159.
[60] FA 2004, s 242.
[61] FA 2004, s 167.

24.9.4.3 Lump Sums

Section 166 deals with the lump sum payments which may be made by a registered pension scheme to a member of the pension scheme; these must fall within the following list: (a) pension commencement; (b) serious ill-health; (c) short service refund lump sum; (d) a refund of excess contributions; (e) trivial commutation; (f) winding up; and (g) a lifetime allowance excess lump sum. The fact that these payments are authorised does not mean that they are necessarily without tax consequences—just that they are safe from the automatic 40% charge under section 208. Section 268 provides rules for lump sums on death benefits, though the actual list is necessarily different and includes a charity lump sum death benefit. Sections 266 *et seq* are supplemented by Schedule 29. Again, the effect of coming within these rules is to escape the automatic 40% charge. Excessive lump sums may lead to the de-registration of the scheme.[62] These rules are supplemented by FA 2004, Schedule 29, as much amended by FA 2005 and FA 2006.

24.9.4.4 Other Payments Authorised and Unauthorised

Transfers to other schemes are permitted, and so section 169 authorises such payments if meeting the conditions for being *recognised transfers*. If the payment is to an overseas scheme and the Revenue do not recognise it, there is right of appeal to the court.[63] Payments to members for administration, eg to pay wages or buy assets, are authorised by section 171. A loan cannot be a valid scheme administration member payment.[64]

The legislation then turns to unauthorised member payments and begins by treating any *assignment of a benefit* (other than of an excluded pension) as if it were a payment to an unauthorised person, and so as an unauthorised payment.[65] There are exceptions for an assignment under a pension-sharing order,[66] or if the pension may continue to be paid after the member's death.[67] The idea of an unauthorised payment is extended to (a) unauthorised benefits in kind[68] and (b) value shifting.[69] The benefit-in-kind rules follow those in ITEPA 2003, Part 3.

24.9.4.5 Payments to Sponsoring Employers

The legislation then turns to the occupational pension scheme, which makes payments to the sponsoring employer. These are public service scheme payments (section 76); authorised surplus payments (section 177); compensation payments (section 178); authorised employer loans (section 179); scheme administration employer payments (section 180); and payments of a description prescribed by regulations made by the Board. The rules in section 179 on authorised employer loans are supplemented by rules in Schedule 30.

Expressly unauthorised payments to a sponsoring employer arise on value shifting (section 181) and unauthorised borrowings (sections 182–185).

---

[62] FA 2004, s 158.
[63] FA 2004, s 170.
[64] FA 2004, s 171(4).
[65] FA 2004, s 172(1).
[66] FA 2004, s 172(2).
[67] FA 2004, s 172(7).
[68] FA 2004, s 173.
[69] FA 2004, s 174.

24.9.5 Chapter 4, Sections 186–205 Registered Pension Schemes: Tax Reliefs and Exemptions

24.9.5.1 Exemption for Fund

Exemption from income tax is given to the scheme by section 186. The exempt income is that derived from investments or deposits held for the purposes of a registered pension scheme, or underwriting commissions applied for the purposes of a registered pension scheme, which would otherwise be chargeable to tax under ITTOIA 2005, Part 5, Chapter 8/the miscellaneous loss rules in CTA 2010, section 91 (ex Case VI of Schedule D). Other parts of section 186 ensure that investments are widely defined and that the exemption covers relevant stock lending fees. The exemption does not apply where the investment or deposit is held as a member of a property investment LLP. The exemption from CGT is given by section 187, which amends TCGA 1992, section 271 and exempts gains accruing to a person on a disposal of investments held for the purposes of a registered pension scheme.

24.9.5.2 Relief for Members' Contributions

Relief for members' contributions is provided by section 188. The payments must be 'relievable pension contributions', ie anything not excluded by section 188(3), such as payments after a person has reached the age of 75. Also excluded are contributions paid by an employer of the individual (which have their own rules) and certain rebate payments by the Revenue. A pension credit which increases the rights of the individual under the pension scheme is treated as a contribution on behalf of the individual only if it derives from a pension scheme that is not a registered pension scheme.[70]

Since the level of contributions is important, other rules go on to provide that certain sums are not treated as contributions for the purpose of FA 2004, Part 4. So one ignores transfers of sums representing accrued rights and any payments recovered by the individual's employer under certain pension schemes regulations.[71] Although the contributions will usually be in the form of money, section 195 allows the transfer of shares acquired under approved SAYE option schemes or under approved share incentive schemes.

Other conditions for relief. The individual must be a relevant UK individual for the tax year, which means satisfying any one of four tests in FA 2004, section 189. The first is having 'relevant UK earnings' chargeable to income tax for that year. The second is being resident in the UK at some time during the year. The third is being resident in the UK both at some time during the five tax years immediately before that year and when the individual became a member of the pension scheme. The fourth is having general earnings from overseas Crown employment subject to UK tax. Section 189(2) then defines 'relevant UK earnings'; for discussion, see the related earned income concepts in *Revenue Law*, §7.8. Section 189(2) lists employment income, income which is chargeable under ITTOIA 2005, Part 2 derived immediately from the carrying on or exercise of a trade, profession or vocation (whether individually, or as a partner acting personally in a partnership), ITTOIA 2005, Part 3 income from furnished holiday letting businesses, and patent income of an

---

[70] FA 2004, s 188(4).
[71] FA 2004, s 188(5), (6).

individual in respect of inventions. Any income that is exempt from UK tax under double taxation agreements is not 'taxable in the UK'.

Section 190 annual limits. Carrying over from the stakeholder pension system, there is a basic amount of £3,600 which may be contributed. Otherwise the limit is the amount of the individual's relevant UK earnings chargeable to income tax for the tax year. Relief is given either by deduction at source (section 192), or under a net pay agreement, ie by deduction from the relevant employment income (section 193). There is also provision for making a claim for deduction from total income (section 194).

Other rules provide relief for employer's contributions (section 196) and for the spreading of the relief in appropriate cases (sections 197–198); so section 197 directs, subject to exceptions, spreading over four years. The deductions are from profits taxed under ITTOIA 2005, Part 2 or, in the case of a company with investment business, as expenses of management under TA 1988, section 75 or under section 76, step 1 for an insurance company (sections 196 and 200). There is a separate rule allowing the deduction of sums required to be added to make good any deficiency in the scheme (section 199). Section 199A, added in 2008, allows certain indirect contributions, ie a payment of a contribution by someone other than the employer, to be spread in the same way.[72] Any minimum contributions made by the Revenue under the Pensions Schemes Act 1993, section 43 are grossed up (section 202).

24.9.5.3 Relevant Earnings

The definition of 'relevant earnings' uses many of the terms and expressions originally used in making the distinction between earned income and investment income, and still important for retirement annuity and personal pension relief calculations. Even though some of the rules were relaxed by FA 2004, the 'relevant earnings' used to calculate such entitlements still use broadly the same categories.[73] It is still important for identifying certain income of husband and wife and civil partners.[74] The distinction is not the same as that in *Revenue Law*, §7.7, ie between savings and other income for tax rate purposes; thus, income from land will be investment income, but is not savings income.

Relevant earnings are defined in three main categories, with one addition:[75]

(1) *Category I* is any employment income charged to tax under ITEPA 2003.[76] In *Dale v IRC*,[77] annuity payments to a trustee 'so long as he acts as trustee' were held by the House of Lords to be earned income. In that case the trustee was to receive the payments; the amount and value of the work actually done was irrelevant.[78] The Revenue argued that since a trustee was not at that time entitled to remuneration for his services as distinct from the reimbursement of expenses, the annuity was a conditional gift. However, the House of Lords held that the income was earned, since the

---

[72] Added by FA 2008, s 90.
[73] FA 2004, s 189(2), ex TA 1988, ss 623(2), 644.
[74] TA 1988, s 282A(4A): earned income cannot fall within s 282A.
[75] FA 2004, s 189(2), TA 1988, s 833(4); the list is supplemented in s 833(5), (6).
[76] FA 2004, s 189(2)(a).
[77] [1953] 2 All ER 671, 34 TC 468.
[78] 34 TC 468, 493 (*per* Lord Normand).

condition of the annuity was compliance with the testator's condition of serving as a trustee.

In *White v Franklin*,[79] dividends were held to be income earned from employment, provided they were a reward for services. However, this case was decided before the introduction of Schedule F in 1965, now ITTOIA 2005, Part 4, Chapter 3. The priority rules in ITTOIA 2005 make it clear that, in general, income taxed under ITEPA 2003 is not taxed under ITTOIA 2005, Part 4 (income from savings and investment); however, they go on to say that this does not apply to Chapter 3 (dividend income from UK-resident companies). It will be interesting to see how the courts get round this nonsense—if it ever comes to court.[80] In *White v Franklin*, the taxpayer (T) was assistant managing director of a company. T's mother and brother settled 50% of the issued share capital on trust to pay the income to the taxpayer, 'so long as he shall be engaged in the management of the company', with remainder to the mother and others. It was held that his income from the trust was earned income. The Commissioners had found that the settlement had been made as an inducement to T to remain with the company, and so the income accrued to him because, and not simply while, he was an active director.[81] It was also important that the trust held a large block of shares in the employing company, so that T's work would produce direct results. These, however, were matters of fact to support the inference that the purpose of the settlement was to keep T interested in the company, and was not simply an arrangement in a family settlement distributing income arising from family property to persons with certain qualifications.[82] This appears to be a borderline case.[83]

If a payment of income is not only in return for services but also for some other consideration, there can be no apportionment of the income so as to treat even a part of it as earned;[84] the question is one of the construction of the arrangement.

The TA 1988 definition of 'earned income' included any income from any property which is attached to or forms part of the employment of any office or employment of profit held by the individual. However, these words are not part of FA 2004, section 189(2). We may therefore exclude them for present purposes. Nevertheless, some see that *White v Franklin* may be justified on this basis. For details, see *Revenue Law*, 5th edition, at §7.8.2.

(2)   *Category II* consists of any income which is charged under ITTOIA 2005, Part 2 (ex Schedule D) and immediately derived by the individual from a trade, profession or vocation carried on by him as an individual or as a partner personally acting in the partnership.[85] This has given rise to some 'nice' distinctions. The earnings will be relevant only if the trade was carried on by the individual. In *Fry v Shiels Trustees*,[86] trustees legally owned and managed a business, the income of which was held for infant beneficiaries. It was held that the income was not earned since the profits were earned by the trustees, and so by individuals who certainly did not own them.

---

[79] [1965] 1 All ER 692, 42 TC 283, [1965] BTR 152.
[80] ITTOIA 2005, s 366(3); the rule may be dated back to 1965 and the start of Sch F.
[81] 42 TC 283, 284.
[82] [1965] 1 All ER 692, 699, 42 TC 283, 297.
[83] See Vinelott J in *O'Leary v McKinlay* [1991] STC 42, 53.
[84] *Hale v Shea* [1965] 1 All ER 155, 42 TC 260.
[85] See the comments of Lindsay J in *Koenigsberger v Mellor* [1993] STC 408, 414.
[86] [1915] SC 159; 6 TC 583.

A trustee-beneficiary would, in such circumstances, presumably be allowed to treat the income as earned and would be allowed to keep the benefit. In a similar vein, it has been held that income received as a name at Lloyds, ie as a member of a syndicate, was not 'relevant earnings' for pension purposes; the taxpayer's activities, which mostly involved deciding with which syndicate he would place his money, were preparatory to a trade which was, in fact, carried on by others on his behalf.[87]

Further difficulties have arisen from the requirement that the profit must be derived immediately from the business. An example is *Northend v White, Leonard and Corbin Greener*,[88] where interest accruing to a solicitor on money deposited at a bank on general deposit account was held to be investment income. The source was not the carrying-on of the profession but rather the loan deposit with the bank. This conclusion has been criticised.[89]

Today, income in the form of dividends may be earned income for ITTOIA 2005. This is because ITTOIA 2005, section 366 makes it clear that the Part 2 classification is to take priority over Part 4, Chapter 3. This is because statute contains a statutory provision that where shares are held as trading assets, the dividends arising from those shares are now treated as part of the trading profits of the business[90] and so may be earned income.

(3) *Category III* is income under ITTOIA 2005, Part 3 from carrying on a UK or EEA furnished holiday letting business.

(4) *Category IV* is patents. FA 2004, as amended, adds patent income, provided the individual, alone or jointly, devised the invention for which the patent was granted. At one time these payments were relevant earnings only if paid to the person who alone devised the invention; this test has been softened.[91]

24.9.6 FA 2004 Part 4, Chapter 5, Registered Pension Schemes: Tax Charges

Chapter 5 (sections 204–242) is the longest and contains details of the tax charges. There are six heads of charge:

- Charges on authorised payments—sections 204–207
- Unauthorised payments charge—sections 208–213
- Lifetime allowance charge—sections 214–226
- Annual allowance charge—sections 227–238
- Scheme sanction charge—sections 239–241
- De-registration charge—section 242.

---

[87] *Koenigsberger v Mellor* [1993] STC 408.

[88] [1975] STC 317; 50 TC 121, the interest belonged to the solicitor thanks to Solicitors Act 1965, s 8(2).

[89] The decision in *Northend* rests on a statement by Pennycuick J in *Bucks v Bowers* [1970] 2 All ER 202, 46 TC 267, which may only be a dictum; the decision in that case was later reversed by statute.

[90] ITTOIA 2005, s 366, ex F(No 2)A 1997, s 24, which applied as from 2 July 1997.

[91] FA 2004, s 189(2A); the test was softened by the removal of TA 1988, s 833(5C) and (5E), ITA 2007, explanatory notes change 125.

Many of these provisions contain rates and financial limits. The legislation usually enables the Treasury to vary these rates and limits by order.

FA 2006 made many detailed changes to ensure that members and former members are treated alike. Thus, an exemption from charge for payments to members extends to payments to former members too—and to payments of wages to former members for work done for the pension scheme itself. Similarly, the charge on unauthorised payments to members also extends to unauthorised payments to former members.[92]

24.9.6.1 Charges on Authorised Payments—Sections 204–207

FA 2004, section 204 begins by enacting rules on when the pensions are taxed as such. Schedule 31 amends the scheme of taxation in ITEPA 2003, Part 9, and in particular inserts Chapter 5A (sections 579A–579D) on pensions under registered pension schemes and so replaces ITEPA 2003, Part 9, Chapters 6–9. It also inserts Chapter 15A (sections 636A–636C) on lump sums under registered pension schemes and so repeals ITEPA 2003, Chapter 16. ITEPA 2003, section 579A charges pensions from registered pension plans (section 579A(1)) unless there is a liability to the unauthorised payments charge under FA 2004, section 208 (section 579A(2)). Sections 579B and 579C charge the pension income on the amount accruing during the year and charge the person receiving or entitled to the sum.

ITEPA 2003, section 636A lists a series of lump sums which are exempt from income tax. These are:

(1) a pension commencement lump sum;
(2) a serious ill-health lump sum;
(3) a refund of excess contributions lump sum;
(4) a defined benefits lump sum death benefit; or
(5) an uncrystallised funds lump sum death benefit.

These terms are defined elsewhere in the legislation. Section 636A goes on to state that it does not limit the operation of the lifetime allowance charge in FA 2004, sections 214 to 226.

FA 2004, section 205 charges short service refund lump sums. In simplified form this charge to income tax arises where a short service refund lump sum is paid by a registered pension scheme; ITEPA 2003, section 636A(2) directs that it is to be charged under section 205 but not otherwise. The charge falls on the scheme administrator. The charge is currently 20% in so far as the sum does not exceed £20,000, and 50% on any balance. Section 205 contains further rules, eg that the charge applied wherever the administrator or person entitled to the payment is resident or domiciled. FA 2011 introduced a serious ill-health lump sum charge of 55% in new section 205A.

Section 206 contains a separate 55% charge (increased from 35% by FA 2011) on special lump sum death benefits. These arise where the scheme pays a pension protection lump sum death benefit, or an annuity protection lump sum death benefit or an unsecured pension fund lump sum death benefit. Again the liability falls on the scheme administrator and non-residence is ignored.

---

[92] FA 2006, Sch 17, paras 1–19.

Lastly, section 207 imposes an authorised surplus payments charge of 35% where an authorised surplus payment is made to a sponsoring employer by an occupational pension scheme that is a registered pension scheme. Again the liability falls on the scheme administrator and non-residence is ignored.

24.9.6.2 The Unauthorised Payments Charge

A charge under FA 2004, section 208 arises where an unauthorised payment is made by a registered pension scheme. The person chargeable may be the member or, if the payment is made after the member's death, the recipient; it may also be a sponsoring employer. Where more than one person is liable, they are liable jointly and severally. As with sections 205–207, non-residence is ignored. The rate of the charge is 40%. The legislation makes it clear that an unauthorised payment may also be subject to the unauthorised payments surcharge under section 209, and the scheme sanction charge under section 239; further, the unauthorised payment is not also to be treated as income for any purpose of the Tax Acts.

The unauthorised payments surcharge in section 209 arises where a surchargeable unauthorised payment is made by the pension scheme. These may be surchargeable unauthorised payments member payments[93] or surchargeable unauthorised employer payments.[94] The persons liable are the same as for section 208. Again non-residence is ignored. The rate is 15%. The surcharge threshold is reached once the amount of the unauthorised payments reaches 25% of the value of the member's rights. The valuation of the member's rights requires one to value the member's crystallised rights[95] and uncrystallised rights.[96]

Unauthorised employer payments, ie payments made to the employer, may also be surcharged.[97] The rate is still 15%,[98] and once more the threshold is reached as the unauthorised payments come to 25%. So it applies once the amount of the unauthorised employer payments exceeds 25% of the aggregate of the amount of the sums and the market value of the assets held for the purposes of the pension scheme at the time when the unauthorised employer payment is made.

24.9.6.3 Lifetime Allowance Charge

This may arise when there is a 'benefit crystallisation event'. The 11 benefit events are set out on section 216, as modified by FA 2006, Schedule 23, adding paragraph 5A, and FA 2011, adding paragraph 5B—along with rules about the amount crystallised, but these have to be read along with Schedule 32. So if it is a money purchase scheme and sums are designated as available for payment to the member, it is the amount of those sums which is the amount crystallised. Where the benefit is a pension, one multiplies the pension by the relevant valuation factor.[99]

The charge arises if the individual's lifetime allowance is available (in whole or in part) but the amount crystallised by the benefit crystallisation event exceeds the amount of the

---

[93] FA 2004, s 210.
[94] FA 2004, s 213.
[95] FA 2004, s 211.
[96] FA 2004, s 212.
[97] FA 2004, s 213.
[98] FA 2004, s 209(6).
[99] FA 2004, s 276.

individual's lifetime allowance then available. On protection of pre-commencement rights, see §24.9.10.2 below. So if the available allowance is £1.5 million, and the amount crystallised is £2 million, there is a potential charge on £500,000. The rate of tax is 55% if the sums are paid out or otherwise treated as a lump sum, and 25% if retained.[100] The section has further magic language, in that an amount 'covered by a scheme payment' is treated as retained.

The persons liable to the lifetime allowance charge are the individual and the scheme administrator; their liability is joint and several. Where the member has died, liability in respect of any lump sum death benefit falls on the recipient. As usual, non-residence is ignored.

The standard lifetime allowance for the tax year 2006–07 was set by FA 2004, section 218 at £1.5 million. The minimum figures for the following four years were £1.6 million, £1.65 million, £1.75 million and, in 2010–11, £1.8 million. From 6 April 2012, however, the allowance dropped back to £1.5 million. Taxpayers can elect to retain the £1.8 million lifetime allowance, subject to additional requirements. The amount of the allowance available on the occurrence of a particular crystallisation event must take account of any part used on a previous event; the rules for this are in section 219, as modified by later Acts.

What may make life even more complicated are the lifetime allowance *enhancement factors*. These affect an individual's lifetime allowance at the time of a benefit crystallisation event. The formula is SLA + (SLA × LAEF), where SLA is the standard lifetime allowance at the time of the benefit crystallisation event, and LAEF is the lifetime allowance enhancement factor which operates with respect to the benefit crystallisation event and the individual or (where more than one so operates) the aggregate of them. FA 2006 added a rule to deal with the situation in which the person has had a benefit crystallisation event but then acquires a new or increased lifetime enhancement factor.[101] FA 2008 added a rule under which certain increases cannot give rise to a charge—these increases are related to the annual threshold rate.[102]

The rules providing the enhancement factors are conveniently listed in section 218(5), section 220 (pension credits from previously crystallised rights), sections 221–223 (individuals who are not always relevant UK individuals), sections 224–226 (transfers from recognised overseas pension schemes), Schedule 36, paragraphs 7–11 (primary protection) and paragraph 18 (pre-commencement pension credits). If an individual is permitted to take pension before normal minimum pension age, the individual's lifetime allowance may be reduced.[103]

The detail of these rules is obviously beyond the scope of this book. Two illustrative policy points may be made. First, the enhancement given by sections 221 *et seq* is designed to recognise that the rights accruing while the individual was not resident have not received UK tax relief; the effect of the enhancement is to remove (ignore) the value of those rights—by increasing the lifetime allowance by a similar amount. Secondly, primary protection;[104] this gives an increase in the lifetime allowance where the value of the rights

---

[100] FA 2004, s 215.
[101] FA 2004, s 219(4A), added by FA 2006, Sch 23, para 31.
[102] FA 2004, Sch 32, paras 10, as amended, and 10A (added). FA 2008, s 92 and Sch 29.
[103] FA 2004, Sch 36, para 19.
[104] FA 2004, Sch 36, para 7.

on 6 April 2006 is greater than £1.5 million. That excess increases the allowance. There are many transitional rules in Schedule 36.

24.9.6.4 The Annual Allowance Charge

This arises where the contributions for a year or 'total pension input amount for a tax year' exceed the amount of the annual allowance for the tax year.[105] The charge is on the individual; any non-residence of the individual or scheme administrator of the pension scheme is ignored. The rate of tax is determined by reference to the taxpayer's marginal income tax rate and is multiplied by the excess, so clawing back the maximum benefit. Section 228 set the annual allowance for 2008–09 at £235,000. The allowance was decreased, however, to its present level of £50,000 with effect from 6 April 2011. Unused allowance may be carried forward.[106]

Section 229 states that the total pension input is the aggregate of pension input amounts for pension input periods ending in the relevant tax year. Under section 238, the pension input period is the 'relevant commencement date' down to the anniversary of that date; the 'relevant commencement date' is defined in a variety of ways in section 238 and includes a date nominated by the individual to the administrator or vice versa.

Under section 229, each arrangement must be brought into account. However, there is no pension input amount in respect of an arrangement if, before the end of the tax year, the individual has become entitled to all the benefits which may be provided to the individual under the particular arrangement, or has died.[107] This means that in that final year, money may be put into the scheme without falling foul of the lifetime allowance charge.[108] Moreover, since it not an 'input' it may exceed the relevant earnings limit. The pension input amounts are specified in detail.[109] FA 2011 added sections 237A–237F on the liability of individuals and scheme administrators where the annual allowance is exceeded.

24.9.6.5 Scheme Sanction Charge

The fifth head of charge (section 239) is the scheme sanction charge, which arises where in any tax year one or more 'scheme chargeable payments' are made by a registered pension scheme. Examples of scheme chargeable payments are unauthorised payments and improper borrowings[110]—see further section 241, which also provides some exceptions.

It will be remembered that section 208(7) expressly states that an unauthorised payment charge under section 208 is without prejudice to any charge under section 239. Section 240 adds that a deduction should be made on account of any payments. However, it is not a full deduction; the deduction is either the amount of tax paid under section 208 or, if less, 25% of the scheme payment.[111] So, if the payment is £1,000 and the tax charged under section 208 is £400, the deduction from the £400 also payable under section 239 is only £250, leaving £150 to pay.

---

[105] FA 2004, s 227.
[106] FA 2004, s 228A.
[107] FA 2004, s 228(3).
[108] *Simon's Finance Act Handbook 2004* (Butterworths, 2004), 224.
[109] FA 2004, ss 230–237.
[110] FA 2004, s 185.
[111] FA 2004, s 208(3).

The person liable to the scheme sanction charge is the scheme administrator, or the person who was the administrator before it was wound up; as usual, any non-residence is ignored.

24.9.6.6 De-registration Charge

This is levied at 40% on the value of the funds at de-registration.[112] It arises where the registration of a registered pension scheme is withdrawn. The person liable is the scheme administrator immediately before the registration was withdrawn. As usual, non-residence is ignored. TCGA 1992, section 239A explains the CGT consequences where a scheme is de-registered; there is an acquisition of any chargeable assets at the value taken for the charge under FA 2004, section 242.

24.9.7 *Schemes That are not Registered Pension Schemes*

Chapter 6 provides rules for schemes that are not registered pension schemes. It begins with section 243, which simply enacts Schedule 33 containing the detailed rules applicable to 'migrant member relief' in respect of contributions under overseas pension schemes; section 244 then enacts Schedule 34 on how certain UK charges apply to non-UK schemes.

Schedule 35 rewrites a number of other tax rules which refer to pension schemes. So FA 2003, Schedule 24, which attacks certain fringe benefit schemes by denying a deduction to the employer for payments made, did not disallow deductions for pension schemes; this is now achieved (section 245) by making an exception for 'employer financed retirement scheme', a phrase which is defined not in the general definition section to Chapter 4 but in ITEPA 2003, Part 6, Chapter 2. The introduction in FA 2011 of the new 'disguised remuneration' rules means that it is now tax-inefficient to provide employee-financed retirement benefit schemes. Section 246 contains a self-standing deferral rule for certain other contributions.

There are further amendments to ITEPA 2003, Chapter 6, including the outright repeal of the charge under Chapter 1[113] and changes to Chapter 2 (taxation of non-pension benefits). The changes to Chapter 2 include a de minimis exception for benefits which do not exceed £100 in that tax year.[114]

Section 248 amends ITEPA 2003, section 307 by imposing a tax charge on the employee where the employer takes out insurance against the risk of non-payment of a pension by reason of the employer's insolvency. The cost of the insurance is a taxable benefit in kind.

24.9.8 *Scheme Administrator*

With Chapter 7 we come to a number of compliance rules, most of which focus on the scheme administrator.[115] Under section 250, the Revenue may issue a notice requiring the scheme administrator to make a return. The return must contain any information

---

[112] FA 2004, s 242.
[113] FA 2004, s 247.
[114] FA 2004, s 249.
[115] Defined in FA 2004, ss 270–274.

reasonably required by the notice and the administrator must deliver any accounts or other documents relating to information contained in the return, which may reasonably be required by the notice. This is followed by a statutory list of matters that can be required, ending with (*k*) 'any other matter relating to the administration of the pension scheme'. The Revenue are then given a power to make regulations requiring persons 'of a prescribed description' to provide further information,[116] and by section 252 for such persons to be required (by notice) to produce documents relating to matters specified later and 'to provide to the Inland Revenue any particulars relating to any of those matters which the Inland Revenue may reasonably require'.[117] These notices have their own procedural rules, time limits and appeals.

Further rules explain how scheme administrators who find themselves liable to income tax under FA 2004 Part 4 must account for that tax; an obligation to account quarterly is imposed by section 254. Again there is a separate regulation-making power.[118] The regulations may, in particular modify the operation of any provision of the Tax Acts, or provide for the application of any provision of the Tax Acts (with or without modification). Enhanced lifetime allowances arise where a person is entitled to a non-standard lifetime allowance.[119] The penalties provisions for breaches of sections 250–254 are in sections 257–260. Enhanced lifetime allowances have their own penalty rules.[120] There follows a general penalty for false statements (max £3,000) in cases of fraud or negligence.

A penalty of £3,000 may be imposed where the Revenue consider that the scheme is being wound up wholly or mainly to facilitate the payment of a lump sum.[121] The £3,000 penalty may also arise if the scheme administrator transfers sums to an insured scheme (one invested in life policies) but does not transfer the sums to the right person (section 266). Sections 266A and 266B provide relief from the unauthorised payment charge for repatriation of money on the order of a court or regulator; section 266A deals with the member and section 266B with the scheme.

There is an interesting two-limbed good faith defence for a scheme administrator liable to the lifetime allowance charge in respect of a benefit crystallisation event:[122]

(1)   The scheme administrator must have reasonably believed that there was no liability to the lifetime allowance charge in respect of the benefit crystallisation event.
(2)   In all the circumstances of the case, it would not be just and reasonable for the scheme administrator to be liable to the lifetime allowance charge in respect of the benefit crystallisation event.

It will be seen that this relief is in respect to the charge to tax arising, not to any penalty. There are similar defences for scheme administrators for certain liabilities for unauthorised

---

[116]   FA 2004, s 251.
[117]   The matters are set out in FA 2004, s 252(3).
[118]   FA 2004, s 255.
[119]   Eg under FA 2004, s 218.
[120]   FA 2004, ss 261–263.
[121]   FA 2004, s 265. *Simon's Finance Act Handbook 2004* (Butterworths, 2004) 252 suggests that this is to counter abuse of the lifetime allowance provisions, as where pension benefits are paid out in lump sums under commutation rules in FA 2004, Sch 29, para 7.
[122]   FA 2004, s 214.

payments surcharge or a scheme sanction.[123] Sections 267 and 268 have their own appeal rules in section 269.

Lastly, the statute address the question of who is treated as a scheme administrator for these rules. Section 270 defines a scheme administrator and lists the required qualifications, eg must be resident in the EU or EEA, and must make a declaration to the Revenue. Section 271 directs what is to happen when there is a change in the scheme administrator. In general, a replacement scheme administrator inherits the existing liabilities of the outgoing one. A person cannot simply escape liability by resigning as a scheme administrator without a replacement (and any replacement must meet the terms of section 270). The Revenue have power to release the scheme administrator in such situations.

If the scheme administrator defaults, there are further rules making trustees of the funds liable as scheme administrator[124] or even, as a last resort and in the case certain liabilities, the members themselves.[125]

24.9.9 Miscellaneous

The legislation concludes with definitions and certain rules as to valuations.[126]

24.9.10 Transitional

24.9.10.1 Deemed Registration

FA 2004, Schedule 36 contains various transitional rules. The first batch are administrative.[127] For example, on 6 April 2006, all schemes approved under the existing legislation were deemed to become registered schemes under the FA 2004 regime.[128] Scheme administrators could opt out of the deemed registration on payment of income tax at 40% on the value of the fund at that date.[129] The Revenue were given the power to modify the rules of existing schemes.[130] Existing scheme administrators became administrators under the FA 2004 regime[131]—with continuing liabilities for any pre-commencement liabilities.[132] The old rules on withdrawal of approval of schemes, eg TA 1988, section 650(1), continue to operate after 6 April 2006.[133]

24.9.10.2 Pre-commencement Rights

The protection of pre-commencement rights from the lifetime allowance charge is governed by FA 2004, Schedule 36, paragraphs 7–20. The FA 2004 rules do not impose an immediate 55% recovery charge on the amount by which an existing fund exceeds the

---

[123] FA 2004, s 268.
[124] FA 2004, s 272.
[125] FA 2004, s 273.
[126] FA 2004, ss 276–278.
[127] FA 2004, Sch 36, paras 1–6.
[128] FA 2004, Sch 36, para 1.
[129] FA 2004, Sch 36, para 2.
[130] FA 2004, Sch 36, para 3.
[131] FA 2004, Sch 36, para 4.
[132] FA 2004, Sch 36, para 6.
[133] FA 2004, Sch 36, para 5.

lifetime allowance of £1.5 million. Instead the actual value of the agreed fund on 6 April 2006 is expressed as a percentage of £1.5 million; this will necessarily be more than 100%, so if X has a personal pension under the old rules, and the value of the fund is £2.5 million, the percentage is 166.66% (and one of £3 million, 200%). This is the personal allowance for X. If X does make any further contribution to the fund, it is safe from any recovery charge. The purpose of this rule is to protect X from any tax risk just because the fund grows in value. The lifetime allowance will then grow, and may catch up with the fund value, at which point further contributions may safely be made.

The person with rights under a defined benefit scheme is in the same position of having a capped lifetime allowance. So if E's rights are valued at £2 million, the percentage for 2006–07 is 133.33%. E cannot count any post-2006 years of service (the analogy of more contributions), but the pension may rise to reflect any increase in salary without risk of a charge under these rules to E.

The protection of pre-commencement benefits rights is governed by FA 2004, Schedule 36, paragraphs 21–36. Other provisions follow dealing with a variety of matters, including pensions taxed pre-commencement but accruing post-commencement[134] and the IHT treatment of a fund which was not a registered pension scheme or superannuation fund but which came within IHTA 1984, section 153 immediately before 6 April 2006 (it may remain within section 151 as long as no contributions are made on or after that date). There is a separate rule on IHT and discretionary trusts; this protects a certain proportion of the assets of the fund.[135]

---

[134] FA 2004, Sch 36, para 45.
[135] FA 2004, Sch 36, paras 57 and 58.

PART IV

Charities

25

Charities

25.1 Introduction[1]

Charities receive generous treatment under many tax codes; such treatments therefore qualify as tax expenditures.[2] The provisional figures for 2010–11[3] show that covenants and gift aid by individuals caused tax repayments of £1,101 million; the payroll giving scheme cost £20 million. Payments by companies are made gross and so do not cause repayments. Repayments in respect of dividend income of charities has ended.[4] Other figures available for 2010–11 are relief from IHT (£435 million), national non-domestic rates (£1,220 million) and VAT (£200 million), giving total relief for charities of £2,640 million. A reason behind the major changes made to the Charities Act 1993 by the Charities Act 2006, was the need to see whether these benefits were justified. The income tax provisions have been rewritten by ITA 2007, and the TA 1988 rules, much amended and rephrased in 2006, were rewritten

---

[1] Among many background tax policy sources, see Inland Revenue, *Discussion Document* (1999); Banks and Tanner, *Taxing Charitable Giving*, IFS Commentary 75 (Institute for Fiscal Studies, 1999); Chesterman (1999) 62 *MLR* 333; Chesterman, *Charities Trusts and Social Welfare* (Weidenfeld & Nicolson, 1979), esp ch 10; Krever and Kewley (eds), *Charities and Philanthropic Organisations: Reforming the Tax Subsidy and Regulatory Regimes* (Australian Tax Research Foundation, 1991); Scharf, Cherniavsky and Hogg, *Canadian Policy Research Network Working Paper* (1996); Surrey (1976) 84 *HLR* 352; Surrey, *Pathways to Tax Reform* (Harvard University Press, 1973); Andrews (1972) 86 *HLR* 309, esp 344–75; Bittker (1969) 78 *Yale LJ* 1285; Bittker (1972) *Tax Law Review* 37; McDaniel (1972) 27 *Tax Law Review* 377; and McNulty (1984) 3 *Virginia Tax Review* 229.

[2] See Surrey, *Pathways to Tax Reform*, esp 20, 223–32; and Feldstein, in Aaron and Boskin (eds), *The Economics of Taxation* (Brookings Institute, 1980). For vigorous criticism of one application of this approach, see Bittker (1969) 78 *Yale LJ* 1285. On US rules for deduction, see Bittker and Lokken, *Federal Taxation of Income, Estates and Gifts* (Warren, Gorman & Lamont, 1989), ch 35; see also Griffith (1989) *Hastings LJ* 343.

[3] HMRC Statistics 2011, ch 10.

[4] F(No 2)A 1997, s 35, see below §25.3.1.

by CTA 2010 for companies. The 2006 changes have been heavily criticised as giving a general impression of attempts to stifle charitable giving and limiting charitable tax relief.[5] The rules on transactions between charities and substantial donors have, it is said, enormous potential for damaging relations between charities and donors, and for increasing administration costs. So much will depend on how the sometimes vague rules are applied by HMRC. One may note that although the rules were reformed in 2006, the 2007 Income Tax Rewrite provisions contain no fewer than nine changes, none addressing these concerns.

Simon says nothing about the charitable deduction in his *Personal Income Taxation*. The Canadian Royal Commission recommended the continuation of the deduction for charitable contributions and the exemption of the income of charities, but also recommended that the beneficiary should be taxed on any benefits received.[6] The 1955 Report of the UK Royal Commission made some suggestions, but its most telling point was that a more restrictive definition of 'charity' was needed; the present law, still unchanged, was hardly less than chaotic and the prevailing uncertainty did not do credit to the tax system.[7] The Meade Committee Report and the Mirrlees Review say virtually nothing on these matters.

The legislation in ITA 2007 talks of a 'charitable trust', with section 519 defining it as 'a trust established for charitable purposes only'. CTA 2010, section 467 (ex TA 1988, section 506) refers to 'a charitable company' as 'any body of persons established for charitable purposes only'. However, these rules are to be replaced once FA 2010, section 30 and Schedule 6 are brought into effect. FA 2010 will introduce new definitions of 'charitable trusts' and 'charitable companies' (paragraphs 1–2). These were necessitated by the extension of reliefs and privileges to charities established elsewhere in Europe resulting from ECJ decisions. The conditions reflect the ECJ's view that the Member States had legitimate interests to protect. The charity must satisfy the UK definition of 'charity' as set out in the Charities Act 2006, section 2 (paragraph 1). It must meet conditions as to the jurisdiction (paragraph 2)—be a Member State of the EU or recognised by statutory instrument. It must be registered with any regulator in its own country analogous to the Charity Commission (paragraph 3), and those in control and management must be fit and proper persons (paragraph 4).

Leaving aside the possibility of registration elsewhere, in the UK a charity must be registered with the Charity Commission unless it is an exempt charity. Such a registration is, however, conclusive evidence that the body is a charity. For this reason the Revenue may object to a registration, as in *IRC v McMullen*,[8] or may ask the Charity Commission to take steps to deregister a charity; they may also refuse relief on the ground that income is not applied for charitable purposes. A trust for foreign purposes may be charitable, but must be under the jurisdiction of a court in the UK.[9]

---

[5] Evans [2006] BTR 531; see also Parry-Wingfield, *The Tax Journal* (14 August 2006) 9, and (21 August 2006) 5.
[6] Carter (chair), Canada Royal Commission on Taxation, *Report*, vol 3 (Ottawa, 1966) 222–27 and *ibid*, vol 4, 131–36.
[7] Royal Commission on the Taxation of Profits and Income, *Final Report*, Cmd 9474 (1955) para 175.
[8] [1981] AC 1, (1981) 54 TC 413.
[9] *Dreyfus Foundation v IRC* [1956] AC 39, 36 TC 126.

In *The Independent Schools Council v The Charity Commission for England and Wales (and others)*,[10] the Upper Tribunal shed some light on the meaning of the 'public benefits' requirement in the Charities Act 2006 as it relates to fee-charging schools. The decision is also relevant to other charities that charge for services. The Tribunal found that the Charity Commission's guidance to fee-charging charities was 'erroneous' in a number of respects. According to the Tribunal, the provision of education by independent schools is not in itself a public benefit, and charitable schools must ensure that children of families who cannot afford the fees are able to benefit from what the schools do in a way that is neither minimal nor token. The Tribunal also decided that it was for the charitable trustees to decide how best to do this in each charity's particular circumstances.

Further tax rules apply to certain well-known public bodies.[11] In addition, the rules on benefits disqualify a gift from qualifying as gift aids are modified for the National Trust and similar bodies.[12] Political parties are not charities, and while there are specific reliefs from CGT and IHT for gifts to them, there is no specific income tax relief. Special but restricted reliefs have been made available to those community amateur sports clubs which do not qualify as charities.[13]

25.2 Tax Treatment of Gifts to Charity

In UK tax law, gifts to charity have been deductible for income tax purposes if they were made in the form of (a) charitable covenants, (b) gift aid, (c) payments under a payroll deduction scheme ((a) is now merged into (b), on which see *Revenue Law*, §10.6).[14] Today the starting point for gifts of money is ITA 2007, sections 520–523 (charitable trusts) and CTA 2010, sections 475–477A (charitable companies). If the gift qualifies for gift aid, it is grossed up at the basic rate and treated as the charity's income of the grossed up amount.[15] If the charity becomes liable to income tax later on, the charge is made under section 521, as envisaged by ITA 2007, section 3(2). Payment by HMRC to the charity is authorised as from the passing of FA 2008; it is not technically a repayment of tax but an authorised payment from public funds.

There are deductions in computing trading income of costs incurred in sending employees to work for charities.[16] Other rules have removed the application of the non-deduction rule for business gifts, etc[17] from gifts to charities.[18] For CGT purposes, a taxpayer who

---

[10] [2011] UKUT 421 (TCC). For a case in which the taxpayer company failed to show that it was established for charitable purposes only, see *Helena Housing Ltd v Revenue & Customs Commissioners* [2011] STC 1307 (UT).

[11] TCGA 1992, s 257(l)(b), applying IHTA 1984, Sch 3.

[12] ITA 2007, s 420, ex FA 1990 s 25(5E)–(5G), as amended FA 2000; for discussion of earlier rule, see Ghosh and Robson [1993] BTR 496, but note that this was before the reform of ss 660 *et seq*.

[13] CTA 2010, ss 658–671, ex FA 2002, s 58 and Sch 18, as amended, eg by FA 2004, s 56. Such clubs that register with HMRC are allowed gift aid repayments, with retroactive effect from 1 April 2010 in relation to gift aid and 6 April 2010 in relation to gift aid claims.

[14] On payroll schemes, see *Revenue Law*, §18.3.4.

[15] ITA 2007, s 520 and CTA 2010, s 475, ex FA 1990, s 25(10) and (12).

[16] ITTOIA 2005, ss 70–71 and CTA 2009, ss 70–71, ex TA 1988, s 86; see also ITTOIA 2005, s 108–110 and CTA 2009, 105–108, ex TA 1988, s 83A (gift in kinds to charity) and 84 (gifts to educational establishments).

[17] Ie ITTOIA 2005, s 45, ITEPA 2003, ss 356–358, CTA 2009, ss 1298–1300, ex TA 1988, s 577 (but not other rules such as ITTOIA 2005, s 34, CTA 2009, s 54, ex TA 1988, s 74(1)(a)).

[18] ITTOIA 2005, s 47(5) and CTA 2009, s 1300(1),(5), ex TA 1988, s 577(9).

makes a gift of an asset to a charity is treated as if the asset were sold for a sum such that no gain, no loss arises on the disposal.[19] The relief exempts a donor from liability to CGT on the gain. It is far less generous than the US rules, which not only exempt the donor from any liability on the gain but also permit the donor to treat the full market value as a contribution to charity for income tax purposes and so as available for deduction against other income.[20] These US rules were wide open to abuse: for example, T would give a car to his church and claim—and get a deduction of—the value of the car ($10,000) even if the church eventually sold it for only $3,000. Restrictions have followed.

Gift rules introduced by FA 2000 were at first confined to shares and other securities; they gave rise to abuse which was countered by legislation in 2004.[21] Relief for gifts of land was introduced by FA 2002.[22] Gifts of other assets, eg pictures or books, do not yet qualify.

The basic UK treatment is also applied for CGT where a taxpayer sells an asset to a charity and the sale consideration received does not exceed the acquisition cost adjusted for any relevant relief or allowance.[23]

This treatment extends also to settled property. Thus, where property has been held in a non-charitable trust and then, under the terms of the trust, a charity becomes absolutely entitled to that property, there is no charge to CGT. This is achieved by the charge on the deemed disposal specified by TCGA 1992, section 71 being treated as if it were a no gain, no loss disposal.[24]

Under the IHT rules, a transfer of value to a charity may be an exempt transfer.

FA 2010, section 32 made amendments to rules for charities, etc for payroll giving (paragraph 1), payments to bodies outside the UK which may be non-charitable expenditure and so disqualified if made in the UK (paragraph 2) and gift aid for donations made by a non UK-resident donor with insufficient UK taxable income (paragraph 3). The remaining paragraphs amended the rules on repayment claims by charitable trusts and charitable companies (paragraphs 4–7). FA 2010, section 31 and Schedule 7 also made a number of technical changes to the rules on gifts of qualifying investments. The relief is normally given on the full market value of the investments at the date of the gift. Avoidance schemes have been devised where the donor acquires investments well below market value as part of a scheme or an arrangement, or where the market value is artificially inflated. In future relief is given only on the true economic cost of the acquisition to the donor.[25] FA 2012, Schedule 14 added new rules governing gifts of pre-eminent property in accordance with a scheme set up by the Secretary of State ('gifts to the nation') and Schedule 15 made further changes to gift aid relief.

---

[19] TCGA 1992, s 257.
[20] See eg Speiller (1980) 80 *Columbia L Rev* 214.
[21] TA 1988, s 587B, added by FA 2000, s 43 and amended by FA 2004, s 139. These rules are now in ITA 2007, ss 431–440 and CTA 2010, ss 206–212. The schemes attracting the Revenue's attention are described in Press Release 2 July 2004, [2004] *Simon's Tax Intelligence* 1573.
[22] ITA 2007, ss 441–442 and CTA 2010, ss 213 and 216, ex TA 1988, s 587C, added by FA 2002, s 97.
[23] TCGA 1992, s 257(2).
[24] TCGA 1992, s 257(3).
[25] See HMRC Explanatory Note, para 30, and see para 31 for examples.

25.3 Reliefs Accruing to the Charity: Income

Income accruing to charities[26] receives privileged treatment. Trading income is dealt with separately, along with miscellaneous income (ex Schedule D, Case VI); see §25.4.1 below. ITA 2007 and CTA 2010 follow the ITTOIA 2005 precedent of considering the trading rules before other types of income. However, as the exemptions are more restricted, we follow the former order in TA 1988. After (a) exemptions for certain types of income of the charity (§25.3.1), we turn to (b) gifts received by the charity (§25.3.2) and then (c) trading and miscellaneous income received by the charity (§25.4).

25.3.1 Exemptions for Certain Types of Income

Various types of income are exempt from income tax and corporation tax.[27] In each case the exemption applies only so far as the income is applied for charitable purposes only:

(1)   Property income. ITA 2007 exempts income under ITTOIA 2005, Part 3 and certain property income taken across to ITTOIA 2005, Part 2 by section 261. Distributions from a REIT is also exempt.[28] The equivalent corporation tax provision is in CTA 2010, section 485.[29]

(2)   ITA 2007 and CTA 2010 exempt most income from savings and investment,[30] public revenue dividends,[31] transaction in deposits,[32] certain miscellaneous income,[33] and income for estates in administration.[34]

(3)   Certain profits from fund-raising events[35] and lotteries.[36]

(4)   Offshore income gains.[37]

This list does not exhaust the range of taxable income, so that the charity is chargeable on any other income it may receive, for example such as falls within ITEPA 2003, or which falls within ITTOIA 2005 and is not yearly interest or other annual payments.

The exemptions are permitted only where the income is actually applied for charitable purposes; this gives the Revenue a policing role. In considering whether money is applied for charitable purposes, the court looks to see how the money has been applied. If it has been applied to charitable purposes, it does not matter that the charity was obliged to apply

---

[26] On position of contemplative orders, see TA 1988, ss 508A and 508B, giving statutory effect to ex ESC B10.

[27] ITA 2007, ss 531–537 and CTA 2010, ss 475–491, ex TA 1988, s 505(1) and s 9(4)). On CGT, see below at §§25.3, 25.6, 25.7. There are also reliefs from VAT under VATA 1994, Sch 8, Group 15 and from stamp duty and NICs (FA 1977, s 57).

[28] ITA 2007, s 531(2A), referring to FA 2006, s 121.

[29] On application for charitable purposes, see *IRC v Helen Slater Charitable Trust Ltd* [1981] STC 471, CA; the scope of that decision is, however, greatly restricted by the rules outlined below at §25.6.

[30] ITA 2007, s 532(2) and CTA 2010, s 486. CTA 2010 excludes non-trading profits from loan relationships as well.

[31] ITA 2007, s 533 and CTA 2010, s 487.

[32] ITA 2007, s 534.

[33] ITA 2007, s 536 and CTA 2010, s 488.

[34] ITA 2007, s 538 and CTA 2010, s 489.

[35] ITA 2007, s 529, CTA 2010, s 484 and ESC C4.

[36] ITA 2007, s 530 and CTA 2010, s 484, ex TA 1988, s 505(1)(f), added by FA 1995, s 138.

[37] ITA 2007, s 535, TA 1988, s 761.

it that way; neither, probably, is it relevant what reason or motive the trustees may have had, nor that they may confer some incidental benefit upon some third person.[38] However, this requirement was not met where a charity established for the public benefit gave all its income to the children of employees of a particular firm which was connected with the managers of the charity.[39]

If charity A gives the money to charity B, the money has been applied for charitable purposes.[40] At one time this entitled charity A to claim any exemptions or repayments whether or not B used the money properly, and even though charities A and B were under common control; this is now restricted (see below §25.6).[41]

25.3.2 Income from Gifts

25.3.2.1 Gift Aid

An individual[42] donor (D) making a qualifying donation is treated as making a payment to charity equal to the amount of the gift grossed up at basic rate (20%).[43] Payment is authorised as from the passing of FA 2008; it is not technically a repayment of tax but an authorised payment from public funds. Thus, a payment of £800 is treated as a gift of £1,000 and the charity recovers £200 tax from the Revenue.[44] If D is a higher-rate taxpayer, D is entitled to total relief of £400, of which £200 is treated as having already been with-held by D; the remaining £200 of relief is given in the self-assessment as a deduction in computing total income. The form allows the taxpayer to direct the Revenue to make this repayment to the charity; the form also allows the taxpayer to direct that any repayment of tax due overall be paid to charity (ITA 2007, section 429).

Where the basic rate tax treated as deducted exceeds the amount of income tax (and CGT) with which D is charged for the year, D is assessable to pay tax at basic rate to make good the shortfall.[45] This rule refers to D's total liability for the year, not to the amount of tax charged on the £1,000 given. So provided D has a taxable income sufficient to generate £200 of tax, it does matter that part of that is at 10% and the rest at 20%. The tax rules for different types of income mean that the tax cost to D of making a gift will vary according to its source.[46]

25.3.2.2 History

For most of the last century the normal form was the charitable covenant. This was a covenant giving rise to income for the charity under Schedule D, Case III as an annuity. The covenantor obtained a deduction for the gross value of the covenant through the basic rate

---

[38] *Campbell v IRC* (1966) 45 TC 427, 443, 444, *per* Buckley J.

[39] *IRC v Educational Grants Association* [1967] 2 All ER 893, (1967) 44 TC 93.

[40] *IRC v Helen Slater Charitable Trust* [1981] STC 471, CA; see Gillard, *In the Name of Charity* (Chatto & Windus, 1987), 20; on recovery of tax, see ITA 2007, s 523 and CTA 2010, s 474, ex TA 1988, s 505(2).

[41] ITA 2007, ss 540, 562, and CTA 2010, ss 492, 393, 515, ex TA 1988, s 505(3).

[42] On the boundary between making a gift as an individual and as PR, see *St Dunstans v Major* [1997] STC (SCD) 212.

[43] ITA 2007, ss 414 and 423(1)–(5), ex FA 1990, s 25(6); the grossing-up rate is tied to the date the payment is made (ITA 2007, s 909 (2)) and no longer when it was due. The 2008 reduction in the basic rate from 22% to 20% would have had the effect of reducing the overall value of a gift aid payment. FA 2008 s 53 and Sch 19 temporarily allowed charities to use a 'notional basic rate' of 22% for payments between 6 April 2008 and 5 April 2011.

[44] FA 1990, s 25(10).

[45] ITA 2007, ss 424(3) and 425, ex FA 1990, s 25(8).

[46] For an example using out-of-date rates but making the essential point, see Lathwood (2000) 145 *Taxation* 118.

mechanism in the now repealed TA 1988, section 348, and a deduction for surtax. In order to escape from the settlement rules in what became TA 1988, section 660A (now ITTOIA 2005, Part 5, Chapter 5), the covenant had to be for a period which was capable of exceeding six years, later reduced to three years. Basic arithmetic tells one that if a covenant is to be capable of exceeding six or three years there must be seven or four payments, and so these became known as seven-year covenants or four-year covenants.[47]

When Schedule D, Case III was reformed by FA 1988, a new category of payment was invented, the covenanted payment to charity. This was similar to the old annual payment but relied on specific rules rather than general Schedule D, Case III principles as they then were, eg as to permissible benefits. Still, however, the covenantor deducted basic rate tax at source (and got a deduction for higher-rate purposes) and the charity reclaimed the basic rate tax from the Revenue.

The 'covenanted payment to charity' was at first supplemented and later superseded by gift aid in FA 1990, section 25. These were single payments, and at first had to be not less than £250 and had to be accompanied by a certificate. Relief for single donations by individuals to charities may be traced back to the payroll deduction scheme originally introduced by FA 1986, section 27 and now in ITEPA 2003, Part 12. As these payments were made gross, there was no question of any tax repayment to the charity; moreover, they were not income of the charity. Relief for single donations by companies was also introduced in 1986 by FA 1986, section 29, which made amendments to TA 1988, section 339; these were supplemented by changes made by FA 1990, section 26. As a result of FA 2000 there is now no minimum sum.[48]

FA 2004 allowed a person entitled to a repayment of tax under the self-assessment regime to elect that the repayment be given to a charity on a list maintained by the Revenue.[49] As with other gift aid payments, the amount is grossed up at basic rate but is then entitled to higher-rate relief. The payment is treated as made in the year in which the repayment arises, not the year to which that repayment relates.

25.3.2.3 Gifts of Shares, Securities and Real Property

A donor making a gift of a qualifying investment or qualifying interest in land (as defined) is entitled to an income tax deduction in computing net income[50] equal to 'the relievable amount', ie the market value of the investments, defined as for CGT and any associated costs of disposal.[51] When the value of the net benefit to the charity is less than the market value, the net benefit is taken instead.[52] Investments qualify if they are quoted shares or securities, units in an authorised unit trust, shares in an OEIC or an interest in an offshore

---

[47] For details see *Revenue Law*, 3rd edn, §§17:42 *et seq* and Tiley and Collison's *UK Tax Guide 1999–2000* (Butterworths, 1999), §§13.28 *et seq*.

[48] FA 1990, s 25 amended by FA 2000, s 39. In 1992–93 the minimum was £600. On millennium aid, see FA 1998, s 47; the list of countries is derived from the World Bank designation of 'low income countries': Inland Revenue Press Release, 14 March 1998, [1998] *Simon's Weekly Tax Intelligence* 393.

[49] FA 2004, s 83.

[50] Step 2, ITA 2007, s 23; see ex TA 1988, s 587B(2)(a)(ii); s 83B added by FA 2000, s 43; on timing, see s 43(3).

[51] ITA 2007, ss 434–436, ex TA 1988, s 587B(10).

[52] ITA 2007, s 434, ex TA 1988, s 587B(4), as amended by FA 2004.

fund.[53] The idea is to give relief where the assets are easy to value and easy to realise.[54] There are equivalent rules for corporation tax.[55]

The relevant amount also takes account of any consideration or benefit received, as where the benefactor sells the shares to the charity at a low price.[56] This relief is distinct from and in addition to the CGT rules exempting the donor from CGT liability. The charity's base cost of the asset is reduced by the relevant amount (or to nil if the base cost is less than the relevant amount).[57] Where the charity becomes subject to a disposal-related obligation, the effect of that obligation must be taken into account in determining the net value to the charity.[58]

The taxpayer may claim a deduction for qualifying gifts of land.[59] Pedants and exasperated legal historians will note that while the legislation applies to qualifying interests in land, including leasehold interests, the section is incorrectly headed 'gifts of real property'. The gift aid treatment applies to a lease carved out of an existing freehold or leasehold interest subsection.[60] Special rules require the individual to provide a certificate. Further rules apply where the land is held jointly or, the opposite case, where there is a joint disposal.[61]

25.3.2.4 Disqualifying Benefits

The gift aid rules require that neither the donor nor any person connected with him may receive a benefit in consequence of making the donation.[62] A saving of IHT has been held to be a benefit.[63] These rules were revised by FA 2007 to provide that the benefit must not exceed 5% of the amount of the gift, subject to a maximum of £500 (which is 5% of £10,000).[64] FA 2011, section 41 further extended the thresholds for the value of benefits from £500 to £2,500. There are also rules which annualise the value of certain benefits and donations, eg where the right to receive benefits extends over a period of less than 12 months.[65]

Like the 1988 rules before them, certain admission rights are disregarded, viz the right to free admission to view property or wildlife where the preservation of property or conservation of wildlife is the sole or main purpose of the charity.[66] As from 6 April 2006 the free admission exclusion is amended, partly to counter the practice of people making a gift aid donation equal to the normal admission price in lieu of simply paying that price, and partly to widen the charities for which the right of admission is not a disqualifying

---

[53] ITA 2007, s 432, ex TA 1988, s 587B(9).

[54] Revenue Notes on Clause 43, para 18.

[55] CTA 2010, ss 203 *et seq*, ex TA 1988, s 587B(a)(ii).

[56] ITA 2007, s 434, ex TA 1988, s 587B.

[57] ITA 2007, s 434, ex TA 1988, s 587B; among the consequential rules are references to total income for s 550 (s 587B(2)(b)).

[58] ITA 2007, ss 437–40, ex TA 1988, ss 587B(8B) *et seq*.

[59] ITA 2007, s 431, ex TA 1988, s 587B(9A)–(9E) and s 587C, both added by FA 2002, s 97.

[60] ITA 2007, s 433, ex TA 1988, s 587B(9C).

[61] ITA 2007, ss 441–443.

[62] ITA 2007, s 418, ex FA 1990, s 25(2)(e); on mechanics, see *Revenue Law*, §10.6.

[63] FA 1990, s 25(5E)–(5G) so as to safeguard benefits such as free admission to National Trust properties, etc. *St Dunstans v Major* [1997] STC (SCD) 212.

[64] FA 1990, s 25(5) and (5A).

[65] ITA 2007, s 419, FA 1990, s 25(5B)–(5D).

[66] ITA 2007, s 420, FA 1990, s 25(5E)–(5G); on earlier law, see FA 1989, s 53.

benefit. The right to make a donation must be open to any member of the public; the right must be to enter or view specified types of property preserved, maintained, kept or created by the charity in pursuance of its charitable objects (no longer just heritage preservation and wildlife conservation). In addition, either the right of admission must be for at least one year at times when the public can come in, or the gift must be for at least 10% more than the normal admission price.[67]

25.4 Trading and Miscellaneous Income

25.4.1 Specific Exemption for Certain Types of Trading Income

ITA 2007, section 524 and CTA 2010, section 478 grant exemption from income tax and corporation tax for 'profits etc' of charitable trades. The exempt profits are, as we shall see, circumscribed. However, they extend to a number of receipts—hence the 'etc'.

If a charity carries on a trade, it will be exempt from the tax on the profits of that trade if the profits are applied solely for the purposes of the charity and the trade is for the relevant period 'a charitable trade'. A trade is a 'charitable trade' if either (a) the trade is exercised in the course of the actual carrying out of a primary purpose of the charity, or (b) the work in connection with the trade is mainly carried out by beneficiaries of the charitable trust.[68] Trading profits now expressly include post-cessation receipts and adjustment income.[69]

An example of requirement (a) is where a charity runs a law surgery and one of its objects is the provision of lectures and general legal education; the profits of conferences for solicitors escape tax. Similarly, if a school or college carries on the trade of education and charges fees, the trade is exercised in the course of the actual carrying-out of a primary purpose of the charity.

Requirement (b) above contemplates 'the basket factory of a blind asylum, the blind inmates being the beneficiaries by whose work the trade of manufacturing baskets for sale is mainly carried on'.[70] However, it has been extended to a charitable association which organised a competitive music festival, the competitors being treated as the beneficiaries.[71] More obviously, the profits of a school run by nuns have been held exempt, the nuns, and not just the pupils, being regarded as the beneficiaries.[72] However, it does not follow that ordinary school teachers are beneficiaries.[73]

It will be seen that commercially-orientated trading, such as the sale of Christmas cards or the organisation of the sales of gifts, gives rise to taxable, not exempt, profits, such sales not being integral parts of the charity's purposes. However, profits from bazaars or jumble sales run by voluntary organisations are not generally charged to tax.[74] A result similar

---

[67] ITA 2007, s 420(8), FA 1990, s 25(5F)–(5H) added by F(No 2)A 2005, s 11.
[68] ITA 2007, ss 524 and 525, and CTA 2010, ss 478 and 479; requirement (b) was introduced by FA 1920, s 30(1)(c) to reverse *Coman v Governors of the Rotunda Hospital* [1921] 1 AC 1.
[69] ITA 2007, s 524(2) and CTA 2010, s 478(2).
[70] *IRC v Glasgow Musical Festival Association* (1926) 11 TC 154, 163, *per* Lord Clyde.
[71] *Ibid.*
[72] *Brighton Convent of the Blessed Sacrament v IRC* (1933) 18 TC 76.
[73] *Brighton College v Marriott* [1926] AC 192, 203; (1926) 10 TC 213, 234, *per* Lord Buckmaster.
[74] ITA 2007 s 529, CTA 2010, s 483 and ESC C4.

to complete exemption of trading income from income tax may be achieved by letting the trade be carried on by a company whose shares are held by the charity and which then covenants to make the payments to the charity equal to its profits; such payments are charges on income of the company[75] and so, in effect, deductible (see above at §4.4). The Revenue have for many years taken the view that such schemes would not usually be challenged provided no circularity is involved; circularity would be involved if the charity provided an interest-free loan to the trading entity, or the trader effectively controlled the charity using it as a tax-free money box.[76] Today the company is able to use gift aid; a qualifying donation is still effective.

Where a charity incurs expense and so a loss on its charitable but non-trading activities, it cannot set off that loss against its profits from a taxable trade.[77] However, if a charity carries on two trades, one exempt, on whom it makes a loss, and the other taxable, on which it makes a profit, the loss may be relieved.[78] This view seems doubtful but has not been tested in the courts. The charity would, in any case, have to surmount ITA 2007, section 66 first.[79] On the other hand, it is perfectly permissible for a loss on a taxable trade to be set off against the profit of another taxable trade. In broad terms, these reliefs apply only if the trade is a charitable trade, ie one qualifying under section 525. If the trade is not within that section, a loss will usually be treated as non-charitable expenditure, so giving rise to a loss of reliefs under the rules at §25.6.

25.4.2 Exemption for Small-scale Trades

To avoid putting charities to the cost of using companies as just described, ITA 2007, section 526 for income tax and CTA 2010, section 480 for corporation tax provide a simpler but limited regime. Income under ITTOIA 2005, Part 2 for income tax and CTA 2009, Part 3 for corporation tax is exempt up to a certain level, called, for corporation tax, the 'requisite limit'.[80] That limit has remained unchanged since 2000–01 and is the greater of (a) £5,000, and (b) whichever is the lesser of (i) £50,000 and (ii) 25% of the charitable trust's (or company's) trading incoming resources for the tax year (or accounting period). So if the income from all sources is £10,000, the limit will be set at £5,000 by rule (a); if the income is £100,000, the limit will be set at £25,000 by rule (b)(ii); while if the income is £1 million, the limit will be set at £50,000 by rule (b)(i). In order to avoid problems of retrospection, the legislation allows the charity to use the exemption if it had a reasonable expectation, at the beginning of the chargeable period, that it would be within the limit.[81] Where a chargeable period is less than 12 months, the limits of £5,000 and £50,000 are reduced proportionately.[82] The equivalent rules for income tax are in ITA 2007,

---

[75] As annual payments; see *R v IT Special Commrs, ex parte Shaftesbury Home and Arethusa Training Ship* [1923] 1 KB 393, (1923) 8 TC 367; distinguishing *Trustees of Psalms and Hymns v Whitwell* (1890) 3 TC 7.

[76] [1985] *Simon's Tax Intelligence* 572; of course, the company must comply with the requirements of TA 1988, Sch 16.

[77] *Religious Tract and Book Society of Scotland v Forbes* (1896) 3 TC 415.

[78] Under ITA 2007, s 64, ex TA 1988, s 380 (see *Revenue Law*, §20.10), or CTA 2010, ss 45 and 37, ex TA 1988, ss 393, 393A (see above at §4.5).

[79] Ex TA 1988, s 384. See *Revenue Law*, §20.10.

[80] CTA 2010, s 482(1).

[81] CTA 2010, s 482(1)(b).

[82] CTA 2010, s 482(7).

section 528. As with other charity exemption rules, the income must be applied solely for the purposes of the charity.[83]

Where a charity has a trade which consists of one activity which is wholly exempt under (for income tax) section 525 and another which must seek exemption under section 526, the statute as amended in 2006 deems there to be separate trades.[84] Thanks to section 527, the limited exemption in section 528 applies also to 'miscellaneous income' of the charitable trust. The heads of miscellaneous income are listed in section 1016, but subject to exclusions in section 527. The figures setting out the limit are applied to the sum of the trading and miscellaneous income (there is one relief, not two). The equivalent rules for corporation tax are in CTA 2010, section 479.

25.5   Capital Gains Realised by a Charity

A gain made by a charity is not a chargeable gain 'if it accrues to a charity and is applicable and applied for charitable purposes'.[85] Thus, where a charity sells an asset for cash and applies the proceeds to its charitable endeavours, no charge to tax arises.[86]

25.5.1 Problems

25.5.1.1 Gifts

Technical problems arise if no actual consideration is received by the charity, since there is nothing to be 'applied'. Thus, if a charity, in the course of carrying out charitable work, gives an asset to a beneficiary, any chargeable gain arising may be assessable on the charity. The Revenue are likely to adopt a generous approach where the gift of the asset was clearly made in the pursuance of the charity's objects.

25.5.1.2 Deemed Disposals

Similar problems arise on a deemed disposal since, again, there is no actual consideration and no gain is 'applied for charitable purposes'. In such cases, the charity is subject to CGT on the gain that arises. Suppose that charity A owns a freehold which it lets for a commercial rent to B, another charity. In order to help B, A reduces the rent from a commercial rent to a peppercorn rent. This alteration of the lease causes a deemed disposal.[87] The charity exemption is not available on this deemed disposal.

25.5.1.3 TCGA 1992, Section 171

If C, a charity, sets up S in the form of a wholly-owned subsidiary, and passes assets to S, TCGA 1992, section 171 should operate to treat the transfer as at no gain, no loss. However, this is specified in statute as applying only where one company is a subsidiary

---

[83] ITA 2007, s 527(5) and CTA 2010, s 480(5).

[84] ITA 2007, s 525(4) ex TA 1988, s 505(1B).

[85] TCGA 1992, s 256(1); there is no requirement that the gain be applied for charitable purposes only.

[86] The exemption is also available where the charity retains the proceeds in its general fund; see *IRC v Helen Slater Charitable Trust* [1981] STC 471 (CA).

[87] Under TCGA 1992, Sch 8, para 3(7).

of another, and it is not clear whether S can be a subsidiary of C since a charity does not have an equitable interest in its assets as such; instead, it holds those assets on trust for the ultimate beneficiaries.[88] If S cannot be a subsidiary, section 171 cannot apply to defer the charge. Moreover, section 256 cannot exempt the gain since, as in the A–B lease problem in §25.5.1.2 above, the gain cannot be said to have been 'applied for charitable purposes' as there is no consideration. In practice, the Revenue allow the use of section 171.

The Revenue view is that a capital payment from an offshore trust which has been realised as 'trust gains' cannot come within section 256 as 'being applied for' charitable purposes. This is because section 87(3) deems a chargeable gain to accrue.[89]

25.6 Restriction of Exemptions: Charitable and Non-charitable Expenditure

There are two groups of rules which may cause a charity to lose the benefit of any exemption to which it is otherwise entitled. One was added in 1986 and was designed to discourage a charity from hoarding its income (§25.6.1). The second was added in 2006 and was designed to counter abuses that might arise as a result of a transaction between the charity and someone who was a substantial donor, or even someone connected with a substantial donor (§25.6.2). When the second group of rules was added in 2006, the original rule was totally recast. The resulting form provides a structure which meets the needs of both. One effect is to make the rules applying in the first situation significantly more severe; thus the disregard of the first £10,000 of non-charitable expenditure has been abolished. In both situations the effect of the rules applying is that the charity loses the benefit of the exception it had hoped to enjoy. The burden thus falls on the charity, which must be ever alert. Where the rules apply there are provisions which allow the charity to decide which parts of its otherwise exempt income, etc should lose the protection.[90] It is these rules which have been criticised (see §25.1 above) as having enormous potential for damaging relations between charities and donors, and for increasing administration costs.

If it appears to the Board that two or more charities are acting in concert, with the avoidance of tax (whether by the charities or by another person) as one of their main aims, the Board must serve notice in writing on the charities, which have the right to appeal against its decision.[91]

25.6.1 Non-charitable Expenditure

This rule is aimed at the charity which makes the wrong sort of expenditures (treating certain investments and loans as expenditures), or which fails to spend enough on the right things. So if a charity incurs (or is treated as incurring) non-charitable expenditure in a relevant period, relief is withdrawn or disallowed for so much of the 'relievable income

---

[88] *Von Ernst v IRC* [1980] STC 111.

[89] Potter and Monroe, *Tax Planning* (Sweet & Maxwell, 1982) §7–10A.

[90] ITA 2007, ss 541 and 542, and CTA 2010, ss 494 and 495, ex TA 1988, s 505(7). Similar rules apply for CGT—see TCGA 1992, ss 256A–256D.

[91] ITA 2007, s 542 and CTA 2010, s 495, ex TA 1988, s 505(7).

and gains' as equals the 'non-charitable expenditure'. ITA 2007, sections 540 and 541, and CTA 2010, sections 493 and 494 refer to the 'exempt' and 'non-exempt' amounts. The rules include a special but common-sense timing rule to deal with the situation in which expenditure actually incurred in one period properly belongs in another.[92]

A payment made (or to be made) to a body situated outside the UK is not charitable expenditure unless the charity concerned takes such steps as may be reasonable in the circumstances to ensure that the payment will be applied for charitable purposes.[93]

The list of non-qualifying expenditure in former TA 1988, section 505 was relatively easy to understand. Study of the rewritten rules in ITA 2007, sections 543–545, and CTA 2010, sections 496–498 shows a number of changes. Some are based on Revenue practice, but the more interesting is the frequent use of the word 'loss' rather than 'expenditure'. Paraphrasing the explanatory notes, two principal points emerge. The first is that it is the losses which may count, rather than expenses taken into account in calculating the losses concerned. The second is that the rules are designed to ensure that losses are not disqualified as a non-charitable expenditure if corresponding profits would have been exempt under the rules in ITA 2007, sections 526 and 529–531, and CTA 2010, sections 480 and 483–485. Any lingering thought that a loss on a charitable trade is necessarily non-charitable expenditure is quashed by the opening part of section 543/section 496. While one may admire the rewrite team for their courage, it is a sad comment that the explanatory notes are much more helpful than the text.

Loans and investments are also treated as non-qualifying expenditure unless they fall within the categories of qualifying loans and qualifying investments. Loans qualify for exemption—in the rewritten language they are 'approved charitable loans'—if:

(1) they are made to another charity for charitable purposes only;
(2) they are made to a beneficiary of the charity in the course of its charitable activities; or
(3) money is placed in a current account with a bank (unless this forms part of an arrangement under which the bank makes a loan to another person).[94]

Investment in non-qualifying investments is non-charitable expenditure; qualifying investments are also elaborately defined.[95] The list of approved investments begins with various types set out in section 558/section 511. Section 559/section 512, which is type 1, lists approved securities, but section 560/section 513 imposes further conditions designed to make sure that the securities are sound. Type 12 of section 558/section 511 allows an officer of HMRC to designate any loan or investment as 'qualifying investment' where, on a claim being made, the officer is satisfied that the loan or investment is made for the benefit of the charity and not for the avoidance of tax.[96]

A further rule ensures that if a non-qualifying investment is made and realised, or loan is made and repaid, during the same chargeable period, the reinvestment of the proceeds

---

[92] ITA 2007, s 546 and CTA 2010, s 499, ex TA 1988, s 506(2).
[93] ITA 2007, s 547 and CTA 2010, s 500, ex TA 1988, s 506(3).
[94] ITA 2007, s 561 and CTA 2010, s 514, ex TA 1988, Sch 20, Pt II.
[95] ITA 2007, ss 558–560 and CTA 2010, ss 511–513, ex TA 1988, Sch, 20, Pt I.
[96] ITA 2007, s 558 and CTA 2010, s 511, ex TA 1988, Sch 20, para 9.

during that chargeable period is left out of account when calculating the amount of 'non-charitable expenditure' incurred by the charity.[97]

25.6.2 *Transactions with Substantial Donor*

ITA 2007, sections 549–557 and CTA 2010, sections 502–510 apply restrictions on reliefs otherwise available where a charity participates in transactions with substantial donors.[98] The effect is to apply a series of arm's-length pricing tests to these transactions; as seen above, the sanction is that the payment is treated as non-charitable expenditure and so gives rise to restriction of available reliefs and a charge on the charity.

Examples of transactions include the sale, exchange or letting of property and the provision of services or of financial assistance by the charity to the substantial donor, or vice versa.[99] An investment by the charity in a business run by the substantial donor is also caught. Any payment by way of remuneration to a substantial donor is caught, unless approved either by the Charity Commission or an equivalent body, or by a court.[100]

The rules in ITA 2007, sections 551 *et seq* and CTA 2010, sections 504 *et seq* try to exclude certain, usually commercial, arrangements. So there is no charge if the charity provides services to the substantial donor in the course of the actual carrying out of a primary purpose of the charity, and on terms which are no more beneficial to the substantial donor than those on which services are provided to others. So when a lifeboat is rescuing someone from an expensive-looking yacht, there is no need to enquire whether the person rescued is a substantial donor to the Royal National Lifeboat Institution.

The converse situation arises where the charity is the recipient, eg of property or services. Here, a typical clause excludes the rules where the transaction:

(1) takes place in the course of a business carried on by the substantial donor;
(2) is on terms which are no less beneficial to the charity than those which might be expected in a transaction at arm's length; and
(3) is not part of an arrangement for the avoidance of any tax.

The rule in (1) does not apply where the substantial donor provides financial assistance.

These rules appear to illustrate the balance the law is trying to strike. There are further rules in section 551/section 506B; certain very particular donors are exempt.[101] Two or more connected charities are treated as one.[102]

In deciding whether a person is a substantial donor, three rules must be considered.[103] First, one who makes relievable gift(s) of at least £25,000 in the period of 12 months in which the charity's chargeable period wholly or partly falls is a substantial donor. So a regular gift of £2,000 a month will not come within these rules, but gifts of £2,084 will. Secondly, one who makes relievable gifts of £100,000 in a period of six years is a substantial

---

[97] ITA 2007, s 548 and CTA 2010, s 501, ex TA 1988, s 506(5).
[98] Originally added by added by FA 2006, s 54; see BN28.
[99] For definitions, see ITA 2007, s 557, and CTA 2010, s 510, ex TA 1988, s 505C.
[100] ITA 2007, s 551(4)–(5) and CTA 2010, s 504(4)–(5), ex TA 1988, s 506A(5).
[101] ITA 2007, s 555 and CTA 2010, s 508, ex TA 1988, s 506B(8)–(9).
[102] ITA 2007, s 556, and CTA 2010, s 509, ex TA 1988, s 506C(5).
[103] ITA 2007, s 549(2)–(4) and CTA 2010, s 502(2)–(4), ex TA 1988, s 506A(2)–(4).

donor. Thirdly, a person who is a substantial donor for a chargeable period remains so for the next five chargeable periods. So if D contributes a chargeable asset worth £100,000 in June 2006, D will be a substantial donor for 2006 and the next five years (rule 2) and, being a substantial donor in 2011, will be so for the next five years as well (rule 3). Interestingly, although the transaction becomes *relevant* only if after 5 April 2006, there is no starting date for gifts, so if the gift had been not in 2006 but in 1999, D would be a substantial donor and subject to rule until the end of 2009.

25.6.3 *Tainted Donations*

FA 2011, Schedule 3 introduced a new, targeted anti-avoidance rule in ITA 2007, Part 13, Chapter 8 and CTA 2010, Part 21C which affects tax relief on donations to charity in circumstances in which benefits received from the charity are connected to the donations. This 'tainted donation' scheme addresses shortcomings in the poorly-targeted 'substantial donor' rules for charities in ITA 2007, section 549 (see above, §25.6.2). Under the new rules, tax relief will be denied if Conditions A and B are met, unless an exemption applies:

- Condition A is that is reasonable to assume that the donation would not have been made and the arrangements would not have been entered into independently of one another.
- Condition B requires that the main purpose, or one of the main purposes, for entering into the arrangements is to obtain a financial advantage.

A number of exemptions are set out in ITA 2007, section 809ZL and CTA 2010, section 939E, such as where the financial advantage is within the threshold limits allowed for gift aid relief, or is applied for charitable purposes only by the person for whom the advantage was obtained. A further exemption (Condition C) provides that the rules will not apply if a donor is a wholly-owned trading subsidiary of the charity or a housing provider which is linked with the charity. TCGA 1992, section 257A similarly disapplies the CGT gift rules in section 257 for tainted donations under the ITA 2007 or CTA 2010 tests.

25.7 CGT Charge if Property Ceases to be held on Charitable Trusts

There is a deemed disposal of property when it ceases to be held on charitable trust and the gain arising on that deemed disposal is chargeable.[104] There is, therefore, no immunity for unrealised capital gains built up behind the screen of charity.[105]

---

[104] TCGA 1992, s 256(2).

[105] On one view, a temporary charitable trust is not really a qualifying charity at all; see Whiteman, *Capital Gains Tax*, 4th edn (Sweet & Maxwell, 2002) 27; there was a concession for a temporary loss of charitable status due to the reverter of a site such as a school and the reversioner cannot be found (ex ESC D47). For problems where gift aid was paid out of dividend income, see Hiddleston, 144 *Taxation* 62 (21 October 1999).

Index

Introductory Note

References such as '178–9' indicate (not necessarily continuous) discussion of a topic across a range of pages. Wherever possible in the case of topics with many references, these have been divided into sub-topics and/or only the most significant discussions of the topic are listed. Because the entire volume is about 'tax', the use of this term as an entry point has been minimised. Information will be found under the corresponding detailed topics.